2089

# TRUDEAU AND OUR TIMES

# TRUDEAU
# AND OUR TIMES

VOLUME 2

---

## THE HEROIC DELUSION

**M&S**

CHRISTINA McCALL &
STEPHEN CLARKSON

Extracts from correspondence by Pierre Trudeau, pp. 46, 48, 50:
Used by kind permission of Rt. Hon. Pierre Elliott Trudeau.

Lines from "Fort Smith," p. 71: From *The Collected Poems of F.R.
Scott*, by F.R. Scott. Used by permission of the Canadian
Publishers, McClelland & Stewart, Toronto.

Lines from "The Six & Five Song," p. 257: Words and music by
Donald Johnston. Used by kind permission of Hon. Donald J.
Johnston.

**Canadian Cataloguing in Publication Data**

Clarkson, Stephen, date
Trudeau and our times

Includes bibliographical references and index.
Contents: v.1. The magnificent obsession. –
v.2. The heroic delusion / Christina McCall,
Stephen Clarkson.
ISBN 0-7710-5414-9 (v.1) ISBN 0-7710-5417-3 (v.2)

1. Trudeau, Pierre Elliott, 1919 –
2. Canada – Politics and government – 1963–1984.★
3. Prime ministers – Canada – Biography.
I. McCall, Christina, date. II. Title.

FC626.T7C52 1990   971.064'4'092   C90-095011-0 rev
F1034.3.T7C52 1990

Printed and bound in Canada

McClelland & Stewart Inc.
*The Canadian Publishers*
481 University Avenue
Toronto, Ontario
M5G 2E9

1 2 3 4 5   98 97 96 95 94

This book is dedicated to
the people who taught us to value
the Canada that was
and to our daughters,
Ashley McCall,
Kyra Clarkson,
Blaise Clarkson,
whose vitality and generosity
make us hopeful about
the Canada that will be

# Contents

FOREWORD                                                                    9

PART I      TRUDEAU AND THE ENGLISH: THE MAKING OF A LIBERAL

    1    A Small-l Liberal Education                                      15
    2    A Large-L Liberal Indoctrination                                 49
    3    The Spectre at the Feast: Economic Decline                       89

PART II     HOPE AGAINST HOPE: DREAMING A NEW LIBERAL DREAM

    4    The Restoration and the Strategic Prime
         Ministership                                                    137
    5    The National Energy Program and National Disunity               162

PART III    TRUDEAU AND THE AMERICANS: LIBERALISM UNDER ATTACK

    6    Hurricane Ronnie: American Retaliation                          187
    7    Ottawa Complains, Compromises, and Complies                     206
    8    The Disastrous Budget and the End of the Dream                  224

PART IV     THE FIGHT FOR LIBERAL SURVIVAL

    9    The Liberals Regroup: Trudeau Gets Going                        243
    10   Restructuring Government, Inc.                                  262
    11   The Last Liberal Optimist Defends the Cause                     284
    12   The Grits Gather in Convention and Contention                   303

PART V      THE END OF THE ERA: LIBERALISM IN DECLINE

    13   One More Time? The International Year of Pierre
         Trudeau                                                         333
    14   The Era Ends: Resignation and Replacement                       379

         CONCLUSION                                                      415
         NOTES                                                           435
         BIBLIOGRAPHY                                                    522
         LIST OF INTERVIEWS                                              552
         ACKNOWLEDGEMENTS                                                555
         INDEX                                                           556

# A Brief Note About This Book, Its Wilful Hero, and His Chroniclers

This book completes a project begun shortly after Pierre Elliott Trudeau retired as prime minister of Canada and the authors set out to analyse his fourth and final ministry, the government he headed from 1980 to 1984.

The work was provisionally titled *The End of the Trudeau Era*, and after we had completed a year's research, we went to Montreal to interview Mr. Trudeau over lunch. Early in the conversation he asked in his mordant style: "Is the emphasis to be on Trudeau? On the era? Or on the end?" It turned out to be on all three with a fourth subject, Canadian Liberalism, providing the conceptual thread that drew together the biographical, historical, and political aspects of the study.

Our original idea had been to write a sequel to Christina McCall's *Grits*, an anatomy of the federal Liberal party of the 1960s and 1970s. But as we examined the Liberals' Restoration government of the 1980s, we realized that the events under scrutiny would have to be placed in a broader context. In the 1980–84 period, the relationships that have defined Canada in the twentieth century – the long conflict between Quebec and English Canada, and the often uneasy interaction between Canada and the United States – clicked into focus in new and dramatic ways. At the epicentre of this turmoil was not the Liberal Party but the wilful self-styled hero, Pierre Trudeau.

The first volume of what came to be called *Trudeau and Our Times* took as its central subject Trudeau's determination to mould his native province into a component of the progressive, cosmopolitan society he believed Canada could become. Drawing on adult development theory, it sought to explain how his complex character was affected by his life experience and affected, in turn, his political action. Subtitled *The Magnificent Obsession*, the book showed how – as a consequence of his upbringing, his education, and his experience as an activist for change – Trudeau was converted to the idea that a legalistic solution could be found to the persistent difficulties between French and English Canadians. Thwarted in this objective by the unexpected successes of Quebec nationalism in the 1970s, he tried in the early 1980s to settle, once and for all, the constitutional problems still plaguing Canada more than a hundred years after the British had cobbled together a handful of their far-flung, querulous colonies into an embryonic state. It was Trudeau's unwavering belief that a new constitution – forged by patriating from the United Kingdom the British North America Act and entrenching within it an amending formula and a charter of rights and freedoms – would provide the means by which he could achieve his dream: a bilingual, multicultural federation, flourishing in the attic of North America as a model for other pluralistic societies around the world.

The critical test of these large ambitions took place between March 1980 and November 1981, when Trudeau and his federalist allies defeated the separatist government of Quebec in a provincial referendum on sovereignty; interpreted this victory as an endorsement of his constitutional position, to the intense irritation of most of the provincial premiers; and then negotiated a compromise accord on patriation to which they all agreed, with the fateful exception of the premier of Quebec.

Volume 1 ended with Trudeau in triumph suggesting – not entirely facetiously and in the face of widespread outrage in his home province – that the accord would last a thousand years.

· · ·

*Trudeau and Our Times: The Heroic Delusion* picks up the story a week after Volume 1 ended in November 1981, and then flashes back to examine the forces that shaped Trudeau's ideas and values. Where the first volume concentrated on Trudeau the Quebecker and his constitutional crusade, this book focuses on Trudeau the liberal Canadian – the man who came to political consciousness as an adherent to the great philosophy of individualism and, after a less than wholehearted flirtation with socialism, ultimately decided to bring his theories about government and society to fruition through the Liberal Party of Canada.

Trudeau was both a small-l and a big-L liberal, as the distinction is expressed in Canadian discourse. As a small-l liberal in his student days, he subscribed to the rich tradition of political thought that coalesced in the nineteenth century to champion individual rights, representative democracy, and free-market economics. By the mid-point of the twentieth century, as a young lawyer seeking societal change, he had embraced modern liberalism's more activist notion that the state could correct the social injustices created by the capitalist market in order to provide equal opportunity and a decent standard of living for all its citizens. Fifteen years later, Trudeau joined the "Government Party" and became a middle-aged adherent to big-L Liberalism, after its supporters had grafted the more interventionist welfare or left liberalism on the old Liberal Party's *laissez-faire* trunk.

Over the next two decades, as Trudeau laboured to bend the Liberal Party and the Canadian state to his will, it became obvious that he was in the grip of a heroic delusion. His very liberal hostility to nationalism of any variety reinforced his stubborn belief that a modern Canada could operate as though it were a fully sovereign nation independent of the United States – a latter-day Atlantis sustained by the magic of federalism and the incantatory power of internationalist idealism.

• • •

Although the two volumes of *Trudeau and Our Times* are intended to fit together as a coherent whole, each book is written so that it can be readily understood on its own. A full treatment of Trudeau's family background and idiosyncratic private life can be found in Volume 1. His biography is recapped here – with many fresh details added – in order to explain his political progress and his attitude towards business. This book also reintroduces several characters described in greater detail in *Grits* and *The Magnificent Obsession*, to which readers may want to refer in order to refresh their memories or to gain other insights into the rich cast of characters who were drawn to Trudeau and his interpretation of the public weal.

*Trudeau and Our Times* can be read in two ways: as a narrative that chronicles for the general reader Trudeau's last ministry, when he experienced, as he told his intimates, more personal satisfaction than he had enjoyed at any other time in his remarkable life; and as a political economy analysis, whose underpinnings the specialist can explore in the extensive notes that document its sources.

We took on this project, as a political writer and political economist who had observed Trudeau closely throughout his public life, convinced that it would be provocative and engrossing. But we had no idea at the time that it would take so long to complete or that the subject would continue to keep us fascinated by his egotistical posturings and altruistic manoeuvrings. For better and for worse, Pierre Trudeau changed Canada. The attempt to understand those changes altered our attitudes and our lives.

# PART I

# TRUDEAU AND THE ENGLISH: THE MAKING OF A LIBERAL

CHAPTER 1

# A Small-l Liberal
# Education

In hindsight the night of November 12, 1981, can be seen as
the zenith of the Trudeau era. Afterwards came the inexorable
decline. But that evening constituted a kind of triumphal celebration. It was a week to the day since the signing of the constitutional
accord that Pierre Trudeau had worked towards throughout his
prime ministerial career, and early doubts about the document's
compromises had given way to sheer relief at its accomplishment.
The minister of finance was about to unveil in the House of Commons at eight o'clock a budget that was rumoured around Ottawa to
be a masterpiece of the fiscal arts. And the prime minister was giving
a reception in honour of King Hussein of Jordan, just the sort of
splendid occasion that fed the streak of grandiosity in Trudeau's
complex character and allowed his acolytes to bask in the glory of
his governing style.

The setting was one of the most beautiful buildings in Trudeau's
Ottawa, the recently reconstructed Bank of Canada, designed by
the architect Arthur Erickson in his romantic modernist mode. The
party was held in a reception area at the top of the Bank's atrium, a
soaring space that looked down six stories on a reflecting pool and a
hundred thousand dollars' worth of illuminated tropical greenery
that defied the dark reality of the approaching northern winter
without.[1]

Standing about in the glittering crowd, enjoying the sound of
revelry by night, were dozens of other old friends and colleagues

of the prime minister, including the chief justice of Canada, the Speaker of the Senate, several Privy Councillors, and the newly named Canadian ambassador to the United States – men appointed to high office by Trudeau, their well-known faces enhanced by the subtle lighting, their familiar mannerisms heightened by the drama of the moment.[2]

Trudeau himself moved easily through the throng, holding his diminutive royal guest by the elbow and introducing him to select members of the company while the official photographers' cameras flashed and the conversational roar rose and fell. "Trudeau looks wonderful still," said an onlooker *sotto voce*. And so he did. At sixty-two he seemed serene, his glamour intact, his great work done, his personal troubles transcended, his *fierté* – always a better word than "arrogance" to describe his attitude on state occasions – justified at last.

But despite the chilled wine and hot talk, the politicians at the party soon began to crane their necks in an attempt to figure out when "Himself," as they called Trudeau, would be ready to depart. It would be bad form to leave before he did and they wanted to take their places in the House of Commons for the budget reading, a pivotal event of the parliamentary year. This evening's performance was expected to prove a coup for the government, reflecting the positive liberalism of the "strategic prime ministership," a phrase Trudeau's supporters had been using to describe the government's agenda ever since the Liberals had returned to power in February 1980, having been briefly out of office, an ignominy that had befallen them only once in the previous forty-five years.

The feeling among the politicians present was that – having dealt with the country's constitutional difficulties – Trudeau was now ready to turn his talents to Canada's economic problems, which would soon be brought under control as the Liberals unveiled the next phase of what was in effect a third National Policy. They hoped this grand design they had concocted to redress the failings of their party's previous dozen years in office would be equal in importance to the John A. Macdonald Conservatives' post-Confederation nation-building scheme or to the Mackenzie King Liberals' ambitious efforts to build a Keynesian welfare state. They expected it to revive not just their own political fortunes but the very spirit of Liberalism itself.

This exuberant mood held as the reception wound down and the guests moved across Wellington Street towards the House of Commons to listen to the minister of finance deliver his speech. Once he had finished, Liberals of all ages and factions could be overheard in the halls of the Commons congratulating themselves on their past successes, their present perspicacity, and their prospects as the natural leaders of a revitalized Canada moving confidently towards the twenty-first century.

A few blocks away in his Rockcliffe house, Jack Pickersgill, the grittiest of old Grits, a man who had served as an adviser to prime ministers for close to half a century, now seventy-six years old and living in lively retirement, turned off his television set after watching the budget broadcast and gave a couple of vigorous nods of satisfaction. "Allan [MacEachen, the finance minister] must be some kind of wizard," Pickersgill said to his wife, Margaret. "That was a first-class document. Everything's back to normal. The government's under control."[3]

Alas for Pickersgill. Alas for Liberalism. And alas for the Trudeauites and their strategic prime ministership. As it turned out, things were neither back to normal nor under control. The budget reading was scarcely over before the hired hands of business big and small joined the opposition parties in denouncing it to every journalist willing to shove a camera, microphone, or notebook in front of their faces. It was the opening round of an unusually vigorous barrage of criticism aimed at Trudeau's handling of the economy, part of a concerted conservative attempt to bring down not just the Liberal Party and its leader but the liberal values that had characterized Canadian governments for two generations – an attempt that had been gathering speed and supporters for close to five years and would soon overwhelm the body politic.

● ● ●

It is one of those pleasing coincidences of history that modern Liberalism – whose decline was being blamed so emphatically on Pierre Trudeau's perfidies in the 1980s – was just beginning to take shape in Canada when he was born in October 1919.

The society into which Joseph Philippe Pierre Yves Elliott Trudeau was ushered in that first autumn after the Great War was riven with conflict and driven by hope. With the slaughter in Europe still the stuff of their night-time terrors, Canadians were already engaging in a multitude of domestic disputes: between the French and the English over their contributions to the war effort; between western farmers and eastern manufacturers over trade and tariffs; between the pro-American and the pro-British over future alliances and allegiances; between conservatives who represented the big interests, and progressives whose advocacy of labour's rights had about it a whiff of the dreaded Bolshevism that was frightening plutocrats throughout the industrialized world.[4]

In the face of this uproar, Sir Robert Borden's Unionist government, an agglomeration of Conservatives and Liberals who had coalesced two years before to contend with the wartime conscription crisis, appeared exhausted and uncertain. They were attempting to govern without a single French-speaking minister in the cabinet or a single new idea for managing this unexpectedly difficult peace. Sir Wilfrid Laurier, the Liberal prime minister who had presided over Canada's passage from the nineteenth into the twentieth century, had died the previous February after eight dark years in opposition, dispirited by the clash between the French and English views of imperialism that had been revealed during the war. There was concern among his followers that his party might suffer the alarming decline that was befalling the Liberals in England. In Ontario, the young dominion's prosperous heartland, the ruling Conservatives were about to be squeezed out of office by a Farmer-Labour coalition; and on the prairies, agrarian progressives were demanding a fundamental restructuring of the economic and political system. In brief, as the great political economist MacGregor

Dawson put it, "the general political situation [in 1919] . . . was confused to a degree hitherto unknown in the Dominion's history."[5]

Also largely unknown in the dominion (unless you counted the clues buried in the prosy thickets of his recently published book, *Industry and Humanity*) was the fact that someone had conceived a plan to solve these sobering problems. His name was William Lyon Mackenzie King; he was forty-four years old and had been engaged with the idea of social and political reform in Canada since early childhood. His mother had burdened him with the name and the myth of his grandfather, William Lyon Mackenzie, the firebrand of the 1837 rebellion in Upper Canada who had challenged the Family Compact, the young colony's ruling oligarchy, and endured years of ignominy and poverty as a consequence. His father was an ineffectual lawyer, often forced to rely on Liberal patronage to make ends meet. King himself had parlayed his family's political connections, along with his Harvard education, into a career in Laurier's government.[6]

In the autumn of 1919 he was just beginning his long tenure as Liberal leader, having been elected Laurier's successor at a convention in August where he had pulled off a double coup: he had bound the Quebec delegates to him through flattery and fear-mongering and had embedded in the party's policy resolutions some of the important ideas on the creative use of the state that he had laboriously worked out over the previous twenty years. While the Liberals were out of office, King had become acutely aware of the polarization between capital and labour that was tearing apart the British Liberal Party and fuelling social unrest in the United States. As a consultant on union-management relations, he had played a direct role in negotiating a truce in the violent conflict that pitted unyielding strikers in Colorado against the American robber-baron businessman John D. Rockefeller. Armed with the fresh insights this experience provided, he was running for Parliament in a by-election called for October 20, with the long-term intention of transforming Laurier Liberalism – that once-successful amalgam of watered-down *patriote* radicalism, Gladstonian reform ideas, and *laissez-faire* economics – into something different: a flexible political formula that would dominate Canadian life for most of the rest of the century and keep him in power for most of the rest of his life.

It's highly unlikely that the vagaries of the Canadian political situation or the schemes of Mackenzie King were playing in the minds of Pierre Trudeau's parents, Charles-Émile and Grace Elliott Trudeau, in their modest Montreal house in October 1919. Charlie Trudeau was thirty-two that autumn, a struggling lawyer whose interest in politics at the time was slight but whose ambition to get on in the world was boundless. The Quebec he had grown up in was still deeply conservative and resistant to British and American ideas about individual rights and free enterprise. Industrialization had made inroads into the province in the previous forty years, but most of the French-speaking population was trapped in its pre-Enlightenment past, in thrall to a resurgent Roman Catholic church that was battling liberalism in all its guises but particularly the politicians who bore the Liberal banner in Quebec and were branded *rouges*, as though they were dangerous revolutionaries. Charlie Trudeau's forebears, unlettered farmers who had been tilling the soil in the countryside south of Montreal for generations, belonged to a class who believed that liberalism was heresy, individual enterprise flew in the face of the good God, and money-making was a grubby activity best left to the Protestant English, who apparently did not care that their materialism meant they would surely roast in Hell.[7]

However densely these ideas were woven into Charlie Trudeau's background, other forces stirring in post-war Quebec were altering his attitudes. His parents had sold their land so their sons could follow the only path to self-betterment acceptable to the Church other than the priesthood: a professional education that would boost them into the bourgeoisie. By 1915 Charlie had managed to graduate from a classical college and to earn a law degree. But the meagre returns from the small practice he set up in Montreal in partnership with his brother and brother-in-law were not what he aspired to in life. He wanted to get rich and had decided the only way to do so was to turn himself into an entrepreneur.

In the milieu where his ambitions could be satisfied – both the little cosmos of Montreal and the larger world beyond its borders – the British were still the dominant economic power despite the horrendous losses they had just suffered in the war to end all wars. As surely as Calcutta or Cape Town, Montreal remained an outpost of empire, a racially stratified city where the French majority was excluded as a matter of course from the gilded garrison the British had created there over the previous century.[8]

There was no question in the minds of English Montrealers in 1919 that they belonged to a superior race. It was their antecedents who had taken over New France in the 1760s as part of the spoils of victory in the Seven Years' War. It was British traders, "close, prudent, quiet . . . strictly faithful to their employers and sordidly avaricious," who had made the fur trade pay in North America in ways the French had never managed. And it was the progeny of those traders, joined by fresh recruits from the Highlands, Loyalist refugees from the American Revolution, and a mixture of other fortune seekers and settlers, who had turned Montreal into a dynamic commercial community that dominated the Canadian economy throughout the nineteenth century and dominated it still on the eve of the 1920s.[9]

Despite the pro-Canadian, anti-imperialist feelings the war had stirred in French-speaking Quebec and other regions of the dominion, Anglo-Montrealers continued to see themselves as proudly English. Regiments of their relatives had marched away and been decimated on the battlefields of France, leaving their survivors with a deepened devotion to the imperial ideal. Their chauvinism was bound up with their religion; the hymns and sermons they heard in their Protestant churches confirmed that God was on their side. Like their counterparts in the Anglo enclaves in Ireland, they had superimposed themselves on a conquered people too stubbornly Catholic to be assimilated. To bolster their authority, they had tried to create on the shores of the St. Lawrence a dreamland replication of British society with its class system, its snobbery, its devotion to the monarchy, to horses, dogs, hunt balls, cricket, clubs, and other English conventions in clothes, conversation, décor, and deportment so arcane they required interpretation by self-appointed arbiters of taste. [10]

The inhabitants of Montreal's Square Mile – a phrase concocted originally to describe the streets on the south side of Mount Royal where a handful of English-speaking plutocrats had built their nineteenth-century mansions but whose meaning later encompassed the whole Anglo-Protestant ascendancy's middle and upper echelons – were happy to live out their lives in this imported, packaged culture. Despite their pretensions, they were mostly the newly prosperous descendants of settlers of modest background. Although a few fortunes had been made in furs and the timber trade in the early 1800s, it was not until after Macdonald's National Policy of 1879 that major blocks of capital were accumulated in Montreal from railway-building, financial institutions, and manufacturing. By 1919, when Pierre Trudeau was born, the Square Mile had put behind it memories of the humble origins and ruthless business practices of its progenitors and established an astonishingly insulated, self-satisfied society. [11]


Anglo Montreal's ideas about how this society should function did not include much contact with French Canadians. Its upper class continued to recruit clergymen, physicians, schoolmasters, accountants, clerks, factory foremen, and skilled labourers in Britain well into the twentieth century. The French Canadians were the backwoods remnant of a conquered settlement they had been saddled with – the "natives" they employed as maids, handymen, unskilled workers in their textile and shoe factories, and stevedores on their docks; people who worked as fishing guides, farmers, loggers, miners, and trappers harvesting the natural resources that had made the Square Mile prosperous. Embracing the "niggers-begin-at-Calais" attitude that characterized the British imperialists at their worst, the Square Mile tried to bar upstart French Canadians from their country-house communities and their city clubs. Most conversations between members of the two language groups took place in the language of the Empire. The English refused to allow Quebec French to be spoken in the presence of their children, even by kitchen maids and yard men. If French were learned, it had to be Parisian French, and the intention was to speak it in Paris.[12]

Seventy years after she formed lifelong friendships among the adolescent daughters of prosperous English Montreal while attending a ladies' college in the nearby Eastern Townships just after World War I, a well-born Toronto woman expressed succinctly the Square Mile's prevailing attitude when she remarked, "Well, it wasn't that [English] Montrealers *meant* to treat the French badly, dear. They just didn't know they were there."[13]

However blinded the privileged young women of the Square Mile may have been to the existence of the several million French Canadians outside their purview, the shrewd businessmen who were their fathers, brothers, and husbands-to-be knew they were there, if only because they were a political reality to be reckoned with and a substantial market to exploit. While the English had prospered in Montreal in the nineteenth century, the French-speaking population – left behind after the Conquest when its élites had mostly decamped to France – had proliferated in the countryside under the protection of a priesthood insisting that their survival as a race depended on their fecundity.[14]

No matter how persuasively the Catholic clergy extolled the joys of pastoralism and procreation, the land could not support the burgeoning population that resulted from their exhortations. Half a million French Canadians migrated south to the mill towns of New England in the last quarter of the nineteenth century and tens of thousands crowded into Montreal, abandoning their impoverished rural communities in search of work in the factories of a rapidly industrializing metropolis. A solid if small French-Canadian urban middle class (doctors, lawyers, judges, notaries, accountants, small businessmen) flourished at the same time. But the English rarely saw them socially or considered them their equals. A few were employed as factotums in their offices or made partners in English law firms, less for the clientele they could bring in than for their knowledge of the Quebec civil code and their connections to the Church hierarchy and to the "local" governments in Montreal and Quebec City, the provincial seat, where French-Canadian legislators practised the self-government they had won through repeated political struggle.[15]

In 1919, French Canadians were still being stereotyped as indifferent to the exigencies of commerce. Only a handful of them had grown prosperous from the new wave of industrialization that had followed the harnessing of Quebec's cheap hydroelectric power just before the Great War. Because the Anglos dominated the large industrial and financial corporations and virtually controlled the province's economy through interlocking directorships, French-Canadian entrepreneurs were hived off into retail and service-sector activities. Even in areas where sheer numbers ought to have made them an important economic force, they were woefully underrepresented. Montreal was Canada's financial capital, but French-Canadian capitalists were excluded from the country's ten largest insurance companies and had a stake in only the smallest of the nine chartered banks. The accepted belief that the English should be left to manage Quebec's financial affairs was expressed in the political tradition of appointing an Anglo-Montrealer as the provincial government's treasurer, as though no French Canadian had the competence to handle the job.[16]

Much of what Charlie Trudeau knew about the English business world by 1919 had been learned from his wife, the former Grace Elliott, a hybrid Quebecker whose mother, Sarah Sauvé, came from French Catholic farming stock and whose father's ancestors were Protestant Scots. Her paternal grandfather, Edward Elliott, had been an illiterate woodsman who spent his life in the lumber country north of Trois-Rivières, felling trees and riding log rafts in the rough company of French and Irish Catholic labourers. Grace's father, Philip Elliott, joined the rural migration to Montreal in the 1870s and scraped together enough money working as a bartender to buy a tavern. After his wife died in 1899, Philip's mother came in from the country to look after his three children, Grace, who was nine, and her younger brothers, Gordon and Allan.

It was a commonplace in mixed marriages for girls to take their mothers' religion and boys their fathers', and Grace Elliott was raised as the only Roman Catholic in an Anglican household. But shortly after her grandmother's death in 1903, she was withdrawn from her Montreal convent school and enrolled as a boarder in an Anglican college. Philip Elliott's reason for effecting this change may simply have been that as a mark of his hard-won prosperity, he wanted his daughter to acquire the superior education available to the English well-to-do. Or it could have been that he thought it prudent to put some distance between her and Charlie Trudeau, the exuberant farm boy turned classical-college student she had recently met at mass. Whatever the motivation, given the mutual hostility of the Catholic and Protestant worlds in Canada in the early years of the century, being wrenched from the bosom of the Mother Church – and from the company of her brothers and father who were living above his downtown saloon – must have had a profound effect on the sensitive adolescent Grace Elliott had become. Suddenly she, a pious Catholic and publican's child, was thrown among the adolescent daughters of the Anglo-Protestant business and professional class.

Her new school, Dunham Ladies' College, had been founded thirty years before under the aegis of the Anglican bishop of Montreal, the Right Reverend Ashton Oxenden, an enlightened Englishman from Kent. It was located in the Eastern Townships south of Montreal in an idyllically beautiful village that was surrounded by wooded hills and enhanced by stone buildings put up a hundred years before by Loyalist settlers from Vermont. The college itself was in a red brick building boasting a huge veranda two hundred feet long, described as "affording an excellent promenade in unfavourable weather." [17]

One of the reasons the privileged girls of English Montreal were sent to country boarding schools was to protect them from the health hazards of a raw port city that still lacked a proper sewage system. A further – and perhaps more fervent – hope was that an education under the direction of schoolmistresses imported from the old country would teach them to be Real English Ladies, as the prospectus for King's Hall, a sister school to Dunham in nearby Compton, described its aims. In those Edwardian days, would-be ladies were not so much educated as "finished" for the marriage market, with classes devoted to instruction in "eating, sleeping and sitting; walking, dress and domestic matters; . . . manners in public assemblies – as in churches, concerts, parties and parlours; manners towards kindred and friends and . . . manners in intercourse with gentlemen." [18]

But Dunham had another, more serious mission. Its stated goal was to provide for its young ladies "a liberal education," as well as the usual classes in ladylike deportment and household management. The Lady Principal, as the school's prospectus described her, boasted a university degree and was intent on preparing her students for university entrance by offering the courses available to young men in other schools: algebra, geometry, history, geography, English literature, French, and Latin.

What the adolescent Grace, who had spent her early life in raucous downtown Montreal, thought of these opportunities can be inferred only from the fact that when she was old and ill her family made an annual donation to the college (renamed St. Helen's School) in memory of her "happy childhood" there. What her schoolmates thought of her is equally obscure. In 1974, Grace MacDougall Pitfield, a near contemporary who was related to several important families in the Square Mile, remembered vaguely, "Some of my friends [were] at school with Grace Elliott. They heard she married a Frenchman nobody knew and of course they never saw her afterwards." [19]

Once she left Dunham, Grace defied the ideal behaviour pattern of Real English Ladies first by studying business procedures at a secretarial college, then by working in an office for several years, and finally by marrying in 1915 the "Frenchman nobody knew," her persistent beau, Charlie Trudeau. Charlie's heavy country accent, haystack hair, and involvement as a semi-pro athlete in lacrosse and boxing were dead give-aways that he was not the sort who typically figured in the rare intermarriages between the French and English among the Montreal bourgeoisie in the early years of the twentieth century. [20]

By the time Pierre Trudeau was born, his parents were settled both physically and psychically *outre-mont* – on the other, French-speaking side of the mountain from the English capitalist class in a row-house on Rue Durocher in the fast-growing suburb of Outremont. Neither of them was content with the French Canadians' lot. Grace's education, her office experience, and the business savvy of her male relatives, who had sold the family tavern and invested profitably in downtown real estate, were an important support to her husband when he decided to branch out from his law practice in 1919. The gimmick Charlie fastened on in launching his Automobile Owners' Association – with its members' insurance scheme and guaranteed mechanics' service in Trudeau's string of corner gas stations – was so successful that within a decade, the association's initials were used in Montreal as slang for an emergency or breakdown, as in "Nous avons eu un Ah-Oh-Ah." [21]

After Charlie sold the AOA in 1932 to Imperial Oil for more than a million dollars, he sought out partners, English as well as French, for other money-making schemes. Bounding onwards as the same country "*jack*" he had always been, a high-spirited roughneck who had worked in his shirt-sleeves alongside the mechanics at the Ah-Oh-Ah, he now ran with a crowd of hard-drinking speculators and sports promoters with backgrounds and ambitions similar to his own – the avant-garde of the French-Canadian entrepreneurial class that was to "reconquer Montreal" half a century later. He never attempted to be a Real English Gent. As a self-styled man of the future, he was aware that it was the Americans who were pumping new capital into Quebec, and that the Square Mile might continue to have social sway in Montreal but that its business dominance was beginning to decline. [22]

He took an energetic part in the efforts being made by the emerging French-Canadian bourgeoisie to develop its own set of institutions parallel to those of the English. He joined the Club Saint-Denis, founded by entrepreneurs who were excluded from the English clubs, and went there regularly to play poker and talk business and sports over whisky and cigars. While the English summered in genteel comfort at Murray Bay and Memphremagog, the Trudeaus and their friends went north to cabins in the Laurentians and then south to Old Orchard Beach on the coast of Maine near Kennebunkport. If the English could make pilgrimages to London for the season in the spring and to Scotland for the salmon fishing in August, then Grace and Charlie were determined to tour the great cities of Europe with their children. When the English rich began to move away from the old Square Mile to Westmount, the Trudeaus moved up the mountain into a larger, more expensive house on McCulloch Avenue in the leafier reaches of Outremont, leaving behind Rue Durocher and its back lanes where tough Irish and Jewish kids played in gangs and taunted the French boys constantly, bloodying their knees and noses, challenging each other at ball games and pick-up hockey.

What the Trudeaus were teaching their offspring by example was a powerful lesson: a colonized people seeking to break the barriers that keep them from equality can refuse to accept the inferior position by which their colonizers have defined them. At the same time as they challenged the exclusivity of English bourgeois privileges, they also rejected the presumed superiority of English educational institutions. Unlike many of their peers among the new rich, the Trudeaus did not seek English schooling for their children. As devout Catholics they saw to it that their daughter, Suzette (who was two years older than Pierre), was educated by nuns and their sons, Pierre and Charles (who was three years younger), by priests. But the children were enrolled at the most progressive Catholic institutions available: for the boys, this meant first the Académie Querbes and then the Collège Jean-de-Brébeuf, recently established equivalents of English Montreal's Selwyn House and Lower Canada College.[23]

Querbes was considered so advanced that Sir Lomer Gouin, the Liberal premier of Quebec for whom educational reform was the keystone of progress, had officiated at its much-heralded opening in 1916. Brébeuf was staffed by Jesuits who were self-consciously training an élite and insisted they were offering their pupils the best education available in North America. Although the intellectually rigorous and culturally enriching classicism they taught excluded consideration of much of what had happened in Europe since the Enlightenment (and in Canada since the Conquest), their staff sheltered at least two closet liberals, Father Robert Bernier and Father Rodolphe Dubé, who later as a laicized writer took the name François Hertel. They were both to have a catalytic influence on Pierre Trudeau and several of his friends who studied at the college in the 1930s.[24]

Bernier had grown up in a French-Canadian community in Manitoba. As a gifted teacher from outside Quebec's cultural stockade, he took pains to ensure that his students were in touch with world culture by recommending they read English and American poets and novelists as well as introducing them to modern music and art. But it was the iconoclast Hertel who had the most intense effect on the young Pierre. Hertel introduced his students to Montaigne, the seventeenth-century essayist whose advocacy of tolerance amidst religious and racial diversity and insistence on the individual's right to work out his own ideas in a time of rigid religious orthodoxies made him the first great exponent of liberal thought in France. With his emphasis on principled tolerance and the thoughtful man's need to master emotion, and his egotistical dismissal of self-doubt, Montaigne's work and life provided the first building block in Trudeau's intellectual structure. [25]

The liberal ideas Bernier and Hertel disseminated – and their insistence that their students read the complete texts of even those authors who were on the Vatican's Index of banned books – ran counter to the ultra-conservative nationalism that surfaced in Quebec in the 1930s. As in other industrializing societies, the Depression created in the province populist heroes who blamed racial scapegoats of one kind or another for the economic misery that was so widespread. With the unemployed roaming the streets of Montreal like a ragged hungry army, it was impossible even in the sheltered atmosphere of Brébeuf to escape the English-French tensions that were growing worse under the Depression's strains. Prominent members of the Catholic clergy were advocating a stridently racist protectionism. The rabidly nationalistic historian Abbé Lionel Groulx was encouraging students at the Université de Montréal (including the older brothers of several Brébeuf boys) to agitate against the domination of English capital and its materialistic values. The college debated another Jesuit school on the topic "To succeed in business, you don't need to speak English." Among themselves, the boys discussed a not-so-thinly veiled anti-Semitic campaign that was being conducted under the slogan "Achat chez nous." "Listes blanches" were circulated to encourage the Catholic faithful to buy canadien and to avoid the Jewish-owned small businesses that were thought to be threatening French-Canadian retailers and their suppliers. [26]

The mostly middle-class adolescents studying at Brébeuf admired and envied their classmates who were the children of the handful of francophone entrepreneurs whose fortunes had been made as suppliers of such consumer goods as soap, cigarettes, and gasoline. But Pierre Trudeau seems to have been the only *gosse de riche* who used the cachet his father's wealth brought him to deliver a liberal socio-political message. He remonstrated with his *copains* who repeated anti-Semitic taunts, saying that the educated should never attack others on the basis of race. Bernier and Hertel had told them again and again that chauvinism and anti-Semitism were retrograde. The modern man embraced pluralism and despised racism. "We don't have to be negative," his friend Charles Lussier remembered Trudeau saying in the yard outside the school. "The English will respect us when we're strong enough to prosper on our own, not when we're attacking others because we're weak."[27]

What the young Trudeau was reflecting was not only his favourite teachers' liberal intellectual vision but his father's can-do capitalist attitude. Charlie Trudeau's politics remained *bleu*, like those of his parents before him. But his zestful expansionist attitudes were the antithesis of their ultramontane conservatism, with its subservience to Rome. After he died suddenly of pneumonia in April 1935, the management of his estate – swollen in three years to an estimated $3 million through his investments in mining companies, an amusement park, and the Montreal Royals ball club – was taken over by Ernest Beaupré, a man thought to be so adept with money that "even though he had a French name, we [Brébeuf] boys just assumed he must be an Anglo," Charles Lussier remembered.[28]

The shock of his father's sudden early death and the changes it brought in the Trudeau household were to have a profound effect on the fifteen-year-old Pierre's development in many ways, including his evolving biracial identity. Charlie Trudeau's fortune enabled his widow, once she had emerged from mourning, to turn her energies to seeking for herself and her children the refinements she had been taught to admire at Dunham thirty years before. With Charlie – and his sporting friends, with their entrepreneurial hustle and crude French – out of the picture, family life for the Elliott Trudeaus, as they began to sign their name, took on a pronounced English flavour. Although Grace spoke French, her mother's language, with her children's friends and her household help, it was

English that she and her adolescent children almost exclusively used with one another. Visitors to their house on McCulloch Avenue were made aware of what Pierre was later to call the "English mores" in the household, that is, the determined gentility practised there. Elocution classes were paid for to perfect the Trudeau children's English diction and to expunge any trace of *joual* from their French. Music and art lessons were arranged, concerts attended, and paintings acquired.[29]

Pierre was sent to Taylor Statten's Camp Ahmek in Algonquin Park, where for two summers in a row, in company with other boys of his age, most of them from southern Ontario, he was inculcated with idealistic notions about living in harmony with the wilderness, as propounded by progressive educators such as Joe McCulley, the headmaster of Lakefield School who was later to become warden of Hart House at the University of Toronto. Native Indian crafts were taught at Ahmek and long canoe trips organized so the campers could commune with nature by cooking over campfires and sheltering under their canoes at night, wrapped in Hudson's Bay blankets. These attitudes were in direct contrast to the general French-Canadian response to native peoples, the turning away in shame from the "long bond of blood and history" between *les Canadiens* and the aboriginals with whom their ancestors had intermingled and intermarried.[30]

After these summertime excursions into the Anglo world, Pierre found student life at the Université de Montréal law school, where he enrolled in 1940, intellectually stultifying, with its emphasis on legal practice as a trade. To counter the narrow curriculum, he read widely on his own and began to quote the ideas of his second liberal hero, Montesquieu, the eighteenth-century *philosophe* who shared with Montaigne a belief in the importance of mastering the emotions through reason. His book *The Spirit of the Laws*, which sang the praises of Britain's parliamentary institutions as guarantors of individual liberty, provided Trudeau with a fixed belief from which he was to lever a life's mission. Among his fellow students engrossed in learning the intricacies of contract and mortgage law, he cultivated a reputation for daring originality by flaunting his familiarity with proscribed texts and by frequenting the avant-garde salon of the anarchist painter Paul-Émile Borduas. He also competed in law-school debates, displaying an enviable talent for dramatic timing, caustic wit, and devastating logic.

His contacts with English Montrealers were still rare and superficial. His close friends could remember only a few isolated incidents when he or they made interracial connections, even though casual acquaintances were misled by his sophisticated posturing and his fluent English into assuming that he had a second, English, social life. They were disabused of this idea during the anti-conscription ferment that flared in 1942 when Trudeau openly defied the authority of Montreal's Anglo establishment, which was exhorting the young of both races to show their patriotic mettle by marching off once more to a European war. He made inflammatory statements at a public rally that were quoted on the front page of *Le Devoir*; challenged to a back-alley fist-fight an Anglo soldier who had razzed him on a streetcar for not being in uniform; and behaved with provocative insubordination in the Canadian Officers Training Corps, which he and many of his contemporaries joined in order to avoid being relegated to a French-Canadian unit in a military machine run by the English. Trudeau began to be talked of among his peers as a champion of French-Canadian rights, most likely a future premier of Quebec, perhaps a second Laurier, a prospect that clearly excited him. Charles Lussier, his friend from Brébeuf days who was also studying law, took it for granted that politics was Trudeau's métier, and they talked far into the night about achieving social reform in Quebec through political action.[31]

The difficulty lay in choosing a political party to serve as a vehicle for Trudeau's ideas and ambitions. The Liberals were in power provincially and federally, but Pierre saw the party as undemocratic, corrupted by power, and distanced from its radical roots. He was even more contemptuous of the connections his father had made among Quebec Conservatives in the 1920s and 1930s. Charlie Trudeau had been involved in raising money for his former law-school classmate, the Conservative leader Maurice Duplessis, who later abandoned the party to form the populist Union Nationale, and in giving campaign donations to Camillien Houde, another Conservative politician who became mayor of Montreal and was jailed in 1940 for advocating civil disobedience as a response to enforced enlistment. [32]

The party that appealed most to both Lussier and Trudeau – ambitious to reform their conservative society and to shock its bourgeoisie at the same time – was the socialist Co-operative Commonwealth Federation, which had been founded in the 1930s. They were deeply impressed by F.R. Scott, a McGill law professor and national president of the CCF, who came to the Université de Montréal campus to deliver a guest lecture eloquently defending the French Canadians' anti-conscriptionist position. Afterwards, they discussed excitedly a radical tract written by Scott and David Lewis, the CCF's national secretary. Not only were the Scott-Lewis ideas doctrinally attractive, they seemed to be gaining public acceptance, since the CCF was now a major political presence in Saskatchewan and Ontario and was challenging the Mackenzie King Liberals nationally in the public opinion polls recently invented by the American social scientist George Gallup. But the party had little chance of making inroads in Quebec, where its Social Gospel–based, Anglo-Protestant egalitarianism was denounced by the ultramontane priests as probably communistic and certainly heretical. [33]

The question of party affiliation was coloured for Trudeau by the fact that his romantic interest at the time was a young woman who belonged to a powerful Liberal family. Fifty years later, Thérèse Gouin was still seen by Trudeau's oldest friends as the woman who evoked the strongest emotional response from him in his long lifetime – with the important exception of his mother. For the twenty-three-year-old Pierre, with his driving need to prove his superiority, the personal and the political came dramatically together in his courtship of Thérèse.

He had encountered her in the early 1940s when he was a law student and she was preparing for her university entrance exams.

(She couldn't remember afterwards exactly which year, and he professed to have forgotten entirely, although he was still able when he was over seventy to recite the phone numbers of his friends of the period.) Thérèse did recall talking to Pierre first during a "musical evening" at his house. In Grace Trudeau's attempt to create an Outremont version of a Square Mile salon – that is, a fantasy of a fantasy of English life – she had bought an expensive phonograph with an automatic turntable so her children and their friends could hear recorded concerts of classical music. A few blocks away in wide-open wartime Montreal, country girls of sixteen who had come to the city to escape the poverty of the Gaspé and the Maurice were standing on street corners hoping to turn fifty-cent tricks with homesick farm boys from Saskatchewan waiting to be shipped out to the battlefields of Europe. Inside the Trudeaus' comfortable (though far from opulent) house, where the Victorian chairs with needlepoint seats were arranged in odd juxtaposition with the abstractions of the French painter Georges Braque, a young coterie was being exposed to the best of the world's music so that the deprivations of war – in this case the dearth of live performances by European musicians – would not keep them from culture. The guests Grace Trudeau encouraged her offspring to invite to these evenings were French Canadians she found acceptably *gentils*, a few from wealthy families linked to English capital, the rest the children of the aspiring professional and small-business class.[34]

Roger Rolland, who squired Thérèse to her first soirée at the Trudeaus', was the younger son of the family who owned the Rolland paper company, one of the rare French-Canadian entrepreneurial successes in the resource sector. He and Pierre had been fast friends since the day he had rolled up a two-dollar bill, thrust it into a roaring fire, and nonchalantly lit a cigarette from the spill. "He liked that a lot," Rolland remembered happily when he and Trudeau were old men. "It was the kind of extravagant gesture that reminded him of his father. From then on we tended to be outrageous together, getting into pranks that made our families furious."[35]

In addition to being rich and insouciant, Rolland was tall and handsome, a student of literature and a ladies' man. Escorting Thérèse Gouin, one of his sister's friends, chez Pierre, he ran straight into his friend's intense competitiveness. Trudeau was working hard to counter his shyness with girls by trying to turn himself into a Lothario, dressing to attract attention, and boasting of physical feats that matched his verbal audacities. One September he returned to class after paddling a canoe to James Bay, sporting a handsome beard that, ever determined to be *un original*, he shaved off as soon as his classmates started to copy him. At parties, he liked to be seen dancing with the best-looking, best-connected girls. And if they were the *petites amies* of men with whom he was rivalrous – well, so much the better. [36]

By any measure, Thérèse Gouin was a catch. Her distinguished family connections made her good looks and intelligence doubly attractive. Her great-grandfather and grandfather had been premiers of Quebec. Her father was a Liberal senator and her uncle a prominent Liberal dissident. The Gouins lived in a big house on McTavish Avenue, inside the Square Mile, where her father, Léon-Mercier Gouin, had settled so his children could be close to their grandfather, Sir Lomer Gouin, who owned a mansion on Peel Street. Thérèse had tobogganed on the McGill campus with English children, attended a bilingual convent, and made other Anglo friends at her family's summer place at Murray Bay. A young woman of demonstrable social conscience as well as good family – she was a volunteer in a church camp for poor children suffering from tuberculosis – she seemed eligible even to Grace Trudeau, who was notoriously sniffy about her son's female friends. [37]

Thérèse first became aware of Pierre's interest in her when he visited her while she was recuperating in hospital from an appendectomy. (Although he was charmingly attentive, he couldn't resist comparing her chemistry marks with his own. She had bested him by half a per cent.) The following summer he drove up to her church camp in the Laurentians. Their romance bloomed when she came back to town in the fall, and at Christmas they went carolling in Westmount with a group of their francophone friends to raise money for the camp. Trudeau rarely talked politics with Thérèse; they read poetry together instead. But he was interested in the discovery that the Gouins' Liberalism was different from the influence-peddling indulged in by his father's buddies and by their counterparts in the Liberal machine that Charlie Trudeau had routinely cursed on election nights.

What the Gouins practised was power politics at quite another level. And although the young Pierre Trudeau may have disdained the Liberal Party, with its compromising connections to English capital, as unworthy of respect from those who were familiar with the *pensées* of Montaigne and Montesquieu, he was intrigued by the political world whose workings he glimpsed at the Gouins' house.

Thérèse's maternal great-grandfather, Honoré Mercier, who embraced a *politique de grandeur* aimed at gaining recognition abroad for his province and himself, had been premier of Quebec from 1887 to 1891, the first Liberal to hold the job. His forceful assertion of provincial rights (he convened the first pan-Canadian premiers' conference) along with his government's heavy borrowing abroad to develop Quebec's infrastructure presaged positions taken by his Liberal successors for a century.[38]

Thérèse's paternal grandfather, Sir Lomer Gouin, was a brilliant young law student with "very advanced ideas for his times" in the anti-clerical *rouge* tradition when he attached himself to Mercier. With a shrewd eye to his own interests, Gouin modified his rhetoric, joined the older man's law firm, and married his daughter. When he became premier in 1905, his greatly tempered radicalism was expressed in progressive legislation that attempted to curb industrial abuses by raising the minimum age for factory employment from twelve to fourteen and imposing a fifty-eight-hour limit on the work week, laws that were seen as daring innovations. But when Gouin also tried to implement educational reforms that challenged the Roman Catholic church – establishing the business college Hautes études commerciales, for instance, or founding technical schools to prepare the work-force for industrial capitalism – he discovered he could make these modest moves only by caving in to the clerical hierarchy's insistence that it control the new institutions.[39]

Unlike his father-in-law, whose meteoric ministry was brought to an abrupt end by scandal, Gouin managed his political career prudently. As a consequence of his talent for accommodation, first with the Church and then with the English, he was knighted by George V, whose son Edward, Prince of Wales, dined at his Murray Bay house while visiting the dominion. The Gouins' household silver, a gift from the Crown, carried the engraved motto "Bien vouloir et faire." And despite his canny opposition to conscription during the Great War, Gouin was included in the imperial delegation to the Versailles peace conference in 1919. His *laissez-faire* approach to investment (based on the belief that the more capital Quebec could attract from abroad, the faster it would develop its natural resources) brought him the approval of Anglo-Montreal businessmen, who appointed him to their boards and made him their champion on the federal issue of tariff protection.[40]

Like Laurier before him, Gouin travelled the classic route from youthful radicalism to middle-aged power and prosperity. When Mackenzie King was elected prime minister in 1921 – just after Gouin handed the provincial party over to his chosen successor, Louis-Alexandre Taschereau, and then ran for office federally – Gouin's weight in the Montreal business community was such that King had little choice but to name him to his cabinet. Gouin had opposed King's candidacy for the leadership but had been unable to control the Quebec delegates who voted for King in large numbers because of his loyalty to Laurier. Now King co-opted Gouin in a move that was prototypical of his guileful efforts over the next twenty years to defuse dissension in Canada by inviting into the federal government powerful regional politicians representing major social forces. Gouin's presence at the cabinet table reassured Montreal business that King would heed its concerns. Later, he named Gouin lieutenant-governor of Quebec, but Sir Lomer died in full regalia on the steps of the Quebec City legislature in 1929, minutes before he was to preside for the first time over the ceremonial opening of the provincial parliament. He was buried with such imperialistic pomp that Thérèse Gouin remembered vividly sixty years later the huge Union Jack that draped the vice-regal coffin she was taken to view as a tremulous five-year-old.[41]

After Sir Lomer's death, the conflict between his sons, Léon-Mercier and Paul-Nérée Gouin, underscored the ideological confusion that roiled away inside the Quebec Liberal Party during the Depression and the early days of World War II. Paul, the younger son, identified with the party's nineteenth-century republican and autonomist tradition. He mounted Action libérale nationale, a protest movement that helped oust Taschereau's corrupt Liberal regime in 1936 in favour of Maurice Duplessis's Union Nationale. He was in turn squeezed out of political action by Duplessis only to resurface briefly in 1942 through his support of the Bloc populaire canadien and its nationalist campaign against the federal Liberals' military and social policies. In contrast, Léon-Mercier Gouin, Thérèse's father, was right of centre in domestic politics and internationalist in world affairs – a double estrangement from his brother, whose ideas he regarded as a veiled attack on their father's political legacy and an open rejection of his own commitment to the Allied effort against fascism.

In recognition of Léon-Mercier Gouin's loyalty and social prominence, he was named to the Senate in 1940, an appointment in keeping with the formula Mackenzie King had developed in his early years as Liberal leader. Its tenets went something like this: hold on by whatever means necessary to the fortress that Laurier had built in French Canada; express pro-British pieties while seeking greater autonomy from Westminster through American associations; cultivate connections in the agrarian west by co-opting populist spokesmen; recruit progressive intellectuals to the federal civil service and draw on their nation-building ideas; and straddle the political middle ground by impressing the business communities in Montreal and Toronto with the government's managerial competence and its responsiveness to their concerns while leaning slightly to the left on social issues in order to appeal to the electorate.

By the early 1940s, King's dream of reconciliation between industry and humanity had been distorted by the Depression's depredations and by the frustrations of brokerage politics – even though he claimed he had never lost sight of his goals. King had resisted the ideological lure of British Fabianism, with its advocacy of a socialist state to relieve the distress engendered by unregulated capitalism. But he had absorbed some of its important tenets, including the rejection of revolutionary change. "All in good time," an aphorism he used so incessantly that it drove his assistants to distraction, reflected his gradualist attitude to reform. Now in wartime, he craftily used the CCF's surging popularity and a parallel increase in labour militancy to push the businessmen in his caucus to accept the welfare program that his supporters in the extra-parliamentary National Liberal Federation endorsed as party policy at his behest in 1943.[42]

Pierre Trudeau's response to King's brand of accommodating Liberalism was ambivalent when he encountered it at the Gouins'. He behaved with studied formality in his face-to-face exchanges with the senator, while joking about Gouin's pomposities to his friends. He once turned up in McTavish Street bearing a roll of anti-conscription stickers and whispered to Thérèse that it might be fun to stick a couple of them surreptitiously on her father's back so the senator could serve as a walking billboard for ideas he cholerically opposed. Trudeau's friends told droll stories about Gouin's fierce pride in his connection with the Royal Canadian Air Force, in whose reserve he served during the war, and about his devotion to the Boy Scouts, whose uniform he often wore even when giving lectures in international jurisprudence to classes at the Université de Montréal law school. Despite his eccentricities, Gouin commanded the students' respect for his learning (he was a linguist as well as a legal scholar) and his reputation as a familiar of the English ascendancy. Mackenzie King had seen to it that he was made chairman of the Senate's international affairs committee, which meant he had a place, if only a minor one, in the tightly woven wartime governing élite in Ottawa.

Although he often professed scorn for the ideological impurities of Senator Gouin's large-L Liberalism – while shrewdly assessing its efficacy – there seemed to be little ambivalence in Pierre Trudeau's attitude to the senator's daughter. He enjoyed Thérèse's company, not least for the envious attention their partnership brought him from his peers. To their friends they seemed a golden couple, striking in appearance and fluent in both languages, their social and intellectual confidence proclaiming a new French-Canadian upper class easily the equal of the English in refinement and ability.

Throughout their five-year-long courtship, Trudeau continued to flirt with socialist ideas. But when Charles Lussier, who had formally joined the CCF partly at Trudeau's urging, asked him to buy a membership in the party, Trudeau answered dismissively, "I don't want to be a missionary all my life. When I join a party, it will be the Liberals." For Lussier, the remark was a revelation. It was as though Trudeau's close contacts with the Gouins had taught him that the Liberal Party was the only possible instrument for his ambitions, but he had not yet determined how or when he would play it. [43]

After his graduation, Trudeau practised law briefly as a junior in the downtown firm of Hyde & Ahern in an office that looked out on the Bank of Montreal's St. James Street head office. His experience there caused him to reject the traditional lawyer's path to political power – the route the Mercier-Gouins had followed for three generations – since it demanded cultivating patronage-besotted party organizers and kowtowing to swollen-headed Anglo businessmen. Having consulted elders as diverse in age and predisposition as Henri Bourassa, the pan-Canadian nationalist, and André Laurendeau, the Bloc populaire politician, anti-conscriptionist, and former editor of *L'Action nationale*, he decided he needed to learn something of modern social science, particularly economics, and to extend his knowledge of liberal thought, still largely untaught in Quebec, which he had come to believe was what gave the English their edge. Mackenzie King had shone at the University of Chicago and at Harvard. Léon-Mercier Gouin had studied at Oxford. Perhaps Pierre Trudeau should also seek an advanced degree abroad, then come home to Montreal to marry Thérèse, teach at the university, and launch his political career from the high ground of academe.[44]

With the English universities still inaccessible because of the war, it was to Harvard that Trudeau repaired in 1944, along with several other intellectually gifted French Canadians of his generation. They were among the first of their compatriots to study abroad not as seminarians under the control of the Church but as laymen, the avant-garde of the post-war cohort that was to modernize Quebec. Determined to excel at graduate work in the United States, Trudeau was apparently confident that he could absorb readily whatever its greatest university had to offer in the fields of economics and political science. But once he took his place among the select few admitted to Harvard to study with some of the most important scholars in the West, his Montreal persona as a swashbuckling, self-directed, would-be Laurier was dealt a serious blow.

The American graduate students he had been conditioned to think of as the product of a heretical, money-grubbing society turned out to be better trained than he was, despite his classical education. The combined legacy of his mother's English-inspired gentility and his father's you-can-do-it! spirit, which had inflated him at home, did not prevent him now from feeling like just another foreigner overwhelmed by his first encounter with an increasingly powerful America in the heady early days of its military and economic dominance and its politically effective New Deal. In response, he holed up in his room at Perkins Hall, refusing to answer the door, working ceaselessly to master the mysteries of economics and to cope with the heavy readings and essay assignments prescribed by his professors in comparative government and political philosophy.[45]

The philosophical system he absorbed at Harvard, through reading such texts as George Sabine's magisterial *History of Political Theory*, was an evolving liberalism that stood on the shoulders of the giants of English political thought – Hobbes and Locke, Bentham and Mill – and that had reached its apogee in late nineteenth-century England. He was also greatly stimulated by the ideas of Louis Hartz, a fellow graduate student, who was shortly to publish landmark analyses of American liberalism. Little of what he read bore directly on Canadian Liberalism, but studying Gladstone's nineteenth-century crusades to right British society's ancient wrongs provided a framework in which to place Laurier's reformist zeal; and understanding T.H. Greene's doctrine that liberty is impossible without an active state ready to provide a reasonable degree of security against the abuses caused by industrialism gave him an intellectual context for Mackenzie King's recently formulated unemployment insurance and family allowance policies. Other than discussing issues of the day with his fellow graduate students over hasty meals in cafeterias and coffee shops – which always took second place to exchanging survival strategies for their demanding courses – Pierre had little contact with the American socio-political world beyond the confines of Harvard's fabled Yard.[46]

To most of the handful of American and English-Canadian graduate students who encountered Trudeau in his Harvard years, he appeared intensely intelligent but tentative, as though he were feeling his way. "I thought he was cultured and sensitive, the kind of other-worldly person you would have never expected to go into politics," the American Sovietologist Adam Ulam remembered. To the American political scientist John Reshetar, who became a close friend, he confided that his interest went beyond the concepts of liberal political theory to a political career. A book that impressed him deeply was *Capitalism, Socialism and Democracy*, the bold analysis made by their economics professor, Joseph Schumpeter, who argued that capitalism was doomed to self-destruct and to be replaced by socialism.[47]

Outside classes, Trudeau was so self-effacing as to be almost invisible, the antithesis of the opinionated law student his friends had looked up to in Montreal. Far from being seen as a Latin lover or a daring athlete or a swaggerer with a great destiny, he was dismissed by the men in Eliot House, a socially superior residence to his, as probably still a virgin and certainly no threat to them, either socially or intellectually. Although some of his classmates' dates found him intriguingly "foreign," with his beret and the French cadence still detectable in his English speech, he showed little interest in American women. He was still in love with Thérèse, who was studying psychology at the Université de Montréal. Only at the occasional party held by the small French-Canadian Harvard contingent did Trudeau display the old panache, describing his efforts to improve his Spanish by lunching with Latin American students; confidently offering Freudian interpretations of his friends' dreams; and discussing his plans for a year in Paris that he and Roger Rolland had promised themselves. Once he passed the oral examinations for the Harvard doctorate, he decided not to pursue a thesis but to settle for a master's degree. He received his Harvard AM on June 6, 1946, standing on the stage with John Reshetar, directly opposite General Dwight D. Eisenhower, who was there to receive an honorary doctorate on this, the second anniversary of D-Day.[48]

Trudeau did move on to Paris after he left behind the Harvard Yard. But he stayed only eight months, auditing courses at the École libre des sciences politiques. Sharing student digs with the ebullient Rolland did not keep Trudeau's diligent side from dominating his days. He made a study plan at the beginning of each week and on Saturdays checked to make sure that he had met his objectives, which included sending home periodically an article for Montreal's Liberal newspaper, Le Canada. He was disappointed by the "reactionary bourgeois" students at Sciences politiques, and by the quality of the courses he sampled there. Far more stimulating were the public lectures given by some of the great intellectuals of post-war France. The most compelling figures Trudeau encountered were the Catholic thinkers Étienne Gilson and Emmanuel Mounier, the

Christian existentialist editor of the review *Esprit*, whose personalist ideas went beyond textbook liberalism to a call for individuals to commit themselves to social action. Trudeau was bold enough to seek an interview with Mounier and to stop the great man when they met by chance on the Boulevard Saint-Michel in order to introduce him to a Montreal acquaintance and fellow student, Vianney Décarie. Unknown to either of them at the time, Décarie was soon to play as significant a role in Trudeau's private life as Mounier would in his philosophical and political development.[49]

By all accounts, Trudeau suffered the worst psychic shock of his young manhood when Thérèse Gouin broke off her relationship with him in the summer of 1947. She married Vianney Décarie eighteen months later amid continuing speculation among their friends about her reasons for jilting Pierre. For years it had seemed a foregone conclusion that Pierre and Thérèse would marry and that she was the perfect mate for an aspiring prime minister.

The problem with this *mise-en-scène* was that the leading lady rejected her role. During his years at graduate school, Pierre had changed. He had written her tortured letters describing his guilt about the privileges his money had brought him and his embarrassment at having missed the significance of World War II as a fight against fascism. In discussions of their future life, he began to stress that if he were to have a great political career, she would have to be "une femme de César" – a wife of irreproachable demeanour, who would devote herself to her husband, manage his household affairs prudently, and raise his children wisely. Not only was the twenty-one-year-old Thérèse disdainful of domesticity – having grown up in a house where such tasks were attended to by a maid, a cook, and a chauffeur – she had career ambitions of her own that went beyond what Pierre considered seemly in a woman. Her mother had been a dramaturge whose work had been produced in Paris; she herself was determined to acquire postgraduate degrees in psychology. After several tense exchanges, she concluded that if she and Pierre were to marry, they would suffer marital misery of a monumental order, "un grand malheur," as she put it.[50]

After spending a post-Paris summer at home in Montreal griev-
ing over his loss, Trudeau decided to continue his studies in London.
Historic change was taking place there as a result of the Labour government's move to establish a welfare state. Registering at the London School of Economics in the autumn of 1947 for *ad hoc* research
and study – which meant that he was not required to sit examinations for a specific degree – he attached himself to Harold Laski, the
famous political theorist. By this time, the peppery champion of
trade unionism and anti-imperialism was a political insider, still battling in the name of democracy to force the Labourite prime minister, Clement Attlee, to stick to his party's socialist program, in
whose formulation Laski had been so instrumental. Trudeau was
later to write that Laski's office "was always open to those who were
hungry and thirsty for justice," particularly students from Britain's
former colonies, many of whom were spellbound by the old radical's wit and daring. [51]

Trudeau himself was touched less by Laski's views on the forms
of social democracy than by the liberal values that underlay them.
Following the decline of the British Liberal Party, its powerful current of reform liberalism, which had endorsed the activist state to
remedy industrialism's evils, had been subsumed in Labour Party
ideology. Trudeau found that Laski's "inquisitive mind . . . forced me
to search deeper and deeper for the answers to social philosophy"
and that observing English politics at first hand was "excellent training," as he wrote to a friend, which made him feel impatient "to get
home and get into it [politics]" since he found himself "more and
more preoccupied with problems of authority, obedience, the foundations of law, etc." [52]

As the months wore on, he was seen only occasionally at the LSE
and made even less of an impact than he had at Harvard. None of his
fellow Commonwealth students – who included the political scientists Rufus Davis and Paul Fox, the legal scholar John McNair, and
the economist Morris Miller – remembered him as being socially or
politically active. Casual conversations caused Miller to believe that

Trudeau was inquisitive about, rather than a convert to, the left. Another Canadian studying at the LSE at the time, the political scientist Robert McKenzie, remembered Trudeau being so contemptuous of parlour pinks that he gave the impression he was a man of the left. But Trudeau didn't attend any of the leftist rallies Miller went to enthusiastically; and in the impassioned debates with Labour ministers that were a regular feature of LSE life, Trudeau's voice was never heard. [53]

Forty years afterwards, Ralph Miliband, one of Laski's teaching assistants and later an important Marxist scholar, could not recall meeting Trudeau at the LSE, although Morris Miller remembered Trudeau contending effectively with Miliband in a Laski seminar. When Trudeau failed to turn up in the graduate common room, the standing joke among his fellow Canadians was that he must be off to Paris on his big scarlet Harley-Davidson, a prospect that made them wildly envious, living as they were on tight budgets in the dingy digs available to students in austerity-locked London. Trudeau chummed with the only other French Canadian in the school, Georges Charpentier, who intended to become a diplomat, and they were seen occasionally at large receptions at the Canadian High Commission in Trafalgar Square. (Student penury was such that when an LSE student from Toronto turned up at a Canada House gathering dressed in a morning coat, he was asked how he could afford to play the toff. "I can't," he responded. "I got married this afternoon. The suit is rented from Moss Bros. And I'm counting on turning this party into a free reception for my bride and the witnesses at our wedding.") [54]

None of the English-Canadian students was close enough to Trudeau to know that he lived in a comfortable flat in Kensington or to guess that he had political ambitions. To Paul Fox, who as a professor of political science was to prove an astute professional observer of the motivations of public men, and his wife, Joan Fox, who was later a film critic in Toronto, Trudeau seemed like "a young nobleman on a Grand Tour, very intelligent but quite disengaged," a demeanour that effectively disguised his concern about what to do with his life now that the future he had planned with Thérèse was no longer possible. [55]

"God only knows what I will be doing next year: possibly pushing a pen in some newspaper office! Or correcting exams . . . the great ahead is a complete mystery, and I enjoy the feeling," he wrote to a friend from London. He sent long letters to Andrée Désautels, a lively young Montrealer studying music in Paris whose mother was a close friend of Grace Trudeau's. They discussed psychology texts he was reading and made arrangements to travel together the following summer in France and Spain, the first lap of a round-the-world trip Trudeau had decided to embark on after the Hilary term ended in July – a last fling before facing up to the need to find gainful employment in Canada. [56]

His years abroad, coupled with his failed romance, changed Trudeau's behaviour significantly and caused him to develop a double mask. With his French-Canadian comrades, he continued to act the swashbuckling hero that he had yearned to become since his schooldays, in the style of the French romantic Cyrano de Bergerac, an audacious adventurer engaged with great ideas and great events, beholden to no one, free to cock his hat at any man, to travel any road under the sun and climb every mountain all alone. But when functioning in English he was watchful and reticent about expressing his beliefs or describing his ambitions. As an unusually privileged member of a still deeply colonized society, he was turning himself into a post-colonial man who rejected British suzerainty – and the inferiority it evoked in its colonials – while appropriating some of its most compelling ideas. [57]

# CHAPTER 2

# A Large-L Liberal Indoctrination

In the process of learning the principles of liberal political theory at Harvard and observing their application in Labourite London, Trudeau had absorbed the post-war style of the trans-Atlantic English-speaking governing élites. A combination of Fabian theory, Oxbridge condescension, and Bloomsbury aestheticism – expressed as a concern for the welfare of "the people" combined with a disdain for their persons – it had adherents in Washington's State Department and Ottawa's External Affairs as well as at the British Foreign Office. [1]

Trudeau had witnessed this generation taking charge in London as the Empire was dismantled, the British class system jolted, and the interventionist state established. Mother England may have been superseded by the United States as the ascendant international power, but the English were comforting themselves with the idea that they could play Greeks to the Americans' Romans – civilized men from an ancient culture influencing the new vulgarians in a rising empire that derived at least part of its strength from their own. [2]

Having learned from these élitist reformers to articulate the axioms of modern government that expressed the left-liberal values he admired, Trudeau was ready for his second encounter with the English in his own country – this time in their role as its Liberal governors. After considering his career options, he had seized on Ottawa as the best place to further his ambitions, and in September 1949 he began work there as a policy analyst in the Privy Council

Office. That the job and the city were not entirely to his taste was reflected in a sardonic card he sent an old friend that Christmas, saying, "The worst has happened to me. I am a civil servant. But I find working for the Cabinet Secretariat very fascinating – especially [when I am] on holiday."[3]

Despite the post-war hustle that gripped the new Liberal government of Louis St. Laurent, Ottawa still bore the dismal air of a British colonial outpost grafted on a lumber town in the bush. Sprawling on the Ontario side of the Ottawa River, criss-crossed with railway tracks, blighted by wartime temporary buildings, it was a cultural wasteland compared with Montreal, let alone the great world cities Trudeau's travels had taught him to savour. Its only architectural glories were the half-dozen government buildings strung out along Wellington Street to the west of the Rideau Canal. Facing these sober neo-Gothic structures were the neo-Federalist U.S. Embassy, the Greek revivalist Bank of Montreal, and the British imperialist Rideau Club, where the local sahibs had enjoyed for nearly eighty years the solace of gin-and-it served under the awnings on the upstairs veranda in summer, and the indoor comforts of oysters, claret, and the London *Times* during the frigid rest of the year.[4]

Though relics from the pre-war period were still to be found there rumbling away at each other from the safety of green leather chairs in the lounge, the club was now more than a refuge for old fogeys, as Trudeau soon found out. It had become the place where a score or so of extraordinarily vital public servants had taken to meeting over lunch or drinks to discuss the concerns of the day and Canada's prospects in the coming decade.[5]

Afterwards, when their power was ebbing away, this group became known as the Ottawa Men or the mandarinate. In 1949 they were still in their vibrant middle age, a group of like-minded intellectuals, most of whom had been educated on the scholarships available to British colonials at Oxford or Cambridge between the wars. They had been recruited by Mackenzie King into the public service when they were unable to find more suitable jobs in the universities or more remunerative ones in business. Many of them had been greatly influenced in the 1930s by the social-democratic ideas of their radical contemporaries, the left-wing academics and political activists whose own educations in England had turned them into anglicized anglophobes and caused them to found, in the early 1930s, the League for Social Reconstruction, a Canadian version of the Fabian Society, and to take part in the formation of the CCF, a political movement partly modelled on the Labour Party. They saw themselves as Canadian nationalists eager to escape British imperialism – while benefitting from the newly formed British Commonwealth's counter-balancing effect on Canada's American relationship.[6]

By the time Trudeau arrived in Ottawa, world events and their own success had modified the mandarinate's views. Between 1939 and 1945, they had experienced the heady pleasures of running what was temporarily a quasi-socialist state through making common cause with the Liberal cabinet and a handful of prominent businessmen who came to the capital for the duration. Proximity, patriotism, and a sense of mission had produced the Anglo-Canadian consociational élites that were to dominate post-war Canada. Proud of the industrialization stimulated through military effort, this close-knit group had carefully considered how the post-war economy should be run in order to avoid a new depression. Although some of its members leaned to the left (the civil servants) and some to the right (the businessmen), and some clung to the magic middle (the Liberal politicians), they had established in the crucible of their intense wartime collaboration a set of goals for Canada to which they could all subscribe.[7]

The mandarins had become so influential with Liberal politicians (and by extension with their business allies, who had returned to entrepreneurial pursuits) that in the years after the war, their ideas were the main engine driving government policy. It was their optimistic conviction that Canada's ordeal by fire had turned the old dominion into a mature nation, no longer dominated by Britain, no longer fearful of annexation by the United States. Now more capitalist than socialist, they were happy to auction off the wartime Crown corporations the government had created so that businessmen regardless of nationality could acquire from the public domain at liquidation-sale prices the productive assets with which to re-create a free-enterprise economy in Canada. As centralists, they still expected to set the economy's overall direction. But they realized that in order to ward off labour unrest – and a further surge of CCF strength – trade unionists would have to be given the protection of collective bargaining rights and all working people social welfare benefits.[8]

Having worked in close collaboration with their British and American counterparts during the war and its immediate aftermath, they believed that Canada could adapt to its new circumstances the best aspects of both mentor nations – the orderliness of the British tradition and the energetic openness of the American progressive spirit – and function as an effective new world power running its own affairs according to modern principles. Reduced to their essence, these principles were rhetorical Keynesianism in economic matters and anti-communist internationalism in foreign affairs.[9]

For the mandarinate, Canada's post-war challenge was not how to resist U.S. domination on the continent but how to cajole the Americans out of sinking back into their instinctual isolationism and into accepting their responsibilities as the world's new hegemonic power. To this end, several important Ottawa Men had recently engrossed themselves in helping their American counterparts build an organizational framework for a reconstructed international order. They were present at the creation of the United Nations, the International Monetary Fund, and the World Bank, plus a host of more specialized organizations to monitor agriculture, culture, health, and even civil aviation and radio transmission. With Canada having emerged from the war as the third- or fourth-largest military and economic power of the time, these officials saw themselves as important players in what was fast becoming a desperate struggle to bolster liberal democracy against the spread of communism on a global basis.[10]

When it came to reviving commerce, Canada supported liberalized tariff reduction under the newly established General Agreement on Tariffs and Trade while expecting to re-establish the pre-war North Atlantic trading triangle. But given a debilitated Britain's failure to restore the pound as a convertible currency in 1947, it became obvious Canada could no longer count on selling more to the U.K. than it bought in order to balance its trading books, despite the huge financial aid it had given the mother country. It would have to turn south and, by exporting more staple commodities, seek to offset its mounting trade deficit in American consumer goods.[11]

This prospect gave the mandarins no pain. Indeed, it scarcely gave them pause. British jingoism was still being expressed nostalgically out there in the old dominion from which they had sprung. But in post-war Liberal Ottawa, pro-Americanism was seen as an expression of Canada's new modernity, confidence, and vitality. Compared with the feelings of resentment aroused by the British, who remained insufferably condescending towards their former colonials, the Americans generated considerably more warmth and considerably less suspicion among the mandarins. They were democrats, not imperialists; denizens of the forward-looking new world, not the backward-turning old; co-operative, not aggressive; progressive risk-takers, not stuffy naysayers. In short, the best of all possible friends and allies for a young country like Canada now beginning to come into its own.

The U.S. was also viewed in Ottawa as disturbingly protectionist, having maintained tariffs against products other than vital resources at such a high level that Canada could not reasonably expect to find an outlet for its manufactured goods south of the border, the only external market in a war-shattered globe that held out a viable prospect for Canadian producers of finished goods. With that concern in mind a few officials had proceeded secretly in 1948 to try to negotiate a reciprocal free-trade treaty with their counterparts in Washington, a deal that had been scotched by Mackenzie King, in the penultimate moment of his long prime ministerial career.[12]

King's new-found qualms about the implications of continental integration – he saw the Americans as "seeking to make this Continent one" and wanting to control "all of North America" – were not shared by his designated successor, Louis St. Laurent. A Quebec City lawyer who had been persuaded to join King's cabinet in the early days of the war, St. Laurent was something of a hero to the wartime consociational élite by the time he succeeded King in 1948. He could be readily idealized by go-ahead businessmen as an unflappable bilingual lawyer who had served business on both sides of the border with courtly ease as a go-between with governments; by intellectual bureaucrats as the even-tempered legal counsel to the Rowell-Sirois royal commission in the 1930s and then the senior cabinet minister in King's cabinets who was most amenable to their ideas; and by Liberal politicians as an efficient administrator who also had electoral appeal in both English Canada and Quebec as a result of his avuncular demeanour. [13]

With St. Laurent ensconced in office, continentalist economic views were the accepted Liberal wisdom. For the most ebullient of St. Laurent's ministers, the American-born C.D. Howe, there never had been any problem: if the country was to thrive, Ottawa needed an economic development strategy geared to the requirements of business. It was clear to him as minister of trade and commerce that, with or without free trade, Canada needed American capital if it was to accelerate the exploitation of its staple resources, whose market in the rearming U.S. economy was sufficiently secure to ensure continuing growth. If U.S. companies wanted to come north to sink wells, dig mines, or cut timber, so much the better: their investment would provide a captive market in their own downstream operations south of the border. If they wanted to move into Canada's tariff-protected market by taking over local companies or establishing branch plants to satisfy the newly prosperous Canadians' apparently insatiable hunger for consumer goods, that was fine too: American investors would bring the benefits of their managerial and technological know-how and ease the pressure on the Canadian balance of payments by substituting local production for imports. [14]

Unlike their Swedish or Japanese counterparts – who were encouraging their nationally owned industries to develop sophisticated, competitive products to sell internationally – the Canadian mandarins felt the start-up costs required to foster a balanced national economy that could compete on its own in world markets were too great to contemplate. Blessed with proximity to the post-war world's most powerful capital market and only industrial giant, they were content to concentrate on the lesser goal of responding to forces driving the American economy by shipping off cheap resources in their unprocessed form. In their eyes, the two economies were complementary rather than competitive, even though the redoubtable University of Toronto political economist Harold Innis had warned twenty years earlier that the U.S. and Canada were turning into Siamese twins in this staples dependency – as he put it, "a very large one linked to a very small one," the policies of the smaller being more and more determined by those of the larger.[15]

Liberal Ottawa was unmoved by Innis's foreboding since most post-war economic analysts believed that in due course a more mature Canadian economy would become better balanced and less dependent. U.S. industrial prosperity was priming the Canadian economic pump with its vigorous demand for iron, pulp and paper, and uranium. U.S. rearmament in the face of the Soviet armed bloc reactivated Canadian military suppliers' hopes for Pentagon contracts. The Cold War, like the hot war that preceded it, was good for continentalism. Canada's assignment of air and land forces to Europe as its contribution to the newly formed North Atlantic Treaty Organization, ostensibly a sign of the country's commitment to the allied struggle against world communism, really meant a commitment to strategic and economic integration in the U.S. war machine.[16]

Of far greater concern in Liberal Ottawa than any fears about staples dependency or continental military integration was how to cope with the oscillations of the business cycle that many feared would repeat the boom-and-bust experience that followed World War I. To mitigate these cyclical extremes, the mandarins and their ministers were relying on the teachings of the liberal economist John Maynard Keynes, whose ideas had captivated them for more than a decade. Keynes was to be far more influential in Canada's development than any home-grown intellectual, however brilliant and pertinent his perceptions. [17]

Reflecting in King's College, Cambridge, during the Depression on how politicians were unwittingly aggravating their populations' hardships by cutting back spending in an effort to balance budgets, Keynes had proclaimed that governments could and should play an active role in modifying the violent swings of the capitalist cycle. In depressed phases, they could incur budgetary deficits by increasing government spending – on infrastructure, for instance, or welfare payments – and expanding aggregate demand in order to encourage entrepreneurs to invest. In boom times, they could raise taxes. This would restrain entrepreneurs' investment and, at the same time, accumulate surpluses to pay down the public debt that had built up in the bad times. [18]

Once these ideas had been propounded in Britain, they were seen by some in the United States as dazzling in their insight, especially by the Harvard economist Seymour Harris. One of his graduate students, a Canadian named Robert Bryce, had sat at the great Keynes's feet in Cambridge and assumed the role of his apostle at Harvard before taking the gospel to the Finance Department in Ottawa in 1938. [19]

By the time Trudeau became a public servant a decade later, versions of Keynes's theories had been taken up by policy-makers in all advanced capitalist countries. "Keynesianism" provided a rationale to justify the abandonment by the federal government of the dominant position assumed under the demands of wartime economic planning, since it prescribed that the private sector should be left largely free of state interference at the micro-level of business decisions. At the same time, Keynesianism preserved for Ottawa's bureaucrats the vital function of macro-economic fine-tuning and gave legitimacy to extending welfare through universal state programs to buttress education and medical facilities and provide assistance to the poor and to pensioners.[20]

For their part, capitalists in manufacturing and the resource sector could now support the expansion of social security because the tax system would redistribute some of the rents collected from the massive commodity exports into the hands of labour, which would, in turn, purchase their industries' products and so maintain consumer demand. Businessmen could even envisage entering into collective bargaining with unions for the kind of higher wages and better working conditions they had formerly repudiated when labour leaders had demanded them in the name of social justice. Their balance sheets would benefit from social peace, and their increased costs would be offset by increased sales, which would justify investing in more efficient technology. The Canadian labour movement, dominated by American business-union ideology, was content to accept the immediate gains of increased material benefits instead of demanding greater power in the country's decision-making institutions. For the élites in post-war democracies, worried about the rise of communism but cognizant of the miseries that unbridled capitalism had caused, "Keynes had a solution without a revolution," as the Harvard economist John Kenneth Galbraith reflected. "Our pleasant world would remain, the unemployment and suffering would go. It seemed a miracle."[21]

None of this positive thinking was alien to the thirty-year-old Pierre Trudeau labouring as a policy analyst in the PCO in 1949. For him these were the most compelling of the political-economy ideas he had spent his years abroad absorbing. Despite the calumnies put about later by his ecclesiastical and political detractors in Quebec, Trudeau was not a communist seeking to overthrow the state when he returned to Canada. He was not even much of a socialist. His postgraduate education had turned him into a left-leaning liberal internationalist who believed that nationalism was the chief cause of the horrific war that had just been fought against fascism and that the territorial nation-state was an obsolescent, if regrettably persistent, reality. Future world crises would be avoided and future prosperity achieved through international economic co-ordination and careful management of national economies by technocrats trained in Keynesian principles.

Before he took the PCO position, Trudeau had been interviewed for a job by Robert Bryce, then the assistant deputy minister in Finance, on the strength of "his Harvard training and his reputation as a very able man," as Bryce put it decades later. "French Canadians [wanting to be public servants] were scarce in those days if they were of good quality, and Trudeau's qualifications were the same as my own." In other words, they had both been trained as Keynesians, even though a decade – and a world war – separated their Harvard experiences. [22]

Trudeau's Harvard transcript showed that in addition to Joseph Schumpeter, he had studied with Alvin Hansen, the most influential American apostle of Keynes and an adviser to American and Canadian governments, and with Wassily Leontief, the future Nobel Prize laureate, as well as old-school economists such as the conservative J.H. Williams, whose hostility to government intervention in the economy ran directly counter to Keynesianism, and Gottfried Haberler. They were all scholars whose work was sufficiently familiar to Bryce that, sight unseen, their former student was deemed capable of comprehending the malevolent as well as the benevolent gods in the Keynesian pantheon. [23]

During their interview, Bryce found Trudeau capable of holding his own in discussing economic issues and decided he would make a valuable addition to his small team of high-powered analysts in Finance. To his surprise – since the job was considered a plum – Trudeau turned him down, giving the impression that he thought the work would prove dull and that he would find it more interesting to be closer to the centre of government in the PCO, which served as the cabinet secretariat and was intertwined with the Prime Minister's Office.

It was a decision that was revealing of Trudeau's character and prophetic of his approach to government. Finance was the real centre of power in Louis St. Laurent's Ottawa. Its officials (in concert with their minister, Douglas Abbott, who represented Anglo-Montreal capital in cabinet) made economic policy without much interference from other bureaucrats or ministers. Had Trudeau really wanted to know how economic theory connected with government practice, working under Bryce's tutelage would have been the best place to begin. He could have gained a detailed knowledge of the broad spectrum of government activity since Bryce was also secretary to the Treasury Board and had a mandate to vet all government expenditures. Plain in physique and calm in manner, Bryce was the most effective public servant in Ottawa. But he was by no means a charismatic figure. His power derived from his job and his acute intelligence, and his way of wielding it was discreet. In eschewing Bryce's offer in favour of the PCO, Trudeau was displaying his distaste for humdrum routine and his attraction to dramatic action.

It was not that he was afraid of hard work. For years he had displayed a capacity for disciplined concentration that confounded his peers. (During one law-school exam period, he had shaved his head so he would not be tempted to abandon his studies to attend a party at the Gouins' house.) Certainly he had the intellectual capacity to become the first French-Canadian clerk of the Privy Council or deputy minister of finance. But he did not have the temperament. An observer who knew the mandarinate well once wrote that for a great public servant the ideal epitaph would read, "He served his minister well." The day-after-day effacement of self, immersion in detail, and devotion to the cause of one's political masters that were required to earn that accolade were antithetical to Trudeau and his self-absorbed search for a heroic mission.[24]

He was attracted instead to St. Laurent's entourage in the East

Block, where the Privy Council Office had recently come under the direction of a new clerk, Norman Robertson, the great romantic figure of the mandarinate era. Robertson was a product of External Affairs, now approaching the zenith of its Cold War glory under the direction of his former colleague and rival, Mike Pearson, who had recently become the department's minister. Robertson had just returned to Ottawa from three years in London as head of the Canadian high commission in Trafalgar Square, where Trudeau had seen him displaying his aplomb in striped pants and morning coat.[25]

The new clerk was given to elliptical language, mannered poses, and cultivated eccentricity in dress, in the manner of the British public servants he had resented and emulated for thirty years. (Robertson wore a black trilby and a cape, not unlike the costume Trudeau made famous twenty years later.) In taking the clerk's job he was very much in the British tradition of the brilliant generalist intellectual plucked from Foreign Office (read External) at apogee of substantial career to keep the occupant of No. 10 (read 24 Sussex) on the right course and thus gain for himself an important place in history.[26]

For the young Trudeau the possibility of observing the interaction between the nation's most prominent public servant and its most powerful politician – the "elbow" of cabinet government, as Sir Ivor Jennings described the relationship – must have been irresistible. If Robertson and Pearson could start out as desk officers seconded from External to the PCO and eventually be whisked away to the capitals of the world as major players in international negotiations (and in Pearson's case be parachuted into a safe Liberal riding and given a cabinet post without having to stoop to petty politics), then maybe Pierre Trudeau could too.

Involvement in St. Laurent's PCO did not work out in the way they had expected, for either Trudeau or the man he chose as mentor. Robertson soon discovered that for him there was "nothing much to do" as clerk. The public servant who pulled the prime minister's strings was John Wesley (Jack) Pickersgill, who was St.

Laurent's chief adviser and ran his prime ministerial office. Pickersgill, too, had been seconded from External. But his governmental
experience involved domestic rather than foreign intrigue, and his
attraction was not to the United Kingdom but to the United States.
From 1937 to 1948 he had served as Mackenzie King's fixer. Aided
by a native shrewdness, already evident when he was growing up as a
widowed schoolteacher's son in rural Manitoba, he had been able to
learn from the grand master of Canadian politics much of what
there was to know about keeping a fractious federation together.
Pickersgill understood better than most members of the mandarinate – and certainly far better then Norman Robertson – what
made Canada tick. And St. Laurent relied on his strategic advice
concerning broad national questions as well as on his tactical suggestions for managing Parliament and the Liberal Party.[27]

Pierre Trudeau soon found that life for a junior official in Pickersgill's orbit was deeply disappointing. Beavering away in an attic
office under the cautious direction of Gordon Robertson, another
External Affairs officer on secondment, turned out to be as humdrum as he had feared the job in Finance might prove. "You have to
remember I was a young guy," Trudeau said later. "They gave me
things that were left over, jobs the more senior policy analysts didn't
have time for. I acted as secretary to the Air Transport Board, for
instance. And I prepared a fifty-page list of federal-provincial agreements, establishing that there was an enormous amount of federal-
provincial co-operation, a terrific overlap between jurisdictions,
rather than watertight compartments. I was also involved in
dominion-provincial conferences at a very low level, certainly not
the strategic thinking level."[28]

Long days in the bat-infested attic of the East Block of the Parliament Buildings, sharing a phone with a fellow French Canadian,
eating lunch at his old wooden desk in the deep chill of winter or on
the lawn outside in the short steamy summer, outings at a downtown bowling alley with the clerical staff, swimming laps in the
Château Laurier's Art Deco pool in the late day, and walking home
at dusk to a room in shabby Sandy Hill did not add up to the career

of his dreams. In this grey town where English mores reigned supreme, Trudeau rarely displayed his exhibitionist's flair, lest he be seen as "unsound," mandarinate code for "overly emotional," an attitude widely attributed to French Canadians, who were scarcely visible in the upper echelons of Ottawa life.[29]

St. Laurent was not turning out to be a Laurier in modern dress, as Trudeau had hoped he might when he was elected leader of the Liberal Party in 1948. Burdened by office, he had become a sad old man, prone to depression and captive to his cabinet and the astute bureaucrats who served it. He had always been bored by party politics, and under his aegis, the Liberal Party hierarchy grew increasingly insensitive to the electorate. Mackenzie King had kept it in a state of alert by means of his uncanny political antennae and his diligent correspondence with Liberals around the country. But now its regional fiefdoms were controlled almost exclusively by cabinet ministers who looked after the dispensation of patronage and the selection of candidates and were mostly indifferent to broader issues of ideology and national development and given to leaving the running of their departments to their trusty deputy ministers. The fusion of the Liberal Party with the Canadian state and the business community was almost taken for granted. Few Liberals bothered to object to the fact that Cockfield, Brown, the government's advertising agency, paid the salary of the party's national director, for instance, or that its fundraising efforts consisted of a systematic dunning of companies that secured government contracts to supply weapons or build infrastructure projects such as the Trans-Canada Highway or the St. Lawrence Seaway.[30]

English-Canadian Liberal MPs were kept in line with promises of advancement, and Quebec Liberal MPs were routinely treated as though they were little more than "trained donkeys," in Trudeau's withering phrase, who could be counted on to vote the way the Liberal whips directed. The capital's indigenous French-Canadian population worked at menial service tasks and were scorned for speaking Quebec French, which the mandarins regarded as an uncivilized backwoods dialect they wouldn't be caught dead under-standing, let alone repeating. (The fact that few of the top public ser-vants could speak French of any flavour did not deter their snobbery. Pickersgill was a rare exception. As a teenager, he had gained a rough command of French from a Franco-Manitoban woman who gave him informal lessons in exchange for milk from his family's cow. Even the great internationalists Robertson and Pearson had never acquired fluency in the language of diplomacy. And despite St. Laurent's presence at the apex of power, the East Block was still a unilingual workplace, right down to briefing notes and way signs.)[31]

In this general atmosphere, French-Canadian public servants, no matter how well educated or fluently bilingual, found that their chances of being admitted to the mandarinate's inner circle were limited. They were subtly ghettoized and given to making wry jokes in private about their lot. Trudeau was caught in an ethnic dilemma. He had come to Ottawa determined to assert his pres-ence as an educated internationalist, only to find a group of gover-nors still too parochially imperialist in their world-view to accept French Canadians as their equals and a group of his confrères still too meekly colonialist to make demands on their own behalf. Despite his own impressive qualifications, senior public servants did not trouble themselves unduly about his personal welfare or career development. (Afterwards, when Trudeau became prime minister, Pickersgill liked to say that he had never even noticed his presence on the small PCO staff.) Younger Anglo public servants, with educations and interests similar to his, men like Fred Gibson and Douglas LePan, remembered only the most superficial of encounters with him.[32]

Trudeau attempted to rouse to political consciousness some of the French-speaking lawyers in the Justice Department on the rare occasions when they met for lunch at Madame Burger's in Hull or at the Canton Inn in Chinatown, hang-outs they preferred to the Château Laurier cafeteria, where the English-speaking aspirants to the mandarinate gathered. He tried out on them the activist rhetoric he was learning through his weekend meetings with personalist Catholics in Montreal, who were involved in the crusade to make Quebec more democratic through founding the magazine *Cité libre*, modelled on Mounier's Paris journal, *Esprit*. But his Ottawa acquaintances, rendered docile by their conditioning and their career hopes, were largely unresponsive. Trudeau could afford to talk about Laski and Mounier, and about liberty, democracy, and the perfidies of Maurice Duplessis, the premier of Quebec, and his involvement with the repressive ultramontane elements in the Church. He had the theoretical education and – far more important – the financial security to indulge in protest. They had to bend their heads to the realities.

For one of Trudeau's colleagues, the young diplomat Jean Fournier, the realities were far from exhilarating. His prospects for advancement were constrained despite the fact that he had earned a law degree at Laval, won a travelling scholarship from the French government, attended the National Defence College in Kingston, served with distinction as a captain in the Canadian army, and married a beautiful young woman named Alice Coote, who was part Irish, part French, and related to the distinguished Taschereaus. Furthermore, he was a childhood friend of Jean Lesage, the MP for Montmagny-L'Islet, who was widely talked about as a coming force in the Liberal Party. But despite these advantages, Fournier was earning $2,400 a year in 1950 at a junior job in the PCO. He had been seconded two years before from External to amass for the cabinet's consideration data on how to ready Canada for World War III. On the day of Mackenzie King's last cabinet meeting, Fournier was waiting in the Privy Council chamber anteroom in case his expertise was needed for the scheduled deliberations. As King left the chamber for the last time, Fournier called out to him, "Bonne chance, monsieur le premier ministre." King did not deign to reply and as the swinging door to the hallway shut behind him, Fournier overheard him asking Pickersgill querulously, "What did that man say?"[33]

In unilingual official Ottawa, Fournier could not expect to advance as rapidly as Anglo-Canadians with qualifications equivalent to his. Trudeau's immediate superior, Gordon Robertson, was three years Fournier's junior but had already served as assistant to the under-secretary of state for external affairs and was soon to be made an assistant secretary to the cabinet. Fournier hoped to be posted to the Canadian embassy in Paris, where Georges Vanier was now the head of mission and French Canadians could be effective. In the meantime, he and his wife endured life in Ottawa with as much wit and optimism as they could muster. For them, Trudeau was an exciting figure, a man who seemed at ease in the English milieu and concerned for his fellow French Canadians' welfare. After they begged him not to ride his motorcycle to Montreal on icy winter weekends, he turned up at their house one Monday morning behind the wheel of a brand-new American car. Their young sons shrieked with pleasure when Trudeau scooped them up and drove them to school.[34]

Trudeau's response to Ottawa, a capital that in his opinion "has never really believed in Canada's bicultural character," was very different from that of his peers in the public service. Its ambiance jolted him into realizing that English Canadians deliberately confined French Canadians, no matter how well educated, to subordinate roles: "The most striking example of this attitude occurs in the federal civil service, where English is, to all intents and purposes, the only working language . . . The federal capital is an English capital," he was to write.[35]

A decade later his anger at this injustice still burned fiercely enough for him to state, "English-speaking Canadians have never given up their condescending attitude to their French-speaking fellows, even to this day." They might "wear the pious mask of democracy" but they "hide their intolerance behind acts of majority rule," such as the "savagely imposed conscription" of 1917 and the "solemn [anti-conscription] promise" broken in 1942. The other side of the equation was the French Canadians' persistent failure to exercise their rights. This stubborn passivity closed the vicious circle that the German philosopher Hannah Arendt described as the complicity of the oppressed. In Trudeau's words, "Ottawa took advantage of Quebec's backwardness, and because of its backwardness that province was unable to participate adequately in the benefits of centralization."[36]

Two years after moving there to work, Trudeau had seen as much of Ottawa as he could tolerate. Canadian Liberalism was still business-oriented and remote from the left liberalism he had ingested abroad; he decided to go home to Quebec to fulminate there in favour of its purer principles. He wrote a formal letter of resignation to the clerk of the Privy Council, complete with a tongue-in-cheek salutation to "Citizen Robertson" and with his own signature rendered as "Citizen Trudeau." He had reached the conclusion, as he was to write later, that French Canadians needed to abandon their role of "oppressed nation," and that "the vicious circle could only be broken if Quebec managed to become a modern society." Effective October 13, Citizen Trudeau, the postcolonial man, was free of his bureaucratic straitjacket and ready to throw his energy into dragging French Canada out of its colonial mentality and into liberal modernity.[37]

The Quebec Trudeau returned to in 1952, after spending several months in Europe and Africa recovering from his PCO experience, was superficially very much like the Quebec he had left behind when he went to Harvard in 1944: a society colonized in almost every aspect of its being. It was culturally colonized by France, since whatever emanated from Paris was seized on with reverence by its small intelligentsia. It was morally colonized by the Vatican through the Roman Catholic clergy who strongly influenced the provincial state. It remained under the immediate economic domination of the Anglo-Montreal business community. And for fifty years it had been experiencing a less obvious colonization by American capitalists eager to exploit Quebec's resources and to supply its consumer market. These colonizers asserted control with the acquiescence of the general population who – except for periodic outbursts of political protest – behaved with the docility typical of the powerless trapped in a learned helplessness. [38]

Underneath this surface sameness, important changes were taking place. The provincial economy, already stimulated by the forced industrialization of the war effort, was being transformed by a surge of American investment that was increasing productivity and employment, particularly in Montreal. The city's prosperity was attracting both a fresh wave of migrants from rural areas and an influx of refugees from Europe. Trade unions were growing in strength. Their social wage had been enhanced by federal old-age pensions, unemployment insurance, and family allowances, and union leaders were now battling employers for higher pay and provincial politicians for better housing, health, and educational facilities. Traditional cultural values were threatened as a result of more intense communication with the North American world begun during the war when Quebec was cut off from Europe. American movies were popular among a populace craving new sensations thanks to the spread of telephones, radios, and cars. [39]

The Church hierarchy and the Union Nationale were heavy-handedly trying to keep these social transformations under control by inciting anti-communist and anti-materialist hysteria among the faithful. Their attempts to contain change were being opposed vigorously by a post-war generation of intellectuals and activists who were seeking ways to achieve greater social, economic, and political equity for French Canadians in a modernized Quebec. [40]

Trudeau's inherited money allowed him to behave differently from most of these reformers, with whom he made common cause in the next few years. With jobs at stake and families to support, they had to be wary about their anti-clerical, anti-Duplessis pronouncements. He was able not only to denounce the corruption of the Union Nationale and the Roman Catholic clergy's abuse of its ecclesiastical power but to bear the consequences: his continuing exclusion from a teaching position at the Université de Montréal.

Readers of his supple prose, which now appeared regularly in *Cité libre* and sporadically in various other publications, were urged to seek the legal redress available to free men against injustice of all kinds. In tone it resembled the passionate polemics of Paul-Émile Borduas's *Refus global*, which had been such a bombshell in Quebec intellectual circles when it was published in 1948. In its bold irreverence Trudeau's writing emulated another of his heroes, the nineteenth-century English liberal thinker Lord Acton, who, as editor of the Catholic journal *The Rambler*, had been courageously critical of the Vatican. He was also affirming in a more sophisticated way an idea he had voiced as a schoolboy: that the weaker group in a social contract (in this case, the French Canadians) can, by banding together to take positive action, refuse to accept the definition of themselves put forward by their overlords. It was an idea that Trudeau was soon to act on as he moved into an intellectual buffer zone between the French and English in Montreal.[41]

Until the mid-1950s, most of the handful of English-speaking Canadians Trudeau knew were Jews or progressive academics or both, people he had met while studying abroad. He had first encountered the economist Morris Miller, for instance, on a train to Montreal when they were both returning from Harvard for the Christmas holidays in December 1945, and they sat up all night together sharing ideas. After meeting again at the LSE, they had travelled together to youth conferences behind the Iron Curtain in 1948 and to Moscow for economic meetings in 1952. Growing up a few blocks from the Trudeaus' house, Miller's main experience with Outremont's French-Canadian majority had been anti-Semitic taunts shouted at him on the street by gangs of schoolboys. He found Trudeau's ardent liberalism fascinating and rare – as did William Kilbourn and Paul Fox, anglophone intellectuals from Ontario whose paths had crossed Trudeau's when they were graduate students abroad. They had even fewer acquaintances among French Canadians than Trudeau had among the English, since the two solitudes prevailed in academe as well as every other segment of Canadian life.[42]

It was not until 1954 that Trudeau established a direct continuing connection with English Montreal through the McGill law professor F.R. Scott. By this time, Scott was a towering figure in the city, having spent his splendid middle age at the bloody crossroads where literature and politics meet. As the son of a well-known Anglican canon, he had grown up a proper little imperialist in Quebec City and had fallen in love with the English as an undergraduate at Oxford in the 1920s. But after he came home to study law and teach at McGill, he had evolved into an anti-imperialist pacifist, a civil libertarian, a modernist poet, and a political activist stubbornly opposed to the capitalist system. [43]

By the time Trudeau came to know him well, Scott was over fifty and in his radical prime, a man of developed intellect and capacious conscience, witty, strikingly good-looking, and physically vital, as he was to remain deep into old age. Later in his life Trudeau was at pains to downplay Scott's influence on his thinking, saying only, "I read him in the 1950s and suddenly discovered there existed in Montreal the kind of progressive thought I had developed on my own in London and at Harvard." To others who knew both men well and had compared their work, Scott's influence on Trudeau seemed profound and of long standing, in both style and content. [44]

Scott's ideas had attracted Trudeau first during the war, when his daring in supporting the French Canadians' right to resist conscription had outraged English Montreal. Later, while Trudeau was working in the PCO, he had observed Scott at constitutional conferences acting as an adviser to Saskatchewan's CCF government, the sole figure at these dismal meetings who seemed to Trudeau to have any panache.

But they did not meet formally until after Trudeau made friends in the 1950s with F.R.'s son, Peter Scott, through Sylvia Knelman Wiseman (later Sylvia Ostry), an instructor in economics at McGill who had met Trudeau at a jazz dance class. Wiseman and Trudeau went out on the town with Peter Scott, who wrote a poem about riding the Ferris wheel with them in Belmont Park, the amusement centre owned by the Trudeau trust. Trudeau began to turn up as a courtroom observer when Scott *père* was acting for the defence in some of the landmark civil liberties cases he took on in the 1950s. Scott was sometimes present at political meetings held at her house by Thérèse Casgrain, the provincial leader of the minuscule Quebec wing of the CCF. The daughter of a well-to-do Liberal family whose husband had served in King's cabinet, Casgrain was a tireless advocate of reform, particularly in the field of women's rights. She was also one of the few members of the French-Canadian bourgeoisie daring enough to try to bridge the two solitudes in Montreal, and Scott was her English counterpart. [45]

Scott's interest in French Canada dated back to papers he had written in the 1930s explaining the attraction to fascism of certain elements in Quebec in terms of the province's political economy. After his wartime opposition to conscription, he became involved with French-Canadian modernist writers by translating and championing the poetry of Anne Hébert and Saint-Denys Garneau. He also founded Recherches sociales, a study group set up with a bequest of a few thousand dollars to foster social science research into French-English problems. A small grant was designated to help the journalist Gérard Pelletier edit a book on the Asbestos strike of 1949, which both men saw as a catalytic event in Quebec's development. When the project bogged down in 1954, Scott asked Trudeau – who had spent a week in the strike town after he came home from his world tour – to take it over. The task absorbed Trudeau's energies for the next two years as he formulated the trenchant analysis – derived in large part from Scott's – of Quebec's reactionary and dysfunctional nationalism that served as the book's introductory and concluding chapters. [46]

In the process, Scott became a cardinal influence on Trudeau's thinking. His stance on the importance of the constitution in a representative democracy, his defiant views on the evils of capitalism, and his vision of a just society were coherent expressions for the Canadian reality of the liberal ideas Trudeau had studied abroad. They were made doubly attractive by Scott's Oxbridge mannerisms and his reputation as a poet and womanizer.

Although he thumbed his aquiline nose at both the Montreal and Ottawa Anglo establishments, Scott's connections to their insular worlds were manifold, and their responses to him were as to one of their own. Among the mandarinate in Liberal Ottawa he held the position of admired thinker and public goad, similar to the role John Kenneth Galbraith played in Democratic Washington. But he continued to evoke apoplectic anger in Westmount, whose elders saw to it that Scott was denied the law dean's job at McGill, even though he was the faculty's most distinguished teacher. ("Westmount" had now supplanted "the Square Mile" as the term Montrealers used not just for the area where the wealthy English lived but as an evocation of the Anglo–Protestant ascendancy in Montreal.)

During their collaboration on the Asbestos strike study, Trudeau was drawn further into Scott's seductively civilized orbit. After the book was published in 1956, the two men travelled to the Arctic together and Scott wrote a poem about Trudeau's feats of physical daring, describing him as:

A man testing his strength
Against the strength of his country.[47]

Over the next few years, Trudeau made friends with several of Scott's students from old Montreal families. The most enduring of these friendships would prove to be with Peter Michael Pitfield, the youngest son of a wealthy family with roots in the Square Mile. Pitfield was neither a social democrat nor a liberal. He was in search of a political philosophy and had become fascinated by Edmund Burke, possibly in order to give intellectual respectability to the Duplessiste conservatism his father, a swashbuckling financier named Ward Pitfield, had espoused enthusiastically in the 1930s. But despite his family's politics, the younger Pitfield admired Scott and had the courage to invite him to Sunday lunch at his family's estate, a proposal that caused his female relatives to suffer what sounded in the recounting very much like Victorian attacks of the vapours.

In this same period, Trudeau also began to date the eligible daughters of Old Mawn-tree-all (as Westmount drawled it), driving them around town in his convertible Jaguar XKE, dancing with them in downtown clubs where he also liked to be seen with the glamorous French-Canadian writers, artists, actresses, and models who had supplanted the genteel girl-friends of his younger years. He sometimes took his dates to North Hatley in the Eastern Townships for the Bloomsbury-in-the-bush-garden gatherings Scott held there at his country place. "He was happier with Scott's coterie than I had ever seen him anywhere else," one of the women remembered afterwards. "The ambiance was completely foreign to me as a French Canadian but Pierre revelled in it. His face glowed."[48]

Beyond his work on the Asbestos book and his contributions to *Cité libre*, Trudeau published a series of polemical essays in *Vrai*, a small reform weekly paper. These weekly provocations devoted to unmasking the abuse of power by church and state in Quebec displayed his knowledge of political theory. He also incorporated into his writings his training in economics by articulating a prescription for Quebec's ills that was tantamount to a blueprint for a Keynesian welfare state at the provincial level. Essentially, he advocated the application to Quebec of what the Labourites were doing in London and the mandarinate was favouring in a more moderate form in Ottawa – the use of Keynes's ideas to buttress a left-of-centre, but hardly revolutionary, liberal vision.[49]

Among his reform-minded French-speaking friends – most of whom had no grounding in economics – Trudeau's familiarity with the dismal science was much prized. He was described in their circles as an economist as well as a lawyer. His grasp of Keynesianism's practical implications was displayed in a closely argued submission he wrote at the request of a trade union for the Tremblay commission on Quebec's constitutional future. Since he quoted at length from this brief in a *Cité libre* article, Trudeau obviously felt he was making a significant intellectual contribution by explaining how Keynesian theory could be applied in a federal state where economic powers were shared between two autonomous levels of government and co-operation between the two was essential for such sophisticated techniques of macro-economic stabilization to work.[50]

Trudeau's admirers remained puzzled by the dichotomy between his burning reformist politics and his disinclination to put them into action. When he returned to Montreal from one of his frequent extended trips abroad, excited about some new author or idea, his friend from Brébeuf days Pierre Vadeboncoeur would ask sarcastically, "Pierre, what are you going to be when you grow up?" The prominent Sorbonne socialist and medievalist Paul Vignaux, who lectured regularly in Montreal, told Trudeau's friends, "There is no one in French politics who can hold a candle to Pierre intellectually." But when Vignaux remarked to Trudeau himself that he needed a political base, Trudeau snapped back, "I know that."[51]

Since he had rejected the idea of leading the Quebec wing of the CCF when this was suggested to him by Thérèse Casgrain, the Liberal Party looked like the only possibility for political action. Even though he had been eyeing it speculatively for nearly twenty years, Trudeau still disliked what he saw. He found it "miserably remiss in its simple political duty. Instead of educating the French-speaking electorate to believe in democracy," he wrote, "the Liberals seemed content to cultivate the ignorance and prejudice of that electorate." Although the provincial Liberals were in the throes of a radical democratization process under a new leader, Georges-Émile Lapalme, Trudeau was unmoved. He stubbornly refrained from making a partisan commitment throughout the 1950s, preferring instead to dabble in socialist rhetoric and citizen activism.[52]

A wealthy left-leaning Montreal Liberal and friend of his mother's, Hector Langevin, provided the financial backing that made possible the establishment of the Institut canadien des affaires publiques, an organization devoted to raising the level of public education on policy questions. Trudeau was prominent in drafting the ICAP's constitution and in running its summer conferences. Then he set up, French-style, a Rassemblement provincial des citoyens, purportedly to rally the citizenry against Duplessis. The failure of this effort in 1956 did not stop him from trying once more in 1958. But again the Union des forces démocratiques he founded proved a hollow shell. Trudeau had not been able to create a political base for himself, for all the democratic manifestos he composed.[53]

The younger intellectual with whom he seemed most at ease in this period was Charles Taylor, who had come home to Montreal to teach philosophy at McGill after several years at Oxford as a fellow of All Souls. Taylor was a Catholic, a social democrat active in the CCF, and a hybrid Quebecker. (His father was a transplanted Torontonian but his mother belonged to the prominent Beaubien family, and Taylor had grown up bilingual in his francophone grandparents' capacious house in Outremont.) In Taylor's view, Trudeau's encounters with Scott's rarefied world taught him "very little more about post-war North America than was known by his friends Pelletier and Marchand – perhaps even less than those two since their involvement with journalism and the labour movement meant they had encountered North American business practice in their work lives."[54]

As he approached forty, Trudeau was still largely unknown in English Canada beyond the confines of Montreal's anglophone intellectual community, British still in its reference points and exclusive in its elegant bohemianism, although anglophilia and exclusion were notions it supposedly abhorred. He had never been in the schoolrooms, common rooms, locker rooms, or boardrooms of post-war Canada. He did not know the country's raw society or its North American hustle. Instead, Trudeau, the post-colonial French Canadian, had joined hands with the prideful post-imperialists of English Canada. They had a meeting of minds on the main lines of the era's mid-Atlantic liberal Keynesian consensus, admirable in its commitment to social and political equity but haughty and facile in its anti-capitalism.

Meanwhile in Liberal Ottawa, everything possible was being done to prolong the post-war expansion, including offering tax relief to business rather than increasing the fiscal levy as Keynes had advised. Under the sway of C.D. Howe's Yankee capitalist impatience to attract investors – particularly from south of the border – generous arrangements were made such as depletion allowances to stimulate the mining of non-renewable resources and accelerated depreciation concessions to encourage industry to buy new capital equipment. These accounting bonanzas saved businessmen hundreds of millions of dollars in taxes, prolonging the boom rather than moderating it. Keynesianism was being honoured more in theory than in practice. When the economy was expanding, the Liberal cabinet was disinclined to apply the darker side of the master's teaching by increasing taxes to restrain consumption and investment or by cutting back the entrepreneurial incentives it had embedded in the tax structure. The politicians' electoral imperatives frequently overruled the mandarins' textbook advice.[55]

Few analysts – inside or outside the government, on the left, right, or centre of the political spectrum – objected to such giveaways because rising incomes had brought a welcome period of social peace. Unions had managed to help workers benefit from the economy's growth and productivity gains by winning for the working class significant wage increases, if not greater political power. Increasing wages without institutionalizing labour or agrarian participation in designing the social security system was an integral part of the uneasy compromise made to secure the quiescence of workers and farmers in a modern industrial state. As long as prosperity continued, as it did from 1947 to 1953, and the various programs for redistributing income stabilized purchasing power in the new consumer economy, industrial peace could prevail. When economic growth did sputter and unemployment rose, as it did in 1954, the government insisted there was little it could do to create jobs and shied away from deficit financing.[56]

Like other industrialized countries, Canada was finding its economy less responsive to Keynesian fine-tuning as capital became more mobile, which meant in this particular case more continentally integrated, as American corporations took advantage of the open season Canada had declared on its resources and markets. The U.S. share of Canadian resource exports increased rapidly at the same time as American branch plants in Canada expanded their imports of components from their parent firms. [57]

A few Canadians raised their voices against this creeping continentalism. The historian Kenneth McNaught had expressed his concern about the dangers of Canada's involvement in the Korean War. Later in the 1950s, a small band of non-partisan activists, led by the retired army general A.G.L. McNaughton, began to make vociferous objections to the proposed Columbia River Treaty, a Canadian-American deal that involved the diversion of Canadian water and hydro power to the United States. Nostalgic Tories periodically decried Ottawa's erosion of Canada's British connection and its ever-cosier relationship with the dangerously expansionist American empire. These public protests went largely unheeded in the consociational élites until a Canadian who was considered a charter member came forward to voice his concerns about the need to defend the country's sovereignty against American economic take-over. [58]

His name was Walter Lockhart Gordon, and as early as 1938, as a partner in Clarkson, Gordon, a century-old Toronto firm of corporate accountants and government consultants, he had begun to feel uneasy about American capital moving unchecked into Canada. He went to London late that year to raise bond capital from British financiers with the idea that whenever a Canadian company was put up for sale, he and a group of businessmen friends would rescue it from American take-over. The idea was intriguing. The timing was terrible. The British backed off once the onset of World War II prevented the export of capital, and Gordon gave up his concerns for the duration.

After the war, there were other obstacles to the expression of his concerns. One was the wave of internationalism that had spread through the Western democracies like a sacred flame and had English-Canadian intellectuals crowding one another to warm their hands at the fire. The other was the conviction among Gordon's peers in the business world and the public service that C.D. Howe's efforts to attract American investment capital were sound. It was not until 1955 that Gordon got up the steam to oppose these twin juggernauts. He voiced his concerns directly to friends in cabinet who, in defiance of Howe, agreed to let Gordon explore them by appointing him chairman of a royal commission on Canada's economic prospects. By the time the commission completed its studies and submitted its final report in 1957, St. Laurent's Liberals had been defeated by John G. Diefenbaker's Progressive Conservatives – the first time the party had lost an election since 1930, when Mackenzie King was thrown out of office for five years. [59]

Although he was wary of the Americans, in the tradition of his party, Diefenbaker as a prairie populist was warier still of Gordon's Bay Street and Liberal connections. He dismissed the Gordon report's warnings about the political implications of the economy's huge levels of U.S.-controlled investment. Ignoring the dangers to Canadian independence from American military domination implicit in his decisions to cancel the Avro Arrow program to build sophisticated fighter-bombers, he proceeded to sign a defence production-sharing agreement with the United States. (In return for Canada's abandonment of its capacity to build competitive aircraft and its commitment to purchase American weapons systems, Washington allowed Canadian firms in the military field – mainly U.S. branch plants in any case – to bid for subcontracts on Pentagon projects.) By this time, the establishment of NORAD had created an integrated command structure for North American air defence so that the Royal Canadian Air Force became an extension of the U.S. Strategic Air Command's defences against Soviet attack. [60]

None of these developments bothered the Ottawa mandarinate very much. They felt Canada was facing the Red menace braced shoulder-to-shoulder with its great wartime ally, still fortunate to share the burden of the free world's defence if only by supplying military components and low-cost unprocessed resources. Among businessmen and academic economists, Gordon's concerns about foreign investment were also dismissed as political fear-mongering.

But the May 1958 issue of *Cité libre* revealed an unexpected ally in Quebec. It carried an article called "On the Question of Economic Domination," signed by Pierre Elliott Trudeau, which commented approvingly on the Gordon commission's major concerns. Canada's "heavily foreign-dominated economy," Trudeau wrote, had led to "the U.S. government's mastery of American capital invested in Canada." Since "political domination and economic domination are inextricably linked," and foreign direct investment through branch plants does not get paid off but "remains indefinitely," giving "non-residents the power to make decisions contrary to the welfare of Canadians," then it followed that "either we will passively submit to our condition as a dominated economy . . . or we will intervene vigorously in the play of economic forces."[61]

It was not Gordon's economic nationalism Trudeau opposed; it was his capitalism. As an economic system, he wrote, "capitalism in our country exploits the worker, and our legislation fails to protect him sufficiently." Trudeau saw Quebec as a class-divided society where the "proletarian condition" of the workers kept them in "a state of insecurity dangerously close to misery" and made Quebec far from "a society of equals."[62]

These socialistic views were repeated in various articles Trudeau wrote in the late 1950s and early 1960s and were consistent with positions he took, inspired by Frank Scott, that advocated the use of the constitutional order to bring greater economic equality to Canadians. Trudeau's writings also showed the influence of C.B. Macpherson, the Marxist political theorist at the University of Toronto, when he wrote in the *McGill Law Journal*, "The liberal idea of property helped to emancipate the bourgeoisie but it is now hampering the march towards economic democracy." Observing how ill protected ordinary people were "against such realities as economic exploitation or massive unemployment," Trudeau noted that the "present private enterprise economy is geared to the satisfaction of individual needs, not to that of collective needs." Incorporating both Schumpeter's gloom about capitalism and Galbraith's more recent critique of the affluent society, he went on to point out that for Quebec "there is a gigantic lag in the provision of educational facilities, hospitals, slum-clearance projects, recreational opportunities, highways, and other public services."[63]

But by the time this article was published in 1962, Trudeau had already begun to distance himself from the anti-capitalism he had affected in the 1950s while he was managing his family's substantial trust. Socialist analysis was being appropriated in a more explicitly Marxist form by the newly emerging Quebec separatists. Trudeau's old reformist friends, who had shared his left-leaning ideas in opposition to Duplessis, had moved closer to the political centre after the Quebec Liberal Party was elected in 1960 on a progressive platform put together by Jean Lesage, Lapalme's successor as provincial leader. Lesage's government had energetically set about modernizing the state, including establishing programs that displaced the Roman Catholic church as the provider of education and welfare. Trudeau himself was now teaching law at the Université de Montréal – the professorial job that had eluded him while Duplessis lived – and had come under the influence of the economist Albert Breton.

Breton belonged to a younger generation of French-Canadian social scientists who had been trained in the United States. The paradigm he used during regular lunchtime discussions with Trudeau was American neo-classical economics, which accepted Keynesian fine-tuning but opposed any more extensive state intervention in the economy as a harmful political distortion of free-market capitalism. Economics, the most abstract and most disconnected from social reality of all the social sciences, was gaining in importance as a profession both in academe, where it had developed into an exclusive discipline centred on highly abstract concepts and mathematical modelling, and in government, where a graduate degree in economics was now the preferred qualification for policy-making positions at a senior level. Economists were turning into the modern state's oracles, with lesser mortals being enjoined to accept their views as pronouncements to be taken on faith.[64]

While studying for a doctorate at Columbia, Breton had learned to emulate the assurance American economists displayed. Since the United States had not experienced dependence for well over a century, its economists had never developed intellectual tools to analyse the phenomenon of domination experienced by subject economies. As a French Canadian from Saskatchewan, Breton had little sympathy for the questions raised by Quebec nationalists. When he found himself teaching economics in a Quebec seething with nationalistic fervour, he was dismayed by popular ideas that seemed to him economically unsound. To explain the discrepancy, he applied the economics he had learned in one kind of society to the social situation he encountered in quite another. It was Breton's novel contention that élites "invest" in nationalism as if it were a "public good" in order to create high-paying jobs and so redistribute income from the working class to themselves. [65]

Trudeau, the evangelical modernist who wanted to bring Quebec and Canada up to date, seems to have had little difficulty shedding his radical anti-capitalism and buckling on Breton's free-enterprise liberalism. Its rationalist, compartmentalized, deductive logic resonated with his own Harvard training in economics. Reducing the social complexities of nationalism to a simple, apparently scientific formulation and categorizing it as both élitist and regressive was so persuasive to Trudeau that it turned into an absolute truth in his mind. He could dismiss the new social-democratic intellectual nationalists of the 1960s, who wanted to use the provincial state to modernize Quebec, in the same way that he had disdained the corrupt parochial nationalists of the Duplessis era, who used the provincial government to oppose progress. This sleight-of-mind allowed him to become economically conservative while still appearing to favour the interests of the working class. He maintained that Quebec nationalists were not concerned with what was best for "the people," they were concerned with what was best for themselves. It also let him draw closer to the Liberal Party since anti-nationalism was a classic Liberal stance. [66]

Trudeau was sufficiently drawn to Breton that he collaborated with him on a couple of articles and joined him, in company with the Montreal lawyer Marc Lalonde and several other young French

Canadians, in drafting a federalist manifesto that was eventually published in 1964 as "Manifeste pour une politique fonctionnelle" and "An Appeal for Realism in Politics." In two years, Trudeau had moved a long way from social-democratic rhetoric. His writing was now more impersonal and technocratic, less populist and democratic. What really matters, he wrote in dismissing Quebec nationalist demands for more political power, "is that per-capita income be increased as quickly as possible. To achieve this, Quebec's economy must become extremely efficient, technologically advanced, quite specialized, and capable of offering the best products at the best prices in all the markets of the world." In adopting the rationalism of economics, Pierre Trudeau was distancing himself from the social-democratic solidarities he had expressed in the 1950s and preparing himself intellectually to enter the Liberal Party.[67]

This prospect was made more palatable to Trudeau because of what had happened in the federal Liberal Party since Louis St. Laurent had stepped down as leader after his government's defeat in 1957. It had become distinctly more progressive in its policy positions and more democratic in its inner workings under the aegis of its new leader, Lester Pearson.

As secretary of state for external affairs under St. Laurent, Pearson had kept as clear of domestic politics as possible in order to continue to exhibit his formidable talents as a diplomatic mediator on the international stage. For a decade it had been expected he would glide smoothly into the prime minister's office, the job at the apex of power that was meant to cap the great career of the greatest charmer of the mandarinate era. More than any Canadian of his generation, Pearson had mastered the style of the post-war trans-Atlantic élite and turned it to his country's advantage and his own. Scant months after he was awarded this élite's ultimate accolade, the Nobel Peace Prize, he found himself in the spring of 1958 the leader of a devastated Liberal Party, which had just lost its second election in nine months.[68]

Instead of hobnobbing in the corridors of the United Nations or sipping Martinis in Georgetown, Pearson was sitting disconsolately on the opposition benches in Ottawa, with virtually no partisan experience, no taste for political debate, no policy vision, and few organizational skills. He turned for help to his old friend Walter Gordon, who had already shown himself ready and willing to come to his aid by intervening on his behalf in the leadership convention and the election that followed immediately.

Gordon decided that if the statist ideas contained in his royal commission report were to be implemented, he would have to work to elect a government more amenable to them than the mercurial Diefenbaker's unpredictable regime, even though this would mean going against his Toronto family's Tory politics and his own professional penchant for remaining non-partisan so he could act as a consultant for governments of every stripe. The Liberal Party under Mike Pearson, whom he had met during the Depression when they served together on a royal commission on price spreads, seemed the best vehicle for his purposes. As a supremely successful careerist whose fortunes had been made by pleasing almost everybody and offending almost no one, Pearson was adept at giving both welfare Liberals and business Liberals the impression that he sympathized with their views by presenting himself as a good-natured, self-deprecating political *tabula rasa*. Since his party's right wing had been decimated in the 1958 election, he was taking policy advice from progressive intellectuals such as Tom Kent, the fiercely reformist editor of the *Winnipeg Free Press*; Maurice Lamontagne, a professor of economics, convinced Keynesian, and federalist who had been a protégé of the radical priest Father Georges-Henri Lévesque at Laval; and Allan MacEachen, another academic economist trained at St. Francis Xavier University in Nova Scotia, where the ideology of the Coady co-operative movement dominated the faculty's thinking. Pearson seemed only too glad to listen to what Gordon had to say about Canada's economic problems and gladder still to give him *carte blanche* to revive his demoralized party.[69]

Gordon accordingly applied his dual talents as experienced management consultant and self-assured policy advocate to restructure, reorient, and reanimate the Liberal Party. He cleared out the dead-wood in the party's national organization, bypassed regional party stalwarts by creating new centralized leader's advisory groups, and supported the efforts of an energetic group of young Toronto Liberals who were determined to supplant the St. Laurent old guard with their own brave-new-era activists who talked excitedly of bringing democracy to the party's internal operations.

Gordon also helped ensure that progressive ideas on social welfare and economic expansion, such as government-financed medicare, income maintenance, regional development, and vocational training – publicly aired by Tom Kent and Maurice Lamontagne at a thinkers' conference held in Kingston, Ontario – were ratified by resolutions passed in January 1961 at the first policy rally the party had seen fit to hold since 1893. With a view to modernizing the Liberals' campaign techniques, he named as national organizer the liveliest of the Toronto Liberals, the advertising salesman Keith Davey, and hired the American pollster Lou Harris – who had been central to the recent presidential victory of John Kennedy – in order to learn new electoral techniques that combined opinion polling with advertising and image-making.[70]

As if these efforts weren't enough, Gordon recruited a new fund-raising team and acted as the Liberals' campaign strategist. He then became a candidate for office himself in the Toronto riding of Davenport. After the Liberals' minority victory in the election of 1963, Gordon prevailed on Pearson to name him minister of finance. But within weeks, the personal power he had built up within the Liberal apparatus was seriously eroded. His reputation for managerial wizardry suffered irreparable harm when his first budget came to grief over its nationalist provision – a 25-per-cent tax to be paid on corporate take-overs by foreigners – which had to be withdrawn because of the combined pressure brought to bear on Pearson by American and Canadian businessmen. When the U.S. introduced a tax later that year to raise the cost of foreign borrowings in Ameri-can capital markets, Gordon, the champion of a more independent Canada, found himself ignominiously following the path of his continentalist predecessors in Finance, rushing off to the American capital to beg for an exemption lest Canadian capital markets go into a spin.[71]

While Gordon was coping unhappily with these Canadian-American realities, Pearson was attempting to deal with that other recurring Canadian difficulty, French-English relations. He desper-ately needed to find a French lieutenant who would arouse federal Liberal energies in Quebec in the face of the growing separatist movement. After several disappointments he approached Jean Marchand, the most popular union leader in Quebec and one of Trudeau's closest allies. Marchand was enough of a political realist to know that Pearson's offer had to be accepted. A basic realignment between the French and English in Canada was under way, and French Canadians in the political class were struggling to find them-selves ideological perches from which to deal with the new realities. Some had become neo-federalists demanding significantly en-hanced powers for Quebec under Jean Lesage's banner. Others were moving in the direction of sovereignty. Still others, including Mar-chand, remained firm federalists, not of the trained-donkey variety Trudeau had so disdained in the 1950s but as adherents of the view that anything the English could do, the French could do better.

If the "anything" involved political action, Marchand main-tained that the best place to do it was in the Liberal Party, which had shown itself the national institution most accommodating to the French fact for more than seventy years. Under Pearson, acting on the ideas of Kent, Lamontagne, MacEachen, and Gordon, the party had stolen the thunder of the old CCF, which had proceeded to recast itself as the New Democratic Party in the vain hope of displac-ing the Grits as the left-leaning alternative to conservatism in Canada.

For Trudeau, joining the Liberal Party in 1965 under Marchand's aegis and in company with his friend the journalist Gérard Pelletier meant climbing on board a political vehicle that had undergone sufficient retooling that he could banish his long-held apprehensions. Bringing his "missionary" period to an end caused him qualms nevertheless, notably because of the alienation of his old social-democratic soulmate, Charles Taylor, the NDP candidate in Mount Royal, the riding Trudeau contested as a Liberal. (It helped that Frank Scott did not censure the move. Scott and several other LSR social democrats were almost as disturbed as Trudeau and Marchand that the NDP at its founding convention in 1961 had endorsed a two-nations view of Confederation.)[72]

On November 8, 1965, Pierre Trudeau was elected to office at last. Fourteen years after he had left Liberal Ottawa in disgust, years when he had analysed the causes and proposed the cures for Quebec's problems, he returned there as a Liberal convert anxious to use Parliament as a "soapbox" from which to declaim his ideas about federalism.[73]


As Pearson's parliamentary secretary and then his justice minister, Trudeau stayed out of the struggle that was raging over democracy and nationalism in the Anglo-Canadian wing of the Liberal Party, which was confronting concerns about American domination of Canada. The election that brought Trudeau to Parliament also ended Gordon's influence with Pearson. When the Liberals failed once more to gain a majority, Gordon resigned from the cabinet although he continued to voice his concerns about foreign control of the Canadian economy. His supporters in the caucus and the extra-parliamentary party were now described as economic nationalists or left Liberals and, in turn, pinned the equally pejorative labels of continentalist or reactionary on their detractors.

Mitchell Sharp, a former member of the mandarinate and stubborn believer in its shibboleths, had replaced Gordon as minister of finance. At a party policy convention in 1966, Gordon's partisans lost out to Sharp's when they confronted each other over the issues of foreign control and free trade. At that same convention, activists won a battle they had been waging to make the caucus and leader "accountable" to the party membership on such policy positions as its demand to strengthen the social security system with universal medical insurance. Trudeau cagily kept himself detached from this fight as well, attending meetings of the reformers but remaining non-committal.[74]

His evasion of these controversies stood him in good stead in his march to the Liberal leadership in 1968. Ostensibly he still believed in a "democracy oriented towards social progress, a federalism that reconciles a strong central power with autonomous, progressive provinces and, finally, a politics open to the left," as he and Gérard Pelletier assured *Cité libre* readers in a jointly written article describing their decision to become Liberals in 1965. This shorthand apparently meant he wanted to use the state to force the redistribution of wealth in favour of the working class. He did not reconcile these statist ideas – let alone his earlier apprehensions about the economic domination and alarming militarism of the United States – with his new-found scepticism about government intervention in the economy. Apparently he had come to politics too soon after his conversion to neo-classical economics to have integrated what were seriously discordant positions into a coherent whole.[75]

That Pierre Trudeau had reached no overarching synthesis resolving the contradictions between economic nationalism and continentalism, between *laissez-faire* financial management and interventionism, seemed to make little difference to Liberals who flocked to his banner once he declared himself a leadership candidate. What mattered to them was his stand on Quebec. Trudeau was bringing to the flexible amalgam of beliefs, nostrums, and everyday practices known as Canadian Liberalism his sharply delineated positions on the importance of official bilingualism and the affirmation of Quebec's place in Confederation under a renewed constitution.

Trudeau temporized when Gordon raised the foreign-ownership question with him during the leadership race by asking what he thought of the study on the branch-plant Canadian economy that

Gordon had inspired following his return to Pearson's cabinet the previous year. The study, which bore the name of the University of Toronto economist Mel Watkins, had recommended that measures be taken to make it easier for Canadian capital to compete in the Canadian market against the massive advantages enjoyed by U.S. firms. Trudeau indicated he had read the report and could "live with it," apparently hoping this neutral response would be enough to gain support for his leadership ambitions from Gordon and his close ally Beland Honderich, the publisher of *The Toronto Star.* And it was. Trudeau also managed to satisfy Mitchell Sharp that he was "sound" – that is, amenable to orthodox economic positions. Sharp's decision just before the leadership convention to abandon his own candidacy in favour of Trudeau's was thought to be crucial to his success because it was a symbolic blessing of this flamboyant French Canadian by the business establishment's favourite Ottawa Man.[76]

In effect, Trudeau and his comrades, Marchand and Pelletier, aided by Marc Lalonde, hijacked the Liberal Party in 1968. "We weren't Liberals," Marchand frankly admitted later, "but we decided to use the Liberal Party." Marchand's experience with trade union politics, Pelletier's writing skills, Lalonde's organizational savvy, and Trudeau's unexpected charismatic appeal to the public made the foursome a formidable team. As a collective, they knew very little more about the English in Canada outside Montreal than Trudeau did as an individual – which was not very much – and virtually nothing about the inner workings of the Liberal Party or the Canadian-American relationship. They seemed to think Trudeau's invocation of "Participatory democracy!" would look after party problems as though the slogan were a formula that would magically transform the brokerage politics of King and St. Laurent – reformed somewhat by Pearson and Gordon – into an instrument of mass democracy flourishing on Rousseauian principles.[77]

It was a measure of Trudeau's triumph that shortly after he was elected leader, Thérèse Gouin Décarie, now a professor of child psychology at the Université de Montréal, asked a mutual friend on the PMO staff if he would be kind enough to take her to her former fiancé's new office so she could offer felicitations in person. When they discovered to her disappointment that Trudeau was out at a meeting, Sir Lomer Gouin's granddaughter gravely planted a lipstick kiss on a sheet of paper, signed it "Thérèse," and left it in the centre of the prime minister's polished desk. He had scaled the heights alone.[78]

That Trudeau's political inexperience and contradictory positions on economic policy ill prepared him to lead a nation that would soon enter a prolonged economic crisis did not bother many Liberals in the heady spring of 1968, since few of them believed that such a misfortune could befall a country as blessed as Canada seemed at the time. The economy was barrelling along, having recovered from the troubles of the early 1960s. Those who expressed apprehensions about its fragility, from either the right or the left, were thought to be outmoded in their thinking. Continuing good fortune was the basic assumption on which public policy decisions had been made for twenty years, and widespread faith in a perpetually healthy economy was a big factor in Trudeau's success in the April leadership race and the election that followed in June. It made the Liberal Party and the broader Canadian public willing to take a risk with him. Prosperity would allow him to get on with his goals of legislating linguistic equality, bringing rationalism to government, experimenting with participatory democracy, and creating a just society. The economy would take care of itself.[79]

# CHAPTER 3

# THE SPECTRE AT THE FEAST: ECONOMIC DECLINE

When the Canadian economy started to go sour in the 1970s and Pierre Trudeau became the scapegoat for its ills, many angry and unfounded statements were made in order to pin culpability on him. Some said flatly that he never had understood economic policy-making and refused to listen to advice because of his invincible arrogance. Others claimed that because he had never been in business himself, he was ignorant of the workings of the free market. And then there were the radicals on the right who purported to believe that he was wrecking the economic climate deliberately because he secretly wanted to transform Canada into a socialist state. [1]

The reality was a good deal more complex than these calumnies. Trudeau was far from ignorant of economics when he became prime minister. No less an authority than Robert Bryce described him as knowing more economic theory than any other politician Bryce had served. Other economic bureaucrats were to report at the end of the Trudeau era that no member of his various cabinets, including his several ministers of finance, was better able to master the material they prepared or to defend it in the House. His intimates asserted that he was well aware of market forces since he had managed his family's trust to good effect after the death in the 1950s of the Trudeaus' financial adviser, Ernest Beaupré. Far from being a socialist, Trudeau had so distanced himself from left-wing economic ideas by 1968 that in the election campaign that year, he dismissed demands for enriched universal social programs by saying he didn't believe there should be "more of this free stuff." And instead of being heedless of others' opinions, Trudeau was open to economic advice – as long as it did not entail adopting a completely new approach to managing the economy.[2]

In his first couple of years in office, the presence in his camp of economic analysts familiar to the old consociational élites mollified business leaders who comforted themselves that it might be possible to get along with him despite their reservations. He was known to consult occasionally on domestic and international issues the eminent – and eminently acceptable – Queen's University economist John Deutsch. Robert Bryce remained in his post as deputy minister of finance. The Bank of Canada's reputation for relaying sound information on the domestic and world economy was unassailable under the direction of its austere governor, Louis Rasminsky; Trudeau was well known at the Bank for posing penetrating questions that went to the heart of the problem under discussion. His daily planning sessions with his personal staff were attended by Marshall Crowe, deputy secretary to the cabinet, whose long experience as a public servant had been augmented by six years in the private sector as an economic adviser to the president of a major bank. Even Trudeau's choice of Edgar Benson as his first finance minister won the cautious approval of the business community. A chartered accountant who had gained solid ministerial experience in the Pearson years, Benson did not fit the old St. James Street–Bay Street ideal minister mould. But he was acceptable to both wings of the Liberal Party – to the adherents of the nationalist Gordon, who had returned to the private sector in Toronto, and the continentalist Sharp, who was now minister of external affairs.

Secure in the common assumption that the country's economic growth was a self-sustaining phenomenon, Trudeau was content to leave its management to these stalwarts. He had come of age in a province where the English Canadians ran the economy, and he had been trained in government procedures in Louis St. Laurent's Ottawa, where the Department of Finance was invincible and omniscient, an almost exclusively anglophone conduit between business and government. When he came to power, Finance was still taking a cautious approach to economic management, by invoking the Keynesian theorems he knew so well while rejecting suggestions that the government should intervene to alter the economy's structural vulnerability in the continental market. Inflation, not growing unemployment, remained Finance's prime concern. The annual rise in the consumer price index was starting to make headlines. At 4 per cent it was double the rate that had prevailed in the previous decade. Finance persuaded first Benson and then Trudeau that the way to address this problem was to worry less about creating jobs than about tightening the supply of credit and establishing a Prices and Incomes Commission in an effort to cajole business and labour into voluntarily restraining price and wage increases.[3]

With these initiatives, Trudeau showed that he was neither uninterested in nor ignorant of the economy. It just was not his main concern. He was learning to cope with the most difficult job in the country, and he had come to office buttressed by his colleagues Marchand and Pelletier and their common commitment to social and political change. He hoped to modernize cabinet procedures, to rethink Canada's foreign policy, to make government more participatory, and to respond to Quebec's aspirations by moving on linguistic and constitutional reform and by promoting the regional redistribution of wealth.[4]

These goals spoke to his principal interests: functionalism in government, anti-war internationalism, constitutional law, and regional equity. They were also the concerns of the two lawyers from Montreal who were to become his most influential advisers: Marc Lalonde, whom he named principal secretary in the PMO, and Michael Pitfield, who, as an assistant deputy secretary in the cabinet office, had ambitions to become clerk of the Privy Council. Lalonde and Pitfield were trusted friends of his and of each other;

they had gained extensive experience of the governmental system in the 1960s; and they were determined to overhaul it. Like their political master, they expected Finance to run the economy, generating the revenues needed to achieve his Just Society.

This delegatory approach to economic management seemed sound, given the sterling reputation of the department in question. Amazingly, Finance let Trudeau down. Within two years of taking office, his government was in deep trouble as a consequence of a tax reform scheme the department devised.

Tax reform was not Trudeau's issue. He had inherited it from the Diefenbaker-Pearson era. Driven by his prairie populist resentment of central Canada, John Diefenbaker had set up a royal commission on taxation under the direction of Kenneth LeMoyne Carter, an accountant from Toronto's Bay Street establishment. Carter's radically simple proposals for an equitable tax system – every increase in wealth, whether from salary or capital gains, in cash or in kind, should be taxed equally – had appalled businessmen grown fat on the tax incentives and concessions Liberal governments had handed out over the years. They raised such an outcry over their friend Ken's inexplicable endorsement of a really free marketplace that Lester Pearson, ever the accommodator, felt obliged to shelve his report when its six volumes were delivered in 1967.

Wary of this contentious issue, Finance under Benson and Bryce decided to tackle it by consulting the public, a seemingly shrewd bow in the direction of participatory democracy. In November 1969, the department published a new set of tax proposals in a discussion paper rather than including them in a budget, a serious strategic mistake. Not surprisingly, the citizens who felt moved to discuss the proposed tax system overhaul were businessmen, and for them participation meant systematic obstruction. Even though the Benson White Paper, as the reform package was known, diluted Carter's original recommendations, the corporate community pumped itself into a rhetorical rage. Changes designed to make the tax system more neutral were denounced. Big businessmen – many of whom had prospered by awarding themselves stock options and then cashing them in when their companies' fortunes rose – claimed taxing such capital gains at the same rate as income amounted to a socialist conspiracy to kill the free-enterprise spirit in Canada. The complementary idea of taxing small businesses at the same rate as large corporations produced another uproar. John Bulloch, a Toronto technical-school teacher and son of a prosperous tailor, became a public figure overnight as the outraged advocate of small business and founder of the Canadian Council for Fair Taxation. The champions of *laissez-faire* were learning to throw tantrums in public at the very thought of losing the special indulgences they had come to expect from the Canadian state. [5]

Even though Trudeau defiantly declared that his government would not "be bullied or blackmailed by hysterical charges or threats," Finance eventually backed down in the face of this orchestrated onslaught. If the acrimonious debate boiled down to a conflict between social equity and economic growth – as Benson put it in the fall of 1970 – his budget of limited tax reforms the following June showed that concerns about growth had triumphed over any lingering hope that the Trudeau regime would usher in a just society. Despite the dramatic retreat from the Carter commission's position that this budget represented, the Benson White Paper continued to be taken as a reflection of Trudeau's real intentions, which were denounced *ad nauseam* in the business press as dangerously left-wing. [6]

To bolster this dubious view, businessmen pointed to what was happening elsewhere in the government. Trudeau had set up the Department of Regional Economic Expansion in 1969 to address underdevelopment in the poorer provinces and appointed as minister Jean Marchand and as deputy minister Tom Kent, the English intellectual who had been bitterly criticized by Bay Street as socialistic when he was chief adviser to Lester Pearson in the 1960s.

Furthermore, Trudeau had made his reform-minded old friend Gérard Pelletier his secretary of state and allowed him to perpetrate – under the direction of Bernard Ostry, another public servant known to have entertained progressive ideas in his youth – Opportunities for Youth and the Local Initiatives Program. Business saw these programs as sapping the spirit of capitalism since they were designed to use government funds to create employment by responding to grass-roots proposals, such as setting up community theatres or establishing self-help projects for the aged or disabled. In a similar vein, the Company of Young Canadians, set up under Pearson, had become a government-funded organization of community workers who supported aboriginal land claims, poor people, and even Quebec separatists.[7]

Even worse, Trudeau was allowing his minister of labour, the gleefully populist former railway man Bryce Mackasey, to liberalize unemployment insurance and turn it into what seemed to business to be a guaranteed income for the ne'er-do-well. Proposals to toughen competition laws put forward by Ron Basford, the minister of consumer and corporate affairs, provoked further anger, as did other measures designed to broaden the scope of collective bargaining and facilitate union certification, all policies that reflected Trudeau's continuing commitment to making Canadian society more equitable and more accountable.[8]

Central to the unease businessmen felt about these innovations was their loss of privileged access in Ottawa. The intricacy of Trudeau's revamped cabinet committee system, with its goal of democratizing the policy process by making cabinet ministers rather than bureaucrats responsible for government initiatives, put businessmen at an unaccustomed remove from government decision-making. It was no longer possible for them to phone up a friendly cabinet minister or an amenable senior official in Finance, voice their complaints, and then sit back while the government responded.[9]

At the same time as this disconnection from government was taking place, the post-war generation of Canadian businessmen was losing touch with the communitarian ethos that had characterized the old élites' interactions. In the process of becoming increasingly Americanized in the 1950s and 1960s, they had acquired ideological reference points and behavioural patterns that were imported and primitive. They returned from business meetings and conferences in the United States spouting the ideas of American biz-think, which had very little to do with their own country's political reality or its long history of consociational relations between business and political leaders. The complexities of Trudeau's ideas and his commitment to capitalism were lost on them, especially since he refused to allay their fears by talking to them regularly in their own language and flattering them on their own ground. He was determined to treat business technocratically as simply one segment of society, albeit a crucially important one.

In his early days in office, he went reluctantly to dinner meetings with corporate men set up by such experienced power brokers as William Bennett, the chairman of the Iron Ore Company of Canada, who had worked for C.D. Howe. At these meetings – particularly after the Benson White Paper was published – Trudeau was usually bored, defensive, or combative. Dismayed by his inability to sway Trudeau, Bennett soon turned his attentions to John Turner, the Liberal justice minister, and to Brian Mulroney, a young Montreal lawyer and Conservative backroom boy, politicians whose accommodating style he understood.[10]

When Trudeau married Margaret Sinclair, the daughter of James Sinclair, a former Liberal cabinet minister, business circles buzzed with damaging gossip. Margaret was caricatured as an out-of-control flower child who had experimented with drugs in Morocco and turned up broke and disoriented in Paris on the doorstep of an executive of Lafarge Cement, the international conglomerate her father represented in Canada. Her dramatic secret wedding in March 1971 to Trudeau, who was nearly thirty years her senior, fed the general corporate view of the prime minister as radical and unreliable. "Probably one of the things that upset CEOs the most," said Ouida Touche, a Calgary art consultant and former journalist with extensive business connections across the country, "was that

Trudeau was living a fantasy most men over fifty can only dream about: he was rich, politically powerful, and the husband of a sexy twenty-two-year-old who seemed to adore him." [11]


As threats to Canadian business, Trudeau's personal style and his government's fiscal and institutional reforms during his first term in office were inconsequential, compared with the structural shift that was taking place in the world economy. Unknown to the Department of Finance — or even to the sages of Bay and St. James Streets—the glory days of the Canadian post-war boom were already numbered by the time he was sworn in as prime minister. Businessmen still believed prosperity had come about in the 1950s and 1960s because of their entrepreneurial hustle. Bureaucrats continued to think it was the result of their Keynesian acumen. Few of them wanted to concede that Canada's remarkable economic growth was really a by-product of the post-war hegemony of the United States. Ever since 1944, when the Bretton Woods Agreement had established the U.S. dollar as the reserve currency for the capitalist world and consecrated the global dominance of the United States, the mighty American industrial engine had dragged Canada behind it like a treasure-laden caboose. But by the late 1960s, swollen by its own élites' belief in their country's manifest destiny to free the world, the U.S. had involved itself ever more deeply in the quagmire of Vietnam, a strategic miscalculation that would contribute significantly to undoing both the Democratic Party's hold on the American presidency and America the Beautiful's position as the world's premier economic power. [12]

The irrefutable proof to Canadian government officials that the Americans' military misadventures had affected their own cosy continental arrangement came on August 15, 1971, when President Richard Nixon unveiled a dramatic change in American global economic and financial policy that marked the breakdown of the Bretton Woods system. By disconnecting the U.S. dollar from the price of gold, the United States forced its global partners to bear the load of its inflation: the dollars they held as reserves to prop up their own currencies had been abruptly devalued by the American president. Nixon's pronouncements caused a shock wave throughout the world, but their effect on Canada was particularly traumatic. [13]

It was bad enough that Washington was unilaterally torpedoing the global monetary system on which the trading economy depended. It was worse when the Nixon administration rudely rebuffed Canada's plea for an exemption from the 10-per-cent surcharge it had imposed on all manufactured imports. More alarming still was a story, leaked to the *Chicago Tribune*, that the president was considering taking a series of further punitive actions specifically aimed at Canada, such as abrogating the Auto Pact, which since its negotiation in 1965 had allowed the subsidiaries of the four big American car companies to rationalize their Canadian assembly plants' production on a continental basis. With American branch plants occupying so much of Canada's economic space, the Trudeau government found itself impotent when Washington offered its transnational corporations tax incentives to increase their U.S.-based production to the detriment of their subsidiaries' operations in Canada and abroad. [14]

Nixonomics showed that the previous three decades of close rapport between Washington and Ottawa had been a historical aberration, reflecting the benign phase of U.S. global economic supremacy. The president's pronouncements in 1971 marked a return to the Americans' earlier strategy towards Canada of maintaining it as a resource-base-cum-market for U.S. firms while keeping in check its capacity to compete as a manufacturing power. The giant next door was no longer quite so jolly. Canada's interests would have to be defended against Washington rather than being defended by it. Clearly, some new plan was needed to replace the King and St. Laurent governments' Keynesian and continentalist prescription for post-war prosperity. [15]

At this crucial point in Canadian history, Pierre Trudeau's stubborn anti-nationalism was a serious impediment to new planning. His best energies as prime minister in his early years in office had been spent in intense discussions about constitutional powers as though Canada were floating buoyantly in a vacuum, unconstrained by its continental ties. He had the fortitude to respond to Nixon's shock tactics but he did not have the knowledge of or the feel for American politics, and his obsession with Quebec blinded him to the need. The crisis of the previous October, when he and his closest francophone colleagues had believed that a separatist insurrection was exploding in their native province, had deepened his antipathy to nationalisms of all stripes. Any criticism by English Canadians of American economic or cultural imperialism was seen as part and parcel of this reprehensible ideology, this "crime against the history of mankind," as he was later to describe it. After ingesting the ideas of Albert Breton in the early 1960s, he apparently had never again considered seriously the prescription for dealing determinedly with American expansionism that he had articulated so clearly in response to the Gordon report. [16]

Trudeau's attitude to nationalism was readily sustained by his contempt for weakness of any kind, and the English-Canadian nationalist movement was unquestionably weak. It was a measure of the country's still-pervasive colonialist mind-set that those who wanted to protect and strengthen its sovereignty were institutionally marginalized and politically enfeebled. In the academic world, the conventional wisdom was continentalist with some residual mourning for the passing of British hegemony. (Claude Bissell, who as president of the University of Toronto in the late 1960s had been confronted with a wave of student radicalism that made one of its targets the Americanization of Canada's largest university, recalled in his memoirs that he was "concerned not so much by the slight increase in American citizens on the staff . . . as by the decline in the staff from the U.K.") By the early 1970s the mainstream social-science disciplines of economics and sociology in most English-Canadian universities were largely staffed by American-born or American-trained academics who had repudiated, in favour of Anglo-American intellectual models, the national school of political economy associated with Harold Innis's pioneering opus. Innis's heirs in Mel Watkins's generation (such as Abraham Rotstein of the University of Toronto, Kari Levitt of McGill, and Patricia Marchak of the University of British Columbia) or in the wave of neo-Marxist political scientists a half-generation behind him (such as Daniel Drache of York or Leo Panitch and Reg Whitaker of Carleton), whose work challenged the value of the American take-over, were disparaged as folkloric at best and subversive at worst. [17]

Outside the universities, public concern had been raised by several incidents that illustrated vividly the nature of American expansionism. An American oil tanker, the U.S.S. *Manhattan*, defiantly pushed its way through the Northwest Passage in order to challenge openly Canada's sovereignty in the Arctic and to threaten its claim to whatever resources might be discovered under the ice floes. The American-controlled Hudson's Bay Oil and Gas Company tried to take over Denison Mines, Canada's principal producer of uranium. Two long-established Canadian publishing firms, W.J. Gage Ltd. and Ryerson Press, were sold to American textbook giants without the Trudeau government showing any awareness of the significance of this shift in national control to English Canada's capacity to sustain its culture. In response, several small Canadian publishing houses were founded by young intellectuals for whom George Grant, a conservative moral philosopher who had written a passionate polemic called *Lament for a Nation*, was a cult hero. These developments were not radically new, but they had a clarifying effect on public opinion much like the clicks of recognition women reported in the early years of feminism. [18]

Neither of the opposition parties was able to make political gains out of this new public dissatisfaction with Ottawa's complicity-as-usual in the Canadian sell-out. Under their new leader, Robert Stanfield, the Progressive Conservatives were distancing themselves as best they could from the visceral anti-Americanism that had characterized their history and kept them out of power for most of the twentieth century. As a former premier of Nova Scotia, and scion of a family that manufactured men's underwear, Stanfield stood in the tradition of protected industrialism of Sir John A.

Macdonald's National Policy. But the rising generation of Tories, particularly those who lived in Ontario and Alberta, were looking to American markets, American investment, and American electoral techniques to bring them to power and the country to greater prosperity. Stanfield was pressured into accepting their point of view as part of the need to modernize his party.[19]

The New Democratic Party, which might have seemed the natural home for left-nationalist feeling, was experiencing serious internal conflict on the issue. As leader of the Waffle, a radical faction in the NDP, Mel Watkins was causing turmoil by preaching nationalism on the grounds that only a Canada freed of American control could establish a non-capitalist order. But older socialists under the newly elected leader, David Lewis, the resolute warrior of its CCF past and principal architect of its NDP present, vehemently rejected these ideas. Their power base lay in the trade union movement, which was mainly an extension of the American AFL-CIO and still vociferously opposed to nationalism.[20]

As a result, the main resistance to continentalism came from inside Trudeau's own party, though even it was desultory and mainly underground. Within his cabinet, most ministers with an eye to career advancement were cowed into quiescence on the American question in the face of Trudeau's anti-nationalist scorn. Eric Kierans, one of the most articulate and economically expert ministers, was so frustrated by the prime minister's indifference to the structural distortions created by Canada's branch-plant economy that he resigned his portfolio in 1971 so that he could speak openly about his nationalist concerns.[21]

A few defiantly nationalist rumblings emanated from the Liberal caucus. The Senate Committee on Mass Media, chaired by Keith Davey, who had been appointed to the upper house by Pearson, called for rescinding tax concessions on the Canadian editions of *Time* magazine and *Reader's Digest* in order to buttress the advertising base for Canadian magazines. Ian Wahn, the member from Toronto–St. Paul's, chaired an investigation by the Commons

Standing Committee on External Affairs and National Defence, which then called for 51-per-cent Canadian ownership of all companies operating in Canada.[22]

In the extra-parliamentary wing of the Liberal Party, where feelings ran high about the American threat to Canadian sovereignty, Davey and Wahn had many supporters. But Trudeau's party loyalists had worked hard to suppress debate on the question of American control in the period when a new policy-making process intended as a practical manifestation of Trudeau's promised participatory democracy was being developed. The ideas of nationalist Liberals such as Mel Hurtig, the Edmonton bookseller, were ignored once they had been indulged with a turn at the convention microphones and their fifteen minutes' worth of attention in the national media.[23]

As a consequence, Liberals concerned about Canadian sovereignty turned for solace to Walter Gordon, who was now seen as the godfather of what had become a nationalist movement. An antipathy had developed between Gordon and Trudeau that was both historic and personal. Gordon's ideas had evolved from his roots in the upper reaches of the old British imperialist class. His father, Colonel Harry Gordon, had moved his family to England in 1915 while he did his duty in the Great War with his regiment, the Mississauga Horse. Walter remembered feeling his first nationalist sentiments stir when he was nine and fending off what he called "the little English snots" who taunted him at school because of his Canadian accent. Over the next fifty years, the focus of his discontent had changed from London to Washington. But as with so many Canadians of his class and generation, Gordon's intellectual reference points and his behavioural style owed a great deal to the English, however much he resented their condescensions. It was the same superior style Trudeau himself, as another kind of colonial, had deplored and then adapted to his needs. In one man, for generational and cultural reasons, this experience had led to an ardent nationalism; in the other, to an equally ardent anti-nationalism.[24]

Added to their ideological differences was the fact that Gordon had harboured ambitions to the Liberal leadership in 1968 that were swept away, as were those of so many others, by Trudeau's meteoric rise. Once Trudeau was elected leader, Gordon continued the habits of a lifetime by trying to influence government policy. When his advice was consistently ignored, he turned away from the Liberal Party to found a citizens' protest group called the Committee for an Independent Canada. Under his direction, the CIC held conferences, published books, and gathered hundreds of thousands of signatures endorsing a petition that called on Trudeau to act before the country lost its capacity to control its own affairs. Despite the publicity it created, the CIC was far from powerful. Because its membership was concentrated in Ontario, it was frequently dismissed in the Atlantic provinces and the west as the proponent of central Canadian, fat-cat ideas. Even more damaging to the CIC's prospects was its inability to build bridges to Quebec. Claude Ryan, the editor of *Le Devoir*, did lend his name to the committee at its inception but withdrew after the October Crisis of 1970, when he decided that English-Canadian nationalists were fully as insensitive as the Trudeauites to Quebec's aspirations.[25]

Weary of all the attention American economic and cultural dominance was drawing in the press, Trudeau decided to investigate whether a genuine policy problem lurked behind the continuing uproar. He referred the question to an understaffed, low-priority task force under the chairmanship of Herb Gray, a junior minister who was concerned about the issue, and appointed Joel Bell, a young lawyer-economist in the PMO, as its research director. Bell's group was still at work when Nixonomics struck, so the job of directing the government's response to this thunderbolt fell to two departments that were trapped in the thinking of a previous era and threatened by the Trudeauites' reorganization of government: Finance and External Affairs.[26]

•  •  •

Finance's position as the fulcrum of government had been under attack ever since the Benson White Paper. Its great mandarin, Robert Bryce, had taken early retirement in 1970, exhausted by the difficulties of coping with a more complex world than the one for which his Keynesian training had prepared him. Trudeau's preferred choice as his successor was Albert Wesley (Al) Johnson, who had joined the department in 1964 as an assistant deputy minister after serving as deputy treasurer to CCF/NDP governments in Saskatchewan. With his prairie Methodist integrity, Harvard doctorate, and impressive experience with the practical problems of tax rates and government expenditures, he seemed a fitting successor to Bryce. But when Trudeau offered him the job, Johnson demurred. He felt temperamentally incapable of withstanding the rage he knew his appointment would trigger in Sol Simon Reisman, the secretary of the Treasury Board, who had made it widely known in Ottawa that he was entitled to Bryce's job by virtue of seniority of service. After months of hesitation, Trudeau acquiesced and appointed Reisman. It was to prove a pivotal decision for the government and the country.[27]

Reisman had grown up in the east end of Montreal, the extroverted, ambitious son of an immigrant Jewish family. He was politicized in the 1930s by the rise of fascism in Europe and joined the Young Communist League, a not unusual act for young men of conscience at the time, given that communist organizations were taking the lead in raising the alarm about Hitler's systematic persecution of German Jewry. In a display of the gutsy whirl-away energy that was to mark his lifelong attitude to work, Reisman made his way through university earning money at a variety of jobs, including jerking sodas in a drugstore, and completed his master's degree in economics *summa cum laude* at a distinctly pre-Keynesian McGill. He enlisted in the Canadian army in 1942 and after the war attended the London School of Economics for six months before returning to Canada to work for the federal government, briefly in the Department of Labour and then in the Department of Finance.[28]

Once Reisman took the measure of the Ottawa establishment in the heady days when Finance was the pinnacle of mandarinate power, he aspired with manic ambition to scale its heights. With post-war American anti-communist hysteria spilling over into Canada and wild charges of subversion being made against Canadian public servants before the Senate Subcommittee on Internal Security in Washington, Reisman abandoned his pre-war radicalism but not his internationalist leanings. He was carefully trained by Bryce and went as a "helper" (the word used for younger economists in those days) to several world trade conferences, including the first round of GATT meetings, before being appointed director of the department's international economics division in 1954. When he was seconded to the Gordon royal commission as assistant research director in 1955, he had the chutzpah to oppose Gordon's views and to take a bold stand as a full-blown free-market continentalist. In his study for the commission, conducted in partnership with the economist Irving Brecher, he argued that even though U.S. companies were shutting Canadian firms out of the economy's most advanced industries, foreign direct investment was an economic asset, whatever its political implications.[29]

After Gordon was appointed minister of finance in 1963, he came to believe that Reisman, who was by then an assistant deputy minister in the department, was relaying information to the financial press that damaged the minister's nationalist plans. He prevailed on Pearson to move Reisman to the newly formed Department of Industry. As deputy there, Reisman was the chief Canadian negotiator for the Auto Pact, which embellished his reputation as a continentalist. Three years later, he moved on to the Treasury Board.[30]

Once Reisman finally achieved the deputy's job in Finance in 1970, he set out to be, in the phrase of his fellow economist Sylvia Ostry, "Bob Bryce with balls." But he soon discovered that the job did not automatically give him the power that had once accrued to Bryce. He continued to fume over Trudeau's long hesitation in appointing him and raged because Trudeau rarely sought his advice directly. For a quarter-century he had longed to whisper in the ear of the prime minister – and thus move the entire government the way he wanted it to go. But he had to settle, given Trudeau's new system for government decision-making, for performing with noisy gusto at cabinet committee meetings, commanding the nervous allegiance of lesser economic bureaucrats, and venting his frustrations by yelling down the telephone at Marshall Crowe, Trudeau's economic adviser in the PCO.[31]

Even though Reisman was attempting to overhaul Finance by bringing in university economists with stronger academic credentials than his own, his department's response to Nixon's disconcerting announcement in the summer of 1971 revealed its intellectual bankruptcy. Faced with the obvious political evidence that massive U.S. control of the Canadian economy held Canada hostage to arbitrary changes of American policy, as Walter Gordon had warned, all Reisman could manage was to change the locus of his hollering. In Washington, where he and a group of Canadian officials repaired immediately after Nixon's announcement, he had less success in browbeating John Connally, the U.S. secretary of the treasury, than he did in bullying his fellow bureaucrats, who nevertheless told admiring stories of how the enraged deputy had flicked ashes from his cigar on the Texan's polished desk. Despite his bluster, Reisman was unable to win an exemption for Canada from Nixon's damaging measures.[32]

Over at External Affairs, Canada's diplomatic élite was almost as ill prepared to recognize the implications of the American government's radically altered attitude. External still believed in "the special relationship" and "quiet diplomacy," euphemistic concepts that had been formulated in the 1950s and 1960s to sweeten the reality of Canada's deepening diplomatic dependence on its neighbour. What these catch-phrases meant in practice was that the United States was willing to give Canada particular consideration in bilateral dealings in return for unquestioning support of its Cold War strategy and open access to Canada's resources and markets. External's adherence to these ideas actually complemented Trudeau's in matters American, so that the extensive foreign policy review it conducted from

1968 to 1970 – intended as a central expression of Trudeau's fresh approach to Canada's role in the world – had produced a report that managed with Trudeau's concurrence to ignore Canada's relationship with the United States. [33]

It was scarcely surprising that its first reaction to the newly rough and definitely tough Nixonian pronouncements was to send carefully crafted diplomatic notes to its Washington embassy officials' cocktail-party friends at the State Department. But unlike Finance under the exhausted Benson and the stubborn Reisman, External had the sensitivity to recognize that new thinking was needed when these pleadings did not produce results.

By the time of Nixon's patronizing declaration to the House of Commons, during a state visit to Ottawa in April 1972, that Canada was henceforth to be considered an independent country – and so could no longer count on special favours from Washington – Mitchell Sharp and his under-secretary of state, Ed Ritchie, had a new strategy to propose to cabinet. They had assigned the department's brilliant policy analyst, Klaus Goldschlag, to study the American relationship and to produce the foreign policy review's embarrassing missing link. There was fresh information for Goldschlag to consider. The Gray report, completed at last, documented in methodical detail the extent to which the branch-plant economy had "truncated" Canada, severely handicapping its capacity for entrepreneurship, research, and self-generated growth, and substantially affecting its politics. Although it recommended that the government transform the economy's structure by taking a more interventionist, European-style approach based on a comprehensive industrial strategy and backed by a powerful screening agency to monitor and direct the performance of foreign investment, Trudeau had been reluctant to concur. [34]

But in the waning days of the federal election race that autumn, when the Liberal campaign was suffering demonstrably from the Trudeauites' inept handling of economic issues over the previous four years, Mitchell Sharp issued a surprise statement on Canada's American relationship. Observers were astonished to learn that

Sharp's new position, drawn from Goldschlag's analysis, complemented what the Gray report had proposed. Ottawa had three options, Sharp said: to maintain the status quo in the Canadian-American relationship; to increase Canada's integration into the U.S. economy; or to try to become more autonomous. This "Third Option" of decreased vulnerability was to be based on a comprehensive economic strategy that would make the Canadian economy more balanced, more efficient, and better able to export competitive goods and services to more foreign markets. In recommending it, the one-time continentalist Mitchell Sharp seemed to have come around to positions that Walter Gordon had articulated in the 1960s.[35]

The timing of Sharp's statement also signalled a classic Liberal manoeuvre. Under pressure from the left, the Grits were appropriating its most appealing ideas, as they had so often in the past. When Trudeau's ill-conceived campaign began in September 1972, his advisers had insisted the prime minister would not stoop to such old-fashioned devices as making promises in order to solicit votes. Instead, he would engage in "conversations with Canadians," and presumably infect them once more with the euphoric spirit that had garnered him a majority in 1968. But when reality struck on the hustings, the Trudeauites had been shocked to find that the opposition leaders, whom they previously had disdained, were having more impact on the electorate than Trudeau's homilies, however high-minded in their conception or graceful in their expression.

Robert Stanfield was doggedly travelling the country addressing economic issues from a centre-right position, accusing the Liberals, in a memorable if misguided phrase, of "chicken socialism." And David Lewis, the scrappy leader of the NDP, was eliciting a vibrant response from the media and the public with a series of solidly researched daily statements that turned the business community's attack against the welfare state on its head. It was not ordinary citizens, Lewis claimed, who benefitted most from government largesse. It was business. Detailing the hundreds of millions of dollars received in hand-outs and tax expenditures by "corporate welfare bums," the NDP's David slung stones at the Liberal Goliath for its accommodating response to their demands.

To counter this unexpected show of opposition strength, the Liberals were forced to start handing out what Trudeau himself facetiously referred to as "goodies," such as a hastily concocted scheme for a people's park on the Toronto harbour. The most coherent last-minute policy statement, the Third Option idea, neatly co-opted the NDP's industrial strategy as well as the Gordonites' nationalism and bolstered the Liberals' sagging campaign. Even so, they emerged from the election with the barest possible minority: 109 seats to the Tories' 107. To govern they needed the support of the 31 New Democrats who held the balance of power in the Commons. Pierre Trudeau would have to eat crow by accommodating his former comrade on the democratic left, the leader of the NDP.

David Lewis's zealotry had been a source of irritation to Trudeau for years. Although Lewis was a decade older, they had come of age in the same inequity-ridden Montreal and had both turned into eloquent advocates of social justice. The difference was one of passion versus reason. Lewis had a visceral hatred for inequity that had caused him to put his life on the line for his principles. His father had been a leather worker and labour organizer in an Eastern European shtetl who emigrated to Canada when his son was twelve. With fierce pride and fiercer industry, David Lewis had propelled himself through the Montreal elementary and secondary school systems in six hard years, having acquired his remarkable command of English by translating Charles Dickens with the aid of a Yiddish/English dictionary. As president of the campus Labour Club at McGill, he had met several of the socialist intellectuals who were instrumental in forming the CCF, notably the elegant and ubiquitous F.R. Scott and his plainer friends, Eugene Forsey and Frank Underhill. They responded to Lewis's fervour and intelligence by helping him win a glittering prize, a Rhodes Scholarship to Oxford.

As a student reading jurisprudence at Lincoln College in the early 1930s, Lewis was elected president of the Oxford Union – a feat never before achieved by a Canadian – by displaying the gifts that were ever afterwards to define his public presence: a voice as richly reverberant as a classical actor's and a talent for sarcasm so charged with social rage it electrified his listeners. Even though his incandescent oratory brought him the offer of a position in the London chambers of the illustrious Labourite barrister Stafford Cripps, Lewis chose to return to Depression-locked Canada to fight the good fight for social democracy.[36]

Twenty years later, still the sturdiest of CCFers, he had challenged Trudeau directly in the Montreal of the 1950s to put his left-wing theorizing into practice, and when he refused, taunted him for what Lewis saw as a failure of nerve. Ever since Trudeau's conversion to Liberalism, he had been skewering him in the Commons, reminding him how CCFers had kept social-democratic ideas alive in the hard years when Stalinists had to be fought off from the left and McCarthyites from the right. It was Lewis who had engineered the rapprochement with the union movement that brought about the CCF's transformation into the NDP. And it was he who had won the party leadership by beating back the young intellectuals in its nationalist faction, led by Jim Laxer, when they attacked him for being out of sync with the society he had been struggling for forty years to reform. Lewis had been in the political trenches up to his knees in gore, while Trudeau had fiddled and fulminated in his Jag and his Mercedes.

Lewis's rhetorical barbs – flung across the Commons floor with the supreme assurance of the righteous man who has sacrificed personal gain for the social good – took their toll on Trudeau partly because Lewis's loathing of Liberalism's vacillations was a sentiment he had himself voiced more than once in the past and still had to suppress on occasion.[37]

The months after the 1972 election were to prove the apogee of Lewis's political life, even though they were fraught with the conundrums that face the radical who gets a chance to wield influence as a reformer. Fresh from the triumph of his corporate-welfare-bum campaign but hobbled by serious divisions within his party, he was willing to keep the Liberals in office – and to prevent the Conservatives from precipitating another election that might decimate the NDP's ranks – for the right price. His conditions pushed the Liberal minority government into cutting personal income taxes, raising old-age pensions, and trebling family allowances.[38]

These social security enrichments were not enough for some of Lewis's younger colleagues, who were under pressure from the new and nationalistic public-sector unions now shifting the balance of power within the NDP away from the American-dominated industrial unions. Recently unionized schoolteachers and civil servants were making Canadian sovereignty, along with feminism and environmentalism, a central issue in social-democratic thinking. With the shock of the Waffle's challenge still sharp in his mind, Lewis's previously unrelenting internationalism began to fade. The threat of exclusionary U.S. protectionism heralded by Nixonomics, and abetted by the American union movement, was a warning he could not ignore. Even though the Waffle's extreme ideas had been extirpated, a moderate nationalism that sought to achieve a Canadian-controlled capitalism seemed appropriate for the NDP.[39]

With the social democrats sniping at them from the other side of the House, the Trudeauites proceeded to strengthen their proposed Foreign Investment Review Agency in the light of continuing public concern about U.S. economic domination; to defend their newly minted Canada Development Corporation's take-over of the American mining company Texas Gulf; and, in response to the OPEC oil crisis, to freeze the domestic price of oil and incorporate Petro-Canada as a state-owned oil company whose purpose was to give Canadians a stake in their energy industry. The final credit Lewis could claim in this period was the appointment of Thomas Berger, the former NDP leader from British Columbia, to investigate how a massive pipeline project, proposed by an American-led consortium to pump natural gas southwards from the Arctic along the Mackenzie River, would affect the native population.[40]

These moves were too cursory and too cynically cosmetic to satisfy most ardent nationalists. But they alienated big businessmen further from a government that seemed to them decidedly out of touch
with the private sector's desire to accelerate, not reverse, Canada's
integration into the U.S. economy. With GATT's trade liberalization
reducing protection for the Canadian market, the direction of continental capital flows had reversed: U.S. capital was less interested in
setting up behind Canada's declining tariff wall, whereas Canadian
entrepreneurs were starting to buy out U.S. branch plants and to
expand their operations to the south.

Trudeau was inclined to dismiss both the nationalist and business
views as irrelevant whining. He believed his government's various
new NDP-inspired regulatory policies and its continuing support for
Canadian cultural institutions were more than adequate concessions
to the nationalists. And he felt he had done what was necessary to
reassure the business community when he replaced Edgar Benson
with John Turner as minister of finance in 1972.[41]

Turner had all the right credentials for the finance portfolio.
His widowed mother, Phyllis Turner, a B.C. coal miner's daughter
who had been trained as an economist in the United States, was
the only woman of her time to penetrate the mandarinate as commissioner of fats and oils in the Wartime Prices and Trade Board.
She later married Frank Ross, one of the businessmen who had
rallied to the government in wartime, and moved with him to
Vancouver, where he made a small fortune in the boom and was
appointed provincial lieutenant-governor. She had goaded her
only son, John, from childhood to go after a great public career.
Always accommodating to her wishes, Turner set out to add the
necessary educational and experiential credentials to his inherited
advantages. After earning a BA at UBC, he went to Oxford as a
Rhodes Scholar; learned French during a further student year in
Paris; gained corporate experience in a Montreal law firm; and
married a handsome woman named Geills McCrae Kilgour whose

father, a Winnipeg businessman, was also an accredited member of the pan-Canadian consociational élites.

After Turner was elected as the member for Westmount in 1962, his rise through Liberal ranks was swift. Mike Pearson, who had known him as a boy, appointed him to his cabinet as registrar general and then as minister of consumer and corporate affairs. As a candidate in the 1968 leadership race, he had put up a stout fight, which was expected to position him well for next time around, when the Liberal tradition of alternating French and English leaders would work in his favour. In recognition of his party power base, Trudeau had made him solicitor general and then minister of justice. Never an independent thinker, Turner was prized by his officials as a politician with a lawyerly capacity to absorb a briefing without raising time-consuming objections. In the blunt assessment of Simon Reisman, Turner ranked as "the best goddam minister a deputy could hope for . . . a man who knew his job and let me do mine."[42]

Turner's job in the difficult 1972–74 minority period was to spout the Finance line, an unusual challenge since the department under Reisman was travelling in a direction somewhat contrary to the one in which the PMO/PCO thought the Trudeau government was heading. Trudeau had appointed as minister of health and welfare his former principal secretary, the newly elected Marc Lalonde, to bring about a fundamental reform of the government's welfare policies – an issue that assumed great importance in his mind after the failed constitutional conference held in Victoria in 1971, where Quebec's demand for full control of social policies created an impasse.

An expanded social security policy had major implications for Finance. NDP-induced fattening of social security payments already meant a budgetary increase of $1.6 billion. Anticipating that Lalonde and his deputy, Al Johnson, would shortly recommend a further quantum leap in Ottawa's spending needs by proposing a guaranteed annual income, Simon Reisman decided to oppose what he felt was the dangerously extravagant thrust of the government's welfare liberalism. In his view – and he now endorsed unreconstructed free-market capitalism with the fervour of the convert – increased social security benefits were as bad for the private sector as any other government intervention. They were also bad for Reisman since they meant Lalonde and Johnson, who were far more compatible with Trudeau than he could ever hope to be, would have the power to undermine his authority. His pride demanded that his department be *the* economic authority in Ottawa, and he insisted that Trudeau disband an advisory group of economists set up in the PMO to provide him with alternative advice.[43]

In the light of the great American conservative economist Milton Friedman's powerful attack on Keynesianism's failure to prevent either unemployment or inflation, Reisman wanted to move towards a "supply-side" approach to economic management that was designed to increase the supply of goods by offering entrepreneurs direct incentives, such as reduced corporate tax rates and accelerated write-offs for new investment. As part of this shift, he had persuaded Turner to adopt a proposal the Progressive Conservatives had espoused in the 1972 campaign, which involved protecting taxpayers from inflation by tying personal income-tax brackets to the cost-of-living index. Besides accomplishing the dexterous feat of borrowing ideas from the emerging right while the prime minister was dependent on support from the social-democratic left, this "indexing" strengthened Reisman's position against the threat from Lalonde and Johnson. Ottawa's tax revenues would no longer escalate as inflation pushed individual citizens' tax payments ever higher. So when Lalonde and Johnson came up with their proposal to solve Canada's poverty problem with a guaranteed annual income, Turner and Reisman would be able to convince the cabinet that the government could not afford the measure: it would have to wait until real economic growth had generated greater tax receipts.[44]

Caught in these economic paradoxes, Trudeau went into the 1974 election with his principles on hold, having increased spending for eighteen months under the influence of the NDP, while his Department of Finance was rejecting Keynes. He was able to rationalize these acrobatics with the support of a new campaign team, a group of savvy Liberals from Toronto who were to prove his last and most enduring English alliance and who assured "the boss," as they took to calling Trudeau, that the kind of accommodation with contradictory ideas he was making was the essence of Canadian Liberalism.

The chief actors in the group were Keith Davey, whom Trudeau appointed campaign chairman in English Canada, and James Coutts, who served as his political tour guide on the hustings. As a duo, they were quite unlike the anglophiliac gentlemen-scholars Trudeau had met in Harold Laski's London, Norman Robertson's Ottawa, and Frank Scott's Montreal. These were post-war, middle-class Canadians on the rise, part of a generation that had been bombarded since early adolescence by the magazines, movies, music, and television of the expanding American imperium. Davey, a native Torontonian with a natural talent for salesmanship, had hustled his way out of the city's small-time advertising world into full-time professional politicking. Coutts had been born, bred, and educated as a lawyer in Alberta, the country's most Americanized province, and was proud of his capacity to manage situations of all kinds in business and politics – and in the netherworld where they meet – with the flair he had learned as an MBA candidate at the Harvard Business School before he returned to Canada to settle in Toronto as a management consultant in 1968.

Coutts and Davey had met during Pearson's opposition years when Coutts, who was twelve years Davey's junior, was a student Liberal. Though they came from conservative backgrounds – Davey's antecedents were Ontario Tories and Coutts's were Alberta Social Crediters – they were both progressive modernists, attracted to the Liberal Party's success at a time when the Progressive Conservatives were seen by the ambitious as an unlikely amalgam of reactionary Bay Street plutocrats and wild-eyed prairie populists, and the CCF as an outmoded movement of woolly-minded dreamers.[45]

The years they spent in Ottawa when Pearson was in power were the happiest of their political lives. Davey, functioning as the party's national director under Walter Gordon's aegis, and Coutts, who was appointments secretary to the prime minister, were catapulted into the world of the powerful at the zenith of the Kennedy era. They treated sleepy Bytown as though their Liberal optimism could turn it into a northern Camelot. They loved Pearson, the most famous Canadian of the post-war era, who could rattle off American League baseball statistics as easily as he recounted funny stories about the foibles of celebrated international figures from Eden to Gromyko, Hammerskjöld to Rusk. He invited them to cosy suppers at 24 Sussex, teased them as though they were his nephews, and advised them on their careers. Best of all he leaned on them for political advice, giving them the feeling that without their know-how, he would be lost in the partisan jungle, easy prey for the retrogressive John Diefenbaker and his prairie Neanderthals.

When the friendship Pearson and Gordon had nourished for more than thirty years came to grief on nationalist issues, Coutts and Davey also diverged, though not as dramatically as their mentors. Davey continued to revere "Mr. Pearson," as he always called the man almost everybody else addressed as "Mike." But he identified himself as a Gordonite while acknowledging that he was "not a policy guy." The apprenticeship he had served with Gordon had taught him primarily how to apply modern management techniques to the electoral process, but he had been sufficiently touched by Gordon's idealism to support nationalist measures, especially as they affected the media.[46]

Coutts was not a policy guy either. And as an Albertan and a doer, he had little interest in nationalist ideas. Gordon's messy performance as finance minister had confirmed his impression that economic nationalists were impractical. Coutts's Liberal friendships were mostly on the business side of the party: he was close to Tony Abbott, for instance, whom he had met while they were both practising law briefly in Calgary. Tony had introduced Jim to his father, Douglas Abbott, the former finance minister turned Supreme Court justice, and the senior Abbott had given him sage advice.

Shortly after Trudeau entered Parliament in 1965, Coutts had decamped to Harvard and then Toronto. Davey had heard Trudeau was a comer and invited him to lunch to give him the benefit of his media-wise moxie. When Trudeau was unmoved by his expert spiel, Davey decided he was "not my kind of guy." He backed the Toronto cabinet minister Paul Hellyer for the Liberal leadership in 1968 and, when his faction of Liberals was displaced by the Montrealers who swept Trudeau to power in 1968, stoically withdrew to the Senate. [47]

Four years later, in the aftermath of the 1972 election, Coutts and Davey and their Toronto Liberal friends had decided pragmatically to come to Trudeau's aid. If he messed up again at the next election and Stanfield's Conservatives took over, they would be cut off entirely from the benefits of power. In choosing them as his advisers, Trudeau was equally calculating. He needed technicians who could manage his campaign in English Canada, and his soundings indicated they were the best in the business. Ever since T.H. White's *The Making of the President 1960* had become their catechism in the early 1960s, Coutts and Davey had honed their electoral skills by pressing their noses against the window of U.S. presidential politics, with its panoply of razzle-dazzle campaign techniques – all the while reiterating truisms about parliamentary democracy as the highest achievement of mankind and national unity as the noblest goal of Canadians. Between them they knew how to draw on the strengths and exploit the ambitions of thousands of their fellow Grits in every part of the country. But the two other key people on the campaign team they put together for Trudeau in 1973–74 were also Torontonians: Martin Goldfarb, an anthropologist turned pollster, and Jerry Grafstein, a voluble communications lawyer who shared Coutts and Davey's fascination with the engineering of consent.

For Grafstein, like so many of the young Liberals in the 1960s who had seen in Pearson's party a vehicle for their ideas, political involvement had become an instrument for professional advantage. His zeal for reforming the judicial system had dissipated as he climbed the Toronto socio-political power structure. By the mid-1970s he was a successful downtown lawyer with a passion for American liberal ideas, an interest in a Toronto television station, and connections throughout the city's advertising industry that he was able to harness to the Liberals' communications efforts at election time. His counterpart as the party's hired surveyor of public opinion was Martin Goldfarb, who, like so many of the post-war generation of Canadian Jews, identified with the Liberal Party as the most ethnically open of Canada's political formations, though he never joined it officially and had polled provincially for other parties.

The campaign the Coutts-and-Davey crowd ran for Trudeau was a *tour de force*. They had cottoned on to the fact that Trudeau was the best actor they had ever seen in public life. "All you had to do was provide him with the script and the costumes," was the way Grafstein described their strategy in presenting their leader. They persuaded Trudeau to use the bourgeois charms of his would-be bohemian wife to bolster his effectiveness at rallies. Acutely aware of the Trudeaus' visual saleability (and Margaret's conversational unpredictability), Coutts and Davey contrived an old-fashioned whistle-stop train tour that kept the curious press at bay while providing plenty of photo ops. They made sure Trudeau stayed off the radio talk shows, with their populist hosts and provocative callers, lest his intolerance for criticism surface for the electorate to hear. In conjunction with Grafstein's advertising advisory group – made up of representatives from firms who had expectations of government contracts – they cagily commissioned television commercials that played up differences between the elegant, athletic Trudeau and the plainer politicians, Robert Stanfield and David Lewis, running once more against him.[48]

The aesthete in Trudeau found the Coutts-and-Davey crowd somewhat distasteful. The pragmatist absorbed what they had to say, followed their directives as far as his conscience would allow (i.e., not *quite* to the letter), and was generous (if somewhat ironic) in his praise after their foxiness, as he described their electoral expertise, brought the Liberals a comfortable majority when the votes were counted on the eighth of July. His irony might have turned acerbic had he known that their advice on how to handle policy questions – which was to ridicule Stanfield's proposal of a ninety-day wage and price freeze for dealing with the economy's problems while announcing an array of policies hastily drafted in response to Gold-farb's public opinion research – would boomerang within a matter of months. [49]

Restored to power for a third ministry, the Trudeau Liberals had to face the unpleasant reality that their patchwork economic policies were not working. In common with governments throughout the industrialized world, they were contending with new dilemmas. The Keynesian panacea had lost its lustre, and the welfare state was in crisis everywhere in the West. Just when rising expectations among better-educated, television-nurtured populations were requiring faster economic growth, governments were losing the capacity to intervene effectively to boost economies that had been hard hit by the inflationary impact of OPEC-induced price increases. International agreements negotiated over the years through the GATT were reducing its member states' ability to protect their local market with tariffs. The prior increase of social security expenditures and the slowdown in government revenue growth exhausted reserves for launching new stimuli in the spirit of Keynes. Citizen activism was broadening demands for government action at a time when the state was losing its practical capability to provide more services. Experts were convening in grave conclaves and publishing dire books warning Western democracies that they were becoming "ungovernable." Although Canada was doing comparatively well in the altered world climate, inflation was still gathering momentum and wage settlements were escalating. Reisman's supply-side budgets had failed to stem the continuing slide in productivity, though they were credited with having prevented unemployment from increasing.[50]

It was in this uneasy atmosphere that the prime minister appointed his friend Michael Pitfield to the job of chief civil servant, with the twin titles of clerk of the Privy Council and secretary to the cabinet. By vaulting Pitfield over the heads of several more senior bureaucrats as the replacement for Gordon Robertson, who had held the job since 1963, the prime minister precipitated a minor revolt in the mandarinate. Even the equanimous Robert Bryce, who had been clerk of the Privy Council when Pitfield first came to work in Ottawa, was dismayed by the choice. It was "imprudent," as he said later. The chief public servant, no matter what his other qualifications, should not be a friend of the prime minister's – or even be *seen* as such. And Pitfield did not have the appropriate qualifications, in any case.[51]

At thirty-seven, he was too young. His education was spotty (a few unhappy months at West Point, the U.S. military academy; a baccalaureate from a college in northern New York State no one had ever heard of; a law degree from McGill and a night-school diploma in public law from the University of Ottawa). His administrative experience was inadequate (fifteen years in Ottawa but only nine within the civil service proper, and only two as a deputy minister in a minor department). And too many of his jobs seemed to have been gained through family or political influence. The meritocratic, basically middle-class mandarinate had come to the conclusion that Pitfield's most important qualification for the role of clerk was his appeal to the anglophiliac snob in P. Elliott Trudeau.

Ever since he had come to Ottawa in 1959, Pitfield's mannerisms and rarefied conversation had signalled that he was a socially superior upper-class man with connections to the American and British élites as well as easy entrée to the upper reaches of the Canadian mosaic. His mother, Grace Pitfield, was the daughter of Hartland C. MacDougall, a St. James Street broker, and the widow of Ward

Chipman Pitfield, who had been a regimental major in the Great War, an associate of the international business barons Max Aitken and Isaak Walton Killam in their Montreal enterprises, and founder of his own brokerage house in the 1920s. In her youth she had been so insistent on her family connections to the ship-owning Refords, the pulp-and-paper Prices, and the beer-brewing Molsons, three Anglo-Quebec dynasties founded before Confederation, that she disdained Westmount as a parvenu's suburb. (Her view of contemporary Toronto went beyond disdain. It was a place, she remarked, where "even the people one *knows* have broadloom in the bawthrooms.")[52]

Pitfield had first met Trudeau casually in the late 1950s at gatherings of the Institut canadien des affaires publiques, when he was a student of Frank Scott's. He had become familiar with Trudeau's federalist thinking when he translated into English for publication in *The Canadian Forum* in 1964 the ideas of the Montreal *manifestistes*, at the request of Marc Lalonde. Later, when Trudeau was first elected to the House of Commons and had an office in the PMO as Pearson's parliamentary secretary, Pitfield was working down the hall in the PCO and offered him expert advice on the intricacies of Pearson's Ottawa. When Trudeau took on the justice portfolio in 1967 and set up a weekly lunch meeting to discuss constitutional reform, Pitfield was part of the group.

Pitfield was also known to have been engrossed more deeply in Trudeau's 1968 leadership campaign than he should have been as a civil servant, a situation that provoked bitter laughter among some of his contemporaries in the Conservative Party, such as Hal Jackman, Brian Mulroney, Lowell Murray, Libby Burnham, and Gordon Sedgwick; they had interpreted Pitfield's first Ottawa job in the office of E. Davie Fulton, Diefenbaker's minister of justice, as a sign that he had embraced his family's conservative politics. ("What these people don't understand is that Michael has never been all that interested in party politics," said Grattan O'Leary, the famously loyal Tory newspaper editor and Pitfield's close friend from the time they had worked together on the Royal Commission on Publishing in 1961 until his death in 1976. "He's interested in power.") [53]

In the early Trudeau years, when Pitfield was still secondary in the PCO pecking order, he had come to be seen by political and bureaucratic insiders as a particular favourite among the prime minister's advisers, a man whose views were given greater weight than were warranted by his titles of assistant deputy and then deputy secretary. Resentment of Pitfield grew when he was chosen as the official who accompanied Trudeau on holidays while they were both bachelors, and was felt more deeply still when Trudeau gave a dinner at 24 Sussex Drive to celebrate Pitfield's marriage in December 1971 to Nancy Snow, a young woman from Toronto (whose family did indeed have broadloom in the bawth-rooms); this was an honour undreamed of by most officials, who had never been invited to any kind of social function at the prime minister's house.

Pitfield's peers were convinced that he competed compulsively for the prime minister's attention, subtly making sure that possible rivals were distanced from Trudeau's presence. Marshall Crowe, also a deputy secretary in the PCO in the early Trudeau years, but with far broader experience than Pitfield's, said later, "If I had stayed in the PCO instead of being persuaded to become head of the Canada Development Corporation, it would have been difficult to pass me over for the job of clerk once Gordon resigned. But Michael would have organized it in some way. He was always able to get that kind of thing done." [54]

Over the years personal disgruntlement had turned into professional hostility towards Pitfield's involvement in the evolution of Trudeau's highly rationalist system of government, which had been a source of controversy in Ottawa since 1968. Even though it was the stalwart Gordon Robertson, not the esoteric Pitfield, who had been ultimately responsible for implementing the reorganization in its early stages, Pitfield was generally understood to have been its principal theorist. Once Trudeau indicated his intention to name him clerk, Pitfield was immediately blamed for the system's imperfections as well as the governmental afflictions for which it was meant to be the cure.

The most forcefully expressive of the new clerk's detractors was none other than Simon Reisman. When he heard about Pitfield's appointment, Reisman decided this represented a further challenge to his power that was untenable. He resigned from the civil service at the age of fifty-five, taking advantage of the uncommonly hand-some retirement package he had caused his department to put together to give senior bureaucrats generous inflation-proofed pen-sions. Reisman invited James Grandy, the deputy minister of indus-try, trade, and commerce, who was also eligible for early retirement, to join him in a pioneering venture, the establishment of a consult-ing business in Ottawa. Over the next decade the Reisman-Grandy firm would serve as a stimulus to the private sector in its opposition to the Liberals' economic policies by providing advice to its clients that drew on its principals' intimate knowledge of government – and on the energy Reisman derived from his anger that his bureau-cratic career had not ended as he had hoped.

With Reisman gone from Finance and Pitfield ensconced in the clerk's job, John Turner became increasingly uncomfortable in his portfolio. His many friends in the business world expected him to champion their point of view in cabinet. But his new deputy minis-ter was neither inclined nor able to offer advice that would allow him to do so. Trudeau had replaced Reisman with T.K. (Tommy) Shoyama, a left-leaning Keynesian who had gained his early bureau-cratic experience working for social-democratic governments in Saskatchewan. Shoyama was the polar opposite of his predecessor, a mild-mannered Japanese Canadian and self-consciously *civil* ser-vant, seeking not to manipulate his political masters but to imple-ment their instructions. The problem that Shoyama faced in the spring of 1975 was that the Liberal ministers knew they wanted to escape their government's economic woes, but neither he nor any other economic bureaucrat was able to produce a grand strategy that would tell them how. Stagflation – the co-existence of inflation with unemployment – was a phenomenon not addressed by Keynes. Trained in the master's paradigm, most Finance officials could see no evil in rising deficits if these helped maintain consumer demand and thereby saved jobs. Without Simon Reisman, the few who were disturbed by deficit financing were not powerful enough to change the dominant view, even though stagflation in the face of government stimulation had revealed that the economic shibboleths in which Ottawa had long placed its confidence no longer worked. [55]

Stagflation was hitting the public in its pocketbook but it was striking economics in its credibility. Suffering from widespread disbelief in their dictums, members of the economic priesthood had taken to quarrelling among themselves. Factions emerged, each claiming exclusive possession of The Truth. Among theorists in the universities, monetarists attacked Keynesians as romantics made obsolete by the realities of politics. Keynesians dismissed monetarists as reactionaries living in a nineteenth-century world of simplistic economic theorems. Neo-classical economists positioned themselves in the middle and preached the virtues of free trade.

For the more empirically inclined, such as the University of Alberta economist Bruce Wilkinson, Canada's structural weakness in manufacturing had become alarming. Measured by the low proportion of finished goods in its exports, the country was only semi-industrialized. It was not competitive in high-tech flexible production fields, and it was threatened by the lower-tech mass production industries now relocating in the NICs, the newly industrializing countries of the Third World where transnational corporations found cheap labour and obliging governments willing to discipline their work-forces. The extraction of diminishing stocks of raw materials was becoming more expensive at the same time as technological breakthroughs were reducing world demand and Third World economies were competing with cheaper supplies. Exporting little-processed resources and importing high-value-added manufactured goods was a formula for a chronic current account deficit and long-run economic decline. This debate took on a further complexity when a few political economists disparaged mainstream economists for ignoring the experience of more economically successful countries, such as Japan and the European social democracies, where the state had intervened to forge consensual industrial strategies that accelerated their economies' adaptation to the new computer-based technologies. [56]

By September 1975, John Turner could no longer tolerate the uncertainties provoked by these controversies. Serving as finance minister under such circumstances was injurious to his self-esteem and his career prospects. He had absorbed the view that Canada was in a state of economic crisis, and he wanted out. After a difficult exchange with the prime minister, during which Turner tried in vain to wring reassurances about his future from Trudeau, he resigned from the cabinet. When he was offered a partnership in the Toronto corporate law firm of McMillan, Binch, he accepted with alacrity, thereby becoming a valuable ally operating in the heart of the anti-Trudeau Bay Street business community. [57]

Donald Macdonald, the Toronto MP who had already served the government in a number of demanding jobs – House leader and defence minister in the first Trudeau regime, energy minister when the OPEC crisis changed the world in the second – gamely agreed to step into the breach in Finance. As the press pumped up the crisis, an emergency damage-control committee of deputy ministers met repeatedly under Macdonald's aegis to discuss new directions but was unable to agree on the basic nature of Canada's economic problems. It did manage to work out a purely mechanical scheme that respected Trudeau's insistence that inflation restraint not look like Stanfield's ninety-day wage-and-price-freeze proposal of the previous year. [58]

Ever sceptical about taking drastic action on the economy, Trudeau was the last member of his cabinet to agree to the deputies' proposals. He was familiar with the arguments of the monetarists and the neo-classicists, as well as the Keynesians. But in the crunch of 1975, he turned out to be most responsive to the supremely confident arguments of John Kenneth Galbraith, who came from a southwestern Ontario farm family but was as much at home in the common rooms of Cambridge, Eng., as he was in the faculty clubs of Cambridge, Mass. Galbraith had moved into a post-Keynesian phase and believed in direct government intervention. Earlier in the year Trudeau had read *Economics and the Public Purpose*, his major new work that made a case for controlling the pricing behaviour of the largest corporations, which constituted America's "technostructure." Galbraith later recalled discussing the practicality of controls with Trudeau, whose "active and unconventional mind's superb response" was resistant to ideologies and open to sensible proposals (such as his own). Once convinced, Trudeau appeared on television on Thanksgiving Day to announce that his government was imposing for an indefinite period a comprehensive system of wage and price controls to tackle the inflationary spiral under the supervision of an Anti-Inflation Board. [59]

To an alienated business community, wage and price controls represented dangerously intensified government intervention in the economy. Corporate control over the allocation and distribution of economic resources was threatened by tripartite business-labour-government decision-making. This politicization of market relations was bound to increase the power of the union movement. [60]

As the autumn wore on, it became apparent that the AIB initiative had not quelled public concern. Disdaining the kind of sweet-talking of major media figures that was being urged on him by James Coutts, who had recently moved from Toronto to Ottawa to become his principal secretary, Trudeau was unable to prevent the AIB from being seen as a cynical flip-flop from the anti-controls position with which he had so recently humiliated Stanfield. The process that led to his about-turn smacked less of rational experts planning than of an inept government blundering. In warding off criticism, Trudeau appeared exhausted intellectually and morally.

To his staff it seemed more likely that he was psychically laid low by the problems of dealing with the unhappiness of his wife, who was suffering a crisis of her own that was to continue for several years and end in their divorce. These domestic difficulties, plus the daily demands of his job, meant that he was too beset to undertake new thinking on his own and too insistent on his intellectual autonomy to fully trust others to do that thinking for him. Vilified in Quebec for his dogmatic federalism by former allies as well as old enemies, and attacked by civil libertarians in English Canada for his tough anti-terrorist position during the October Crisis of 1970, he was largely cut off from intellectuals outside the bureaucracy, people who might have produced fresh ideas to help in his government's struggle to contend with new world economic conditions.[61]

Apart from talking to his old friend Albert Breton, who came to Ottawa almost every week throughout the 1970s to advise Trudeau directly on economic issues, he was largely isolated within the vortex of the political storms. His incapacity to admit uncertainty and his obsessive need to show superiority in all fields had caused him to rebuff the intellectual talent that was available to him within government circles. He seemed to onlookers to suffer from the Chomsky syndrome, to be a man who purported to know it all. While he could draw on a substantial body of independent, if orthodox, economic research done at the Economic Council of Canada, he usually dismissed its reports since they were often critical of his government. The Science Council's work was too tainted by its nationalist aura even to be considered. The establishment of the Institute for Research on Public Policy, a think tank modelled on the Brookings Institution in Washington, was his personal project, but he paid little attention either to its start-up problems or to its eventual flood of publications.[62]

With little time to read anything apart from the endless cabinet documents supplied by his bureaucrats, Trudeau attempted to ride out the post-AIB difficulties by relying on his rhetorical prowess in the Commons and his compelling presence on television. This tactic backfired at the end of the year when he caused another brouhaha in the boardrooms by publicly giving voice on television to Galbraith's maverick views on the failure of the free market. His remarks were read by a paranoid business community as a revelation of his covert socialism rather than as the dose of realism he intended them to be.[63]

This episode made it apparent that Trudeau had not recognized the importance of maintaining a coalition of interests sufficiently broad to support the government's economic policies. It was as though he took a perverse pride in governing *against* the views of the main forces in his society, including labour, the media, and academe, as well as business. The former apostle of participatory democracy had become frankly authoritarian: governments, he indicated, were elected to govern as rationally as possible until they presented themselves to the atomized voters to seek their support once more. Between elections, the public should mind its own business and the elected should not compromise themselves by responding to pressure. Citizen activists were dismissed as defending vested interests, which by definition could not have the common good at heart.

Just as disconcerting was the realization that even if there were a clear solution to Canada's economic dilemmas, Trudeau had a limited capacity to bring it about as prime minister. The Bank of Canada – which significantly affected the behaviour of the economy by regulating the supply of money – was beyond his control. Relations between governments and their central banks are frequently uncomfortable, but the attitude of the Trudeau government towards the Bank of Canada after the mid-1970s went beyond discomfort to agonized ambivalence. Partly it was a question of turf. Who was in charge of monetary policy: the accountable government or the independent Bank? Implicit at the Bank's founding in the 1930s was its predominant role in managing the credit supply, an authority that had become virtually absolute after a bitter dispute in the early 1960s between Diefenbaker and James Coyne, the Bank's obdurate governor. The spectacle of Coyne's forced resignation paradoxically led to a strengthening of the governor's role, which accorded his institution near autonomy from political interference.[64]

The current incumbent, Gerald Bouey, had come to the job secure in this expectation. He had joined the Bank with only a BA from Queen's after serving in the RCAF during the war. Having worked in the same institution for almost thirty years, his attitudes by the mid-1970s were a perfect reflection of the Bank's insularity, its unwavering celebration of theoretical modelling, and its attraction to the latest economic theories being propounded in the United States. Bouey's conversion to monetarism had been signalled in 1974 when, after expanding the money supply for years, he adopted the beliefs of Milton Friedman that were gaining credence with nervous central bankers everywhere, particularly at the Federal Reserve Board in Washington. Deeply concerned about inflation, Bouey came to accept what Friedman had been preaching for decades: the only way to curb it was to restrict the supply of money available for business investment and consumer spending.[65]

Since the Liberal cabinet did not have the nerve to adopt a tight fiscal policy by increasing taxes, Bouey made it clear that the Bank would defy the government and go it alone by constricting growth in the money supply. If making credit hard to get deflated the economy and aggravated unemployment, this was an unfortunate but necessary cost. Unhappily, contracting output and increasing unemployment did not stop inflation. So Bouey decided to follow the Americans' lead once more by raising interest rates. This pushed up the value of the Canadian dollar by attracting footloose foreign capital. The high dollar made Canadian exports costlier and so reduced the country's foreign earnings, while demand for imports held steady. The resulting balance-of-payments problem, combined with increasing capital outflows from subsidiaries to head offices, aggravated the current account deficit. This alarmed the labour movement.[66]

Organized labour was experiencing its own turmoil because of changing global conditions. Investment capital was now flowing out of Canada rather than into it, taking jobs with it to the Third World or the American Sun Belt. As a consequence, productivity had stalled, and without gains in that area that would offset rising inflation, it was impossible to stop Canada's competitive position from degenerating, or to prevent real wages from declining. At the same time, the union movement had lost public sympathy (because of its ever-higher wage demands and continuing public-sector strikes, which harmed a broad spectrum of Canadians), suasion in government circles (because of its hostile rhetoric), and clout at the bargaining table (because business profits were down). Although the high-wage skilled work-force was defended by unions, conditions among unskilled part-time workers – mostly women and youths who moved in and out of the labour market – were deteriorating as their numbers swelled. In the face of these changes, union leaders blamed the government, interpreting the introduction of wage controls as a significant move to the right. For them it marked a breakdown of the social contract and a provocative return to prewar class warfare, since limiting wages proved easier to effect than constraining price increases.[67]

Buffeted by these conflicts, Donald Macdonald gave up the finance portfolio after only two years and ducked out of government to follow John Turner to Bay Street, as a partner in a rival corporate law firm, McCarthy & McCarthy. Both men were immediately described in the business media as sterling candidates for the Liberal leadership if only Trudeau could be forced out.

Trudeau responded with predictable stubbornness. A separatist government had been elected in Quebec the previous year; the pundits in his own province were saying his federalism-through-bilingualism theory was a failure. Now English Canada was saying his government was a managerial fiasco and French power had failed. He decided to defy this judgement by appointing the first francophone finance minister in Canadian history. His options were limited, his choice difficult. He had already moved his most able cabinet colleague, Marc Lalonde, to Federal-Provincial Relations to oversee the volatile constitutional dossier. His sometime minister of industry, trade, and commerce, Jean-Luc Pepin, who had established a rapport with pan-Canadian business, had been rejected by the voters in his Quebec riding in 1974 and was now serving as chairman of the Anti-Inflation Board. The remaining possibility, Jean Chrétien, gave him pause.

An old-fashioned *rouge* politician who styled himself "the little guy from Shawinigan," Chrétien had been eyeing the finance job ever since he had served as parliamentary secretary to Mitchell Sharp when he was minister in the 1960s. But it was a ministry for which he was ill suited at this confusing moment in economic history. A hinterland lawyer without training in either business or economics, his real forte was giving rousing speeches to audiences in small-town Canada, not fronting for the Canadian government at international conclaves on global economic conditions. Trudeau decided to appoint Chrétien anyway, reasoning that his great personal charm would work with the business community. But under Chrétien's aegis, Finance fell to a new low in influence.[68]

In the late summer of 1978 Trudeau's patience snapped. For the past two years, he had been attending the annual economic summits of the seven most powerful nations and participating in the newly emerging multilateral management and disciplining of the world economy's members. That summer the summit was held in Bonn, the capital of the Federal Republic of Germany, where the host was Chancellor Helmut Schmidt. As Europe's leading social democrat, Schmidt had great suasion with Trudeau when he explained at general meetings and in private conversations on his yacht the need for governmental restraint in a time of stagflation. Flying back to Canada with Schmidt's ideas vividly in mind, Trudeau worked out, with the help of James Coutts, a dramatic if desperate plan for his personal intervention in economic affairs. Without consulting either the minister or the deputy minister of finance, Trudeau announced that his government would make a $2-billion cut in its spending programs. Auditor General James Macdonell's much-publicized recent pronouncement that the government was "close to losing effective control of the public purse" was embarrassingly confirmed by the revelation that Trudeau himself was directing this drastic pruning. The system's failure to control the growth of its own spending – which the Lambert royal commission on financial management had described as "a serious lack of accountability" by the government to Parliament – was evident for all to see. The ensuing débâcle, as ministers and deputies lobbied against the belt-tightening and predicted disaster if their favourite programs were truncated, managed to lower morale in Finance further but did nothing to improve Canada's economic situation or the public's belief that the Liberals were in control.[69]

Bureaucrats in other parts of the Ottawa system had been no more successful than Finance in developing a coherent economic strategy. The giant staples corporations had no interest in the federal government intervening with a grand plan that might well divert some of their huge economic rents into industrial development. For its part the manufacturing sector was too fragmented between branch plants and Canadian-owned firms and too balkanized by region to be able to agree on a common overarching position. Small wonder then that in the Department of Industry, Trade and Commerce a decade's worth of discussion about an industrial strategy for the country had produced nothing more than a series of studies to investigate what the twenty-three main sectors of the economy wanted government to do for them.

Beyond making statements about the need for Canada to spend more on research and development to acquire competence in the industries of the future, ministers publicly expressed doubts about the very concept of a government-led industrial development policy. The only concrete action the government managed to take – and this was in response to pressure from a group of backbenchers furious that the government was failing to cope – was organizational: the creation of a new super-ministry, the Board of Economic Development Ministers. But BEDM (pronounced like "bedlam" without the l) had little time before the coming election to do much more than prepare for the transfer of power that the public opinion polls were showing was inevitable. By early 1979, with the OPEC cartel pushing up world oil prices still further, the Trudeau government was on the ropes. It had been battered less by the opposition parties (even though they had been energized by the election of new leaders, the Conservative Joe Clark and the New Democrat Ed Broadbent) than by all the unresolved problems of the dismal decade now coming to an end. [70]

As far as Trudeau was concerned, there was little more he could do beyond shrug in weary frustration. He had taken Canada's economic dilemmas seriously. He had refrained from scoring easy points by blaming the Americans for the country's woes. Who knew what he should have done when no two economic advisers could agree on what course to take? Was it his fault that these problems were as intractable as they were universal? Every other government in the West had confronted the same international recession, the same incapacity to meet all the demands for increased benefits that kept pressing on the welfare state. Besides, Canada had actually fared well in comparison with its competitors among the industrialized nations. In the second half of the 1970s, Canada's annual deficits were proportionally among the lowest in the industrialized economies; its inflation rate was close to and its growth rate a shade better than the OECD averages. Only in two indices – its productivity performance and its unemployment rate – was Canada among the worst performers. Trudeau tried to make this case during the 1979 election campaign, with the help of Philippe Deane Gigantes, a former journalist now in his PMO entourage, who skilfully cranked out positive data for him to use on the hustings. [71]

But Trudeau's efforts at self-justification by international comparison were in vain, despite the accuracy of Gigantes's statistics and the dexterity with which the Liberal speech-writers wove them into the texts they prepared for him to deliver. For Canada to do much better in such complex circumstances would require a prime minister who had not only a broad grasp of the emerging problems and a coherent plan to deal with them, but also a passionate determination to implement the plan and a committed national constituency to support it. Trudeau had none of these. His protestations about his valiant efforts and good intentions, whatever their validity, were beside the point. The electorate had come to believe that he and his cohort could not manage the economy. And on May 22, 1979, it turfed them out of office.

# PART II

# HOPE AGAINST HOPE: DREAMING A NEW LIBERAL DREAM

# THE RESTORATION AND THE STRATEGIC PRIME MINISTERSHIP

During the six months following the election of 1979 – when Pierre Trudeau was suffering the final breakdown of his ill-fated marriage as well as the ignominy of electoral defeat – a small band of his loyalists set out to recoup his political fortunes and to revive Canadian Liberalism at the same time. At the centre of this plot were two unlikely conspirators: James Coutts and his sidekick, Thomas Axworthy, who were holed up in the Leader of the Opposition's Office as Trudeau's principal secretary and senior policy analyst respectively.[1]

Because of the too-clever-by-half image-making schemes he had devised as Trudeau's political chief aide in the 1970s, Coutts found himself in the election's wake much disparaged by disaffected Liberals and political journalists, who fed each other's discontents. Liberalism of the Trudeau variety would soon be defunct in Canada, they assured one another – and Jimmy Coutts along with it. For several years the media had been carrying analytical pieces saying that not only was Trudeau's once-great popularity dissipated forever but the Liberal Party itself had run out of steam, its principles discarded, its ideas outmoded, its adherents disillusioned. The party was out of power in every province as well as in Ottawa, reviled by union leaders and farmers' groups, its very name anathema to the kind of businessmen who had once admired its power and efficiency. Academics with a deep interest in the Canadian body politic, including John Meisel of Queen's and Michael Bliss of the University of Toronto, were suggesting that the May election had been a "systems-altering" contest and the Liberal Party could well be suffering from "a fatal illness." The conventional wisdom in political circles had it that the new prime minister, Joe Clark, was riding a conservative tide that had begun to flow with Margaret Thatcher's election in Britain that spring and with the further discrediting of Jimmy Carter–style liberalism in the United States, where the Democratic Party was losing its white middle-class adherents to the renascent Republicans. Given this trend, the Tories would be in office in Canada until the century's end. The Liberals were irrelevant, finished, kaput.[2]

The way Jim Coutts dealt with these portents was very much in character. He weighed their validity in private, dismissed them in public, and determined to overcome his troubles with a resolute show of good cheer, defiantly telling anybody who asked after his health and his party's, "We were defeated, not destroyed."[3]

Coutts had belonged to the Liberal Party for so long, he had made its myths his own. For him, the Liberals were still the can-do party, the party of progress, prosperity, and a benevolent welfare state, the party of federalism and national unity, the party that had formed modern Canada and that deserved the success it had enjoyed for so long. In his view, there was nothing wrong with the way he had behaved during his stint as principal secretary in the PMO. He had simply been applying to the business of politics the managerial techniques he had acquired at Harvard. Politics was about power, and he was willing to consider whatever accommodations had to be made to retain it. When the disasters of the late 1970s crowded in on Pierre Trudeau, Coutts had soldiered on, refusing to admit that the Liberal hour was over. Coutts had a strategy. Coutts had a life plan. And he was damned if he was going to give up on it now.[4]

Central to the plan were his own ambitions. He had intended to stand for office himself since early adolescence and had run federally in a hopeless Alberta seat when he was twenty-four in order to learn from the experience and to show his Liberal loyalty. Fifteen years later, while toiling during the week for Trudeau in the PMO, he had busied himself on weekends and holidays with trying to find a winnable riding in his home province. His dream was to bring Alberta back into the Liberal fold after half a century of disaffection and to use it in the way that Jimmy Gardiner had used Saskatchewan as a power base when he was a minister in the governments of King and St. Laurent. When this task proved too daunting, Coutts had turned to his adopted city of Toronto as the place where electoral success might be achieved, reasoning that Parkdale, a west-end riding rich in ethnic voters, would be a safer bet than any Alberta constituency and might provide him with a base as a champion of the city's immigrants, a role roughly comparable to the one Ernest Lapointe had played in consolidating support for Mackenzie King in Quebec. These careful calculations had been abandoned reluctantly, if temporarily, when he was needed at Trudeau's side to try to stem the Tory tide in the 1979 election campaign. In the long run-up to that campaign, while all around him Grits were wringing their hands and waiting for the Conservative deluge, Coutts had conceived a grand strategy for recovery – his leader's, his party's, and his own. He had driven the Liberal machine relentlessly as the spring campaign unfolded, figuring that if the party ran full out, using all the technical skills at its command, it would be possible to hold the Tories to a minority.[5]

This first goal had been reached on May 22. Even though the Tories gained a small plurality of seats in the Commons, the Liberals won a plurality of the popular vote. Exiled now in the LOO (his sobriquet for the Leader of the Opposition's Office), Coutts began work on the next part of his plan. His immediate concern was to prevent Trudeau from resigning, since he was still the party's best asset despite the electorate's love-hate reaction to his peccadilloes. Then the Liberals would have to topple the Tory government and propel Trudeau back into office so that he could patriate the constitution and leave public life having fulfilled his personal agenda: the reconciliation of Quebec within a bilingual Canadian federation. Next, Coutts needed to get himself elected and appointed to a cabinet portfolio so he could enter the race for the Liberal succession once Trudeau stepped down.[6]

It was an ambitious scheme by anybody's measure; and for it to come to fruition, Coutts knew that Liberalism had to be restored as a political force. The party needed an infusion of fresh ideas in order to recover its popularity, and the resources at hand were meagre. In the ignominy and isolation of opposition, he would have to rely on the advice of his associate Tom Axworthy, who shared his western roots and had been his faithful helper since 1973.


Tom Axworthy was thirty-two in the summer of 1979 and still ideal-istic enough to be a happy warrior in the Liberal cause, although he had been observing and absorbing the lessons of Coutts's pragmatic approach to politics for half a dozen years. He had grown up in a close-knit family in the multi-ethnic north end of Winnipeg, the second of the four sons of Norman Axworthy, an insurance agent, and his wife, Gwen, an energetic community activist committed to the progressive ideas of the United Church. Her oldest boy, Lloyd, was her pride, a good student and star athlete at Winnipeg's United College, where he studied political science and won a Woodrow Wilson Fellowship to Princeton. Tom, who was seven years younger, was different. Looking back, he liked to say that since he was too fat to run and too myopic to fight, he had been forced to learn to talk fast in order to fend off the gangs of immigrant kids who roamed the Axworthys' neighbourhood, "where being a WASP was to suffer as a visible minority." When Lloyd fell in love with the civil rights movement in all its 1960s glory while taking part in the Stu-dents for a Democratic Society protest marches that enlivened American campuses with their we-can-change-society idealism, Tom fell in love from a distance with American-style activist ideas, too, and began to dream up ways to bring citizen participation to Canada. He decided Lester Pearson's Liberals were admirably pro-gressive and campaigned for them in the 1962 election when he was only fifteen.[7]

When Lloyd returned to Winnipeg with a brand-new PhD in 1966, he still saw himself as unequivocally left of centre, but conversations with Tom convinced him he would never be happy in the NDP. The social democrats were too self-righteous to achieve the consensus they needed to put their ideas into effect. They didn't have the American Democrats' political smarts or the British Labour Party's solid base in the working class. When Lloyd decided to seek a seat in the Manitoba legislature as a Liberal, his family mobilized their friends on Lloyd's behalf – people typical of many middle-class Anglo-Canadians of the times who, having survived both the Depression and the war, were benefitting from the boom but had not forgotten their commitment to social equity or their belief that government should help achieve it. When Lloyd lost that election, he declared that he had learned invaluable lessons about practical politics all the same, and moved to Ottawa to work as an executive assistant to John Turner, then a junior minister in Pearson's cabinet. [8]

By this time, Tom was active in the University of Winnipeg's Liberal Club and had been captivated by Walter Gordon's nationalist ideas. As a student delegate to the Liberals' policy convention in Ottawa in 1966 – the meeting where the federal party engaged in its heated debate over economic nationalism – he had jumped to his feet in the Château Laurier ballroom and made an impassioned speech on Gordon's behalf, despite the former finance minister's unpopularity among senior Liberals in the west. His bravado brought him to the attention of Keith Davey, who marked Axworthy down as a good kid, smart, funny, and malleable, just the sort of recruit older Liberals had been encouraging ever since Sir William Mulock had shown an interest in the young Mackenzie King, seventy-five years before "mentoring" became a climber's cliché. Summer work was found for Tom on Mel Watkins's Task Force on Foreign Ownership that Gordon had formed with Pearson's reluctant acquiescence, a dream job for a budding nationalist and a flaming Liberal.

The Axworthy family had been described in Winnipeg as resembling the Massachusetts Kennedys – but "without the looks, charm, or money," as Tom explained in a typical self-deprecating joke. Still, with Lloyd and Tom both beavering away in Ottawa, it looked as though they really might turn into the Jack and Bobby of the North. Canada was changing, and they were at the leading edge of the new participatory consciousness. A year later, the Axworthy brand of reform Liberalism was eclipsed by the passionate federalism of the Trudeauites when they took over the Liberal Party with a zealotry of purpose that reflected their personalist Catholicism. Lloyd stayed in Trudeau's Ottawa for only a few months and then retreated to Manitoba to teach at his alma mater. Tom took himself off to Queen's University to prepare an MA thesis on Walter Gordon's impact on the Liberal Party, an exercise that gave his nationalism an intellectual grounding and made him familiar with Liberal history and liberal thought.[9]

He then spent a year at Oxford's Nuffield College and began work on a doctorate in political science. But when Trudeau made common cause with the Coutts-and-Davey Toronto Liberals in order to win the 1974 election, Axworthy set aside his academic work at their request to act as an advance man in western Canada. Being part of that winning campaign was such a heady experience, Tom decided to plunge into a political career immediately rather than return to academe. He worked for a few months as a ministerial assistant in Ottawa, but since it was an important maxim of modern Liberalism that private-sector experience was vital for the politically ambitious, Axworthy took a job in Coutts's Toronto consulting firm. A few months later, when Trudeau appointed Coutts as his principal secretary, Axworthy came along to the PMO as a speech-writer and general intellectual roustabout.

Over the next four years, Tom learned the language of public policy issues by researching and drafting dozens of speeches for the prime minister as a junior in the PMO/PCO hierarchy. He was distanced from Trudeau by his immediate boss, Coutts, the cabinet secretary, Michael Pitfield, and Richard O'Hagan, the prime minister's media adviser. (O'Hagan was a communications wizard with a background in journalism and advertising who had worked for Pearson as his press secretary in the 1960s before being appointed minister-counsellor at the Canadian embassy in Washington. He had been recalled to Ottawa in 1975 to help Trudeau deal with the serious image problems created by his flip-flop on wage and price controls.) This high-powered trio met Trudeau every weekday morning in the late 1970s and conveyed whatever fresh ideas their associates and assistants, including Axworthy, had to impart.

Tom didn't mind playing a secondary role. For him, this was a career-building phase, a time to expand his network and his expertise. Everybody liked Tom. Tom was loyal. Tom was witty. Tom was shrewd enough to disguise his doubts and his ambitions. He was drawing on long experience at such dissembling. His mother had always favoured Lloyd. By this time, Lloyd had made a name for himself in Manitoba as an urban activist and member of the Manitoba legislature, the only strong Liberal opposition voice in a region where Liberalism was on the wane. In time of electoral need, Tom would repair to Winnipeg to knock on doors in Lloyd's constituency in the company of their younger brothers, Bob and Trevor. In the PMO, Tom's strengths were his knowledge of Liberal history and western politics, his easy writing style, and his endorsement of the enthusiasms of his generation – big-league baseball, rock 'n' roll, and progressive ideas. (His abiding heroes were Catfish Hunter, the Beatles, and Walter Lockhart Gordon.) When Tom was around, older Liberals could still imagine that their party – though entrenched in power for much of the previous half-century – was a vehicle for change.

In temperament and experience Tom was very different from the austere Trudeau. But after drafting and re-drafting scores of prime ministerial speeches and memoranda – and watching how Trudeau reacted to them – he began to feel he understood the way the prime minister's mind worked. He was fascinated by the way Trudeau could take a speech-writer's text, read it intently, note the four or five main points and a few of the key phrases, close his eyes for several minutes to ruminate on them, and then declare himself ready to deliver it. Hours later, when he rose to his feet to speak in some banquet hall or school auditorium, Trudeau would take inspiration from the crowd for an opening comment – the sight of a turbaned Sikh, for instance, would give him an introduction to a national unity speech. He would begin with this multicultural observation, then wing it from there, weaving the phrases and points he had memorized earlier into a seamless whole. At least, this was the sort of oratorical feat Trudeau could accomplish when he was "on," in his staff's parlance, as in "The old man is really on tonight." But when he was "off" – that is, tired or irascible – he would read in a monotone directly from the printed text, to the dismay of Axworthy, who, as an accomplished speaker himself, wanted every prime ministerial performance to be a star turn.

This apprenticeship phase of Tom's career came to an end during the 1979 election, when he found himself for the first time "one on one with the boss" for a protracted period. In the last week of that difficult campaign, Coutts had left the leader's entourage to tend to pressing matters in Toronto. Tom was delegated to take over his functions on a swing through southwestern Ontario. Sitting in the back of a limousine with Trudeau, he briefed him on upcoming campaign events and described the passing farmland in historical terms. It was home territory for the original English-Canadian Liberals, the nineteenth-century Clear Grits, a group of stubbornly Protestant Scottish farmers and stonemasons who saw in American democratic politics a model for their republican hostility to the Family Compact, the Tory oligarchy in colonial Upper Canada.

As the long campaign day wore on, Axworthy moved on from talking about Liberal history to describing some of the ideas he had been formulating on what had gone wrong with Liberalism in the 1970s, linking the party's situation now to the problems that Laurier's *rouges* had encountered in their alliance with the Grits nearly a century before. Trudeau listened carefully, seemingly captivated by these links between English-Canadian reformers and the radical French Canadians he had learned about in his youth. Axworthy felt he had passed some unspoken test and become real to Trudeau in a way he had not been before, a genuine man of ideas instead of an unknown factotum.

After the Liberals' defeat a few days later, Tom's good humour had buoyed the morale of Trudeau's staff during the move into the LOO. His connections with younger Liberals around the country, his familiarity with the party's glorious past, his empathy with its present dissatisfactions, and his capacity to write strategic papers as well as clever speeches made him particularly valuable to Coutts as he struggled with the task of trying to restore the Liberal Party's fortunes.

In his ruminations on the party's difficulties, Axworthy had come to believe that the only way to postulate a Liberal future was to revive an old axiom from the Liberal past: in times of trouble, turn left. In this particular time of trouble – with neo-conservatism an important force in Canada's mentor nations and Canadian Liberalism's critics saying that the party did not stand for anything beyond power-mongering any more – turning left in Axworthy's view meant turning to Canadian nationalism.

His own left-liberal values were a pastiche of 1930s American New Deal bromides, 1960s American New Left idealism, Canadian prairie populism, Clear Grit radicalism, CCF-style Fabianism, and the United Church version of the Social Gospel – all glued together with a fervent belief in the importance for Canada of greater economic and cultural sovereignty. Despite his admiration for Walter Gordon's central-Canadian nationalist ideas, Axworthy was convinced as a westerner that the Liberals had become too dependent on Ontario's volatile voters. He believed the party needed to reforge Mackenzie King's alliance between Quebec and the western provinces, where, apart from brief gains in 1968 due to Trudeaumania, Liberals had been steadily losing ground since the 1950s to Tory populism and the social-democratic reformism of the CCF/NDP. Coutts's flirtation with the right in the late 1970s – when he had enticed the Alberta redneck Conservative Jack Horner to cross the floor and had encouraged Trudeau to make ambiguous statements about holding a referendum to reinstate the death penalty

– had been a media disaster and had not won any support in the west. Axworthy decided that the way to regain Liberal strength in Manitoba and Saskatchewan was to dismiss the Tories as reactionaries and to outmanoeuvre the NDP on the "people issues," particularly on foreign ownership and energy development. At the same time, this interventionist thinking might help satisfy policy-oriented Liberal activists in Ontario who had been complaining bitterly for years that their ideas had been ignored in the Trudeau PMO.[10]

That Axworthy's ideas – redolent as they were of economic nationalism and participatory democracy – were even a possibility for serious contemplation in the entourage of the still stubbornly anti-nationalist and autocratic Trudeau, let alone an acceptable basis for making Liberal policy, was due to the fact that Coutts was operating on his own in the LOO, detached from his business-Liberal base and bereft of any alternative source of coherent partisan policy advice. He could not be described as either a nationalist or a participatory democrat, having dismissed Walter Gordon's economic nationalism as ineffectual in 1963 and Pierre Trudeau's participatory idealism as unworkable in 1968. As Trudeau's principal secretary from 1975 to 1979 he had proven the bane of activists in the extra-parliamentary party by blocking their access to the leader. But as an Albertan by birth, he had warmed to the logic of Axworthy's ideas about expanding Petro-Canada; and as a Torontonian by transplant, he was sufficiently attracted by cultural nationalism to be interested in Canadian literature and engrossed in amassing a sophisticated collection of Canadian art.

Coutts's closest colleagues from his PMO days were preoccupied with trying to resuscitate their careers outside Ottawa. Michael Pitfield, having been fired from his job by Joe Clark even though his further reforms of the governmental system had found favour with the Tories, had repaired to Harvard and the John F. Kennedy School of Government. Richard O'Hagan had been appointed a vice-president of the Bank of Montreal several months before the election. Keith Davey was back in the advertising business in Toronto.

And so it went, down the scale of influence to the secretaries and administrative assistants, who were trying to find work elsewhere in the government service.

Most Liberals beyond their small circle did not give a damn about what Coutts and Axworthy were doing in the LOO in any case. They had been written off as powerless, a couple of backroom boys with nowhere else to turn, making a last brave stand before Trudeau's inevitable retirement. Trudeau himself was largely absent from Coutts and Axworthy's deliberations as they went about plotting a Liberal revival. Depressed by his personal and political troubles, Trudeau had become a front man with barely enough physical energy or political commitment to fill even that undemanding role. In speaking to an academic interviewer after a heated party national executive meeting in Toronto in July, he talked dismissively about its activists as "second-rate men of action," with whom he had formed a symbiotic alliance through Coutts and Davey but who were now of very little interest to him. When Axworthy convened a party advisory group later in the summer, Trudeau's indifference verged on the insulting. He arrived for a scheduled meeting very late on a sweltering Ottawa afternoon, turned a jaundiced eye on his parched guests, who looked on longingly while he drank iced Perrier, and then proceeded to belch repeatedly as they discussed their ideas for reviving Liberalism. ("It was like one of those cartoons where you see a guy crawling through the desert under the burning sun trying to reach an oasis mirage," David Walker, the University of Winnipeg political scientist, remembered. "I couldn't decide whether I wanted to grab the Perrier bottle to take a swig or use it to bop Trudeau on the head.")[11]

This kind of rudeness did not faze Coutts and Axworthy. They were used to it. They figured "the boss" needed some "down time" in order to "get his act together," and they were determined to pursue their plan to propel him – and themselves – back to power. Their immediate concern was to gather policy material so the Liberals could use it to do battle in the new parliament scheduled to convene in the early autumn. They decided to set up a small research unit in the LOO, mixing some of the old PMO staff with some suitably progressive policy analysts Axworthy had hired. Its purpose was twofold: to prepare briefing notes for the leader in the manner to which Trudeau had become accustomed as prime minister, and to provide the Liberal caucus with professional policy-making advice. They also put together a shadow cabinet list and prevailed on Trudeau to accept their suggestions. Of the 1970s Liberal caucus, more left-wingers than right-wingers had survived the party's defeat in May, and Coutts and Axworthy wanted to make sure that the most prominent opposition critics' jobs went to them in order to give their Liberal revival plan the best chance.

For finance critic, they settled on the only Liberal MP with experience in an economic portfolio whose reputation had not been compromised by the disasters of the late 1970s: Herb Gray, who had languished on the backbenches between 1974 and 1979 after falling out of favour with Trudeau because of his nationalism. Comparable concern was shown in the choice of other critics, with Lloyd Axworthy assigned to Housing, Monique Bégin to Health, Jean Chrétien to Federal-Provincial Relations, Roméo LeBlanc to Welfare and Pensions, Allan MacEachen to External Affairs, and Jeanne Sauvé to Communications. Once confirmed in these roles, the critics were instructed to set up consultative committees that would involve both caucus colleagues and extra-parliamentary Liberals in the reformulation of policy positions. [12]

For what they regarded as the most important assignment of all, Coutts and Axworthy had convinced Trudeau he needed to make an especially canny appointment. With world energy prices doubling once more, and with Petro-Canada, the popular public oil company the Liberals had established in 1975, under attack from the Tory government, the energy critic would be a key figure in the new parliament. In their view, the man for the job was Marc Lalonde, the MP for Montreal-Outremont, who had the best mind and toughest hide in the new caucus and whose loyalty to Trudeau was beyond question. Lalonde was also one of the few Liberals who actually believed in the scenario for a quick recovery of power that Coutts and Axworthy outlined to a few of their closest colleagues in the summer of 1979. What is more, he agreed with their argument that energy was Canada's most pressing economic problem, that he was the man who could solve it, and that federalism would be strengthened in Quebec as a result.

"When we lost the election, I made up my mind as a result that if we ever got another kick at the can, we were really going to kick it," Lalonde said afterwards, "and I wanted to be ready for the chance." Over the summer and early fall he directed the activities of the caucus committee set up to take a fresh look at energy questions, with the help of a single staff member, a young analyst with an MA in resource policy named Barbara Sulzenko, who had been hired by Tom Axworthy. He also made contact with several policy activists in the extra-parliamentary wing of the Liberal Party and decided to tour the country extensively to talk with energy experts.[13]

By the time Parliament finally convened in October, Liberal caucus members had begun to adjust to their new status in opposition, although few of them were able to refrain from calling Trudeau "Prime Minister," a difficulty that afflicted almost everybody else in Ottawa as well, including Joe Clark, the man who actually held the job. Despite such slips of the tongue, the Liberal MPs had decided to take Clark at his word when he said he intended to govern as though he had a majority – that is, to hang on to office for at least two years. Few were privy to the Coutts-Axworthy scheme for restoring Trudeau to power, and if they had been, they would have dismissed it. Most of them accepted the media's conviction that Trudeau's day was done.

Once they settled into their new places in the Commons, across the aisle from the government benches they had occupied for so long, the Liberals' mood shifted subtly. Freed from the demands of hectoring business lobbyists and from the constricting advice of cautious economic bureaucrats, they had the luxury of indulging their own reformist instincts. They began to relish inflicting on the

Clark government the kind of savage attacks they themselves had suffered throughout the 1970s. They grew bolder as the inexperienced Tories struggled with their tentative neo-conservative ideas, such as the privatization of Crown corporations, or tried to fulfil their contradictory promises to give home-owners mortgage payment relief and reduce the budget deficit at the same time. Deft criticism based on the Liberals' inside knowledge of decisions made earlier in the year – along with the zesty opposition mounted by the NDP – began to unhinge the Conservative front bench. The program-slashing far-right ideas of Sinclair Stevens, the secretary of the Treasury Board and a rich man from rich Ontario, were clearly at odds with the more moderate notions of John Crosbie, the minister of finance and former Liberal from the have-not province of Newfoundland, who favoured maintaining social programs and increasing the tax burden carried by the prosperous in central Canada.[14]

The Tories' discomfort sustained Liberal morale throughout the early autumn, but the mood was broken by the unexpected news of Trudeau's resignation in late November. Coutts's best efforts to persuade him to the contrary had been to no avail. The Liberals were just beginning to line up behind potential leadership candidates when the Conservatives produced their first budget on December 11, promising the "long-term gain" of a reduced deficit in return for the "short-term pain" of higher energy prices for consumers. To the Liberals' delight, the Tories had boxed themselves into a corner, inadvertently giving them the "people issue" that Tom Axworthy was persuaded the party needed. Crosbie's budget broke popular Tory campaign promises of the previous spring and proposed genuinely regressive taxes at the same time. Emboldened by their renewed liberalism – and by the prospect of a swift return to power – the Liberals came together in a spasm of solidarity they had not felt for nearly a decade and precipitated an election by supporting a no-confidence motion moved by the NDP.[15]

Once Trudeau had been persuaded to withdraw his resignation, the Liberals had to switch their attention from planning a leadership convention to mounting an election campaign. Despite the caucus's show of solidarity in defeating the Tories and reinstating Trudeau as leader, the extra-parliamentary party was riven by discord. The French were fighting with the English, the right wing of the party was murmuring darkly about the ascendancy of the left, and Liberals from the west apparently felt as disaffected from the centre as ever.

Whatever their ideological or regional views, there was a widespread belief among extra-parliamentary Liberals of all persuasions that some sort of skulduggery by Coutts was involved in Trudeau's resurrection. This suspicion was felt most acutely in the national executive, whose members believed their rights, as laid out in the party constitution, had been violated. The only real power they could claim – control over the leadership renewal process – had been usurped.[16]

In high dudgeon, they demanded a voice in deciding campaign policy in order to make sure that the Coutts-and-Davey clique did not totally control the Liberal future. Faced with a possible revolt in the ranks, Coutts accepted a participatory idea thought up by Axworthy and agreed to the establishment of an election platform committee representing the party's main constituencies. Its members met on two successive weekends in late December and early January to hammer out proposals for the Liberal platform.[17]

Excitement was intense. The assembled Liberals believed both that the party could win the election and – since Trudeau had given his blessing to this ambitious platform-building process – that the ideas they adopted would soon become government policy. Their discourse lost the air of futility that habitually clouded party policy discussions and took on the urgency of *realpolitik*. Two substantial papers had been prepared. The first, a critique of the Crosbie budget, had been written by Nate Laurie, an economist who worked for Tom Axworthy in the LOO, and was adopted as the basis for a campaign pledge to reduce the deficit. The second was an ambitious proposal to restructure the oil and gas industry, worked out by Marc

Lalonde's caucus-party committee on energy, which he presented with all the force of his commanding personality. Western Liberals were able to amend a couple of measures that they considered particularly offensive, but they could not prevail against its interventionist thrust. Their fellow militants from Quebec and Ontario believed Canadians had to be protected from the world energy supply crisis even if it meant defying the Americans and their Alberta provisioners to do so. [18]

After the deficit and energy questions had been dealt with, reaching agreement became more difficult. Lloyd Axworthy's plan for a massive housing program was accepted in principle but set aside, as was a proposal for a guaranteed annual income to complete the social security system. Both were deemed inconsistent with gradual deficit reduction. Tax reform, involving the review of tax expenditures and loopholes, was suggested and discarded for want of a hefty background paper. Tom Axworthy and Herb Gray tried to promote an industrial strategy, but the idea was blocked by Don Johnston and Roy MacLaren, MPs with strong ties to business, who argued against increased government intervention of any kind. In the end all proposals were taken under advisement on behalf of the leader's campaign group, which meant Trudeau himself, Coutts, and the national campaign co-chairmen, Marc Lalonde and Keith Davey. But the co-operative mood among the Liberals present was such that they assumed their ideas would become solid party planks. Once the campaign was in full swing, this goal turned out to be surprisingly difficult to achieve, even for a Liberal as powerful as Lalonde. [19]

Although Goldfarb's polling confirmed that Lalonde's energy policy would be useful in consolidating the Liberal vote in central and Atlantic Canada, Coutts was not convinced Trudeau really had to announce a detailed energy position in order to win the election. Goldfarb's data showed the public was sufficiently disenchanted with Joe Clark and alarmed by the Tories' proposed 18-cent-per-gallon surcharge at the fuel pumps to want to punish them at the polls. Why should the Grits close off their options on energy if they didn't really need to? For Axworthy and Lalonde, closing options was precisely the point. Trudeau had to announce the energy policy so the Liberals *would* be obligated to act once they were elected. They were determined to get a formal commitment from the party leader and a formal mandate from the electorate.[20]

Once Lalonde had insisted that Coutts pencil into the leader's schedule a major energy speech, he decided to fly to Winnipeg, which had been tentatively chosen as the place for Trudeau to deliver it, so he could respond to media questions on the proposed policy in careful detail. To his chagrin, he found out after arriving in the city that the energy text had been blocked by Trudeau's campaign staff and a routine speech substituted instead. The leader's next scheduled stop was Halifax, and Lalonde proceeded there grimly determined to monitor every step leading up to Trudeau's planned speech in order to make sure it involved a major energy announcement. His first move was to take Trudeau out to dinner so he could lead him through the rationale for each of the seven points in his energy policy package. He was determined – as he told his leader and federalist comrade-in-arms – to apply to Canada's energy crisis what he had learned by studying its medicare program when he was minister of health: that prevention was longer-lasting and more effective than surgery.

Trudeau already had a substantial background on the subject, having become intensely interested in energy at the time of the first OPEC crisis in 1973. (He had shown prescience even earlier by appointing Jack Austin, a lawyer and private-sector resource expert from Vancouver, as deputy minister of energy so he could assess Canada's future needs.) Throughout the OPEC crisis, Trudeau stayed directly involved with the issue until concrete policy proposals were announced by the energy minister, Donald Macdonald.[21]

Distracted by the 1974 election and his myriad political difficulties after it, Trudeau had let energy policy drift until the second OPEC crisis, which redoubled the world price of oil just in time for the 1979 election. With that campaign issue engraved in his mind, Trudeau was immediately responsive to Lalonde's advocacy because it was expressed in terms of their principal mutual interest: beating back the separatists in Quebec. He agreed with the premise that if the federalists were to win the referendum campaign on sovereignty-association that the Parti Québécois intended to mount later in 1980, they would have to offer Quebeckers blandishments that went beyond flag-waving. A guaranteed supply of oil and gas below world prices was a concrete benefit Quebeckers could identify with federalism and contrast with the economic difficulties a sovereign Quebec would face, dependent as it would be on the uncertain supplies and unstable prices offered by the world market. For such redoubtable anti-nationalists as Trudeau and Lalonde to favour the Canadianization of the petroleum industry was less difficult than might have been expected. At stake was the need for security of supply in the cause of national unity. Since the transnationals' Canadian subsidiaries had recently proven they could not guarantee oil shipments from the Middle East when their head offices wanted fuel diverted to the U.S., Lalonde and Trudeau had no qualms about endorsing energy self-sufficiency and greater Canadian ownership of the industry.[22]

Back in the Liberal campaign suite after dinner, Lalonde was angered to find that Trudeau's speech-writers were still debating the pros and cons of his energy ideas. He dressed them down like the rector of a classical college reprimanding delinquent schoolboys, demanded they produce a text forthwith, and stormed off to bed, after making sure that he would be roused at 4:30 A.M. to go over their draft text. This time Lalonde prevailed, and within twenty-four hours news services were flashing reports that Trudeau had promised in a speech to the Halifax Board of Trade a comprehensive energy policy that included a "made-in-Canada" blended price, energy security, an expanded Petro-Canada, greater conservation, and stepped-up Canadianization. Full-page advertisements promptly appeared in newspapers across the country, dense with the text of Trudeau's energy speech, projecting to voters the message that the Liberals were once again the take-charge party they had elected so often in the past.[23]

Despite Lalonde's success in pushing his energy initiative, Coutts continued to argue against using the rest of the platform committee's policies. Goldfarb's daily polls showed Liberal popularity fell every time Trudeau made speeches that went beyond scornful attacks on Joe Clark's pratfalls or the Conservatives' punitive budget. ("[The Tories] may even tax your mouth if it continues moving," he shot back at a heckler, displaying the brio Liberal crowds loved.) Media coverage of Liberal policy initiatives was redirecting the public's general frustration with politicians from Clark, who was viewed as too weak, to Trudeau, who was seen as too strong. Those who had hated him were reminded of their dislike; those who revered him, of their past disappointments. Coutts decided that the only way to hold on to the Liberals' lead was to run a battened-down campaign that would prevent mistakes and avoid voter backlash. He refused most requests for media interviews and stonewalled when the Liberals were pressed to participate in a three-party television debate, fabricating picayune objections to the proposed format in order to scupper an encounter that might have turned the voters' ambivalence towards Trudeau back into support for Clark.

Keith Davey went along reluctantly with this downplaying of the party platform and "low-bridging" of the leader – a piece of jazzy jargon current in the American political class that he had picked up while he was briefly reimmersed in the ad business during the opposition hiatus. The strategic plan he had sent to party candidates as campaign chairman in English Canada urged them to "constantly link Tory programs and policies to Mr. Clark" and promised that a Liberal platform would shortly be announced that was "progressive, tough, fair and nationalistic" enough to get a good press and cut off possible NDP gains. Now with the election alarmingly close, the platform had yet to be unveiled. Davey was taking so much flak from Liberals in the field over the campaign's lack of positive content that he decided Trudeau must announce some policy positions despite Coutts's cavils. The goodwill of party workers as well as Davey's credibility with *The Toronto Star* was at stake. He had assured the paper's publisher, Beland Honderich, that Trudeau had become genuinely more concerned about Canadian sovereignty. If Trudeau failed to deliver, the Star's editorial support – which Davey had cultivated throughout his political career – would be lost once more as it had been in 1972, and along with it the Ontario votes that would bring the Liberals a majority.[24]

Coutts capitulated and let loose Tom Axworthy's policy team, whose strong suit was youthful idealism, not bureaucratic experience or extensive knowledge of the continental economy. With Barbara Sulzenko and Nate Laurie fleshing out the platform committee's controverted policy suggestions along with some left-over ideas from the fruitless industrial-strategy debate of the 1970s, Axworthy drafted a series of texts for the leader to deliver. Amid the whirling uncertainties of electoral battle, Trudeau was pressured to adopt the interventionist positions his handlers were urging on him. Jean Chrétien's political assistant, Eddie Goldenberg, was lobbying against a nationalist shift in the campaign's thrust, but in the absence of cautionary counsel from more familiar advisers, Trudeau was ready to acquiesce. The Coutts-and-Davey Liberals had stuck with him in the humiliation of his defeat the previous year. They had promised they would snatch power back for him if he would do his part on the hustings. In late December, they had recommended that he change his campaign wardrobe and he had agreed, provided the party paid for the clothes. In January, they had said he should keep his speeches under eighteen minutes, refraining from any free-ranging expression of ideas in the presence of the media, and he had complied. Now in early February, they were advising a radical change in policy and he concurred – as long as it could be framed in language consistent with his personal philosophy.

"With Trudeau, everything depends on how you present ideas," Axworthy explained later. "You have to relate a policy proposal to one of his early reference points, such as Schumpeter or Lord Acton. You have to be part of his paradigm." Axworthy had deliberately used his knowledge of Trudeau's intellectual roots to find ways to persuade him that the proposed energy and industrial-strategy policies did not reflect the old negative nationalism but were portents of a new positive Canadianization – and the economic prerequisite for the realization of Trudeau's national unity mission. Canadianizing the energy industry was a way to offset the excessive power of Alberta and the multinational petroleum cartel, a means of redistributing wealth to the less fortunate populations of central and eastern Canada. Playing on themes from Trudeau's early writings in *Cité libre*, Axworthy offered him a parallel rationale for dropping his economic conservatism and accepting the value to Canada's vulnerable federation of an expanded role for the federal government: the growing power of the business sector and the provincial governments needed to be countervailed.[25]

In the dying days of the campaign, Trudeau made a concerted pitch for Ontario support by delivering several speeches that went beyond derisive remarks about Clark's Tories and committed the Liberals to an industrial strategy that would include an expanded FIRA, new targets for research and development spending, procurement policies to stimulate industrial restructuring under increased Canadian ownership, and a strengthened automobile industry.[26]

Once the election returns on February 18 confirmed that their gamble had paid off, the Trudeauites eagerly turned to the serious task of deciding how best to fulfil their ambitions for their renewed mandate. During the first weeks of the new Liberal ministry, there was an almost euphoric sense in the PMO that everything Coutts and Axworthy had hoped for in the LOO was possible. The Liberals' impressive parliamentary majority meant they could push back against the forces – provincial, international, and entrepreneurial – that had threatened to overwhelm the Liberal view of Canada. They were bringing a new enthusiasm, a new vision, and a new ruthlessness to the exercise of power.

With minimum disruption in his office ensured by the return of Pitfield as clerk of the Privy Council and of Coutts as principal secretary, Trudeau himself was ready to govern with a zest he had not displayed for years. Pitfield had convinced him that in order to succeed, his new government would have to be run as a "strategic prime ministership," which would mean blending his constitutional objectives and the party's interventionist campaign positions into a coherent government agenda and then focusing his own energies on two or three top priorities before planning his retirement.[27]

No anglophone had been more influential in articulating the new government's policy thrust than "young Tom," as Axworthy was still called, even though he had been named assistant principal secretary in the reclaimed PMO. Intent on making sure that Trudeau's campaign promises were translated into official commitments, he seized the chance to draft the speech from the throne when it was offered to him. By this public showcasing of the new government's long-term plans, Axworthy hoped to overcome the bureaucracy's natural resistance to change – a problem that had plagued the Liberals throughout the 1970s and surfaced again when the deputy ministers were assembled immediately after the February election to discuss the government's agenda, and none of them thought it was practicable.[28]

The immediate impact of Axworthy's carefully crafted throne speech was dampened by the lifeless reading Governor General Edward Schreyer gave it when the new parliament opened on April 14. But it was seen by professional analysts as a bold document outlining a resolutely left-Liberal program. Social policy was given pride of place with pension reform; new job programs for women, native people, and the handicapped; and an increase of $35 a month in the guaranteed income supplement for the elderly poor. Next came the Lalonde group's proposed actions on energy, which conjured up a new national dream. Then there were promises of a vigorous industrial policy, greater access to information, and, of course, constitutional reform, complete with an entrenched "bill of civil and human rights, including language rights." As though these grandiose plans were not enough for the government's first year in office, the speech described an "active" (though ambivalent) foreign policy that offered a new fighter aircraft as an indicator of Canada's commitment to NATO, while establishing an ambassador for disarmament as a token of the government's dedication to peace.[29]

Besides heralding new vitality in the Trudeau camp, the speech was a dramatic attempt to overturn the Liberals' recently acquired image of managerial ineptitude. Some observers even saw it as outlining a third National Policy for Canada, on the scale of Sir John A. Macdonald's original National Policy a century earlier and the great King–St. Laurent Keynesian reconstruction strategy of the immediate post-war period. Macdonald had offered railroads, tariffs, and immigration. King and St. Laurent promised expanded social security, macro-economic management, and full employment. Now the Trudeau government was offering another kind of policy trinity: liberty through energy independence, fraternity through a regionally balanced industrial strategy, and equality through a charter of individual rights in a patriated constitution.[30]

It was a formula designed to generate a new Liberal coalition to replace the one that had been undermined in the earlier Trudeau years and to crowd out the Tories and the NDP by positioning the Liberals as a moderate left-of-centre party straddling the magic middle. In his stubborn idealism – which was only later seen as naïveté – Tom Axworthy still believed it was possible for the Liberal Party to become more of a movement and less of a haven for careerists. His new Liberal alliance would include federalist Quebeckers, the co-op movement in the west, workers below the level of the union leadership, women, ethnic Canadians in big urban centres, small businessmen, and the disadvantaged who needed the social security system to protect them from poverty – a working-class/middle-class agglomeration of the kind that Lloyd Axworthy had put together in Winnipeg–Fort Garry and that pointedly left out any connection to big business.

Tom Axworthy was so delighted with his handiwork and the grand ideas behind it that he sent a copy of the throne speech, fresh

from the Queen's Printer, to his old friend Walter Gordon. He had
given Gordon the Trudeau campaign speech promising nationalistic measures that he had written with the inscription "This one is for
you, Walter." Now he signed a card he attached to the throne speech
with "You'll be glad to see we're going to do what we promised" –
an irony that did not escape Gordon's notice. Twenty years after he
had failed to persuade the Liberal Party under his seemingly malleable friend Lester Pearson to bolster Canadian sovereignty, it looked
as though his elusive dream might be realized under the aegis of his
obstinate anti-nationalist opponent, Pierre Trudeau.

The new Liberal program revealed the Trudeauites as having
renewed their commitment to a philosophy of governance already
in deep trouble around the world, as democratic administrations
encountered increasing difficulty in funding social programs and
sheltering their entrepreneurs and workers from the competitive
pressures of rival economies. Trying on a new style at the age of
sixty, Trudeau was endorsing what some were calling a post-
Keynesian view of the state's economic role, one that went beyond
the magisterial demand management so popular in the 1950s to a
more interventionist approach that saw the state actively engaging
in micro-economic measures designed to alter the structure and
productivity of specific sectors and industries. In addition, the two
main facets of the government's economic approach – the energy
program and the projected industrial policy – were meant to
complement Trudeau's constitutional agenda. Building a new "economic union" – a pan-Canadian common market without provincial protectionism – would put flesh and blood on the constitution's
legal skeleton for a reborn nation.[31]

Despite its ambitious scope, the program was deeply flawed.
Trudeau's piecemeal campaign promises boasted neither internal
consistency nor consensus within Liberal ranks. Its individual elements had merit, but their hasty assembly meant there had not been
time to integrate them into a comprehensive, long-term program.

Assumptions had been made about the behaviour of world markets over which Ottawa had no control. No one could tell whether pro-active neo-Keynesianism would work better in the 1980s than the reactive approach to the economy the Liberals had taken in the 1970s.

In the excitement of their glorious return to power, when the sky seemed scarcely high enough to contain their ambitions to reshape Canada, the Trudeauites had no way of knowing what Fortuna had in store for them.

# CHAPTER 5

# THE NATIONAL ENERGY
# PROGRAM AND NATIONAL
# DISUNITY

The man charged with fulfilling the most immediate of the new government's bold commitments – although their real audacity was not clearly understood at the time of the speech from the throne – was Trudeau's truculent Talleyrand, the Honourable Marc Lalonde. From the time he allied himself with Trudeau in the fall and winter of 1963–64 to produce their manifesto for a new federalism, Lalonde had been ready to do whatever was necessary to realize their shared goals. It was as though Trudeau was the pope of the new Canada they wanted to establish and Lalonde his efficacious cardinal.

Lalonde was born in 1929 into a family of Quebec farmers who had been working the same land on Île Perrot, southwest of Montreal, for generations. He was an unusual child, intensely intelligent as well as deeply devout, the only student in his class to complete public school in a district where most boys dropped out early to work on the farms. His family sent him on to a classical college in Ville Saint-Laurent run by the Fathers of the Holy Cross, a rare privilege for a boy of his background. Lalonde consistently stood first in his baccalaureate class, then studied law at the Université de Montréal and won a scholarship to Oxford, where he read philosophy, politics, and economics, the course that prepared young Brits for Whitehall and Westminster.[1]

What animated Lalonde was his faith, his personalist interpretation of Catholicism. He had become involved with Jeunesse étudiante catholique when he was in his teens, then worked full-time for the movement for two years between college and law school. Lalonde saw party politics not as "an epiphenomenon, a carbuncle on society," as so many of his Jéciste colleagues believed, but as a means for the faithful to do God's work in the world.[2]

Observers who watched Lalonde and Trudeau closely over the long period of their involvement together in politics came to think of them as the closest of partners. Lalonde, who was ten years younger, first met Trudeau in 1951 when personalist friends suggested he ask Trudeau's advice about his career; Trudeau told him to study both law and social sciences so he could bring a breadth of knowledge to his work. After that encounter, he devoured every article Trudeau wrote in *Cité libre* and was greatly influenced by his ideas because of their reformist passion, their rationalism, and the elegance of their expression. When Trudeau excoriated Duplessis, so did Lalonde. When Trudeau espoused federalism, so did Lalonde. More than anyone other than Jean Marchand, it was Lalonde who was convinced of the importance of turning the Liberal Party's power to their purposes. When Trudeau ran for Parliament, became a parliamentary secretary, then a cabinet minister and finally prime minister, Lalonde was there in the background, proposing strategies and personnel, taking on the hard tasks Trudeau needed to have done. In this loyalty there was nothing whatever of the acolyte's deference. Lalonde was his own man. He knew Trudeau's faults but he judged them to be far less important than his strengths, most particularly his strength of purpose, which Lalonde saw as rooted not in egotism but in faith.

Their relationship was far from intimate. Lalonde remarked once that he and his wife, Claire, had never dined with the Trudeaus at 24 Sussex Drive in the Margaret years, that he and Trudeau had never discussed the breakdown of his marriage, that Trudeau was the least forthcoming man he knew. "He is not your typical Rotarian," Lalonde once said sardonically, smiling his wide grin at the thought of comparing Trudeau to the small-town optimists whose service-club funds had paid for his scholarship to Oxford.

"He's never been easy to work with. But he is a man with a developed social conscience, a rationalist committed to change for the greater good."[3]

On that high-minded basis, the two men's acceptance of each other was total. On his father's side Trudeau came from the same stock as Lalonde – their families' farms were only thirty miles apart – but Lalonde had remained more rooted in French-Canadian society, was earthier and less complex. He had not suffered the confusions of Trudeau's cross-cultural conflicts, the strain of his family's upward mobility, or the trauma of an early parental death. His education was not as eclectic as Trudeau's nor his interests so esoteric. And his early adult life had involved more sustained self-sacrifice and more concrete accomplishments. Trudeau had studied in Paris and London, playing with socialist ideas at the Sorbonne and the LSE without completing a degree. Despite his lesser ability in English, Lalonde had managed to "work like a horse" at Oxford, achieving graduate degrees in social science and law. Lalonde had gone to work in a Montreal law firm and acted as an adviser to governments, while Trudeau had dabbled in advocacy law and protest marches. Lalonde had built an exemplary marriage while Trudeau danced in discos with showy women he referred to as "babes." Lalonde went to Île Perrot in haying time for his holidays; Trudeau went to Gstaad and Marrakesh. Trudeau was the performer, the dazzler, the lightning rod. Lalonde was the organizer and the work-horse, Trudeau's conscience, goad, and ally.

And what an ally to be able to count on. By 1979 Lalonde's experience in government spanned a quarter-century. He had worked on the Fulton-Favreau constitutional amending formula in the Diefenbaker years as a Justice Department lawyer; he had been legal counsel to a royal commission, an adviser to Lester Pearson, and principal secretary in Trudeau's first government before being elected to Parliament himself in 1972. Besides serving as minister of health and welfare and then of federal-provincial relations in the wake of the PQ victory in 1976, he had functioned as the Liberals' election campaign co-chairman, Quebec caucus leader, and party boss. In these demanding overlapping jobs he had endured exhaustion and come close to the sin of despair. But he had not crumpled, as had so many of the Trudeau cohort from Quebec in the 1970s. He had lashed on the Liberal machine in his home province in the 1979 campaign, delivering to Trudeau, even in that dismal season, sixty-seven of a possible seventy-five Quebec seats. In the 1980 election he had raised the total to seventy-four, with one lone Tory holding out against the red tide.[4]

Having been given his pick of portfolios in the new cabinet, Lalonde had chosen Energy, Mines and Resources, in order to ensure the implementation of the energy policy he had been working on with such single-minded intent over the previous eight months. Anyone less confident would have been daunted by the prospect of tackling this contentious issue. But in the late winter and early spring of 1980, Lalonde was in the state of elation that comes to those reaffirmed in the belief that God is on their side. He had hated what had happened to him and to his alter ego, Trudeau, in the late 1970s – hated the sense of events spinning out of control; hated the success their separatist enemies were enjoying in Quebec under the Parti Québécois government of René Lévesque; hated having Trudeau's personal reputation sullied in the voyeuristic hysteria that surrounded the breakdown of his marriage; hated the fact that he had been unable as minister of health and welfare to bring about the guaranteed annual income that would have completed the post-war welfare state; hated the feeling that the interminable intergovernmental wrangling over the constitution had not yielded to his prescriptions no matter how determinedly he had tackled the problem as the minister of state for federal-provincial relations from 1977 to 1979.[5]

But now in this fresh political season, he was experiencing a renaissance. He gladly gave over leadership of the federalist forces in the upcoming referendum fight to the prime minister and his scrappy minister of justice, Jean Chrétien, and turned his formidable talents to a new field. As a young man he had absorbed the message at the heart of personalist Catholicism: the Christian should govern his life on the basis of three imperatives: *Voir! Juger! Agir!* In his months in opposition, he had looked at the energy issue carefully and judged it to be soluble. Now was the time to act.

After twenty years' experience in Ottawa, he was sure the city's economic technocrats would be doctrinally opposed to the interventionism he had in mind. The major departments concerned with the business community – Finance, External Affairs, and Industry, Trade and Commerce, as well as the energy industry's regulatory body, the National Energy Board – had resisted the establishment of Petro-Canada on the grounds that a state-owned energy company would strain relations with the oil industry and, *ipso facto*, with the United States. The chances were that the public servants running these institutions in 1980 could be counted on to pick holes in Lalonde's grand design. It was an opportunity he intended to deny them.[6]

He decided that his first problem after being sworn in on March 4 would be to animate the bureaucrats in his new department, a task that turned out to be easier than expected. Energy, Mines and Resources had been through a federal-provincial battle of its own over the previous decade that had made its officials suspicious of the Ottawa bureaucracy's usual dogma of *laissez-faire*. The years they had spent struggling with a seemingly impossible situation meant they were fed up with the federal government's incapacity to act in Canada's interests on the vital issue of energy supplies.

Oil and natural gas were two of the rich store of staples Canadians had treated with reckless extravagance through ignorance of their potential importance to the country's long-term development. Petroleum had been discovered in elephantine proportions in Alberta in 1947 as a direct response to U.S. Cold War strategy. Washington's concern for a secure supply of raw materials in the face of the communist threat had led it to offer American transnational oil companies generous tax write-offs for exploration costs abroad. Since

Canada was politically reliable and geographically accessible, U.S. corporations focused their prospecting efforts for several years on the Western Canada Sedimentary Basin, most of which lay within Alberta's boundaries.

The provincial government of the day, a right-wing Social Credit administration rooted in the funny-money populism brought to Alberta by waves of American homesteaders from the prairie states to the south, was left to manage its burgeoning oil patch without significant federal government involvement. As a result, petroleum was the most Americanized sector of the Canadian economy next to the auto industry. Since Calgary and Edmonton had closer ties with Dallas and Tulsa than with any Canadian metropolis, the regulatory regime the Socreds adopted was modelled directly on the one created to service American oil companies in Texas and Oklahoma.[7]

Even at the federal level, petroleum policy was formulated in response to advice from the U.S. companies that dominated the Canadian industry and were the conduit for Washington's strategic objectives. The Borden royal commission, established by Diefenbaker in 1957, rejected the idea of piping oil to Montreal and obligingly accepted the Americans' suggestion for splitting the Canadian market in half. According to this formula, western oil would be shipped only as far east as Ontario, and Alberta would maintain a large market in the northwestern United States to keep its outlook continental. The Canadian market east of the Ottawa River was reserved for lower-priced offshore crude oil from Venezuela, a plan that was consistent with the American strategic goal of keeping Canada from developing an integrated market on east-west lines. Apart from a lonely voice or two raised to lament the take-over of the few Canadian-owned companies distributing gasoline to the public, a consensus enveloped business and government on both sides of the border. As energy exporters Canadians were proud to be part of a continental industry pumping cheap oil and natural gas as fuel for the free world.[8]

It was not until 1973, when OPEC forced the doubling and redoubling of the world market price of oil, that the turmoil of the international energy economy had a direct impact on the Canadian consciousness. Suddenly, petroleum was said to be so scarce – although Imperial Oil, the subsidiary of the giant Exxon, had been claiming only recently that Canada had several hundred years' supply – that many Canadians wondered whether there would be enough oil to heat their houses through the winter. A commodity that had been treated like just another staple for export had become a precious dwindling resource vital to the country's survival.[9]

Although the OPEC shock reverberated world-wide, it caused a particularly acute controversy in Canada because most of the country's proven petroleum reserves were situated in Alberta. Since the provinces had constitutional jurisdiction over natural resources, Canada turned into a microcosm of the global confrontation between energy producers and consumers. Alberta understandably wanted the highest possible price and largest possible market for its depleting assets. But governments of most other provinces, as well as central Canadian manufacturing industries and individual consumers, were objecting to the prospect of paying higher prices for an essential commodity whose production costs had not increased and whose reserves they believed should be husbanded to ensure a long-term, low-cost supply for all Canadian consumers.

Caught in this polarized situation, the minority Trudeau government of 1972–74 took sides. Alberta was barren territory for them politically, and it made economic sense to utilize cheap petroleum as an industrial input in order to improve the Canadian economy's overall international competitiveness. Under strong pressure from the NDP, the Liberals proceeded to intervene in a provincial arena they had previously left largely alone. By freezing the price Canadians paid for domestic petroleum products, they limited both the oil industry's profits and the Alberta government's royalties. They also promised to set up Petro-Canada as a public-sector petroleum corporation and increased the oil and gas companies' federal taxes in two ways – by disallowing royalty deductions and by increasing rates as an attempt to divert funds from the west to pay for eastern Canadians' forced consumption of more expensive offshore oil.

For his part Alberta's feisty Conservative premier, Peter Lougheed, eagerly grasped the opportunity that OPEC's price increases presented. He expanded his government's bureaucratic capacity and strengthened the provincial regulatory agencies to gain greater control over the petroleum industry. He raised royalties to increase the province's share of the petroleum industry's cascading revenues and set aside a portion in the Alberta Heritage Fund, intended to provide the investment capital with which the province could ultimately diversify its staple-based economy. Lougheed also worked hard to build alliances with other provinces in the west so he could better withstand Ottawa's threatened incursions in the energy policy field. [10]

Because he was extremely sensitive to any hint that his oil-rich, go-ahead province was still subject to its pre-oil-boom quasi-colonial dependency on Ottawa, Lougheed was incensed in September 1973, when Donald Macdonald, the abrasive federal minister of energy, peremptorily summoned his Alberta counter-part, Bill Dickie, to Ottawa to hear him announce the imposition of an oil price freeze and an export tax on western crude destined for American markets. A Toronto lawyer with little personal experi-ence of the west, Macdonald came across as rude, arrogant, and ignorant of Alberta's needs – the very model of an uncaring central Canadian. Lougheed viewed the federal tax as tantamount to a dec-laration of fiscal war and responded by resisting further federal initia-tives vigorously in an embittering Ottawa-versus-Edmonton energy battle that lasted throughout the 1970s. [11]

Despite various concessions made by Ottawa to accommodate Lougheed's concerns, the decade closed without any sign of peace in sight. By this time the federal Energy Department had beefed up its expertise with a high-powered group run by Ed Clark, a brilliant young bureaucrat who had proven his fiscal fealty to federalism in

Finance before being dispatched along with Ian Stewart and George Tough to EMR to wrestle with the petroleum problem. They had advised the Clark government to let petroleum prices rise to world levels in order to force efficiency on central Canadian manufacturers and conservation on consumers across the country.[12]

As it was, Ottawa was paying the difference between the world price for imported offshore oil and the domestic price the Liberals had established. But this gigantic subsidy had turned Canadian energy consumers into the most wasteful in the industrialized world and was costing the federal government $3 billion annually. In 1979, world petroleum prices had shot up again, threatening new chaos on international markets and further upheaval in Canada. Oil had gone from $15 U.S. per barrel in April to $25 in November, promising new riches for Alberta and new crises for Ottawa. Appalled by the indecisiveness of the Conservative energy minister, Ray Hnatyshyn, and shamed by the way Peter Lougheed had managed to bully Joe Clark, senior EMR officials had already begun to express privately the belief that if Ottawa wanted to achieve an energy policy advantageous to the whole country, it would have to get tougher with Alberta.[13]

Marc Lalonde's appointment – with the signal it gave to the governmental system that the new regime was taking energy problems seriously – had heartened rather than alarmed the energy bureaucrats. In Lalonde they had the public servant's dream minister, a politician who knew exactly what he wanted and who had the clout with the prime minister to get it. Instead of resisting his directives, they welcomed the chance to formulate a definitive solution to problems that had dogged them for nearly a decade.[14]

Lalonde let his officials know immediately that he was not looking for a series of incremental policy changes to be announced *seriatim* so they could be torn apart by the Alberta government and Ottawa's economic mandarinate. What he had in mind was a mammoth legislative package that would implement the Liberal campaign promises on energy in one swoop. EMR would have to divert into federal coffers even more substantial financial flows from the cash-rich oil industry and fat Alberta treasury. Furthermore, it would have to rejig several facets of the many-sided energy problem simultaneously – consumer demand, industrial supply, ownership patterns, the distribution system, and conservation incentives. Lalonde made these large demands knowing very well that translating his comprehensive energy scheme into legislation would depend only partly on how well his departmental technicians handled their policy-making task. Success would also hang on whether his bold proposals could be exempted from the complex policy-review process known in Ottawa as the Pitfield system, in mock tribute to its brooding progenitor.

Ironically, Pitfield's process represented the kind of government by technocracy Lalonde and Trudeau had talked about as a logical solution to chronic Canadian problems before they came to power. They had observed with scorn the muddling-through that characterized the governments of Diefenbaker and Pearson. In their view, the shameless manipulation of elected ministers by their mandarins, dismayingly casual policy-making carried out in the bureaucracy, and the crisis-driven decision-making in cabinet that characterized those regimes made a mockery of democratic accountability and managerial rationality. Lalonde and Trudeau had determined to transform Canada by applying advanced technology and scientific investigation to government. Functionalism – a notion they loved as Cartesians – would cause Canadian federalism to realize its dazzling potential, and in the process, the French would show themselves superior to the English at the governing game.[15]

They set their young Montreal establishment friend, Michael Pitfield, to work out the reforms they wanted. He shared their zeal for revamping government and had familiarized himself with the latest scientific management theory when he was sent to Europe in 1967 to study how other parliamentary systems coped with the problem of maintaining collegial co-ordination in an expanding bureaucratic apparatus. Armed with this research, he then produced a blueprint for government policy-making, aimed at setting long-range priorities, requiring interdepartmental consultation, and imposing cost-benefit evaluation. Trudeau approved of Pitfield's proposals for policy-making by cabinet committees serviced by secretariats, because they promised democratic control by the elected ministers over their professional bureaucrats and a modernization of the welfare state's administrative machinery. Lalonde liked the formal demarcation between the public servants' policy function in the PCO and the explicitly partisan mandate of the PMO. [16]

As principal secretary from 1968 to 1972, Lalonde saw to it that Pitfield's planning procedures worked to consolidate Trudeau's power. But as a minister from 1972 to 1979, he learned – particularly from his unhappy experience in trying to reform the social security system – that ambitious and imaginative legislative proposals could suffer dissipation of momentum and dilution of substance as they went through exhausting departmental reviews. The complicated process Pitfield had devised had turned into an administrative maze, frustrating both the elected and the appointed. [17]

Now as a reinstated minister in 1980, Lalonde was acutely conscious (as were Trudeau and Pitfield himself) of the threat the system posed to their new priorities. They no longer wanted to play philosopher-kings but to achieve constitutional reform and restructure the energy sector. Pitfield was not only willing to exempt these big items from the constraints of his system, he was willing to show the politicians how to do it. The newly appointed minister of justice, Jean Chrétien, had already been given the power to run the referendum battle as a freelance exercise that used the government apparatus without deference to the Pitfield system. And Trudeau was setting up his own constitution-making unit, led by a politically astute Liberal named Michael Kirby who was charged with keeping virtually everyone else ignorant of its proceedings.

Lalonde's energy program presented a more difficult problem. Because it involved billions of dollars, it had to be part of the government's new "envelope" approach to expenditure management, which had been conceived by Pitfield and put in place by the Clark government after Pitfield was fired in 1979. In an effort to discipline apparently uncontrollable increases in the government's spending that had been severely criticized in the late 1970s, this Policy and Expenditure Management System allotted a fixed annual sum called an envelope to broad expenditure areas rather than specific departments. External Affairs was lumped in with National Defence, and social development covered several departments dealing with social issues. Each envelope was administered by a cabinet committee, which was made responsible for divvying up the contents of its envelope among its ministers' departments. If the ministers wanted to bring in new policies that cost more than their envelope contained, they could not ask Finance for more money. They would have to find it by agreeing among themselves to cut back some of their existing programs. Putting Lalonde's energy package through an envelope committee's scrutiny would slow it down and make it vulnerable to sabotage by other ministers. Bureaucratic objections would proliferate as soon as it became clear that energy legislation would involve making fundamental changes in the tax system.[18]

Pitfield found a solution to these difficulties by resurrecting EnFin, a group of high-level bureaucrats from the Energy and Finance Departments that Clark had set up the previous year to facilitate his negotiations with Lougheed. The revived EnFin was exempted from the regular procedure of submitting policy drafts and budget proposals for consideration by the Cabinet Committee on Economic Development. Instead, it was granted its own multi-billion-dollar envelope and the right to report directly to P&P, the Priorities and Planning Committee, which functioned as the prime minister's small and very powerful inner cabinet. When pronounced *en français*, EnFin sounded the real message: Finally! the energy nettle was about to be grasped.[19]

At the Ministry of State for Economic Development, the new envelope system's central agency for co-ordinating economic policy-making, its secretary, Gordon Osbaldeston, was livid about being kept in the dark. As the bureaucrat who normally would have been consulted at every point along the way, he felt that, under its new minister, EMR had become paranoid, refusing to divulge its plans lest they be scuppered by their critics, inside Ottawa or outside. Even the inner cabinet was largely excluded from EnFin's deliberations. Lalonde fended off complaints from his ministerial colleagues by bringing to P&P in the early autumn a condensed version of his energy policy in the form of a slide show. But they were never given a chance to read a complete draft of what became the National Energy Program.[20]

In the meantime EnFin was busy working out the bureaucratic problems attached to the massive energy policy. Finance disliked using taxes as policy instruments. EMR wanted to use changes in the tax system as incentives to transform the structure of the petroleum industry. Without the understanding and active support of Ian Stewart, the new deputy in Finance, the NEP might have foundered on this issue. Stewart, who had been an economic adviser to Trudeau in the 1970s and had served as deputy minister of energy during the Tory interregnum, saw that so many tax changes were being proposed, it made sense to merge the energy document with the Finance Department's annual budget. He agreed to make the NEP the core of the first budget that his minister, Allan MacEachen, would present. As a result Finance and EMR were able to work more closely than ever before, though there was still tension over the appropriate use of tax measures. From Lalonde's point of view, the official secrecy that came from "budgetizing" the NEP gave it still further protection from bureaucratic predators. He had in effect managed a reverse take-over of his department's potential competitors.[21]

Oil industry spokesmen were later to argue that it was the young EMR official Ed Clark who had masterminded the NEP as a socialist experiment, brainwashed his immediate associates, and then intimidated the deputy ministers at Energy and Finance with his misbegotten brilliance. The reality was far more collegial. Lalonde's ambitious plan meshed closely with that of the seventy-odd economists whom Ed Clark had forged into an impressive analytical team at EMR. As the son of the great sociologist S.D. Clark, who had been a colleague of Harold Innis's and a member of that handful of original thinkers who had created the short-lived Canadian school of political economy in the 1930s and 1940s, William Edmund Clark could claim to belong to an intellectually exciting but very Canadian tradition. After studying economics at Toronto, he had gone on to complete his doctoral work at Harvard on the problems of achieving socialism in Tanzania and was now making his meteoric way in the federal government service, having joined Finance in 1974 and worked on wage and price controls for the Anti-Inflation Board.[22]

The man in charge of the economic team Ed Clark had assembled in EMR was Lalonde's hand-picked deputy minister, Mickey Cohen, a shrewd tax lawyer with ten years' experience in Finance. Cohen acted as the NEP's chief negotiator and expediter, with Ed Clark designing the policy components and orchestrating them into a coherent whole while his colleague George Tough directed most of the actual drafting of legislation. They worked with their small support group in a feverish atmosphere under security that kept even the department's senior geologists out of their deliberations.[23]

Every weekday evening before he went home for the night, Lalonde was briefed on their progress. He read every draft of every proposed measure – the document went through eighteen rewrites, from draft A to draft R – making innumerable changes and suggestions, relishing his authority and purpose. As he told his caucus colleagues, "We're going to make hard decisions. If we're defeated again [as a government], it will be for good reason."[24]


There were two ways to read the thick booklet with the straightforward title *National Energy Program* that accompanied the new government's first budget when it was presented to the House of Commons on October 28, 1980. The cool view recognized the NEP as a logical extension of the framework established by federal policies throughout the 1970s, when four goals had been articulated:

achieve security from foreign disruption of supplies; increase Ottawa's power to regulate this strategic industry in order to give price protection to consumers; raise levels of Canadian ownership; and use the development of giant energy projects to spark Canada's overall industrial development.[25]

But Lalonde wanted the NEP to be seen in another, hotter light. He personally drafted the document's polemical opening chapter to catch the attention of the electorate, stating that the effect of OPEC's price increases was a massive transfer of wealth from Canadian taxpayers and consumers to foreign-owned producers; he warned that unless something drastic was done without delay, Canada would be left "with no choice but to accept a permanent foreign domination." His daring approach succeeded dramatically. The document detonated like a bomb over Alberta, stunning the petroleum province momentarily, while its fall-out spread slowly across the continent.[26]

Not since the industrial mobilization of World War II had such an all-encompassing governmental economic intervention been tried. Detailed regulations were proposed to keep prices controlled at "blended" levels, with cheaper "old" oil fetching far less than more expensive, recently discovered "new" oil. (This scheme was meant to force the pace of development outside Alberta by encouraging exploration on the "Canada lands," the areas beyond the provinces' boundaries stretching out into the Arctic, Pacific, and Atlantic Oceans, which came under federal jurisdiction.) The state oil company, Petro-Canada, was to become the chosen instrument for increased Canadianization through a "back-in" provision, which gave it automatic ownership of a 25-per-cent "Crown interest" in every new oil development on the Canada lands. It would also be assigned capital to buy up more foreign-owned petroleum companies.[27]

Furthermore, a range of new taxes would divert the expected flood of petrodollars into the federal treasury by the billions. The petroleum and gas revenue tax, or PGRT, would tap oil and gas as it gushed out of the ground; a tax on gasoline as it came from the refinery would pay for Petro-Canada's foreign acquisitions; and another tax on gasoline at the pump would involve consumers in financing the subsidy on imported oil themselves. With these new revenues the government would be able to spend billions in order to have its way with the oil industry. Petroleum Incentive Payments, called PIP grants, would replace depletion allowances as the government's main lure to shift exploration from Alberta to the Canada lands. Grants would give householders a good reason to convert their furnaces from oil to a more abundant energy source, like natural gas or hydroelectricity.[28]

By the time this detailed final version of the NEP was released with the 1980 budget, the EnFin group's members were exhausted by their labours. They made the mistake of assuming that the battle was over. As it turned out, publishing the policy was the first, not the last, shot in a new energy war. The NEP soon became a target for all those connected with the energy industry who had been waiting to strike back at Ottawa ever since Tom Axworthy's speech from the throne had reaffirmed the Liberals' intentions to act. The province of Alberta, the petroleum industry, and even the United States government were ready to defend turf threatened by the NEP. In the six months leading up to its announcement, Lalonde's negotiations with the Alberta government on energy questions had been pro forma and his consultations with the oil industry negligible. Now both reacted with ferocity.

Lalonde had realized from the beginning that he would have to negotiate the NEP with the Alberta government and that he would be hampered by the old animosities between Ottawa and Edmonton. He had contributed to this antagonism himself when he was health minister in the 1970s by publicly expressing the contemptuous attitude towards provinces and their premiers that had jelled in the minds of his generation of Quebec federalists when they came to political consciousness in the Duplessis era. "I must state quite clearly that the . . . theory of provincial duchies which we refused to endorse when it applied to Quebec we are not about to accept . . . for the rest of the country," he told a reporter. For him provinces were parochial and reactionary. They had to be brought into the light of federalism.[29]

The Lougheed government had been preparing for confrontation from the moment it became apparent that Trudeau would be returned to office early in 1980. Even so, they were dumbfounded by the audacity of the NEP when its details were finally unveiled. Its effect was heightened by the fact that it was released in the same month that Trudeau announced his provocative unilateral constitutional initiative. Having won the Quebec referendum, he was pressing on to resolve this problem that had plagued the country for so long by threatening to ignore the provinces entirely and enforce his own solution.[30]

In the face of these twin aggressions, Lougheed saw no option but to retaliate. Within two days he was denouncing Ottawa's "outright attempt to take over the resources of this Province." His diatribes — charging Ottawa's socialist bureaucrats with plotting to nationalize the oil industry as part of Trudeau's scheme to turn the Canadian federation into a unitary state — were warmly received on his home ground. So was his proposed program of reprisals. He announced a cutback in oil production by 180,000 barrels per day in three stages over the next nine months in order to slow down shipments to central Canada; withheld approval for the Alsands and Cold Lake tar-sands megaprojects; and initiated a constitutional challenge to the proposed federal tax on natural gas.[31]

For several weeks the Lougheed government played on Alberta's alienation, whipping up anger at central Canada with speeches and pamphlets that found popular echoes in bumper stickers and radio phone-in shows. The premier dismissed the NEP as economically stupid, predicting a severe economic downturn, increased dependence on offshore oil, and a loss of exploration initiatives and jobs to the United States. In rallying his electorate against the federal program, Lougheed was trying to strengthen his negotiating position before coming to the bargaining table.[32]

Lalonde himself exacerbated the situation by remarking sarcastically to journalists that Ottawa had not fought the recent Quebec referendum to defeat the Quebec separatists' aspirations to political sovereignty with economic association, in order to acquiesce to the Alberta government's demands for economic sovereignty with political association. But despite rhetorical extremism on both sides, relations between the two governments did not break down. "We never got to the point where we couldn't have a drink together," was the way the behind-the-headlines situation was described by Merv Leitch, Lougheed's soft-spoken energy minister. Leitch, Lalonde, and their entourages had been sparring while the NEP was gestating. Once it was released, both sides knew they would have to start serious negotiations.[33]

Even before the NEP was tabled in the House of Commons, Lougheed had instructed Barry Mellon, the Alberta deputy minister of energy, to meet Mickey Cohen and get down to business as soon as possible. In November, only days after the NEP announcement, the two bureaucrats dined together at the Four Seasons in Ottawa to assess the situation. By December they had agreed on a rough agenda. Alberta had insisted the negotiations start with price increases, reasoning that if oil profits got bigger, their respective tax shares would be larger too; the exact division could be negotiated later. In the new year enough progress was made – with the officials' initial achievement being an agreement on whose figures to use – that a ministerial meeting between Lalonde and Leitch was scheduled for April, to be held on neutral ground in Winnipeg.[34]

"Let's get to work," Lalonde said briskly, once the meeting's twenty-point agenda of differences had been drawn up. Lougheed had stipulated to his officials that Alberta must come out of the negotiations with a revenue share larger than Ottawa's. But Lalonde kept badgering Leitch, wittily and forcefully, about Alberta's Arabian Nights wealth, and its backroom deals with Quebec and Newfoundland on the constitution, until even Leitch's own officials began to think the province had gone too far in its furious response to the NEP. "We had to recognize that we *were* fabulously wealthy as a province," one of them recalled, and "that we wanted to get back into the [Canadian] family." With both sides using rising price forecasts supplied by the petroleum giants, the Albertans came to believe that the province could afford a new set of rules for the oil industry. [35]

In the end, the detailed negotiating came down to the question of who could outfox whom. Mickey Cohen played on Alberta's phobia about federal intervention. Conjuring up the spectre of seven hundred federal bureaucrats doling out PIP grants in the Calgary oil patch, Cohen invited Alberta to administer the program itself – at a price, of course. "If you want power, you have to pay," he told them. "What have you got to worry about, anyway, when you're so rich? If you don't want us to run the PIP grant system, then take it on yourselves." The Albertans lunged at this bait and landed themselves with a federal program to administer at the cost of $600 million a year. [36]

The federal negotiators were also under pressure to make concessions. Some mutually acceptable price schedules had to be drawn up quickly if Finance officials, now busy preparing the 1981 federal budget, were to have reliable figures on Ottawa's share of petroleum revenues in order to make their fiscal projections. Further pressure came from Trudeau. In the general war still raging over the constitution, an Edmonton-Ottawa energy settlement that mollified Lougheed might well pave the way for an accord on his patriation package. [37]

When the negotiations, held in Montreal late in August, yielded a deal, the Albertans had reason to be pleased. They had caused Ottawa to retreat from the proposed export tax on natural gas and to agree to accelerate the rise of Canadian oil and gas prices towards the world market level. On September 1 Lougheed signed what he called this "balanced agreement" and posed with Trudeau for the cameras, champagne glass in hand. It looked as though the NEP battle was over. [38]

In Ottawa there was jubilation. With Alberta administering the PIP grant system, Canadianization could forge ahead at Edmonton's expense. As for the oil price increases, giving in to Alberta's pressure took the Liberals off the hook on which they had impaled themselves in the 1980 campaign by promising Canadians low-price petroleum. Furthermore, if prices were to rise faster than the NEP had anticipated, Ottawa's proposed energy megaprojects would become easier to finance. Energy revenues would yield the federal treasury an expected $65 billion in the next five years. "We've won!" was the way Tom Axworthy, whose ideas had instigated the whole operation, summed up the deal. [39]

Nick Taylor, a maverick oilman who also led the minuscule Alberta Liberal Party, viewed the deal differently. "Lougheed has taught Trudeau how to rob the stage-coach and split the profits," he said in explaining why these doughty opponents were happy at the outcome. Since both would benefit from steadily increasing prices, the two governments had expanded their take at the expense of the once-omnipotent petroleum industry. [40]

For the most part, Lalonde had refused to involve the industry in his deliberations while his department was formulating the NEP. Only a few resolutely pro-Canadianization oilmen – Bob Blair of Nova, Bill Hopper and Joel Bell of Petro-Canada, and to a lesser extent Jack Gallagher of Dome Petroleum – knew what was transpiring. Lalonde had sour memories of how the Trudeauites had bent over backwards to give Canadian business what it wanted only to find the country's executives and entrepreneurs consistently denouncing the Liberals and supporting the Tories. And the oilmen, mainly right-wingers who hated governments with religious fervour, were more vociferous than most. As far as Lalonde was concerned, there was no use talking to them. His people at EMR knew what the industry wanted, but what it wanted was not necessarily what was good for it. Its profits were far higher than could be justified. What other industry could finance growth from its own cash flow? Lalonde knew oilmen would be mad as hell when they first read the NEP. He expected them to calm down when they realized Canada still had a politically favourable climate by international standards. He would then work co-operatively with the better firms. [41]

When oil executives made speeches denouncing Ottawa, or the Canadian Petroleum Association issued statements blasting the NEP, they only served to confirm widespread public satisfaction with the policy and to stiffen Lalonde's determination to defend it. At this stage the Lougheed government was not getting on with the industry much better than Lalonde was. The oilmen had been trying to pressure Edmonton to make a quick deal with Ottawa, and Lougheed had instructed his officials to limit contacts with them in case his negotiating strategy leaked out and reached federal ears. [42]

Into this incendiary situation the brazen Lalonde had marched resolutely in the run-up to the intergovernmental agreement. He had flown out to Edmonton and addressed an oil industry audience so hysterical he could hardly make himself heard above the jeers and catcalls. He responded to this abuse by producing figures that showed the NEP was designed to promote a healthy, capitalist petroleum industry in which even foreign firms could make more money in Canada than they would by drilling elsewhere. He had been keeping in close touch with Jack Gallagher, who was promising that Dome Petroleum would be pumping 600,000 barrels per day from the Canada lands in the Beaufort Sea by 1986, so he felt confident in taunting Alberta that the province's near-monopoly as the country's oil supplier was in jeopardy. Lalonde even spent several days at the Calgary Stampede talking with oilmen, reasoning that it was worth wearing a cowboy hat and drinking whisky if he could neutralize what should have been Edmonton's main weapon in the intergovernmental tussle: its alliance with the private sector. [43]

Neutralize he might, but convert he could not. The oilmen's rage was too powerful, their free-market beliefs too fundamentalist, and their hatred for central Canada too rabid for them to admit that something good could come out of government, particularly the federal government. There was some resignation over Ottawa getting a bigger share of petroleum revenues, but the fact remained that even the "juniors" and the "independents" – the small Canadian firms that the NEP was supposed to help – were vituperative in criticizing it.

The small firms' hostility was understandable because Ottawa, while giving Canadianization incentives with one hand, had taken away other benefits with the other. The Finance Department had inserted into the 1980 budget a tax change ending a fast write-off of natural gas well-development costs without fully explaining its implications to EMR bureaucrats. Although small when compared with the billions involved in the PIP grant system, this write-off was the way the small firms were financing their operations. It took their trade group, the Independent Petroleum Association of Canada, a year and a half of lobbying with EMR and Finance to get the matter corrected. During this crucial period the NEP was deprived of political support from the very people that Ottawa had counted on from the beginning.[44]

The feds also underestimated the extent to which the Canadian-owned juniors and independents identified with the foreign-owned majors. Partly this was because they shared the giants' free-market ideology and empathized with the Americans' angry charge that the NEP had lowered their net worth – by $1.3 billion in Gulf Canada's case and $1 billion in Imperial's. But it was also because many of them were too small to exploit PIP grants on their own. They depended on the majors, who had long acquired a near-monopoly grip on the bulk of the explorable land, for the chance to "farm in" on exploration plays. As the economy moved towards a recession and strenuous objections to the NEP mushroomed, some of the oilmen decided to conduct a capital strike. In highly publicized acts of defiance staged for the television cameras to give the impression that the Canadian oil industry would be shut down because of the NEP, they moved their drilling rigs, their capital, and their outrage south of the border to the land of free enterprise – where, given the *laissez-faire* mood of Reagan's America, they expected to flourish.[45]

# PART III

# Trudeau and the Americans: Liberalism Under Attack

# CHAPTER 6

# HURRICANE RONNIE: AMERICAN RETALIATION

W hile this feverish activity was going on in the summer of 1981 – with federal and provincial bureaucrats working towards an intergovernmental energy agreement and Marc Lalonde contending with the distemper of the Alberta oil industry – serious concerns were developing in Ottawa about the new Reagan administration in Washington.

Canadian-American relations had been relatively tranquil during the previous four years while Jimmy Carter was in the White House. The Liberal government, which had been assured by its diplomats in Washington that Carter would be re-elected, was ill prepared for the shock of Ronald Reagan and his right-wing revolutionaries taking power in January 1981. The America that was most congenial to Ottawa's government élite was the old liberal America and its eastern seaboard internationalism, the America of Foggy Bottom and the Harvard Yard, of FDR, JFK, J.K. Galbraith, the Council on Foreign Relations, and *The New York Times*.

In that America, the New Right, whose triumph the Reagan election represented, had been seen as an aberration, merely the "ethical afterglow of feudalism," in the dismissive words of the great liberal historian Arthur Schlesinger, Jr. Some notice had been taken of Reagan's astonishing career – his rise from mediocre movie actor and anti-communist president of the Screen Actors Guild in the 1940s, to television host and lecture-circuit apologist for corporate America in the 1950s, to governor of California and Republican presidential aspirant in the 1960s and 1970s. But there was little understanding, even after he finally won the Republican nomination in the summer of 1980, that Reagan would be able to mobilize a new conservative coalition that had been forming in the United States in the years since Richard Nixon had been elected president in 1968. An unlikely alliance of Wall Street money men, southern fundamentalists, New York Jewish intellectuals, committed Cold Warriors, *Reader's Digest* devotees, Texas oilmen, and disaffected Democrats in the Sun Belt and the Midwest, the new conservatives were variously enraged or threatened by the failure of welfarism to contain black poverty, the horrors of drug abuse, the spread of sexual permissiveness, urban decay, and the decline of American hegemony in the world – all of which they blamed on the liberalism of the political and intellectual élites who had been dominant in the United States for nearly half a century.[1]

In dismissing Ronald Reagan before the 1980 presidential election as nothing but a front man, an amateur so inadequately prepared for public life that as governor of California he had to be "goof-proofed" by his staff before appearing at important events, Liberal Ottawa was ignoring the strength of the forces that were using Reagan's skills as a communicator to capture the White House. Just how zealous those forces were, how great an impact they were having on American life, and how damaging an effect they could have on Canada took several months for the Trudeau government to recognize.

Even Coutts and Axworthy, who were fascinated by American politics, saw Reagan as a bit of a joke, the guy who had played second lead to a chimpanzee in the 1950s movie *Bedtime for Bonzo*. When it came to planning the events for his first presidential visit to Ottawa in March 1981, they decided to mount an extravagant gala at the National Arts Centre, taking their cue from the lavish inaugural celebrations held in Washington in January. "Obviously, this guy likes a spectac'," Axworthy said to Coutts, "So let's give him one. Bring out the Mounties – it's Nelson Eddy time."[2]

Trudeau's first meetings with Reagan were expected to be pro forma, an opportunity for the two leaders to establish a personal rapport rather than to engage in a serious discussion of policy issues. But a few days before Reagan was to arrive, this benign illusion was shattered when Washington administered three sharp slaps to Ottawa. On March 5 a threatening note objecting to the National Energy Program and signed by the U.S. secretary of state, Alexander Haig, was delivered to Peter Towe, the Canadian ambassador in the American capital. On March 6, the White House withdrew the U.S.-Canada East Coast Fishery Treaty from the U.S. Senate, where it had been sent for ratification by President Carter, thereby wiping out several years of painstaking but successful negotiations over a historically contentious bilateral problem. On March 7, the American delegation to the United Nations Law of the Sea Conference was abruptly withdrawn, an act that threatened to abort more than fifteen years of international negotiations at which Canada had made important gains in sovereignty over its coastal waters and entitlement to the resources under them. [3]

Trudeau's staff was still trying, in concert with the Department of External Affairs, to assess what these provocative moves meant when Reagan and his entourage arrived on March 10. Not knowing exactly what to think about the tempestuous situation in Washington – where the new administration was shaking up the entire government system in an even more radical manner than was usual with the changing of the presidential guard – or what the new president's precise role was in this particular Canadian-American contretemps, the Canadians decided to play it cool. Trudeau was restrained but courteous, on his best statesmanlike behaviour.

Reagan seemed anxious to advance the cause of what he had been calling in campaign speeches the previous autumn "a new North American Accord" that would unite the United States with its immediate neighbours, Mexico and Canada. At the same time, he was apprehensive about Trudeau's reputation as an intellectual and a little confused by the heavy briefing on Canada he had been given by State Department officials, who had not yet learned that "the new president [did not] read" so "you [had] to talk to him and show him pictures," as an American diplomat said later. His handlers expected him to deploy his legendary charm in order to make up for his embarrassing ignorance of foreign policy detail. [4]

Both attributes were soon displayed in Ottawa. At a small lunch at 24 Sussex Drive on the first day of Reagan's visit, there was talk about the Arab-Israeli conflict, which Trudeau had re-examined at first hand during a recent trip to the Middle East. A vigorous discussion developed between Trudeau, on the one hand, and Alexander Haig and William Brock, the U.S. trade representative, on the other.

"Then the president weighed in with a story," an American official recalled. "It went something like this. There were a couple of Israelis in the '73 war who were tooling around in a Jeep in the desert. They were man-hunting because they had heard the government would pay a bounty for the capture of Egyptian prisoners. But by the time night came, they hadn't found any. So they rolled out their sleeping bags and turned in. Early next morning, one of them woke up to find they were surrounded by the Egyptian army. He nudged his sleeping buddy awake and said, 'Hey! Get a move on, dopey! We're rich!'

"When Reagan and his sidekicks started laughing uproariously at this joke," the official continued, "you should have seen Trudeau's face! He didn't know how to react. He seemed to be wondering, What am I dealing with? Obviously, this was his first exposure to the anecdotal Reagan that Washington was already getting used to." [5]

"Anecdotal" was not exactly the way the Canadians present viewed the presidential performance. One of them described Reagan as continuing this bilateral discussion of international relations – after waiting while his entourage chuckled obligingly at his hoary story – by delivering his own prescription for peace in the Middle East.

"I don't understand," said the president of the most powerful nation on earth, "why we can't solve what's wrong out there anyway. I mean, you have three kinds of peoples involved, right? There's the Jewish peoples. There's the Arab peoples. And then, there's us, the Christian peoples. And we're all God-fearing peoples, right? So why can't we just get together and fight the communists?" It was this display of sunny simplicity, according to the Canadian, that surprised Trudeau rather than Reagan's story about Israeli chutzpah in the face of adversity. He remembered Trudeau's responding diplomatically to Reagan's remarkable scheme by saying gently, "From what I have observed in the Middle East, it would be quite an achievement to get the *Arab* peoples together."[6]

Further exchanges between the two leaders went smoothly enough at this superficial level that the visit was officially pronounced a success by both sides, despite public demonstrations against Reagan on Parliament Hill that included a huge sheet with large letters spelling out STOP ACID RAIN. ("What's acid rain?" the puzzled president asked his host.) When Reagan returned to Washington, he told Vice-President George Bush that Trudeau was not as bad as he had been led to expect. [7]

Shortly afterwards, the bilateral situation deteriorated markedly. Sharp exchanges of notes on the NEP and FIRA between ministers and officials in the two capitals continued throughout the spring and early summer. And when Trudeau visited the White House for his second meeting with Reagan in early July, on a courtesy call in advance of the economic summit at which he was to play host later that month in Montebello, Quebec, he was ambushed. Expecting to discuss the agenda for the summit, he found his interlocutors bent on attacking him over the NEP.

George Bush, who had made his money in Texas oil, led the attack. The American viewpoint was straightforward. In openly discriminating against foreign companies, the NEP was lowering the value of the petroleum assets of U.S. firms in Alberta, and making them targets for take-overs by Canadian companies. Nearly every day stories were appearing in the U.S. business press about Canadian take-over attempts on American companies in other fields, and this situation was alarming business leaders across the country, not just the oilmen in Texas and Oklahoma. Furthermore, U.S. oil companies were objecting vociferously to what they called the gross unfairness of the "back-in" provision in the NEP, the 25-per-cent "Crown interest" that the Canadian government intended to allot Petro-Canada in every project on the Canada lands once it had shifted from the exploration to the development stage.[8]

To Canadians who had worked on the energy policy, these complaints seemed hysterically overstated and dangerously one-sided. Canadian take-over fever had bid up the price of oil company shares, yielding big gains for U.S. shareholders. Far from harming American oil companies, Canadian energy policy had helped them make bigger profits. Thanks to Canadian government exploration incentives, for instance, the American firm Mobil had discovered the huge underwater oil field called Hibernia off the coast of Newfoundland. Now Mobil was crying foul at the prospect of Petro-Canada's getting a 25-per-cent share of its equity in the operation. But its real concern was that Petro-Canada would secure a place on Mobil's board and so give the Canadian government access to its corporate intelligence. Canadian public enterprise was muscling in on American private enterprise. The spectre of socialism loomed.

Even though they were blatantly self-serving, these objections to the NEP by U.S. big business were enough to focus on Canada the Reaganites' neo-conservative paranoia about world-wide dangers to American interests, and to confirm the consensus – which had hardened by now in Reagan's Washington – that Trudeau was an unreliable maverick, the "odd man out in the industrial club," the leader of "an industrialized nation with Third World policies."[9]

The Reaganites had come to Washington subscribing to the general, vague American view of Canada as a trustworthy neighbour and admirable ally-in-arms that had been formulated during the Depression and World War II, when a remarkable rapport had grown up between Mackenzie King and Franklin Delano Roosevelt. They knew nothing of the Canadian-American problems of the 1960s, when there were skirmishes on defence questions – first between John Diefenbaker and John Kennedy during the

Cuban Missile Crisis, and then between Lester Pearson and Lyndon Johnson over the bombing of North Vietnam. Certainly they had not realized how much their Republican predecessor in the White House, Richard Nixon, had disliked Trudeau, since Nixon had kept up the façade of smooth relations as usual with Canada. Once ensconced in office, however, the Reaganites discovered that their ideas about Canada were alarmingly out of date.[10]

In the previous fifteen years, that handful of officials who were concerned with Canada in the U.S. Departments of State and Defense had altered their collective view of their neighbour. At State, there had been a deliberate muting of the benign imperialism towards Canada that George Ball, the powerful under-secretary in the Kennedy and Johnson eras, had freely articulated: the idea that in the post-war years the U.S. had helped Western Europe towards integration and would now do the same for the Anglo-Saxon world. Ball believed that the U.S. should form "a political confederation" of Britain and the English-speaking white dominions – Canada, Australia, and New Zealand. Through resisting such a union, he wrote in a notorious statement, Canada was "fighting a rearguard action against the inevitable." This kind of thinking had already led to North American bilateral agreements, such as defence produc- tion-sharing and the Auto Pact, which were seen as interim stages in the development of a genuine continental market. But with the advent of the Republican regime of Richard Nixon in Washington and the Liberal government of Pierre Trudeau in Ottawa, such plans wĕre shelved. Not abandoned – just shelved. It was recognized at State in the early 1970s that hopes for a continental energy arrange- ment, for instance, couldn't be realized immediately, given the "obstacle" of "Canadian sensitivities," meaning the resurgence of nationalism in Canada. American officials who shared Ball's views, such as Willis Armstrong and Philip Trezise, recognized that the Canadian officials who agreed with them – Jake Warren in External and Simon Reisman in Finance, among others – had to fit in with the prevailing mood in Canada, which, if not exactly hostile to the

United States, was both more independent and more inward-looking. "We knew," said one of them, "that we would just have to wait out this period, wait out the nationalist mood and the Canadian navel-gazing."[11]

State was relatively sophisticated in its knowledge of Trudeau and of Canada. Officials there saw his travels to Moscow and Beijing and his anti-nuclear stance in *Cité libre* in the 1950s as a young man's intellectual posturing that was outweighed by his strengths on the Quebec question. "We realized," said a State Department official, "that there would be nothing but trouble for us if Quebec separated, that it was much better for the United States to deal with a united Canada rather than a fragmented one. We decided to proceed with a businesslike relationship, whatever our reservations about Trudeau, an attitude with which Nixon was in agreement." In this vein, the State Department saw Nixonomics as a dose of hard reality that would do Canada good and shrugged off the Third Option, produced by External Affairs in response, as "not very sensible," that is, bound to prove impractical in the face of continental realities.[12]

Among U.S. Department of Defense officials in their Pentagon fortress, the consensus on Trudeau was less sanguine. They regarded as perverse his decision in 1969 to cut Canada's contribution to NATO's European forces by half, and still resented his less than enthusiastic support of American initiatives in Vietnam and Cambodia. Such actions and attitudes created the view among the Pentagon's intelligence-gatherers that Canada was no longer a serious military nation and that this "slide down the slippery slope to disarmament," in the words of one Pentagon official, was a direct reflection of Trudeau's "soft, almost socialist attitude to the communist world."[13]

During the Carter era, both State and Defense held back their criticisms of Canada, since the Democratic president got on well with Trudeau on a personal level and it was evident to everyone concerned in Washington – once the Parti Québécois was elected in Quebec in 1976, just days after Carter's own election to the presidency – that Trudeau's role in fending off the separatist threat was more important than ever. Four years later, when Reagan came to power, the separatist threat had receded. And the very fact that Trudeau had developed a mutual understanding with Carter made him automatically suspect to the Reaganites, who considered the Carter White House a direct cause of the declining strength of the United States in the world. They were belligerent in their foreign policy stance, since they realized that Reagan had been elected not because of a mass conversion to neo-conservatism but because a majority of Americans had voted against Carter's personal weakness. The Republicans feared that liberalism would reassert itself immediately, giving them only a single term in the White Office in which to bring about their revolution at home and its corollary, the restoration of American standing abroad.

In Reaganite terms, the United States had been playing Lady Bountiful to an ungrateful world. It had been too generous with its post-war aid programs, which had allowed foreign entrepreneurs – abetted by complicit governments who protected their home markets from U.S. products but subsidized their own countries' exports – to grow strong enough to make inroads into the American market. In order to counter their worsening international competitive position and to compete successfully again with other trading nations, all American entrepreneurs needed was the famous "level playing field" – a trading game with fair (i.e., American) rules. Under Reagan, the U.S. government was ready to get tough with trading partners it believed were discriminating against U.S. companies.

In the early months of his administration, thousands of Republican appointees who had learned to believe in the magic of the level playing field took over significant jobs in Washington. Many of them knew very little about the capital's workings, let alone those of foreign states. They came to their jobs with almost no training in dealing with other countries, whose institutions and attitudes were different from their own. This inexperience extended into Reagan's close circle. A Canadian official seconded to work on arrangements for the 1981 economic summit at Montebello remembered showing the conference site to an advance party from Washington led by Michael Deaver, Reagan's California confidant and a key member of the team running his White House. The Canadian suggested that Deaver should pose the substantive questions he was asking about the event to his own country's "sherpa," a trade expert named Myer Rashish, the Reagan appointee in the State Department who, as assistant under-secretary for economic affairs, was in charge of the Canadian dossier in this crucial period. "What the hell is a sherpa?" asked Deaver. "And who the hell is Rashish? And why can't *you* tell me what I want to know?"[14]

One of the things the Reaganites wanted to know – and fast – was what Canada was going to do about the NEP. They seemed unhinged by the atrocity stories they were hearing from their corporate friends about both the National Energy Program and the Foreign Investment Review Agency. At one point several multinational oil executives were called to a meeting on Canada at the State Department so that they could vent their grievances. Many of the Republican appointees charged with assuaging such angers had not yet developed a context within which to place the "new" information they were receiving about Canada. ("I only heard about it yesterday," a very senior official in the U.S. Treasury said to a Canadian academic who asked him in the summer of 1981 why he was so upset about FIRA, since it had been tolerated for seven years by previous administrations.)[15]

It was as though the Reaganites' limited world-view could encompass only good guys (themselves, along with Margaret Thatcher and her merry men in London) and bad guys (those who did not support them 100 per cent). And what they were hearing about Trudeau made it sound as though he was consorting with the latter. According to Myer Rashish, "It was obvious that Trudeau was playing ball with some fellas [mostly in the Third World] who wanted to kick us in the balls. We thought, 'This guy is going to go nationalistic, cut off U.S. investment, and stick it to us with high prices for oil.' We were particularly mad that Canada would set a bad example for other countries – madder than we would have been if we hadn't thought of the country as being such a close ally. It was the difference between the way you treat a mistress and a wife. The mistress gets a bauble every once in a while if she shows signs of acting sassy; a wife's not expected to show independence, and if she dares to, she has to be brought into line."[16]

In this atmosphere, pent-up rage against the Trudeau government in a Canadian business community that was becoming more and more integrated along continental lines echoed back and forth across the border and fed the Washington mood. Insiders heard from their friends in the Texas oil industry (who in turn got their information from *their* friends in Alberta) that Ottawa was out of control. Reinforcing old canards still circulating about Trudeau as an "egghead com-symp" was the shrill hectoring of the American business press. Even *The Wall Street Journal* warned its readers about "the xenophobic passions of Canadian officials."[17]

These overwrought and under-researched responses were unleashed on the National Energy Program, particularly on its Crown-interest or back-in provision, which was seen as a particularly heinous example of the kind of unfair practice that was undermining U.S. interests abroad. Oddly enough, this provision was not a measure to which Marc Lalonde was deeply committed as the minister responsible for the NEP, although it was he who had ultimately approved it. But once American officials began to make accusatory statements in public about it as discriminatory, a form of retroactive expropriation, it became impossible for Lalonde to withdraw it without serious loss of face for the Trudeau government. Lalonde had been bamboozled by U.S. tactics in May into agreeing to make an *ex gratia* payment to affected companies, a symbolic contribution to the costs of the Crown asserting its ownership right in Hibernia, only to find that the inch he had given led Washington to demand a further mile: full compensation based on the future value of the Hibernia reserves. [18]

Lalonde's public response to the Americans' aggression was to dismiss it. "Ce n'est pas une crise," he said, pooh-poohing the confrontation when Washington's mounting campaign to gut the NEP was reaching a climax. "C'est une crisette." Lalonde obviously wanted to give the impression that this mini-crisis was of minor import, something the Department of External Affairs could handle through normal diplomatic channels, though behind the scenes he admitted to a concerned supporter, "You wouldn't believe the pressure the Americans are putting on us." [19]

The Reaganites were also displaying marked pugnacity towards the Foreign Investment Review Agency. Previously accepted in Washington for the tame bear it actually was, FIRA suddenly became a wild beast in Reaganite demonology. It was alleged to be unfairly protecting predatory Canadian corporations from counter-attack while they bought out U.S. operations in Canada at "fire-sale prices." With Canadian capitalists being painted as latter-day barbarians, swooping down from the north to pillage innocent America, Canada had suddenly become the test case for the new administration's campaign to save the world for free enterprise. [20]

That Canada put less onerous a burden on foreign oil companies than Norway did, let alone Indonesia, did not impress the Reagan ideologues. For them, Canada was not a foreign country. It was a neighbouring territory that by an accident of history was politically separate from the United States – a lucky accident, as it had turned out, since the U.S. had gained almost unrestricted access to Canada's rich resources and burgeoning market without the problems of governing its unruly people. As Willis Armstrong, the former State Department Canadianist, advised the Reagan transition team, "Canada [is] part of our economy and [will] have to adjust to it." Accordingly, Canada was expected to grant U.S. capitalists the same rights they enjoyed in Texas, including respect for the Fifth Amendment, which prohibited the taking of private property without compensation. If it refused, then it would be treated the way the U.S. treated other miscreant nations. In Washington in the summer and early fall of 1981, dossiers on bilateral issues were studied intently as the U.S. trade representative's office searched for ways to bring Trudeau and his government to heel.[21]

In its early stages, Trudeau had revelled in the NEP crisis. The fight with Alberta was a challenge he enjoyed because there was an important point of principle at stake on federal-provincial relations. In his mind, the NEP had not been formulated to grab control of the energy industry from Alberta and enrich the central government's treasury. It was meant to be a major step towards building the "economic union" that had become a central theme in Trudeau's discourse on national unity. In tandem with a patriated constitution and a charter of rights, the NEP would strengthen pan-Canadianism. Its comprehensive nature suited Trudeau's political temperament. It was his regime's best attempt ever at taking a *tabula rasa* approach and boldly redesigning an entire industry's dynamics. The crisis this confrontational action precipitated could be seen as something that Fortuna had offered for exploitation by those who showed Virtù, in Machiavelli's famous formulation. It even gave Trudeau a chance to answer the rhetorical question he had posed so often during the 1980 election campaign about who would speak for Canada: We will! his government seemed to be saying. We Liberals whose strength is as the strength of ten because our hearts are pure![22]

The implicit nationalism of an energy policy that emphasized the Canadianization of a foreign-controlled sector seemed to have escaped Trudeau or at least not to have troubled him very much. In his view, the object of the NEP was to increase energy self-sufficiency and strengthen national unity, not to attack the Americans. Besides, its passage involved the kind of political fight he loved, a fight where the issues could be readily dramatized. Once again he could play Cyrano de Bergerac, battling on behalf of the disadvantaged against the big interests, whether in the guise of Alberta politicians, or transnational oilmen, or Uncle Sam himself.[23]

When the Reagan administration started pushing Canada aggressively, Trudeau was more than ready to stand his ground. He did not have the deference to all things American that Canadian politicians normally displayed. His graduate studies at Harvard, rather than turning him into an Americanophile, seemed to have immunized him to the blandishments of the American myth. The anti-Americanism of his French spiritual mentor, Emmanuel Mounier, had not affected him either. Trudeau's *Cité libre* polemics had expressed a social-democratic anti-militarism that showed an all-embracing disgust with the spectre of nuclear war, not the America-as-the-imperialist-aggressor rhetoric heard among student radicals in Paris and London.[24]

As prime minister Trudeau had learned to get on with American presidents, even when they were narrower intellectually and less sophisticated culturally than he was. Lyndon Johnson was already a lame-duck president when Trudeau first came to power, and their contacts were minimal. Trudeau had respected Richard Nixon's acuity in international affairs, even though this respect was not reciprocated, as was later revealed when Nixon's tape-recorded references to Trudeau as an "asshole" were made public. For Trudeau the interesting Republican was Nixon's heavy-duty strategist, Henry Kissinger. The caretaker president, Gerald Ford, had been of marginal concern during his short tenure, but Jimmy Carter's high regard for Trudeau, whom he phoned on occasion for foreign policy advice, had been appreciated and reciprocated. It was of great importance to Trudeau that Carter openly supported his position on national unity against the Quebec separatist government and that Carter's vice-president, Walter Mondale, played the role of Canada's best friend in the U.S. administration, calling Trudeau "a priceless asset to the industrialized world."[25]

"Trudeau was in harmony with Carter's general outlook on the world," a Canadian official explained later, "though he shared [German chancellor] Helmut Schmidt's disappointment at Carter's weak performance on the international stage. But even during the Carter presidency, Trudeau was mainly interested in the U.S. when its actions were relevant to his own agenda . . . For him, his finest hour [in Canadian-American relations] was when he spoke to the Congress on national unity in March 1977. The Americans' sympathy was important to him then and he really turned on to them. At other times, he tuned out."[26]

In brief, whatever their personal strengths and weaknesses, none of the American leaders whose presidencies overlapped with Trudeau's prime ministership had affected his basic lack of interest in American ideas, American culture, and American internal politics. This indifference was evident to his anglophone intimates – from his wife to the members of his PMO staff – who discovered to their surprise that, unlike the vast majority of English-speaking Canadians, he was largely unaware of what was going on in the United States. Its popular entertainment idols were unknown to him. He responded with puzzlement to Margaret Trudeau's references to the celebrated denizens of the rock 'n' coke 'n' boogie world she frequented in Los Angeles and Manhattan in the late 1970s as though she had taken to speaking Swahili. He was even less familiar with American sports heroes and media personalities past and present. Tom Axworthy was amazed by Trudeau's incapacity to master the references to pop culture that he regularly inserted into drafts of prime ministerial speeches in order to lighten their content. "At first I felt it was weird that Trudeau didn't know who Walter Cronkite or Ty Cobb was," he said. "But then I realized that he wasn't interested in mass culture celebrities in Canada, either. You also had to check before he went on stage that he had heard of Bobby Hull and Allan Fotheringham."[27]

Trudeau's ascetic devotion to high culture might explain his ignorance of popular icons, but his indifference to Americana was apparently more profound than that. Jean Le Moyne, who had known him for most of their adult lives, realized early in their friendship that American culture at any level did not interest him very much. Le Moyne had an unusually broad knowledge of

American literature, particularly of the New England transcenden-
talists, and once persuaded Trudeau to make a pilgrimage with him
to Ralph Waldo Emerson's New England house. He was disappointed by Trudeau's passive response to his enthusiasm for the great
American poet and philosopher. "I think Pierre was in fact not
much interested in North American ideas in any form. It was the
great ideas of the classicists in the literary and political spheres that
moved him; it was Europe where he felt culturally at home and Asia
where his interest in the exotic was piqued."[28]

Trudeau was also dismissive of American political lore, unlike
most English-Canadian politicians, who immersed themselves in it.
Whenever Keith Davey, in his role as campaign chairman, tried to
get him to read T.H. White or David Halberstam or Robert Caro –
or any of the other hagiographers of the American political system –
Trudeau would categorically refuse. In the summer of 1979, Davey
was excited by David Halberstam's book *The Powers That Be*,
because it described the effect of the media on modern American
politics. After Trudeau refused to accept a copy, Davey tried to leave
it surreptitiously on a table in his office, only to have Trudeau call
out to him as he was leaving, "Keith, take that [book] with you. You
know damn well I'm never going to read it." Richard O'Hagan,
who had worked in Washington for a decade before becoming Trudeau's communications director, found that he could rarely persuade the prime minister to read American magazines or to watch
American television. "He could be affected by reports in *The New
York Times* on international issues and he was willing to grant interviews to American political analysts of the first rank – people like
James Reston and Joseph Kraft – not because he read them regularly
but because he could be convinced of the seriousness of their reputations in a way that you could not convince him that he ought to
pay heed to the ideas of Dalton Camp in the *Star* or Geoffrey Stevens
and Jeffrey Simpson in the *Globe*. But most American publications
didn't interest him any more than English-Canadian newspapers
did. For international news he would far sooner read *Le Monde* or
*The Times* [of London] or *The Guardian*."[29]

No one who worked closely with Trudeau on foreign affairs issues over the years felt he had any overall vision of how Canada should develop economically alongside the United States, let alone any strategic view about how the country could cope politically with its superpower neighbour or react to its overwhelming cultural power. He had come into politics without a considered intellectual position on Canadian-American relations and had not developed one while in office. A legalist in international affairs, as in every other sphere, Trudeau accepted the right of the United States as a great power to its dominance in world councils and never had indulged in the anti-American sentiments voiced by Anglo-Canadian nationalists who embraced the attitudes of the American New Left in the wake of the Vietnam War.

Once he had abandoned his concerns of the late 1950s about U.S. economic domination, he seemed to have spent little time worrying about the obvious fact that Canada was falling ever more deeply into trade, investment, and cultural dependence upon the United States. He had never shown any embarrassment that the laborious review of Canada's foreign policy he had initiated in 1968 – which was openly admitted in External Affairs to reflect his views more than anyone else's – left the relationship with the United States out of its analysis. A few years later, the Third Option policy generated by External received no perceptible support from Trudeau once it had served its purpose as a slogan in the 1972 election campaign. It had virtually no impact on the major economic departments that dealt closely with the U.S. on a daily basis and was visible only in Trudeau's ineffectual efforts to develop a special relationship with the European Community and Japan.[30]

For Trudeau, dealing with the United States was like dealing with any other foreign relationship: occasional difficulties were best handled on an *ad hoc* basis. In effect, he subscribed to the post-war Ottawa mandarinates' notion that Canada was an independent state.

•  •  •

This belief – and the corollary, that he was a world leader among world leaders – was very much in evidence at Trudeau's third meeting with Reagan, which took place at Montebello, Quebec, in late July 1981, when Canada was for the first time the host country to the annual economic summit of the industrialized nations. The performer in Trudeau rose to the occasion. Arrangements for the gathering had been meticulously drawn up over many months. At his insistence, he was kept closely informed about everything from the band music and the sculptures carved out of lard to decorate tables laden with delicacies, to the helicopters that shuttled his international colleagues from the Montebello meeting rooms to a party on the green lawns of Government House so they could mingle with hundreds of guests. Chosen by Trudeau himself, they included such disparate, distinguished Canadians as Gordon Robertson, the good, grey public servant who had been his immediate superior in the PCO of 1949, and Conrad Black, the bad, bold young newspaper tycoon and biographer of his old enemy Maurice Duplessis.

As the Montebello meetings unfolded, Trudeau looked every inch the world statesman at the peak of his powers, trying as doyen of the group to engage his guests in fruitful discussion. When he pleaded with the assembled leaders of the world's richest states to embrace the cause of alleviating Third World poverty, Ronald Reagan took this interest in altering "North-South" interchanges as a prime example of his host's "woolly-minded, impractical, liberal thinking." Reagan's unease was triggered by more than his host's bleeding-heart liberalism. Few of the participants in this, his first major international gathering of heads of government, were to Reagan's taste. They were less anti-communist than he had expected his NATO allies would be. François Mitterrand, the recently elected French president, was an outright socialist, and Helmut Schmidt, the German chancellor, was a social democrat. The West Germans actually wanted to *help* the Soviet Union to build a pipeline so it could sell natural gas to Western Europe. Furthermore, the Europeans were highly exercised by skyrocketing

U.S. interest rates that were damaging their economies. Only Margaret Thatcher displayed the pro-American, the-market-knows-best responses that made Reagan feel comfortable. [31]

Despite the American president's general discomfort, there was not much overt evidence at the multilateral meetings of Canadian-American tensions. Ed Meese, the White House counsellor, turned aside questions about the seriousness of the American response to the NEP. But behind the scenes Reagan's cabinet secretaries, White House aides, and State Department appointees were hectoring their Ottawa counterparts, as part of their concerted effort "to scare the shit out of the Canadians." [32]

One of many well-publicized congressional bills introduced to beat back the Canucks during that summer of 1981 proposed a nine-month retroactive moratorium on Canadian acquisitions of more than 5 per cent of any U.S. energy company. In its efforts to help orchestrate the U.S. administration's disciplining of Canada, *The Wall Street Journal* quoted an unnamed official who indicated that Canada had become a test case for the Reagan administration's economic foreign policy: "'If the U.S. allows Canada to get away with its new [interventionist] policies,' he asked, 'what about Mexico? It's not something we can just sit by and not fight.'" As the summer wore on, Reagan's strategists continued to leak anti-Canadian stories to the business press, mounted a survey of the Fortune 500 companies through the U.S. Department of Commerce to find out which of them were suffering from Canadian "protectionism," and generally made it clear they were serious in their belief that if they could not control their own neighbour, their attempt to "stand tall in the saddle again" would collapse. [33]

As a former State Department official said afterwards, "It took the new [Reagan] administration a while to recognize the truth of Averell Harriman's dictum that 'the United States doesn't own the Pacific Ocean,' let alone the rest of the world. Canada bore the brunt of this early ignorance." [34]

# CHAPTER 7

# OTTAWA COMPLAINS, COMPROMISES, AND COMPLIES

It was at this crucial moment in Canadian–American relations that what came to be known in Liberal circles as the Jim Coutts Spadina caper focused the Canadian electorate's attention on the Trudeau government's management of domestic problems in a way that was to prove permanently damaging to its image.

After the 1980 election victory, Coutts had continued to work hard as Trudeau's faithful counsellor for over a year before springing on him the news that he wanted to run for Parliament and join the cabinet. Because Coutts had promised to stay on in the PMO until Trudeau retired, it had fallen to his old crony, Keith Davey, to broach this novel idea. Trudeau's first response was one of astonishment. Why would Jim want to do that, Trudeau asked Davey, when as principal secretary he already has more power than any minister? The point, of course, was that Coutts did not have more power than the *prime* minister, and his influence in the Liberal Party would not last five minutes beyond Trudeau's eventual resignation, as he had learned to his dismay in November 1979 when neither John Turner nor Donald Macdonald, the major candidates in the quickly aborted leadership race, was interested in Coutts's services.

However self-evident these truths, Davey still felt uncomfortable about expressing them even obliquely in the prime minister's presence. Since his exile in opposition, Trudeau had become hypersensitive to any sign of disloyalty, of which the mere mention of the leadership succession was one. When he went to see him to break the news about Coutts, Davey equivocated, joked, and cajoled until somehow his creamy diplomacy worked. Trudeau appeared convinced that Coutts's gallant run for office would prove good for national unity, good for the Liberal Party, and good for Pierre Trudeau. He agreed to open up the Toronto riding of Spadina by appointing to the Senate the incumbent MP, Peter Stollery, who could look forward to thirty years in the red chamber, or what amounted to an annuity worth some $4 million. (Coutts and Davey had become aware that Stollery, the eccentric son of an old Toronto family of haberdashers, could be persuaded to resign when they heard his seat had been offered to Donald Macdonald during the brief 1979 leadership campaign.)[1]

Coutts's plan was the one he had been refining for years. He would enter Parliament as a westerner with private-sector experience and a base in the Toronto ethnic community, credentials that could not help but appeal to several sectors of the Liberal alliance. Once in cabinet he would command national media attention as minister of federal-provincial relations, a secondary portfolio that would allow him to bask in Trudeau's reflected glory as a defender of strong central government and the father of the about-to-be-patriated constitution, while leaving him free to cultivate possible delegates in the run-up to the Liberal succession race. It seemed like a critical path to 24 Sussex, once Coutts had been propelled into Parliament – a step along the way to glory that he thought would be a cakewalk.

Spadina, an ethnically rich Toronto riding, had been a Liberal stronghold since 1945, and Stollery had been racking up large majorities there for a decade. It was ideally situated scant blocks from the fashionable area where Coutts had lived for several years in an impeccably refurbished workingman's cottage around the corner from the Park Plaza Hotel at Bloor and Avenue Road, his favourite place for power breakfasts and late-day drinks.

On July 5, the cloudless summer day when Coutts's intentions were announced, no one knew how swiftly his plan would come to grief. In the next six weeks, his candidacy had to bear the weight of an agglomeration of misfortunes beyond the Canadian-American contretemps. Painfully high interest rates. Layoffs by the thousands. Bankruptcies and mortgage defaults by the hundreds. Strikes in the postal service. Reignited anger at the Liberals for not having fixed the economy in the 1970s or the 1980s. Irritation in the west over the NEP, and everywhere in the country over the interminable constitutional negotiations. All these problems were rolled into one big wad and hurled at Coutts. The media oozed vitriol in retaliation for the countless times he had obstructed journalists over the years on Trudeau's behalf, demonstrating in his refusal to answer their questions forthrightly what they saw as the arrogance of power and what he saw as the discretion of command.

At the beginning of the Spadina campaign, that confidence motivated dozens of eager Liberals in and out of Parliament to canvass for Coutts, raise cash for Coutts, cheerlead for Coutts. At first they believed the Davey-doctored theory that the media's dyspepsia would not affect the by-election's outcome. But well before the campaign was over, a nagging unease took hold of the electorally experienced among the Liberal canvassers. When the sociologist Lorna Marsden, who had worked on several Liberal campaigns in downtown Toronto, finished her door-knocking stint in late July, she tried to discuss her apprehensions with the candidate's executive assistant, George Wilson, by pointing out that there weren't any children hanging around Coutts's campaign office despite the school holidays and the superb summer weather. Wilson missed the point of her professional reading of the portents and wrote on his must-do list: "Get kids for HQ."[2]

On August 18, the day after Coutts lost the election by a few hundred votes – to the NDP's Dan Heap, an Anglican worker-priest and city alderman whose radical views made even his own party uneasy – many Liberal careerists claimed they had known all along Spadina would turn into a bummer. Coutts had got his comeuppance, they said to one another, but better him than us.

After a consolation lunch with Davey and Wilson at the Park Plaza, Coutts let it be known that he was not going to give up on his dream; he would run again another day. Workers were dispatched around the constituency to collect the sign stakes for next time. Meanwhile, he intended to spend most of the working week in Toronto, tending his would-be riding in anticipation of the next election and travelling up to Ottawa regularly to advise the prime minister. By keeping his cool, Coutts was acting in the liberal optimist belief that his career plans could be rescued after the humiliation he had precipitated for himself, his party, and his boss. But Spadina's rejection of Trudeau's Machiavelli was a blow that reverberated throughout the country, and nowhere more intensely than in the upper reaches of the federal civil service.

The senior official who was perhaps most discomfited by the portents was the under-secretary of state for external affairs, Allan Gotlieb. A fifty-three-year-old legal scholar turned career public servant, Gotlieb had acted as Trudeau's sherpa for the Montebello summit, and what he saw behind the scenes there added to the unease he had been feeling for years over the Liberals' failure to develop a bilateral strategy vis-à-vis the United States. Although Gotlieb had served the Trudeau government in several important posts, he had never had the policy influence that many people in Ottawa – Gotlieb prominent among them – believed his talents warranted.

He had joined External Affairs in 1957, the year that Lester Pearson won the Nobel Peace Prize in recognition of his diplomatic talents and of the role he had developed for Canada in the post-war world as a peacekeeping middle power marginally less anticommunist than the United States. External was at the apex of its influence at home and abroad in the mid-1950s, and countless young Canadians with impressive educations and rarefied ambitions were eager to join its ranks. What they did not know was that the department was on the cusp of its long decline. Over the next fifteen years, External would steadily lose influence at home under the prime ministerships of John Diefenbaker, Lester Pearson, and Pierre

Trudeau; and Canada would just as steadily lose influence abroad, as the country's economic ranking fell in relation to the resurgent economies of Europe and Asia, and its good offices became less valued as the East-West conflict altered in nature.

These melancholy trends were still in the future when Gotlieb, a wunderkind from an affluent Winnipeg family, joined the public service. He came to Ottawa with a reputation for academic brilliance earned at the University of California; at the Harvard Law School, where he was editor of the *Law Review*; and at Oxford, where he was elected a fellow of Wadham College and named Vinerian Law Scholar. His rise through External's ranks was rapid, so rapid in fact that it ruffled some of the department's senior members, who were still pretending that External's glory days could be prolonged if the department would only conserve the style that they had copied from their hated mentors in Whitehall. According to these standards, patience and respectful reticence were the correct stances for a young officer to adopt, and it was suggested to Gotlieb that he contain his ambitions, emulate his elders, and bide his time. [3]

Gotlieb pressed on nonetheless, searching for areas of expertise where his scholarly skills could be applied. Showing remarkable prescience, he attached himself to Marcel Cadieux, the only French Canadian with power in the department at a time when French Canadians were beginning their struggle for parity in Ottawa. They were both acutely aware that they were outsiders in External, that haunt of the mid-Atlantic Canadians who had sprung from the old WASP middle class. Gotlieb was a secular Jew, Cadieux a working-class Roman Catholic from Quebec, and in their unease, they made common cause. When Cadieux became under-secretary and appointed Gotlieb assistant under-secretary after only a decade's service, it was conceded that he was not just intellectually impressive but a shrewd player of the power game as well – a man to be watched if not imitated. [4]

As Pierre Trudeau's fortunes flourished in this period, Allan Gotlieb's future looked ever brighter, since the two men were thought to be close. They had met in 1966 when Trudeau, as the newly appointed parliamentary secretary to Pearson, was tackling the question of how to block Quebec's quest for an independent international role, and Gotlieb, as External's legal expert, was called on to give advice. Gotlieb's capacity to apply international law effectively to the complex question of provincial jurisdiction impressed Trudeau sufficiently that the next year he asked to have him seconded from External to chair the task force on the constitution he had set up as minister of justice. The year after that, when Trudeau as a Liberal leadership candidate expressed his dismissive views of Canada's foreign service – whose global aspirations he saw as pretentious, out of date, and contributory to divisiveness between French and English Canadians – it was clear that External was no longer the place for an ambitious man. Gotlieb left its ranks to serve as a deputy minister, first in the newly formed Department of Communications and then in the Department of Manpower and Immigration, both difficult portfolios and secondary constellations in Ottawa's firmament.[5]

As Gotlieb took on one tough, unrewarding departmental task after another, it was whispered around town that he was deliberately being squeezed out of the important central agencies because he had run afoul of Michael Pitfield, whose views on policy and personnel were so influential with Trudeau. One official who observed the interactions of the three men throughout their Ottawa careers said later, "Michael apparently thought there was room for only one dazzling intellect in Trudeau's orbit, and he certainly was not going to cede that role easily to Allan, who had a far better education and the confidence that comes from jousting with Oxford dons in senior common rooms and their imitators in External Affairs. But Pitfield had the boss's ear and an uncanny capacity for defending his turf. Gotlieb was not the only rival he kept out of Trudeau's inner circle. But he was probably the most serious threat."[6]

In response to his vicissitudes, Gotlieb soothed himself with creature comforts: chess, a collection of Tissot prints impressive enough to merit a show at the National Gallery, the glorious food provided by his wife, Sondra, who was an inspired cook, an aspiring writer, and a madcap talker. But when his career did not improve after several years of hard slogging, Gotlieb began to consider returning to academe. He even went so far as to let his name stand for the dean's job at the University of Toronto Law School and to spend a year in Oxford as a visiting fellow at All Souls. Suddenly in 1977, to the surprise of *le tout Ottawa*, Gotlieb was asked to return to External as under-secretary. Even though Pitfield was heard pontificating what a great pleasure it was for him, as clerk of the Privy Council, to be able to appoint a man with a first-class mind to such an important post, it was surmised that Gotlieb's dissatisfactions had been made known to Trudeau, who had continued to respect his intellect even though their paths had crossed infrequently in the previous eight years. ("Sondra and I never dined at Sussex," Gotlieb said later. "We were never really friends after Pierre became prime minister." It was a complaint that was echoed over the years in the conversations of many Canadians who had thought they were Trudeau's familiars and then found themselves inexplicably distanced from him. But in Gotlieb's case it had a particularly plaintive ring.)[7]

Once he had returned to his old department as under-secretary of state, Gotlieb began to wonder whether his lot had changed after all. He found External "dispirited and disorganized," as he described it, "after nearly a decade of being destabilized by Michael, who was playing one of his exotic games in trying to cut the department down to size in order to please Pierre. By the later 1970s he realized that a weak foreign service was bad for the government, but by then the damage had been done."[8]

In Pitfield's system, External's traditional job of providing officials to brief the prime minister on foreign policy matters had been assigned instead to Ivan Head, a former law professor and another alumnus of Trudeau's advisory group on the constitution, who operated within the Prime Minister's Office as a foreign policy adviser on the Kissinger model. From 1970 to 1978, much of the information gathered by External's diplomats abroad and analysed by its desk officers at home was "back-channelled" through

"Mini-Kiss," as Head was nicknamed. In Trudeau's Ottawa, External officials were seen as "fancy-pants" whose work was largely representational and irrelevant to the government's central concerns. In the troika of Finance, Industry, Trade and Commerce, and External – the departments involved in making foreign economic policy – External was perceived as lacking in expertise on the economic side. It was consulted formally on trade questions that were actually handled in IT&C. It was even distanced from foreign aid questions, which were dealt with by the Canadian International Development Agency and the International Development Research Centre.[9]

Confronting this institutional competition, Gotlieb set out to make External Affairs a central agency once more, expending energy in trying to achieve "a coherent context for a new Canadian foreign policy through the establishment within the department of the necessary instruments to achieve that end." Or as he sometimes put it more forthrightly, "It was my attempt at bureaucratic imperialism." Empire-building is slow work, and Gotlieb's plans and aplomb were seriously shaken during the brief Clark regime in 1979 when Flora MacDonald, the Conservative minister assigned to External, made no secret of her distrust of him because of his Liberal connections, proclaiming frequently to her intimates that she would like to have him removed from his post.[10]

Even after Trudeau was restored to office in 1980, Gotlieb felt uneasy. He was not invited to participate with senior officials from the most important departments in the deputies' mirror committee of the Priorities and Planning Committee of cabinet, a sign that External had not yet regained its old prominence. His exclusion from the centre of power was particularly evident when he was not consulted on the National Energy Program, despite its obvious foreign policy implications. "The EnFin people thought External would be 'soft' on the Americans and would counsel modification of the energy policy," Gotlieb observed. "That's the kind of a charge that is made against foreign ministries throughout the Western world by officials who don't actually have to deal with the U.S. and can hide behind an intellectual defiance of reality. The NEP was put together in locked rooms, and in some ways the secrecy surrounding it proved its undoing. It could have been sold to the Americans if they had enlisted External's help."[11]

Despite his chagrin, Gotlieb continued to work hard to overcome the "multilateralism" with which External had been mesmerized since its golden age immediately after World War II, and persuaded his new Liberal minister, Mark MacGuigan, to push "bilateralism": the idea that Canada should concentrate on its most important individual international connections, the American relationship first of all. At first, his efforts had little effect. MacGuigan was regarded as a weak minister, put in place so Trudeau could control his own foreign policy. For an old hand like Gotlieb, the situation was puzzling, since the born-again Trudeau of the 1980s appeared to be pursuing the kind of Pearsonian global influence for Canada that Trudeau had so scorned in the past. Gotlieb became convinced that Trudeau's new "romanticism" on North-South issues meant he was actively seeking a new career in an international agency where Third World support would be crucial to his effectiveness. In the light of these developments, Gotlieb decided that he had better look to his own future. "My life was going by and I was doing the same old things, fighting the same old battles," he remembered. He resolved to extract a promise from Pitfield that once the summit was over, he would recommend that Trudeau appoint Gotlieb ambassador to the United States.[12]

In the aftermath of the Montebello meetings, which had engrossed Gotlieb's energies for months – and were widely conceded to have been an organizational *tour de force* – Gotlieb realized just how tough the Washington job would prove if the government persisted on its interventionist course. At one point, he was sitting in a meeting beside Myer Rashish of the U.S. State Department when Rashish was handed a phone message from Caspar Weinberger, the U.S. defence secretary. "Gotlieb was so tense [about the Canadian-American altercations], he turned pale, and I tried to spook him further by saying, 'Don't worry, Allan, we're not going to invade *anybody* this week,'" Rashish remembered with relish. Gotlieb's fears escalated when William Brock, the U.S. trade representative, threatened that Canada would be excluded from the next quadrilateral meeting on trade, which normally involved representatives from Canada as well as the United States, Japan, and the European Community.[13]

To make matters worse, almost every day in that difficult summer of 1981, Paul Heron Robinson, Jr., the newly appointed U.S. ambassador to Canada, was making his presence felt in Ottawa by speaking out in flamboyant language against the NEP and FIRA. Robinson had come to Canada fresh from his prosperous insurance brokerage business in Chicago, his chief qualification apparently being his ability to raise money for the Republican Party in his native Illinois. Innocent of subtleties, a stranger to guile, Robinson saw himself as a Reaganaut, not a diplomat, a man who loved free enterprise, baseball, the U.S. Navy, his horse, his western holiday ranch, his wife, who had been his high school sweetheart, and their prepubescent daughter, who, he proudly said, "looked on Canada as one big Idaho." He had an abiding faith in the old chimera of an Anglo-Saxon union and prided himself on doing business only in English-speaking countries, an idea he felt would appeal to Canadians if only they could be convinced of its possibilities.

Within weeks of having his appointment confirmed by the U.S. Senate, Robinson set out to jaw his way up and down the nation, ad-libbing to a Canadian Club here and haranguing a news reporter there, expressing his enthusiasms and excoriating democracy's detractors. He gave voice to the firm opinion that Canadians should spend more money on defence and less on welfare so they could once again enjoy the reputation as stout men and true that they had earned in two world wars. He pronounced the metric system to be rubbish and the Foreign Investment Review Agency to be staffed by nitpickers. He declared the back-in provision of the NEP a violation of the American constitution and maintained that things could not help but get better between our two big beautiful countries because in the crunch Canadians and Americans were one and the same, two peoples with interchangeable parts.[14]

In the face of these undiplomatic volleys, Allan Gotlieb convened in the late summer an interdepartmental committee of senior officials in an attempt at crisis control. At a series of Tuesday breakfast meetings, he set out to convince his colleagues that his fears about Canada's losing control of its American relationship were justified. "Gotlieb was the strongest intellectual force in Ottawa calling for 'making peace with the United States,'" said a fellow official later. "He really got carried away by his anxieties."[15]

At the time, most members of the senior mandarinate were preoccupied with indications of trouble on the domestic front, from labour unrest to intergovernmental hassles over the constitution. It looked as though the positive atmosphere that had prevailed during the first eighteen months of the fourth Trudeau regime was disintegrating.[16]

Now there was a dangerous new problem to add to the persistent old ones. Canada's powerful neighbour was signalling an attitude that was uncomfortably close to rage. When Myer Rashish decided in early September "to take a two-by-four to Canada," in his phrase, by proclaiming in a public speech in New York City that the U.S.-Canada relationship was approaching a crisis point, the Ottawa bureaucracy was more than ready to heed his message. Something would have to be done to mollify Washington. Canada would have to show itself willing once more to be the accommodating partner in the most unbalanced bilateral relationship in the Western world.[17]

It was obvious that neither Trudeau nor Lalonde — "both of whom were stubborn buggers," as one official remarked — would agree to back down on the NEP itself, especially after their highly publicized federal-provincial energy deal was struck with Alberta on September 1. Some other means would have to be found to show Washington that Canada was willing to mend its ways. The perfect sacrifice was the putative industrial strategy that had been promised by Trudeau in the 1980 campaign but had not yet come to fruition. "That Canada might spawn a 'son of NEP,' and was talking of expanding FIRA, was rattling the hell out of them in Washington," Allan Gotlieb said later. Had the Reaganites better understood the weakness of nationalism and the strength of continentalism within the federal government, they would have known that the industrial strategy was a paper tiger. But since they were so lathered up about the threat of further interventionism, the time seemed ripe to Gotlieb and certain of his continentalist colleagues to immolate this weak offspring of nationalist desires on the altar of North American amity. [18]

Ever since the early 1970s, political economists in the Innis tradition had been arguing that an industrial strategy was the obvious alternative to Canada's basic economic dilemma: an improvident reliance on exporting relatively cheap raw materials in order to finance the importing of the expensive high-technology goods that its own inefficient manufacturers could not supply. It was an entrenched problem that had created a unique anomaly: a country with a Third World economic structure and a First World standard of living. If Canadians could only correct this, they could become both more prosperous and more autonomous. Or so the argument went. As Canada's economy grew sicker throughout the 1970s, "industrial strategy" had become a code phrase for a position most persuasively propounded by the Science Council of Canada, and then endorsed by the Canadian Labour Congress, which argued for a new economic policy mix aimed at reducing foreign investment and increasing the "technological sovereignty" – and therefore world-market competitiveness – of Canadian-based manufacturing. [19]

Advocates of an industrial strategy liked to refer to European models of development, particularly that of Sweden, which had been able to develop – with a small population, northern forests, mineral-rich geology, and a vulnerable geopolitical location – a highly competitive manufacturing economy. Sweden's own resources were processed internally into high-quality products that competed effectively on world markets, while providing an admirable quality of life for the Swedes. Key to this success was Sweden's stable social-democratic government, whose partnership with business and labour had forged a consensus that protective tariffs should be kept low and foreign ownership restricted, especially in industries crucial to the country's military capacity as an armed neutral state on the Soviet Union's western border.[20]

The chief Liberal proponent of these ideas was Herb Gray, the member of Parliament from Windsor, Ontario, who had sponsored the basic exegesis of the industrial strategy position in the Gray report nearly a decade before. Gray's persona as a tenacious if humourless nationalist, which had dragged him down as a member of earlier Trudeau governments, had proven an effective asset while he was finance critic in the 1979 opposition period. His policy positions had been used to formulate what Tom Axworthy called the 1980 election campaign's "coup d'état" – the surprising speech Trudeau delivered to the Toronto Ad & Sales Club on February 12, 1980, when he promised to introduce some elements of an industrial strategy by strengthening FIRA's capacity to discipline foreign-owned corporations and by helping Canadian firms beat back take-over attempts.[21]

Sitting in the noon-hour audience at the Royal York Hotel that day, with a Liberal victory less than a week away, the normally morose Gray was glowing with gratification. "For the first time he has been really listening!" he said, in a simple sentence that summed up a decade of frustration. And for a while, it looked as though Trudeau would continue to listen. He invited Gray into his new cabinet as minister in Industry, Trade and Commerce, the department responsible for FIRA and industrial policy; and he formally confirmed his legislative intentions in the April speech from the throne, which spoke of energy and resource policy in terms of their value for industrial development. The text went on to promise new levels of government intervention to encourage Canadianization of the economy: the strategic use of FIRA, tougher rules for assuring government procurement contracts that would favour Canadian firms, and a new State Trading Corporation to help sell the products of smaller Canadian companies to centrally planned economies.[22]

Four months later, Gray brought to a late-summer cabinet think-in at Lake Louise a document prepared by his officials that was meant to flesh out the throne speech promises – a frankly interventionist strategy to revamp Canada's industrial structure. It had two basic premises: Keynesian fine-tuning had failed to generate economic growth in the 1970s, and the market was no longer able to perform effectively in Canada under high levels of foreign ownership and behind high levels of tariff protection. Gray had a remedy: the federal government must play an active remedial role as regulator, intervener, or investor, depending on the circumstances. Vigorous efforts should be made to push potential winners into the global marketplace. This would mean going far beyond FIRA's inadequate mandate in order to review the often lamentable performance of foreign-controlled subsidiaries and force them to "perform to world standards in terms of innovation and export freedom." Canadian-owned companies also needed to be prodded to compete internationally, using the traditional tools of government grants, procurement contracts, and tax incentives. At the same time weak performers in mature sectors – such as textiles and clothing, propped up over the years by trade barriers and government handouts – would have to fend for themselves. The message from government to business would be clear: rationalize and compete, or decline and disappear.[23]

The ideas were bold. The packaging and presentation were dismal. Even Gray's ideological allies in the cabinet considered his paper unacceptable. Its coherence was confused by the reappearance, in more expensive form, of a number of old IT&C programs that made Gray look as though he was making – in the guise of an industrial strategy – an opportunistic $2.75-billion power grab for his notoriously ill-co-ordinated department. For Gray's enemies on the Liberal right wing, his attack on the market and foreign investment and his call for still more government intervention were outrageous. They even questioned his ministerial competence, knowing that his nationalist initiatives were opposed by some of his own department's officials, including the deputy minister, Robert Johnstone. (Gray was even having trouble with Gorse Howarth, the director of FIRA, because he had increased the agency's backlog of take-over applications by insisting on personally reviewing each file.) [24]

Gray, who was bereft of diplomatic talent, had never developed a personal constituency in the party, so he was without loyalists among his colleagues to defend him in his hour of need. Even Marc Lalonde, whose energy project was no less interventionist, failed to offer support, since this seemingly complementary plan, if approved, could become a rival claimant for funding by the treasury. [25]

Faced with this cabinet dissension, Trudeau adopted an air of bored detachment, his normal stance on contentious economic issues. If he had really wanted to honour his ambitious made-in-Toronto promises, he would have equipped Gray with the personnel resources and administrative clout necessary to circumvent bureaucratic resistance, just as he had set up a special structure so Lalonde could bring off the NEP. But Trudeau had never warmed to Gray's personality or his ideology, and he did nothing at Lake Louise to protect him from his colleagues' scorn. With Trudeau's own priorities for the autumn of 1980 focused on energy and the constitution, dissension in cabinet meant that Gray's strategic initiative was sidelined.

The following June the issue flared up again when Bud Olson, a former Social Crediter from Alberta who was minister of state for economic development, brought to another cabinet retreat an alternative economic-development strategy prepared by his deputy, Gordon Osbaldeston. Where the Gray document had used the language of Harold Innis and political economy, Osbaldeston's paper was written in the vocabulary of W.A. Mackintosh and mainstream economics: Canada's comparative advantage lay in its traditional staples. Osbaldeston was convinced that rising price trends meant the country's agricultural, energy, mineral, and forestry resources were escalating in value. This buoyant prediction complemented the call for a stupendous program of resource megaprojects made in the recently completed report of a business-labour task force headed by Bob Blair, the Alberta oilman, and Shirley Carr, the trade union leader. Since these huge construction projects would provide billion-dollar markets for central Canadian industry, the Osbaldeston paper argued that a market-driven expansion of staples production could act as the engine of Canada's continued economic development.[26]

Howls of protest greeted Osbaldeston's paper. The activists in cabinet – Lloyd Axworthy, Pierre De Bané, John Roberts, and a still determined Herb Gray – denounced it for violating the industrial strategy promises contained in the government's speech from the throne and savaged its bureaucratic author for thumbing his nose at the democratic process. Osbaldeston was mortified by the attacks on his person and his position, but his senior assistants, David Bond and Hal Kroeker, immediately started manoeuvring in the corridors of bureaucratic power to "unblight" their boss. They suggested to Michael Pitfield and Robert Rabinovitch, his chief lieutenant in the PCO, that to resolve the cabinet impasse an *ad hoc* committee should be struck that would include the nationalist ministers but be chaired by the anti-interventionist finance minister, Allan MacEachen, with Osbaldeston in the crucial post of secretary. Pitfield and Rabinovitch agreed. Their policy system was overloaded and could not cope with another major program. They wanted cabinet infighting muted and Gray effectively silenced. Bond drafted a letter, which, with a significant addition, was sent out over Pierre Trudeau's signature.[27]

"All Ministers appear to agree that the promotion of economic growth and improved Canadian economic performance are of vital and prime concern," Pierre Trudeau wrote in his invitation to Olson, Roberts, Axworthy, Gray, De Bané, and Ed Lumley, his minister of international trade, to serve on the proposed committee. "The other impression which I have," he continued euphemistically, "is that a considerable range of views also exist within the Cabinet about . . . how active a leadership role the Government wishes to have in economic development, . . . the degree of government intervention required in the marketplace and the priority to be placed on Canadian ownership and control." Lest the committee wonder where he stood, Trudeau made his own position perfectly clear: "Personally, I remain convinced that the primary engine of economic development must be a dynamic private sector and that the marketplace is in most circumstances the best allocator of scarce resources. The role of government must be to complement these functions . . . and where necessary supplement private initiative."[28]

The letter, with its endorsement of the market, put the economic policy agenda back under the control of Osbaldeston, the most ideologically committed and most powerfully situated of the Ottawa bureaucrats who believed in the importance of shrinking government. Still angry that the NEP had been exempted from his purview, Osbaldeston was determined to scotch any other expressions of interventionism. He asked David Bond to draft a new strategic overview document proposing a range of economic strategy options weighted towards the centre-right. It passed a July meeting of cabinet without a reprise of the previous month's bureaucrat-bashing: the ministers had taken note of the prime minister's signal.[29]

What followed that summer was a masterfully manipulative squeeze play worthy of a *Yes, Minister* episode, in which Osbaldeston killed off Gray's industrial policy hopes entirely by making sure the IT&C bureaucrats were on his side; fighting off a rival official in the Finance Department who attempted to control the drafting process; ignoring a number of position papers from the committee's cabinet members; and appropriating a proposal made by Pierre De Bané to merge his department, DREE, with IT&C.[30]

Osbaldeston almost went too far in his attempt to block the politicians. As one of his assistants warned, his final draft had become "a rather namby-pamby . . . very bland document that really says very little on the policy options." Another objected, "Ministers may get the feeling that we are once again steering them a bit too obviously; this will be especially so given the combined attack by both us and External on the FIRA Nationalist wing." Lloyd Axworthy did indeed criticize the section of Osbaldeston's policy paper dealing with Canadianization, objecting that it apologized too abjectly for the NEP and welcomed foreign capital too heartily, but it was all to no avail.[31]

Osbaldeston's document, *Economic Development for Canada*, provided, in the sardonic words of a fellow civil servant, "leadership without dirigisme, and more visibility without more intervention." When it was published three months later with the 1981 budget, it was revealed as extraordinarily limp. Its rhetoric about comparative advantage, megaprojects, high-technology research, and industrial development was an all-things-to-all-people mishmash of measures that only displayed the government's continuing intellectual confusion.[32]

As such, it entirely suited Osbaldeston's colleague Allan Gotlieb, who was anticipating his forthcoming move to Washington, as well as the powerful finance minister, Allan MacEachen, who had been trying all summer to slow down the Canadianization process in the energy sector by asking the banks not to extend more loans to firms using the NEP's incentives to buy out foreign petroleum companies.[33]

Heeding Gotlieb's urgings that he give a soothing message to the Americans, MacEachen flew to Washington early in September and reported to the U.S. secretary of the treasury, Donald Regan, that the industrial strategy idea had been ditched and its corollary, the expansion of FIRA, would be quietly set aside as well. There was to be no "son of NEP." The nationalist Liberals had been routed by the prime minister's indifference, their own right-wing cabinet colleagues, and the manoeuvrings of their intractably continentalist economic bureaucrats.[34]

# CHAPTER 8

# THE DISASTROUS BUDGET
# AND THE END OF THE DREAM

Finessing domestic and international dissension was the kind of task Allan MacEachen had been shouldering on behalf of Liberal leaders for nearly thirty years. For most of that time he had been seen in political circles as an odd figure, a lonely bachelor for whom silence was a tool, party loyalty a creed, and devout Catholicism a shield and solace. He had been born poor (or "pore" as they said in the Maritimes, where he came from), the second of three sons of a Cape Breton coal miner, the descendant of proud Gaelic-speaking Scots from the western Highlands. "Allan J.," as he was called, was an intelligent child, "a little tick, just the sort who always knew his Scripture and had his hand up in class with the answer," one of his cousins remembered. The priests noticed his diligence early. They helped him on his way to an advanced education that was rare for a boy of his background: at St. Francis Xavier University in Antigonish, Nova Scotia, the Universities of Toronto and Chicago, and the Massachusetts Institute of Technology near Boston. In between work on a master's degree in economics at Toronto and Chicago, and doctoral studies at MIT, MacEachen taught briefly at St. FX, as his alma mater was popularly called, an experience that left him marked forever by the plight of his own people and by some of the ideas for alleviating their poverty that were being propounded at the university.[1]

At the time, St. Francis Xavier was the centre of the Antigonish Movement, which had been founded in the 1930s by Father Moses

Coady. Enraged by the awful hardships of the Depression, and drawing inspiration from the socially radical papal encyclicals of the
period, Coady had inveighed against the evils of economic forces
that were squeezing out the largely self-sufficient way of life that had
persisted in rural Nova Scotia for generations. He helped establish
worker-owned credit unions and co-operatives for fishermen,
farmers, and miners in the hope of preventing them from being
turned into a dispossessed class of semi-employed proletarians.
Coady was radical in resisting free-market capitalism. But he was
also conservative – and very Canadian – in his effort to shore up an
old order. His ideas enlivened debates at the university and caught
the idealistic fancy of many young Catholics who were studying
there. In MacEachen's case, Coady was part of what compelled him
to become a politician and a Liberal. "He taught me that things
could be changed," MacEachen said, looking back, "that all things
in this world were not immutable."[2]

After a tenacious battle for the federal Liberal nomination in his
home riding of Inverness–Richmond, MacEachen was elected to
Parliament and served on Louis St. Laurent's backbench from 1953
to 1958. By watching party and parliamentary proceedings carefully,
he ingested Liberal nostrums about loyalty, progressivism, and the
importance of the Canadian duality. After his defeat in the Conservative sweep of 1958, he was hired by Lester Pearson, who had taken
an interest in his progress, to work as a special assistant and consultant on economic affairs in his small opposition office. Over the next
four years, while the Liberals battled the huge Conservative majority in the Commons, MacEachen attended daily meetings to decide
tactics for Question Period and began to learn the procedural tricks
that were to form the basis of his reputation as a shrewd parliamentarian. Once re-elected in 1962, he held on to his riding through
thick and thin thereafter, though its boundaries were altered and its
name changed to Cape Breton–Highlands–Canso.[3]

Pearson prided himself on the advisers he gathered around him,
and MacEachen had a special place in his circle, developing a reputation for saying little in private and less in public. Occasionally when

he had been drinking rum or malt whisky, he would wax eloquent, even sentimental, a habit that inspired his fellow Pearsonian, Keith Davey, himself a strict teetotaller though an effusive talker, to remark: "I've always thought that Allan J. was born two Scotches under par." As a minister MacEachen developed a reputation for laziness, caution, and inattention to detail. Ever the loner, he was given to abrupt, inexplicable withdrawals from conversations, from his office, and even from the capital city itself when the political pressure became too heavy. However protracted his silences or entrenched his caution, he usually voted with the left Liberals in Pearson's cabinet on social, though not on economic, issues. He supported Walter Gordon at the party's 1966 convention when Gordon was opposing Mitchell Sharp's move to delay the implementation of medicare – but not on questions concerning foreign investment, where his inbred Maritime north-south bias and distrust of central Canadian protectionism showed. As minister of labour and then of health and welfare, he did yeoman service in shepherding through the House several landmark social-policy innovations, including a federal labour code with Ottawa's first minimum-wage provision; the supplementary old-age pension, which gave the poorest among the aged special assistance; the Canada Assistance Plan for those of all ages in dire need; and medicare, the health system that was to become the envy of American liberal politicians.[4]

None of these measures – important as they were – made MacEachen a political star. To the astonishment of most of his acquaintances, he bravely declared himself a candidate to succeed Pearson in the Liberal leadership race in 1968, apparently expecting to garner support from progressive Liberals across the country, and from Maritime delegates as a favourite-son candidate. Despite an attempt to package him as a mystic though canny Celt, with pipers in his entourage and an early version of a pocket-diary-cum-organizer as a give-away to delegates, he came across at the convention as a solid, stolid man in a too-tight suit, sweating under the ubiquitous television lights, earnest about his beliefs and traditional in his rhetoric, noticeably out of place in the newly Americanized politics of modern central Canada. He seemed old and awkward, though at forty-six he was two years younger than Pierre Trudeau and far more experienced politically. The progressive delegates went to Trudeau nevertheless and the Maritime votes to the other Nova Scotian in the race, Robert Winters, who was also the favourite of business Liberals. When the first ballots were counted, MacEachen came second to last in a field of eight serious candidates.[5]

He withdrew immediately and threw his votes to Trudeau, who made him minister of manpower and immigration in his first cabinet – a sidetracking of sorts, since much of the innovative work in the social policy area was designated for other portfolios. MacEachen forbore, paying careful attention to parliamentary proceedings and consolidating his political reputation in his own region. In Cape Breton he was a patriarchal figure, a man who never forgot his constituents' needs, whether it was his presence at local wakes and Highland games – ever at the ready with lilting speeches that reflected his familiarity with their common Scottish heritage – or the infusion of government grants for building a heavy-water plant, restructuring the coal industry, or refinancing the steel industry, efforts co-ordinated through the Cape Breton Development Corporation, a new body MacEachen was instrumental in establishing in the 1970s to give his craggy peninsula a share in the Canadian federation's economic growth. "We've been in a recession here since the boat-building industry peaked a couple of centuries ago, and Allan J. always tries to help," another Cape Breton cousin said of him with pride. "Of course, down here, we call him Allan G. instead of Allan J. The G stands for God."[6]

As the 1970s wore on, MacEachen developed a reputation with the Trudeauites as a man of many parts, despite (or perhaps because of ) his old-fashioned loyalties and capacity for dissembling. "There were all sorts of intellectual dazzlers around Ottawa in the early Trudeau years," Keith Davey remarked, "and Allan was nothing but a black backdrop. But he survived when the dazzlers had departed."

MacEachen loved the Commons and was obviously so at home there that Trudeau made him Liberal House leader, a tricky job he had held under Pearson. In the difficult minority period of 1972–74 he showed himself so adept at managing the government's business through the Commons that Trudeau rewarded him with the external affairs portfolio in 1974 because he wanted some international glamour after all the years of domestic drudgery.[7]

MacEachen did not get to indulge himself in the diplomatic life for long. External was peremptorily taken away from him in 1976 when Trudeau once again had need of his skills as House leader. He raged in private briefly, then bent his head to the familiar task of coming to the aid of the party, mollified by the honorific title of deputy prime minister. In the political crucible of the late 1970s, MacEachen functioned as Trudeau's right-hand man in Parliament, the rock on whom the prime minister depended in trying times. "They were very different types, and it was fascinating to see the symbiosis they achieved," said Senator John Stewart, another Maritimer. "MacEachen appreciated Trudeau's boldness and self-confidence, his willingness to gamble on any kind of procedural ploy that MacEachen conjured up. And Trudeau appreciated his loyalty. He seemed to know MacEachen's mastery of procedural rules was important for his survival in politics."[8]

Just how important became publicly obvious in December of 1979 during Trudeau's temporary resignation as Liberal leader. In concert with Coutts, Axworthy, and Trudeau's legislative assistant, Joyce Fairbairn, MacEachen skilfully engineered the Clark government's defeat in the Commons, then persuaded a dubious caucus to call Trudeau back from retirement by making two passionate speeches about what it meant to be a Liberal. By all accounts those speeches were Allan J.'s finest moments in public life. He was persuasive, poignant, and personal beyond anything ever heard from him in Ottawa before, playing on the emotions of the Liberal MPs whose weaknesses and strengths he knew very well. If re-elected, he declared, the Conservatives would reinstate their scandalous budget and bilk the disadvantaged in favour of the rich. "None of us who heard those speeches will ever forget their electric effect," a caucus member said. "For the first time in many years, Liberals seemed to know what they stood for, and the idealism Allan expressed was like a shot of helium gas that pumped us up for the campaign that followed."[9]

MacEachen went on to play a key role on the platform committee, and when the 1980 election campaign succeeded, his career was at its high point. It was as though his political reputation, so slowly and painfully built, had turned into solid gold. His dry wit was now widely appreciated, and the urbane self-confidence of his late middle age was remarked on by people who had formerly dismissed him as nothing but a dull old pol with a solid regional base. Trudeau had stated he would stay on as leader only until the constitution was formally patriated, and rumours abounded that he would step down well in advance of a leadership convention and name MacEachen interim leader so Allan J. could realize his old dream of becoming prime minister. It was an improbable scenario. Trudeau, being Trudeau, was rarely aware of other men's ambitions; and MacEachen, being MacEachen, was entirely unlikely to inform Trudeau of his desires. In any case, he seemed content with having been named deputy prime minister again and given the finance portfolio, the most important and most difficult job in any cabinet.[10]

For Trudeau the appointment of MacEachen to Finance seemed to be the solution to economic management problems that had evaded him throughout the previous decade. Despite serious attempts to decentralize economic decision-making in the government by assigning professional economists to such departments as Energy, the only agency with the capacity to respond to Trudeau's political needs was still the Department of Finance, whose historic task was to provide the government with funds by levying imposts on the public, the corporations, and their imports. The targeting and timing of these taxes was the one remaining lever the government could use to alter the country's economic performance, since the stick of tax increases and the carrot of tax relief altered the behaviour of both producers and consumers.

Trudeau had never been able to achieve a symbiosis with Finance. He had been told again and again by economic experts – as disparate in their views as Walter Gordon and Grant Reuber, an economics professor who was briefly an adviser to Trudeau in the mid-1970s and deputy minister of finance under Joe Clark – that the relationship between a prime minister and his minister of finance was the most important in any government. On one occasion when Gordon raised with Trudeau the thorny question of his lack of rapport with Finance, Trudeau remarked that the department's power had to be contained, otherwise the minister there would be as powerful as he was. [11]

Over the years Trudeau and his close lieutenants had come to see Finance as a fiefdom that stubbornly resisted their control. It had a strong institutional culture that they believed made it servile to business. None of the various combinations of politicians and bureaucrats they had put in place there had managed to contain the problems of high inflation, high interest rates, high unemployment, and constant public dissatisfaction with his government's economic performance, for which Trudeau's alleged indifference was so frequently blamed. [12]

After their return to office in 1980, Trudeau and his closest advisers determined to get it right at last. When they put MacEachen in Finance, they were conscious that in addition to his proven political skills, he was that rarity, a trained economist who believed wholeheartedly in social justice. They decided to team him with a deputy minister, Ian Stewart, whose thinking on the econ-omy was highly attractive in their eyes. Even though Stewart had impressive training as an economist (a BA from Queen's, an MA earned at Oxford on a Rhodes Scholarship, and a doctorate from Cornell) he was not confined by his profession's conventions. He had a broad interest in new ideas that he was able to synthesize and reformulate clearly and persuasively. Even better, he could be trusted, because he was "one of us" rather than "one of them" – that is, a product of the Trudeau PMO/PCO rather than of the Finance Department's hierarchy. [13]

In 1966 Stewart had given up an assistant professorship at Dartmouth College to become an economist at the Bank of Canada, where he managed the development of a macro-economic computer model. Following a stint at the Treasury Board, whose bureaucrats were charged with imposing strict economic criteria on politically inspired projects, he was transferred to the Energy Department in 1973 just in time for the OPEC crisis. Jack Austin, the deputy in Energy, was impressed by Stewart's capacities and recommended he be named the prime minister's PCO economic adviser in 1974. Stewart proved to be proficient at explaining economic issues in conceptual terms, a talent guaranteed to endear him to Trudeau and Pitfield, who disliked discussing the dreary details of fiscal policy as much as they loved the tour of the theoretical horizon that Stewart was so good at providing. He had also shown his ability to translate the grand intellectual sweep into measured prose by writing *The Way Ahead*, a brochure explaining how the government intended to manage the economy after wage and price controls were removed. Just as important, Stewart was atypically modest for an economist, an attitude that had allowed him to climb the Ottawa ladder without making enemies and to advise the mighty without appearing to condescend. [14]

Not long before the fall of the Liberal government, Trudeau appointed Stewart deputy minister in Energy. He soon revealed a capacity to adapt to changing circumstances that was seen in bureaucratic circles as clear proof of professionalism: he was as smoothly capable at briefing Joe Clark, who called on his advice at the Tokyo economic summit in 1979, as he had been at counselling his predecessor. In short, Stewart was an unusually well qualified economic bureaucrat, just the man for a difficult job in a difficult time. He would be able to reconcile, if anyone could, Trudeau's constitutional goals, Lalonde's energy plan, and his own tax reform ideas and glue them together with a refurbished version of the Keynesianism that his political master still seemed to espouse. In tandem with

MacEachen, Stewart seemed exactly the right choice to keep the economy off Trudeau's agenda while he dealt with the personal priorities of his strategic prime ministership.

This plan worked well for a time. The first MacEachen-Stewart budget of October 1980, which was dominated by the NEP, demonstrated unprecedented co-operation between Finance and Energy, because of Stewart's willingness to collaborate with his former department and MacEachen's willingness to let Marc Lalonde claim the glory for his first budget. Official Ottawa assumed that MacEachen was staying out of the limelight deliberately in order to cogitate on how to contain the deeply entrenched problem of inflation. He turned aside flak about rising interest rates by pointing to international factors beyond Canada's control. For the first eighteen months of the Restoration his cautious stance succeeded, and his reputation for wizardry held through the summer of 1981, despite the generalized alarm about American hostility, soaring interest rates, and a declining Canadian dollar. Canadian-American relations were not the finance minister's responsibility, and everyone knew that monetary policy fell within the bailiwick of the Bank of Canada, where the governor carefully guarded his independence from political direction. [15]

In September, when it came time for the semi-annual cabinet think-in, held – not coincidentally – in Cape Breton's Keltic Lodge, MacEachen played host with the air of a tomcat who knew just where his next bird was coming from. He spoke persuasively about the budget preparations his department was engaged in, and explained how he proposed to make it possible for his colleagues to achieve some of their expensive policy objectives despite the government's commitment to hold the line on spending and refrain from raising taxes. He had looked at their requests for funding new programs and found they amounted to a colossal $10 billion. Since deficit reduction had formed a significant part of the Liberals' 1980 platform, they would have to restrain their hopes. But he did offer a partial solution. Two billion dollars could be found by cutting

federal government transfers to the provinces, and another two billion could be generated by closing tax loopholes for the rich in the
name of social equity. This would produce $4 billion for new pro-
grams without creating new taxes or raising old rates. MacEachen
believed his upcoming budget would prove a superior document in
both political and economic terms.[16]

MacEachen was convinced by now that Ian Stewart was as brilliant as Trudeau and Pitfield had claimed in proposing his appointment. Stewart had developed a solution to the economists' dilemma
of the 1970s (the failure of Keynesianism plus the failure of monetarism) that he called a post-Keynesian stance: the view that in addition
to managing aggregate demand, government should intervene to
correct problems on the supply side. Unlike his predecessor Simon
Reisman, he believed the government had to be concerned with
questions of social equity as much as with those of economic efficiency. As a liberal economist serving a Liberal government, Stewart
was determined to eliminate the many tax breaks created in the early
1970s when Reisman had persuaded John Turner to load the tax
system with incentives to business. Their aim had been to stimulate
investment by – and to win political support from – particular
groups, such as real estate developers and high-income professionals, who were given generous schemes to direct their liquid assets
into housing construction, resource development, or corporate
financing and at the same time cut their taxable incomes. These
loopholes – or "tax expenditures," as economists were calling them,
as though the government figuratively spent the hundreds of millions in forgone revenue that they represented – had proliferated in
the 1970s to the point where they were distorting the economy's
capacity to perform efficiently. Surplus capital was responding less to
general market signals than to tax gimmicks and business deductions, which led to excessive construction of luxury condominiums
for high-income investors and an undue expansion of gourmet
restaurants where executives could charge their self-indulgence as
tax-deductible expenses.[17]

Stewart believed that once these distortions were removed, the more neutral tax system that resulted would lead to greater economic efficiency on the supply side. At the same time, cutting tax expenditures would produce greater fairness and thus greater social equality, because the high-income-earners' capacity to exploit the loopholes meant that Canada's tax burden was shifting from the shoulders of those who could most afford to pay to those who could least. Closing the loopholes would help contain the government's debt by increasing revenues and so reduce the burden of interest payments, which were expected to escalate during 1981 by some $4 billion. Greater fiscal responsibility coupled with greater social equity sounded wonderfully close to the old Liberal formula for efficient management and progressive government. Surely even fat-cat professionals and businessmen would have reason to be pleased in the long term, because their tax rate would be cut from 65 per cent to 50 per cent to keep it in line with Reagan's tax cuts. Conceptually, the Stewart budget was a *tour de force.* [18]

Small wonder then that MacEachen was feeling so self-assured at Keltic Lodge, or that his confidence in Stewart's formulations for the upcoming budget held throughout the early autumn, when the cabinet's attention continued to be focused on constitutional brinkmanship, energy dealings with Alberta, and the Reaganites' bullying. So when MacEachen rose in the Commons on the night of November 12, it was easy for Trudeau and his ministers, fresh from the lavish party at the Bank of Canada for King Hussein, to believe that this occasion would prove another triumph for the man Lester Pearson had called "the old smoothie." As MacEachen read through his speech their expectations appeared to be fulfilled. He shifted from English to French with surprising ease, pausing occasionally for effect to sip water from his glass or to acknowledge with a small smile the enthusiastic applause of his supporters. When his reading was over, he did a perfunctory turn in front of the television cameras, dismissed his critics ably, and then retired to his office where his deputy, Ian Stewart, was taking bows of his own at the traditional budget-night party. [19]

The generally happy mood was disturbed when Michael Pitfield suddenly appeared at the party like the ghost at Macbeth's feast, grave of eye, trench coat flapping. Pitfield had been at home in Rockcliffe watching the budget reading on the CBC and listening with mounting dismay to the cutting attacks made on it by the business lobbyists hired as critics by the state network. Eventually, his alarm had overwhelmed his reticence and he had dressed hurriedly, driven down to Parliament Hill, rushed into the minister's office, and pulled Stewart to the periphery of the crowd to ask hoarsely, "My God, Ian, what have you done?"[20]

For months thereafter, this question echoed through the Canadian body politic, although it was usually phrased as "What has Allan MacEachen done?" Day after day, newspaper headlines trumpeted the dissatisfactions of the business community. Night after night, on television news shows, representatives of interest groups, labour unions, and even charitable foundations could be heard lambasting the government, each of them implying that the Liberals intended to destroy them. It got so bad that MacEachen went incommunicado, retreating to a hide-away his staff could not reach, refusing to meet the press, resisting the prime minister's pressure on him to embark on a national speaking tour, trying to distance himself from what had so suddenly become a fiasco.

Ottawa insiders began to say snidely that Trudeau was reaping the whirlwind he had sown by appointing to Finance two men whose virtues were negated by their inexperience in the department, where neither of them had ever served before, and by their lack of familiarity with the business community, where neither of them had close connections. Stewart was a generalist, not a specialist of the kind who could tell instinctively when a technical issue had been properly resolved. Driven on by his passion for theory, he had squandered precious departmental time in the summer of 1981 by asking his officials to explore the new tax-based income policy approach to controlling inflation that the economist Arthur Donner was espousing in *The Globe and Mail*. As Stewart saw it, inflation in the 1980s was caused by the maldistribution of power:

the inequitable appropriation of more assets by strong individuals and corporations who, to the detriment of the weaker and less well organized, prevented the government from taxing them. He agreed with J.K. Galbraith that it was not an abstract equilibrium-seeking "market" but rather the big players – big governments along with giant corporations – that drove the economy in the post-industrial state. Inflation was produced when these core institutions drove prices or wages up faster than productivity. The scores of expert hours spent proving to Stewart's satisfaction that Donner's proposal was impractical had diverted middle-level Finance bureaucrats from careful nuts-and-bolts work on the budget.[21]

More serious, Finance was in worse shape than its reputation as the country's best economics faculty implied, since several officials who had been recruited from university campuses, mostly by Simon Reisman, had left the department. The directorship of the tax policy section, for instance, had been vacant since 1979, when Ed Neufeld went to work for the Royal Bank. Stewart had managed to fill Neufeld's job only in September 1981, a mere two months before the budget's release. He also had failed to consult with economic bureaucrats outside his own department, depriving himself of the normal bureaucratic filters that would check and double-check whether a proposed budget measure was well conceived. Even his former colleagues in Energy, for instance, Ed Clark and George Tough, were appalled to discover that the main incentive they were relying on to channel the savings of high-income Canadians into Canadian-controlled petroleum firms had been scrapped, a mistake that could have been avoided if Stewart or his drafters had discussed it with them for a quarter of an hour.[22]

Stewart lacked the caution that would have come naturally had he risen through the ranks of Finance. The tax loopholes to be closed were chosen by adding up how much revenue they would yield without considering how much political risk they would incur. His main concern was to reach MacEachen's reduction target of $2 billion, not to anticipate the reactions of those whose benefits were cut. Some 150 separate tax changes were proposed – four times as many as normal for a budget. Implementing them was bound to put tremendous pressure on his department, which had not managed to work out in advance the requisite technical details, including designing transitional measures so that taxpayers could be eased from the old system to the new without undue dislocation. Gérard Veilleux, a senior official in the department's federal-provincial relations branch, warned Stewart not to attempt so much in one swoop, but Stewart rejected this advice as old Finance group-think. He wanted to go for the big bang. Not only was "vertical equity" – reduced disparities between rich and poor – important to him, so was "horizontal equity." It would be unfair to close some business loopholes while ignoring those that others could still exploit. Technical glitches could be dealt with by the usual process of making adjustments when the budget measures came to the Senate for detailed review. [23]

The trouble with this approach was that the interest groups affected were not inclined to wait for the senators. When they found mistakes that would create anomalies or injustices – charitable foundations claimed they would be effectively put out of business, for instance – their lobbyists were able to say the budget was not just punitive, it was unworkable. It's not that we're self-seeking, they whined, it's just that we want a fair deal, sensible procedures, due process, a favourable climate for investment, etc., etc. With Finance's technical expertise discredited by the budget's revealed ineptitudes, the media were able to add to the left-wing label they had taken to pinning on the Trudeauites charges that they were incompetent. Morale in the Place Bell Canada building, where Finance officials worked, plummeted. They felt bruised because they believed they had produced a budget that was similar to the supply-side efforts of the Reaganites but was fairer to the tax-paying public. After a brief period of harmony following a decade of tension with the PMO/PCO, they had become the focus of the country's anger and derision. [24]

A couple of blocks away, in the offices housing the prime minister's entourage, there was no contingency plan for dealing with this uproar. The budget had been kept secret during its preparatory stages even from Trudeau's closest advisers. Robert Rabinovitch, the deputy clerk in the Privy Council Office, subsequently accepted some of the blame. "We had had big successes with the NEP and the constitution," he explained. "But we let the side down by not being tough enough on Ian [Stewart] and MacEachen. We didn't make Finance check its budget by putting it through our normal ministerial and administrative hoops, so I only realized a few hours before it was released that we had a disaster on our hands."[25]

When Rabinovitch, who had a doctorate in economics from the University of Pennsylvania, read an advance copy of the budget he raised the political question of how the government was going to handle the "coalition of losers" that the loophole-closing would create, and found to his astonishment that the old political wizard, MacEachen, had not concerned himself with this immediate problem. MacEachen's eye was on a longer-term prospect, his own chances of becoming prime minister. After a lifetime of caution, he had taken a gigantic gamble, having come to believe in his political genius – a myth the press had been amplifying for months. A brilliant coup at Finance could prove the stepping-stone not just to the interim leadership but to the main prize itself. His budget would rejig the old Liberal formula of competent but compassionate economic management – socially liberal, fiscally conservative – the formula from the 1950s that he still believed was feasible. But in his eagerness to assume the guise of a financial Robin Hood, MacEachen had grown careless. He had rejected the proposal to build into the budget tangible goodies that would give middle- and lower-income groups a reason to support the government's initiative and so create some allies for the government against the onslaught of the well-heeled.[26]

Allan J. was a parliamentary expert and an adept regional politician. But he was far from nimble as a political player on the national stage. He knew little about interest groups beyond the depressed Maritimes and was unable to understand that what looked to him like a political master stroke could become a self-inflicted *coup de grâce* for the Trudeau Liberals. He had not consulted representatives of the interest groups who would be most affected by his budget's changes, his natural shyness complementing the secretiveness of the budgetary process. Nor did he prepare the general public for the budget. There was no orchestrated build-up of ministerial hints and backbenchers' warnings that the tax burden was going to be shifted from the shoulders of the weak to those of the strong. Newspaper editors and columnists, caught up with the outrage of a few thousand paper capitalists in the investment business who were about to lose the right to deduct the interest they paid when borrowing funds for their speculations, never grasped the complex budget's basic free-market reform logic. Small wonder that the vast majority of ordinary voters – those who were to have benefitted from the fairer system – did not understand how it would improve their lot. If they read expert comments, they found that independent economists were dumping on the budget for quite a different, Keynesian reason: because the economy was entering a recession, investors needed encouragement to speed up economic activity. Cutting investment incentives should have been postponed.[27]

As the private sector's counter-attack grew in vehemence, consternation built up in the Liberal cabinet and caucus. Twenty thousand letters were pouring into Ottawa every day as insurance companies mobilized their policy-holders to complain that their previously inviolate benefits were now going to be taxed. Trudeau refused to admit that his government had goofed. When he addressed a fundraising dinner in Vancouver where prosperous Liberals were expecting some reasoned explanation for the tax reform measures that were going to nip them in the wallet, Trudeau treated them instead with contempt, haranguing them for being parochial.[28]

Since the prime minister also declined to repudiate his humiliated finance minister by relieving him of his position, the Liberal caucus grew restive, urging that MacEachen beat a retreat as hastily as possible. Finance called on David Hilton, one of its most capable officers, to help the minister respond to the media. But Hilton's qualifications for the assignment – that he had not been involved in the budget-making process, had developed diplomatic skills as a member of the trade commissioner service, and had worked briefly as a journalist in his younger days – were of only marginal help in stemming the onslaught from the angry losers' coalition. MacEachen was forced to back down. Over the next two months – in a slow-motion series of provisional exemptions, delays in implementation, clarifications, grandfathering of existing practices, and amendments to proposed measures – he withdrew from his budget the bulk of the proposed "loopholectomies," until nothing remained either of that document's reformist thrust or of the Liberals' Restoration momentum. [29]

# PART IV

# The Fight for Liberal Survival

# CHAPTER 9

# THE LIBERALS REGROUP: TRUDEAU GETS GOING

February is the low ebb of the Ottawa year, a month when only the very young or the happily deluded can summon optimism in the face of winter. But even in that bleak context, February of 1982 in Ottawa was awful in its own way. When Sylvia Ostry, a Canadian economist who was then head of the Department of Economics and Statistics at the Organisation for Economic Co-operation and Development in Paris, came back in mid-month to spend a week in the city where she had previously worked as a public servant for fifteen years, she was appalled both by Canada's deteriorating economic situation and by the torpid nature of the government's response. With her was a team of OECD researchers who fanned out through the bureaucratic reaches of the capital, bent on producing one of that organization's detailed reports on a member nation's economy. From the perspective of two years as an international public servant dealing with global rather than national issues, Ostry quickly decided that demoralization in government circles had reached a new depth. The city seemed riddled with suspicion, the Liberal politicians sunk in despair, the senior bureaucrats disoriented, the structures of the Canadian state out of kilter.[1]

Ostry had been appointed to the OECD during Joe Clark's brief term in office and had missed the euphoria of the Trudeau Restoration. What she was witnessing in the MacEachen budget's aftershock was the hangover from the elation that the idea of a strategic prime ministership had produced in official Ottawa. Public servants in the Finance Department were taking a daily drubbing from professional economists in the private sector, who were blaming them for having misunderstood the country's economic dilemma – blame they felt rightfully belonged to the politicians. Senior bureaucrats of Gordon Osbaldeston's persuasion were saying openly that if they had not been excluded from the formulation of the National Energy Program they might have saved Lalonde and the government from a colossal embarrassment. World oil prices had not continued to rise, as the formulators of the NEP had blithely assumed, but had levelled off and were actually starting to decline. Revenues were poised to fall billions of dollars short of projections, jeopardizing the government's entire fiscal framework.

Equally alarming was the fact that the Bank of Canada's attempt to throttle inflation by tightening credit had not worked. Post-war records were being set in unemployment figures, as well as in the budgetary and current account deficits. It was cold comfort to argue that a world-wide economic downturn had cut the demand for Canadian staple exports abroad. The government was being blamed by the public for an inflation rate that was pushing up the cost of living by over 12 per cent a year, and by business for the decline in international confidence in the Canadian dollar, which had fallen to an unprecedented low of 76.8 cents U.S. The Canadian-American relationship continued to be shaky, with Washington still threatening retaliation against the NEP and launching a formal complaint at the GATT against FIRA, developments that were making the always skittish Canadian business community increasingly nervous. There was no one to whom the bureaucrats felt they could express their grievances and fears, since no one seemed to be steering the ship of state.[2]

Michael Pitfield, the man who ought to have been providing the public service with leadership and a sense of stability, was instead indulging in one of his periodic departmental reorganizations – the recasting and merging of the Departments of Industry, Trade and Commerce, Regional Economic Expansion, and External Affairs – which had been sprung on the senior bureaucracy in January with minimal prior consultation. Allan MacEachen, the deputy prime minister, had settled into sullen defensiveness. He had missed six consecutive meetings of the cabinet's Priorities and Planning Committee and had given a maddeningly opaque performance at a day-long meeting with provincial finance ministers, who went home aggrieved by Ottawa's arrogance and ignorance of their needs. Himself, as the prime minister was caustically described, was still indulging his obsessive involvement with Quebec and the constitution. Even though the federal-provincial accord had been signed three months before and an enabling resolution had been passed by Parliament, barriers to the patriation of the British North America Act remained. The British government's amendment to the act – the final recognition that the Dominion of Canada was no longer bound to its erstwhile imperial centre – was still winding its tortuous way through the mother of parliaments in London, with Parti Québécois representatives lobbying peers in the House of Lords and native groups launching appeals in the British courts. Trudeau's active direction of federal constitutional strategy, which had consumed so much of his energies in the previous two years, meant that he had time to pay only glancing attention to economic issues.[3]

While Ostry's OECD team was fact-finding in Ottawa, Trudeau appeared on CTV in an hour-long interview with the British television star David Frost, who posed deferential questions that for the most part elicited obfuscatory answers. The prime minister's judgement was once again being called into question on the private as well as the public front as a result of the posturings of his estranged wife. Two weeks before, deep in the winter of Canada's economic discontent, Margaret Trudeau had produced a second ghost-written book about her marriage, an expansion on *Beyond Reason*, which had been published during the 1979 election campaign. Called *Consequences*, the new book proclaimed her present emotional equilibrium while revealing further sensational details about an abortion she had undergone as a teenager, her most recent sexual adventures with rock stars and actors in limousines and hotel lavatories, and the many dreamy dreams of fame and fortune she had enjoyed while spending money wildly on clothes and caviar in great cities on three continents, aided in her musings by hallucinogens of several varieties.[4]

When Frost asked Trudeau discreetly about his family – his three young sons were living with him in the official residence at 24 Sussex and visiting their mother and her live-in lover in her nearby townhouse on weekends – he responded with grace, saying only that his children had wrought such a transformation in his life that it made him eternally grateful for the miracle of their existence and for the mother who had borne them. More revealing was a reference Trudeau made to the way his commitment to personalism had transformed his life. As he talked about the importance of his activist Catholic faith, his face took on the luminous look that high emotion often evoked in him. Sylvia Ostry had known Trudeau for nearly thirty years, and when she was told about this look – which was likened to that of a monk coming out of a meditative high – she responded by saying, "There is a terrible irony here. Reality has finally caught up with Canada. Our deferment of economic pain went on too long. Every other industrialized country came to understand in the 1970s that the post-war era was over. But we continued to live in a bubble. And now, when the world crisis has hit us, Pierre isn't a presence. He always wanted to transcend the ordinary. Now he's transcending everything. Trudeau Transcendent. It ought to be on our coat of arms."[5]

The disconsolate mood that Ostry found so dispiriting hung on in Ottawa throughout the winter and early spring, marring the festivities surrounding the constitution's homecoming in mid-April. Once the British politicians had done their constitutional duty by Canada by amending the British North America Act with the new charter and amending formula and turning it into the Constitution Acts, 1867 to 1982, elaborate preparations were made in honour of what ought to have been the Trudeau era's greatest triumph. Scores of distinguished Canadians and platoons of the Liberal faithful were called to the capital for formal dinners, a gala at the National Arts

Centre, a full-fledged ceremony on Parliament Hill in the presence of the Queen, and the quaffing of countless *coupes de champagne*.[6]

Despite the glitter, the celebrations fell flat. At the outdoor ceremony for the actual signing over to Canada of the country's 115-year-old constitution in the presence of the monarch, the Privy Councillors on the platform looked solemn, the crowds gathered to see the show were muted rather than joyous, and the Queen had the air of a disapproving Visitor presiding over a college prize-giving where the upper-form prefects were in disgrace. Her pursed mouth was said to reflect her discomfort with the fact that Quebec had been left out of the constitutional accord, as the journalistic cliché had it, and that its premier, René Lévesque, was leading a counter-demonstration in Montreal. *And No One Cheered*, the title of a book by Richard Simeon and Keith Banting commenting on the fractious process by which the BNA Act was finally brought home to Canada, was an apt description of the general ambiance in Ottawa. Only the prime minister looked as though he was deriving real pleasure from the celebrations. Trudeau's face was once more radiant, his air of other-worldliness remarkable.[7]

In the fortnight that followed, the political journalists were in full cry, anticipating his resignation as prime minister now that he had accomplished his mission of entrenching a charter of rights and freedoms in a patriated Canadian constitution. They knew that supporters of the perennial aspirants for his job, John Turner and Donald Macdonald, were muttering darkly in the locker rooms of their Toronto fitness clubs that it was time for Trudeau to go.

Opinion polls were affirming that the public had lost faith in the Liberal Party, and the business press was reporting that a new conservative majority, similar to the one that had vaulted Ronald Reagan into the White House the year before, was forming in Canada. Buoyed by the Liberals' troubles, Joe Clark and his Conservatives had set up a travelling task force to collect complaints about the budget in public hearings held from coast to coast and had mounted an unrelenting barrage of criticism in the Commons, intended to exploit the obvious unhappiness on the Liberals' front and back benches. For a fortnight in March, the Tories had managed to paralyse the House by keeping the division bells ringing with their stubborn refusal to vote on Marc Lalonde's omnibus bill, a huge legislative package whose purpose was to write the government's controversial energy program into law.

The *Toronto Star* columnist Richard Gwyn, whose 1980 biography had portrayed Trudeau as a political magician, published a series of pieces describing the death watch in Ottawa. Douglas Fisher, whose animosity towards the Liberal Party had been a driving force in his professional life as a CCF/NDP politician and multi-media pundit for a quarter of a century, wrote in his syndicated column that Trudeau had turned into "a charismatic without anything to radiate," that his "era was over," and that the Liberal Party was probably finished as a national force. Elsewhere in the press, Trudeau was berated for his arrogant insistence that his friend the flamboyant modernist Arthur Erickson be given the contract to design the new Canadian embassy in Washington, despite the recommendations of a committee of experts who had picked other architects for the job in an arduous professional competition. His reputation for practising favouritism and condoning extravagance was further embellished by the revelation that Michael Pitfield had travelled back and forth from Boston to Ottawa first-class at government expense nearly every week during the early months of the Restoration, when he was still lecturing at Harvard and serving as Trudeau's principal bureaucratic adviser at the same time. Trudeau's once-fervent ally the respected constitutionalist Eugene Forsey renounced his Liberal allegiance, saying he intended to sit in the Senate as an Independent because of his disagreement with the Trudeau government's "imperfect understanding of the rule of law," as displayed in the report of the McDonald commission on RCMP wrongdoing.[8]

"We were at our nadir around that time," Tom Axworthy remembered. "But as the spring advanced, things began to stir."[9]

• • •

To the surprise of official Ottawa the principal stir involved the active participation in economic policy-making of the radiant Trudeau. Even before the constitutional celebrations, the prime minister and his close colleagues had decided that he could not give in to his detractors by resigning his position and moving home to Montreal with his sons. Before he could retire with honour, they would have to find a way out of the morass into which his government had floundered. With the decline in GNP now stretching into a third quarter and no end to the economy's downturn in sight, there was little point in denying that Canada was suffering the worst recession in forty years.[10]

The men ostensibly in charge of sorting out this mess – the minister of finance and his deputy – were the very people who had been in charge as it developed. Even though MacEachen and Stewart had steered the government to the brink of ruin, the prime minister loyally insisted that they were to remain in their jobs in the hope that, later on, a less ignominious retreat could be arranged. But the decision taken in early 1980 to leave the economy to them while his own energies were focused on constitutional concerns and energy had to be revoked. Brought to earth by the prospect of a daunting challenge, he resolved to turn his full attention to the aspect of government that had frustrated him throughout his tenure in office.

In the PCO, where the government's economic difficulties had been anxiously monitored all winter long, his staff was ready to provide him with the policy support he needed. The deputy cabinet secretary, Robert Rabinovitch, had assembled a small team of capable analysts. Formally their role was to help the prime minister ask the right questions of Finance officials, not to do that department's work. But with Finance discombobulated, Rabinovitch realized the PCO would have to move into the vacuum. Accordingly, he asked Nate Laurie to write a briefing note for Trudeau to serve as a guide to the maze of economic conundrums his government faced.

Laurie had been hired away from the Conference Board of Canada by Tom Axworthy in 1979 to advise the Liberals in the LOO. After the 1980 election he had been dispatched to Finance as a liaison officer for the PMO/PCO but had found himself unwelcome among the department's cagey bureaucrats, who were jealously guarding their turf against a rival agency's intrusion. When Laurie was invited to come in from the cold and join Rabinovitch's economic policy team, his reaction was one of relief. He quickly produced fifteen densely argued pages intended to give Trudeau an overview of the government's precarious position, a memorandum that laid out the main elements at issue in the economic crisis and then suggested how a series of trade-offs might reconcile the sharply differentiated positions being expressed within a badly divided cabinet.[11]

Basic tensions between welfare Liberals and business Liberals had sharpened as the Trudeau ministers discussed solutions to the government's unnerving economic problems. Few in number but firm in conviction, the business Liberals were resentful of the marginal role they had played in the previous two years. Don Johnston, a Montreal tax lawyer and a vociferous exponent of business concerns, had been fobbed off with the treasury secretariat when he had been expecting the finance portfolio. Ed Lumley, an energetic businessman from Cornwall, Ontario, had been slotted into the junior ministry of international trade. Jean-Luc Pepin, a former professor of political science and veteran politician who had accomplished the considerable feat in the 1970s of earning respect in the corporate world as minister at Industry, Trade and Commerce and chairman of the Anti-Inflation Board, had been sidelined to the Department of Transport. Now, with the Liberals' historic reputation for managerial competence in tatters, the business Liberals began to assert their authority at every cabinet meeting.

They were out-talked initially by its left-leaning faction under the insistent leadership of Tom Axworthy's brother Lloyd. Although he was new to cabinet, Axworthy was not readily intimidated. The decade he had spent in the rough world of opposition politics in Manitoba, culminating in a stint as leader of the beleaguered provincial Liberal Party, had turned him from a reformer with an intellectual edge into a hard-nosed pol with an inner-city populist base and a pugnacious debating style. After shifting to federal politics in 1979, he had proven so effective in opposition that when Trudeau resigned briefly in November that year, he was seen by many left Liberals as their best hope in the coming leadership contest. The Conservatives' collapse and the unexpected return of Trudeau to office had changed the scenario drastically. As one of only two Grits elected west of the Ontario border in 1980, he was a sure bet for a cabinet job. Employment and Immigration, the portfolio he was appointed to, along with his responsibility for the status of women and membership on the important P&P committee, made him a rising star. But the glow on his reform reputation was dimmed by his clumsy handling of women's rights issues during the constitutional negotiations, and his ambition to make his mark as a policy pioneer by launching a thorough review of the labour market had been stalled by the recession.[12]

Instead of playing midwife to a reborn Canadian economy in a historic wave of high-tech resource megaprojects linked to high-value-added industry with high-skill jobs, Axworthy found himself besieged by the public clamour for work of any kind. He did not endear himself to his envious cabinet colleagues just after MacEachen brought down his ill-fated budget when he short-circuited the envelope system by wresting $400 million directly from the finance minister for emergency programs to relieve unemployment. But he earned their respect by going into a recession-management mode, using every makework trick and every existing community-support program his staff could think of to save jobs. When Trudeau turned his full attention to the economy in the late spring of 1982, Axworthy took the lead in pressing the welfare Liberals' case. Strongly supported by Herb Gray, Roméo LeBlanc, and Monique Bégin, who agonized about the human suffering caused by widespread bankruptcies, mortgage foreclosures, and plant closings, he pressed for billions to be spent on a Keynesian-style stimulation of the economy.[13]

The welfare Liberals' rhetorical fire was directed more at Ian Stewart than at Allan MacEachen. Even Axworthy was chary of taking on the redoubtable minister, who had been pulled out of his paralysis by Trudeau's reaffirmed confidence in his capacities and was turning up regularly at P&P once more. MacEachen was standing tough with the provinces, unilaterally imposing his budget's new limits on Ottawa's fiscal transfers to them despite the concerted protests of the premiers, their finance ministers, the Economic Council, and *The Globe and Mail*. Supported in cabinet by Don Johnston, and in the media by the lobbyist Tom d'Aquino on behalf of the Business Council on National Issues, MacEachen retreated from his reform stance and doggedly resisted his impatient colleagues' desire to spend their way out of the recession. The expanding federal debt was the most pressing problem. The government deficit was in the process of trebling, as revenues fell and welfare costs rose to record levels – from the range of $7 to $9 billion he had predicted in November, to over $20 billion. Finance's fiscal framework could not be violated any further. Whatever rescue measures his colleagues decided on, their net result would have to be fiscally neutral so as not to require still more government borrowing.[14]

Armed with Nate Laurie's comprehensive guide, Trudeau presided assiduously over P&P's tempestuous debates. To the relief of his ministers, his Socratic style of conducting their deliberations – so often criticized in the past for turning executive decision-making meetings into endless academic seminars – proved highly effective in this exercise, largely because he knew what he wanted the cabinet's ultimate position to be. Trudeau's familiarity with both Keynesian and monetarist economic theory proved invaluable. He was able to persuade the interventionists to recognize the seriousness of the inflationary threat. At the same time, he managed to get the program slashers to acknowledge that the cyclical deficit should not be cut during the recession. Patiently he guided his peers through long meetings and carefully staged reviews of the options until by early June they had discovered a new policy direction around which to reaffirm their solidarity. [15]

The overarching objective was to change the way Ottawa's own policies contributed to the deficit by driving up government expenses and driving down government income. In order to protect welfare recipients against the ravages of inflation, social security payments had been rising for a decade to keep pace with the cost of living. During the same period, "indexing" – the policy of linking the rates of the progressive income-tax ladder to the consumer price index – had eased the load on individual taxpayers but had prevented the government's revenues from rising. As beneficiaries of the state's safety net, all citizens received inflation-proof support. But as taxpayers who financed this welfare system, the middle- and upper-income citizens were partially exempted from paying for the growing costs. As the recession drove ever-greater numbers of the jobless to seek relief from the public purse and transferred more workers to lower tax brackets, the combination of structural and cyclical factors created a budgetary disaster. [16]

P&P's first proposal was to put a limit or "cap" on inflation-pegged increases in social security payments, transfers to the provinces, and public service wages. A second capping would keep increases of federally administered prices such as phone rates below the inflation rate. A third measure would allow government revenue from income taxes to grow faster by de-indexing personal tax rates. Finally, money saved by capping along with money raised by de-indexing would be redirected to create jobs. There would be no Keynesian stimulus. Savings would balance new expenditures so the impact on the deficit would be neutral: the fiscal framework would remain intact. [17]

It was a measure of Trudeau's leadership skills that this complex set of trade-offs agreed upon by his quarrelsome ministers turned out to be virtually the same package Nate Laurie had outlined back in April. On the surface, it seemed to be a classic Liberal compromise between the program boosters on the left and the deficit cutters on the right. For the moment, both welfare and business Liberals were satisfied. The welfare state would have to be reined in unless Canada could get relief from the major cause of its economic woes, the high levels of world interest rates.

All over the world, economists were expressing their consternation at the damaging effect of American economic policies. The Reaganites' refusal to raise taxes to pay for their giddy spending on armaments had created a U.S. deficit that was being financed by borrowing foreign capital. To attract this capital the chairman of the Federal Reserve Board, Paul Volcker, had raised interest rates to the highest point "since the birth of Jesus Christ," as the German chancellor, Helmut Schmidt, despairingly described the situation.[18]

If Germany's Bundesbank could not deviate from made-in-Washington interest rates because U.S. financial markets still dominated the global monetary system, there was obviously nothing Trudeau could do but hope that multilateral pressure would bring the Americans to their senses. His own complaints in Washington that high and erratic U.S. rates were "having a very damaging effect on us" had fallen on deaf ears. But after world leaders attending their annual economic summit at Versailles in early June failed to convince Reagan to renounce his aberrant ways, the Trudeauites realized they could expect no salvation from central bankers abroad. Even their own central banker remained aloof from their desperate concerns. Prohibitively high interest rates may have been accelerating bankruptcies and throwing thousands of workers on the dole, but they were also propping up the value of the Canadian dollar, as the governor of the Bank of Canada intended they should.[19]

Gerald Bouey was still fixated on inflation. At 13 per cent, the annual increase in the cost of living in Canada was running four points ahead of the American rate. Since the governor continued to insist that a lower dollar would push inflation higher still, he would not take steps to reduce interest rates, since lower rates would scare away international capital and the Canadian dollar would plummet.

Bouey was determined to keep rates up, whatever the immediate damage to the economy. In effect the priority he assigned to combatting inflation locked Canada into adherence to Paul Volcker's harsh deflationary strategy.[20]

In many ways it was politically convenient for the Trudeauites to let the blame for bad times fall on Bouey, a man whose persona was so constrained and whose thinking so conventional that a conversation with him was often described as the best soporific in town. "It's awkward for politicians, you know," Bouey remarked drily in response to a question about how it felt to be the most disliked public figure in the country. "When they are in opposition, they always complain about interest rates in order to be seen to be on the side of the voters. But once in power, they have to be responsible. Even if they defer to the Bank's reasoning, they may prefer to wash their hands of the issues and let the Bank's governor take the blame."[21]

Equanimous as the governor sounded about playing the scapegoat, he was in no mood in the late spring of 1982 to offer succour to a Liberal government concerned about political survival. He was still sufficiently miffed at the Trudeauites for having gone ahead with the National Energy Program without heeding his advice on its exchange-rate implications that he was unperturbed at the sight of them taking the heat for the social pain inflicted on flesh-and-blood Canadians by the Bank's hard line on inflation.[22]

Sitting in the deputy minister's office at the Department of Finance, Ian Stewart could not afford so Olympian a disregard for the human misery caused by the stalled economy. Nor could he do anything about what he thought of as the governor's compulsions. He was obliged to accept the Bank's monetary restraint even though he could not ignore how high interest rates were increasing the budgetary burden of the rapidly escalating national debt. His chief comfort in these vicissitudes was the change in his immediate personal situation. Even though PCO officials and P&P ministers had hijacked the budgetary process, the prime minister had managed the take-over with such finesse that Stewart had been able to recover his nerve. He could take pride in having proposed the idea of capping public-sector wages and programs in the first place. He strongly disagreed with the P&P ministers' decision to de-index tax rates, but his own minister had lost the final hard-fought battle over the prospect when Trudeau – prepped by Nate Laurie on how to refute Finance's position – had confronted MacEachen with a cabinet consensus. Since big business would probably object even more vociferously than it had in 1975 to the imposition of any kind of price controls by a Trudeau government, Finance would have to accept a course of action that offended Stewart's Galbraithian sense of fairness. Employees of the government and its Crown corporations would unfortunately have to bear the brunt of the wage-capping, but it was hoped that this action would suggest a path for provincial governments to follow and at the same time offer the private sector an example to use in its collective bargaining with labour.[23]

The final issue was to determine at what level the cap should be set. When Stewart originally suggested the idea, he thought a limit on benefits and wage increases to 9 per cent in the first year and 8 per cent in the second was as far as it was politically feasible to go. But by early June, when P&P handed down its capping directive, growing unemployment and falling production were finally sapping inflation's momentum. In light of these changed conditions Stewart thought that 6 per cent for 1982–83 and 5 per cent for 1983–84 were caps that could be tried. Even though this target seemed Draconian to some ministers, they acknowledged that the lower figures would curry greater favour with the private sector by showing the government taking decidedly bold action to cut costs. They would also yield savings when applied to family allowance and old-age security payments and thereby provide a tidy $2 billion that could be funnelled into job creation. Capping at 6 and then 5 per cent was certainly a blow to the welfare system. But left-Liberal ministers could comfort themselves that they had managed to enrich a couple of programs. Impoverished old people would get a guaranteed income supplement, and destitute single-parent families a child tax credit.[24]

The success of Pierre Trudeau's backstage leadership and of Ian Stewart's calculations was signalled by an unusual phenomenon. When the P&P package was turned into a new budget and tabled by Allan MacEachen on June 28, ministers, backbenchers, and senators from the Liberal left, right, and centre rushed to claim credit for its tough measures, which had won the approval of the business community in extensive pre-budget consultations. Don Johnston even wrote a ditty in celebration of the Liberals' modest attempt to bring government spending under control. [25]

> What does it take to beat inflation?
> What does it take to make us thrive?
> How will we be a stronger nation?
> The answer, my friend, is "Six & Five."

(His admirers claimed that to enjoy its full effect, Johnston's doggerel had to be heard in his Commons office, sung by a chorus of revivified Grits while the affable minister pounded out the tune on an upright piano.) [26]

Trudeau did not join the chorus but sang his own solo, making speeches that extolled a third way between total government control over the economy and widespread social misery caused by too free a market. To ensure that Six & Five survived the test of public opinion, he pressed into service his secretary of state, Serge Joyal, and his campaign manager, Keith Davey, to sell the program and forestall any repetition of the public relations nightmare that had followed the 1981 budget. Backed by the PCO's staff, Davey quickly displayed his salesman's prowess. MPs were revved up to blitz their constituencies armed with cardboard cases containing draft speeches, texts for the local media, pre-packaged questions-and-answers, and a 45-r.p.m. recording of Don Johnston's chorus in a rendition of his musical masterpiece. [27]

For the next few weeks Six & Five seemed like a magic wand. When Bell Canada turned up in Ottawa with a request for telephone rate increases of 32 and 25 per cent for the next two years, it won a mere 6 and 5 per cent. Trudeau publicly boasted of the government's pressure on business to conform: "If Bombardier expects us to help them get other contracts like we helped them get the New York [subway car] one, we would first be interested in looking at the possibility of Bombardier and the unions at Bombardier looking at the Six & Five per cent society in their prices, in their wages, in their incomes, and so on . . . Maybe that is 'twisting arms,' but I think it is just using the powers of persuasion." The business world, which had escaped the imposition of constraints on its price increases, started to use the formula as a benchmark for wage increases, and union leaders found themselves up against this limit. Premiers who had angrily dismissed public-sector wage controls as unthinkable in February began to announce equivalent measures in their own jurisdictions. By midsummer the phrase "Six & Five" was imprinted on the nation's consciousness at the same time that inflation had begun to recede. The Liberals appeared to be weathering the economy's storm.[28]

The hold-out from the general enthusiasm for Six & Five was organized labour. For union leaders the June budget was nothing less than "a declaration of war against the nation's workers," as Louis Laberge, president of Quebec's Confédération des syndicats nationaux, described it. And a phoney war at that. World energy prices, U.S. interest rates, and mounting levels of imports were all pushing up costs. But wages had been lagging behind inflation, not leading it, in recent years, although the media kept repeating the business community's mantra that the culprit was still the wage-price spiral. Labour leaders, who found themselves negotiating against a psychological ceiling of 6- and 5-per-cent increases, protested that the government had deliberately provoked class polarization by fighting inflation on the backs of workers, shifting resources from wages to capital, and – through high interest rates – transferring wealth from borrowers to lenders.[29]

Union leaders no longer expected satisfaction from a government headed by Pierre Trudeau. Thirty years before he had been their champion; the rich kid who cared, who was willing to serve as itinerant teacher, economic analyst, courtroom advocate, and public protester on their behalf. But the October Crisis of 1970, during which so many Quebec union organizers were indiscriminately arrested, had alienated francophone labour leaders from him permanently. He had lost the support of their anglophone counterparts as a result of the gradual whittling away during the 1970s of the generous unemployment insurance regime that had been greatly enriched by Bryce Mackasey, Trudeau's first minister of labour. Their enmity was deepened with the imposition of wage and price controls in 1975, which they saw as jeopardizing their hard-won collective bargaining rights. It did not help that the Liberals were able to shrug off these protests knowing that, however hostile the unions' leadership might be, their members continued to vote for Trudeau. Even when he was on the political skids in May 1979, the Liberals still pulled over 50 per cent more support from union households than the NDP under Ed Broadbent.[30]

By the time of the Restoration there was little reason for union leaders to believe that anything had changed for the better in their relationship with Trudeau's government. The labour movement was stronger in Canada than ever before. The successful spread of public-sector unions through provincial and municipal governments meant it had expanded to include two-fifths of the workforce at the same time as the American labour movement had declined to half that figure. The articulate, activist, and nationalist leadership in the public-sector unions, backed by the labour movement's umbrella organization, the Canadian Labour Congress, had encouraged industrial unions towards greater autonomy from their American parent organizations.[31]

While these empowered unionists were advocating more interventionist industrial-strategy policies and pressing for reforms to deal with sexism and racism on behalf of their increasingly female and immigrant membership, the Canadian government was becoming more reactionary. The minister of labour appointed in 1980 was Gerald Regan, whose policies while he was premier of Nova Scotia had deliberately frustrated union aspirations. The new Trudeau government was as deeply committed as the old to the view that the rate of inflation was more important than the rate of unemployment, and that government had to become more efficient, not more expansive. The Trudeauites might be spouting a new nationalism, but their basic language was capitalist: scarce public funds were needed more for capital development than for social programs; labour-market bottlenecks had to be broken and greater mobility achieved so that workers would be pushed to leave their communities in such high unemployment areas as the Atlantic provinces and head for dynamic sites such as the projected megaprojects on the prairies. The much-maligned market was to be fired up and made to work again.[32]

Surprisingly, many of these views were shared by Lloyd Axworthy, who by temperament and ideological bent ought to have been a friend of organized labour. While Axworthy was trying to use innovative measures to "pull the sting out of unemployment," as he phrased it, he was also pulling the sting out of the union leaders' rhetoric. As a left Liberal whose political experience was earned in opposing an NDP government in Manitoba, Axworthy had little love for the NDP's comrades-in-politics. His token consultations with labour representatives during the formulation of the National Training Act was typical: in offering direct services to workers for retraining, Axworthy achieved greater visibility for the Trudeau government while ignoring the union leadership.[33]

The truth was that the Restoration Liberals had become antipathetic to union leaders, who had dumped on MacEachen's egalitarian budget of 1981 because their members would have had to pay taxes on such fringe benefits as company contributions to employees' private dental plans. Even though their policy positions on the need for government intervention to spur industry were more in sync with the Liberals' policies than they had been for twenty years, labour leaders were as angry as business at the budget's curtailment of their prosperity. It could be argued that the CLC's choleric president, Dennis McDermott, displayed the most extravagant post-budget anti-government belligerence of any Canadian. At a mass protest against high interest rates on November 21, 1981, he called Trudeau and MacEachen "turkeys [who] have their heads so far up their backsides, they wouldn't see very much even if they opened their eyes." In a closed meeting with eight federal cabinet ministers three weeks later, he launched into a tirade, calling them "shitheads" and "assholes" during a fruitless two-hour exchange.[34]

As a consequence, union leaders found that they had no clout in Ottawa when they tried to resist the imposition of Six & Five on public-sector unions by Don Johnston. As the most committed right-winger in Trudeau's cabinet, Johnston wanted not just to curb wage increases, but to take back the bargaining rights that had been conceded in the late 1960s and to curtail the unions' capacity to launch strikes in such crucial public services as air traffic control. By using the courts to designate larger numbers of workers as essential to government services, and so forbidden to strike, he was tilting the field markedly against union power.[35]

By this time it was clear that a fundamental shift was under way within the government. It had begun subtly enough, as the Liberals adjusted their agenda to harsher economic realities during the free fall the economy suffered in the first half of the year. Now at the end of "the terrible summer of 1982," as Monique Bégin called it, the Liberals were still up against the wall despite the public relations success of Six & Five. There was general recognition that their original program for the Restoration would have to be revised drastically. Their energies would have to be directed at regaining the favour of constituencies that their heady interventionism had offended in 1980 and 1981. Their opponents might be saying that Liberalism was dead, the Liberal era over, and Trudeau's second coming a mere historical blip. But after nearly fifty years of managing the Canadian federation, the Government Party was not prepared to give up its hold on power without one hell of a fight.[36]

# CHAPTER 10

# RESTRUCTURING GOVERNMENT, INC.

Trudeau had decided to take part in this fight for survival not for the love of Liberalism but because his pride dictated that he could not abandon his job while his government's reputation was in jeopardy. He would have to wait until the economy picked up and the electorate was amenable to the Liberals once more. By the late summer of 1982 four men were engaged with him in a strategic attempt to recover the party's fortunes and their own: his abiding loyalists in cabinet, Marc Lalonde and Allan MacEachen; his young Sancho Panza in the PMO, Tom Axworthy; and his *éminence grise* in the PCO, Michael Pitfield. Despite their several shortcomings as individuals, they represented as a quartet a formidable combination of experience, intelligence, and devotion.

This inner circle knew very well that the Trudeau government was suffering the consequences of the aggressive strategy they had adopted in 1980. Back in power by a fluke of fate, they had realized that their time was short, their credibility limited, and their goals daunting. They were determined to resolve the country's constitutional impasse, tackle its energy dilemma, and wrestle inflation to the ground. If allies could be found in provincial governments or interest groups, well and good. If not, they would act alone. If their determined unilateralism and centralism were successful, they might be so disliked it would be difficult to win another victory at the polls; a different team would have to be found with a new vision for Canada.

Two and a half years later, they were not quite so sanguine. The provincial Liberals in Quebec were livid over Trudeau's constitutional manoeuvring; the energy scene was a shambles; inflation was still a severe problem; and their government was being lambasted by voters from one end of the country to the other. To safeguard their reputations and their legacy, each of them must do his part to rebuild support for their unpopular regime. [1]

Between them, MacEachen and Lalonde would have to deal with the continuing hostility of Reagan's Washington and Canada's business community. Pitfield acknowledged it was time for him to leave the clerk's job, but he was concerned that his contribution to the "science of government" be defended and preserved and his devotion to Canada be recognized. Axworthy was saddled with managing the prime minister's relationship with the Liberal Party, whose restless ranks were abuzz with the view that the sooner Trudeau stepped down, the better the party's prospects.

The obvious first move was to shuffle the cabinet, a phase of the recovery plan that depended on easing Allan MacEachen out of Finance. Having been given the chance to save face with the Six & Five effort, MacEachen accepted Trudeau's offer to rebuild his career in the external affairs portfolio he had vacated reluctantly six years before. And Lalonde, who had been fighting a rearguard action to preserve the essential thrust of the NEP despite the remorseless decline of world oil prices, was delighted to take on a new challenge in Finance.

The rest of the shuffle, announced in two parts in the autumn, reflected the Trudeauites' shift away from the nationalist, left-leaning positions they had embraced so brazenly in 1980. Rationalizing that they could return to their social reform agenda once the economy was sturdier, they strengthened the right wing of the cabinet at the expense of the left.

Herb Gray, the bane of the Reaganites, was moved to the Treasury Board, where he could do little more than play accountant to the government – a subtle way of signalling the Trudeauites' turning away from statism. He was replaced in the newly constituted

Department of Regional and Industrial Expansion by Ed Lumley, the only minister with direct business experience among the thirty-three around the cabinet table. (Lumley had managed the Coca-Cola franchise in Cornwall, Ontario, an industrial town on the St. Lawrence where he had been mayor for a term before running for federal office in 1974.) While he vigorously rejected the notion that he was right-wing, Lumley had a reputation as a persistent critic of Gray's nationalist stands. Once installed in DRIE, he quickly moved to speed up FIRA's review of foreign take-over proposals and to increase its acceptance rate. [2]

Even more significant was Don Johnston's transfer from the Treasury Board, where he had been chafing at his inability to affect economy policy, to the Ministry of State for Economic and Regional Development, the rejigged central agency where he could forcefully express his pro-business views. Jean Chrétien's move to Marc Lalonde's still-warm seat in Energy was interpreted in the bureaucracy as part of the same ideological shift. Although Lalonde told Energy officials that he intended to keep a hawk-eye on his successor lest the NEP be unravelled further, they were given a different message almost immediately by their new minister. Chrétien's first question when introducing himself to senior bureaucrats was "What did you do on the NEP?" The implication was that if they had been important in formulating or implementing that dirigiste program, their glory days were numbered. [3]

Similarly, Roméo LeBlanc's replacement by Pierre De Bané in the Department of Fisheries and Oceans heralded the imposition of a tough new approach to the Atlantic provinces in which economic criteria would prevail over social welfare priorities in managing the East Coast fisheries. Jean-Luc Pepin was left in Transport, where he and his deputy, Arthur Kroeger, had been working for two years on a daring program to alter the central role the railroads had played for most of the century in the prairie wheat economy by emphasizing market forces rather than government subsidies. [4]

There were limits to the government's capacity or desire to shift to the right. Most Liberals in the parliamentary caucus were still decidedly centre-left and believed that the social distress caused by the economic crisis cried out for generous rather than tough measures. (Statistics Canada had just reported that unemployment had reached a post-Depression record of 12.2 per cent in August, and that the economy had shrunk for the fourth consecutive quarter, making the recession the sharpest and most prolonged decline in overall real output and aggregate demand in the post–World War II period.) Accordingly, Lloyd Axworthy was left to soldier on trying to save jobs at Employment and Immigration. Eugene Whelan, the Ontario farmer famous for his fractured syntax and green Stetson, remained in the Department of Agriculture so he could push his ideas for a grand agri-food strategy to protect Canadian farming from the vagaries of the world market. [5]

André Ouellet stayed in Consumer and Corporate Affairs to deal with the merger mania gripping the private sector, and John Roberts continued in Environment to attack the intransigent American administration for not limiting the causes of acid rain. The appointment of left-leaning Jack Austin, now a senator, to the Ministry of State for Social Development, the central agency in charge of the social security envelope, indicated that welfare liberalism still had some clout in cabinet. And Monique Bégin, the passionate Quebec feminist for whom medicare symbolized left Liberalism's finest achievement, continued her struggle at Health and Welfare to save a health care system threatened by escalating costs, delinquent provinces, and defecting doctors. [6]

The motivation behind the crucial move of Marc Lalonde to the Department of Finance was not so much ideological as pragmatic. If they were to save their skins, the Liberals had to revive their claim to competence in managing the economy. Finance was still the fulcrum of government, and in putting Lalonde in charge, Trudeau was dispatching his seasoned general to the sector of the political front where low morale was most dangerous. Even though the Conservative leader, Joe Clark, saw "this appointment of a dangerous statist" as "the worst possible move Mr. Trudeau could make" in difficult times, it was to prove a brilliant if audacious piece of cabinet-making.[7]

Despite the NEP's unpopularity in business circles, Lalonde's reputation as the most capable of Trudeau's ministers flourished there as it did everywhere else. Even Alberta oilmen, who spat out the initials "N-E-P" as though they were fragments of wormwood, were respectful of his capacities. "That's one smart frog," was the view expressed in downtown Calgary. (Lalonde returned the compliment by displaying prominently in his office a collection of frogs, made of every sort of material from glazed china to nylon plush and given to him by admiring detractors and distraught admirers.)[8]

In taking on Finance, Lalonde knew he had to be seen to understand the business point of view. "I needed to re-establish Finance as the main interlocutor for financial interests in the country," he explained. "I had to provide them with leadership." In his opinion, this emphatically did not mean that he was shifting to the right. His Catholic activist philosophy allowed him to move with ease from social-democratic interventionism to neo-liberal collaboration with business. He was committed to Trudeau's government because Trudeau was committed to God and to keeping Quebec in Confederation. "Fundamentally, [Trudeau and I] are two strongly religious people with strong ethical norms . . . We have to show our people [Quebeckers] they have a role to play in Canada, if they want to play it," he had said in explaining why the NEP was good for Quebec. Now his mission demanded that he turn his talents to managing the economy so Canada and Quebec could prosper, and he went at the task with his usual zeal.[9]

"I was on the road within twenty-four hours of my appointment," he said afterwards, grinning at the memory. "I had a signal to send out." Over the next few weeks, he consulted frenetically with CEOs, with business lobby groups, with everybody who thought he had something to contribute to the rethinking of the government's economic strategy. Finance officials reacted unfavourably to their new minister's determination to seek the views of outsiders, particularly when he set up an advisory panel of academic and corporate economists. "They balked because they were clinging to the department's traditional attitude," said Lalonde. "They knew all and they wanted to control all. This hadn't been literally true for many years. Finance needed fresh thinking, if only for the sake of stimulus."[10]

At the same time, there was no doubt in Lalonde's mind that for his actions to be credible with business, Finance had to be restored to primacy in the Ottawa firmament. He had to show the corporate world that he was powerful in the government world by changing his department's style as well as its policy direction. To do this, he asked Trudeau to appoint Mickey Cohen as Ian Stewart's replacement in Finance.[11]

Originally a Toronto tax lawyer, Cohen had joined Finance in 1970 as an assistant deputy minister. He had busied himself, under the direction of Simon Reisman, with restoring the tax concessions to business that the Benson reforms had withdrawn. Later in the decade, he had displayed administrative talents as a deputy minister himself, first in Industry, Trade and Commerce and then as Lalonde's right hand in Energy. Back in Finance as deputy in the autumn of 1982, with Lalonde's stentorian instructions to restore its reputation ringing in his head, he assembled a new roster of senior officials – increasing to five the number of assistant deputy ministers and installing two associate deputy ministers to carry out the actual economic policy-making for which he had neither the training nor the patience.

Cohen's connections in the business world were such that he enjoyed an unusual immunity from the criticisms heaped on most of his bureaucratic colleagues. He was rarely censured for the NEP, for instance, although it had been developed in his department by bureaucrats under his direction. Once he was back in Finance, his role in its formulation was not just forgiven, it was forgotten. Businessmen were mollified further by the appointment as minister of state for finance – in effect, a cabinet assistant to Lalonde – of Roy

MacLaren, a Toronto MP and publisher of *Canadian Business*. They were happy that "the kind of guy we can communicate with" had been put in place to "listen to reason."[12]

Certainly in the prevailing climate, the business version of "reason" was more attractive to the Trudeauites than it had ever been before. In the previous two years, three rival government plans for economic salvation had failed. Herb Gray's high-tech, industrial strategy approach was stillborn. Gordon Osbaldeston's resource-exporting alternative, based on government-targeted investment in energy megaprojects, had fallen victim to an unco-operative world commodities market, where prices had failed to rise as Osbaldeston's scenario had predicted. Faltering petroleum prices had also sealed the fate of the NEP, the boldest plan of all. Six & Five had been seen for what it was: a makeshift income-restraint program hyped into a grand crusade to convince voters that their government was taking action. Apart from this temporizing device, Ottawa appeared to have nothing more in the way of economic policy than the Bank of Canada's determination to throttle inflation.

It was the ideal opportunity for the corporate world to impose on the government the policy views it had been developing carefully for nearly a decade. As early as the mid-1970s, when economies all over the Western world were suffering the death throes of Keynesianism, and when GATT tariff reductions had left much of the Canadian market wide open to foreign competition, business as a collective had come to the conclusion that free enterprise could no longer thrive within a national framework. Its future depended not on resisting the forces of globalization but on adapting to them. Canada's proximity to the world's largest market meant its entrepreneurs would have to target particular niches so that the economies of specialization could be realized on a continental scale.

As Canadian businessmen developed their capital expansion programs continentally in accordance with this theory, they were disconcerted to find that Ottawa was reinforcing the boundaries of the Canadian state and attempting to bolster the vitality of the Canadian economic union by creating such pan-Canadian economic institutions as the CDC, FIRA, and Petro-Canada. The country's industries, which had developed in their infancy under the stimulus of the first National Policy of 1879 and matured under the second National Policy after World War II, now wanted to act in the wider world on their own. Having been dependent on government protection and support since Confederation, they now chafed at measures that got in the way of their continental aspirations and fretted about their inability to convey their dissatisfaction. Government seemed to them like an overbearing parent trying to keep them at home with bribes, admonitions, and incentives. Everywhere in industrialized countries, political structures had grown more complex as governments had become more involved in almost every facet of society. In Canada, the Pitfield system was a focus for businessmen's complaints that they could no longer express their views "one on one" to key governmental figures, as they had in the simpler days of C.D. Howe and Louis St. Laurent.

When these grievances were relayed to Pitfield himself in the 1970s by disaffected businessmen opportuning him at parties in the houses of his friends and relatives in Montreal and Toronto, he responded that if the message they were trying to convey was not getting through to the Trudeau government, it was their fault, not his system's. Their discordant views were being expressed as specific industries' narrow self-interests, and their manner of communicating them was so combative that the politicians tuned out. If you want to be heard, he told them, organize yourselves so that you speak with one voice, and a reasonable voice at that.[13]

The Business Council on National Issues was big capital's response. The country's major Canadian-owned and foreign-controlled businesses (including resource companies and the big banks), with an operational scope that was continental if not global, decided to band together. Taking as their model the Business Roundtable, which gave U.S. corporations a powerful voice in Washington, they coalesced 150 strong in an organization designed to develop a broad consensus on national issues. The avowed purpose of this new lobby group was to forge better connections with

Trudeau's elaborate government structure; its hope was to publicize effectively the need for a more highly concentrated capitalism in Canada.[14]

Working groups involving corporate CEOs were set up to develop policies, area by area, issue by issue, that expressed continental capital's program for the Canadian political economy. The impact of these ideas was heightened in the early 1980s when Thomas d'Aquino was named president and the BCNI's offices were moved from Toronto to Ottawa. A lawyer with European as well as Canadian experience, d'Aquino had spent three years as a special adviser in Trudeau's PMO before becoming a lobbyist for such clients as *Time* magazine. He knew Trudeau's Ottawa intimately and agreed with his employers entirely: the government had to be awakened to its statist delusions.

Under his shrewd management, the BCNI made efforts to avoid its American counterpart's crudely expressed neo-conservatism. Instead of attacking the unions, d'Aquino made a point of engaging labour leaders in discussions of BCNI positions, which were moderated in the process. Instead of denouncing social welfare holus-bolus, his organization took the centre-right position that Canada could no longer afford universal programs that paid bank presidents the same baby bonuses as single mothers on welfare. Those below the poverty line should be supported more generously, while those who did not need help could be cut out of welfare programs without hardship.[15]

The BCNI burnished its image by seeming to address the national interest in this and other subtle ways, such as proposing reforms to make the parliamentary system more democratic. It was a sophisticated strategy to present a complete agenda for government action, developed in a low-key, non-confrontational – i.e., very Canadian – manner. "We want to be your partners," was the BCNI's message to the Liberal government. "This is the consensus you urged us to develop, and now we want to share it with you." And share they did. In dozens of meetings arranged with heavy hitters in high places, from the prime minister and key members of his cabinet to senior officials in the state apparatus, the BCNI persistently purveyed its positions, its solutions, its advice. By the autumn of 1982 the council's anti-interventionist, pro-business ideas had been articulated so often they appeared reassuringly coherent and highly credible to a government desperate for direction.[16]

D'Aquino, who had worked in the PMO when Lalonde was running it, invited several important CEOs to his house, including the chairman of the Royal Bank and the head of the Southam newspaper chain, to meet the new minister of finance over lunch. A few weeks later, an "economic statement" that Lalonde made in the House of Commons illustrated the BCNI's influence. The speech was a mini-budget, complete with revised estimates of the economy's projected growth (3 per cent) and the size of the government's deficit ("only" $22.3 billion) – estimates that business economists, such as William Mackness at the Bank of Nova Scotia, called "first class." More important, as far as the private sector was concerned, ten items still on the books from MacEachen's 1981 budget were, in the words of *The Globe and Mail*, "scrapped, deferred, reverted or modified." In short, Lalonde's speech "reflected a noteworthy change in the federal Government's attitude toward business."[17]

Not only was Lalonde demonstrably on side, as business liked to say, Trudeau himself was persuaded to take part in public acts of contrition and conversion. His PCO advisers had decided that spending in the country had veered out of control and Six & Five had not sufficed to bring it back on course. With inflationary expectations breeding inflationary behaviour, it was not enough for the federal government to mend its own profligate ways or to hold consultations with provincial and municipal politicians to persuade them to do likewise or to give tough signals to the private sector. (Striking B.C. dockworkers, who had been demanding 15-per-cent wage increases, had settled for 8 per cent once the government threatened to impose on them its rule-of-thumb 6 per cent.) Still needed was a sea change in the attitude of the citizenry as a whole. If the prime minister's charisma could be revved up, he might be able to achieve the required transformation of the public consciousness.

Trudeau agreed that solving the country's economic dilemmas demanded an act of national will if Canada was to escape the Scylla of rigid price controls and the Charybdis of drastic program cuts. In three speeches to the nation, broadcast on CBC-TV in late October, he preached a new economic Darwinism: "Our country is in trouble . . . Our challenge is to restore Canada's fitness to survive economically in a world where the survival of the fittest nations has become the rule of life . . . [in] a harder, leaner world, hungrier for customers, for investment, and for advantage." Trudeau looked acutely uncomfortable while delivering these homilies, his face wooden, his voice strained, his message as flat as his speech-writers' prose. He was admitting that his government's power to rescue the Canadian economy was limited and that Canadians needed to pull together in their time of troubles. This uninspired sermonizing was linked to the conciliatory attitude Trudeau's government had been obliged to assume vis-à-vis the United States.[18]

While Marc Lalonde was taking charge decisively in Finance, Allan MacEachen had been installing himself quietly at External Affairs, where an organizational uproar had been created by Michael Pitfield's latest reform, which had added the government's trade commissioner service to the department's responsibilities. The Canadian-American question continued to be the most troubling issue on External's agenda. By now exchanges between Washington and Ottawa had mellowed a little, and MacEachen, whose education had made him an Americanophile, was determined to improve them further.

His visit to Washington in September 1981 and his budget two months later had included important signals to Washington that American concerns were being heeded in Ottawa. Far from being mollified, William Brock, the U.S. trade representative, fired off the Reagan administration's umpteenth imperious letter to the Canadian government, setting out dozens of changes that still had to be made in both FIRA and the NEP for these programs to be acceptable to imperial Washington. Officials in Ottawa, who believed they had gone more than the extra mile to appease the American bullies, were appalled. Allan Gotlieb, who was just beginning his seven-year stint as Canadian ambassador to the United States at the time, put his name to a strong diplomatic retort that, translated into plain English, meant, Quit trying to strong-arm us. If you don't like what we're doing, take us to Geneva with a formal complaint, which can be dealt with by the GATT's dispute settlement mechanisms. [19]

This burst of Canadian self-assertion cleared the air. Throughout 1982 the atmosphere improved further. Myer Rashish was eased out of the State Department, where he was thought to be too intemperate in his dealings with Canada. When Alexander Haig's much-repeated threat to resign as secretary of state was finally accepted by President Reagan on June 25, George Shultz took his place. Shultz brought to the administration a rare familiarity with Canada. He had first gained insight into the Canadian economy and its importance to the United States through a study of U.S. resource needs conducted for President Nixon in 1970, and had come to know the country even better as president of the Bechtel Group, a giant engineering firm with a dominant position in the Canadian market. He was on familiar terms with important Canadian business figures, including John Turner, whom he had asked to write a position paper for the Republican campaign in 1980 and had subsequently invited onto Bechtel's board of directors. Best of all, Shultz had studied economics at the Massachusetts Institute of Technology at the same time as MacEachen. Much was made in the media of their rapport as alumni of that institution, especially since it was soon obvious they had more in common than nostalgia. They were both strong-minded, able, and given to long silences and laconic statements. They both wanted to deal expeditiously with the many problems generated by the world's largest trading relationship. [20]

In the aftermath of the aggressive bullying Canada had suffered in 1981, the bilateral issues to be resolved were legion. They ranged from large (White House intractability on acid rain, the U.S. moratorium on issuing licences to Canadian trucking firms, continuing

U.S. pressure to remove the "back-in" from the NEP); through medium-sized (U.S. anger at legislation that discouraged Canadian businesses from buying ads on border-town television stations); to small (province-state co-operation in fighting forest fires, the claim by members of Congress that Canada was unfairly subsidizing the successful bid by the Quebec firm Bombardier to build subway cars for New York City). Shultz signalled his approach by making his first official visit abroad to Ottawa, where he and MacEachen agreed to meet on a quarterly basis.[21]

Trudeau was brought into MacEachen's calm-the-Yanks effort when he gave a series of interviews to important American journalists, notably James Reston of *The New York Times*, and actively participated in a visitation to Ottawa by a score of important senior executives from major American corporations. Arranged by a continentalist business group called the Niagara Institute under the aegis of Donald Macdonald, the former finance minister, this was a spectacular communications exercise aimed at showing American businessmen that Canada had not turned into the Cuba of the North and that Trudeau was no Castro. In his session with the executives, the prime minister assured them that he himself had never been an economic nationalist. He distanced himself from his government's nationalist actions by saying they had been forced on him by the Ontario Liberals in his caucus. These efforts at improving the optics went so well that the American ambassador, Paul Heron Robinson, Jr., was soon able to assure a black-tie audience in his home town of Chicago that FIRA was a lapdog and the situation in Ottawa was back under control.[22]

It was a curiosity of the federal Liberals' predicament in the early autumn of 1982 that while Lalonde and MacEachen were making dramatic personal recoveries in their new portfolios, the regime's chief civil servant, Michael Pitfield – who presumably acted only at the bidding of his political masters – continued to be scapegoated for the government's ills. Vilification of Pitfield, which had been rife for years, had grown markedly worse during the MacEachen-Stewart budget brouhaha. After he played a prominent part in the constitutional patriation ceremonies in April 1982 – looking wan in the spring light as he punctiliously presented documents to the Queen at the signing on Parliament Hill – speculation that he would soon be giving up his onerous job had become frenzied.

Every aspect of Pitfield's life was scrutinized by journalists trying to determine when he would resign. His wife's casual remarks made at the tables of close friends were reported in newspaper columns; his facial tics at cabinet committee meetings were analysed on radio shows. Would he go back to Harvard where he had been lecturing when Trudeau recalled him to Ottawa at the Restoration? Or would he return to Montreal to practise law? Perhaps he would have the temerity to engineer an appointment for himself as an ambassador or as head of a Crown corporation? Where, oh where, would Pitfield land?

Conjecture about Pitfield's future was almost invariably linked with rumours about Trudeau's departure from office – the assumption being that the two men would leave their jobs at the same time – and was marked by a pervasive, poisonous animosity. In the little world of the capital, errors made by Lalonde and MacEachen were forgiven readily. Their behaviour was condoned partly because they had struggled mightily against socio-economic odds to achieve positions of power and because they had offered themselves for election, repeatedly risking rejection by the voters and forgoing large salaries in the private sector. But Pitfield, who was seen as having been wafted into high places on wings of privilege and to have been protected in his job because of his friendship with the prime minister, was the target of a visceral hostility that loaded onto him responsibility for ills of far greater magnitude than any one civil servant, however powerful, could possibly have created.

Pitfield was being treated as the personification of all that had gone wrong with government in the Trudeau era and blamed for the arrogance, extravagance, impracticality, and rampant statism that were now seen to be its hallmarks. Outside the PMO/PCO where his ideas held sway, and the farther shores of academe where public administration specialists analysed the inner workings of government, Pitfield was without advocates. Cabinet ministers readily expressed dislike for the systemic reforms he had brought about in Ottawa, and so did other members of the Liberal caucus, the opposition parties, and many of his peers in the public service. It was as though the political class were projecting onto a single man their hostility towards a government that was in deeper trouble than any of the discontented could bear to admit or knew how to fix. It was far easier to sum up complex problems by saying, "Pitfield is a disaster. Pitfield must go."

This situation both puzzled and pained the clerk, since he saw himself as having done exemplary duty in the service of his country at considerable financial and emotional cost. Against the wishes of his family, he had decided not to practise law or go into the Montreal financial world, where the Pitfield name was well known and his own prospects bright. Instead, he had resolved when he was barely twenty to "help save Canada" by becoming a professional administrator in Ottawa – an aspiration that was expressed by many young men of his generation, though few carried it out with as much fervour as he and none with as much success.

For Pitfield, his friendship with the prime minister was a non-issue. He had continued to see himself as non-partisan, a public servant devoted to the public interest. When Joe Clark dismissed him from his job in 1979, he was devastated. He withdrew to Harvard hoping to make a second career as an academic expert on government procedures. It was this role he saw himself as playing when various Liberals – including Michael Kirby, Marc Lalonde, and Pierre Trudeau himself – had sought his advice during the Liberals' period in opposition. And when Trudeau asked him to return to Ottawa as his clerk in early 1980, Pitfield claimed he "wasn't wildly keen on the idea." He had understandable misgivings about returning to what could only be a temporary perch since Trudeau was unlikely to contest another election. He felt his dismissal by the

Conservatives – not his own behaviour while performing his job as clerk – had "politicized" him, so that he had no long-term future in his "beloved public service."[23]

But because Trudeau wanted to continue using the cabinet committee system – in its Mach II variant as modified by Pitfield in 1979 and road-tested under the Tories – he wanted it run by the man who knew it best. Pitfield realized, "I would have to come back . . . because of the constitution's importance to Canada and because I was asked. It wasn't for my career."[24]

Ever since his return, Pitfield had been sensitive to the Ottawa animus against him. He occasionally told PCO officials, in self-indulgent monologues he delivered like some overwrought professor departing from his lecture notes, that he did not intend to stay long enough to be fired again. Some of his listeners were heartened by this news and began to wonder how long they would have to endure the administration of a man who remained as inadequate at two of his job's three functions (managing the civil service and servicing the cabinet) as he was indispensable in the third (acting as the prime minister's deputy).

As Trudeau's chief adviser on governmental matters, Pitfield had amply justified the prime minister's confidence. He had created a system that was tailored to the personality of an unusual politician. Trudeau preferred to deal with problems on paper rather than in personal encounters, where he would have to cope with human tensions and conflicts. He could annotate and assimilate banker's boxes full of documents overnight, and handle masterfully in cabinet next day discussions of the complex issues with which they were concerned. A system that required long-term priorities to be set at biannual ministerial think-ins, that restored Finance's power to discipline department spending, that obliged departmental proposals to be scrutinized by a central agency before getting cabinet approval, that delegated run-of-the-mill policy problems to cabinet committees for resolution – all in order to let the prime minister's own inner cabinet, the Priorities and Planning Committee, deal with the two or three burning issues of the day – was a system that was well suited to the cerebral Trudeau with his lawyerly capacity to compartmentalize problems and master briefs. [25]

Pitfield's wizardry at managing the extraordinary intricacies of his planning system in Trudeau's interest and his remarkable capacity for strategic political thinking were much admired within the PMO/PCO. James Coutts, Michael Kirby, and Tom Axworthy, who worked with him closely, saw him as brilliant, informed, and devoted to Canada – by which they meant Trudeau's federalist cause. [26]

But what pleased Trudeau's in-group rankled with cabinet. The new "envelope" system, the current manifestation of the Pitfield-style rationalism in government, had been a focus for ministerial bitching ever since it was introduced in 1979. Designed to control spending by tying expenditure decisions to policy-making, it forced ministers to fight one another for their department's share of a fixed envelope of funds. They lost faith in the goal of collective decision-making, especially when severe budgetary constraints scotched the new projects on which they had pinned their own political prospects. In frustrating their efforts to create new programs, the envelope system was proving its effectiveness – but further increasing Pitfield's unpopularity. For Gerald Regan, who as premier of Nova Scotia had been used to a much simpler governmental structure, the Pitfield system was an "unmitigated disaster" that used up intolerable amounts of scarce ministerial time. Far from having recaptured decision-making power for the elected, it caused most ministers to feel they were in an uphill battle against central-agency bureaucrats who could block ministerial initiatives they disliked. [27]

Pitfield was also faulted by some ministers because he had never managed to convince them that he was meeting their needs for bureaucratic support half so well as he was tending to those of the prime minister. When the Newfoundland MP William Rompkey was newly appointed to cabinet as minister of revenue, he felt disempowered by his deputy, who ignored his instructions and carried on as though he, not Rompkey, were in charge. Rompkey complained to the PCO, but Michael Pitfield declined to take action. Rompkey's successor in Revenue, Pierre Bussières, was also unable to discipline the deputy and found that Trudeau supported Pitfield against him and in favour of the bureaucrat. (Lloyd Axworthy's aggressive response to similar situations was more effective. He bypassed obstruction from senior bureaucrats by seconding their immediate subordinates to his personal staff and ordering them to pursue his objectives.)[28]

Senior bureaucrats were even less enthusiastic about Pitfield in his role as personnel manager of the upper civil service, the clerk's third traditional function. Deputies complained that Pitfield appointed them to a department without giving proper guidance about government objectives, then harangued them later for failing to accomplish some specific task they had never been assigned. They found that Pitfield's handling of personnel appointments created a we-versus-they atmosphere. Those getting the best jobs were generally drawn from the central agencies, where Pitfield developed pets whose careers he boosted at the expense of officials who had only line-department experience.

Pitfield's manner did little to appease his detractors. Essentially shy, he was always uncertain in groups. He had been isolated from his peers in childhood by his precocity (he was ready for college at the age of fourteen) and alienated from his government colleagues in early adulthood because of his social connections. (As a young public servant in the 1960s, Pitfield was such an inveterate name-dropper that it was not uncommon for him to quote in a single conversation remarks made to him by Averell Harriman, Walter Lippmann, Duff Cooper, Henrietta Lodge, and his uncle, Senator Hartland Molson.) During his tenure as clerk, his introversion was perceived as arrogant and devious. He rarely went out to parties in a city where business was often done over drinks. He was deliberately excluded from the Five Lakes Fishing Club, the mandarinate retreat in the Gatineau. He was notorious for delegating the same task to several underlings in what was seen as a desire to create rivalries among them, and for sequestering himself in his office where his secretary served Earl Grey tea in bone china to the favoured few. Douglas Hartle, an economist who had served at the Treasury Board, saw him as "an inveterate manipulator, always jockeying for advantage."[29]

The deputies resented the interminable meetings required by the envelope system fully as much as their political masters. Long-smouldering anger at the clerk was exacerbated by the two new ministries of state. Gordon Osbaldeston of the Ministry of State for Economic Development and Gordon Smith of the Ministry of State for Social Development wrote patronizing critiques of the departmental documents produced by deputies under their purview "as though [we] were lowly assistant deputy ministers," as one of them complained. Having to spend up to twelve hours a week at as many as five mirror-committee meetings sapped their energies. Donald Tansley, the deputy in Fisheries, received 18.5 kilograms of material for one week's meetings, most of it the night before it was to be discussed. The time expended on this co-ordinating activity interfered with their main job of managing their departments, which was taxing enough in itself.[30]

When Osbaldeston appropriated De Bané's proposal from the summer of 1981 and persuaded Pitfield to expand his ministry of state's powers and to introduce a new category of senior bureaucrats, the Federal Economic Development Coordinators, or "Fedsies," who were charged with representing the federal government in provincial capitals, his bureaucratic colleagues were dismayed. Even in normal times, it would have taken at least a year to work out the transfers of personnel and redefinitions of function this reorganization demanded. But the trauma induced by the recession, the MacEachen budget, and the sense that the Trudeau government's days were numbered kept Ottawa in a chronic state of high stress, ill suited to major structural adjustments.

Years after he left the PCO, Michael Pitfield asked an interviewer why he thought Canadian public servants had lost a sense of the national interest. The question was revelatory of the former clerk's disinclination to acknowledge responsibility for what had happened to the bureaucracy during the decade and a half when he and Trudeau had indulged their infatuation with cybernetics. The massive expansion in the ranks required to introduce new programs, staff new departments, and co-ordinate their operation had changed the nature of the federal bureaucracy. The feeling of belonging to a select community committed to the national interest that inspired the old mandarinate had vanished. Senior personnel were circulated at an unprecedented rate without having time to master any dossier. Officials found themselves appointed as deputies in departments where they had never served, only to be moved on in a year or two to other responsibilities. Not unnaturally, they responded to the system's imperatives in terms of their own needs. "You did what you could," one reflected later. "You knew you wouldn't solve much, but the better you used the system, the more you were personally rewarded."[31]

Old Ottawa hands such as the crusty Eugene Forsey bemoaned the "exaltation of management" during the Pitfield era at the cost of a national perspective. "U.S. business-school whiz kids came in and reorganized departments, and then moved on. The Justice Department hired lawyers who were ignorant of Canada's constitutional history," he said. Most state managers agreed that they had no collective agenda and considered it small wonder that Pitfield's system, which gave priority to process over policy, had been taken over by careerists without an overarching view of the national interest.[32]

Pitfield remained the guardian of Trudeau's door, constantly interpreting his master's wishes, while no one knew for sure whether "The prime minister wants . . ." really expressed the desires of Trudeau or of Pitfield himself. It was as though Pitfield and Trudeau in concert had produced another oligarchy instead of a greater democracy, one in which the prime minister's power – along with that of the central agencies where Pitfield presided as clerk – was enhanced at the expense of the elected ministers and their deputies in the line departments that worked directly with the public. The two men had become inextricably identified with each other, with the revamped governmental system, and with the widely held notion that its high-handed rationalism had produced an irrationally complex process.[33]

On October 26, 1982, Trudeau's office issued a surprise statement: Michael Pitfield was to be replaced as clerk of the Privy Council and secretary to the cabinet by Gordon Osbaldeston. Ottawa was amazed. Trudeau had given no sign that his own departure was imminent. And even more bewildering, when he was questioned in the Commons, he expressed little regret at the departure of his loyalist of twenty-five years' standing and made no mention of another assignment for him. Was Trudeau fed up with the organizational schemes of his clerk? Or with the emotionalism that Pitfield could no longer contain? Was Pitfield jumping from the apex of power without having prepared a landing?

Only PMO/PCO insiders knew that Trudeau and Pitfield had come up with the ideal job for the retiring clerk. Ever since the Restoration, the Trudeauites had been talking about the need for a new agenda for Canada once their immediate goals had been accomplished. They had agreed that a royal commission on Canada's future would be a good way to provoke a national debate, stimulate new thinking, and possibly attract a new team of politicians and policy-makers to the Liberal Party, in the way that Walter Gordon's royal commission on Canada's economic prospects in the 1950s had sparked some of the ideas and recruited some of the talent that drove the Pearsonian Liberals in the 1960s.

In the late summer of 1982, it was decided that the time to establish this royal commission was ripe, and that Pitfield had the ideal qualifications to head it. But no sooner had Pitfield made plans to leave the PCO in order to set up the commission than *Saturday Night* published a cover story on him that, while far gentler in its assessment of his performance and personality than most of his critics, nevertheless exposed to public view the less than exemplary record of his governmental system. In the context of the anti-Pitfield feel-ings that pervaded the bureaucracy and the cabinet, this article was the final blow to Pitfield's hopes. "I would have given my right arm to do [the royal commissioner's job]," Pitfield said eight years later. "But the more I talked to people, the more I concluded I did not have the credibility."[34]

On November 5, 1982, the task of chairman of the Royal Com-mission on the Economic Union and Development Prospects for Canada was bestowed on the Honourable Donald S. Macdonald. And on December 22, Peter Michael Pitfield was called to the Sen-ate of Canada. Still insisting on his non-partisanship, he entered the red chamber as an Independent.

# CHAPTER 11

# THE LAST LIBERAL OPTIMIST
# DEFENDS THE CAUSE

Unlike the newly minted Senator Pitfield, Tom Axworthy would never dream of describing himself as an Independent. Political neutrality in his eyes was an oxymoron: to be involved in public life meant being philosophically and emotionally engaged with a political party.

Axworthy had been grappling with the conundrums of Canadian Liberalism ever since he had written his MA thesis on the subject a dozen years before. When Jim Coutts charged him with the job of assessing the party's prospects in the late 1970s, he had produced the memo suggesting that the Liberals become more interventionist and more nationalist. Even after the third National Policy legislation that resulted had come to grief, Axworthy continued to believe that sticking to progressive principles was the only way for the Liberals to recover their popularity. "Liberals are on the run everywhere in the world," he was given to saying with surprising good cheer. "We're swimming against a right-wing tide." [1]

"Everywhere in the world" was hardly an exaggeration when it came to liberalism's vicissitudes. Mackenzie King's great Liberal balancing act – sustaining a belief in free enterprise while using government programs to redress inequities created by capitalism – was a feat of accommodation that had proven impossible for British Liberals, who had not been able to form a government for more than sixty years. It had never even been attempted under a Liberal banner in Europe, where Liberal parties remained narrowly bourgeois in their membership and largely *laissez-faire* in their ideology, leaning towards the anti-statist ideas of Friedrich von Hayek and playing an ambivalent role in the struggle for improved working conditions and state-provided educational and medical services. Conservative in economic affairs but progressive in their commitment to civil liberties, Old World Liberals distrusted policies that smacked of collectivism, centralism, or statism. At meetings of the Liberal International, their umbrella organization, they welcomed participation by their successful Canadian cousins, although in the Trudeau era they considered them to be covert social democrats rather than proper liberals. [2]

By 1982, when the Trudeauites were retreating from their bold left-liberal venture, there was even less comfort to be found in the plight of European social democrats. Left-leaning parties, whatever their label, were running into serious trouble in Scandinavia and elsewhere. The hard-line socialist François Mitterrand had managed to capture the presidency of France in 1981. But his enthusiastic pro-labour agenda and splurge of nationalizations had caused such a flight of capital that he was forced to adopt economic orthodoxies that made him appear more conservative than Helmut Schmidt, his social-democratic counterpart in West Germany, whose days in government were numbered. [3]

The important pressures on Canadian Liberalism in the early 1980s came not from the beleaguered European left but from the resurgent right in the United Kingdom and the United States. Margaret Thatcher's fierce attack on the very idea of a benevolent state had been unrelenting since her election in 1979. In her open contempt for "wets" who embraced the ideological middle, the fiercely Conservative Thatcher had heartened the zealots of the American right, who had been gaining ground on their liberal enemies for a decade. The message that helped rally Americans to Ronald Reagan's extremism was direct: if the Brits can accept a prime minister who preaches the survival of the fittest, surely the American people are ready to forsake the bromides of Rooseveltian interventionism and embrace once more the values of unreconstructed free enterprise.[4]

The crisis of the American imperium had undermined the incantatory power of even the most sacred of liberal talismans. Mainstream Democrats had no answers to the inflation generated by their Keynesianism, the alienation caused by their Vietnam adventurism, or the legislative paralysis produced by their factionalism. Used admiringly for decades to describe American political culture, the very word "liberal" had become a pejorative by the end of the Carter presidency – often embellished by descriptive phrases such as "lily-livered," "soft-on-communism," or "tax-and-spend," implying that liberals were unpatriotic, decadent, and dependent for re-election on ruinous government hand-outs.[5]

The l-word had also taken on negative connotations in the universities, where political philosophers on both the left and the right were blaming on liberalism most of the social evils – including recurrent anti-Semitism – that had developed in the Atlantic world since the Enlightenment. Social theorists criticized the decline of self-reliance and the excesses of state meddling for producing a culture of narcissism. Liberalism was being described as an individualism so perverted by consumerism that families were losing their values, universities their integrity, communities their cohesion, politics its dignity, and society its stability.[6]

In Canada, by way of contrast, liberalism continued to enjoy a more positive reputation. Nowhere in the world had it been so enduringly successful or so broadly embraced. For almost ninety years, its tenets had defined the country's public philosophy by containing the tensions between its capitalist and humanist variants. As the decades of Liberal dominance piled up, conservatives and socialists alike had been forced to modify their principles and change their names – to *Progressive* Conservatives and *New* Democrats – in order to survive by poaching on liberal territory.[7]

Under Mackenzie King and his hand-picked successors, St. Laurent and Pearson, the two main strains of liberal thought had been mirrored in the party's business and interventionist factions. The dialectic between them had generated an internal dynamic that energized the party for decades and was the basis of its proud centrism. By choosing Trudeau, with his multicultural federalist fervour, as their leader at the very moment when liberalism began to decline elsewhere, Canadian Liberalism had injected itself with a new ideological vitality that extended its political hegemony into the next decade.

In his first years in office Trudeau had shown himself to be fully as supportive of free enterprise as his predecessors. But his marked lack of interest in the business community – based on disdain for its intellectual and ethical standards rather than disagreement with its basic ideology – made it appear to some observers that the Liberal Party had veered dramatically to the left. Paradoxically, it was argued elsewhere that the party's public support declined because the Liberal lurch was not nearly leftward enough. When the postwar Keynesian consensus was shattered by monetarism and the imposition of wage and price controls in the mid-1970s, the Trudeau government's failure to countervail these shifts to the right by replacing the patchwork social-security system with a comprehensive guaranteed annual income eroded its left-of-centre constituency.[8]

Liberalism's renewed popularity in the first eighteen months of the Restoration – achieved through Trudeau's defeat of the separatists in the Quebec referendum, the entrenchment of his eminently liberal charter of rights and freedoms in the constitution, and the attempted Canadianization of the energy industry – was startlingly short-lived. The MacEachen-Stewart budget alienated upper-income, better-educated Canadians, and the ensuing severe recession shattered the trust of middle- and lower-income citizens. In the wake of these misfortunes, it was apparent that with their preference for action and confrontation over compromise and consensus, the born-again Trudeauites had abandoned their party's original governing formula. As a result they were in danger of losing their electoral alliance – an impending disaster that weighed heavily on the spirits of the normally ebullient Tom Axworthy in the autumn of 1982.[9]

By then, Axworthy had served as Trudeau's principal secretary for over a year, having inherited the job when Coutts left the PMO for his electoral gambol in the summer of 1981. It was an uncomfortable role in an uncomfortable time. In Coutts's scheme of things, Axworthy was very much a junior player, designated to serve as the Toronto Liberals' duty officer in the PMO while Coutts was building his leadership momentum during the brief period Trudeau was expected to remain in office. After the Spadina by-election loss, a very different dynamic was established. It was Jim Coutts who was marooned in Toronto most of the week. And it was Tom Axworthy who was advising the prime minister daily on political matters great and small.

As the first of Trudeau's principal secretaries who had come up through the ranks of the PMO, Axworthy had definite ideas on how the job should be handled that differed from those of his strongman precursors, Lalonde and Coutts. In Axworthy's view, the Trudeau PMO in its first configuration under Lalonde had been all policy and no politics, an agency run by a disciplinarian given to setting governmental priorities without concern for building coalitions in the electorate. Under Coutts's direction from 1975 to 1981, it had suffered from the converse: too much politics and too little policy, with considerations of substance submerged by a concerted effort to control the government's media image and to manipulate electoral consent. (In the period between Lalonde's departure in 1972 and Coutts's arrival in 1975, the PMO had been run on an *ad hoc* basis, with no one staying long enough in the principal secretary's job to leave a lasting mark.)[10]

Axworthy believed that policy and politics were interdependent, and he took on the principal secretary's job determined to run a tighter, happier PMO. His experience in hiring and directing policy-makers in the Leader of the Opposition's Office in 1979 had demonstrated to him how effective a small team could be. As associate principal secretary in the first eighteen months of the Restoration, he had urged Coutts to reduce the size of the PMO and sharpen its focus. The idea was that the office would become a "political central agency," imposing an explicitly partisan direction on the bureaucratic process through its interaction with the PCO and making sure at the same time that connections between the prime minister and the Liberal Party were frequent and productive. The first of these goals had been realized before Coutts relinquished the job. But the second remained Axworthy's major challenge. [11]

He was quick to admit that the Liberal Party was in sorry shape organizationally as well as ideologically despite its 1980 victory. The government's recent sharp decline in the polls was only the outward and visible sign of the party's inner decay. The regional alliances that Mackenzie King had built up with painstaking calculation had begun to disintegrate in the 1950s as the political dynamic of Canada changed. With the western provinces dead set against them after a brief upsurge in support in 1968, Liberals in the Trudeau era could be sure only of their fortress in Quebec. Their historic vote in the Atlantic region, where a stable population still adhered to inherited political loyalties, now depended more on the dispensation of government largesse than on ideological commitment. Gaining federal power meant holding on to Quebec by fair means or foul and continually wooing the volatile voters of Ontario, where predetermined party affiliations had almost disappeared because of massive immigration, galloping suburbanization, and the disruptive effect on the collective memory of the electronic media's relentless hyping of the crises of the moment to the exclusion of the meaning of the Canadian past. [12]

Even in its basic role as a fundraising and vote-garnering machine, the party was functioning poorly. The Liberals had fallen behind both the Tories and the New Democrats financially because of their surprising inability to exploit the comprehensive election-expenses reforms they had introduced in 1974. Long gone were the days when a Liberal lawyer with a partnership in a Bay Street firm and a seat in the Senate could raise the bulk of a campaign budget – and nurture the party's role as a vital link between business and government at the same time – with a dozen phone calls and a few double Scotches in clubland. In recent years, the Tories had become twice as successful as the Liberals at extracting money from big business. Far more galling to progressive Liberals, who thought of themselves as belonging to a reform-minded party responsive to the needs of ordinary people, the Conservatives were also besting them at soliciting donations from the general public through direct-mail techniques they had learned from the Republicans. With the NDP still solidly in command of whatever could be raised from committed social democrats, the once-mighty Government Party was unable to raise enough money to pay its operating expenses and discharge its election debts. [13]

Faced with these realities, Liberal careerists – and at this point in the waning Trudeau era they outnumbered the party's ideologues by far – were beginning to consider a horrifying possibility: could it be that they belonged to a party of losers? Young idealists were attracted to the NDP. Young comers aspiring to be part of the governing class were joining the Tories if they were politically ambitious, or provincial governments if they were interested in public administration. With the Liberals shut out of office in every province and the federal party in decline, the lawyers, lobbyists, accountants, architects, and advertising men who had supported it in the hope that a contract or a Senate seat would ultimately come their way were aghast. (Although patronage was a self-defeating practice, draining the party of its political energy as its most talented adherents were appointed to the bench or to the boards of public corporations, pressure from the party's hopeful activists to maintain this reward system had stymied efforts to reform government appointment procedures for decades.)

Among Liberals still preoccupied more with principles and policy than with power and patronage, there was deep anxiety that the party had degenerated into little more than a one-man magic show. "After Trudeau, what?" was the question Liberals kept asking themselves. "What will we stand for once *he* is gone?" Trudeau's intellectual dominance had suffocated creativity in party ranks for more than a decade. Liberals of long standing believed that new thinking about the party's direction would be futile until he finally announced his retirement and the renewal process could begin.[14]

All these woes, clearly evident in 1979 but camouflaged briefly by the early triumphs of the Restoration, had re-emerged in a more noxious form when the fortunes of the fourth Trudeau ministry went into reverse just as Axworthy replaced Coutts in the PMO. Within a few weeks of his appointment, Axworthy commented laconically, "So far I find the job a delight – we have lost two by-elections, dropped several points in the Gallup, and have an economic crisis on our hands. However, the only way to go is up!" A year later, it was alarmingly evident that the only way his party was heading was further down – to 28 per cent in the polls, its lowest rating in the post-war period. The PMO was once more the symbolic focus for party grievances, as it had been under Coutts's direction in the late 1970s, and Axworthy was struggling valiantly to cope. He knew when he took the job that a different name on the principal secretary's door would not in itself alleviate festering resentments in both the parliamentary and the extra-parliamentary wings of the party. But true to his nature as a doer, he was trying energetically to ameliorate the situation.[15]

Individual Liberals' problems varied considerably, depending on where they stood in the party hierarchy. Among the rank and file across the country, alienation was intense and in need of concerted attention. On Parliament Hill, where the backbenchers felt condemned to second-class status, morale was mixed but manageable. In the Privy Council chamber, the joy of power still held most cabinet ministers in its embrace, however vociferously they might complain about their lot, particularly the demands made on their time by endless meetings.

Only ministers important enough to be appointed to the key

Priorities and Planning Committee of cabinet, chaired by the prime minister, relished going to such meetings since P&P was "where all the real action takes place," with ministers sharing in the collegiality of power and "receiving the deepest briefings and the most thorough discussions." Collegiality was less common elsewhere, even on the two super-committees of the envelope system. In the Committee on Social Development, ministers ganged up on the chair, Jean Chrétien, who was seen as a policeman blocking the line departments' schemes on behalf of the central-agency bureaucrats. Similarly, when Don Johnston took over direction of the Committee on Economic and Regional Development from Bud Olson in 1982, the atmosphere quickly became conflictual. Like Olson, Johnston was deeply committed to restraining government spending. But unlike him, he had leadership ambitions, which created suspicions of mixed motivations and aggravated turf wars between Lloyd Axworthy and Ed Lumley over who would get to spend the larger share of the fixed envelope.[16]

That such strains were not in evidence at P&P's deliberations had to be credited to Pierre Trudeau. He had given up running cabinet meetings in the mode of a professor more interested in theoretical discussions than practical decision-making, as the Six & Five exercise had proven. After fourteen years as chief executive of the Government of Canada, Trudeau had become adept at managing his colleagues. According to Ed Lumley, his minister of international trade, he was quite simply the "best man I ever worked for in my life" because he believed "in giving freedom to people, and if you knew your stuff, and could sell your case on the basis of logic, he supported you loyally." As an example, Lumley recalled that "he stood behind me when I was stalling the importing of Japanese cars," even though this protectionist action offended his liberal principles.[17]

At both P&P meetings and the weekly sessions of full cabinet, Trudeau was in complete control of the agenda and generally unchallenged by powerful personalities with dissenting views. The giants of the past had departed, opponents and allies alike. Paul Hellyer, Eric Kierans, and Paul Martin, who had opposed him for the leadership in 1968, had been shunted aside years before. Bud Drury, Otto Lang, Donald Macdonald, Jean Marchand, Gérard Pelletier, Mitchell Sharp, and John Turner, mainstays of his early years in office, had withdrawn. The long-serving Toronto ministers Barney Danson and Alastair Gillespie, who had close connections with the business community, had returned to the private sector. Of the surviving veterans – Jean Chrétien, Marc Lalonde, Allan MacEachen, and André Ouellet – only Lalonde would stand up to Trudeau, but he did so judiciously and from the acknowledged position of total loyalty.

However experienced they were at cabinet discussions, ministers had to be on their toes to contend with Trudeau's superior capacity to master background material and his complete intolerance of incompetence. Apart from Lalonde and MacEachen, whose interventions Trudeau listened to with respect, and Gene Whelan and Monique Bégin, whose interruptions he indulged because of their shared role as the cabinet's social conscience, Trudeau gave no quarter in the rigour of his response to ministers. He pounced on the slightest error and insisted on making a disciplined, productive meeting out of every cabinet gathering. If Jean Chrétien started one of his folksy rambles, Trudeau would shut him up in mid-sentence. Mark MacGuigan, who lacked confidence rather than experience or intelligence, could be completely thrown by one prime ministerial probe. Lloyd Axworthy could hold his own with Trudeau, armed with his Princeton degree, his populist pol's up-to-date information about the west, and the toughness he had gained as a scrapper in the Manitoba legislature. But even he was wary of crossing Trudeau and planned his interventions with care.[18]

Those ministers who were neither on P&P nor otherwise designated as favourites of the prime minister took part sparingly in the cabinet's major discussions. Jean-Luc Pepin and Francis Fox, both men of superior ability, stuck to their departmental fiefdoms, having run afoul of Trudeau in the 1970s – Pepin because of his contrary constitutional views and Fox because of a scandal that had caused him to resign from cabinet.

Trudeau was able to tolerate considerable intercollegial disagreement within the Privy Council chamber, but his hypersensitivity to the least hint of overt disloyalty to his leadership remained. After Serge Joyal and Monique Bégin broke cabinet solidarity in early 1982 by making public, along with eight other Montreal MPs who co-signed it, a letter calling for immediate job-creating measures of the kind the government had been resisting, Trudeau reprimanded them severely. He then stated coolly that instigators of any other such public criticism would be fired from their posts immediately. [19]

When Jim Fleming, the minister of state for multiculturalism, invited half a dozen colleagues to dinner later in the year to discuss collective resistance to the government's rightward turn, one of his guests' wives phoned Ilona Fleming to say how daring it was for her husband to host such a gathering. For the Flemings the implicit message was that, according to some unwritten code of behaviour, ministers were expected to "do their own thing and keep their heads down in order to stay out of trouble with the PMO." It may have been his audacity in convening a second such dinner that brought Fleming into disfavour with Trudeau, but the former broadcast journalist thought his transgressions were of a different order. [20]

As chair of the cabinet's communications committee, he was nominally in charge of the government's $60-million advertising budget. His view that ad agencies outside Toronto should be given a chance to compete for a share in this largesse was a direct threat to Keith Davey's power as intermediary between the government and a tight little group of agencies in Toronto (Vickers & Benson, Ronalds-Reynolds, and MacLaren) who had worked on the party's English-language advertising campaigns in every election since 1974 under the direction of the communications lawyer Jerry Grafstein. As a reward for their political support, it was understood that these agencies were entitled to the lion's share of federal advertising dollars, an arrangement that Fleming had the effrontery to question.

In another display of independence of mind, Fleming had publicly described Coutts's Spadina adventure as obscene.[21]

Whether or not Fleming's defiance of the Toronto insiders was the cause of his fall from grace – Davey dismissed him as a "big disappointment" and "not a team player" – his responsibilities steadily declined: loss of the chairmanship and membership on the communications committee, loss of his place on P&P, loss of membership in the caucus communications group. When he managed to waylay a discomfited Trudeau to ask him directly about his declining fortunes, the prime minister brushed him off by saying, "Trust me, Jim." This assurance was soon proven hollow when Fleming was replaced as minister of state for multiculturalism by David Collenette, a Toronto MP who also had a reputation for defying Coutts and Davey but who had protected his career prospects by working hard outside their bailiwick as deputy to the government House leader, Yvon Pinard.[22]

From his perch in the PMO, Tom Axworthy observed these manifestations of cabinet infighting with mixed feelings: he knew what was going on, but he had little capacity to affect it. It fell to him to tell Fleming he was being turfed out of cabinet – the kind of emotionally charged task Trudeau disliked – and to sound him out about whether he would accept a face-saving appointment to the Senate or the Canadian Radio-television and Telecommunications Commission, offers that Fleming refused. Otherwise, Axworthy had little direct contact with cabinet politics, except for briefing ministers on the public mood as interpreted by Martin Goldfarb or expounding on his own schemes for pulling the government out of its long slump in the polls – some of which involved reanimating the Liberal caucus.

From the beginning of his tenure as principal secretary, caucus morale had been one of Axworthy's primary concerns. After inviting backbenchers for weekly tea-and-empathy sessions in his office over a period of several months, it was clear to him that their feelings varied from a resigned recognition of the party's decline to a simmering frustration at the PMO's apparent inability to do anything about it. What most agitated the MPs – aside from chronic anxiety that they might not be re-elected – was their incapacity to affect government policy. Like the Canada they represented, they were more acute in their understanding of the political process and more demanding in their expectations of government than their counterparts of thirty years before. Many of them boasted post-graduate degrees and a few held doctorates from international institutions, educational qualifications that were far beyond those of the provincial lawyers and prosperous farmers who had crowded the Liberal backbenches in the St. Laurent era. As a cohort, they were more likely to belong to Amnesty International than to the Masonic Order, more apt to holiday in the Caribbean than at Sainte-Agathe.

Despite their greater worldliness, they were remarkably similar in gender, racial background, religious adherence, and social status to the complacent Liberals of earlier times. Most of them were male, upper-middle-class, Christian, and French or British in origin. (The Liberal caucus of the early 1980s included only three Jews and eleven women, compared with one and none in the early 1950s.) Dangerously few represented other ethnic groups, considering that the party counted on the votes of post-war immigrants from southern Europe, the Caribbean, and Asia. And despite their protestations to the contrary, the Trudeau MPs were just as bound by party discipline – just as docile, in other words – as their predecessors, who had been characterized by Trudeau as "trained donkeys."[23]

Most of the MPs of the 1980s had first run for office under Trudeau's banner, expecting to have a direct impact on government. Once elected, they had found that the bulk of their time was spent acting as unsung ombudsmen for their constituents, looking into immigration problems, disability pensions, passport difficulties, and a host of other concerns vital to voters but notably lacking in stimulus or glamour. Their involvement in the grander affairs of state amounted to little more than harried stints on Commons standing committees, where, under revised rules instituted in the 1970s, opposition MPs had plenty of leeway to criticize draft legislation but government backbenchers were forced – often reluctantly and with inadequate briefing – to defend cabinet proposals against partisan attack.[24]

A few, notably the diligent Herb Breau from Tracadie, New Brunswick, were able to make substantial contributions to public policy by chairing a Commons committee. But the prodigious effort required to produce a document as influential as Breau's much-quoted report on federal-provincial fiscal relations was regarded by many of his peers as wasted, since he had not been rewarded with a ministry. (The logic of regionalism dictated that Breau could not be given a portfolio as long as Roméo LeBlanc, Trudeau's former press secretary, represented francophone New Brunswick in the cabinet.)[25]

Marginalized in modern Ottawa's ponderous governmental system, backbenchers found that their only regular access to power occurred on Wednesday mornings, when they met in caucus with the full cabinet and the Liberal senators. Even then, they could expect to command the floor for only a few minutes each. Performing effectively was more difficult than ever at the calamity-clouded caucuses of 1982, which combined football-team morale-boosting with family-style group therapy, as the disaffected blew off steam and the anxious reported on their constituents' soured attitudes. Because they were able to "fan out on the weekends all over the country" and "speak to journalists, political organizers, provincial members, mayors, union leaders, and businessmen" – as one parliamentarian solemnly described his routine local intelligence-gathering – they believed their graphic views of the political realities were more compelling than the professional pollsters' impersonal statistics, which had displaced them as the eyes and ears of the Ottawa technostructure.[26]

Unlike Lalonde and Coutts, Axworthy was quick to acknowledge the validity of the MPs' claims. In his experience, the weekly caucus overview "was as good a reading [of public opinion] as you could get; it presaged what Goldfarb would tell us a month later." Because there were no bureaucrats present, no minutes taken, and no press releases issued, official Ottawa dismissed these weekly sessions as partisan hand-holding, a condescension that only deepened the MPs' frustration with their condition.[27]

Part of what sustained their commitment was the excitement of the trench warfare that had prevailed in the Commons since the Restoration. Bitter wrangling over the constitution's patriation had kept them fighting for the Liberal vision of Canada throughout 1980 and early 1981, when they were able to push the cabinet to extend the rights included in the draft charter. Then they had rallied to the defence of the National Energy Program against the stubbornly resistant Conservatives, who obstructed parliamentary business for sixteen days during the notorious division-bell-ringing episode of March 1981. Once that battle was won, they had endorsed the Six & Five exercise by publicizing the program in their regions, equipped like itinerant evangelists with uplifting material to bring Liberalism's new message to the masses.[28]

However lively and concerted these efforts had proven, the backbenchers knew that when it came to government action, they could only propose or oppose. It was the cabinet that disposed. Wednesday after Wednesday, once the MPs had had their say in caucus, ministers would put up a smooth defence of the policies under debate until the prime minister intervened, first among unequals, demonstrating his extraordinary ability to knit together the themes from the morning's discussions and extract from them a consensus defining the party's general will for that week.[29]

Trudeau's response to caucus discontent varied from bristling self-justification to an acceptance, almost Buddhist in its calm, of the impossibility of realizing the participatory ideal he had espoused in 1968. He believed he had done well by parliamentarians when he agreed early in his first ministry to provide technical and research resources designed to help them represent their voters more expeditiously and to engage more successfully with the complexity of the modern governmental process. Instead of working in cramped quarters and sharing one overworked secretary with another backbencher, MPs from all parties had the budget and space for two assistants and two secretaries each in Ottawa, as well as staff for their constituency offices and travel allowances to visit their ridings regularly. [30]

"I [also] made sure that the structures were there so that the caucus would be involved in . . . major decisions," Trudeau insisted, when reflecting on his contribution to parliamentary reform. As far as he was concerned, he had democratized caucus by giving up his prerogative as leader to appoint its committee chairmen in favour of having the MPs elect their own national, regional, or policy chairs.

"In response to complaints that, 'Geez, we hadn't been involved in a bill on such-and-such a subject, which was vital to the people of Toronto,'" he explained, "I would tell the caucus chairman, 'Okay, get out the statistics.' And he'd go back and find that the [relevant] cabinet document . . . verified that . . . there had been a caucus committee meeting on that particular subject, and it had been attended by perhaps nine members out of a hundred and forty . . . Then you'd have caucus members say, 'Well, yeah, but when you were meeting on . . . immigration, I was busy on another committee on finance or was active in the external affairs caucus consultative group.' . . . In response, I used to make a speech at least once every parliament saying: 'You can't bear all the problems on your shoulders. I can't as prime minister, either. I have to trust ministers in the cabinet committee on such-and-such to go through the details. I can't read all the documents and I can't attend all the cabinet committees. No more should you want to be present at every caucus subcommittee meeting . . . We're a party and there has to be a division of labour.'" [31]

Despite these exhortations, ambitious backbenchers continued to feel disgruntled by their inability to wield real power. This feeling was particularly prevalent among a younger group of talented and feisty Quebec MPs (including Rémi Bujold, Pierre Deniger, Dennis Dawson, Louis Duclos, and Jean Lapierre), whose hopes for political change and personal progress were blocked once Trudeau reappointed Marc Lalonde as the party boss in Quebec after the

1980 election, and the two men allotted the province's share of ministerial posts to old-guard MPs.[32]

Lalonde's dominance of the Quebec caucus had been supreme since he took over from Jean Marchand as the province's party boss in 1975. It derived as much from his implacable will as from his capacity to affect virtually any government decision in any area because of Trudeau's respect for his judgement. Showing himself as shrewd about the wielding of temporal power as any Jesuit, he controlled personnel and patronage in Quebec absolutely, from the selection of candidates and parliamentary secretaries to the allocation of government funds. Lalonde had pursued so effectively Jean Marchand's original strategy of promising federal regional-development funds to ridings held by the Liberals' opponents in order to seduce electors to vote *rouge* that by 1980, the party's enemies were all but wiped out when the Liberals won seventy-four of Quebec's seventy-five seats. With the province's representation larger than all the other regional caucuses combined, Lalonde could demand a lion's share of federal largesse. At regular Thursday-morning meetings of the Quebec ministers he presided over hotly contested discussions about new projects. Should there be a biotechnology research centre in Jean Chrétien's Saint-Maurice riding? A data processing plant in Pierre De Bané's Matapédia-Matane district? Few discussants escaped his probing questions or his pervasive scorn.[33]

In his treatment of individual backbenchers, Lalonde behaved with an authoritarianism that suppressed dissent – an attitude that suited those who were in politics for the perks, which Lalonde handed out on the basis of seniority and loyalty rather than competence or promise. Among the ambitious and the independent of mind, his message was as well understood as it was resented. "Sois belle et tais-toi!" was the formula for advancement: if you defied Lalonde you would wreck your career. Described behind his back as the whipping priest ("le père fouettard"), Lalonde treated MPs who had divergent ideas about what was good for Quebec – such as Louis Duclos, who opposed the government repeatedly during Trudeau's constitutional initiative in 1980 and 1981 – as though they were insufficiently devout acolytes who needed the threat of excommunication to keep them in line.[34]

By comparison, the anglophone regional caucuses had neither coherence nor clout. Herb Gray, the minister for Ontario, was rarely heeded by his province's MPs, partly because of his unassertive personality and partly because of the greater influence over personnel and patronage decisions of the Toronto backroom boys, who had privileged access to Trudeau, the ultimate dispenser of political favours. Lloyd Axworthy was seen as a strong regional minister because he was able to direct federal funds to Winnipeg. But because his Manitoba caucus had only two members – Robert Bockstael from francophone St. Boniface was the second – it had little impact on the party as a whole, particularly since the Liberals were shut out of the other western provinces electorally. Roméo LeBlanc had proven equally adept as a regional minister working the system on behalf of New Brunswick fishermen. Even after his shift from the fisheries portfolio to Public Works, he had retained his position as regional minister and was able to exploit the new federal economic development coordinator's office to influence other government departments in their spending.

But neither Axworthy, LeBlanc, nor Allan MacEachen, the third minister with a regional mission, could command a deeply rooted partisan organization linked to a provincial base. None of them was a regional baron in the manner of Jimmy Gardiner, King's unrepentantly partisan minister from Saskatchewan, who was committed to building the Liberal Party over the long haul. As political capos equating their regions' interests with their own, they did little to boost morale among Liberals outside their territories.[35]

At first, Tom Axworthy had tried to address the various causes of caucus alienation by arranging for MPs to lunch with Trudeau in small groups at 24 Sussex Drive. He was dismayed to find that the honour of breaking bread with the prime minister did not always soothe frustrations or end alienation. If a backbencher – particularly one who was intellectually acute, progressive, nationalistic, a Quebecker, or all four – used the occasion to issue a challenge on some issue or other, Trudeau's compulsive competitiveness would click into gear. Fixing his interlocutor with a sceptical eye, Trudeau would devastate his argument, sometimes energetically, sometimes lazily, depending on the mood of the hour and the gravity of the challenge. A favourite stratagem was to provoke a general argument by teasing out disagreements among the other guests and then to turn on the unhappy dissenter and say mockingly that the government could hardly comply with *his* views since they did not even represent a caucus consensus. [36]

Most MPs would retreat to their offices from these encounters realizing – once the glow brought on by good food, good drink, and an hour of power proximity had faded – that their impact on government policy was as slight as their hopes for advancement to cabinet. The realists took comfort from the reminder that their status in their ridings was considerable and their perks more than generous, ranging as they did from occasional junkets abroad to extraordinarily rich, fully indexed pensions. Full meals at $2.75 in the parliamentary restaurant, $1 haircuts, free VIA Rail and Air Canada passes, long-distance phone privileges, and French immersion courses were just a few tangible manifestations of the rich subculture they inhabited. Dramatic late-night sittings of the House, long-running poker games, insider gossip about their peers and their betters added to their self-esteem. Theirs was a pressured existence, with dozens of meetings to attend, an endless stream of importuning constituents to placate, and exhausting weekends spent travelling to their home territories and attending to community business. [37]

Camaraderie and partisan loyalty kept them going. Despite their disappointments, most backbenchers believed that Liberalism was a cause worth espousing and Trudeau a leader worth following. They respected him as much for his mastery of the power game as for the integrity of his vision, which they were called on to defend again and again in the Commons and in their constituencies. As one MP from a Toronto riding put it, "Trudeau's intelligence was the cement that held the parliamentary party together. He was a giant among pygmies." [38]

# CHAPTER 12

# The Grits Gather in Convention and Contention

Tom Axworthy's concerns about Liberalism and its discontents in the late autumn of 1982 extended beyond Parliament Hill across the country to the loose federation of ten provincial, two territorial, and 282 riding organizations that made up what he thought of as "the lay party." As a man who still believed that the participatory ideal Trudeau had conjured up in 1968 was feasible, Axworthy disagreed with the Coutts-and-Davey view of the party faithful as a bunch of amateurs who had to be stroked occasionally so they would work hard during election campaigns. For him, Liberal loyalists were a crucial political factor at every season of the electoral cycle. Axworthy had been soliciting new ideas from rank-and-file Liberals and liberal intellectuals for years, convinced that Liberalism could be renewed and party tensions assuaged by encouraging the Trudeau government to become more responsive to grass-roots thinking.[1]

During his long apprenticeship as an assistant to Coutts, he had made a point of attending party executive meetings in every province, adding Liberals from Ontario and the Maritimes to his network of contacts in the west. Since becoming principal secretary, he had kept in touch with his contacts by schmoozing with them on the phone regularly and seeing to it that they were invited periodically to grand events – state receptions in Ottawa, official dinners in their home towns – so they would feel needed, maybe even heeded

by the party leadership. His soundings convinced him that alienation among extra-parliamentary Liberals was far stronger than
caucus discontent and less amenable to an easy fix.

The causes of activist disaffection were profound. Among lay
Liberals interested in influencing the nation's destiny, the memory
of their betrayal a decade earlier by the failure of Trudeau's promise
to bring about a participatory democracy lingered like a sulphurous
smell. During the 1968 leadership race he had had "a subjective
reason" for making his ardent participatory pitch to convention
delegates: his roots in the party at the time were so shallow he
needed to make a distinctive appeal to the aspirations of Liberal
"militants" – as he called party members in the French style. Displaying his remarkable talent for adapting the ideas of others,
Trudeau had turned the American radical student movement's call
for participatory democracy into a seductive appeal to bring "the
party rank and file more directly into the decision-making processes
. . . letting them participate in government and public affairs before
the final decisions [are] taken." Once elected, he pumped up the
rhetoric by invoking Rousseau's eighteenth-century vision of citizens in a utopian society collectively creating the general will.
Calling on Liberals to exercise "real, organic power and political
action," he encouraged the party president, Richard Stanbury, and
the policy chairman, Allen Linden, in their ambitious scheme to
create a "modern mass party." [2]

In private, he spoke at length with Stanbury and Linden about
his need to take a couple of years to clear up inherited unfinished
business – such as determining how to pay for social programs established during the Pearson years – and to set up a new government
structure before he could move the country in a new direction. By
that time he would be ready to "shock the nation" by asking radically new questions about "the basic issues confronting [us]."
Inspired by the new prime minister's visionary timetable, Stanbury
and Linden launched the most ambitious effort at extra-
governmental policy-making ever attempted in Canadian party
politics. [3]

Designed to improve on the pathbreaking venture of the early Pearson period, when Walter Gordon had recruited Liberal activists rather than Ottawa bureaucrats to create the party's 1962 and 1963 election platforms, the process was broken down into three components – a thinkers' conference, a grass-roots response, and a policy convention. Dozens of specialists were invited to begin the exercise by offering their frequently conflicting ideas at a three-day meeting at Harrison Hot Springs, a spa hotel in British Columbia. Trudeau flattered the assembled participants by calling the Liberal Party "society's radar," but his metaphor conveniently ignored the organizers' efforts to exclude discussion of issues known to be anathema to the prime minister, in particular the knotty questions of Quebec nationalism and American control of the Canadian economy. In a second phase, concentrated efforts were made to involve party adherents across the country, but when it came to policy discussion at the community level, the Liberal rank and file tended to defer to its elected members. "Policy is for nuts," exclaimed one riding president testily when pushed to encourage his constituency stalwarts to submit resolutions for consideration.[4]

At the climactic policy convention in Ottawa, over a thousand delegates assembled nevertheless to debate, amend, veto, or approve several hundred sometimes contradictory resolutions during an intense few days under the chandeliers of the Château Laurier ballroom. They managed to withstand the cabinet's efforts to squelch views that diverged from government policy, most notably the neutralist foreign-policy positions advocated by the Edmonton publisher Mel Hurtig. But editing the intellectual hodge-podge that resulted from the convention's deliberations into a draft election platform turned out to be so much wasted effort for the militants, who had squandered energy on the participatory exercise from its high-spirited start in 1968 to its dismal finish in 1971. When Trudeau's ministers rebuffed the product of their earnest labours, their morale sank, never to be buoyed again. ("Who the fuck do you think you are?" John Turner asked Stanbury and Linden when they presented their proposed campaign document to the cabinet. There was to be no party-member-inspired campaign platform after all. In describing the exchange afterwards to a fellow activist, Linden remarked grimly, "We've been had.")[5]

When Trudeau himself also insulted Liberal activists who remonstrated with him privately in his office a few months later for abandoning his participatory promise, many of them withdrew from party activity. "I don't think the Parliamentary wing of the Government gives a damn about the Party or what it thinks," one activist answered in response to a researcher's questionnaire on grass-roots participation. Party activity "hardly seems to matter," wrote another: "Is anyone listening anymore?" The answer, of course, was no. And it continued to be no for the rest of the decade.[6]

As an ardent participatory democrat, Tom Axworthy had witnessed with dismay this period of party demobilization and demoralization. He believed the party rank and file had gone limp in both the 1979 and 1980 campaigns, with only Joe Clark's perceived inadequacies and Pierre Trudeau's residual charismatic appeal sustaining the Liberals' electoral strength. After the Restoration, he had tried to revive Liberal activist interest by reconvening the party platform committee from the 1980 campaign and listening carefully to its members' views before writing the speech from the throne. Once he became principal secretary he determined that a key aspect of his tenure would be an attempt to reverse the antagonistic attitudes that had grown up between the PMO and the lay party and to stop activists and organizers, the party's blood and bone, from being treated in Ottawa like so many barbarians hammering at the gates of power.

In this goal, he had the resolute support of Lorna Marsden, one of the rare academics in the country still willing to be identified as Liberals. Marsden had grown up on Vancouver Island as Lorna Bosher, the youngest child in a family whose antecedents from Manchester had lived "in poverty so dire it was almost Dickensian," as she described it, before they emigrated to Canada in 1911. Inspired by her feisty English grandmother, whose maiden name and feminist politics she adopted, she moved east to study at the University of Toronto in 1960 but dropped out before graduating to marry another student from British Columbia named Edward Harvey and to work at a variety of jobs while he pursued a PhD in sociology. She finally finished her BA at Toronto in 1968 when she was twenty-six and earned a doctorate in sociology from Princeton four years later.[7]

When one of her professors suggested she take a hard look at the grossly unfair conditions women worked under in academe, Marsden began to research and advocate pay and pension equity for women and returned to Toronto as an assistant professor, determined "not to end up being dismissed as somebody's wife." Rapidly promoted to a full professorship, she became the first woman to head her department, then associate dean of arts, and eventually vice-provost of the university. She also managed to publish three academic texts, two in collaboration with Edward Harvey, turning upside down the usual marital arrangement between professionals, where the man is the public figure and his partner the self-effacing helpmate.[8]

A male colleague remarked admiringly, "The thing about Lorna is that she looks like a woman and acts like a man. There's the blonded hair that suits the long Modigliani face. The glimpse of black lace under the tailored skirt. The measured voice that turneth away wrath. The steadiness that steadies others. It throws men off kilter and allows her to navigate adroitly the trickier shoals of sexual politics so she can give her energies to important matters. In intellectual output, she's not outstanding, but in managing human interactions, she has unbeatable skills. She's smart enough, as the old saw has it, to conceal how smart she really is."[9]

As though shinnying up the academic greasy pole in jig time were not enough, Marsden worked just as hard as a political activist. Her Princeton years had coincided with the consciousness-raising phase of the women's liberation movement, the beginnings of what was later called the second wave of feminism. When she came back

to Toronto to teach, Marsden found that feminists in her own country were unlike the radical American women who had learned their
activist style from men in the anti-war movement. The Canadians
were an eclectic group whose roots were mostly in the gentler
home-grown social protest movements and staid mainstream
women's associations and whose instincts were to turn to government with their grievances, not to take to the streets.

Their determined lobbying of the Pearson Liberals in the
mid-1960s, backed by the editorializing of Doris Anderson, the
most effective feminist of the day, in the mass-circulation women's
magazine *Chatelaine*, had led to the establishment of the Royal
Commission on the Status of Women. After three years of careful
research, inquiry, and cogitation, its recommendations were
published in late 1970 only to be ridiculed or ignored by media
commentators and politicians. Without a champion in the Trudeau
cabinet, the SOW report seemed destined to go the way of so many
such worthy documents: straight into the boneyard of the political
process. [10]

Only briefly daunted, the feminists banded together to push
governments to turn the commission's recommendations into law.
Marsden became prominent in the Ontario Committee on the Status of Women and the National Action Committee, an umbrella
lobby for a variety of women's organizations. She learned so much
about the nature of male power structures by skirmishing with them
successfully as a lobbyist for OCSOW and NAC that in 1974, she
decided to join the Liberal Party – a clear indication that she
intended to pursue her equity goals in a way that was markedly different from the passionate theatricality and dedication to feminist
purity that characterized the sisterhood in the U.S. and the rare radical feminists in Canada who adopted the American style. The
debate during the first feminist wave more than half a century before
over whether to join men in partisan activity had taken the suffrag-
ette Nellie McClung many years to resolve; it took the very modern
Marsden only a matter of months. [11]

In her opinion, the way for women to achieve personal progress and political change was not to confront men adversarily but to analyse their behaviour and influence them by taking an active part in the male-dominated party process – an attitude that made some of her feminist friends uneasy even before it was described as liberal feminism. Marsden deftly turned aside incipient sisterly anger by saying that sociologically it was "typical of those on the verge of achieving power to display envy and outrage" towards those who already have it. [12]

The focused energy that had worked so well for her in academe soon brought her to the attention of leading Liberals, notably the Axworthy brothers, whose family background, progressive ideas, and hard-won graduate-school educations were similar to her own. The advice she offered to women on how to use the party system for change was analogous to the truisms the Axworthys themselves had absorbed as they turned partisan involvement into high-flying careers: avoid becoming a single-issue advocate by developing expertise on diverse policy problems; gain practical political experience at the constituency level; pick out people in the party hierarchy who can benefit from your strengths and help you at the same time; recognize that you're in it for the long haul and set up a buddy system so you and your allies can defend each other's interests at party meetings. Marsden applied these precepts herself by canvassing doggedly for progressive Grits regardless of gender during election campaigns; taking on onerous party chores in between; and listening patiently to every Liberal bore who buttonholed her, determined above all to avoid being labelled an impractical, woolly-minded egghead – the standard putdown of academics among party hacks.

Not that there were many professors waiting to be put down in the period when Marsden first came to Liberal prominence. Partly this was because of academic disdain for the Liberal Party. Partly it had to do with the combative attitude towards other thinkers on the part of the Liberals' philosopher-king, Pierre Trudeau. "Once Pierre got into office," said Bernard Ostry, who had been a friend in the 1950s and early 1960s when they were both active critics of Canadian society, "he seemed to think all the intellectual stimulus he needed was the sound of his own voice declaiming his ideas to Gérard Pelletier or Michael Pitfield or Ivan Head. The work-load he carried meant he was cut off from what was happening in intellectual circles in Europe as well as North America. He didn't know who Jean-Jacques Servan-Schreiber was or Christopher Lasch. He didn't see his old friends any more, people who could have told him what was going on and presented an overview that was different from that of the yes-men who surrounded him." (A few of Trudeau's old intellectual friends did keep in touch, notably the historian Ramsay Cook and Madeleine Gobeil, a former professor of French literature, who became a UNESCO official in Paris.) [13]

But he did not seek out Liberal policy-makers, and the lay party fell into a virtual coma after the failure of the participatory exercise, with its disheartened members merely going through the motions of conducting policy discussions at their biennial conventions. There was plenty of carousing, gossiping, and philandering at those meetings. (The 1975 convention had been set to convene under the slogan "Coming Together" until it was pointed out that using a rallying cry with such orgiastic implications might not be the best way to embellish the party's image among those concerned with family values.) But most convention delegates showed minimal policy interest and less staying power in the post-participatory 1970s. The turnover rate from one meeting to another was so high that few of them had any sense of how new resolutions contradicted or extended party positions taken at previous conventions. Given the general belief that the Trudeau cabinet scorned advice emanating from any but their own bureaucrats, policy debates were perfunctory and resolutions were passed by the hundreds simply because no one bothered to oppose them. [14]

Lorna Marsden's response to the Liberals' moribund participatory capacity when she first joined the party was to avoid policy and concentrate on organization. After developing a national network of progressive allies, she got herself elected to the party executive as a vice-president; provided Ontario candidates with advice on how to answer media questions during the 1979 campaign; worked hard at consensus-building during the trying autumn of 1979 when the extra-parliamentary party fight between francophones and anglophones over Trudeau's leadership almost broke into the open; supported Lloyd Axworthy's cause in the manoeuvring for the succession that warmed up briefly after Trudeau resigned temporarily in November; and then moved the crucial motion at the December meeting of the national executive urging Trudeau to return to his job. Displaying her mediating talents, Marsden was able to facilitate the executive's quid-pro-quo demand that the party have a real voice in the 1980 election by working with Tom Axworthy to convene and then co-chair the hastily invented platform committee.[15]

By this time she was an acknowledged backroom broker, a woman who had decided that she could best influence the party leadership on behalf of women not by running for office but by joining with other ambitious activists, most of them men, in a classic power combine. A few years as an activist observer had shown her how brutal electoral politics could be for those intrepid women who managed to become MPs. With her connections to the Trudeau PMO and her party bona fides consolidated, she continued her partisan involvement by going after the job of national policy chair at the first post-Restoration party convention. Held in Winnipeg in July 1980 as a symbol of the party's determination to reach out to the electorate in the west, the meeting turned into a love-in for the victorious Trudeau, the happiest gathering of its kind since 1968. Marsden was elected to the policy post by promising to make the lay party's role more effective forthwith.[16]

Even in the early afterglow of that convention, she was realistic about what could be achieved with the meagre resources available to her. Her only full-time help was provided by Audrey Gill, the director of policy development at Liberal Party headquarters in Ottawa, and a lone secretarial assistant. A former journalist, Gill had close connections to some serious-minded, centrist Liberals who had come to be called the Grindstone Group, after the island resort near

Ottawa where they met in the late 1970s to ponder the party's declining fortunes. Since Gill was fully as determined as Marsden to
produce demonstrable gains in participatory policy-making before
the next party convention, the two women set to work with a will.

To give substance to the notion of leader accountability that had
been adopted as part of the uncompleted push for party democracy
in the Pearson era, Marsden decided to forward the resolutions
passed at the 1980 convention to ministers who might be expected
to bring about their implementation. At the same time she shrewdly
requested a timetable for their consideration in individual departments and then by cabinet as a whole. The goal was to compile a
document describing actions taken on each resolution, to have it
signed by Trudeau himself, and then to send copies to every delegate
so that lay Liberals could see the impact of their policy decisions on
the government. At the same time, regular phone surveys of key
party members were instituted in order to offer the caucus a
monthly digest of grass-roots views. Gill also mailed out "viewpoint
papers" on topical issues, established a regular *Liberal Policy Newsletter* to keep convention delegates in touch with government initiatives, and offered to help them formulate policy resolutions for the
next biennial gathering. [17]

While the two women were preoccupied with these activities, their
party's commitment to greater participation in the political process
by women – and Lorna Marsden's credentials as a feminist leader –
came under serious question. Marsden's closest friend in cabinet,
Lloyd Axworthy, had taken on, in addition to the employment and
immigration portfolio, ministerial responsibility for the status of
women, a job Marc Lalonde had shouldered in the 1970s along with
his other tasks. (Although there were highly capable women in cabinet in both periods – Jeanne Sauvé, Monique Bégin, and Iona
Campagnolo in the 1970s and Bégin and Judy Erola after the 1980
election, when Sauvé was made Speaker of the House – the role was
thought to be too tricky for a woman politician to handle.)

When federal-provincial exchanges over Trudeau's plans for constitutional change grew increasingly abrasive in late 1980, Lloyd Axworthy peremptorily cancelled a women's conference on the issue sponsored by the Canadian Advisory Council on the Status of Women, on the dubious grounds that its deliberations might prove embarrassing to the government. The council's president was none other than the redoubtable feminist and former *Chatelaine* editor Doris Anderson, who quit her job in protest after angry denunciations of Axworthy's behaviour. Feminists of every hue were roused by the controversy to take part in a show of collective strength. Thirteen hundred of them turned up in Ottawa on Valentine's Day in 1981 and staged their own constitutional conference with the support of women MPs who crossed party lines to give them practical support. By the time the reverberations from this event had subsided later in the year, the wording of several sections of the charter of rights had been altered to guarantee a fuller measure of equality for women.[18]

In the course of the uproar, Marsden was seen as a lapsed feminist who had crossed over into the no-woman's-land of male-identified careerists. She publicly rebuked the protesters, saying she thought the whole exercise was a waste of political energy, since she could have won the changes the feminists wanted in two hours behind closed doors with the legal team drafting the charter in the Department of Justice. She stood by Axworthy when the status-of-women responsibility was taken away from him – and bestowed on Judy Erola, the tough-minded minister of mines – then refused to be diverted further from her participatory purposes by feminist infighting, saying it demeaned women and their democratic cause.

In her determination to do something about the weak position in the Liberal constellation of power of both men and women from the lay party, Marsden had developed a smooth plan to involve them with Privy Councillors and other pooh-bahs who made government policy in a wide-ranging discussion of where the Canadian state should be heading in the 1980s. She and Gill invited a hundred leading Liberals to meet for a weekend at Carleton University in June 1981 to create a thematic agenda for the 1982 convention. In setting it up, they made sure that parliamentarians would exchange ideas with party activists while they considered position papers together in workshops.[19]

This evidence of renewed participatory zeal so impressed party mavens that even the jaundiced Jim Coutts – whose planned candidacy in Spadina was still a secret – was careful to take time away from the PMO and turn up at Carleton disguised as just another optimistic Grit. Looking cherubic but sounding crafty, he suggested in the weekend's last plenary session that the best possible media spin could be had from the closing press conference by stressing not the assembled Liberals' considered ideas but the process whereby they had reached them – that is, the style and not the substance of the think-in, a notion so Couttsian that Hugh Faulkner, the former cabinet minister chairing the session, responded with a quip that produced general hilarity. "Is that the kind of advice you give the PM, Jim?" he asked in mock innocence.[20]

By the end of the weekend, Marsden, Gill, and their ally Tom Axworthy had every reason to hope that the 1982 convention process might produce a new intellectual thrust for Liberalism. But a few weeks later, with the public revelation of Coutts's Spadina power play and its intimations of continuing inner-circle arrogance, their spirits were flattened. In the wake of the party's plunge in the polls that autumn, there were overt signs of renewed unrest in Liberal ranks.

A Toronto law student named Alf Apps wrote an outraged letter to Tom Axworthy, saying that the party was in a shambles, overloaded with political has-beens, its leadership numb to new ideas, its rank and file sycophantic to the leader and uninterested in functioning as anything other than cogs in a successful election machine. The letter summed up party members' accumulated cynicism about participation, which apparently had been assuaged only superficially by the respectful treatment accorded the 1980 platform committee and the post-election efforts of Marsden and Gill. When Apps's letter was leaked to the media early in 1982, its message encouraged the handful of dissidents in the Liberal caucus and provided new ammunition for the business community's calumnies against the government. Not only was the Trudeau administration inept at managing the economy, it was anti-democratic.[21]

Marsden and Gill kept on nurturing their networks and refining their plans for holding regional policy forums, hoping that substantial and practicable thinking would emerge from party members' deliberations on economic policy. But they were increasingly apprehensive that the convention – now postponed until November 1982 in the expectation that the Six & Five exercise would improve party morale – would turn into a forum for disunity.

There was little prospect of an organized revolt against Trudeau since the party constitution ruled out a leadership review vote at any convention other than the first one following an election. But their policy-making process was in danger of looking irrelevant in the light of factional warfare. Marsden had been racking her brains for weeks trying to find a way to defuse party tensions and to display her commitment to feminism at the same time. On a return flight from a late-summer meeting of the Liberal International in Europe, she hit upon the idea of persuading Iona Campagnolo, the former minister of fitness and amateur sport, to run for party president. Campagnolo was popular with party activists as a dynamic politician from Prince Rupert, British Columbia, who could claim to be both a westerner and a northerner; and she had great appeal to the Coutts-and-Davey crowd because her striking good looks and vibrant speaking style made her unusually telegenic. Her candidacy would turn the presidential election into a lively race and possibly give the media something else to chew on beyond the government's economic troubles. She seemed the ideal person to boost the party's bedraggled public image and raise its members' spirits at the same time.[22]

The incumbent president, Norman MacLeod, had been the party establishment's candidate in 1980. Under normal circumstances, he could expect to be acclaimed for a second two-year term in 1982 and to follow his presidential predecessors into the Senate as a reward for his labours. But circumstances were far from normal. Not only was the party in unprecedented disfavour with the public, it was nearly a million dollars in debt. Even though MacLeod was vice-president of a branch-plant finance company in Toronto, he had proven no better at fundraising than his immediate predecessor, the Nova Scotia senator Alasdair Graham. Since MacLeod was also thought to be a covert Turnerite, the challenge from Campagnolo, who had been involved in raising money for Third World causes since her defeat at the polls in 1979, would give the party a proxy fight on which to focus activist angers. With these encouraging possibilities in mind, Marsden initiated a chain of conversations that resulted in Marc Lalonde's telephoning Campagnolo and persuading her to run for the presidency.[23]

Successful as Marsden was in precipitating the Campagnolo challenge to MacLeod, she was unable to prevent party malcontents from turning her carefully planned policy-making process to their own ends once the convention began. Alf Apps's youth wing snookered her by extracting an exception to the rule that required the party's constituent bodies to submit months in advance the drafts of three "priority resolutions" that would command mandatory consideration by the full convention. When the young Liberals presented her with their priority resolutions on the evening before the three-day convention was to open in Ottawa on Friday, November 5, Marsden had no choice but to allow them to put forward their text, however incendiary its language. To refuse, she reasoned, would bring them even more media attention, the primary goal of their protest.

The youth wing's Priority Resolution 40 seemed at first glance to be just another long-winded call for pure democracy by idealistic young Liberals who had absorbed their political science lectures on the iron law of oligarchy. Couched in debating society pomposities, it resolved "that this convention: a) condemn manipulative electoral shams; b) condemn the view that non-accountable, non-legitimate, non-elected members of the Party should have direct informal roles in advising the government which totally bypass the democratically accountable executive of the Party." [24]

As media observers were obligingly quick to point out, the resolution could be construed as a straight castigation of the Coutts-and-Davey group for the influence they had wielded over the political process during the previous decade. But Alf Apps, the resolution's principal author, was not leading a grass-roots revolt. He was part of a yeasty group of would-be politicians in their twenties who had already tasted the delights of party patronage as ministerial executive assistants or summer interns in government departments and were impatient for Trudeau to resign so that they could benefit from the circulation of élites that occurs when a new leader brings his own troupe into the party's power structure. Apps was also seen as a stalking-horse for business Liberals who wanted to replace the interventionist Trudeau with the more amenable John Turner. His Young Turk's indignation about the power of the backroom boys and their abuse of "polls, propaganda and patronage," as Resolution 40 had it, was a cover for an indirect attack on Trudeau by a faction of the party's old turkeys – Liberals on the outs and on the right who wanted to promote Turner, their perpetual undeclared candidate for the succession, so they could be the ins again. Turner discreetly let it be known that he agreed with Resolution 40. His muted support caused delegates to swarm around him in such numbers when he turned up at the convention on Saturday that his challenge to Trudeau's leadership seemed all but launched. [25]

But by the end of the day, it was clear that "all but" was really "not just yet." Turner was reluctant to take on Trudeau openly. Trained from childhood to be courteous to all comers, he was unable to act without determining whether the party's left-right divide could be straddled – as it had been in Mackenzie King's time when his mother had invited both the right-wing C.D. Howe and the left-leaning Brooke Claxton for cosy dinners at her Ottawa house and got along famously with both. Having first presented himself in the 1960s as a crusading progressive, Turner was now being touted as a Liberal saviour in Toronto by his right-of-centre law partner, William Macdonald; in Montreal by his communications consultant, John Payne; and in Ottawa by the sometime ministerial assistant and now full-time lobbyist William Lee.

Under nearly intolerable pressure to front an anti-Trudeau coup, Turner went into an automatist state. He was too caught up in the Liberal axiom that you never attack the leader to let his backers do any hard strategizing or direct proselytizing on his behalf. His business friends did not have the guts to confront the prime minister either and reserved their diatribes against him for boardroom meetings and corporate newsletters. Former Turner supporters, such as Jerry Grafstein and the Axworthy brothers, who had been drawn to him by his progressive stance at the 1968 convention, were mostly in it with the prime minister for the duration, as one of them told Turner, content to let Trudeau make his own decision on when to depart.

A further reason for Turner's reluctance to mount a direct challenge to Trudeau was the perplexing question of the other dauphin. Donald Macdonald's putative candidacy for the succession seemed to have been given a boost on the eve of the convention when he was asked by the prime minister to chair the new royal commission to investigate "the economic union and development prospects for Canada." This appointment was seen in Turner's camp as a not-so-subtle way for the PMO to provide Macdonald with a carefully researched progressive agenda at government expense, should he choose to go after the leadership when Trudeau finally gave up on it.

In response to these confusing cross-currents, Turner fell back on his charm. He worked the convention energetically by greeting well-wishers in the hallways of the Château Laurier with tender pats on the back, sympathetic flashes from his amazing blue eyes, and noisy cries of "How-ya-doin' boy?" To show his serious intent, Turner also sat down briefly in various hotel salons to listen in on policy debates and exchanged guarded banter with old cronies from the parliamentary press gallery who were trying to inflate the Turner excitement into the opening act of a great revolt against Trudeau.[26]

As had happened with discouraging regularity in the past, Turner found himself outshone by the prime minister, who managed several star turns in the party spotlight over the convention weekend. Flagged on by Tom Axworthy, Trudeau presented himself to the delegates as responsive to their needs and pugnacious on their behalf, the leader who must be a leader. His formal speech praised the Liberal Party as "perhaps the greatest success story in the history of modern democracies"; described its ranks as being "crowded with men and women bursting with ideas, eager to reform, and anxious to make Canada a better place"; reminded delegates of his attendance at the preparatory regional meetings leading up to the convention; and promised that "the deliberations and conclusions of this great assembly" would be seriously considered by his government so that the next speech from the throne would "represent all that is innovative, bold, and dynamic about the Liberal Party." He also made himself "accountable" in a bear-pit session, sparring with those brave enough to criticize him, admitting that his government had made mistakes, and mocking Joe Clark and his fractious Conservatives. As usual with Liberal crowds, whenever he showed his fair form in the flesh, Trudeau was mobbed.[27]

As far as Axworthy and Marsden were concerned, the prime minister's performance only partially countered the damage that open dissent had inflicted on the policy process in the previous several months. The Apps uproar diverted attention from the substantial debates on economic issues that went on at the convention, although the media did pick up on the delegates' rebuff to Marc Lalonde when he floated a trial balloon suggesting governments might no longer be able to afford universal medicare. Axworthy and Marsden had agreed at the outset that there was nothing to be gained by precipitating a showdown with Apps or Turner. Apps's reform fervour represented the kind of young energy the party needed. Turner was part of the Liberal family, and one of its rare remaining connections to the world of business. His strutting of his political stuff and Apps's defiantly worded Resolution 40 had to be endured for what they were – unwelcome evidence of party troubles given embarrassing play by the media – and then rationalized as a venting of concerns that made activists feel they counted and showed that the party was democratically inclined.[28]

When Apps rose to bring forward his resolution before a packed auditorium at the convention's Saturday-evening plenary session, the air was already escaping from his balloon. In order to make it absolutely plain that he was *not* trashing the prime minister, he asserted his personal loyalty in flowery terms, which promptly set off a round of "Trudeau! Trudeau! Trudeau!" chanting among the delegates. Apps then elaborated on his critique of the leader's advisers. Forty-five minutes later – after four short speeches had been given in favour of his resolution and four against – his motion passed to general exultation in the Château Laurier ballroom. The backroom boys had been duly rapped on their oligarchic knuckles but left in place all the same.[29]

If the sparks set off by Resolution 40 did not ignite a conflagration, it was partly because Marsden and Gill had managed to create such an open atmosphere that there were few grounds for complaint about the policy process. Dissension had been dissipated further by the contest for the presidency. After a fiery speech, Iona Campagnolo was elected president of the Liberal Party of Canada, the first woman to win the position. Her closing address to the assembly was calculated to send the militants happily homeward, warmed by her promise to address their grievances by establishing a reform commission to study the party's internal governance and to propose appropriate changes to its structure and constitution.

By the time the convention adjourned, minimal cosmetic surgery and a few primal screams had improved the party's image of itself and dealt with the emotions of the moment. The Liberal élite had shown once again its ability to conciliate and conquer. But two basic questions remained: given the conservative temper of the times, where should the Liberals be heading, and was Pierre Elliott Trudeau still the man to lead them there?

Far more difficult for Trudeau than carrying out Tom Axworthy's carefully choreographed convention performance aimed at defusing Liberal Party discontent was the need to contemplate the next phase of his life. Most of his contemporaries were engaged in the process that social psychologists define as the transition to older age, when men in their sixties add up what they have accomplished in their careers and prepare to move into retirement. By the time his government's mandate ran out he would have served longer as prime minister than any of his predecessors in the job other than Sir John A. Macdonald and Mackenzie King. Within months, he would have to decide whether to keep the promise he had made in 1980 *not* to lead the Liberals into another election campaign – a promise he had hedged recently by remarking to a television interviewer: "Who knows? Something might happen that I'll have to run again . . . Everything is possible."[30]

Concerned about the decline in his popularity and mindful of how unhappy he had been in 1979 during his exile in opposition, his oldest political allies, Jean Marchand and Marc Lalonde, wanted him to find another challenge. Given the high regard he enjoyed among liberal-minded heads of state all over the world, there was a possibility he might be offered a post in an important international institution. On the other hand, should he decide to retreat into graceful contemplation of the universe unfolding as it should, he could decamp with his sons at any moment to the splendid Art Deco house he had acquired on Montreal's Avenue des Pins and become once more a polemicist, teacher, and traveller. Once ensconced there – all passion presumably spent – he might even act the elder statesman by writing his memoirs. By his own calculation, he had changed Canada along the lines he had been advocating for fifteen years with the Constitution Act of 1982. The provincial Liberals' hostility to its provisions and the flat refusal of the governing Péquistes to sanction it had not yet diminished the Quebec public's support for Trudeau's patriation package.[31]

When the budget crisis of early 1982 threatened to obscure his historic gains at the constitutional bargaining table, Trudeau had responded with alacrity. But the struggle with economic issues had been frustrating: inflation and unemployment continued to resist the government's most imaginative and concerted counter-measures. Even as he applied himself diligently to the economy's complexities, his closest associates believed he was constantly assessing his record and trying to decide his future. Entrusting Donald Macdonald with a sweeping royal-commission mandate to investigate Canada's prospects was a tacit admission that he and his policy strategists no longer believed they had the answers to the Canadian federation's worsening social, economic, and political problems.

His young staff's penchant for describing him in conversation as "the old man" – a nervous reflex since he could still intellectually outmanoeuvre and physically outlast most of them – reflected the way he was widely viewed in official Ottawa: as a lame-duck politician increasingly isolated in a city where communal life centred less on nation-building concerns and prime ministerial grandiosities than on toy-strewn family rooms in gentrified Sandy Hill and New Edinburgh. These were the neighbourhoods that housed the upper-middle-level civil servants in their thirties and forties who were assiduously engaged in contemplating their own career paths and whose devotion to Canada was very different from that of the post-war mandarinate who had helped form Trudeau's idea of the public weal. For them, policy-making was a job, not a mission.

Emotionally sustained by his attachment to his three sons and preoccupied privately with their concerns, Trudeau now only occasionally displayed in public his famous sexual braggadocio. His appearances with showy women as young as or younger than his estranged wife, Margaret, were rarer than they had been in the late 1970s and seemed contrived to burnish his old image as the consummate dance-away lover.

The ironies of his life abounded. The once-pugnacious advocate of an oppressed working class was now repudiated bitterly by trade union leaders and left-wing intellectuals as an aging version of the kind of uncaring, overprivileged sell-out to vested interests he had so disdained in his youth. In the eyes of nationalist intellectuals in Quebec, he had become what he had chafed against in the 1950s: a political figure almost as authoritarian and annihilating to dissent as his bête noire, Maurice Duplessis. Heartily hated by the Quebec élites for keeping the province in its constitutional place, he was maintained in power electorally by the very tribalism he had once reviled. Quebeckers at every social level continued to reaffirm, whenever they were asked by pollsters, their intention to vote for him as the province's most illustrious native son. "The people," as he described his compatriots, saw him as a *p'tit coq* – the kind of tough scrapper you would want on your side in a brawl – admired not so much for his ideas as for his unshakeable self-assurance in expressing them. His sartorial and rhetorical style were made piquant by the contrast between his habitual elegance in dress and manner and his occasional vulgarisms in gesture and speech. (Up yours! Eat shit! Fuck off! were phrases as closely identified with Trudeau in Quebec as his lofty aphorisms defining Canada's need for a just society, a participatory democracy, and a multicultural federalist state whose rupture would be a crime against the history of mankind.) René Lévesque may have been the politician Quebeckers loved, but Pierre Elliott Trudeau was the man they wanted to be, as the Péquistes' *enfant terrible*, Claude Charron, once remarked.[32]

Still combative in first ministers' meetings, still a formidable debater in the House at Question Period, still a great performer on the public stage, at sixty-three he remained a contender in the political arena – more formidable, Tom Axworthy kept telling him in the wake of his success at the November convention, than any aspirant to his office from any party, including his own.

●   ●   ●

It had taken Trudeau many months to come to trust Axworthy's judgement. He had been reluctant to take him on as principal secretary when Keith Davey suggested him as a replacement for Coutts in the late spring of 1981. Although undeniably well educated (he had completed his doctoral thesis in 1979) and broadly experienced in backroom politics, Axworthy lacked training in economics, knew very little about the business world, and had only a superficial understanding of Quebec.

He and Trudeau were poles apart in background and sensibility. Axworthy was Margaret Trudeau's contemporary – a baby-boomer nearly thirty years younger than Pierre Trudeau – and, like her, a product of non-exclusive, co-educational, multi-ethnic public schools in the rough and readily democratic west. His experience of political history, political theory, and political action, despite his brief stint at Oxford and his admiration for the old mandarinate's anglophile style, was intuitively North American and very different from Trudeau's cerebral European approach.

Over time, Axworthy's apparent liabilities had turned out to be assets. After a difficult six or eight months when Trudeau was perceived as missing the formidable talents of Coutts, the two men developed a working rapport, re-forming the relationships of their own family configurations, with Trudeau as the older brother expecting deference, and Axworthy as the younger sibling, eager and willing to endure Trudeau's testiness and insensitivity to others and to learn from his experience. Years of adapting himself to Trudeau's needs as a speech-writer had made Axworthy adroit at fitting in with his thinking. Had Tom been self-aggrandizing, Trudeau might have been compelled to contradict rather than to welcome his clear-headed ideas. As it was, no less a personage than Michael Pitfield claimed the prime minister was notably easier to get along with once Axworthy's unflappable good cheer had set a new tone in the PMO.

What the two men had in common was a basically Christian commitment to social activism that had led them both into politics. Axworthy's sunny Methodism found resonance in Trudeau's messianic personalism. His still-youthful exuberance and wit appealed to Trudeau's own sense of fun, which had been buried for years under the weight of his personal and political troubles. Trudeau apparently liked Axworthy's engaging idealism about Canada, his tenacious commitment to Liberalism, his belief in the Aristotelian maxim that politics is the honourable profession, and his ability to formulate a comprehensive strategy from which progressive policies and clever tactics could logically be derived.[33]

With the Coutts-and-Davey Liberals – who had presented themselves as his electoral saviours in English Canada when they came to offer him their campaign services in 1973 – he was always a little wary. "What's in it for you guys, anyway?" he had asked the group at the time, and several of its members believed the same scepticism played in his mind whenever they put forward new proposals for his approval despite the demonstrable success of their political schemes. With Tom Axworthy, who was not so obviously "foxy" – Trudeau's word for Coutts – he was more accepting. He ceased to grumble about party commitments such as meeting riding presidents and local heroes or giving speeches at annual fundraisers. Instead, he fulfilled these routine tasks with ease, playing his part wholeheartedly in Axworthy's determined drive to recover the Liberals' popularity.[34]

By the end of 1982, with Pitfield in the Senate and Coutts's influence in Ottawa steadily diminishing (although he kept an office in the Langevin Block), Axworthy had become the English-speaking adviser closest to Trudeau. But even with Axworthy, he remained opaque about his future plans, refusing to divulge whether he meant to contest another election.

Trudeau's continuing coyness about his future created a dilemma for Axworthy in his role as the party's chief election strategist. By early 1983, the cabinet, caucus, and national party executive were generally persuaded to his view that the way for the Liberals to survive once the economy had improved was to become even more progressive in their policy thrust. But no powerful figure had yet emerged around whom left-leaning Liberals could coalesce. The Spadina by-election loss, coupled with Alf Apps's Resolution 40, had convinced every hard-headed pol in the party – other than Coutts himself – that his audacious dream of succeeding Trudeau was unlikely to be "do-able," a favourite Couttsian word. Lloyd Axworthy's star had been eclipsed by his constitutional fight with the feminists. Herb Gray was seen as too doggedly dull to be leadership material. Allan MacEachen, felled by his bold budget, was merely holding on at External. The hip Toronto MP John Roberts had proven disappointing as a minister, his reputation for intellectual acuity on policy matters having been damaged by an inattention to the routine detail of constituency politics that was perceived in the PMO as laziness.

Even if the party tradition of alternating French and English leaders could be overcome, it would take a miracle to transform the iron man Lalonde into a popular figure. Jean Chrétien, something of a caucus loner despite his huge public appeal, was patently eager to succeed the boss but was seen as an anachronism in his attachment to pre-Trudeau Liberal values. And none of the other francophone ministers, Monique Bégin, Jean-Luc Pepin, and Roméo LeBlanc, who enjoyed regional or interest-group support had a national following. With Donald Macdonald out of the running for the immediate future with his royal commission task, John Turner looked like the sure winner in an early leadership race and his accession a sure end to the sort of progressive liberalism Axworthy was advocating.

Irascible, unpredictable, and long in the tooth he might be, but Pierre Trudeau remained the left Liberals' best hope. The voters were weirdly ambivalent about him, but he had never been dismissed as inept or laughed at in the way the opposition leader, Joe Clark, was constantly being mocked. Whatever they thought of his ideas, Trudeau's advocates and opponents alike had no doubt about his strength of purpose or of mind.

In order to counter the advice the prime minister was hearing from his old francophone friends that now was the time to step down, Axworthy realized he would need to play a Machiavellian Mephistopheles to Trudeau's princely Faust. Coutts had tempted Trudeau back to the leadership in 1979 with the chance to beat the Quebec separatists at their referendum game. Now some equally attractive challenge would have to be found to entice him to stay on – some mission unaccomplished that would appeal to his demanding intellect and dramatic sense of self.

It was high time, in any case, for Axworthy as principal secretary to think about preparations for the next election, which would have to be called within two years. The Restoration government's original priorities – on the constitution, energy policy, and inflation – had been tackled for better or for worse. Inflation had not been wrestled to the ground, but the cabinet had given it their best shot with the Six & Five initiative. Aside from monitoring indicators of the economy's expected recovery, nothing more could be done for the moment. The energy dossier held out little prospect for electoral gain. Petroleum prices were still falling, and as the minister in charge, Jean Chrétien was under pressure from Newfoundland to cede control over offshore resources and from Alberta to gut what little remained of the NEP's incentives for Canadian-owned companies. Even the necessary follow-up to the 1982 Constitution Act was uninspiring: a series of federal-provincial conferences on aboriginal rights and the allocation of funds to disadvantaged groups so they could mount pro-active court cases that would define the charter's provisions more specifically.

Beyond these big issues, the Liberals were struggling with two historically intractable problems, western freight rates and the East Coast fishery crisis. While undoubtedly important to the regions in question, neither issue was politically sexy enough to appeal to Trudeau or to the national electorate. Lloyd Axworthy, who had replaced Jean-Luc Pepin in Transport in the hope that, as a westerner, he could achieve a political solution to the Crow Rate issue, was making repeated concessions to western grain growers and Quebec livestock farmers with the aim of getting the Western Grain Transportation Act passed at last. Michael Kirby was acting as a plenipotentiary with the mandate to restructure the Atlantic fish economy and to relieve the government of its growing subsidy obligations. He had managed to negotiate a deal with the Newfoundland government that created one potentially viable fish corporation there. But he was still trying to find a way to keep Nova Scotia's failing fish processing companies in private hands.[35]

In addition to freight rates and fish, there were a dozen sidelined policy issues that had been deemed minor in relation to the grand schemes of the third National Policy. Robert Kaplan, the solicitor general, had a controversial bill in the works to create a civilian authority to direct the country's spy service. André Ouellet's long-overdue plan to reform federal competition legislation was on hold, having been squelched by Marc Lalonde when he began to court the business community as finance minister. The report from the task force on unemployment insurance – a reflection of Lloyd Axworthy's scheme to bring the Canadian workplace into the high-tech, post-industrial era – had been set aside in response to the recession's depredations.[36]

Other ministries were developing new policy initiatives. Michael Pitfield's former right-hand man in the PCO, Robert Rabinovitch, had become the deputy in Communications, where he was working with his minister, Francis Fox, on a new set of cultural policies to support Canadian film and television broadcasting. In Health and Welfare, Monique Bégin was still trying to save the universal health care system from the threat of extra-billing. The minister of agriculture, Eugene Whelan, was impatient to unveil a comprehensive food strategy for Canada. Charles Caccia, the Toronto MP who had become minister of the environment in August, had fired up his department to increase the moral pressure on the Reaganites to control acid rain by persuading nine European countries to commit themselves to cutting their emissions of airborne pollutants by 30 per cent.[37]

Many of these were initiatives that would have been do-able and saleable in the decades when economic growth was a given. But in a political climate where the Conservatives were already adopting the anti-government rhetoric of their role models, the Reagan Republicans, Axworthy realized that heightened government intervention in the marketplace would no longer play with the electorate. Goldfarb's polling data showed that the 1981–82 recession had brought about a sea change: for the first time in the forty years since survey research had been invented, more Canadian voters identified themselves as Conservatives than as Liberals. Axworthy believed it was no longer realistic to hope, as John Turner and Jean Chrétien did, that the Liberal Party could bridge the divide between left and right by commanding the mythic centre. It was time to take sides.

In Axworthy's view his party's best hope was to adopt a position he had proposed to Trudeau the previous year: the Liberals should return to the historic mission of their nineteenth-century forebears, the *rouges* and the Grits, and govern on behalf of the oppressed, the poor, and the otherwise disadvantaged. This was a left-wing twist on what was becoming a formula for political success on the ideological right. Whereas Thatcher and Reagan had won power by questioning the *raison d'être* of the very governments they wanted to control, Axworthy was proposing to attack the big interests whose support twentieth-century Liberals had relied on to gain office. A more equitable distribution of the nation's wealth through a multifaceted war on poverty was just the sort of idea that had appealed to Trudeau in his salad days and might appeal to him again as a means of political rejuvenation. It was also the way, in Axworthy's view, to distance the Liberals dramatically from the Tories and, at the same time, outflank the NDP on the muzzy left.

An expansion of the pension system to include homemakers, for instance, would appeal to women, the impoverished, immigrants, and the aged, people who leaned to the Liberals in any case and could be bound to them by this initiative. Democratization of the workplace might also prove a saleable policy, one that would appeal to labour and the rising lower middle class by promising profit-sharing and issuing stock to workers, moves that could energize the economy and transform labour-management relations by turning resentful, disinterested employees into eager, highly motivated co-owners. Similarly, selling Crown corporations to their employees would provide an example of privatization, not for the benefit of the rich but as a democratic means of giving punch to the economy.

When Axworthy had first broached the subject of this new social-policy thinking in late 1981, Trudeau was not persuaded that he (rather than his Liberal successor) should be the one to front it. But a year later when retirement from public life loomed larger, the adventurer in him was roused by young Tom's happy notion that he could forge a new Liberalism against the odds of a neo-conservative era. It had rankled with them both that the government had been forced to zig to the right over the previous year. Now Axworthy was offering Trudeau a way to zag back towards the left.

Apparently unaware of how incompatible these ideas were with the harsh economic realities the government had been forced to face – or how revelatory of intellectual muddle in the Liberal middle – he sweetened the original proposal by suggesting that Trudeau extend the scope of his mission by reactivating his old internationalist idealism. Not only could he turn himself into the champion of a new coalition of disadvantaged Canadians, he could try once more to become the advocate of the dispossessed all over the world, a lyrical left-Liberal voice shouting into a conservative gale. What was needed was some kind of international forum or initiative that would bring Trudeau applause from abroad and put a shine on his leadership credentials at home.

# PART V

# The End of the Era:
# Liberalism in Decline

# ONE MORE TIME?
# THE INTERNATIONAL YEAR
# OF PIERRE TRUDEAU

There was more than a modicum of Couttsian foxiness in Tom Axworthy's hope that some new foray into international affairs might be the way to induce his boss to stay on as Liberal leader. He knew it rankled with Trudeau that his accomplishments as an international statesman fell short of his ambitions and that his ambitions in this area were greater than in any other beyond his fervid mission to keep Quebec in Canada.

Trudeau had come to office as the least parochial of Canadian prime ministers: a politician more adept at foreign languages and more familiar with foreign cultures than any of his predecessors, including the country's premier diplomat and Nobel laureate, Lester Pearson. This cosmopolitanism had accrued during a quarter-century of travelling the globe; of hobnobbing with scholars and assorted gurus wherever he went; and of dropping in on weighty conferences in the First, Second, and Third Worlds bearing various intellectual credentials, the most important of them his keen curiosity about the workings of different societies. Although he had never studied international affairs in a formal way, he nevertheless had developed a world-view that aspired to a global community at peace, with interdependent nations managing the heritage of humankind and avoiding the horrors of atomic war. [1]

These were standard ideas among liberal Canadians of his class and cohort, freely and frequently expressed in cafés in downtown

Montreal by artists, intellectuals, poets, and poseurs and at impassioned university think-ins in Toronto and earnest summer conferences in the countryside north of both cities. Trudeau was unusually intense in his exposition of them, partly because he had evolved a critique of the old Ottawa establishment and its foreign policy postures as a result of his experience as a public servant under St. Laurent, as a polemicist in Quebec, and as Pearson's parliamentary secretary and justice minister.

His starting point was that Canada's foreign service was swollen, arrogant, and outmoded in its thinking and that the country's foreign policy as it had developed under Pearson's aegis needed to be reviewed. It should become less pretentious and more realistic by reflecting Canada's domestic interests and responding to an international situation very different from that of the immediate post-war period. Europe had been rebuilt and Soviet communism had been contained, Asia was burgeoning, and Canada's position in the world had greatly altered as a consequence. The challenge in 1968 was not – as it had been at mid-century when Pearson was in his heyday – to animate the North Atlantic alliance or to behave as a helpful fixer by peacekeeping in trouble spots. The Cold War alliances had generated two armed camps that were now as great a threat to peace as they were a deterrent to war. Canada's ultimate international interest involved dealing with humanity's double jeopardy: the plight of the impoverished in the Third World and the possibility of an accidentally triggered atomic apocalypse. Canada's immediate need was to survive as a federal entity against the threat of Quebec separatism, now vigorously supported by President de Gaulle of France. Within the context of these global and domestic urgencies, its defence posture should be rethought and its foreign aid efforts expanded. Through public and private statements to this effect, Trudeau's supporters were led to believe he would make substantial changes in Canada's role in world affairs.[2]

He made a determined effort to act on his beliefs during his first ministry with Ivan Head, his special assistant on foreign affairs, providing him with policy advice to offset External's Pearsonian thinking. Expanding aid to francophone Africa and establishing embassies there in order to outflank Quebec's international aspirations; opening a legation in the Vatican to affirm French Canada's Catholic presence abroad; declaring Canada's interest in and affinity with Latin America; defying the United States by asserting Canadian sovereignty over the Northwest Passage in the guise of preventing Arctic pollution; making an official visit to the Soviet Union in a show of diplomatic autonomy from the United States; and trying to extricate Canada from the untenable peacekeeping commitments Pearson had made in Vietnam: these were moves that sprang directly from Trudeau's personal agenda. But even as these successes unfolded, there were signs that Trudeau's approach to world affairs, with its buoyant perception of Canada as an autonomous nation-state, was neither realistic nor unpretentious. Although he acknowledged on occasion the impact on Canada of U.S. economic power, he acted as though it need not constrain Canada internationally. [3]

It was as though his adherence to personalism – with its central tenet that the individual has a duty to act boldly to change the world – caused him to believe he could overcome with his high intelligence the strictures put on Canada by the post-war phenomenon of American hegemony in much the same way as he and his personalist friends had transcended the strictures that had hobbled Quebec under Duplessis. The way to challenge regressive authority was to appeal to chaste reason and the law. The best style was calculated audacity modulated by studied civility. A brave man could refuse to submit to entrenched power while respecting its legitimacy and, by persevering, succeed in effecting gradual change.


An early indication that Trudeau's approach to world affairs was faulty came on the defence front. He had intended to redefine Canada's military commitments in the name of peace and the new global realities. He believed that Pearson had skewed his government's foreign policy thinking by allowing Canada's commitment to collective security through the North Atlantic Treaty Organization to remain his overriding priority. It was no longer reasonable, Trudeau argued in 1968, for Canada's foreign policy to be derived from its military policy or for its military policy to be determined by a mindset mired in the early days of the Cold War. His inability to take a clear-eyed look at the Canadian-American relationship meant he could not push this critique to its logical conclusion by acknowledging that Canada's foreign policy options were basically determined by the imperatives set by the United States. Instead, he proceeded on the legalistic assumption that the two nations were equal and sovereign. His reasoning was that since the sophistication of modern weaponry made North America the likely locale for the next world war, Canada would be better served by disengaging from the North Atlantic alliance and having "something to say about what will happen here and the way in which we shall defend ourselves" by collaborating with the United States on continental defence through NORAD, whose rationale he accepted, rather than in preparing for a war in Europe.[4]

For a brief period he stood his ground against warnings from parliamentarians and bureaucrats that dire consequences would follow from any tampering with the country's long-standing involvement in NATO, not least because of the Americans' dominant position in the alliance and the expectation in Washington that Canada would continue to pull its weight. But his resolve dissipated after extensive consultations had been held with academics and other outside experts, and all the options, from neutrality and non-alignment to rearmament, had been examined in concert with his ministers, who were deeply divided on the issue. By the end of the process all he was able to manage was the withdrawal of a portion of Canada's forces from their NATO bases in Europe – a compromise that owed more to the dithering continentalist liberalism of Mackenzie King than to the unyielding internationalist idealism of Pierre Trudeau but that damaged his reputation in the European capitals as well as in Washington nevertheless.[5]

A more significant demonstration of Trudeau's over-confidence in his own and Canada's autonomy was his defiance of Richard Nixon on the question of China. Having travelled there twice in his wandering years, Trudeau was convinced that the exclusion from international councils of the world's most populous power was a serious threat to world stability. External Affairs had wanted to recognize the People's Republic ever since Mao Zedong's revolutionary armies had pushed Chiang Kai-shek's nationalists off the mainland in 1949. But for twenty years it had reluctantly deferred to Washington's insistence that Chiang's government in Taiwan legitimately represented the Chinese people, and Canada routinely lined up behind the U.S. to block Communist China's membership in the United Nations.

Trudeau was determined to recognize Beijing, and Mitchell Sharp, as his first secretary of state for external affairs, proceeded to direct his department's painstaking negotiations to achieve this end despite objections that Nixon made to Trudeau privately. (Nixon was concerned that independent action by Canada would interfere with complex schemes he was cooking up with his chief foreign affairs adviser in the White House, Henry Kissinger, for his own historic breakthrough on China.) Canada's recognition of the communist regime in 1971 was hailed as a significant accomplishment that helped bring about China's admission to the United Nations shortly thereafter. But even as Trudeau was basking in this international acclaim, one of the underlying costs of defying Nixon was being revealed obliquely in an angered Washington, where the administration was refusing Ottawa exemptions from the ravages of Nixonomics and aborting the special relationship Canada had developed with the United States.[6]

Trudeau had managed to engender a deep antipathy in the American president because of his incapacity to understand fully how his detachment from the ideological fervour of Cold War politics was perceived among the hard-line Republicans in the White House and his inability to defuse Richard Nixon's bitter resentment of most intellectuals (especially those he thought of as effete "swells" in the eastern seaboard liberal tradition that Trudeau fitted into by virtue of his Harvard degree and polished demeanour).[7]

That Trudeau rejoiced in Nixon's extraordinarily condescending declaration in Ottawa in April 1972 that Canada was independent of the United States was further proof of his naïveté about the nature of the Canadian-American relationship and of his misreading of the superficial rapport he and Ivan Head had achieved with Henry Kissinger. They seemed to believe that the way to get on with the U.S. was to contend gracefully with Kissinger in Washington on a donnish level, to bow knowingly to his cultivated media image as a womanizer by arranging a date with a blonde, the television interviewer Charlotte Gobeil, when he accompanied Nixon on his official visit to Ottawa, and then to sit back while he ran interference for Canada with the president. This century's most skilful practitioner of *realpolitik* was respectful of Trudeau's intelligence – they had been schooled by the same professors of government at Harvard, after all – but he knew that Trudeau irritated Nixon intensely, however correctly the two men might behave in their rare face-to-face meetings, and that Canada was tangential to the big East-West issues that concerned the president. Powerful empire-builders do not want charm or intellectual stimulus from the leaders of their dependent states. They want compliance.[8]

The Watergate scandal and Nixon's disgrace gave Trudeau a reprieve from dealing directly with the implications of the sea change Nixonomics represented in Ottawa's connection with Washington, an opportunity that was squandered over the next few years with his failure to reorient the economy in the more autonomous direction prescribed by Mitchell Sharp's ambitious Third Option strategy.[9]

Trudeau had little time to advance his foreign policy thinking during this period in any case because he was snowed under by domestic problems of various kinds. Coping with minority-government politics in 1972–74, responding to the gathering fiscal crisis, containing René Lévesque's Péquistes, and managing his emerging marital difficulties diverted him from paying anything but occasional attention to international questions for the rest of the decade. Under the direction of Sharp's successors, the stolid Allan MacEachen and the Americanophile Don Jamieson, neither of whom was given to innovative thinking or bold action, External Affairs remained marginal in the Ottawa power structure and its senior officers assumed an air of resentful caution, as Allan Gotlieb found out when he returned there as under-secretary in 1977 and tried to restore its lustre. Ironically, Canada's standing abroad improved for a time, partly because of the appreciation in an energy-conscious international community of the country's rich resources and partly because of Trudeau's improved performance as a statesman. [10]

Trudeau's early sorties abroad as prime minister had been marred by his flamboyant bad-boy style. By flaunting his disdain for dull convention on official visits to London, Tokyo, and Moscow, he was able to cover up his inexperience and his unease at joining an international élite whose paradigm he had been scoffing at for twenty years. His behaviour created problems for External officials abroad, who were busy with their own kind of posturing. Nervous inheritors of a great tradition without the wherewithal to sustain it, they had good cause to believe that Trudeau was contemptuous of their abilities. In his first years in office, he was renowned for displaying his lack of regard for their efforts by complaining tersely on his arrival in far-flung capitals that their briefing papers were inadequate and the proposed schedule unacceptable, obliging the frantic diplomats to reorganize his itinerary and to apologize to their local contacts for the prime ministerial no-show at events long since carefully prepared. In Tokyo in 1970, for instance, he refused to inspect a steel factory or to witness a demonstration by black belts at a judo club where he had once stayed as a private traveller. This time he wanted to try kendo and to commune with an old Zen master. Once these additional activities were laid on, he agreed to a compromise that involved taking part in the judo demonstration rather than merely watching it and alleviating his boredom during a foreshortened steel-mill tour by pelting a television cameraman with a handful of the Alberta coal used to fuel its furnaces. [11]

As he gained international experience, he left behind this Arrogant Abroad pose and applied himself to polishing his performance as a cultured adventurer-statesman, the André Malraux of the New World. (Trudeau had met the originator of the act when Malraux was visiting Montreal in 1953. A quarter of a century later, he had another close encounter with Malraux in France, and the onlookers were intrigued by the ease with which the two old romantics discussed Baudelaire before moving on to a wide-ranging exchange on the parlous state of the world.) [12]

As early as 1971, at a Commonwealth meeting in Singapore, he had begun to display a capacity for managing international exchanges by patching over a dangerous dispute between the British prime minister, Edward Heath, and the Commonwealth's Third World leaders. His trip to Beijing in the autumn of 1973, with its personal reward for his foresight in championing China's recognition – an exchange of elegant compliments with the polished Zhou Enlai, an audience with the Buddha-like Mao in a darkened room in the Forbidden City, and a Ming vase as a gift from the great one – was unmistakably a public relations triumph. As the decade progressed, increasingly frequent top-level meetings abroad – NATO consultations and, after 1975, annual economic summits as well as biennial Commonwealth conferences – began to institutionalize an ever-larger role for heads of government in international relations in a move towards global management by committee. (Canada gained entry to the economic summit meetings thanks to Kissinger's advice to President Gerald Ford to invite Trudeau to the second such gathering, held at Puerto Rico in 1976. This intervention was seen as a vindication of Head's courting of Kissinger. It was also a further sign of Kissinger's brilliance at diplomacy: the presence at the summits of a regional partner, rich in strategic commodities, particularly energy, would bolster America's position in consultations with its industrialized rivals.) [13]

Trudeau loved these top-level gatherings. They provided intellectual challenge, cultural stimulus, and rarefied camaraderie in the company of empathetic colleagues such as James Callaghan of the United Kingdom and Helmut Schmidt of West Germany. Joining as an equal in the discourse of powerful statesmen allowed him to exercise his big brain and gratify his big ego while providing welcome, if brief, escapes from problems at home. His pride in his prowess was enhanced by the stature his seniority brought him as new heads of government displaced the old. Eventually, he attained such an expansive self-confidence that he was able to hearten other statesmen in the circle. (After an economic summit session in London, Jimmy Carter astonished Canadian officials by jumping into their limousine in order to hitch a ride to the next event. He wanted the reassurance of talking to his North American allies after being intimidated by a heavy round of economic deliberations dominated by their European and Japanese counterparts. Unlike Nixon, Carter respected Trudeau's views and conferred with him periodically by phone.) [14]

Trudeau's star performances at heads-of-state conferences in the middle and late 1970s rarely translated into perceptible gains for Canada on the economic front. He enjoyed suavely negotiating a new framework for trade between Canada and the European Economic Community with officials and politicians at the highest levels. But the follow-up needed to give commercial substance to this contractual link was left mostly to the private sector, which was too comfortably integrated in the familiar North American market to take the necessary risks, and the hoped-for breakthrough in greater trade with Western Europe never materialized. His delight in international encounters, coupled with the duress he was under in Canada over the wage-and-price-control flip-flop, apparently obscured for him how little of his original foreign policy agenda had been achieved. It was not until he had to confront the premature obituaries on the Trudeau era published at the time of his resignation in 1979 that he came to realize that history would judge as disappointing his efforts abroad. He returned to office in 1980 determined to overturn this critique by bringing to foreign policy the same vigorous, focused attention he expected to devote to his constitutional patriation drive. In these two areas above all others, he saw the possibility of a lasting legacy.

It had been particularly galling for Trudeau to realize that even in the field of international development, his record was deemed far from outstanding. Under the influence of Ivan Head he had emphasized again and again in the 1970s the gravity of Third World poverty. The most notable of the eloquent speeches on the subject crafted for him by Head was delivered at London's Mansion House in 1975, where he expressed his empathy with the "frustration and anger" behind the developing countries' demands for "a comprehensive restructuring of all the components – fiscal, monetary, trade, transport and investment" – of their dependency on the industrial world. Canadian foreign aid had grown substantially after it had been entrusted to the specially constituted Canadian International Development Agency. But his original commitment to raise Canada's official development assistance to 1 per cent of GNP had remained a chimera; and the effectiveness of much of Canada's assistance to the Third World was reduced because it was tied to what Canadian companies could sell and Canadian engineers could build in the recipient nations.[15]

Even when moral rectitude came at minimal cost – imposing sanctions on trade, investment, and athletic relations with South Africa would have endangered only 0.3 per cent of Canadian exports – the Trudeau governments had proven cautious rather than courageous. Despite the prime minister's own statement that Canada "should either stop trading or stop condemning" South Africa, his government continued to support the Johannesburg regime by tolerating trade, investment, and the export of advanced armaments technology, while declaring sweeping embargoes on South Africa and endorsing anti-apartheid resolutions at the UN. Such contradictions between rhetoric and reality meant that by the time the Liberals were defeated in 1979, Canada's moral and material record in the Third World was markedly worse than that of the Scandinavian or Benelux countries with which it could appropriately be compared, although it was marginally better than that of the great powers.[16]

As the Restoration government got under way, fresh alarums about world poverty seemed to present an ideal opportunity for Trudeau to recoup his reputation. In March 1980, an international commission headed by the former German chancellor Willy Brandt published a report urging an international emergency program to transfer resources from the rich to the poor nations. *North-South: A Program for Survival* amounted to a clarion call to the conscience of the First World. With the crusading optimism that marked his return to power, Trudeau responded by setting up a secretariat within CIDA to raise public consciousness on the issue and announcing that Canada would increase its official development assistance targets to 0.5 per cent of GNP by 1985 as part of an effort to reach a target of 0.7 by 1990.[17]

When Canada's turn to host the annual economic summit came in 1981, he determined to seize the opportunity to encourage this club of the northern hemisphere's richest states to accept as an urgent priority the Third World's demand for action to alleviate the terrible poverty of much of the southern hemisphere. Even though he was heavily engaged in constitutional negotiations at home, he took the trouble during the period leading up to the summit to visit two dozen countries, including Mexico, Brazil, Senegal, Nigeria, Kenya, Tanzania, and the Arab states, to learn more about their governments' views. The South was demanding structural change on a global scale to get a fair chance to sell its products at stable prices in the protected markets of the North. "Trade Not Aid" had become its slogan. In his peripatetic conversations with Third World leaders, Trudeau was able to build trust by demonstrating his informed concern while trying to persuade the leading spokesmen for the South to moderate their negotiating stance.[18]

The trouble was one of timing. Even as Trudeau sought renewed rapport with leaders in the Third World, continuing economic distress was changing the political mood in the industrialized nations. Trudeau's friend Helmut Schmidt, under pressure from conservatives at home, was responding guardedly to the ideologues Thatcher and Reagan, who had vanquished James Callaghan and Jimmy Carter, his summit sympathizers on development in the 1970s. Even the newly elected French president, François Mitterrand, was cautiously feeling his way on Third World issues, a socialist lion among the capitalist tigers trying to adjust to post-modern realities.

As a consequence, when Trudeau pleaded the grievances of the developing world at Montebello in July 1981, his colleagues were markedly unresponsive. He did manage to persuade a reluctant Reagan to attend the international conference on co-operation and development, recommended by the Brandt report and scheduled for September in the Mexican resort city of Cancún. It proved a futile effort. Although Trudeau co-chaired the large gathering with trilingual aplomb, the Anglo-American message was unyielding in the face of the developing countries' intransigent demands: if they would only unleash the competitive forces of the free market, their problems would resolve themselves. The lack of agreement even on an agenda for further negotiations delighted the Reaganites, who saw it as a defeat for the liberal Trudeau. They made no effort to hide their glee from Trudeau's entourage: "Up against our guy, your guy's bleeding-heart liberalism is a joke," was the sentiment they conveyed.[19]

During the fifteen months following the Cancún conference, Trudeau again found that pressing domestic issues left him little time for independent initiatives in international relations. The last spasms of his constitutional patriation effort engrossed him until the early spring of 1982, and the economic crisis set off by the recession and the MacEachen-Stewart budget fiasco kept him tied to Ottawa for the rest of the year. All he could manage was the quick-trip states-manship involved in attending the economic summit that Mitter-rand hosted at Versailles in June 1982, and the NATO meeting that followed immediately afterwards in Bonn.

As chairman of the Bonn conference, Trudeau made a thought-ful statement about the sterility of such gatherings, but his carefully considered ideas were treated with far less interest by the media than a sarcastic quip he let slip that was interpreted as a reference to Ronald Reagan's chronic state of befuddlement. During a photo-op mêlée Trudeau responded to a reporter's shouted inquiry about U.S. defence policy directed at Reagan by pointing to his secretary of state, Alexander Haig, and saying, "Ask Al," the implication being that Haig was better able to articulate White House thinking than the president himself.[20]

For his Liberal handlers at home, the reaction this episode inspired brought with it a peculiar kind of heartburn. On the one hand, it made the lippy Trudeau once more the object of opposition attack. On the other hand, such flashes of audacity gave the elector-ate a renewed sense of his vitality and originality as a leader. The effect on Trudeau's domestic reputation of his performances abroad had always been double-edged. Goldfarb's polling showed that Anglo-Canadians alternated between indignation at his inflated self-importance and admiration for his stylish bravado. Trudeau made it possible to be a Canadian cosmopolite, a phrase that before his appearance on the world stage had been a contradiction in terms. In Quebec, the reaction was different. He was regarded in his home province as a not unusual – though extraordinarily visible – example of a French-Canadian type, the inveterate traveller, a *coureur de bois* of the twentieth century, projecting the adventurous spirit that was the converse of the stay-at-home stability of the *habitant*.[21]

The ambiguities inherent in the "Ask Al" incident prompted Tom Axworthy, in consultation with Martin Goldfarb and Keith Davey, to persuade the prime minister to postpone for a second time the extensive trip to the Far East that had been planned as his next big initiative abroad. Davey, who was busy promoting Six & Five, believed it would be a mistake for Liberal MPs to be urging their constituents to make sacrifices for the national good while their leader was appearing in television news clips emerging from limousines in far-away places, wearing tropical suits that made him look like a throwback to the last days of the Raj. However serious the intent of his mission, he would be charged with globe-trotting at public expense while his fellow citizens were being urged to scrimp and save.

Beyond the Liberal operatives' preoccupation with media images were other, more substantial concerns about the prime minister's global efforts. An interdepartmental group of Ottawa economic policy-makers was arguing that Trade Not Aid was a notion that Canada might well apply to its own problems. Dismay about the country's deteriorating economic position had already prompted the organizational reform of January 1982, designed to subordinate External Affairs fancy-pants discussions of high politics to a new focus on the nitty-gritty of trade. In hard times, charity had to begin at home. Canada could no longer afford to ignore its trade imbalance, and the prime minister needed to demonstrate that he understood this new fact of global life.

This reasoning was a key factor late in 1982 – when the Six & Five exercise had been deemed a success and the Liberal policy convention was over – in his political advisers' decision that the moment had come to unleash Trudeau on the world once more. This time, trade would be the focus of his efforts. Canada's commerce with Asia had overtaken its dealings with the whole of Europe. A prime ministerial visit to the "little dragons," the newly industrializing countries of Southeast Asia, during the Christmas–New Year parliamentary break might help to improve the Liberals' standing with the corporate community and to quicken Trudeau's interest in holding on to his job.

When the prime minister took off in January 1983 to court markets for Canada in seven Asian states, he was trying on an unaccustomed role: that of high-priced pedlar for his country's wares in the world's fastest-growing market. Lotus petals and brass bands at airports; motorcades, cannon fire, and miles of red carpet; hectic twelve- to fourteen-hour days; newspaper photos and television film of Trudeau's middle son, Sacha, falling asleep on Daddy's shoulder while watching a kick-boxing match or a sumo bout: all these images were aimed at drawing attention to the home of the brave Mounties and the land of the snowbound Inuit in order to gain access for its entrepreneurs to the Southeast Asian politicians and civil servants who might sign contracts for new subways for their teeming cities or fibre-optics technologies for their communications systems. Trudeau took on this new job with zest, closeting himself with Canadian executives in each country he visited, and asking how he could help them open doors. He even tried to drum up business in the tiny oil-rich Islamic autocracy of Brunei, the former British protectorate known as the Shellfare state, in reference to the prosperity generated there by Royal Dutch Shell.[22]

Although Canadian entrepreneurs working these distant territories were pleased at the boost that Trudeau's presence gave their prospects, for his partisans at home there was little comfort to be drawn from the trip's outcome despite all the strategizing that had gone into its timing and itinerary. Media coverage of the Asian tour in Canada was a public relations fiasco. It started badly at the first stop in Thailand. Having been told by the prime minister that he was taking an evening off, journalists covering the tour were enraged the next morning to find they had been scooped by images splashed all over the Bangkok media of Trudeau at a Thai boxing match. In Singapore he fobbed off his media pursuers a second time by telling them he was attending a private dinner with friends. Once again the Canadian reporters were confronted with local coverage of him feasting publicly in a restaurant, brandishing chopsticks he had been given by the establishment when he had eaten there twelve years before.

When Trudeau went out of his way to be unobliging, the media people went out of their way to minimize his accomplishments. After he spent one Sunday afternoon relaxing on a beach in Malaysia and his staff created further hostility by prohibiting the only photographer on the trip from using his camera, they retaliated. The stories they filed described Trudeau as goofing off, even though this was his first real break from his arduous performance as trade ambassador and it lasted only a few hours.[23]

Irritated by Trudeau's ill-concealed dislike and given little time in the whirlwind schedule to analyse the complexities of international trade or the subtleties of Pacific diplomacy, the journalists were looking for easy putdowns. Citing a scathing report on the Philippines by Amnesty International, which held the Marcos government responsible for dozens of arbitrary killings, torturings, and other rights violations during the previous year alone, they put the Canadian delegation on the defensive in Manila. An official in the Trudeau party made headlines by dismissing an inquiry based on the Amnesty findings with the considered opinion that Canada could not afford to "increase unemployment in Sudbury to free a nun in the Philippines."[24]

Although he reprimanded his aide for this indiscretion, Trudeau himself declared that he had not come to visit other countries "with the intention of telling them how they should run their own affairs." Beyond mutual antipathy, there were grounds for the journalistic scepticism with which Trudeau's stance was reported. His proclamation of impeccable respect for his host countries' autonomy patently contradicted his government's actual record. Canada had long supported the International Monetary Fund and the World Bank in dictating to the Third World Draconian programs to restructure their economies and to submit them to the harsh discipline of global capitalism.[25]

Back in Ottawa in early February after his not-so-triumphal progress through the Far East, Trudeau found himself once more in the hurly-burly of domestic politics. While he was away, the Conservatives in convention had committed an audacious act. After eighteen months of outdistancing the Liberals in the popularity polls and

with less than two years to go until the next election, they had
entered into a leadership race. Ottawa was awash with rumours that
Joe Clark was too progressive a Conservative for certain elements in
the Toronto, Montreal, and Calgary business communities, who
were attempting to oust him by responding favourably to the relentless manoeuvring to succeed Clark of one of their own: the Montreal lawyer and comprador beyond compare, Brian Mulroney,
president of the Iron Ore Company of Canada, a subsidiary of the
Hanna Mining Company of Cleveland, Ohio.

In the PMO, Trudeau's staff was busy concocting a suitably sunny
interpretation of this turn of events. "These turkeys have decided to
self-immolate once more," Tom Axworthy was saying to his friends
as he contemplated with relish the prospect of the Conservatives
perpetuating the factional feuding, policy quarrels, and savage
attacks on their leadership that had kept them out of office federally
for much of the twentieth century. "It's the Tory syndrome," he
explained, evoking the analysis of this self-destructive pattern developed by his colleague from his days at Queen's, the political scientist
George Perlin.[26]

Axworthy hoped the Liberals could benefit from the Conservatives' folly by continuing to pursue their recovery agenda quietly
while the media concentrated their ferocious energies on the
Tories' infighting. But soon after Trudeau's return from Asia, a contentious issue of the Liberals' own making resurfaced to threaten this
equanimous attitude. It was in the foreign policy area that had
caused Trudeau the greatest difficulty from the beginning: national
defence.

After he had been defeated on the NATO question in 1969, Trudeau had persuaded himself that Canada could continue in its
nuclear-based military alliances (this was the necessary practice of
*realpolitik*) while eagerly pursuing negotiations on disarmament and
nuclear non-proliferation as its special mission (this was the altruistic
pursuit of peace). Accordingly, he directed External Affairs to contribute vigorously to international discussions designed to achieve a
comprehensive test ban. But at every such forum, Canadian officials

came up against the wall of their country's impotence. Canada might want to act the moralist in the nuclear club, but as representatives of a country that was without atomic armaments of its own and dependent for protection on the American arsenal, their reasoned positions were dismissed as self-serving do-goodism. Proof positive of this powerlessness was Trudeau's failure in 1972 to convince Nixon to abandon plans for a nuclear test on the Alaskan island of Amchitka, despite having scientific and public opinion in both countries on his side.[27]

Even in efforts to block nuclear proliferation, Canada had turned out to be less effective than Trudeau had hoped, as illustrated by the unhappy experience of providing India with a Canadian-designed nuclear reactor, the CANDU, which was intended to generate electricity solely for peaceable use. But Indian scientists extracted fissionable material from the CANDU in order to produce their own bomb, in defiance of the spirit of the original agreement between India and Canada and the tough safeguards that Canada subsequently attempted to impose. Trudeau's angry exchanges with the Indian prime minister, Indira Gandhi, did little to rectify the situation. A further disillusionment was in store when West Germany was able to sell a reactor to Argentina as a result of *not* insisting on the rigorous controls Canada had pioneered.[28]

Trudeau did manage to secure the denuclearization of Canadian fighter-bombers deployed in Europe. Using to his advantage the technocratic logic of deterrence theory, he made the case that nuclear bombs turned the planes into first-strike weapons, which made them inherently destabilizing. But when he engaged in these issues, he found that the ill will caused by Canada's partial troop withdrawals from NATO was still reverberating. The Brits, the French, the Dutch, the Belgians, the Germans, and the commissars at the European Commission in Brussels all gave him to understand that the price for expanded Canadian economic relations with Europe was a greater military contribution to NATO, if not of troops then of equipment. Opting for hardware over humanware required Ottawa to replace weaponry that had become obsolescent. This meant that defence spending, frozen since 1969 as a sign of the Liberals' half-hearted anti-militarism, would have to be increased. Accordingly, National Defence was granted a substantial annual increase of 12 per cent for its capital budget, to be effective for five years from 1975 and rendered inflation-proof for good measure. Because Canada no longer had the capacity to manufacture complete weapons systems, equipment would have to be purchased elsewhere. Armaments for NATO deployment had to fit into the alliance's integrated military planning, which meant buying them principally in the United States, where the most advanced military hardware was available thanks to the Pentagon's control of Western defence strategy and technology.[29]

By this tortuous route, the Trudeau government reverted to the logic of Cold War continentalism, and Trudeau himself was transmuted from the peace-promoting polemicist who had attacked Pearson in *Cité libre* for even considering a nuclear capacity for Canadian forces into a complicit, though reluctant, participant in the U.S. Department of Defense's nuclear-based strategizing. By the late 1970s, when some officials in the administration indicated the Pentagon might shift from subscribing to the deterrence doctrine labelled MAD – for "mutually assured destruction" – to the even madder notion that a nuclear war started by the Soviets could actually be won by the United States, his government was too tied in to the American military-industrial complex to demur.[30]

It was in this context that American defence officials approached their opposite numbers in Ottawa to suggest testing over Canadian territory the Cruise – a new missile that was more accurate because of its ability to read enemy terrain and was capable of cruising so close to the ground that it could obliterate its targets undetected in advance by enemy radar. The Dr. Strangelovian dream of vaporizing the West's enemies while enjoying ice-cold Coke in comfort was about to come true. To the Canadian military, this looked like an offer that might make life next to the nuclear giant worth living again. Canada's importance to the Pentagon had been in decline ever since intercontinental and submarine-launched ballistic missiles had displaced long-range bombers as the chief nuclear threat. These new aircraft-launched Cruise missiles could return Canada to its rightful place as the strategic battleground in U.S.S.R.-versus-U.S.A. war-games. At virtually no cost, National Defence had a chance to regain direct access to the latest data on weapons development as well as to intensify their rapport with the American military.[31]

Officials in other government departments had their own reasons for welcoming the idea of testing the Cruise. The Canadian arms industry contributed only 0.5 per cent to Canada's GNP, but its sophisticated products yielded the kind of high-tech jobs prized by industrial policy-makers. Even better, Canadian production of arms components was almost entirely for export and accounted for the slight balance-of-payments surplus that Canada enjoyed in that category. The Cruise could also serve as a showpiece for the government's dogged effort to co-operate with entrepreneurial winners rather than to continue propping up business losers. The inertial guidance system for the Cruise had been developed by Litton Industries, the Metro Toronto–based subsidiary of an American corporation, with the help of $26 million in research-and-development funding provided by Ottawa's venerable Defence Industries Productivity Program, set up by C.D. Howe a quarter of a century earlier. Litton International was willing to give this Cruise component "a world-product mandate," which meant it would be manufactured in Canada for marketing around the globe – an important consideration since the device could be adapted to civil aviation and might generate an estimated $1.2 billion in world sales.[32]

Given what was at stake, it was no wonder that the community of interests centred on the tiny Canadian defence industry was poised to deliver concerted support to the Cruise project. The Canadian Defence Association could guarantee solid backing from veterans and armed forces personnel. And the Business Council on National Issues, which normally attacked the Trudeauites for their profligacy with the public purse, had no difficulty recommending, given the Soviet arms build-up, that Ottawa double the annual increase in its military budget.[33]

But even though the value of the Cruise was unquestioned in this community, the political risk involved in testing it put a premium on bureaucratic guile. Public sensitivity to any escalation of the arms race at a time when hard-liners were in the ascendancy in the U.S.S.R. as well as the U.S.A. could provoke a public outcry. A major uproar might scare off Trudeau and his cabinet. To pre-empt this possibility, Canadian officials proposed to their American counterparts that they negotiate an umbrella accord on joint weapons trials that would elide specific mention of missile testing. CANUSTEP, the Canada–United States Test and Evaluation Program, was duly formulated, along with a public relations campaign that could be activated in case of need.[34]

Because of this careful backstage manoeuvring, when U.S. Secretary of Defense Caspar Weinberger made a formal request for a new weapons-testing agreement to Minister of National Defence Gilles Lamontagne on April 15, 1981, the way had been cleared for the proposal to slide smoothly through the Ottawa system. It passed the two relevant cabinet committees during the late summer and fall of 1981, when ministerial attention was conveniently focused on the constitutional negotiations and the crisis in the Canadian-American relationship over the NEP. By December of that year, when Trudeau signed a letter addressed to Reagan confirming the Canadian government's concurrence in principle with an agreement on testing new weapons, it looked as though National Defence officials had succeeded in having their way with the Cruise by finessing the issue past the unsuspecting politicians.[35]

Within weeks, this cosy arrangement was inadvertently exposed. A casual comment made by a Pentagon official at a Washington gathering led a Canadian journalist to break the story of a secret deal to test in Canadian airspace a new addition to the Americans' nuclear arsenal. Trudeau initially denied that anything of the kind had transpired, apparently believing this to be the case. In

CANUSTEP, he thought he had kept Canada's options open by insisting that there be "no agreement [for testing specific weapons] except in certain circumstances." Instead, he found that the program was an elaborate ploy to prevent the Canadian military from "looking so palsy-walsy with the U.S.," in his phrase, while behaving in precisely that manner. "That's the way they operate!" he exclaimed in frustration when reflecting later on the defence officials' capacity to create irreversible situations *sub rosa*. His unwitting endorsement of CANUSTEP's full implications naturally caused the Reaganites to assume that his government would be willing to test the Cruise. Once the scheme became public in Canada, it threatened to make a mockery of his reputation as an activist for *détente*, particularly his original 1978 proposal to a United Nations special session on disarmament of a four-point program of arms control based on the suffocation of new weapons development.[36]

When Mark MacGuigan acknowledged shortly afterwards that CANUSTEP existed as a formal document, he promised that the government would not agree to test any specific weapon before the next United Nations special session on disarmament, scheduled for June. The UN session failed to achieve a breakthrough. Ironically, Trudeau's speech to the assembled delegates, which called for a package of measures including a ban on testing new delivery vehicles, helped link the Cruise – itself a new delivery system – to the anti-nuclear protest that was spreading through Western Europe. Public concern was rising there about the NATO allies' own escalating arms build-up, and the Soviets under their new leader, Yuri Andropov, who had recently succeeded the bellicose Leonid Brezhnev, were adeptly playing on it. In a remarkable peace offensive, Andropov was offering to reduce Soviet nuclear strategic arsenals, freeze deployment of all new nuclear weapons, and cut back the threatening new-generation ss-20 missiles Brezhnev had installed in Eastern Europe. In January 1983, Andropov went further by proposing a nuclear-free zone in the Mediterranean, a cut in Soviet deployment, a ban on further nuclear tests, and even a halt in arms sales to the Third World.[37]

In response to Andropov's propaganda for peace, Ronald Reagan stepped up his use of the rhetoric of war, describing the Soviet Union as an "evil empire" as though he were a stalwart space commander dealing with a mythical diabolical force in the movie *Star Wars*. His frighteningly simplistic attitude helped trigger massive public demonstrations in Germany, Italy, and Holland against the new intermediate-range nuclear-tipped American missiles that NATO was installing there to counter the ss-20s.[38]

European anti-Americanism reached a crescendo after Reagan unveiled in late March 1983 his Strategic Defense Initiative, a plan to develop a space-based anti-missile system that would make the United States impervious to nuclear attack. Star Wars, as SDI was immediately dubbed, appalled even mainstream security analysts, who expressed concern that shifting America's missile defences into space was at the very least destabilizing to the East-West balance, if not patently provocative to the Soviets. Since the Soviets had little reason to trust Reagan's professed commitment to share SDI technology at some time in the future, the prospect of an "invulnerable" United States of America could well prompt the hard-line old guard in the Kremlin to override Andropov and launch a pre-emptive strike while American defences could still be penetrated.[39]

This was the unavoidable reality Trudeau faced in the late winter of 1983. Canada's involvement in testing the Cruise meant he was caught *in flagrante contradictio*, after managing to keep military matters by and large out of the limelight for more than a decade.

Trudeau's distress at the damage the international controversy over the Cruise was inflicting on his record as a peace advocate was made worse by his long-held, but now intensified, anxieties about accidental nuclear catastrophe. Far from being willing to suffocate arms development, the Reaganites were pushing ahead with massive increases in military research. Their scarcely veiled contempt for NATO's "two-track" approach – simultaneously negotiating arms control agreements at Geneva while modernizing nuclear missiles –

was alarming their allies as well as their enemies. Tensions caused by the Soviet interventions in Afghanistan and the military take-over of the Polish government paled in the face of concerns being expressed in European capitals that the Reaganites' Manichean view of world problems might trigger an outbreak of hostilities between the Pentagon and the Kremlin. The survival of the planet was at stake, and Trudeau urgently wanted the leaders of the industrialized world to address the threat when they met at Williamsburg, Virginia, where Reagan was to host the 1983 economic summit meeting in late May.[40]

He knew that the co-religionists Thatcher and Reagan would oppose him and that, in concert, their strength at Williamsburg could be irresistible. Helmut Schmidt had been defeated in March by the conservative Helmut Kohl. Amintore Fanfani of Italy wanted to avoid confronting the United States on military matters because such controversies were not in his country's economic interest. Only François Mitterrand was a possible ally, and at that, he might prove an ambivalent one. A committed socialist who had battled pro-Soviet French communists for decades, Mitterrand was deeply suspicious of the U.S.S.R. He was at the same time a committed chauvinist, jealously guarding the French military autonomy built up by Charles de Gaulle. France's nuclear weapons may have been more *farce* than *force de frappe*, but their existence made Mitterrand reluctant to support disarmament proposals that might call into question these symbols of his glorious nation's glorious past. Furthermore, he was developing an odd admiration for Thatcher – "Elle a les yeux de Caligule, mais elle a la bouche de Marilyn Monroe" – and her intractability along with her ancient nation's importance in the European Community appealed to his undogmatic pragmatism.[41]

Trudeau had another problem with Mitterrand. He needed his co-operation to lay to rest Gaullism's other legacy, French support for Quebec's international aspirations. Trudeau's determination to contain Quebec separatism had coloured his approach to Canada's foreign policy from the early years of his political career. When de Gaulle shouted his "Vive le Québec libre!" from the balcony of Montreal's city hall in 1967, Trudeau had been among the hawks in Pearson's cabinet insisting the French president be denounced. Later he had picked a quarrel with de Gaulle by objecting to France's use of its former colony Gabon as a pawn in inviting Quebec to an international conference as though it were a sovereign state. To counteract further encouragement of Quebec independence by de Gaulle's successors, he had sent his close friend Gérard Pelletier to France as a watch-dog ambassador. But the Élysée Palace had continued to be captive to a small group of separatist sympathizers in the Quai d'Orsay, despite Ottawa's initiatives. Trudeau had hoped that the election of the Fifth Republic's first socialist president might allow this festering issue to be resolved. But he had not yet won concessions from Mitterrand on the Quebec question, and until this was the case, he could not count on his support at Williamsburg. [42]

He could at least assume a procedural advantage there, gained as a result of the criticism he had made as chairman of the NATO summit in Bonn, when he had expressed his annoyance with the meaningless formality of meetings where heads of government gathered to read aloud their bureaucrats' texts and then comment to the press on communiqués negotiated before the statesmen had even convened. His protest had helped persuade Reagan to plan a less formal summit for Williamsburg, where the participants would be able to interact more spontaneously and to draft communiqués reflecting whatever consensus was reached. Such a relaxation of protocol could allow Trudeau to exploit his intellectual prowess and confront his ideological opponents over their misbegotten positions. [43]

Still at issue was the NATO two-track approach to arms control and the balance to be struck between the first track of installing the new American missiles and the second track of pursuing arms control talks. Trudeau wanted to show that Canada was in tune with the Europeans' desire to lower East-West tensions by persuading the U.S. to be less irresponsibly confrontational with the Soviets. But once Reagan introduced the question of global security at the summit's opening dinner, Margaret Thatcher – in an apparently pre-arranged response – began lecturing her fellow heads of government on the need to endorse a tough, even provocative, line towards the Kremlin.[44]

This kind of approach appalled the Iron Lady's foreign affairs advisers, who found she remained impervious to their frequently expressed view that it would be better for her to be more temperate, that international relations was a ceaseless process of negotiations among interests. When she had first ventured abroad as prime minister in 1979, Thatcher had disliked international exchanges intensely, largely because she had found it difficult to bully her allies abroad the way she could her ministers at home. She found the aristocratic Valéry Giscard d'Estaing insufferably patronizing, and he dismissed her as "that grocer's daughter." Helmut Schmidt's firm grasp of financial matters was too strong for her to best him in disputes; he had been known to defend himself against her volubility by feigning sleep in her presence.[45]

By the time of the 1983 summit, she had gained in self-assurance and authority thanks, in part, to her close relationship with Reagan, which had flourished during the previous two years. With his unreconstructed view of the communist menace, Reagan was a wonder in Thatcher's view, and he was heartened by her total agreement with his beliefs and the fervour of her Anglo-American jingoism. She had arrived at Williamsburg as a reincarnated Boadicea in teased blonde hair and high-heeled pumps, exultant because the British victory over the Argentinians in the Falklands had caused her political stock at home to climb. That very weekend, she was half-way through her second winning election campaign, energetically smiting her political foes on the left and confounding her enemies within her party's ranks. It was in this bellicose spirit that she spoke at the summit's opening dinner. Far from responding to the world-wide concern among women for international peace and social security, she had turned out to be the ur-example of a male-identifying upwardly mobile careerist, proud to be the best man in her cabinet, and as hawkish as any Pentagon general.

Undaunted by her belligerence, Trudeau objected to these sentiments at the dinner and again the next morning when, along with Mitterrand, he took issue with the confrontational tone of the draft communiqué the Americans had produced. He argued that Western leaders should speak more softly if they really wanted to be heard in Moscow. Although his words were aimed at Reagan, Trudeau found himself in an acrimonious fight with Thatcher. The clash between the two prime ministers precipitated a debate so heated that the meeting continued for an hour beyond the scheduled break for lunch. Thatcher dismissed Trudeau's reluctance to take a strong line on deterrence, accusing him of being "a solace to the Soviets." In the face of her scorn – at one point Reagan thought that she was going to order Trudeau to stand in a corner – Trudeau persisted with his argument for moderation. Reagan himself was roused from his genial torpor and launched into a vigorous defence of his position for twenty minutes without using his cue cards – to the wonderment and relief of his advisers, who knew he had put aside his briefing books the night before so he could watch *The Sound of Music* on television. [46]

Observing this unwelcome spat, U.S. officials feared that their carefully calculated agenda was being hijacked by Trudeau. "Who does this asshole think he is?" a State Department official was overheard asking in exasperation as Trudeau kept arguing his points. By the end of the afternoon, after the foreign ministers had joined the discussions, Trudeau and Mitterrand won some concessions. (This was the beginning of a greater rapport between the two leaders, who were equally appalled at what they saw as Reagan's ignorance.) The communiqué on security, drafted to convey to Moscow a strong affirmation of Western solidarity and resolve, was amended so its tone would be less provocative. And at Trudeau's urging, a final point was added pledging the summit leaders to "devote our full political resources to reducing the threat of war." The meeting then moved on to economic issues and concluded with civility restored and Trudeau congratulating Reagan on the vigour and informality of the proceedings.[47]

The momentary satisfaction Trudeau felt as a result of his gains at Williamsburg scarcely survived the return flight to Ottawa. He told his PMO advisers and cabinet ministers that he found the intractability of the Reagan-Thatcher attitude to the Soviets deeply disturbing. He had cause to feel gloomier still a fortnight later, when the formal announcement of the U.S. government's request to test the Cruise over the Canadian northscape triggered a new series of protests by Canadian peace activists. The impact of their agitations was heightened by a continuing flood of protest mail to parliamentarians and by polls that showed Canadian public opinion had evolved from the automatic pro-Americanism of twenty years before. There was a pervasive sense that, although the danger of a nuclear holocaust had increased, creating new weapons was futile. Despite the recent Soviet invasion of Afghanistan, Canadians expressed less fear of nuclear attack by the Soviets and a reduced tendency to blame East-West tensions exclusively on Moscow. The U.S. under Ronald Reagan was held to be at least as great a threat to peace. By this time, the Cruise had become a seriously divisive issue. "Natural allies [of Liberalism] like the United Church were deserting us," Tom Axworthy recalled later. "Our own caucus was split down the middle." And for a few weeks, it even seemed possible that the cabinet might refuse the U.S. request.[48]

Once Washington realized that Ottawa was wavering, it mobilized its bilateral resources. The Pentagon cagily kept out of the controversy, knowing that the Canadian military was on side. Since the problem lay with the politicians, the arm-twisting was left to the White House, in acknowledgement of its successful exercise in disciplining the Trudeauites over the NEP and FIRA. The administration merely had to decide which hints to drop and which anxieties to raise on Canadian-American issues. Countervailing the softwood lumber exports that were causing problems for forestry operators in the American northwest was a possibility. So was harassing Canadian steel manufacturers, whose success in exporting their products to the United States was a perennially touchy topic on Capitol Hill. Stalling the Alaska natural gas pipeline so dear to Calgary's Petroleum Club could mobilize Alberta against Ottawa. Reopening the Auto Pact would alarm Ontario. Reviving the moratorium on regulations preventing Canadian truckers from driving loads across the border into the U.S. would anger Canadian exporters and Canadian unions. By subtly and not-so-subtly linking support for the Cruise to these and other bilateral issues, the Reaganites implied that retaliation would be swift if Ottawa – as NATO's notorious free rider and gratuitous moralist – had the gall to stand in the way on a military matter the U.S. deemed essential to its security. "They were pounding the shit out of us," a PMO official revealed.[49]

For Washington it became a question of commitment: was Canada for freedom or against it? "They're testing us, not the Cruise," Iona Campagnolo observed from her vantage point in the Liberal Party's national office. As threats coming from the White House and Congress were relayed to the cabinet, some ministers urged capitulation while others resented the American pressure.[50]

Only Lloyd Axworthy and half a dozen others were unequivocally opposed to the testing. "Nothing else took so much ministerial time in that period," Axworthy remembered, crediting Trudeau with permitting an exhaustive debate and chairing it with resolute fairness. Eventually the majority of Trudeau's ministers decided Canada was in too deeply to get out. How could they suddenly nix a project Ottawa was funding? Marc Lalonde summed up the dilemma: "Why should we go out of our way to make difficulties with the Americans? We just couldn't afford to antagonize them on a subject they felt so strongly about." Eventually the cabinet lined up behind Lalonde and Allan MacEachen, who had already assured George Shultz that Canada would permit the testing.[51]

Having agonized privately over this conundrum, Trudeau turned his rationalizing machine on high once the cabinet decision was made. He told several colleagues and friends he was acquiescing to the Cruise tests as a result of discussions with Helmut Schmidt, the originator of the NATO two-track strategy. Though no document was produced to justify this assertion, he maintained in public that testing the Cruise was a question of honouring Canada's international commitments. Canada's credibility with its NATO allies was at stake; it had to pull its weight in the alliance. These statements echoed the way in which he had eased his pride earlier in the year by boldly telling George Bush when the American vice-president was visiting Ottawa that Canada wouldn't test the Cruise as a favour to the United States; it would do it for Europe. [52]

Characteristically, once the Cruise decision was made, Trudeau admitted to no regrets and displayed no sign of humiliation or embarrassment even though the gap between his words on disarmament and his government's deeds had become an abyss. But there were indications that he was still concerned about the peace issue. When the Prince of Wales during a visit to Ottawa in June piqued Trudeau's interest by lauding the National Film Board documentary *If You Love This Planet*, he asked Tom Axworthy to screen it for him. The passionate anti-nuclear pleading of its subject, the Australian physician and pacifist Helen Caldicott, had been branded propaganda by the U.S. Justice Department.

Throughout the spring and summer in their early-morning meetings, Trudeau and Axworthy had been discussing whether – since his private advocacy at the summits had yielded no significant softening of the West's hard line – Trudeau should take on the disarmament issue more assertively. Some of their Liberal colleagues felt that the Canadian economy was still in such bad shape that they would be criticized for trying to divert attention from the country's internal problems. Trudeau himself insisted he wasn't going "to play politics with peace." [53]

As a left Liberal who had been nearly as incensed as his brother Lloyd over the Cruise decision, Tom Axworthy kept searching for some legitimate reason for Trudeau to go public, some peg on which to hang a prime ministerial initiative. He set up a lunch for Trudeau with Helen Caldicott and the actress Margot Kidder, an anti-nuclear activist who was romantically interested in Trudeau. He arranged for Trudeau to meet John F. Kennedy's secretary of defence, Robert McNamara, who was urging NATO to renounce the first use of nuclear weapons and who advised the prime minister to act while he still enjoyed the power and prestige of office. He synchronized Trudeau's summer holiday with a meeting of scientists in Sicily where he could absorb – and be duly horrified by – the message propounded there by Edward Teller, the White House's real-life Dr. Strangelove, who had conceived Star Wars and who matter-of-factly explained the calculus of annihilating the Soviets in space-based nuclear warfare. [54]

Axworthy also organized a ministerial seminar at Val Morin in the Laurentians so that Allan MacEachen and Gilles Lamontagne could get a direct sense of the gravity of the international situation by discussing it with a score of academic and political experts from Canada and the United States. Although no specific recommendation emerged from the weekend meeting, there was agreement that the East-West stand-off was extremely dangerous. The Soviets and the Americans had worked themselves into such paranoid states of mind that something needed to be done to help them back down from their hardened positions. What was that something? Could Canada help? The answer came with a bolt from the blue. [55]

The bolt was a missile fired on September 1 by a Soviet SU-15 fighter, its target a regular Korean Airlines flight (KAL 007) from New York to Seoul. The loss of life was total – 269 passengers and crew, including ten Canadians. The shock was global and the world braced for nuclear war.

Trudeau knew from Canada's access to American intelligence monitoring of radio traffic between the fighter pilot and his ground control that the Soviet military believed the Korean plane had penetrated Soviet airspace deliberately on an American spy mission. Despite this intelligence, the Reaganites decided to turn the incident to their ideological purposes; the president of the United States denounced the Soviets' heartless disregard for innocent human life and raised the level of international tension by several alarming notches. This was the kind of disaster-in-the-making that Trudeau had been warning could happen in his orations at Williamsburg, a catalytic event that could trigger global annihilation once human error combined with technologically sophisticated weaponry. The world had inched closer to the brink of nuclear catastrophe than at any time since the Cuban Missile Crisis. [56]

Ivan Head, keeping a watching brief on reaction to the KAL crisis from his perch at the International Development Research Centre in Ottawa, which he had been directing since 1978, felt that something had to be done to defuse this powder keg and that Trudeau could be the man to do it. Over lunch at 24 Sussex, he urged the prime minister to intervene with the superpowers by embarking on a private one-man peace mission to the Kremlin and the White House. It should be short, sweet, and secret; a plea for reason and understanding on both sides for the sake of the planet's survival. Trudeau was intrigued but wary. [57]

Axworthy was also energized by this fortuitous development. He set up more meetings for the prime minister: Trudeau with General Bernard Rogers, the Supreme Allied Commander in Europe; Trudeau with General Brent Scowcroft, former head of the White House's National Security Council; Trudeau with George Kennan, the State Department elder who was seriously concerned about the deepening East-West crisis; Trudeau with the Harvard Nuclear Study Group; Trudeau with Georgii Arbatov of Moscow's Institute for the Study of the U.S.A. and Canada. [58]

As with all big decisions affecting his life and image, Trudeau proceeded with caution – ruminating in private, consulting widely, playing the devil's acerbic advocate by grilling those who proposed he take action even more intently than those who counselled reticence. "Why me? Why should I do it?" he asked Allan Gotlieb, his ambassador to the United States. When Gotlieb responded that he thought the context was propitious for him to make a contribution to world peace and then added the caveat "But you're not unique," Trudeau was vexed. He seemed to want to be told what Helen Caldicott had said to him earlier in the summer: "You are the one person in the world who can bring East and West together." It was as though if enough people made this extravagant statement, and he demurred with sufficient reluctance in order to provoke still more fervent pleas for his intervention, he could then – diffidently but bravely – buckle on his armour and set off on a hero's quest.[59]

After playing coy for more than a fortnight, Trudeau finally made up his mind to act and, having done so, turned for help to the two departments of government whose workings and expertise he had been depreciating for years: External Affairs and National Defence. On September 21, he summoned their ministers, Allan MacEachen and Gilles Lamontagne, to say he had decided to mount a solo peace mission, and he gave them ten days to work out the strategy and tactics.

When the ministers returned with this news to their departments, their senior officials – seeing Trudeau's proposed initiative as quixotic – decided the best way to satisfy his needs would be to keep a safe distance from the operation while setting up a joint committee of younger, middle-level bureaucrats and letting them draw up a plan. Excited by the chance to have their ideas fed directly into the PMO/PCO, these unjaundiced policy analysts under the direction of Louis Delvoie, director general of External's General Bureau of International Security and Arms Control, produced twenty-six proposals to be considered at a special meeting at the Meech Lake government centre in the Gatineau. It was chaired by Trudeau himself with participation by several Canadian ambassadors he had summoned from their posts to give him advice: Allan Gotlieb from Washington, Gérard Pelletier from the UN in New York, Si Taylor from NATO headquarters in Brussels, Michel Dupuy from Paris, and Geoffrey Pearson from Moscow. In the charged atmosphere created by this gathering of diplomatic heavyweights, the working group's ideas were shaped into a plan of action. Rather than make secret trips to Moscow and Washington, Trudeau would embark on a round-the-world journey, using his prestige as a statesman to engage other heads of government in discussions about East-West issues by putting forward half a dozen disarmament proposals, specific enough to make sense technologically but not so radical as to provoke either outright rejection by communist leaders or angry dismissal from the Western nuclear powers, the U.S., the U.K., and France.

The initiative would be launched with a major speech, Trudeau's favourite form of performance art, at a modest conference scheduled to be held near Toronto at the University of Guelph, after months of careful planning by George Ignatieff, a retired mandarin from External's glory days who had made an important place for himself in the Canadian peace movement. The prime ministerial writing team was asked to produce a speech as portentous as Trudeau's orations in the 1980 referendum, only this time his aim would be not to save Quebec from the crime of separatism but to save the world from Armageddon.[60]

On October 27 – eight weeks after the KAL disaster and two days after Reagan had unleashed the armed might of the United States to rescue the tiny Caribbean island of Grenada from Marxism – Trudeau told the Guelph audience of earnest peace-makers, startled by his glamorous presence in their midst: "There is today an ominous rhythm of crisis . . . a crisis of confidence in ourselves, a crisis of faith in others." Affirming that "the relationship between the superpowers may have become too charged with animosity for East-West relations to be entrusted to them alone" and invoking the Williamsburg summit's injunction to "devote our full political resources to reducing the threat of war," he announced he had "begun a process of close discussion with President Reagan" and was setting off to talk to the heads of government of France, Holland, Belgium, Italy, and West Germany about his specific suggestions for "a strategy of political confidence-building."[61]

Despite the jolt of energy with which this exciting rhetorical send-off endowed his European journey, the results were disappointing. The problem was not commitment to his task, which was now total, but haste and inadequate preparation. Canadian diplomats in Paris, The Hague, Brussels, Rome, and Bonn had not been able to mount efforts through back channels to reach a consensus with the host governments before his arrival. Heads of government could hardly proffer unqualified endorsements for Trudeau's mission when they had not been given time to consider his recommendations, however vociferously the accompanying Canadian reporters demanded their reactions. As NATO members they did not quite understand why Trudeau was acting outside the normal processes of consultation and lobbying and were suspicious of the precipitate scheduling. Was this a personal vendetta against Reagan? A retiring politician's last-minute bid for a Nobel Peace Prize? An attempt to position himself for a high-level international job? Trudeau had to settle for closed-door tête-à-têtes everywhere he went, with the Germans turning out to be the most receptive since he was expressing out loud ideas Helmut Kohl had been wanting to convey to Reagan but did not care (or dare) to say publicly. Mitterrand was also sympathetic but felt the timing was wrong. However well the private discussions went, they generated virtually no interest in the European media, even in the serious press.[62]

Trudeau had not intended to visit London, having argued East-West issues fruitlessly with Margaret Thatcher twice that year, first at Williamsburg in May and then in September when she came to Canada to preach the gospel of neo-conservatism. Normally a speaking tour by a British prime minister would have been a low-key affair, but Thatcher was a dangerous figure for the Liberals, with their mandate running out and the Progressive Conservatives under their new leader Brian Mulroney at 55 per cent in the polls. Trudeau had followed her around the country, apparently trying to contain any damage she might cause.

The lady was neither for turning nor for learning. Her attitudes had been inculcated by her father the grocer (a nineteenth-century free-market Liberal and stern Methodist who endorsed, among other plain truths, the belief that the French were inherently corrupt) and fixed by her education at Oxford, where she was a hyperactive young Tory among the post-war Labourites, and by her marriage to the Conservative businessman Denis Thatcher (whose money allowed her to abandon a career as an industrial chemist testing cake fillings so she could study law and use it as the route to political power).[63]

Thatcher understood viscerally the striving classes who voted for her, from the working people who were able to buy their municipal council houses thanks to her privatization program, to the self-made suburbanites with the leased Jaguars parked on the crunchy gravel outside their pseudo-Tudor houses in the Home Counties, who admired her transcendence of her class origins. The post-war Labourite dons such as Harold Laski, who had so influenced the development of Trudeau's ideas, were anathema to her, people whose maunderings had brought brave England to its knees. She loathed twentieth-century liberals in any form – the people she called "wets" – and none more than the man she had appointed foreign minister in her first term in office, Sir Francis Pym, with his aggravating old-Etonian manner and his Tory concern for the well-being of the world. For his part, Pym cordially returned her dislike. "We've got a corporal at the top, not a cavalry officer," he once remarked. It did not enhance Trudeau in Thatcher's eyes that Pym – whom she had failed to reappoint to her cabinet following her second election victory in June and was in the process of destroying politically as her main rival for control of the Conservative Party – respected the Canadian prime minister, with whose constitutional patriation problems he had empathized two years before in secret meetings between them in Ottawa.[64]

Since Trudeau was both a Frenchman and a wet, she found his behaviour generally repugnant and entirely predictable. Her high commissioner to Canada had even suggested he might harbour a desire to make Canada a republic. He would persist in taking the side of the Africans and Asians at the Commonwealth conferences that Thatcher so disliked because the white countries were outnumbered and often outmanoeuvred there although they were paying the lion's share of the bills. Margaret Trudeau's escapades in London in the late 1970s, which gained her notoriety in the British tabloid press just as Thatcher came to power, were a further blot on Trudeau's copy-book: his unsuitable marriage was simply proof positive that he was unsound in his private life as well as in his political attitudes.[65]

These antipathies were generally suppressed in her public treatment of Trudeau. She had sought punctiliously to meet his needs on the patriation of the constitution, and their debates over the KAL 007 incident during her Canadian tour in September 1983 were civil, if tough. "Occasionally we disagree, but only when you are wrong, Prime Minister," she jibed at him in front of a Toronto business audience she had moved to cheers with her praise of free enterprise. Her pitch was palpably more popular than Trudeau's sober statements about living "under the threat of the mushroom cloud" and the need for political leaders to get involved in promoting disarmament between East and West. Trudeau obviously took pleasure from their spirited exchange, scoring a point of his own by quoting Lord Carrington, Thatcher's first foreign minister, back at her: "We cannot go on facing down the Russians in a silent war of nerves, punctuated by periods of megaphone diplomacy."[66]

She was decidedly less temperate about Trudeau in private, complaining afterwards to her press secretary and confidant, Bernard Ingham, that Trudeau was horning in on her tour. "Mr. Trudeau was always a problem [for Mrs. Thatcher]," explained Ingham, a blunt ex-newspaperman from Yorkshire, who was her most enduring close adviser. "He was seen to be a bit exhibitionist . . . a spectacle in himself, adept at the theatricality of politics. He had got himself into the position of being a half-way house between the undeveloped and the developed worlds by a lot of do-gooding and

Third-Worlding. Nasty people here [in Britain] would say this was the French in him and not the Scot. We soon figured out what kind of animal we were dealing with . . . a man at the wet end of everything . . . and in this we were thoroughly briefed by the British high commission in Ottawa."[67]

When Thatcher heard Trudeau was in Europe in November, pursuing his dream, she summoned him to London. He turned up at No. 10 to find her disturbed that Reagan had intervened in Grenada without so much as asking her leave, although it was a Commonwealth country. Simple courtesy – let alone her expectation of Reagan's trust in her good judgement on matters of war and peace – should have caused him to consult her in advance. Still, the rapport between No. 10 Downing Street and the White House throughout the overlapping terms in office of Thatcher and Reagan was such – closer than it had been even in the days of FDR and Winston Churchill or JFK and Harold Macmillan – that her dismay with her great friend Ronnie turned out to be momentary, while her disagreement with Trudeau was nearly total. For his part, he found her position on nuclear war as horrifyingly wrong-headed as Reagan's. Grass was growing in Hiroshima a year after the bomb was dropped, she told him blithely over tea.

Spurred on by this evidence of unreality in high places, Trudeau flew home to reveal his peace proposals to the Canadian public. He gave a well-wrought speech that first summarized how the increasing resort to the use of force, the growing proliferation of nuclear weapons, and the worsening state of relations between the two superpowers were creating a "sinister composite trend-line." He then went on to outline a five-part program for the political management of the current crisis, suggesting that East-West trust could be fostered in Europe by having "high-level political representation" at the forthcoming Stockholm conference on European security and by reanimating talks in Vienna to "raise the nuclear threshold" by achieving better balanced and reduced levels of the Warsaw Pact's and NATO's conventional military forces. He further proposed that the two superpowers and three other nuclear powers convene a conference to discuss setting "global limits" to their strategic arsenals; that all nations agree to ban the testing and deployment of anti-satellite weapons at high altitude; and that the non-proliferation treaty be shored up.[68]

Trudeau's intervention constituted a "well-crafted and balanced set of proposals . . . designed to probe all areas where East-West dialogue and cooperation might be possible," in the words of the University of Toronto international relations expert John Kirton, whose authority on the issue was heightened by the fact that he had never been involved in the several professors-for-peace organizations that had existed on Canadian campuses since the 1950s and were now ecstatically welcoming Trudeau back to the fold. But there were a number of problems inherent in Trudeau's peace package despite the usefulness of his ideas and the clarity of their expression.[69]

The occasion he used to unveil his arms control suggestions – a Liberal Party fundraising dinner in Montreal on November 13 – marred the altruistic spirit of his mission since it fed speculation that he was being driven by the need to boost his political popularity. If he was targeting an audience beyond the Canadian electorate, it was not clear who it was meant to be. The British were scornful. The Europeans, who might have been expected to respond favourably to his arguments, had been polite but publicly non-committal. Perhaps the non-white leaders of the Third World with whom he had developed such a strong rapport would be more responsive to his message. "Trudeau was intoxicated by the admiration of the Africans," Allan Gotlieb said later. "It can be argued that it was their warm regard as expressed in the 1970s that skewed his view of what Canada could achieve in foreign policy in his later years in office."[70]

With renewed expectations Trudeau flew to Tokyo and Dacca on his way to India for the biennial Commonwealth conference, which opened on November 23. But his disarmament remarks were poorly delivered in New Delhi and badly received in the face of strong objections from his old opponent Indira Gandhi. She saw his proposal to strengthen controls on nuclear proliferation as a cover for the industrialized nations' desire to perpetuate their military and economic dominance over the nations of the South.

This disappointment was barely swallowed when Trudeau's spirits were raised again by some unexpected good news. Geoffrey Pearson had been able to wangle an invitation for him to visit Beijing on the basis of his courageous early support for China's admission to the United Nations. But again the goodwill did not translate into positive results: Trudeau's audience with the prime minister and president of the most uncommunicative of the five nuclear powers was unproductive. The Chinese leaders conceded they would lose hundreds of millions of their citizens in a nuclear war but insisted that China itself would survive. They showed no interest whatsoever in participating in a conference with the four other nuclear powers to discuss collective controls. Still without any dramatic breakthrough, Trudeau flew back to India to try to salvage his Commonwealth sortie with the tepid declaration of support for his efforts negotiated by Sonny Ramphal, the organization's admiring secretary general.

With his round of overseas consultations completed, he then returned to home base to take stock. The original plan had been for him to start his odyssey by arranging a tête-à-tête with Andropov in Moscow in order to have some calming message to bring to Reagan in Washington. But the Kremlin was not receiving visitors, however eminent their reputation or benign their intent. Andropov was seriously ill, and the Soviets' paranoia had reached such a height that NATO's joint war exercise, Able Archer 83, had been thought by the KGB to be a cover for an actual pre-emptive American nuclear attack. Still stymied on the Moscow front despite Geoffrey Pearson's best efforts over a period of several weeks, Trudeau's peace-initiative team decided he should press on to the United States as planned, however inauspicious the circumstances.[71]

Ottawa's understanding of what was going on in the White House – while still far from acute – was better than it had been for decades, because of the efforts of Allan Gotlieb. With relentless

energy and political shrewdness, Gotlieb in his two years as ambassador in Washington had managed to overcome his lack of familiarity
with the American governmental system and to change the nature
of Canadian diplomacy there. Instead of behaving like overly polite
pale clones of British Foreign Office stereotypes – the stance taken
by most of their predecessors over the previous half-century – he
and his wife, Sondra, had infiltrated the administration's inner circles
by cultivating, with a flair that old External types disdained as
unseemly, both the powerful Washington press corps and Reagan's
most important and amenable advisers, particularly Michael
Deaver, his deputy chief of staff.[72]

The State Department had given Gotlieb no hint of the hostility
the Reaganites felt towards Trudeau when he arrived in late 1981.
But he soon learned from Deaver that the president had been greatly
troubled by an article he had read in William Buckley's *National
Review* maintaining that Trudeau was a communist. Later, others in
Reagan's circle told the Gotliebs that the president's suspicions
about Trudeau's ideological bent had deepened his resentment of
the prime minister's behaviour, particularly his aggressive debating
style at summit meetings. Reagan perceived Trudeau as condescending towards him at the best of times and at worst, downright
dismissive of his cherished beliefs about the nature of Cold War conflict. The Reaganites were convinced that Trudeau had called the
president "an idiot," and when Gotlieb remonstrated that this could
not possibly be so, their response was along the lines of, "Well, even
if he didn't actually say it, that's what he thinks, isn't it?"[73]

The Trudeauites' back-down on FIRA, along with the recent
general harmony achieved at the quarterly bilateral meetings
between Allan MacEachen and George Shultz, had helped alleviate
Canadian-American tensions. This much Gotlieb knew from his
State Department sources. What he had not fully realized was that
Trudeau's proselytizing at Williamsburg as well as his reaction to
the KAL 007 disaster had revived and exacerbated the Reaganites'
original view of him as an unreliable ally and, if not a communist,

certainly a fellow-traveller in the way right-wing Republicans had come to understand that term in the McCarthy and Goldwater eras.

Reagan's closest advisers were no longer raw novices at dealing with foreign governments, as they had been in 1981 when Canada was "on the front end of their learning experience." But their view of their northern neighbour's international role under Trudeau's direction had hardened, although they were now far less open in expressing it. In their nearly three years in office, they had absorbed the Pentagon hard line on Canada, rejecting the more liberal State Department position that had prevailed in the Carter years. The Pentagon's view was that Canada under Pearson the peacekeeper and Trudeau the peacenik had turned into a wimp among nations. Pearson's opposition to the Vietnam War and his unification of the Canadian Armed Forces had started the country on the slippery slope to neutrality that Trudeau had slid down further with his reduction of Canadian forces in Europe. The decision forced on him in the 1970s to buy more military hardware and support the NATO two-track strategy had not redeemed his reputation. And his vacillations over testing the Cruise followed by his recent prancings for peace had reinforced the Pentagon's position that whatever the State Department might say, this guy was soft on communism.[74]

Richard Perle, the assistant secretary for international security policy at the Pentagon and the architect of its extra-hard line on the Soviets, was viciously sarcastic about Trudeau's peace proposals. "So they're going to give away all their nukes?" he sneered. "Iceland might as well propose naval disarmament as Canada propose nuclear controls." As Perle saw it, the Canadian prime minister was under-mining the American stand-tough negotiating position with the Soviets.[75]

Perle's idea of arms control – as demonstrated over a decade of backroom campaigning on Capitol Hill, first against the Nixon-Kissinger efforts at *détente*, then against Carter's strategic arms limi-tation efforts – was to achieve strategic nuclear superiority for the United States. He was behind the "zero option" that Reagan had proposed two years before in the guise of a disarmament proposal: in exchange for the United States agreeing not to install its new Pershing and Cruise missiles in Europe, the Soviet Union would have to dismantle all its existing ss-4s, ss-5s, and ss-20s everywhere – an idea that was so obviously unacceptable that Moscow was bound to reject it, thereby helping to legitimize Washington's massive arms build-up aimed at winning a nuclear war.[76]

Perle's forcefully argued positions had given policy weight to Reagan's intuitive response to the evil empire and his heightened dismay over the way Trudeau had treated him at Versailles, Bonn, and Williamsburg on international issues. White House anger at the NEP in 1981 had been stirred up by Republican oilmen, mostly the friends of George Bush and James Baker. This time the anger was the president's own; it had to do with his feeling that he was being treated like a dumb actor who knew nothing about the world. He resented Trudeau's detached criticism of both the superpowers and his use of Lord Carrington's "megaphone diplomacy" phrase, with its insulting implication that the United States was morally equivalent to the Soviet Union. It wasn't Reagan's style, or his policy advisers' strategy, for him to express his upset. The Pentagon had advised the White House that the United States did not have to make overt moves against Trudeau's peace initiative, that America's loyal allies would take care of the Canadian's preposterous pretensions. Margaret Thatcher would inform her counterparts in the capitals of Europe that Trudeau was not to be taken seriously. "There goes that nut sounding off again," would be the gist of her message. This is the man who had hugged Fidel Castro and been given a reception in Cuba second only to the one put on for Brezhnev. How could anyone who understood Washington's view of East-West relations take him seriously as a go-between?[77]

Unaware of the depth of these feelings, Gotlieb used his White House connections to seek an appointment for Trudeau with the president, and the Reaganites went along with his request. Officials at State, the Pentagon, and the National Security Council involved with the Canadian dossier realized that Reagan could not publicly be seen to disavow the importance of peace by refusing to hear his neighbour's pleas, even though Trudeau's self-aggrandizing chase around the world could potentially disturb their own Soviet strategy. In a few months, they told one another, Trudeau would be toast. Whoever replaced him – whether it was Brian Mulroney or John Turner – Ottawa would return to acting "sensibly," a favourite State Department word to describe the behaviour it preferred in the leaders of client states. They decided the thing to do was for Reagan to receive Trudeau and to kill his initiative with kindness.[78]

Trudeau realized his trip to Washington involved a tricky situation. Influencing the two superpowers was the prime goal of his peace initiative. Yet previous exchanges on East-West issues with Reagan had been counter-productive, as Gotlieb had been telling him gently for many months. He would have to alter his approach if he hoped to affect the president's attitude. On a working visit Trudeau had made to Washington the previous spring at the height of the Cruise controversy, the Gotliebs had invited the cream of their "A" list, including Michael Deaver, to a dinner in his honour. The only guest Trudeau had asked them to include was Margot Kidder, and he had looked on imperturbably as she lambasted Deaver at table for what she described as the Republicans' shameless war-mongering. Afterwards, Trudeau and Kidder had danced to Cole Porter songs in a display of sophisticated grace à la Fred and Ginger that charmed the assembled company of powerful Washingtonians, many of whom had star quality of their own and recognized it immediately when they saw it in others. On his peace-initiative visit to Reagan, Trudeau would have to avoid the kind of confrontation Margot Kidder had forced and display the grace that Reagan possessed in abundance and found reassuring in others.[79]

To Gotlieb's relief, Trudeau had refrained from making speeches around the U.S. to arouse American public opinion against the White House, as some peace activists had suggested he should. He had also shown restraint in not criticizing U.S. interventionism in Central America or the Caribbean. (Though he had been outraged at the American invasion of Grenada in October, Marc Lalonde, newly mindful of the attitudes of the bilateral business community, had prevailed upon him to hold his tongue.) Now he would have to stifle his distaste for Reagan's simplicities on global issues. Gotlieb persuaded him to watch videos of Reagan's presidential press conferences and State of the Union addresses in preparation for their meeting. Trudeau, who had never seen Reagan on television, was impressed by his mastery of the medium, as he was with Gotlieb's careful argument that the way to reach Reagan would be to talk to him about matters of sentiment and style rather than discussing substantive ideas.[80]

When Trudeau was finally seated in the Oval Office on December 15 with Gotlieb backing him up, he ignored the American cabinet secretaries and senior aides who had been assembled for the occasion and addressed the president directly with persuasive passion rather than cold reason.

"Ron, I know you are a man of peace," he began – as he and Gotlieb had agreed he should. I also know you are a great communicator, he continued. But something's gone wrong. Only part of your message is being heard. Your tough talk about re-establishing a strong America with increased defence forces is coming through but not your hopes for peace. You obviously do believe in arms control. You told the Japanese Diet you don't personally think a nuclear war can be won. If it were possible to modify the rhetoric, perhaps you could be seen for what you are by an anxious world: a man of great power who is also a man of peace.[81]

The approach Gotlieb had suggested seemed to work. Trudeau, the confronter, was non-confrontational. Reagan, the communicator, responded to his subtle flattery by telling stories rather than turning the meeting over to George Shultz or Caspar Weinberger, the usual signal that an issue was too abstruse for him to handle. The president had been deeply shaken to learn through the CIA that the Soviets had genuinely believed the United States was about to launch a nuclear attack, which made him more responsive to Trudeau. To the relief of everyone present, the two leaders seemed to be having a real exchange of views, and the hour of presidential time allotted to Trudeau sped by.

The president's staff had agreed after considerable advance pleading from Gotlieb to give the visit an aura of importance by having
the two leaders appear for a few minutes together in front of the
cameras on the White House East Lawn. Reagan duly called their
discussion "very useful," declared that he fully shared Trudeau's
"concerns for peace," appreciated "his strong statements . . . [on]
meaningful arms reductions and . . . dialogue with other nations,"
and wished the Canadian prime minister "Godspeed in your efforts
to help build a durable peace."[82]

Trudeau waxed effusive in response, calling the meeting a "great
step forward" because "the president agrees that we should not seek
military superiority in NATO, . . . that we do not think a nuclear war
can be won; that we think the ideal would be to see an end to all
nuclear arms." But as the prime minister walked to his limousine his
new placatory persona came unstuck. He yelled back defiantly at a
reporter's question about some Pentagon official's dismissive remark
before his arrival, saying his detractors were "third-rate, third-level
pipsqueaks." To make sure Trudeau's visit did not cause undue mis-
chief, the presidential entourage had let the word out that the meeting was not a big deal, an impression confirmed when Trudeau
admitted to the senior reporters convened for a debriefing in the
Gotliebs' official residence that he had not discussed with Reagan
the substantive elements of his peace proposals. Having hoped for
major coverage, the embassy staff had to take comfort from a mention of the visit buried on page 8 of *The Washington Post*.[83]

Trudeau's international year was over. And no one yet knew
what – if anything – had been achieved by his frenetic travelling and
high-minded hopes.

# CHAPTER 14

# THE ERA ENDS: RESIGNATION AND REPLACEMENT

The talk in the Canadian governing class at the holiday parties that followed Trudeau's return from Washington in mid-December was not about world peace, of course, but about federal politics and Trudeau's future. As the nation prepared to face the year that George Orwell had etched on the twentieth-century consciousness as prophetic for the human race, the speculation about the prime minister's plans reached a new intensity, particularly in the upper echelons of the federal bureaucracy, and among the political operatives in the Liberal Party whose futures hung on Trudeau's decision to stay or not to stay.

Some repeated what they had overheard a senator say to a PMO type about the business community's lukewarm response to the new Conservative leader, Brian Mulroney. Some relayed what a cabinet minister had told them about the dissension in John Turner's camp and the confusion on Donald Macdonald's royal commission. Some speculated that the January Gallup poll would confirm that the prime minister's commitment to peace had improved the voters' regard for the Liberals to such a degree that Trudeau might be willing to lead the party into another election.

Having heard his umpteenth such discussion, Bernard Ostry, who had left Ottawa in 1980 to work first in Europe and then as a deputy minister in the provincial government of Tory Ontario, remarked, "Forget about the opinion polls. Forget about Turner's gang, Macdonald's troubles, and Mulroney's prospects. The way to tell what will happen with Pierre is to watch the guys who don't eat without him. When enough of *them* are appointed to safe havens, you'll know he's ready to go." [1]

By that standard, the end was nigh. Nineteen eighty-four had barely begun when Michael Kirby, Jerry Grafstein, Philip Deane Gigantes, and Lorna Marsden were appointed to the Senate, to join Jacques Hébert, the Montreal publisher and Trudeau's old civil-libertarian ally, who had taken his seat there a few months before. For his part, Jean Marchand, who had been Speaker of the Senate for nearly four years, wanted *out* of the red chamber and was duly appointed chairman of the Canadian Transport Commission. Jeanne Sauvé, the Speaker of the Commons, was to be installed as the next governor general. Gérard Pelletier was leaving the United Nations to take up the chairmanship of the board of the National Museums of Canada. Ian Stewart had been made chairman of the Canada Mortgage and Housing Corporation. Barney Danson, the former minister of defence, was set to become the Canadian consul general in Boston, and Nate Laurie the government appointee to the International Monetary Fund in Washington. Bryce Mackasey, the ex-minister of labour and controversial Irish charmer from Verdun, was haunting the corridors of Parliament Hill, brogue as thick as any boyo's, beseeching everybody he knew to help him get the job that would cushion his retirement. And so it went, up and down the ladder of loyalty, as favours were called in and credentials dusted off for fear of the darkness that might descend should Trudeau finally depart. [2]

Beyond the nervous concerns of individuals seeking to secure their futures, there was a pervasive unease in the body politic. The old liberal Canada was in decline. The new conservative Canada was pressing to displace it. Lined up on one side were people of a left-liberal cast of mind who were thrilled by Trudeau's peace efforts and had let him know this in thousands of phone calls and letters to the PMO. The attitudes they expressed belonged to the Canada of another era, the quasi-colonial nation that had sent its young to fight in foreign wars for the sake of unattainable imperial ideals but had never itself been warlike, the naïvely moralistic country whose do-gooders a Third World politician in one of Margaret Atwood's novels characterized as the dumb "sweet Canadians." These people were cheering on Trudeau's peace initiative in community college and high-school staff rooms, and at the coffee hours after Sunday services in churches across the country. They still believed that Canada had a role to play in the world that was truly disinterested, and that the privilege of its prosperity brought with it obligations.[3]

On the other side of the widening political divide were the new pragmatists, Canadians from across the social spectrum, but mostly clustered in the clamouring middle class, who agreed with the U.S. State Department under-secretary Lawrence Eagleburger that Trudeau's peace pronouncements made him sound as though he were high on pot. These were the citizens whose prospects had been diminished by punishing interest rates and escalating inflation, and whose apprehensions had curdled into anger during the recession of 1981–82. They espoused the corporate world-view – as disseminated by the business sections of the dailies, the populist tabloids, and the radio phone-in shows – that Canada needed to come to grips with the realities of the late twentieth century, to learn to compete in the marketplace, to forget its utopian involvement with peace, social security, and economic justice for all. Their mantras were privatization, deregulation, and globalization. In their eyes, governments got things wrong, business did things right. They saw Canada's place in the world as that of junior economic and military partner to the United States. By now they had cynically, even sullenly, dismissed the Trudeau Liberals as woolly-minded, soft-hearted, and terminally extravagant with the public purse and had come to believe that the Mulroney Conservatives were better equipped to deal with the tough international conditions that threatened the economic base of the old sheltered Canada.[4]

For the first few weeks of 1984, Trudeau managed to remain detached from the political pressures that this new and growing opposition consensus created, even though they threatened to engulf his party. Some of his closest advisers thought that his international initiative had caused him to enter into such a transcendent state that partisan concerns no longer affected him. What was on his mind, they told inquirers, was still peace, disarmament, and his place in history. Having spent twenty years in mainstream politics, mastering a hardbitten trade, Trudeau had again put on the whole armour of God and returned to the messianic altruism that had motivated his activism in the 1950s. The global consultations he had undertaken in the late autumn and early winter constituted one of the greatest spiritual, intellectual, and emotional epiphanies of his political life – rivalling his referendum and constitutional victories in intensity – and he was reluctant to see them end. [5]

Accordingly, after the turn of the year he went to Manhattan to try to persuade the secretary general of the United Nations to convene a meeting of the nuclear powers, and to induce the editorial board of *The New York Times* to endorse his position on arms control. Unsuccessful in New York, he flew to Switzerland to take on the global corporate and government élites at their annual powwow in Davos. Once there, he soon lost his senior statesman's bearing by involving himself in a spat over the validity of NATO's deterrence theory, and in the process outraged the former French prime minister Raymond Barre by boldly questioning whether the Americans would really risk a nuclear war to defend Europe. Still shut out of Moscow, he repaired to East Berlin and Bucharest, where he won endorsements for his peace agenda from the leaders of two of the most repressive regimes in the Soviet bloc. These sideshows, along with a concomitant visit to Prague, confirmed the views of both his anti-nuclear supporters at home and his conservative critics in Washington. "He's back to his old self, the way he was before he joined the Liberal Party," is what they were saying in the Canadian peace movement and among the social democrats in the university common rooms. "He's broken ranks and shown his true colors," is how they were responding in the Pentagon. [6]

Trudeau finally brought this disjointed round of his proselytizing-for-peace efforts to an indecisive close by delivering a summary report to Parliament on February 9. In it, he suggested "ten principles [forming] a common bond between East and West." Cast as a new catechism for the world to adopt, it began: "1. Both sides agree that a nuclear war cannot be won. 2. Both sides agree that a nuclear war must never be fought," and continued through eight more points phrased in a similar vein. The speech ended with an elegant peroration:

> And let it be said of Canada, and of Canadians: that we saw the crisis; that we did act; that we took risks; that we were loyal to our friends and open with our adversaries; that we lived up to our ideals; and that we have done what we could to lift the shadow of war.[7]

Four days later, an unexpected event provided an addendum. After suffering for many months, the Soviet leader Yuri Andropov died, providing Trudeau with the chance to reach Moscow at last. He journeyed to the U.S.S.R. to attend the state funeral on February 14 and was granted a half-hour in the Kremlin the next day with the new general secretary, Konstantin Chernenko.

The exchange had Chekhovian overtones in that it came too late. The pearls of wisdom that fell from Chernenko's lips on the virtues of world peace and superpower harmony were as readily available to George Bush, who was also in Moscow, and to the other official mourners from the West, as they were to the Canadian prime minister. The restoration of a more civilized East–West dialogue at the Stockholm conference on European security the month before, when Andrei Gromyko and George Shultz had engaged in a long exchange, and the marked moderation of the rhetoric emanating from the Reagan and Thatcher camps, had already taken the edge off the autumn's frightening confrontation. There was no special message left for the Canadian to bring from the Kremlin's ramparts to the White House lawn.[8]

Trudeau's contribution to these first steps towards the new *détente* that resulted eventually in the end of the Cold War was assessed in dramatically different ways. Admirers praised his courage in stubbornly calling for reason to prevail against the reckless ideological belligerence of the American and British leaders. "No one else among the summiteers even tried at that time to confront the large questions," the University of Toronto peace and conflict expert Janice Stein observed. "In the face of the obstructionism of the [military and diplomatic] bureaucracies, Trudeau made it legitimate to talk about the immediate risk of nuclear war."[9]

Critics were loath to accord him any credit, interpreting his improvised travelling as little more than a last desperate grasp at history's skirts. To them it was a detriment rather than an aid to the strategy of the United States, with its emphasis on hanging tough on armaments in order to destroy the Soviet economy by forcing the Kremlin into ever more crippling defence expenditures.[10]

Outside the professional circles where the nuances of this debate were explored, many Canadians had difficulty deciding what to think about Trudeau's peace initiative, with its fresh revelations of his strengths, weaknesses, and contradictions. His venture had been at the same time egotistic (as though only he could do this) and altruistic (but it was for the good of humanity); extravagant (careering in a government jet from one world capital to another for months on end) and non-confrontational (listening respectfully to the Chinese leaders' long orations and the American president's sentimental monologue). He had used his stature as head of a NATO government to gain access to other heads of state, then thumbed his nose at the alliance's rationale. He had endorsed old-style Canadian diplomacy (taking on a Pearsonian mien by offering his mediatory services) while at the same time playing international Lone Ranger (ignoring the foreign-service officialdom whose ethos had made Pearson's successes possible). He had defended the rights of Canadians to be heard on the nuclear question, but had done so by staging a drama starring himself as a kind of post-national citizen of the world. He had traded on his international celebrity (a status enhanced by his wife's notoriety and by the fame of the actresses who were his dates and co-agitators for peace, Margot Kidder and Barbra Streisand) in the service of a morally uplifting ideal. [11]

The successes he could tentatively claim – reducing the strident nature of Anglo-American discourse on the nuclear threat and persuading NATO's foreign ministers to attend the Stockholm meetings – had been achieved by the time he left the White House after meeting Ronald Reagan on December 15. In the following months, his credibility on the issue began to wane. The longer he took to wind up his initiative, the more the value of his courageous acts of the autumn depreciated. [12]

Considering the confusions created by these ambiguous signals, Canadians had responded more favourably to his mission than might have been expected. Although the Liberals still trailed the Conservatives by 20 per cent in a Gallup poll taken in January and released on February 9, this was a reduction in the chasm of 29 per cent that had separated them from the Tories in October before the peace initiative was launched. [13]

True to form, Trudeau refused to respond to such epiphenomena as public opinion polls or professional critiques of his progress. "My destiny is so complex," he commented to Canadian reporters pressing him about his plans while he was abroad, "that I don't think I'd like to tie it to any particular aspect of my many interests in life." [14]

Once he was back on home ground on Thursday, February 16, such airy unconcern was not easy to sustain. The coming weekend would mark the fourth anniversary of the Liberals' restoration to office in 1980. An election would have to be called before the year was out, and the need to make firm campaign plans meant he would have to decide whether he was the right man to lead the Liberals into it.

"I had been determined for two years to protect him from the yahoos in the party who were trying to push him out," Tom

Axworthy commented later. "I wanted him to be able to make up his own mind about whether and when to retire." Over the next fortnight, this is precisely what Trudeau set out to do. Displaying the self-containment and political shrewdness that caused his old CCF friend the philosopher Charles Taylor to remark that he had "the mind of a superior lawyer," he began to take soundings.[15]

Of those whose judgement on governmental matters he trusted, the most important was Marc Lalonde. Over the previous several months, when Trudeau had been so often absent from Ottawa on his international quest, Lalonde had effectively taken his place, commanding the government's major decisions from the Department of Finance in a concerted attempt to improve both the government's and the economy's performance.[16]

Lalonde's general strategy of trying to foster greater confidence in government among the advocates of free enterprise had been moderately successful. The most obvious example of Ottawa's new deference to business was the Liberals' altered attitude on competition policy. Although the rate of corporate mergers had reached an all-time high and was still rising, Lalonde had managed early in 1983 to block André Ouellet's tough competition bill for a second time. In the autumn, Ouellet's replacement in the consumer and corporate affairs portfolio, Judy Erola, instructed her department's bureaucrats to negotiate the bill's details directly with the three major business lobbies, the Canadian Manufacturers' Association, the Canadian Chamber of Commerce, and the Business Council on National Issues. The BCNI had already published a 177-page draft Competition Act, expressing in legislative format its considered position that Canada needed to encourage, not block, corporate concentration at home if it wanted its private sector to be competitive abroad. This argument had won over Erola, a Finnish Canadian who had become a Liberal when she went to work as an account executive at a Sudbury radio station twenty years before. With Lalonde's blessing she "bent over backwards" to accommodate the trinity of business lobbies.[17]

The finance minister had also taken into account business opposition to the broad public demand for a substantial reform of the country's pension system. A 1980 federal study on retirement income had shown that large gaps in the coverage provided by private and public plans were causing poverty among the aged, particularly older women. But after Lalonde took over in Finance, the only minister gutsy enough to continue to champion the need for action on retirement income was Monique Bégin. The others were persuaded by Lalonde's argument that business was dead set against significant improvements in either the private or public-sector income security systems. After a second government report and a parliamentary task force had re-examined the issue in the light of these objections, pension reform was effectively jettisoned.[18]

While the interests of free enterprise were being vigorously defended in social policy areas, direct pro-business legislation was being formulated in Lalonde's own department. Some sixty foreign bank subsidiaries had been complaining about the ceiling put on their assets and hence on their capacity to expand. An amendment to the Bank Act, now in the works, would soon double the allowable quotas.[19]

Finance had tried hard in other ways to become the good news department. Lalonde's second budget, tabled while Trudeau was still in Moscow, claimed that the terrible recession had bottomed out, thanks to the "recovery budget" he had brought down in April 1983. Although both unemployment and interest rates remained alarmingly high, the economy was growing again and inflation had reached a ten-year low, with the downward trend expected to continue. Still a Keynesian optimist, the minister avoided making big cuts to government spending programs, although the shortfall between Ottawa's expenses and revenues was to be $31 billion in 1983/84, a deficit that would bring the national debt to $157 billion. Lalonde's carefully constructed package of measures was at once cautious (the Six & Five program was to be phased out gradually), stimulative (half a billion dollars would be put into job creation), and progressive ("profit participation" for employees would be encouraged by tax incentives). It was also electorally smart, with its $50-per-month increase in the guaranteed income supplement, which would benefit 750,000 seniors.[20]

The initial response to his budget showed that, on the whole, Lalonde's bold initiatives and discreet retreats had mollified business. In his view, Trudeau could stay on as leader and face down the Tories without having to apologize for his government's economic performance. Or he could resign without feeling that he was abandoning the Liberal Party when times were tough.[21]

Trudeau's next consultation was with his English lieutenants, Tom Axworthy and Jim Coutts. The old soft-shoe shufflers from the PMO were invited to dinner at 24 Sussex to give him their assessment of the pan-Canadian political situation. (It was reported that Senator Pitfield had joined them at table, but since he continued to be skittish about any involvement with Liberal activities, the story went unconfirmed.)[22]

Using the briefing style they had developed during a decade of working closely with Trudeau, Coutts and Axworthy told him what they wanted to hear. Canada was still a small-l liberal country, they claimed. If the Liberals kept to the progressive strategy Axworthy had been refining over the previous four years, they had a good chance of winning back the electorate. True, they had trailed the Tories in the polls since the late summer of 1981, when the recession had taken hold. But their ratings had been climbing steadily since the previous October, thanks to the economic recovery and Trudeau's peace initiative. Goldfarb's data showed that Canadians, other than the disaffected middle-class baby-boomers who had deserted to the Tories, were much more optimistic than they had been even a year before. Some of them were even sophisticated enough to blame external factors – not the Canadian government – for the recession.[23]

The objective of the detailed election strategy Axworthy had prepared was to rebuild the Liberal coalition by focusing on the needs of three groups: first-time voters who had tended historically to vote Liberal and who in the next election would comprise 363,000 new Canadians and two million young adults between eighteen and twenty-two; women, whose majority support for the party had been an important factor in returning it to power in four of the five elections Trudeau had contested as leader; and the fickle urban middle class, whose votes determined the outcome in crucial swing ridings in southern Ontario and who would have to be wooed anew.[24]

The interests of these groups had been targeted in the December speech from the throne, with its promise to create a Youth Opportunity Fund and its genuflection to multiculturalism (continued support for heritage-language instruction and a task force on visible minorities); its reforms of divorce and pornography laws, aimed at meeting the needs of women; and its proposals for helping distressed mortgage holders and small-business victims of bankruptcy, directed at members of the middle class who had been hurt by high interest rates. Action was already under way on more than forty of the ninety items in the throne speech, with Lalonde's budget providing increased funding for women's organizations and the enrichment of the registered retirement savings scheme to allow the self-employed to contribute larger amounts.[25]

None of these ideas was new to Trudeau. But the passion Axworthy and Coutts projected in their presentation of them was unusual. In dealing with him the tone they normally strove for was cool. This time they felt, as Axworthy put it, "full of emotional conflict. I wanted to see him out in style if he insisted on leaving. But at the same time I was afraid that without him everything we had stood for, in terms of trying to forge a new Liberalism, was in danger of being destroyed." Both men were concerned that "a quantum shift in the country's approach to public life was taking place," Coutts recalled, and both believed that Trudeau would be better able than any other Liberal to withstand the Tory onslaught.[26]

They knew that the onus was on them to dissuade him from a course of action that had been agreed upon from the time of the Restoration and that had permitted his government to pursue unpopular policies without flinching. "I won in 1980 on the basis of resigning before the next election: how would I now justify staying on?" was what he was asking them. In response, variations were played on the theme of "Only You." You are still needed to scotch the separatist threat. You can achieve more on disarmament. There is still an unfinished Liberal agenda. You're the best man for the job. You could kick the stuffing out of Mulroney. Trudeau listened carefully, clearly relishing these assessments of his prowess. But Coutts and Axworthy left the prime ministerial residence uncertain about whether he had been convinced by their arguments.

They gathered he would be spending Saturday and Sunday in Quebec, although exactly what he intended to do was outside their purview. Both Axworthy and Ted Johnson, the young lawyer who acted as Trudeau's executive assistant in the 1980s, had been careful not to become involved in his personal life, making particularly sure that his weekend privacy was sacrosanct. It was only when he was planning to travel outside Ottawa on a Monday that Axworthy would intrude on his Sunday quiet. Realizing that Trudeau rarely read a paper or turned on the news, Axworthy would telephone him to be sure he knew that some new war had broken out, some political leader had been elected or assassinated, or some less cataclysmic event had occurred that he might be quizzed about at his destination.[27]

Whatever else Trudeau was planning for the last weekend in February, his Anglo loyalists suspected he wanted to ponder the counsel of his francophone friends. Whichever of his intimates he consulted – and the possibilities included his sister, Suzette Rouleau; Marc Lalonde, in his role as commander of the federal forces in their continuing campaign to bludgeon the PQ government to pulp; Gérard Pelletier; Jacques Hébert; and Jean Marchand, who had advised him earlier to continue in his job until he had taken his peace crusade to Moscow – when he returned to his office on Monday morning, his demeanour had changed. He seemed to have been reminded of how he had loathed being in opposition in 1979 and had determined then never to risk such an indignity again; and to have been told how much better it would be for his sons to be removed from the gossipy glare of the capital, where New Edinburgh was agog with the news that Margaret Trudeau had filed for divorce and would soon marry a wealthy real estate broker named Fried Kemper.[28]

Positive reasons for retiring now apparently had been called up as well. Federalism in Quebec was on firmer ground than it had been for years. René Lévesque's erratic behaviour had become a serious embarrassment to the separatist cause, and his Parti Québécois government was in disarray. Robert Bourassa, who had become leader of the Quebec Liberal Party for a second time when he replaced Claude Ryan in 1983, would soon be premier again. These ideas about the state of Quebec were in harmony with those of Michael Pitfield, who believed that in fairness to the next generation of francophone federalists, the natural cycle of leadership renewal – interrupted by the extraordinary circumstances of the Restoration – should be re-established.[29]

Furthermore, despite his English-Canadian militants' attempt to rouse Trudeau's competitiveness by touting his capacity to outclass Mulroney in a campaign, many francophone federalists believed that it might not be so bad for their cause if the Tories won. However distasteful Mulroney's opportunism might be, however venal some of his political associates, he had shown himself to be sound on federalism, staunch on bilingualism, and even courageous on the universality principle for health care. In brief, he was easily as amenable as John Turner might be on these issues, which were central to Trudeau's Liberalism.

As for an important international job, Pelletier had denied firmly that Trudeau was seeking one. In response to rumours that he had been appointed ambassador to the United Nations in 1981 so he could lobby for the appointment of Trudeau as its secretary general, Pelletier remarked, "That was never true. As [Trudeau] said at the time, 'I want out of one tough job, so do you think I would seek a tougher one?'"[30]

On all these grounds, Trudeau could retire with equanimity. A good life awaited him in Montreal. His elegant Art Deco mansion beckoned, as did his weekend camp in the Laurentians. He had fought many great battles and endured many lasting hurts. It was time to come home.

To counter these disconcerting arguments, Keith Davey's persuasive wiles were called into play. An hour-long meeting with the senator was slotted into the prime minister's schedule for the afternoon of Monday, February 27. Five years before, Trudeau had told an interviewer privately that much of his fondness for Davey was based on his unabashed presentation of himself as a good old pol, a man without pretensions, glad to say that his value to any Liberal leader sprang from his determination to remain just an ordinary guy who knew what ordinary people thought.[31]

Apart from his role in promoting Six & Five and chairing a generally inert election readiness committee, Davey's gift for interpreting public opinion had not been called on often by Trudeau in the 1980s. The senator had enjoyed the period hugely all the same. Now in his advancing fifties, married for a second time, to a Toronto Liberal organizer named Dorothy Petrie, he had managed to take off the twenty-five pounds he had been gaining and losing for the previous twenty years. ("If I can just stay away from the odd piece of pie," he would say every time he began a new diet, "I'll be in shape again in no time.") He still affected the sideburns he had grown in the Pearson period. But they were now so out of date, they looked like an assumed eccentricity since they complemented the handsome fleshy face and the three-piece, broad-striped navy-blue suit he habitually wore, a get-up that satisfied ideas about dress he had acquired thirty years before as a Toronto radio station's young sales manager, eager to make it in the big time.[32]

With the passing years, Davey had come to look more and more like a U.S. senator from some dimly remembered 1950s black-and-white movie, a fitting image since his fascination with American political techniques and American gimmicks had never waned, despite his loyalty to Walter Gordon. He loved American baseball, American magazines, and most of all, American liberal Democrats. One of the best-ever days of his life had occurred in 1981 when he had visited Washington to make a speech at the request of the Canadian embassy and had called on Senator Edward Kennedy on Capitol Hill, as well as Ben Bradlee and Katherine Graham at *The Washington Post*, in order to explain Canadian nationalism to them. If Trudeau were to resign, such "super" times, to use a favourite Davey word, might not be replicable; in fact, they might not be possible at all, given the wariness with which the leading candidates to succeed Trudeau as Liberal leader had been treating him since their hopes were dashed in 1979.[33]

The fact that Trudeau missed entirely most of Davey's media and sports-world references had not fazed the senator for years, and neither had his tendency to react with exasperation to many of Davey's ideas. "Okay, okay," Trudeau had said sardonically on one occasion, when Davey was carrying on about the need to please the publisher of *The Toronto Star*, "I'll have lunch with Honderich every week for the next six months if that will make you happy!"[34]

On this cold afternoon in February 1984, Davey had brought the leader a message that could not possibly be misunderstood. The gist of what he had to say was that only Trudeau could save Liberalism in Canada. And only Trudeau could save the world, which amounted to pretty much the same thing in Davey's mind. "The Canadian public is with you on your peace thing, Prime Minister," he remarked with super sincerity, "and on your Third World thing, too. And they will vote us back into office on that basis."[35]

At the same time as he was delivering this upbeat message, Davey downplayed all the aspects of electioneering that Trudeau loathed, particularly the daily necessity of dealing with the media on the campaign trail. By now, the senator had realized that he could not persuade Trudeau to respond to the cavils of *The Globe and Mail* by inviting its editorial board to lunch. Nor could he make him deploy his charms to win the allegiance of Barbara Frum, the celebrated interviewer on the CBC-TV news show *The Journal*, whose executive producer, Mark Starowicz, had made the program into English Canada's national daily. Trudeau continued to react to Frum's interrogations with bristling irritation no matter how often he was told of her importance. In fact, there were only three or four media people he actually would talk to without a fight – notably Peter Gzowski, the host of the CBC Radio program *Morningside*, who had written a long profile of Trudeau when he was still teaching law in Montreal and Gzowski was the Quebec editor of the old monthly *Maclean's Magazine*; and George Radwanski, the author of a biography of Trudeau, who had become editor-in-chief of *The Toronto Star*. The prime minister's media aversion did not matter any more, was the idea Davey now conveyed. He and Axworthy would handle them and low-bridge the leader the way they had in 1980. Once Trudeau was emoting for the cameras on the hustings, the voters would come out of their funk. [36]

Having run through the points he had planned to make, Davey extracted a promise that Trudeau would not decide definitively on his retirement before talking to Martin Goldfarb, who could give him a detailed explanation of why the polls were moving in his favour. Delighted by his own palaver, the senator departed "in great spirits," as he wrote in his memoir, *The Rainmaker*. "I honestly thought he was going to stay." [37]

What he had not reckoned with was the impact on Trudeau of a conversation with another Liberal that Davey had been unable to prevent.

The Liberal was the party president, Iona Campagnolo, whose view of the political realities was very different from Keith Davey's, as was her experience of Liberalism and of Canadian society.

Campagnolo was born in 1932 on a remote island in northern British Columbia, the oldest of four children in a fishing family of modest means. At the impressionable age of ten, she had taken her place on the production line alongside the native and Japanese-Canadian children working for a pittance in a fish canning factory. Later, she had to unlearn the mangled English she picked up there and to push back constantly against the defeatism that was expressed by her family and friends about making it "outside," as they called the cities of southern Canada. After graduating from high school, she married a fisherman, had two children, then divorced, and set about with a will to make a better life for her family and herself. She found a job in a radio station, read voraciously, ran for office as a school trustee and then alderman in Prince Rupert, and then left local radio for local television.

By the time she was recruited in 1974 by the nearly moribund British Columbia wing of the Liberal Party to run federally as a sacrificial lamb in the huge riding of Skeena, Campagnolo was more than ready for the political limelight. Her drive, the wide recognition she enjoyed in the riding as a community activist, and her unusual beauty – "She could have been a movie star easily," was the way the B.C. Liberal organizer Paul Plant described her – helped her defeat the incumbent NDP MP, Frank Howard, and to roll on to Ottawa, determined to do good and to do well. She was immediately made parliamentary secretary to Judd Buchanan, the minister of Indian and northern affairs, then given the junior portfolio of fitness and amateur sport, where she made her mark. Gaining Trudeau's attention thanks to her striking appearance and his personal interest in physical prowess, she developed a high profile as both the champion of Canadian athletes in international competition and the advocate of public fitness through a program called Participaction. Keith Davey talked about her at the time as "dynamite," "pure political gold," possibly the next prime minister.[38]

When Campagnolo lost her riding in the 1979 election, she turned to volunteer work in Africa, took courses at Simon Fraser University, and made some television shows in Vancouver. But she missed politics and responded with alacrity to the idea that she run for party president in 1982. Then and later, she resented the assumption made by many Liberals and repeated in the media that Davey helped her get elected. She insisted the help had come from Lauris Talmey, a dynamic Liberal activist from Vancouver who was president of the National Liberal Women's Commission, and from Marc Lalonde and Jean Chrétien, who had acted as her mentors when she was a novice parliamentarian and cabinet minister.[39]

Campagnolo had barely moved into her Ottawa office on Bank Street when she fell out with the PMO crowd, as she called the Coutts-Davey-Axworthy trio and their political friends. As a woman and a westerner, she had always felt like "an alien" among the central Canadian power players in Ottawa. But the immediate reason for the animosity that flared between her and the PMO was the firing of Gordon Ashworth, who had been the party's national director since 1979 and had worked under Davey's direction in the two previous federal election campaigns.[40]

Although it was Gordon Dryden, the party's devoted treasurer, who had brought about Ashworth's dismissal over bookkeeping irregularities, Davey and Axworthy believed Campagnolo was waging a struggle for control at party headquarters and blamed the quarrel with Ashworth on her emotionalism. This chauvinistic cliché, combined with Axworthy's prompt hiring of Ashworth for a job in the PMO, exacerbated Campagnolo's feeling that the men she called "the bosses" were treating her unfairly. Apart from MacLeod, previous party presidents had been awarded a seat in the Senate with tenure until age seventy-five and a handsome pension to follow. All she was guaranteed was an annual salary of $60,000. Despite her resentments, Campagnolo soon proved herself effective both at retiring the party's debt and at travelling the country tirelessly in an effort to rally the Liberal faithful. As relations between party headquarters and the PMO continued to be frosty, Davey set up a liaison committee between the two, but he remained convinced Campagnolo was a loose cannon – that is, not controllable.[41]

She had become shrewd enough to have requested an appointment with Trudeau through his assistant Ted Johnson rather than through Tom Axworthy, whom she believed Davey had charged with guarding the gate against party members bearing different views from his. When, with two hours' notice, she joined Trudeau for lunch at 24 Sussex on February 28, he talked to her about the sense of obligation he felt towards the Liberal Party, which had "taken him in as a political orphan," and then asked her to give him her perception of its current state of mind.[42]

What followed was a dispassionate analysis in which she reported that, quite apart from those who were already backing potential successors, there was a consensus among thoughtful Liberals – and not just the yahoos, as Axworthy characterized dissenters – that Trudeau had outstayed his time. He had completed the agenda that had brought him to power and was no longer giving leadership on such crucial domestic issues as the alarming deficit and the escalating national debt. Those who respected him preferred to see him leave as a champion rather than suffer defeat in the Liberal rout they anticipated.

Campagnolo's province-by-province report on party sentiment was both unsettling and useful. It aroused again the deep mistrust of the anglophone militants that he had developed in 1979 when he and his Quebec loyalists had bitterly resented the pressures put on him to resign in the wake of his electoral defeat. "I swim in a sea of disloyalty," he had confided to Philippe Deane Gigantes only a few weeks before. It also gave Trudeau the ammunition to counter the arguments made by Coutts, Davey, and Axworthy and to stick with his original plan to retire before another election.[43]

Their conversation was long and detailed, covering such minutiae as the timing problems involved in calling a leadership convention. Trudeau told Campagnolo that on the previous weekend he had spent several hours thinking through his decision and that it was as difficult to make up his mind to leave as it had been to enter the leadership race in 1968. She told him that, if he decided to go, the public would expect some departure "drama" from him. After lunch, the prime minister's chauffeur drove them both back downtown, stopping first on Parliament Hill so Trudeau could get back to work on preparations for a constitutional conference on native issues planned for early March. As he prepared to get out of the car, "with his karate gee rolled under his arm, wrapped in its black belt, I patted his hand and wished him luck in his decision. He looked at me intently and with a dazzling smile and not a word, moved into the snowstorm, and I went back to work in the party office on Bank Street."[44]

The House of Commons was in recess that week and Ottawa was unusually quiet. By late afternoon the city was shutting down in the face of the blizzard. Trudeau left his office early and joined his sons at their martial arts class, where they had the master to themselves because of the weather. Later, after the children had eaten their dinner and been tucked into bed, he had the promised talk with Martin Goldfarb, a conversation that was subsequently described as having convinced him to resign since it sowed further doubts about whether he could win another election. This suggestion so aroused Trudeau's ire that he still resented it more than a year afterwards.

"Things are written about polls that are not always true," he remarked with some heat in June of 1985. "The story is that I asked Goldfarb that night about my position in the polls and then decided not to run again. That's nonsense. Keith Davey had been pleading with me for months to run again, using Goldfarb's data in favour of his argument. Goldfarb didn't know that night that I was thinking about resigning immediately. No one knew. He called me at dinner. I had a girl-friend there, and the call was an unwelcome interruption. My recollection is that Goldfarb's message once more was that I could win."[45]

This statement seemed to his listeners *echt* Trudeau. The casual aside about the girl-friend, with its hint of trysts and roses, and the insistence that the polls had not affected his decision one whit were intrinsic to his self-image as an always reluctant politician, self-directed, self-contained, and rarely intimidated by a challenge or impressed by an orthodoxy. Goldfarb had once said ruefully he could never convince Trudeau that polls were an extension of democracy since he found them manipulative and repugnant. "What can you do?" Goldfarb asked. "The guy's a romantic."[46]

The difference between Trudeau's account of the conversation and Goldfarb's was also revelatory of the cultural dissonance between his attitudes and those of the political technicians from English Canada with whom he had made common cause for more than a decade. Goldfarb remembered thinking as he prepared to deliver his one-more-time argument by long-distance phone that what he had to say as a cultural anthropologist could change Trudeau's life and the nation's. He proceeded to talk for forty-five minutes, putting the most optimistic spin possible on his findings, and failing to realize that the statesman listening to his arguments on the other end of the line had decided the whole process of modern politicking was a pain, one that he was soon to be free of forever – or at least until the next time the sovereign asked him on bended knee to come to the aid of his country.[47]

When Trudeau talked briefly to journalists the following day about the evening of February 28, he said nothing about Goldfarb or the girl-friend. He did describe going for a long, solitary walk in the blizzard that was still raging, coming home for a long, solitary sauna, and then sleeping soundly in his solitary bed, having made his decision to resign.[48]

Next morning, he still felt resolute, and the first to be given the news were his sons. At nine o'clock, he telephoned Tom Axworthy at the PMO. After he arrived at the office, they drafted a "Dear Iona" letter together. Trudeau phoned Campagnolo to tell her the resignation was coming, and Axworthy had it hand-delivered to Liberal headquarters by ten-thirty. Then Trudeau called in Ted Johnson, Joyce Fairbairn, and his secretary, Céline Viau, to tell them privately about his decision. Next, he placed calls to Jim Coutts, Keith Davey, and Marc Lalonde before addressing a hastily assembled gathering of his large PMO staff, many of whom were misty-eyed. Having skirmished for a few minutes with reporters gathered outside his office, he drove off home for lunch. After months of vacillating, the deed was done.

The opposition was caught off guard. Both Brian Mulroney and Ed Broadbent were spending the parliamentary break in Florida, soaking up the sun against the rigours of the Ottawa winter, and were unavailable for immediate comment. Trudeau himself refused to be interviewed on television or to submit to other encounters with the reporters he so disdained. "Will you give a news conference?" Iona Campagnolo had asked him when he telephoned his news. "No, I don't have to do that any more. You do it!" was the tart reply.[49]

The media went wild without him, seeking assessments of his prime ministership from great and small. Interviews with men and women in the street were evenly divided between those who were deeply regretful to hear of his resignation and those who felt it was high time. Davis of Ontario believed history would call him a great man. Lévesque of Quebec said he had been a worthy opponent but a political disaster. Willy Brandt and Abba Eban, Harold Wilson and James Callaghan, Richard Nixon and Henry Kissinger, all praised him as a statesman of remarkable talents. But Reagan's White House was silent, leaving it to the State Department to issue an oblique statement: "The American people and government wish him well in his future endeavors."[50]

Trudeau's own assessment was unsentimental and succinct: "I was my best successor, but I decided not to succeed myself."[51]

Over the next six months, the Liberal Party proceeded to prove him right as it went about the titillating business of selecting another leader and running another election campaign.

As had been predicted for weeks, the chief contenders for the succession were John Turner and Jean Chrétien, both Liberals steeped in the traditions of the party's distant pre-Trudeau past. Turner, the Bay Street lawyer from Ottawa, Vancouver, Westmount, and Forest Hill, was the very model of a St. Laurent–era consociational élitist. Chrétien, the Main Street lawyer from Shawinigan, came out of an even older tradition as a Laurier Liberal with a pan-Canadian vision.

They were joined by a flock of what one expert commentator called the seriously deluded, five cabinet ministers who had little hope of winning but remained determined to tell Canadians how they would transform the ailing body politic: two from the party's left-Liberal wing, John Roberts and John Munro; one centrist,

Mark MacGuigan, who was economically conservative but socially progressive; one business Liberal, Don Johnston; and the minister from the south cow pasture, Eugene Whelan, who talked engagingly about Canadian agriculture and how it could alleviate the miseries of the Third World.[52]

Three extra-parliamentary Liberals, all of them better known in the media than this quintet of Privy Councillors, decided not to run. Donald Macdonald was still tied up with his royal commission and was rumoured to have been put off the whole process by the disappointment he had suffered in 1979 when Trudeau unexpectedly returned to his job. Iona Campagnolo declined because she was committed to managing the coming leadership convention from the high ground of presidential neutrality, or so she said in public. In private, her friends admitted ruefully that although dozens of grassroots Liberals had come forward to support her candidacy, her French was inadequate, and despite support from Nick Taylor, the wealthy oilman who was the maverick leader of the Alberta wing of the Liberal Party, she could not raise the $1.5 million necessary to mount a serious campaign. Jim Coutts issued a brave statement claiming that he had decided not to run because his priority was winning the election in Spadina and representing his constituents in the next parliament. His friends whispered that, having wanted to be prime minister forever, Coutts had bowed out of the race in response to the bad news tendered by his erstwhile supporters, principally Keith Davey, who had told him regretfully that even an overflowing campaign chest could not guarantee him more than a handful of first-ballot votes.[53]

Despite the range of views represented by the declared contenders, it was the Liberalism of the late Trudeau era that dominated their discussions from the first time they appeared together before a crowd of potential delegates – at the Liberal Party of Ontario's annual meeting in Toronto on March 24, where Tom Axworthy, having been invited to talk about election readiness, seized the day and turned it to his purposes. After mounting a slide show that used Goldfarb's data to bolster his case for a left-Liberal campaign strategy, he made a powerful speech that defended the Trudeau record. It combined his definition of a Liberalism that could survive the 1980s – which fudged the accommodation with principle that the party had been making for fifty years – with an astute identification of its supporters and enemies. He ended with a call to the barricades. Adapting several lines from Robert Browning's poem "The Lost Leader" as a tribute to Trudeau and his politics of purpose and using the stirring tones that had won him elocution prizes in high school, he declaimed:

> We that have loved him so, followed him, honoured him,
> Lived in his mild and magnificent eye,
> Learned his great language, caught his clear accents,
> Will make him our pattern to live and to die! [54]

Axworthy's oration won the loudest applause and the best press of the day despite the schmaltz. The candidates moved on to five cross-country policy conferences and frantic efforts to win delegates. He went back to Ottawa, determined to oversee last-ditch efforts to make Trudeau's liberalizing effect on Canada "irreversible – the way Roosevelt's New Deal was irreversible." This involved winding up operations on three prime ministerial fronts: the legislative, the governmental, and the international. [55]

There were still several pieces of legislation before Parliament of vital interest to the PMO. A pet scheme of Axworthy's was about to be realized in a bill establishing a Canadian Institute for International Peace and Security, with a capacity to provide more substantial advice on peace issues than had been available when Trudeau's initiative was first contemplated. He was also keen to see Monique Bégin's new Canada Health Act passed because it defended the Pearsonian principle of universality for medicare. Her proposed legislation to penalize provinces that allowed user fees for hospital services and extra-billing by doctors was popular with the public but anathema to provincial premiers, who were already complaining about restraints on the growth of transfer payments. Bégin had first raised the issue in 1979 and had met strong resistance from cabinet colleagues and senior bureaucrats reluctant to provoke further provincial hostility. She had ultimately prevailed by gaining Trudeau's personal support, on the grounds that if the bill pleased the voters and irritated the premiers, it was a sure political winner – just as the patriation of the constitution had been.[56]

Then there was the Canadian Security and Intelligence Service Act, whose passage had top priority for Trudeau. Beyond wanting to repair the damage to his reputation as a civil libertarian caused by the RCMP's illegal acts against the Parti Québécois, the prime minister had deep convictions about the need to clarify the interrelated roles of politicians, police, and judges. The Commission of Inquiry Concerning Certain Activities of the Royal Canadian Mounted Police had recommended making the RCMP's intelligence function a separate service accountable to Parliament, and Trudeau was keen to see it established while he was still prime minister. Michael Pitfield, as chairman of a special committee of the Senate and Trudeau's ally on these issues as on so many others, had rewritten the solicitor general's disappointing "spy act," Bill C-157, which they both considered retrograde, to ensure that the spy service would be brought under political control. The new bill was now ready for final passage through Parliament. The government was also preparing to proclaim the Department of Justice's quintessentially liberal reform – the 1982 Young Offenders Act – aimed at making young people more responsible for their behaviour but keeping them out of adult courts and jails.[57]

Still to be addressed was the matter of end-of-the-era appointments, the placing in government jobs of men and women who could help keep the values of the Trudeau era green and act as moles for liberalism in the neo-conservative age that Axworthy saw coming. Patronage was a subject that was both fascinating and fraught for Liberals at every level. Some decisions – principally choosing judges for the Supreme Court – were regarded as beyond political favouritism. The inviolability of the law was one of Trudeau's absolutes, and his interest in the high court profound because of its role in interpreting the Charter of Rights and Freedoms. Intellectual prowess was his sine qua non for such appointments, though he was bound by custom to maintain a regional balance on the court.[58]

On most other appointments, he subscribed to the general Liberal view that patronage was part of the political game, an attitude that, for quite different reasons, enraged Tories, New Democrats, long-suffering bureaucrats, and political scientists interested in systemic government reform. Some Order-in-Council appointments involved showy, well-paid jobs that attracted the unwelcome attention of the press and the opposition, as had the selection earlier in the year of well-known Trudeau loyalists for senatorial and diplomatic plums. But most appointments were to the lesser posts that made up the nitty-gritty of patronage, the cement that had held the party system together since Confederation. Hundreds of full- and part-time jobs were described in an appointments list, kept in the PMO and involving everything from the prestigious and remunerative chairmanship of the state-owned Air Canada to directorships on the Canadian Livestock Feed Board. Bootlegged copies of the list, which featured the dates when positions were due to come free, were passed from hand to hand among Liberals hoping to find suitable perches so they could lobby appropriate cabinet members and PMO insiders to help them in their quests. Prime responsibility for choosing candidates for most positions belonged to individual ministers, while regional ministers were charged with monitoring the political implications of these choices for their provinces.

Two hundred and twenty-five appointments were due to be made by the time Trudeau stepped down in June. The leadership renewal process was barely under way when the prime minister raised with the candidates as a group the question of how to time the announcements: should he release the news during the race, or did they want him to wait? To a man they counselled delay, in part because of subtle promises they might be able to offer potential delegates but also because they realized that published reports of the large salaries available to some of those appointed to government posts would reinforce opposition charges of Liberal arrogance and extravagance. As Order-in-Council notices piled up in the PMO, Axworthy was trying to keep a watchful eye on all of them, worrying about placing the liberally inclined on academic councils as well as on a plethora of boards and tribunals. [59]

One appointment already processed was cause for mounting "a spectac'," as Axworthy continued to call splashy official occasions, this one to take place on Parliament Hill with a band, an honour guard, and a horse-drawn carriage. The swearing-in of a new governor general was always a stately ceremony, but this time there was a difference. Since Jeanne Sauvé was the first woman to be elevated to the vice-regal post, her installation on May 14 gave the government a chance for nervous self-congratulation on the gender equality issue.

For a liberal reformer, Trudeau had been remarkably slow in his response to the feminist revolution. His disparaging attitude to the aspirations of women had earned him the enmity of the Pearsonian Liberals Judy LaMarsh and Pauline Jewett. During his first decade as prime minister, his close advisers had been exclusively male, except for his legislative assistant, Joyce Fairbairn; and as late as the winter campaign of 1980, he had dismissed the concerns of aboriginal women in a tense discussion with a group from NAC. But in the years since the Restoration, under the influence of Axworthy, who was vocal on the need to appoint women to government posts, his attitude had altered. There was now a woman serving as his economic adviser in the PMO, Denise Chong; a woman as party liaison officer, Heather Peterson; and, since the previous summer, a full-time adviser on women's issues, Maude Barlow. But Jeanne Sauvé's appointment – along with that of Madam Justice Bertha Wilson, the first woman elevated to the Supreme Court – was a matter of particular pride. It was intended as a reminder that Trudeau had opened the gates of power a fraction wider, not just to French Canadians but to other disadvantaged groups: Jews, who had been appointed to crucial positions in the cabinet, the judiciary, and the diplomatic service from which they had previously been excluded; and women, who had been doing the service jobs in government for generations and were now gaining access to its inner circles.

The next big events on Trudeau's calendar in the countdown to his retirement were international. Accompanied by his summit sherpa, Sylvia Ostry, and his foreign policy adviser, Robert Fowler, he flew off in early June for a last bittersweet taste of life at the top, stopping first for a final prime ministerial tango in Paris at ceremonies marking the fortieth anniversary of D-Day, and then proceeding to London for the annual economic summit meetings, where he conducted a last Liberal wrangle with his neo-conservative opponents in the resplendent setting of Lancaster House.

The repetition of his now familiar views on disarmament and *détente*, put forward in tandem with François Mitterrand, once again displeased Reagan and Thatcher. Richard Burt of the State Department recalled Trudeau "making a big peacenik statement," which was roundly criticized and peremptorily rejected by the British prime minister. Reagan wrote in his memoirs, "Pierre bitterly lit into Margaret, the chairman of the meeting, and told her she was being heavy-handed and undemocratic . . . I was horrified by his rudeness and the insulting way that he spoke to her." Unchastened by Thatcher's reprimands, Trudeau also pushed Reagan on the peace issue to the point that the president blurted out in frustration, "For God's sake, Pierre, what more do you want me to do?" The ideological hostility was palpable.[60]

Unlike the good-natured American, who generously wished Trudeau good luck for the future in a private conversation before the meetings broke up, Thatcher pointedly refused to do so. She failed to even mention in her closing public statement that this was Trudeau's eighth and final summit. When Reagan expressed his shock at Trudeau's behaviour, she replied, "We women know when men are being childish."

Nanny Thatcher was relegating her Canadian colleague to the nursery while she and her admired friend Ronnie pressed on with the adult task of defending the free world. None of them yet had an inkling that East–West peace was about to break out and that the hawks Reagan and Thatcher would soon be boosters of the future Soviet leader Mikhail Gorbachev.

Four days after Trudeau's return from London, the Liberal delegates, thirty-five hundred strong, gathered in Ottawa to choose his successor. With his leave-taking imminent, the capital had fallen into a mood that the recently widowed Judy Erola described as "a state of collective grief that affected even the commissionaires at the Senate door and the waitresses in the parliamentary restaurant." Trudeau's obduracy and frequent insensitivity to others' needs were forgotten, his strength of purpose and occasional expressions of empathy remembered and inflated.[61]

In contrast, among lay Liberals who were arriving from across the country and calling greetings to one another in the jammed lobbies of every hotel in town, there was an air of hopeful anticipation, aided by the wonderful June weather and the unexpected good news that the party was once again number one in the voters' affections. In the months since Trudeau's resignation, the Liberals had climbed ten points in the Gallup and were now ahead of the Conservatives for the first time in three hard years.[62]

The media were floating stories that this reversal of fortune was causing deep dismay among the Conservatives. Even the normally feisty former finance minister, John Crosbie, who had been taunting Trudeau to resign for months, sounded glum at the prospect of a Liberal resurgence when he turned up at the Civic Centre as one of the pundits corralled by the television networks to provide commentary on the convention. The faster the news of the Tories' discomfort spread, the better the Grits began to feel.[63]

They congratulated themselves that throughout the succession race the candidates had been able to adhere to basic party maxims

about never savaging fellow Liberals publicly on personal or ideological issues. The policy debates, held in five cities across the country, organized by the new senators Kirby and Marsden and chaired
by the aspiring business Liberal Paul Martin, Jr., had been designed
to garner maximum publicity, not to polarize the candidates or to
develop specific party positions. By the time the contenders
emerged from a dozen weeks of exhausting encounters with one
another and the delegates, and converged on Ottawa for the convention, all of them, even the business community's white-haired
hope, John Turner, had been pushed towards the vaguely progressive, mildly nationalistic Liberal centre.[64]

Since Turner had forbidden his supporters to organize in
advance, his campaign headquarters had been a disaster area,
swamped as it was by volunteers who had rushed forward to align
themselves with the sure winner. His loyalists, Alf Apps and Norman MacLeod, were crowded out as ministers from Trudeau's cabinet, including Monique Bégin, declared their support. "Trudeau
left us no other choice when he delayed his resignation for so long
for his own purposes," Bégin explained. "In those last years, it was
like being led by a dead man." Other pragmatic reformers in the
Quebec caucus, including Dennis Dawson and Jean-Claude
Malépart, jumped on the Turner express along with such staunch
anglophone nationalists as Herb Gray and Lloyd Axworthy. Since
Turner was expected to walk away with the succession, they
reasoned, their ideas were needed to counter-balance the influence
of his businessmen buddies who had been haranguing him for years
over long Martini-and-steak lunches at Winston's in Toronto.

In the early stages of his campaign, Turner had been revealed as
unexpectedly wooden in his self-presentation and astonishingly
rusty in his grasp of current issues. He had made a couple of serious
bloopers on language rights in Quebec and Manitoba and had been
indiscreet enough in talking to journalists about the details of his resignation in 1975 to trigger a sharp public rebuke from Trudeau.
Observing these ineptitudes, the journalists who had previously
idealized him now mocked him as a disappointment. It took several

weeks of listening to the experienced politicians in his camp before he was able to pull himself together. Gradually, Lloyd Axworthy and John Payne, a Pearsonian Liberal who had been Turner's political adviser in Quebec since the 1960s, prevailed over Simon Reisman and William Macdonald on campaign strategy and policy. The left Liberals even persuaded Turner – a man's man, as he liked to call himself, who was famous among party feminists for his chauvinism – to agree with the rest of the leadership pack on women's issues in his support of contract compliance and universal day care.[65]

Garnering support among Quebeckers, rather than among women, had turned out to be Jean Chrétien's main difficulty. The Quebec referendum and the constitutional conferences of the early 1980s had made him a star in English Canada but caused him to be seen in his home province as an Uncle Tom. Nationalist intellectuals dismissed him in the Montreal media as the hit man for Trudeau's hated offensive against greater powers for Quebec. Even among those Liberals who appreciated his distinction between good patriotism and bad nationalism, and acknowledged his winning ways and *rouge* roots, Chrétien's candidacy was dogged by the belief in *alternance*, the first among the Liberals' many shibboleths. As Céline Hervieux-Payette, his Quebec caucus colleague, put it to him, "The English outnumber us four to one. If we break the rule and don't let them have the leadership this time, we will have a hundred years of anglophone leaders."[66]

Despite having been drawn inexorably to the centre by the campaign's demands, Turner had managed to insert code phrases into his public spiels (ministerial accountability, business confidence, broad consensus) to signal his intent to distance himself from the Trudeau legacy, with its Pitfieldian governmental complexities, its economic crises and federal-provincial confrontations. Chrétien, on the other hand, presented himself as a loyalist who was proud of the Trudeau government's accomplishments: peace, a strong federal government, and the patriated constitution. Without Trudeau, "Canada would not be together today," he said over and over again, appealing to federalist sentiment, and reiterating that his was a people's party open to all Canadians, not an establishment party for the few. Turner might be the darling of the urban business élite, but he was the guy with a heart from the hinterland – which gave the Liberals a choice, according to an acid piece in the conservative London *Times*, between "Mr. Blunder and Mr. Backwoods."[67]

What Chrétien wanted was a keep-things-as-they-are Liberalism, not Turner's turn-the-clock-back variety. His pea-souper French and "p'tit gars" style were an embarrassment to Quebeckers who had grown used to more sophisticated political leaders in the previous quarter-century. But his inspired reductions of complex issues to homely images, his anti-bureaucratic and anti-intellectual jokes, and professions of love for the Rockies as well as the St. Lawrence cemented his popularity in English Canada, particularly in the reluctant west.

Chrétien's sentimental appeal to Liberal delegates had also played well among journalists, who appreciated his good nature and his unwavering belief in what he was saying, as much as they laughed at his oratorical style and disparaged his self-disparagements. His candidacy made this event a race and produced better copy than a stately coronation of Turner would have provided. For party members, Chrétien's sure-footed campaigning proved the value of his long years as a minister and of his willingness to travel any distance to make speeches on behalf of Liberalism. He was able to call in credits and activate loyalties around the country: in Ontario, the tight little network of the former provincial leader Robert Nixon, as well as his cabinet colleagues Charles Caccia and David Collenette from Toronto, and Ron Irwin from northern Ontario; the oil-patch Liberals in Alberta, who had always liked his unpretentious style and were more appreciative of his amiability than ever because of his conciliatory stance as energy minister; friends of the gutsy new Liberal leader in Manitoba, Sharon Carstairs; and almost the entire Newfoundland delegation, thanks to the support of the MPs William Rompkey and Brian Tobin.[68]

For Liberal delegates of every stripe, Chrétien was by far the more likeable of the front-runners, as an academic survey of

incoming delegates showed. But despite his mistakes and incon-
sistencies, Turner had remained well ahead on every other
criterion of leadership – image, policy, competence, and most
important of all, electability.[69]

A mood of almost goofy optimism took hold in the crowd as Liberals assembled in Ottawa's Civic Centre on the convention's opening
night to witness the last best spectac' of the Trudeau years, listed in a
glossy souvenir album as *A Tribute to the Right Hon. P.E. Trudeau.*
Staged by the PMO crowd for prime-time television, with a lot of
help from their ad agency friends, and hosted by Keith Davey and
Marc Lalonde dressed up in white dinner jackets like MCs of
showgirl extravaganzas in Las Vegas hotels, it succeeded in
"re-inventing the TV variety show," in the inspired analysis of *The
Globe and Mail*'s television critic, Rick Groen, by combining a
Roman fête for a departing emperor with a modern sitcom featur-
ing a Canadian version of *My Three Sons.*[70]

What moved the crowd most was not the expatriate Canadian
entertainers (Rich Little doing hilarious impressions of Dick Nixon
and Ron Reagan, or Paul Anka crooning, "He Did It His Way," or
Norman Jewison claiming Trudeau had given the best speech that
Senator George McGovern had ever heard in Congress); not the
extravagant praise in both official languages by Trudeau's party eulogists ("a magic man . . . you have given reality a new dimension . . .
you are nobility"); but the brilliantly manipulated footage taken
from the television archives of the era.[71]

The Trudeau years unfolded on a huge screen in the arena, and
the audience was there again for the leadership campaign of 1968,
for the Saint-Jean-Baptiste Day riot that followed it, for the October
Crisis and its traumas, for the several elections dramatically won and
nearly lost, for the spirited travelling to the capitals of the world, all
of it interspersed with still shots of Trudeau with the Beatles, Trudeau with world statesmen, Trudeau on the Great Wall and in the
great white North, Trudeau with his children, and even, for a brief

moment, Trudeau with the lovely, long-lost Margaret, who otherwise went unseen and unmentioned at the convention.

At the end of the tribute, Trudeau gave one of his very best renderings of the Axworthy-inspired "I'm a Liberal and I love you" speech. Alone on the stage without a prop, he paid tribute first to his predecessors, Laurier (for his reforming zeal and vision), King (for giving Canada old-age pensions and family allowances), St. Laurent (for helping to found NATO and disseminating foreign aid), and Pearson (for believing in medicare and peacekeeping); then to Liberals as a caste ("They confront the powerful, they confound the secure, they challenge the conventional"); and finally, to his own heroic leadership.

> I found that if our cause was right all we had to do to win was to talk over the heads of the premiers, over the heads of the multinationals, over the heads of the superpowers to the people of this land, to the people of Canada.

It was an anti-consociationalist valedictory address delivered by the abiding élitist from Brébeuf, Harvard, Sciences Pô, and the LSE, a man who had been so un-Canadian as to aspire to greatness, and it ended with a flourish:

> Our hopes are high. Our faith in the people is great. Our courage is strong and our dreams for this beautiful country will never die. [72]

When his children, Justin, Sacha, and Michel, joined him on the platform for the finale, wearing baseball caps marked TRUDEAU, the Liberal crowd roared its adoration. After the Trudeaus finally disappeared offstage, it emitted a collective cathartic sigh and trailed out of the arena for a street dance.

The next two days were anti-climactic. It was as though the Grits were suffering a hangover, not just from the Trudeau tribute but from the glories of the Trudeau era, as they soberly, doggedly, determinedly proceeded to choose another leader. On the Friday, they endured hour upon hour of forums on youth and women's issues, provincial and territorial caucuses, and the numbing experience of sitting through the seven candidates' speeches, each of them repeating the familiar promises and dependable clichés perfected during the policy forums, but this time with bands and balloons as distractions.

On Saturday came the voting for party officers in the morning, when Iona Campagnolo was acclaimed for another two-year term, and for the new leader in the afternoon. As the delegates filed into the Civic Centre after lunch, there was a brief buzz of excitement. In the great heat of the convention, Chrétien and his ardent campaign team, directed by the Montreal businessman John Rae and Chrétien's ministerial assistant, Eddie Goldenberg, had worked themselves into a state of exalted exhaustion, fuelled by computerized calculations that showed them they could win. But before the voting even began, their hopes suffered a blow. It had been rumoured for two days that Marc Lalonde was now advising Turner on Quebec, which meant that just about the entire party establishment was with him. Now at 2:20 P.M., with the voting about to begin, Allan MacEachen, who had been making a display of his neutrality in the race, moved to join Turner in his box, telling the journalists importuning him in the crush that Turner was "a real Liberal." As a statement, it had all the spontaneity of a penance, and instead of uniting the crowd, it seemed to make it sullen. On television, John Crosbie called it "the final shaft up poor Chrétien's fundament."[73]

In the Chrétien box, his family and friends tried to keep up their spirits until the first-ballot results were announced at five o'clock: 1,593 for Turner, 1,067 for Chrétien, with the other five splitting the remaining 775 votes. MacGuigan moved to Turner immediately, with Whelan, Munro, and Roberts going to Chrétien, and Johnston stubbornly hanging in even though he had only 8 per cent of the vote. Up to the final hour, Rae and Goldenberg struggled to make second-ballot deals, to shake loose Turner delegates dismayed by the plastic quality of his campaign, and to spread news of their candidate's winnability among the television reporters still trying to turn the inevitable into a cliff-hanger.[74]

Finally, at eight-thirty, in the prime of prime time, Iona Campagnolo announced the second-ballot results: 1,862 for Turner, 1,368 for Chrétien. Hard-headed calculation had ruled the delegates but there was a pervasive sourness in the crowd, a perfunctory quality about the cheering. From the podium, Iona Campagnolo made things worse by trying to make them better, expressing a generosity Turner had not managed to summon up in his first remarks as leader. After a shattered Chrétien made his way to the stage to move that the vote be declared unanimous, Campagnolo told the crowd that John may have been first in the balloting but Jean was first in their hearts.

Throughout this two-day ordeal, Trudeau had been sitting high in the stands, the lost leader surrounded by his loyalists. On Friday, Lalonde and MacEachen had flanked him. Now only Tom Axworthy and Joyce Fairbairn remained. When the moment came for him to go down to the platform to make the gesture of handing over the leadership to Turner, as Pearson had handed it over to him sixteen years before, his RCMP security officers came forward to lead the way. Trudeau rose to his feet and started down the stairs towards the stage with the Mounties running interference for him. When he reached the first landing, he paused, looked back, and saluted his companions.

"Until that moment, I hadn't considered fully what was happening," Axworthy said afterwards. "I had been so busy all spring with the summit, with the tribute night, with the briefing books for the new prime minister, that I just hadn't taken the time to think about it much. I had been telling myself, 'It ain't over 'til it's over.' But when he gave that last little wave, the finality of it hit me. And I knew it was really over."[75]

# TRUDEAU IN THE AFTERLIFE, CANADA AFTER TRUDEAU

It was not just the Trudeau years that were over when Canada's fifteenth prime minister got up from his seat in the Civic Centre to go down to the bunting-draped platform below to shake hands with his successor. The confident Liberalism of the prosperous post-war era was over too.

As the painful events of the summer of 1984 played themselves out, and the new Liberal leader led the great party of Canada's twentieth century to electoral ruin, almost everything the Trudeau loyalists had predicted in their hyperbolic, self-fulfilling fear of losing power came true. Under John Turner, the Liberal Party fell apart. Without Pierre Trudeau, its centre could not hold.

Turner, and the men who had kept alive his political ambitions in his opulent exile, came to office as the ragtag remnant of an old Liberalism, based on a combine of élites that had broken down as Canadian society fragmented regionally and integrated continentally. For the best part of ten years they had been acting as an opposition within the Government Party's expansive circle, a cell of malcontents blaming on the omnipotent Trudeau everything that had gone wrong in Canada during the sixteen years he had been in office. In their vengeful triumph after Turner's victory, it was impossible for them to believe that anything the Trudeauites had wrought was worth preserving. [1]

Rather than executing an orderly transition from his regime to theirs, they created an almost comic chaos. They went into the PMO and dismissed the senior staff, took out their rage at Pitfield's governmental system by unceremoniously axing two of the central agencies he had set up, and refused to pay heed to the briefing books that had been painstakingly prepared by the Privy Council Office bureaucracy under the joint direction of Tom Axworthy and Gordon Osbaldeston.[2]

Once they had rejected the Trudeauites' approach to government as too clever by half, the Turnerites displayed their own, which was too naïve to be believed. It had been predicated on a view of John Turner as a superman whose reappearance on the Ottawa scene would put the political world to rights. As a consequence, they came to power without a plan for governing or a strategy for getting themselves elected, and their champion, whose great successes in life had come about as a result of following others' advice, proved unable to provide the leadership necessary to develop either.

Having promised to banish the Trudeau backroom boys in favour of a collegial management style, the new prime minister allowed so many would-be advisers to crowd around him that he could not make sense of the cacophony that resulted. Having criticized Trudeau's cabinets as badly made and poorly run, Turner proved dismayingly ineffectual at deploying and directing his own ministers. Although he pared down the number of Privy Councillors in his cabinet to show his faith in leaner government – and embittered several of his own supporters in the process – he failed to bring in the businessmen and westerners whose presence he had so emphatically stated was necessary to make the Liberals representative of the country as a whole.[3]

Raised on the truism that the Liberal Party's strength lay in its historic accommodation of the French fact, he proceeded to alienate the two most important Quebeckers in his caucus. Turner the great conciliator, the man who boasted he knew how to get on with other men in a way that Trudeau never could, was unable to persuade his chief rival, Jean Chrétien, that he could play a role in the new government commensurate with his proven strengths. His negotiations with Chrétien were so inept that they perpetuated the factional hostilities roused by the leadership campaign and created new antagonisms that would dog Turner throughout his tenure. Just as disturbing to the Liberal apparatus was his failure to appreciate Marc Lalonde's mastery of the governmental process and his dominance of the federal party's organization in Quebec. Within weeks of Turner's ascendancy, Lalonde, who had favoured his candidacy over Chrétien's, quit government altogether to return to the practice of law, after pronouncing that the new prime minister was weak, weak, weak.[4]

Impervious to the counsel of caution coming from Chrétien and from his own advisers, John Payne and Bill Lee, Turner succumbed to pressure from his other courtiers and a panicky Quebec caucus, and called an immediate election. In the ego-expanding aftermath of his leadership victory, which brought the Liberals a ten-point lead in the polls, he seemed to believe that, as a politician of superior talent, nobly devoted to the mission of reconciling government and business, he could prevail over the Conservatives' inferior leader, even though the Liberals were far from ready for a campaign. Nothing had been done about nominating candidates in the constituencies, or recruiting staff for the campaign headquarters, or renting a plane for the leader's tour, or deciding on a slogan for the as yet non-existent platform. Manically Turner plunged, exhausted and unprepared, into the next act in his drama of self-destruction.[5]

At the same press conference at which he announced there would be an election on September 4, he named seventeen retiring MPs to the Senate, the diplomatic service, and the bench, the last and most blatantly offensive of the many Order-in-Council appointments that Trudeau's PMO had readied but had deferred at the request of the leadership candidates. Distributing patronage during an election campaign – and saying he had no choice in the matter – associated Turner with the worst of the Trudeau regime's arrogant style. At the same time, he dissociated himself from the best of its substance, the social policies that were still popular with the electorate and with the Liberal delegates who had voted for him. Heedless of such concerns, he reverted to conservative turf, making pronouncements that sounded the chords of fiscal responsibility and deficit reduction in order to please his former business associates, who had been alarmed by his slide to the centre during the leadership campaign.

Rather than offering the public a new man with a new plan, he appeared on the hustings to be an old man with a predisposition to pratfalls, fronting a party he did not agree with or understand. He appointed as his campaign manager Bill Lee, one of his most obsessively anti-Trudeau cronies, whose main qualification for the job was that he had been tour manager for the Trudeau election campaign in 1968. After Lee fought with Jerry Grafstein over the advertising budget and with Turner's aides over the leader's agenda, Turner replaced him half-way through the campaign with Keith Davey, the hoariest of Trudeau's backroom boys.[6]

The media obligingly helped dismantle Turner's reputation, and his party's, with their almost gleeful transmission of his every blooper, large and small. When a public uproar ensued after a television camera caught him patting Iona Campagnolo on her posterior at an election event, reporters christened his campaign plane Derri-Air. But Turner's most self-destructive acts were performed live and unassisted during the nationally televised leaders' debates. Foolishly accepting the opposition parties' challenge to debate in his rusty Paris-learned French, Turner offered the colloquially bilingual Mulroney the perfect chance to present himself as Quebec's native son by promising reconciliation and honour to the province he described as having been humiliated by Trudeau's constitution. On the return engagement in English the following night, Turner appeared nervous, indecisive, and awkward in the face of Mulroney's confident attack on the Liberal record. Although he had reformed the old pork-barrel system of selecting judges when he was a minister in the first Trudeau government, he managed to arrogate to himself the blame for Trudeau's departing appointments orgy and to allow Mulroney, probably the most patronage-obsessed federal politician in Canada in modern times, to pose as Mr. Clean.[7]

As a result of the debate débâcle, Mulroney replaced Turner in the public's eye as the better successor to Pierre Trudeau. The Tory campaign had been readied over a period of ten months by expert politicians from the Ontario Conservatives' Big Blue Machine, who knew how to play the media and how to put together an organizational team representing all factions of their party. Exhaustive public opinion research conducted by their pollster, Allan Gregg, had confirmed that although the voters were fed up with the Liberals, they still liked their liberal policies. These findings persuaded Mulroney to work hard at assuring Canadians that his government would not undermine Pierre Trudeau's legacy and to come out four-square for universal social programs, bilingualism in Manitoba, and peace in our time.[8]

While promising continuity to Canadians, Mulroney guaranteed change to the Americans. A pre-campaign trip to Washington, with appointments in high places and an "A"-list dinner at the ambassador's residence arranged by Allan and Sondra Gotlieb, had allowed Mulroney to display his Irish amiability to the Reaganites. At the White House he disavowed Pierre Trudeau's critical attitude towards U.S. policy and promised to put the Canadian-American relationship back on a friendly footing. This cheery undertaking reassured the continental business community's heavy hitters, who put aside their earlier concerns about Mulroney as a lightweight and a toady to the liberal media.[9]

The combination of the Turnerites' stupidities and the Tories' smarts produced a Liberal rout: from 49 per cent in the polls and 146 seats in the House on July 9, when the election was called, the Liberals fell to 28 per cent and 40 seats on September 4. The once-invincible Liberal machine in Quebec had proven to be a hollow shell without its strongman leaders. With 211 Conservative members, 58 of them from his home province, Mulroney had won the largest number of seats of any prime minister in Canadian history.[10]

Once he had taken this terrible beating, Turner summoned the courage in adversity that was part of the creed dinned into him since childhood and held on to the Liberal leadership for five years. But he was never able to recover from the disaster of 1984. Nothing he tried could put the Liberal alliance back together again. Not winning a seat in Vancouver-Quadra in order to attract support in the west. Not trying to persuade business leaders to join him in the struggle to renew Liberalism. Not hoping to ingratiate Quebec by disavowing Trudeau and supporting the decentralizing ideas of the former provincial Liberal minister Raymond Garneau. Not opening up the Liberal Party to the new ethnic groups who were demanding their share of influence. Not hoping to attract a new generation of Grits by relying on Iona Campagnolo's attempt to reform the extra-parliamentary party.

The rage in the western provinces against Liberalism – and its centralizing interventionism – seemed to be irreversible. Mulroney commanded the allegiance of Quebeckers, including the Liberal premier, Robert Bourassa. Neo-conservatism had the governments of the United Kingdom and the United States in its grip and the Canadian business community in its thrall. It did not matter that Turner had so lately been that community's darling. It now had a better front man in the comprador from Baie Comeau, who was backing off the progressive stance that had won him the election of 1984 and embracing wholeheartedly the market-centred agenda of his finance minister, Michael Wilson. [11]

Turner was dealing with a world that had assumed a Hobbesian hue. A world where transnational capital was becoming increasingly powerful and Canadian business increasingly hostile to an activist welfare state. Where huge deficits meant that social policies and national institutions were in jeopardy. Where the press was cynical to the point of surliness and regional leaders dismissive of calls for solidarity. And where policy wonks were pursuing their careers not by making contacts in the back rooms of the Liberal Party but by making big money in slick consulting firms that had become go-betweens for business in the new era of the downsizing, deregulation, and privatization of the state's functions. [12]

The horrors that befell John Turner as he struggled with these new political and economic realities were imprinted on the Canadian consciousness like some awful upside-down morality tale in which the would-be saviour is destroyed rather than vindicated by his valour and his toil. Party uprisings, caucus divisions, feuds over nominations, financial travails, staff betrayals, private humiliations, and the assorted other woes he suffered laid to rest the notion that Liberalism meant competence and loyalty. It was enough to make even John Turner question the premises of the past. And when the Mulroney government adopted free trade with the United States as its main agenda, he began to do just that.[13]

Free trade had been a panacea that mainstream economists had been advocating for decades. Turner's former cabinet colleague Donald Macdonald, a sometime nationalist, had converted to the cause as a Bay Street lawyer under the influence of his clients in the formerly protectionist, now continentalist Toronto business community. Once Macdonald displayed his doubts about the positive state and his faith in the powers of the continental market as chairman of the royal commission on Canada's prospects, he was given enthusiastic support by the U.S. ambassador in Ottawa, the Business Council on National Issues, and trade policy officials from the Department of External Affairs, who had been pushing free trade with little success since 1981. When the Macdonald commission's final report in 1985 declared aggressive American protectionism to be a critical danger to Canada and recommended that Ottawa subordinate its traditional reliance on the GATT's rules in favour of a broad one-on-one economic deal with Washington, Brian Mulroney was delighted. Accepting Macdonald's proposal meant he could appropriate a well-known Liberal's agenda for Canadian prosperity, forge closer ties with his beloved United States, and deprive John Turner of one of his closest advisers by appointing the belligerent Simon Reisman as Canada's chief free trade negotiator.[14]

The Americans skilfully outmuscled the high-powered Canadian team led by Reisman and imposed unprecedented constraints on Canada's policy-making capacities without restricting their own freedom to harass Canadian exports. A close reading of the draft Canada–United States Free Trade Agreement, published in October 1987, convinced Turner that the country he had been brought up to serve was unlikely to survive what President Reagan hailed as the economic constitution of North America. As Turner saw it, institutionalizing asymmetrical integration with the United States was a historically fateful act. The FTA would bind federal and provincial governments into a straitjacket and lead to Canada's inevitable cultural absorption, economic decline, and political disintegration. That the FTA had been dictated by Turner's former clients in the corporate world (because it amounted to a charter of rights for continental business to move investment wherever it wanted), was espoused by his former political allies in Quebec (because it would weaken Ottawa), and was hailed by provincial politicians in the west (because it would prevent another NEP) added to the shock. From Turner's point of view, the Canadian political, bureaucratic, and business élites were no longer combining benignly to run the country. They were conniving to sell it out. [15]

Over the next year and a half he turned himself into a champion of the pro-Canada movement, a broad coalition of farm organizations, labour unions, the women's movement, and church, ethnic, cultural, environmental, and aboriginal groups, whose position – that the FTA threatened the integrity of the Canadian state on which their well-being depended – was articulated best by the political economists Duncan Cameron and Marjorie Cohen. Calling his anti-free-trade crusade, in a defiant tone that nobody had heard him use before, "the cause of my life," Turner began to display the political astuteness for which he had been respected twenty years before. He used the Liberals' majority in the Senate to block the passage of the FTA so that an election could give the public a chance to vote on this momentous question. During the 1988 federal campaign precipitated by his stratagem, he broke through the media mystification surrounding free trade to communicate directly to the voters his outrage that its insidious costs would entail the further, perhaps fatal, Americanization of Canada. This time he slugged it out with

Mulroney in the televised leadership debates and came close to transforming the election into a referendum on free trade.[16]

But Turner's passionate pleas on behalf of the historic Canada he believed in were only briefly effective. His dreadful leadership record was exploited in the counter-attack mounted by the Conservatives and the free trade propaganda paid for by their big business allies. With Ed Broadbent undermining the anti-FTA forces by directing the NDP's campaign against the Liberals rather than the Tories, Turner lost the election and with it any hope of future political success. His last-ditch effort to recast his beliefs – which redeemed him as a man if not as a politician – left his fellow Grits divided. Disoriented by Turner's nationalism, exhausted by the struggle to supplant him that had gone on since Jean Chrétien quit the Commons in 1986, they had been unable to reach a consensus about what Liberalism was in the late 1980s or where it should be going.

In the middle of the last, worst caucus revolt that Turner suffered, an old Liberal friend from the Pearson years phoned him late one night to find out how he was faring. He discovered Turner, with his family away and his aides gone home, all alone at Stornoway, the opposition leader's residence in Rockcliffe, working on his speech for the annual press gallery dinner. When the friend expressed commiseration on the latest round of betrayals, Turner responded with the mixture of gentlemanly fortitude and wild-eyed optimism that sustained his last years in politics. "Don't worry, fella," he said. "Everything's going to be fine."[17]

Nothing ever was fine, of course, in Turner's years as leader. But in his response to his vicissitudes, he displayed a grace under pressure that did the old Liberalism proud.


Throughout these politically eventful years, living in an opulent exile of his own, Pierre Trudeau appeared not to care about the Liberal Party's disintegration or Canada's continental slide. For him, retirement meant a return to the discreet charms of bourgeois

Montreal. Installed with his three children in his Art Deco mauso-
leum just inside the northern boundary of the old Square Mile and
working downtown as a trophy lawyer in the small firm of Heenan
Blaikie, he moved confidently through a city that was greatly
changed since he had lived there last. Now assertively francophone,
with a business community dominated by French-Canadian entrepreneurs who saw themselves as international titans of the future,
Montreal had become a place where the English were a dwindling
minority hived off into a few old haunts. [18]

For the first few years after Trudeau's return, Quebec was in a
state of quiescence. The traumas wrought by the referendum debate
of 1980 were healing. Quebeckers seemed to be in love with life,
with their heritage, and with their hopes for the future, and they
welcomed Trudeau back as a celebrated prodigal son. Socially, he
reverted to the behaviour patterns he had developed a quarter-
century before, turning up with showy women at private parties and
cultural events, wearing buckskins or cowboy outfits or elegant suits
from Brisson & Brisson. He turned to the friends of his youth for
moral and intellectual support and to the youth of the new day to
help him deny the truth about his advancing years. He began dating
women only a little older than his adolescent sons – students, artists,
actresses, and the daughters of both the French and English élites.
Montrealers talked delightedly about having sat behind him at an
experimental theatre production, seen him with his sons at a hockey
game, observed him lunching at a tiny Chinese restaurant, in the
faculty club at McGill, or in the dining room of the Ritz. He
displayed his continuing physical prowess by skiing in the Laurentians and scuba-diving in the South Seas, indulged his taste for the
exotic by accompanying rich businessmen on voyages to the Far
East or group treks in the Himalayas, and cultivated his international
interests by calling on François Mitterrand at the Élysée Palace or
discussing world events with Helmut Schmidt and Jimmy Carter. [19]

His old boosters tried to keep alive the hope that he might
return, like de Gaulle from his voluntary exile in Colombey-les-
Deux-Églises, to save Canada from its gathering crisis. Perhaps

nurturing this notion himself – he sometimes reminded acquaintances that the British Liberal leader William Gladstone had been
re-elected prime minister for the last time at the age of eighty-two –
Trudeau was careful to maintain his distance from everyday events,
reserving his political energy for what he called "polemics," should
the cause or the occasion arise.[20]

The moment came in the spring of 1987 when the prime minister of Canada and the nine anglophone premiers met at Meech Lake
in the Gatineau Hills north of Ottawa and, in the course of striking a
deal, agreed to the five demands made by the premier of Quebec as
the sine qua non for his formal acceptance of the constitution that
had been made the supreme law of the land in 1982. Trudeau
ruminated on this development briefly and then erupted in a diatribe published with great éclat in the French and English media.
The Meech Lake Accord was reprehensible, in his view. Not only
did it surrender important federal powers to all the provinces, it
moved Quebec a giant step towards sovereignty by declaring it to be
a distinct society.[21]

With Trudeau's intervention, the defence of the constitutional
status quo, which had begun as an eccentric and seemingly futile
effort by a handful of professors and retired mandarins, became a
popular phenomenon. Because a provision in the constitution's
amending formula gave legislatures three years in which to ratify the
Meech agreement, resistance to it had time to grow. The Conservative premiers Richard Hatfield of New Brunswick and Brian Peckford of Newfoundland, who had sanctioned the deal, were defeated
in provincial elections by the Liberals Frank McKenna and Clyde
Wells, whose substantial doubts about Meech made them chary of
giving it legislative approval. Dozens of debates and discussions on
the complex issues involved were held across the country, with
aboriginal and feminist groups expressing particularly vociferous
objections. By the time Mulroney realized how serious a threat the
anti-Meech movement had become and tried to adjust the agreement at another first ministers' meeting in June of 1990, his cause
was lost. Although Frank McKenna finally rallied to Meech, two

provincial legislatures failed to ratify the agreement, in last-minute displays of defiance by an aboriginal MLA named Elijah Harper in Manitoba and by the persistently pro-Trudeau premier Clyde Wells in Newfoundland. [22]

Trudeau, the icy federalist, had bested Mulroney, the gladsome decentralist, at enormous cost to national unity. During the period of the Meech imbroglio, anti-Quebec feelings in English Canada and anti-Canada feelings in Quebec were exacerbated further by a Supreme Court decision overturning Quebec's French-only sign law and by the Bourassa government's invocation of the 1982 constitution's notwithstanding clause to nullify the federal judges' ruling.

Divisive sentiments deepened over the next two years as the increasingly unpopular Mulroney blundered and blarneyed his way through a further round of constitutional wrangles. After extensive public debate and enormous exertion by Joe Clark, acting as Mulroney's plenipotentiary with the provinces, a new accord was reached at Charlottetown in the summer of 1992. It was then presented to the electorates in Quebec and the rest of Canada for their approval in separate though simultaneous referendums. But a well-publicized denunciation by Trudeau of the new document as destructive to the federal state – made at a session organized by contributors to the reconstituted journal *Cité libre* in the Montreal restaurant La Maison Eggroll – tipped the scales once more against constitutional change. On October 26, 1992, the Charlottetown Accord was soundly defeated in Quebec and in much of the rest of Canada. [23]

These paralysing debates darkened the national mood and leached energy from the body politic for five interminable years. While they raged, the fury of Quebec nationalists at Trudeau, and his contempt for them, took on a fresh intensity, attracting adherents to the separatist cause and creating severe problems for Trudeau's one-time faithful foot-soldier in the constitutional wars, the new Liberal leader, Jean Chrétien.

• • •

When Chrétien succeeded Turner in 1990, he was no longer the folksy, jokey populist whose sweet patriotism had made him so popular during his first leadership race six years before. Beset by family troubles – his adopted son was arrested on a sexual assault charge in Montreal only a few weeks before the convention – and with his reputation as a shrewd politician damaged by the confusion he had displayed during the Meech controversy by trying to please both Trudeau and popular opinion in Quebec, he seemed defensive and intellectually out of his depth. His chief rivals for the leadership prize were both more attractive than he was to voters in Quebec. Paul Martin, a protégé of the Montreal tycoon Paul Desmarais, whose son was married to Chrétien's daughter, had campaigned on a coherent economic program to provide business with less-intrusive state support. The only woman in the race, the Ontario MP Sheila Copps, had proven an unexpectedly appealing candidate for Quebeckers because of her fluent French and unqualified support for Meech.[24]

Even the date of Chrétien's victory seemed ill-omened: the Liberal delegates cast their ballots for him on June 23, 1990, the day after the Meech Lake Accord came to grief and the day before the traditional Saint-Jean-Baptiste celebrations were expected to produce dramatic anti-federalist demonstrations in Montreal. Transferring the blame for their disappointment over Meech to Chrétien's shoulders, two angry Quebec Liberals left his caucus immediately to join Lucien Bouchard, the Chicoutimi lawyer who had quit Mulroney's cabinet to establish a dissident Bloc Québécois of sovereigntist MPs.

For Chrétien, there was worse to come. The shock of re-entry into political life after four years as a corporate lawyer was traumatizing. While mainstreeting in small-town Quebec he found his outstretched hand ignored, his friendly greetings accorded insults or indifference. The Ottawa media treated him as another doomed Liberal leader, deriding his federalist beliefs as outdated and his turn of phrase as embarrassing. For months after his return to Parliament, he stumbled through speeches as though he did not fully comprehend the sentences he was reading. The party he inherited was some

$5 million in debt, its structures still unreformed despite Campagnolo's best efforts, its members demoralized by apparently unbridgeable policy divisions on Quebec, free trade, and the deficit. Two senior Liberal activists from the Grindstone Group, the lobbyist Rick Anderson and the political scientist Blair Williams, quit the party in disgust to join the western protest Reform Party led by Preston Manning. As though this weren't enough, Chrétien suffered serious health problems that caused the Ottawa rumour mill to predict his early replacement.

In the face of these trials, Chrétien summoned his Liberal optimism and began to regroup. He installed Jean Pelletier, the former mayor of Quebec City, in the Leader of the Opposition's Office and charged him with imposing order on its operations. He recruited Peter Donolo, an energetic young Liberal from Montreal, to manage communications. He brought into his entourage Chaviva Hošek, a talented academic, feminist, and former Ontario cabinet minister, and asked her to direct, in tandem with his finance critic, Paul Martin, the development of new policies through a thinkers' conference, a party convention, and a consultative platform-drafting process. He also took control of riding nominations so that he could field a respectable election team that included candidates who were solid cabinet material. [25]

Ridiculed in the political class as yesterday's man and a sure loser in the upcoming election, Chrétien kept a low profile while Brian Mulroney struggled to save himself from the furore raised by his constitutional adventures, the hated goods and services tax his finance minister introduced in 1991, and the negotiation of a North American Free Trade Agreement, which extended the original FTA to include Mexico and put further constraints on Canadian sovereignty. After Mulroney resigned reluctantly, still boasting he had been a great success, and his successor, Kim Campbell, revived the Conservatives' popularity briefly in the summer of 1993, Chrétien kept his cool and continued pre-testing the Liberal organization on regional tours. [26]

When Campbell called the election for October 25, she was faced by an expertly organized Liberal team backing up an experienced campaigner. Chrétien's platform turned out to be a thoroughly researched, carefully produced "red book," a smooth document that balanced Paul Martin's pro-business neo-liberalism with Chaviva Hošek's welfare-Liberal concerns for aboriginals, women, and the maintenance of medicare. As the campaign unfolded, Chrétien's confidence and good humour returned. He held his own during the leaders' debates and benefitted from the media's concentration on Campbell's myriad mistakes, Bouchard's sovereigntist eloquence, and Manning's simplistic bromides.[27]

A combination of disgust with the Conservatives, nostalgia for the Liberal past, and the collapse of the New Democrats helped Chrétien win an impressive majority with strong representation from every anglophone province. But his surprising triumph was tempered by the success of Bouchard, who captured fifty-two of Quebec's seventy-five seats by exploiting nationalist anger at Chrétien and invoking a utopian future for Quebec as a sovereign state.

In the election's wake, it quickly became evident that although Chrétien had emphasized on the hustings the *rouge* aspect of his platform, he would have to govern as a blue Grit. Fronting a government with such a large foreign debt that economic and social policies had to be made with an anxious eye on the international bond market, Chrétien found his options limited. In his first year in office, he benefitted from the reduced expectations of government that so many Canadians had been forced into during the Mulroney years. Determined to trust him, the public seemed to accept that the good old days of bountiful Liberalism were no more and that Canada would not be able to pay down its debt without pruning government services.

Even in the 1980–81 constitutional battles, Chrétien had shown a distaste for confrontational politics. His style was to seek common ground and to strike a deal. As befitted a protégé of the business

Liberal Mitchell Sharp, he naturally took a brokerage approach to government by straddling the centre of the political spectrum and leaning to the left or right as circumstances dictated. With the social-democratic movement in disarray, there was no pressure on Chrétien as prime minister to lean left. He could situate himself where a little guy from a resource town was most comfortable: on the continentalist and right-of-centre side of the Liberal spectrum. What he was peddling as the Liberalism of the 1990s was hope in adversity and competence in a time of crisis. By saying that he meant to govern according to Canadian values, what he seemed to be seeking was social harmony and political peace in the face of dire millennialist warnings that Canada would never be the same again and, given the distemper in Quebec, might shortly cease to exist. Certain that Quebeckers, like other Canadians, were more interested in jobs than the constitution, he determined to answer the sovereigntist challenge by governing soberly, keeping his campaign promises as far as prudent budget-making would allow, and forging a cautious new Liberalism appropriate to the times.

In his heady internationalist days, Pierre Trudeau liked to tell a story about his intellectual sparring partner Henry Kissinger. The version he recited during an unscripted speech he gave to a packed audience of students at the University of Toronto in March 1984 went something like this.

At an official dinner in Paris, held during the Vietnam peace negotiations in 1972, the host asked Nixon's national security adviser to describe the impact of the French Revolution on his society. Kissinger launched into a magisterial exposition of the influence of the French Enlightenment on American political thought, weaving philosophical, historical, and cultural allusions into a seamless whole. After he had finished, attention at the table turned belatedly to the diplomat sitting silently on the host's other side, the representative from Beijing, who was asked politely how the events of 1789 had affected China. Puffing thoughtfully on his pipe, the envoy voiced the laconic opinion: "Too early to tell."[28]

Ten years after Trudeau left office, it was still too early to tell whether his mission to keep Quebec in Canada would ultimately succeed or fail. As separatist forces mounted their most sophisticated assault on federalism in thirty years of seeking independence, their nemesis was not the new francophone prime minister of Canada but the old one. Pierre Elliott Trudeau was still the enemy that sovereigntists feared the most and the leader that federalists turned to for salvation when contemplating yet another referendum battle on sovereignty. If Canada survived as an entity, the lion's share of the credit would go to Trudeau – for his determined inflexibility in fighting for his all-provinces-must-be-equal concept of federalism. If Canada failed, the lion's share of the blame would fall on Trudeau, too, for his dogmatic inflexibility in refusing to accommodate the neo-federalism of the Quebec Liberals under Claude Ryan and Robert Bourassa.

It was *not* too early to tell, a decade after his retirement, that Trudeau's effect on the Canadian polity had been profound.

• By negotiating with the provincial premiers an agreement that allowed Canada to achieve full sovereignty through patriating its constitution, he completed the country's formal development from colony to nation-state.

• By persisting in his efforts to achieve official bilingualism and to afford francophones a fair share of senior positions in the federal government, he righted the balance of power between the French and English in Canada.

• By effecting the liberalization of immigration and refugee policies that made Asian, African, Latin American, and Caribbean applicants as eligible for Canadian citizenship as Europeans, he altered the ethnic make-up of the nation.

• By entrenching a charter of rights and freedoms in the new constitution, he reoriented the Canadian political system, shifting to the courts for resolution by appointed judges many issues that previously were dealt with by elected politicians, and granting minority groups of all kinds the legal means by which to assert their equality as citizens.

Through such significant acts, Trudeau helped transform the authoritarian, parochial, British, white dominion of his youth into a more equitable, tolerant, and pluralistic society. But in other efforts to modernize his country's institutions and manage its affairs, he met with less success.

• The cabinet committee system contrived for him by Michael Pitfield, while honest in its attempt to rationalize the decision-making process and put the elected ministers in charge, created such complexity and disharmony that much of it was subsequently abandoned. By the end of the Trudeau years, the enlarged state apparatus had become so difficult to control that its senior bureaucrats, who were resistant to Liberal policies, particularly in the economic field, were preparing the way for a neo-conservative attack on the Trudeau legacy.

• In trying to achieve his goal of a balanced federalism through institutionalizing first ministers' conferences, Trudeau altered the character of intergovernmental relations in Canada and gave provincial premiers a greater say in national affairs. But he was unable to reconcile his commitment to strong central government with Ottawa's inability to maintain its financial contributions to the shared-cost programs on which federal suasion with the provinces was based.

• The unresolved conflict between his pan-Canadianism and his anti-nationalism resulted in serious contradictions. Despite his obsessive concern with federal government power, he had remained strangely indifferent to external threats to Ottawa's autonomy. His heroic delusion that he could make Canada fully sovereign by force of will alone led him to deny rather than confront the pervasive pressure of the American hegemony and left Canadians susceptible to continentalism's siren call when it came in the form of Brian Mulroney's extravagant promises that free trade would bring better jobs, cheaper goods, and a rosy future.

• Paradoxically, by regaining power in 1980 and using it to achieve the liberal goals that he had failed to realize earlier, Trudeau delayed the coming of neo-conservatism to Canada through the party system and blunted its impact when it arrived. The many policies that were implemented by the Trudeauites during the 1980-84 period embedded in the public consciousness a deep commitment to liberal values that increased voter resistance to the Mulroney Conservatives' efforts to dismantle the welfare state.

More than Trudeau's liberal values lingered after he had gone. His intellectual brilliance, moral integrity, toughness of will, spiritual intensity, and physical prowess made him a model for many Canadians aspiring to excellence in politics and other fields. For the big generation of Canadians who came of age while he was prime minister, he defined political leadership for good and for ill, and his advancing years failed to stale their interest in his life's infinite variety. When he fathered a daughter with one of their cohort, the constitutional lawyer Deborah Coyne, and both parents refused to discuss their relationship publicly, the national media suffered paroxysms of frustration at not being able to bring their readers every titillating detail of their romance. When he was persuaded to collaborate with interviewers in order to produce the memoirs that he had vowed he would never undertake, disappointment in the contents of both the television series and the heavily illustrated print versions that resulted was widely expressed by reviewers. But their great success in the ratings and on the bestseller lists showed that for many Canadians, the Trudeau era had taken on the glow of a golden age: what they were watching or buying was not just a film or a book but a piece of their past. [29]

Volume 1 of this study, which was published in 1990, began with the statement "He haunts us still." Four years later, as Volume 2 was delivered to the printers, Pierre Trudeau was still a live political force in Canada, dangerous, provocative, and unpredictable. At the age of seventy-five, he continued to daunt his enemies, inspire his allies, and enliven the public discourse he had dominated for so long as the most compelling and controversial Canadian of his times.

# NOTES

## Chapter 1
## A Small-l Liberal Education

1. Details of the Bank of Canada party are from the authors' observations and from Zena Cherry, "Jordan's King Visits Trudeau," *Globe and Mail* (Nov. 14, 1981), p. 19. Details of the expanded Bank of Canada building are from interviews with Louis Rasminsky, the governor who presided over the planning for its expansion, July 22, 1991; Toronto architect Ronald Dick, whose firm designed the original 1936 building and collaborated with Arthur Erickson on its 1979 modernization, July 4, 1991; and Jean-Michel Catta, public information officer at the Bank, Apr. 22, 1991.

2. Sound of revelry: In hindsight, the Bank of Canada party on budget night 1981 took on the aura of the ball given before the Battle of Waterloo, as described in Lord Byron's famous stanzas from *Childe Harold's Pilgrimage* (canto III, verse 21), which begin:

> There was a sound of revelry by night,
> And Belgium's capital had gather'd then
> Her Beauty and her Chivalry, and bright
> The lamps shone o'er fair women and brave men . . .
> A thousand hearts beat happily; and when
> Music arose with its voluptuous swell,
> Soft eyes look'd love to eyes which spake again,
> And all went merry as a marriage bell;
> But hush! hark! a deep sound strikes like a rising knell!

3. "Under control": Authors' interview with J.W. Pickersgill, Nov. 13, 1981.

4. On French and English contributions to the war effort: Morton and Granatstein, *Marching to Armageddon*, pp. 32–34.

5. On the decline of the Liberals in England: The British Liberal Party of the late nineteenth century had embodied the ideas of progress and individualism, free trade and anti-imperialism, which so appealed to the rising middle class of industrial England. Under its towering leader, William Ewart Gladstone, it had also championed the values of human rights and social emancipation on behalf of the working class, which was pressing for enfranchisement. Gladstone's long record of social-reform legislation – a national system of education, the secret ballot, the legalization of trade unions, the reconstruction of the judicial system – made him an ideological model for Wilfrid Laurier in the 1890s when he was seeking to transform the opposition Liberals into a governing party. The British Liberals' ventures before World War I into state insurance against sickness and unemployment, old-age pensions, workmen's compensation, the regulation of sweated trades, and progressive taxation were equally important as an inspiration for Mackenzie King when he was charting his political path between industry and humanity.

   After 1914, blocked on the right by the House of Lords, outflanked on the left by

435

the emerging Labour Party, held hostage by the Irish question, and besieged by the women's rebellion, the Liberals – described in Dangerfield's ironic *Strange Death of Liberal England* as that "capitalist left wing [which] advanced upon social reform with noisy mouths and mouselike feet" (p. 15) – declined steadily, to the dismay of their Canadian cousins, who proved under King's leadership to be more adept at steering a middle way between labour and capital and at mastering the pressures of change while fending off the forces of reaction. See Cook, *Short History of the Liberal Party*, chs. 7–9; and, for a review of the theories about the party's decline, Cregier, *Decline of the British Liberal Party*. For a literary liberal mind at work, see the novels of E.M. Forster and the authorized biography by Furbank, *E.M. Forster*, which discusses how Forster struck the great American analyst of the liberal imagination, Lionel Trilling, pp. 244–45.

"The general political situation": Dawson, *Mackenzie King*, p. 271.

6. On Mackenzie as firebrand: Kilbourn, *Firebrand*. Mackenzie is more often called "the little rebel." The published material on King is extraordinarily rich. The basic biography of the younger King is MacGregor Dawson's authoritative *William Lyon Mackenzie King*. After Dawson's death, four volumes covering his later career as part of the same project were produced by H. Blair Neatby, J.W. Pickersgill, and D.F. Forster. For a radical revision of the story, see Ferns and Ostry, *Age of Mackenzie King*. The liberal historian who set the tone for pouring scorn on wily Willie was C.P. Stacey in his *A Very Double Life*. Two interesting studies by political scientists are the psychobiography in the manner of Erik Erikson by Joy Esberey, *Knight of the Holy Spirit*, and the vivid description of King as prime minister by H.S. Ferns in his memoir, *Reading from Left to Right*.

7. On anti-liberalism of Catholic church: Linteau et al., *Quebec: A History*, pp. 198–204, 454–60.

8. On British hegemonic power: See Barzini, *Europeans*, pp. 35–65, and James Morris's superb trilogy on the Empire, *Heaven's Command*, *Pax Britannica*, and *Farewell the Trumpets*.

9. "Sordidly avaricious": Morris, *Heaven's Command*, p. 126.

In ways the French had never managed: "Few French Canadians had the contacts, experience or opportunities to enter the international commercial networks that the new [British traders] were creating. Few were able to use the patronage system erected by the new foreign governors. The Canadiens' situation became more difficult with time . . . [They] were not at all equipped to rival the pushing young Scotsmen who poured into the colonies as agents-on-the-make." Bliss, *Northern Enterprise*, p. 115.

Dynamic commercial community: Other sources of wealth beyond resource extraction involved the servicing of the transportation (canals, railroads, shipping), financial (banking, insurance), and consumption (tobacco and alcohol) needs of the staple economy.

On Montreal's dominant position: Although Toronto's population overtook that of Montreal in the 1970s, "Toronto supplanted Montreal as Canada's chief economic centre considerably before that, probably even before 1960." Jacobs, *Canadian Cities*, p. 9.

10. Pro-Canadian, anti-imperialist feelings: Carl Berger in *Sense of Power* describes Toronto as the ideological centre for Canadian imperialist thinking in the decades bracketing the turn of the century, with the McGill economist Stephen Leacock the only significant intellectual in the movement from Montreal. English-Canadian nationalism emerged from imperialism, whereas French-Canadian nationalism of the Henri Bourassa school was anti-imperialist in origin. Berger, *Imperialism and Nationalism*.

Dreamland replication of British society: Authors' interviews with Isobel Barclay Dobell, curator emeritus of Montreal's McCord Museum, who rescued the McCord and Notman collections in the 1950s and 1960s, June 1, 1991; Colin Dobell, May 18, 1991; and Pamela Miller, Sept. 3, 1991.

On Montreal's Anglo-Protestant élite: Westley, *Remembrance of Grandeur*. Also Newman, *Flame of Power* and *Canadian Establishment*.

Although they took as their collective ideal the English aristocracy, the behaviour of the denizens of the Square Mile was classic *nouveau riche*. Their suits, boots, riding habits, and guns were ordered from bespoke tradesmen in London; their china, linen, books, magazines, butlers, and nannies were spewed out on the Montreal docks from ships arriving from Southampton. The network of schools set up for their offspring were mock-British to the core. They dispatched American architects to copy the plans of English country houses and French châteaux for their mansions. And they stuffed those dwellings with European art and artefacts, collected with an acquisitive zest very nearly equal to that of the English lords they were emulating.

On the Square Mile's European art collections: Brooke, *Discerning Tastes*.

On the scorn for the products of local craftsmen that this imperialism entailed: "It was the proud boast of the grandest Anglo-Canadian mansions that not a stick of furniture in the house, not a knife, not a single painting of Highland cattle in a gloomy brownish glen, was home-produced – all came, as they liked to say, from the Old Country." Morris, *Pax Britannica*, p. 389. A notable exception was Donald Ross McCord, whose mania for collecting produced the invaluable record of Montreal life in the museum that bears his family name.

11. The Square Mile was formally defined as the area bounded by Bleury in the east, Dorchester (now René-Lévesque) to the south, Guy on the west, and Pine.

12. On the Square Mile's hiring and linguistic practices: Westley, *Remembrance of Grandeur*, pp. 34–41.

"Niggers begin at Calais": Morris, *Pax Britannica*, p. 132. The phrase is sometimes rendered as "Wogs begin at Calais."

13. "They just didn't know": Authors' confidential interview, Sept. 1991.

14. On the economic, social, and political history of Quebec and Montreal: Hamelin and Provencher, *Brève histoire du Québec*; Daniel Latouche, "Quebec," in *Canadian Encyclopedia*, 2nd ed.; Paul-André Linteau, "Montreal," in *Canadian Encyclopedia*, 2nd ed.; Linteau et al., *Quebec: A History*; and Wade, *French Canadians*, vols. 1 and 2.

On the Church's utopian rural ideology: Trudeau, *Asbestos Strike*, ch. 1.

15. The land could not support: "The failure of wheat as both staple crop and basic consumption item" accounted for the stagnation of Lower Canada's agriculture. McCallum, *Unequal Beginnings*, pp. 25ff. Paradoxically, Montreal's rural hinterland in the

first two-thirds of the nineteenth century lay more in Upper Canada, where the wheat economy had prospered and found an export route through the St. Lawrence River. McCallum, *Unequal Beginnings*, p. 4.

Urban middle class: "What our educational system produced was priests, priests, priests. And lawyers, lawyers, lawyers," Jean Fournier, the distinguished former federal and provincial public servant, remarked as he reviewed the progress of his generation of Quebeckers. "What we didn't produce [until the late twentieth century] was people who knew how to do well in business, because business was outside our experience." Authors' interview, June 4, 1991.

On the ethnic and linguistic division of labour in Montreal: Henri Bourassa described the English Montrealers "living in this city and province as a group of isolated Uitlanders, wealthy, self-satisfied, and self-contained, with no care for their French-speaking neighbours – except on such occasions as when French votes are needed to elect an English-speaking mayor." Quoted from Bourassa, *French and English Frictions*, pp. 22–23, in Wade, *French Canadians*, vol. 2, p. 638.

Self-government: The Quebec Act of 1774 had guaranteed Canadiens the right to continue to use French civil law, had retained the seigneurial system, and had confirmed the Catholic church's right to tithe its adherents and have them hold public office. An assembly, elected but with little real power, was established by the Constitution Act of 1791, which split Upper Canada from Lower Canada until 1840, when, following the advice of the Durham Report, the Act of Union reunited the two troubled provinces in a futile attempt to assimilate the Canadiens into the culture of the English-speaking majority. With Confederation, Durham's political strategy for Britain's white dominions – gradual progress towards self-government – was extended to the Empire's French-speaking subjects.

16. Stereotyped: The English Montrealers' view of French Canadians as poor at business but good at law is captured by the novelist Hugh MacLennan in the language of clubland gossip: "'Damned good lawyers though, I have one for a partner, clever little devil. Don't know what I'd do without him.'" *Two Solitudes*, p. 218.

On those who grew prosperous: In the 1930s the five major French-Canadian family groups of Simard, Bienvenu, Raymond, Brillant, and Lévesque controlled the only large French-Canadian businesses: Levine, *Reconquest of Montreal*, pp. 22–23.

On Anglo domination in business: Bélanger and Fournier, *L'entreprise québécoise*, pp. 48–52. In the Montreal of 1935, where 61 per cent of the population was francophone, English-speakers held 73.8 per cent of managerial positions, while French-speakers held only 22.6 per cent of these positions. Hughes and McDonald, "French and English," pp. 495–96.

Interlocking directorships: Hughes and McDonald, "French and English," p. 500; Linteau et al., *Quebec: A History*, pp. 403–4; and Westley, *Remembrance of Grandeur*, pp. 186, 202.

On French-Canadian businesses: Hughes and McDonald, "French and English," pp. 499, 502–3.

On ownership of banks and insurance companies: Linteau et al., *Quebec Since 1930*, pp. 147, 158.

The English as the managers both of business and of the Quebec ministry of finance: Levine, *Reconquest of Montreal*, pp. 1–2, 18, 31; and Wade, *French Canadians*, vol. 2, p. 638. "A citizen who wished to correspond with the department of the provincial treasurer could do so only in English": Linteau et al., *Quebec: A History*, p. 538.

17. Huge veranda: Dunham Ladies' College, *Calendar, School Year 1899-1900*, McCord Museum archives, Montreal; Dunham Ladies' College, *Prospectus, Academic Year 1911-12*, authors' archive; Edgar Andrew Collard, "The Story of St. Helen's School," *Montreal Gazette* (May 6, 1972), p. 6; and C. Gossage, *Question of Privilege*, pp. 10, 64, 117–19. Also authors' interview with William Westfall, Mar. 4, 1993.

18. Health hazards: Regular garbage collection was not instituted in Montreal until 1914: Hamelin and Provencher, *Brève histoire du Québec*, p. 111.

On manners at King's Hall: C. Gossage, *Question of Privilege*, p. 64.

19. "Frenchman nobody knew": Authors' interview with Grace Pitfield, Oct. 26, 1974.

20. On Charlie Trudeau and Grace Elliott: Breslin, "The Other Trudeaus," supplemented by authors' interviews with I.M.B. Dobell, June 1, 1991; Grace Pitfield, Oct. 26, 1974; Jeanne and Maurice Sauvé, Nov. 27, 1986; and Charles Lussier, June 15, 1991.

21. "Ah-Oh-Ah": Authors' interview with Charles Lussier, June 6, 1991.

22. *Jack*: Joual meaning strong guy – "individu de forte taille": Léandre Bergeron, *Dictionnaire de la langue québécoise* (Montreal: VLB, 1980).

American direct investment exceeded British directly controlled investment in Canada from 1926. Aitken et al., *American Economic Impact*, table 8, p. 156.

23. Break the barriers: Janeway, *Powers of the Weak*, ch. 14.

Recently established equivalents: The construction by French Canadians of these institutions in response to their exclusion from those of the English turned out to be the beginning of the long march to take back economic, social, and cultural control of Montreal, a slow campaign that would take another fifty years to succeed. Levine, *Reconquest of Montreal*.

24. On Sir Lomer Gouin and Querbes: "Inauguration de l'Académie Querbes à Outremont demain," *La Presse* (Oct. 21, 1916), p. 17.

Training an élite: Authors' interviews with Camille Laurin, Jan. 23, 1991; Jean de Grandpré, Jan. 30, 1987; and James Reed, Feb. 10, 1994.

25. On Hertel and Bernier: Authors' interview with Charles Lussier, Oct. 21, 1992.

On Bernier at Brébeuf: Iglauer, *Strangers Next Door*, pp. 172–75.

26. On Abbé Groulx: Delisle, *Traitor and the Jew*.

"Achat chez nous" and "listes blanches": Authors' interview with Georges-Henri Lévesque, Jan. 25, 1991; Trudeau, *Asbestos Strike*, p. 32; and Delisle, *Traitor and the Jew*, pp. 187–88.

On Jewish businesses: The ten-fold expansion of the Jewish population of Montreal in the first decade of the twentieth century made it the largest such community in Canada and contributed to the French Canadians' fears. Wade, *French Canadians*, vol. 1, p. 546.

27. On admiration of classmates and Trudeau's rejection of anti-Semitism at Brébeuf: Authors' interview with Charles Lussier, June 6, 1991.

28. On Beaupré: Authors' interview with Charles Lussier, June 6, 1991.

29. Biracial identity: For Pierre Trudeau's psychological development, see vol. 1, chs. 2 and 3.

"English mores": Interview with Pierre Trudeau cited in Radwanski, *Trudeau*, p. 56.

30. Two summers: Letter to the authors from the Taylor Statten Camps, Oct. 24, 1991; and interview with Dr. A.W. Beairsto, July 12, 1991.

On Canadiens and Indians: Professor Jean Morriset of the Université de Montréal, as quoted in Pauline Couture, "Québécois Voices," *Globe and Mail* (Mar. 10, 1992), p. A19.

31. On Trudeau at law school: Authors' interviews with Pierre Carignan, Jan. 26, 1991; and Charles Lussier, June 6, 1991.

The Canadian armed forces demanded equality of sacrifice from French Canadians without granting them equality of opportunity. Linteau et al., *Quebec Since 1930*, p. 94.

Prospect that clearly excited him: Authors' interview with Charles Lussier, June 6, 1991. Lussier was editor of *Le Quartier latin*, a university literary journal, and remembered realizing it would not be suitable to ask Trudeau to write for it since his great interest was in politics, not the arts. Fifty years later Trudeau denied he had any political interests at the time. *Memoirs*, pp. 24, 31.

32. Charlie Trudeau and Duplessis: Black, *Duplessis*, p. 559, n. 9.

33. Radical tract: "No CCF government will rest content until it has eradicated capitalism and put into operation the full programme of socialized planning which will lead to the establishment in Canada of the Co-operative Commonwealth." Lewis and Scott, *Make This Your Canada*, p. 207.

34. Wide-open wartime Montreal: Authors' interview with Jeanne Sauvé, Nov. 27, 1986; and Victor-Levy Beaulieu, *Montréal, P.Q.*, téléroman, broadcast by Radio-Canada, Oct. 1992.

35. On Trudeau and Rolland: Authors' interview with Roger Rolland, Jan. 30, 1991.

36. James Bay: Trudeau went with three friends including his Brébeuf classmate Guy Viau. Trudeau, *Memoirs*, pp. 26–27.

37. Thérèse Gouin's father's law firm, Beaulieu & Gouin, was bipartisan; Gouin's partner, Beaulieu, was Duplessis's lawyer.

On Thérèse Gouin's youth: Authors' interview with Thérèse Décarie, Sept. 7, 1992.

38. On Mercier and provincial rights: Linteau et al., *Quebec: A History*, pp. 249–52.

39. "Very advanced ideas": Gouin, *Sir Lomer Gouin*, p. 28.

40. On Sir Lomer as premier: Linteau et al., *Quebec: A History*, pp. 486–87, 506–11.

41. On Sir Lomer and King: Dawson, *Mackenzie King*, pp. 360–73.

On Gouin's funeral: Authors' interview with Thérèse Décarie, Sept. 7, 1992.

42. Fabianism: Holroyd, *Bernard Shaw*, vol. 1, pp. 124–90.

On King's rejection of Fabianism: Dawson, *Mackenzie King*, p. 85.

On King and the NLF: Reginald Whitaker, *Government Party*, pp. 146–52.

43. "I don't want": Authors' interview with Charles Lussier, June 6, 1991.

44. Having consulted elders: Trudeau, *Memoirs*, pp. 38–39.

45. On Trudeau at Harvard: Authors' interviews with Pierre Carignan, Jan. 26, 1991; Fred Gibson, July 22, 1991; Kenneth McRae, June 2, 1991; Morris Miller, July 23, 1991; John Reshetar, Mar. 8, 1992; and Adam Ulam, Oct. 10, 1991.

Later, when he became famous, English Canadians who had been at Harvard at the same time as Trudeau but were not his friends or classmates circulated stories that he had never worked hard, that he was a dilettante, a kind of retroactive reading into his behaviour as a graduate student of the nonsense that was being circulated in the press in the late 1960s and 1970s by his separatist and business opponents.

46. Liberalism was "the present-day culmination of the whole 'Western political tradition'": Sabine, *History of Political Theory*, p. 741.

47. "Cultured and sensitive": Authors' interview with Adam Ulam, Oct. 10, 1991.
   Political career: Letter to the authors from John Reshetar, Jan. 1992.

48. The occasional party: Authors' interview with Pierre Carignan, Jan. 26, 1990.

49. "Reactionary bourgeois": "Compte-rendu de la conférence de M. Trudeau," Sept. 22, 1947, in "Le livre-album du Club de Relations Internationales," n.d., p. 92. We are grateful to D'Iberville Fortier for supplying this document.
   Trudeau on Mounier: *Memoirs*, p. 40.
   On meeting Mounier: Authors' interview with Vianney Décarie, Sept. 9, 1991.

50. "Un grand malheur": Authors' interview with Thérèse Décarie, Sept. 7, 1992.

51. Laski was besieged by eager acolytes, and his stature as the Labour Party's guru sometimes lured him away from the mundane obligations of academe. On one occasion, he fetched up late for a two o'clock seminar, his face mottled, eyes bright, and looking around as though not quite sure where he was, said in measured tones, "Ahh, yes, gentlemen. Who is giving the paper today? And *what*, pray tell, is the topic?"
   "I am, sir," piped up Ralph Miliband, one of Laski's protégés, later to become a renowned Marxist scholar. "And the subject is Russian foreign policy from World War I to 1939."
   "Right, Miliband," said Laski. "I've just come from lunch with Molotov [the Soviet foreign minister]. *Do* proceed."
   In the face of such donnish one-upmanship even the cocky Miliband was daunted. Lesser lights among Laski's students did not even achieve name recognition though the most promising of them were invited, half a dozen at a time, to his house in Putney for evening discussions with the leading intellectual and political figures who converged on his illustrious salon. Authors' interview with Paul Fox, Sept. 26, 1991.
   "Hungry and thirsty": Trudeau, "Faites vos jeux," p. 38.

52. Decline of the British Liberal Party: Cregier, *Decline of the British Liberal Party*, and Dutton, "Brink of Oblivion." The great Cambridge economist John Maynard Keynes and Sir William Beveridge, the father of the welfare state, were two of the most influential academic Liberals in the party's period of continuing decline.
   Laski's appeal for Trudeau would have been due in part to his great fame as a lively and challenging professor who was on intimate terms with the world leaders of the time, and in part to his ideas, which were at once federalist, liberal, and radical, as the 1934 preface to his phenomenally successful text indicated:

   The necessarily federal character of society; the incompatibility of the sovereign State with that economic world-order so painfully struggling to be born; the antithesis between individual property rights in the essential means of production and the fulfilment of the democratic idea; the thesis that liberty is a concept devoid of real meaning except in the context of equality; the refusal to regard law as valid merely in terms of the formal authority from which it emanates; the argument that in any society, even when based on equal and universal suffrage, the existence of serious economic inequalities biases the incidence of government in favour of the rich . . . There cannot, in a word, be democracy unless there is socialism. (Laski, *A Grammar of Politics*, n.p.)

Laski's positions on functionalism, federalism, pluralism, egalitarianism, anti-nationalism, and liberalism were to find a clear echo in Trudeau's own intellectual opus in the 1950s.

"Inquisitive mind" and "excellent training": Trudeau to John Reshetar, Jan. 6, 1948, and May 1, 1948.

53. On Trudeau at the LSE: Authors' interviews with Anne Bohm, Apr. 2, 1992; Paul Fox, Sept. 26, 1991; Ralph Miliband, May 30, 1991; and Morris Miller, July 23, 1991; and a letter to the authors from Rufus Davis, Mar. 16, 1992.

On Robert Mackenzie's dissenting opinion: Jeffrey Simpson, "Card-Carrying Canadian Is a British Institution," *Globe and Mail* (July 20, 1981), p. 7.

54. By the end of the session his work with Laski had taken the more general direction of "Studies on liberty, authority and obedience" on which he had completed five chapters, work that was probably the raw material for what became the short essays he was to write in 1957 for the Montreal weekly *Vrai*, which were published subsequently as *Approaches to Politics*. Letter to the authors from the Academic Registrar of the LSE, Oct. 4, 1988.

Moss Bros.: Authors' interview with Paul Fox, Nov. 10, 1991.

55. "Young nobleman": Authors' interviews with Joan Fox and Paul Fox, Nov. 10, 1991.

56. "God only knows": Trudeau to John Reshetar, May 1, 1948.

Psychology texts: These included Charles Odier's *Les deux sources consciente et inconsciente de la vie morale*, a densely reasoned work that attempts a reconciliation of the views of Freud and Bergson. On the voyage from New York to Le Havre in 1946 he had pored over Emmanuel Mounier's *Traité du caractère*, showing that his intellectual interests at the time went well beyond mastering the main ideas of political economy: Authors' interviews with Roger Rolland, Jan. 23, 1991, and Andrée Désautels, Jan. 23, 1991.

57. Cyrano de Bergerac: For the influence on Trudeau of Edmond Rostand's play of the same name, see vol. 1, pp. 43–44. In the French-language television version of his *Memoirs*, Trudeau remembers his father receiving from a friend a copy of the play with an inscription describing Charlie Trudeau as the Cyrano of French-Canadian business. In the English version, he mentions memorizing Cyrano's great monologues or *tirades* for recitation at school. He still knew them by heart when he was in his late sixties. Authors' interview with Pierre Trudeau, June 6, 1985.

# Chapter 2
# A Large-L Liberal Indoctrination

1. On concern and disdain for the people: As Harold Nicolson put it, "But how diffi-cult the proletariat are! . . . They destroy the grass . . . Yes, I fear my socialism is purely cerebral: I do not like the masses in the flesh." Nicolson, *Vita and Harold*, pp. 322–33.

2. For the ideas of the English-speaking post-war generation: Annan, *Our Age*, and Hitchens, *Blood, Class and Nostalgia*.

    Mother England: From his exposure to Enlightenment thinking at Brébeuf, Trudeau knew that England had already been deemed by Montesquieu to be the "one nation in the world whose constitution's main objective is political liberty." Montesquieu, *De l'esprit des lois*, livre XI, ch. 5, authors' translation.

3. "The worst": Postcard to John Reshetar, Nov. 13, 1950.

4. On Ottawa's urban blight: Woods, *Ottawa*, p. 281.

    Architectural glories: The neo-Gothic piles on Parliament Hill, divided like Gaul into three parts, the Centre, West, and East Blocks; the austere Art Deco Bank of Canada building; and the grandiose Supreme Court, which together represented Ottawa's bow to the modern century.

    For the prevalence of the Gothic style in the outposts of Empire and the impor-tance of the Rideau Canal as an engineering feat, see Morris, *Heaven's Command*, pp. 208–9, 265.

5. Rideau Club: S. Gwyn, *Private Capital*, p. 90.

6. Ottawa Men: The phrase was first coined in 1962 by Christina [McCall] Newman in *Maclean's*, "How to Spot the Ottawa Man: A Concise Guide."

    On the shaping of this influential cohort: Owram, *Government Generation*.

7. Quasi-socialist state: "The second war placed Canada on a basis of state socialism. The state was by long odds the most important force in Canadian life, private initia-tive being almost entirely subordinated to state policy." Lower, "Second Great War," p. 97.

    Consociational élites: Noel's "Consociational Democracy and Canadian Feder-alism" applied Arend Lijphart's notion in "Cultural Diversity and Theories of Politi-cal Integration" of élite accommodation in ethnically divided political systems.

8. On the Liberals and the civil service: J.L. Granatstein wrote that "as good tacticians they were wisely unwilling to go too far out in front of their Cabinet ministers, and almost none ever did." Granatstein, *Ottawa Men*, p. 280. Also Reginald Whitaker, *Government Party*, p. 143: "The Liberal party was by now the Government party, and as such its ability to draw on the expertise and new ideas of the civil service and to put them into effect in an electorally successful manner was an integral part of its func-tioning as a political organization." And John Meisel: "Much of what had, in the years immediately before the [1957] election, been called Liberal policies or the Lib-eral programme was actually the product of the intimate co-operation of leading civil servants and their ministers." Meisel, "Liberal and Conservative Programmes," p. 565.

    Ordeal by fire: Allen, *Ordeal by Fire*.

On the privatization of military-industrial assets: Bothwell and Kilbourn, *Howe*, pp. 188–90. Also Borins, "World War Two Crown Corporations."

On civil servants as centralists: "The Ottawa men were centralists first and foremost. The Depression had demonstrated that Canada could work satisfactorily only if the central government had the power to create and implement national programs, to equalize services across the land, and to establish and maintain a national minimum standard of social services." Granatstein, *Ottawa Men*, p. 273.

On the threat from the left: "The high tide of CCF popularity was only a symptom of a massive shift of public opinion toward the left – a shift which was, on a much smaller scale, even sweeping a few Communists to electoral success in some of the larger cities." Reginald Whitaker, *Government Party*, p. 137.

On post-war industrial relations: MacDowell, "Canadian Industrial Relations System," and Webber, "Compulsory Conciliation."

9. On Canadian-American co-operation during the war: Cuff and Granatstein, *American Dollars*, ch. 1; and R.W. James, *Wartime Economic Co-operation*.

New world power: Writing of how, through the war effort, her country became a manufacturing giant, a creditor nation, the world's third sea power, and its fourth air power, Louisa Piet concluded that, while Canada might be "a little dazed at the very heights to which she has leaped in this sudden metamorphosis of being . . . her sense of moral rectitude protects her from fear." *New World Power*, pp. 9, 280.

10. On Canadian mandarins' world-view: Bothwell, Drummond, and English, *Canada Since 1945*, p. 63; Plumptre, *Three Decades of Decision*; Holmes, *Shaping of Peace*; and E. Reid, *Time of Fear and Hope* and *Radical Mandarin*.

On the commonality of outlook between Canadian and American officials in the post-war years: Cuff and Granatstein, *Canadian-American Relations*, ch. 6, "Corporal Pearson, General Acheson and the Cold War." Lester Pearson recalled that very little thought was given to the question of economic sovereignty in Canada's relations with the U.S. "A major omission also was the need to ensure our survival as a separate state against powerful, if friendly, social and economic pressures from our American neighbour." *Mike*, vol. 2, p. 25.

Present at the creation: Holmes, *Living with Uncle*, ch. 1.

Among the UN specialized agencies of which Canada was an active participant: Food and Agriculture Organization (1944); United Nations Educational, Scientific and Cultural Organization (1946); World Health Organization (1946); International Labour Organization (reorganized 1946); International Bank for Reconstruction (1946); International Monetary Fund (1946); International Civil Aviation Organization (1947); International Refugee Organization (1947); Universal Postal Union (special agency status, 1948); International Telecommunications Union (special agency status, 1949). Soward, *Canada in World Affairs*, pp. 168ff., and Spencer, *Canada in World Affairs*, pp. 167ff.

11. Support for the GATT (established in 1947): Stone, *International Trade System*, p. 22.

Balance its trading books: Although Canada's trade deficit of $488 million with the U.S. in the first half of 1947 was theoretically offset by its surplus with Britain, the bulk of this surplus was still being financed by Canadian loans. Cuff and Granatstein, "Canadian-American Free Trade," p. 463. See also Granatstein, *Man of Influence*, pp. 215–37; Granatstein, *Britain's Weakness*, ch. 2; and Muirhead, *Postwar Canadian Trade Policy* and "Trials and Tribulations."

Huge financial aid: During the war, the total of Canadian aid to Britain was $3.468 billion, almost one-fifth of the total $18-billion cost of the war to Canada. Granatstein, *Britain's Weakness*, pp. 38–39. In 1946, Ottawa cancelled $425 million in debt and lent Britain an additional $1.25 billion. This latter amount equalled more than 10 per cent of Canada's gross national product in 1946, and was one-third the size of U.S. loans to Britain that had to be repaid. Soward, *Canada in World Affairs*, p. 106; and Cuff and Granatstein, "Rise and Fall," p. 462.

12. On U.S. protectionism: The American tariff channelled Canadian development "along lines complementary to the economy of the United States. This casts Canada, in its relations with the United States, in the role of a supplier of unmanufactured or semimanufactured products." Aitken, "Changing Structure," pp. 11–12. This concern was dismissed by the great economist W.A. Mackintosh, who declared: "We need United States markets. We need United States capital. We need United States industrial 'know-how.' Clearly our economic policies will be shaped by our needs." Mackintosh, "Canadian Economic Policy," p. 67.

On the preoccupation with exports: Mackintosh, "Export Markets Overseas"; Plumptre, "Exports to the United States"; and Deutsch, "Recent American Influence in Canada," p. 43.

On the free trade episode: Cuff and Granatstein, "Rise and Fall," especially n. 72. Also Hart, "Almost but Not Quite."

Scotched by Mackenzie King: King fretted that, while the economists in the Department of Finance were persuasive about the benefits that would accrue from free trade, the political danger to Liberals of being vilified as wanting "to sell Canada to the United States for a mess of pottage" was too great to risk. The prime minister was aided in his decision to reject free trade by "guidance from Beyond. [F]eeling I ought to look at some book, I drew out from my shelves a volume entitled 'Studies in Colonial Nationalism' . . . Was amazed to see how completely the views there expressed accorded with my own." These views were mainly sentimental verses steeped in the romantic imperialism of Rudyard Kipling.

> Here, in Canadian hearth, and home, and name –
> This name which yet shall grow
> Till all the nations know
> Us for a patriot people, heart and hand,
> Loyal to our native earth, our own Canadian land!
> (Jebb, *Studies in Colonial Nationalism*, p. 331)

13. King's new-found qualms: "I get alarmed beyond measure at the casual way in which a few officials take it into their hands to try and settle the great national policies; force the hands of the Government, etc. without having the least knowledge of the political side of matters." Recording a conversation he had in Washington with the Canadian ambassador, King reflected that the issue "unquestionably came back to what the future of Canada either in the British Commonwealth or as a part of the United States will be." Pickersgill, *Mackenzie King Record*, vol. 1, pp. 261–69, 272–73.

The American diplomatic historian Gordon T. Stewart provided confirmation of King's qualms about U.S. strategic designs on Canada. "America's Canadian Policy."

In step with St. Laurent, Canadian officials also thought continentally. As a State Department diplomat reported, they "tend to the view that Canada's ultimate destiny is inevitably linked with ours and that the integration of the economies which was effected during the war should be continued and developed further." Cuff and Granatstein, *American Dollars*, p. 71. C.D. Howe, too, "was convinced that Canadian industry would do well if allowed to enter the vast American market." Bothwell and Kilbourn, *Howe*, p. 239.

14. On Howe's business-government alliance: "The federal government was now an ally, not a distant enemy. From Victoria to Halifax, businessmen were reaching the same conclusion: business had found a capital and a home – and the head of the household was C.D. Howe." Bothwell and Kilbourn, *Howe*, p. 179. Also: "To the end of his career, Mackenzie King had kept insisting that, in Canada, the Liberals were friends of the 'little man' and the Conservative party was the party of 'big business.' This worn-out fiction was moribund even before the war; but by 1951, it survived only as a kind of Greek myth, with all the irrelevance of a Greek myth and none of its charm. Howe had not merely linked big business and the Liberal Party; he had virtually identified them." Creighton, *Forked Road*, pp. 222–23.

By 1954, the proportion of U.S.-controlled capital in the petroleum and natural gas sector in Canada totalled 67 per cent, while that figure was 49 per cent in mining and smelting. Aitken, *American Capital*, pp. 83ff. In 1967, these figures were 60 per cent and 56 per cent, respectively. *Foreign Direct Investment*, table 4, p. 20. Also Clement, *Canadian Corporate Elite*, pp. 89–92.

The consequences of this integration for the structure of the Canadian economy, however, were ominous. "The latent purposes of an overall continental resource strategy, and of stockpiling in particular, appear to favour large resource companies with American links and the establishment of secondary processing in the United States rather than Canada – hence the crystallization of Canadian-resource dependence." Clark-Jones, *Staple State*, p. 20.

On Canada's import substitution strategy: Williams, *Not for Export*, chs. 6–7.

15. Start-up costs: "Developing an industrial sector to serve the needs of the resource industry would have required tariff protection for the new suppliers, but such protection . . . would have raised at least in the short-run, the costs of production of raw materials." Gillies, *Facing Reality*, p. xxviii. Also Aitken, "Defensive Expansionism."

Siamese twins: Innis, "Economic Trends," p. 238.

16. On U.S. imports of Canadian resources: Goodman, *Industrial Materials*, p. 11; and Brecher and Reisman, *Canada-United States Economic Relations*, pp. 177–78.

On the U.S. military market: Canada, Royal Commission on Canada's Economic Prospects, *Final Report*, p. 91.

On the Cold War and continentalism: "In negotiations with the new empire, the Russian threat served the Canadian interest." Cuff and Granatstein, *American Dollars*, p. 217. Also Aitken, *American Capital*, ch. 3; Clark-Jones, *Staple State*, ch. 1; and Scheinberg, "Indispensable Ally."

On Canada and the anti-communist crusade: Bothwell, Drummond, and

English, *Canada Since 1945*, pp. 132–33. "On the whole the Canadian attitude to Soviet policy and Soviet intentions was less categorical. There were more doubts. We tried immoderately to be moderate." Holmes, *Living with Uncle*, p. 35. Also Stairs, *Diplomacy of Constraint*, pp. 332–33.

17. On post-war concerns about recession: R.M. Campbell, *Grand Illusions*, pp. 19–21; and Owram, *Government Generation*, ch. 11.

18. On the development of Keynes's general theory: Moggridge, *Keynes*, ch. 5; and P. Clarke, *Keynesian Revolution*, chs. 10–12.

19. On Harvard economists: Harvard became the centre for the adaptation and exposition of Lord Keynes's theory in North America in the late 1930s. Alvin Hansen joined the faculty in 1937 and became an apostle in due course.

   "Robert Bryce, fresh from Keynes's seminar in England . . . had been able to say with final authority what Keynes really meant. 'Keynes is Allah,' Schumpeter once observed, 'and Bryce is his prophet.'" Galbraith, *Life in Our Times*, p. 90. Upon its publication Bryce organized the shipment of copies of the *General Theory* to Harvard, where Harris organized a seminar on it. Letter to the authors from Donald Moggridge, Mar. 1994.

   "More than anyone else [Bryce] made Canada the first country . . . to commit itself fully to the Keynesian compensatory faith." Galbraith, *Life in Our Times*, p. 90. Bryce considered the 1939 budget, in whose formulation he played a role, to be the first Canadian exercise in economic policy (as against tariff policy) and a precursor of the post-war Keynesianism prevalent in Ottawa. Authors' interview with Robert Bryce, Nov. 21, 1979; and Bryce, *Maturing in Hard Times*, p. 121. The deputy, W.C. Clark, was an "unacademic Keynesian whose growing faith in government interventionism led him down an increasingly Keynesian path." Owram, *Government Generation*, p. 295.

20. All advanced capitalist countries: Hall, *Political Power*.

   On the mandarins' economic vision: The federal government's 1945 White Paper and its Green Book, *Proposals of the Government of Canada* to the Dominion-Provincial Conference on Reconstruction in August 1945, "were designed to place the Government of Canada in a position of leadership and effective control in policy related to economic development and fluctuation." Mackintosh, "Canadian Economic Policy," p. 61.

21. "A solution": Galbraith, *Age of Uncertainty*, p. 217.

22. Trudeau's job interview: Authors' interview with Robert Bryce, July 2, 1991. Bryce's view of Trudeau's suitability could have had something to do with the fact that a decade earlier he had also studied under Schumpeter, Leontief, Haberler, and Seymour Harris, the most interventionist liberal on the Harvard faculty, who argued for a broad social security system and a progressive income tax. Granatstein, *Ottawa Men*, p. 258. Trudeau had also taken a "reading and research" course with Harris.

23. Trudeau had been impressed with Hansen and had recommended his course "Economic Analysis and Public Policy" to his friend Pierre Carignan, when he asked Trudeau's advice about studying social science. He was particularly enthusiastic about Hansen's writings, which explained how economic collapse could be prevented and full employment achieved as long as governments would aggressively exploit both their ability to set monetary policy and their taxation power to dampen the upswings

and mitigate the downswings of the business cycle. See Hansen, *Fiscal Policy and Business Cycles*, especially ch. 15, "Price Flexibility and Full Employment of Resources," and ch. 24, "Fiscal Policy and International Stability." Authors' interview with Pierre Carignan, Jan. 26, 1991.

On Trudeau's economics courses and professors: Letter to the authors from Nancy Boyden, Office of the Dean, Harvard University Graduate School of Arts and Sciences, Aug. 11, 1989; authors' interviews with Professors Myron Gordon and Stefan Dupré, Mar. 20, 1990; and letter from D.E. Moggridge, Mar. 11, 1994.

24. "He served his minister well": [McCall] Newman, "How to Spot," p. 3.

25. Cold War glory: External was dealing with the great issues of world politics abroad by helping to set up a North Atlantic military organization to contain the threat of an expansionary Soviet Union in Europe and by helping mount a desperate military action alongside the United States to thwart Stalin's North Korean puppets in their attempt to take over the whole peninsula and perhaps unleash a third, nuclear war. Escott Reid reminisces: "Within five years [1947-51] Canada's defence expenditures had tripled; for the first time in its history, it became in peace-time a member of a military alliance; as a member of that alliance, it had armed forces stationed in Germany as part of the North Atlantic forces; as a member of the United Nations it had an army brigade and naval units fighting in Korea under the United Nations command; and it had become a member of the Colombo Plan for cooperative economic development in South and Southeast Asia." E. Reid, *Radical Mandarin*, p. 245. Authors' interview with Allan Gotlieb, Oct. 31, 1989.

26. The manner of the British public servants: "A gentleman disguised his abilities as much as he disguised his emotions. The key to recognition was good manners – unceremonious, relaxed behaviour, designed to put others at ease. Men should be judged by their conduct rather than their ideas." Annan, *Our Age*, p. 20.

27. On Pickersgill and St. Laurent: D.C. Thomson, *St. Laurent*, pp. 263–64, 324–25, and Pickersgill, *My Years*.

28. "I was a young guy": Conversation with the authors, Dec. 11, 1986.

29. Sandy Hill: The 1950 Ottawa phone book listed P.E. Trudeau at 593 Besserer, the home of Col. Shuldham H. Hill.

30. On the fusion of the Liberal Party with state and business: Reginald Whitaker, *Government Party*, ch. 5.

31. "Trained donkeys": Trudeau, "Some Obstacles," p. 120.

On the unilingual East Block: "When I was there," Trudeau recounted much later, "there was a bloody great fight to have a sign put up saying 'Bureau du Premier Ministre' alongside 'Prime Minister's Office.' It was unbelievable." Authors' notes of Trudeau speech to the Ontario Liberals' policy conference, Oct. 2, 1976.

32. On English Canadians' indifference to Trudeau: Authors' interviews with Jack Pickersgill, Nov. 30, 1986; Fred Gibson, July 22, 1991; and Doug LePan, May 16, 1991.

33. French Canadians in External: Authors' interview with Jean Fournier, June 2, 1991. "The 1951 External Affairs Register showed 258 Canadians of British origin against 50 of French origin. This was the highest ratio of the latter in any government department. The figures show the influence of a classical education on those who chose diplomacy as a career." Letter to the authors from Jean Fournier, June 4, 1991.

34. Exciting figure: Trudeau was also a practical joker and Fournier decided to pay him

back one day. It had been announced that the so-called Red Dean of Canterbury would be speaking at Carleton College. Trudeau urged Fournier to come with him to hear the famous left-wing Anglican, but Fournier reminded him that the Roman Catholic bishop of Ottawa had warned from the pulpit the previous Sunday that it would be unwise for Catholics to attend. This made Trudeau all the more determined. The next day Fournier phoned his attic office and said in English, "This is Inspector Mitchell of the RCMP. We understand you went to hear the Dean of Canterbury last night. This is a warning. Your job puts you in a vulnerable position. You should not be seen at such gatherings." Trudeau remonstrated hotly, "What do you mean? This is my right as a citizen. Listening to other ideas doesn't mean you espouse them," etc. etc. In his reply to this outburst, Fournier to his chagrin inadvertently pronounced a "th" as "d," and Trudeau, recognizing him immediately, responded with good humour, "Merde, Fournier. Tu m'as eu!" Authors' interview with Jean Fournier, June 2, 1991.

35. "Never really believed": Trudeau, "De libro," p. 69.

"An English capital": Trudeau, "Quebec and the Constitutional Problem," p. 5.

36. "Hide their intolerance": Trudeau, "New Treason," p. 162.

The complicity of the oppressed: Young-Bruehl, *Arendt*, pp. 328–78.

"Ottawa took advantage": Trudeau, "Federalism, Nationalism," p. 200.

37. "Citizen Robertson": Quoted in Harbron, *This Is Trudeau*, p. 23.

"Oppressed nation": Trudeau, "Quebec and the Constitutional Problem," p. 31.

"Vicious circle": Trudeau, "Federalism, Nationalism," p. 200.

38. On the colonized mentality: Janeway, *Powers of the Weak*, p. 207; Eisler, *Chalice and the Blade*; and Mannoni, *Prospero and Caliban*. Trudeau made an extensive reference to Fanon's classic on the subject, *The Wretched of the Earth*, in "Separatist Counter-Revolutionaries," pp. 211–12.

39. Social wage: The non-cash benefits provided by the state, such as schools and health care, that increase an individual's well-being.

40. For an overview of economic and social changes in Quebec during and after World War II: Linteau et al., *Quebec Since 1930*, chs. 12–27.

41. Exclusion from a teaching position: Authors' interview with Vianney Décarie, Sept. 9, 1991.

On Lord Acton's radical Catholicism and his English Catholic periodical, *The Rambler*: Gertrude Hemelfarb's introduction to Acton, *Essays on Freedom and Power*, p. 10.

42. On Miller's friendship with Trudeau: Authors' interview with Morris Miller, July 23, 1991.

43. As with so many of his peers in Canada's small intelligentsia, Scott's change of attitude to the British came about mostly in response to the horrors and futilities of World War I, which became more fully apparent as the 1920s unfolded. Canadian anti-imperialism was derived in part from English intellectuals such as the poet Robert Graves, whose 1929 memoir *Good-Bye to All That* masterfully catalogued the passionate disillusionment of those who had survived the trenches but had come to hate the British class system.

44. Trudeau on Scott: Authors' interview, Dec. 11, 1986.

On Scott's relationship with Trudeau: Djwa, *Politics of the Imagination*, ch. 19.

45. On Trudeau and Peter Scott: Authors' interview with Peter Scott, Nov. 18, 1988.
46. On fascism in Quebec: F.R. Scott, "Nationalism in French Canada" and "Embryo Fascism in Quebec."
47. On Scott and Trudeau: Authors' interviews with Pierre Trudeau, Dec. 11, 1986; Michael Pitfield, June 10, 1961, and Feb. 23, 1979; and Grace Pitfield, Oct. 26, 1975.
    Scott's poem "Fort Smith": Quoted in Djwa, *Politics of the Imagination*, p. 324.
48. On Trudeau at Scott's country house: Confidential interview, June 1991.
49. Trudeau's columns in *Vrai* were compiled and translated by I.M. Owen for Trudeau, *Approaches to Politics*.
50. Trudeau's brief: *Mémoire*. The *Cité libre* article: "De libro," pp. 9–12.
51. "Hold a candle": Authors' interview with Vianney Décarie, Sept. 7, 1992.
52. "Miserably remiss": Trudeau, "Some Obstacles," p. 119.
53. Hector Langevin: "We used to say to him that he was a capitalist from 9 o'clock to 5 and a socialist from 5 to 9." Letter from Léon Dion to the authors, Oct. 12, 1992. His furniture store, N.G. Valiquette, on Sainte-Catherine went bankrupt after his death.
54. "Perhaps even less": Authors' interview with Charles Taylor, Jan. 21, 1991.
55. Under the sway: "The real Liberal plan, whether by accident or design, was Howe's . . . It would not be the economic abstractions of doctrinaire planners in Ottawa that would shape post-war Canada . . . Post-war Canada would be a free enterprise society." Bothwell, Drummond, and English, *Canada Since 1945*, p. 69. In 1949, the government introduced a capital cost allowance scheme, which incorporated into the new Income Tax Act many features of Howe's accelerated depreciation rates of 1944. Between 1945 and 1960, an estimated $1.154 billion was transferred to foreign-owned corporations through this provision of the tax act. Wolfe, "Economic Growth," pp. 9ff.
    More in theory than in practice: "The postwar Liberal government adopted a somewhat partial view of Keynes that emphasized the more expansionary policy implications of his theory . . . through public support of private enterprise." Wolfe, "Economic Growth," p. 9. Robert Campbell shows counter-cyclical macroeconomic policy was not really applied at all in Canada, either theoretically or practically. R.M. Campbell, *Grand Illusions*, p. 202, and *Full-Employment Objective*, p. 8.
56. Legislation establishing the unemployment insurance program was passed in the summer of 1940. Legislation on family allowances was passed during 1944. Other elements of the welfare state established in 1944 were the expansion of the National Housing Act, the passage of the Farm Improvements Loans Act, and the creation of the Industrial Development Bank. Struthers, *No Fault of Their Own*, ch. 6; and Mackintosh, "Canadian Economic Policy," pp. 57–58.
57. Economy less responsive: "Domestic economic stabilization policy has, at best, a small effect in Canada." Paul Phillips, "National Policy," p. 26. Cooper analyses the various factors besides capital mobility that undermined the responsiveness of economies to Keynesian controls in *The Economics of Interdependence*.
    Resource exports: "The overwhelming bulk of Canada's exports to the United States is made up of primary or semifabricated products. More than 70 per cent of the total represents raw materials for United States industry." Aitken, *American Capital*, pp. 74–75. Also Cuff and Granatstein, *American Dollars*, p. 143.
58. Kenneth McNaught's *cri de coeur*: "CCF Failure in Foreign Policy."

A.G.L. McNaughton's protest: "Proposed Columbia River Treaty." Also Higgins, "Alienation of Canadian Resources," and Holmes, *Shaping of Peace*, pp. 263ff.

Economic take-over: U.S. investment in Canadian manufacturing in 1939 accounted for 28 per cent of total capital, while U.S. capital in mining and smelting (including oil and gas) accounted for only 6 per cent of the Canadian total. By 1957, these proportions were, respectively, 30 per cent and 29 per cent. Aitken, *American Capital*, p. 54. James Coyne, the governor of the Bank of Canada in the mid-1950s, made a number of speeches calling for "a greater measure of autonomy and independence on the part of Canadian management." Resnick, *Land of Cain*, p. 103.

59. "'Internationalism' was almost a religion in the decade after the Second World War ... For [Canadian foreign service officers], NATO was a good club to belong to. The association was new, but the members for the most part had breeding and tradition." Holmes, *Shaping of Peace*, pp. 119–20.

On Gordon's opposition: "Early in 1955, I decided to try to start a debate about this ... The validity of a number of our economic policies, including especially the question of selling control of our business enterprises to foreigners and the effect this could have upon Canada's independence ... C.D. Howe was furious. He had been away when it was decided to set up the commission and had always been opposed to the idea. Now he interpreted its findings as a criticism of policies for which he had been responsible, and to some extent this was quite true." Gordon, *Political Memoir*, pp. 59, 64.

On the Gordon commission: [McCall] Newman, "Growing Up Reluctantly" and "Year They Created."

60. By the mid-1950s unmistakable signs of structural weaknesses were appearing in the economy. "Canada was exporting less in 1952 (or 1957 for that matter) than in 1945 ... As a result, Canada rang up a massive deficit in its foreign trade. The difference in the balance of payments was made up by foreign investment." Bothwell and Kilbourn, *Howe*, p. 271. The Diefenbaker government was concerned that the "outflow of interest and dividend payments to the United States, coupled with the inflow of manufactured goods, more than offset the export of Canadian raw materials. The net imbalance then had to be financed again by foreign capital imports, thereby perpetuating a vicious circle." R.M. Campbell, *Grand Illusions*, p. 137.

The decision to cancel the Avro Arrow remains highly controversial, Michael Bliss's claim to the contrary in *Northern Enterprise*, p. 612, notwithstanding. Several works – Dow, *The Arrow*; Peden, *Fall of an Arrow*; Shaw, *There Never Was an Arrow*; Greig Stewart, *Shutting Down the National Dream* – argue that this dealt a crippling blow to Canada's high-tech industrial development and its military autonomy. The contrary perspective is given in McLin, *Canada's Changing Defense Policy*.

On the military-industrial relationship: Kirton, "Consequences of Integration"; Middlemiss, "Economic Defence Co-operation"; Byers, "Canadian Defence and Defence Procurement"; and Van Steenburg, "Defence Economic Cooperation."

61. Academic economists: Harry Johnson dismissed Gordon's concerns in scathing style. "It is difficult to see in the Commission's argument anything more than another attempt to blackmail successful alien risk-takers into paying tribute to unenterprising but powerful local capitalists as the price for controlling the mob; so far, in contrast to other developing nations, Canada has gained by abstaining from such behaviour."

"Canada's Economic Prospects," p. 108. Also Brecher, "Flow of United States Investment Funds."

Trudeau quotes: "À propos." Authors' translation.

62. Trudeau was hedging his radicalism by citing the anti-capitalism of a left-wing pastoral letter from 1941: *Approaches to Politics*, p. 86.

Trudeau's class-war vocabulary: *Mémoire*, pp. 11 and 8.

63. Inspired by Frank Scott: Djwa, *Politics of the Imagination*, ch. 19.

Trudeau quotes: "Economic Rights," pp. 125, 121, 123. The influence of C.B. Macpherson, whom he had come to know through the London School of Economics in the 1950s, on his position on property appears striking. Trudeau rewrote his famous paper "Federalism, Nationalism, and Reason" for Macpherson's book *The Future of Federalism*; authors' interview with Kay Macpherson, Nov. 6, 1992. (Reg Whitaker believes it is Hobbes's influence that is dominant in this article; "Reason, Passion and Interest.")

Galbraith's *Affluent Society* had made a sensation throughout the English-speaking world when published in 1958.

64. On economists: Already in 1941 Harold Innis could write: "The voice of the economist is heard throughout the land . . . They have captured crucial positions in the civil service, especially with the Bank of Canada, and the discussion of the problems of Canadian recovery has taken on the air of rational calculation. Every large organization concerned with business has its economist. A new religion has emerged." Innis, "Recent Developments in the Canadian Economy," p. 292. According to Granatstein, "In the late 1950s there were still only a handful of economists in Ottawa; but by 1975, Bryce reported, there were 2,374 civil servants classified as economists." *Ottawa Men*, p. 279.

A large, if uninfluential, literature has generated a powerful indictment of conventional economics, tracing its difficulty in coping with the complexities of real-world problems to its radically unreal assumptions. However convincing to the already sceptical, this critique has done little to dislodge economists as voices behind the policy-makers' thrones. Kuttner, "Poverty of Economics," pp. 74–80ff.

65. Elites "invest" in nationalism: Breton developed this theory in discussions with two sociologists trained at Johns Hopkins – his brother, Raymond Breton, and Maurice Pinard – and Harry Johnson, the internationally influential Canadian economist. Johnson leaned on Breton's theory to propound his own thesis on the irrationality of nationalist policies, which established an important anti-interventionist tenet in the credo of mainstream economists in English Canada. Breton, "Economics of Nationalism," and H.G. Johnson, "Theoretical Model."

66. On Breton's influence on Trudeau's anti-nationalism: Many years later, during a meeting of student Liberals at the University of Toronto, Trudeau defended himself from the charge that he had failed to protect the Canadian economy from American control by citing Albert Breton as his authority for the proposition that nationalism constitutes a "transfer of wealth from the lower to the rising middle classes." Authors' notes, Mar. 24, 1977.

67. Collaborated: Trudeau, "Manifeste" and "L'agriculture."

"Per-capita income": Trudeau, "Quebec and the Constitutional Problem," p. 22.

68. On Pearson's background: English, *Shadow of Heaven*, pp. 329–33, and *Worldly Years*, pp. 154–63.

69. Taking policy advice: Kent, *Public Purpose*, chs. 8–12; Gordon, *Political Memoir*, ch. 5. There was a strong affinity between the two activist priests, Lévesque and Coady.

70. The Kingston conference was organized by another future Liberal stalwart who turned out to be Gordon's nemesis, Mitchell Sharp: *Which Reminds Me*, pp. 88–93. On its ideas as adopted by the Liberals' rally: Kent, *Public Purpose*, pp. 82–84, 90–93.

    On hiring Lou Harris: Davey, *Rainmaker*, p. 46; Denis Smith, *Gentle Patriot*, p. 87.

71. On Gordon's loss of power: Denis Smith, *Gentle Patriot*, ch. 8.

    Combined pressure: "During the two-and-one half years I held that office [minister of finance], the influence that financial and business interests in the United States had on Canadian policy and opinion was continually brought home to me. On occasion, this influence was reinforced by representations from the State Department and the American Administration as a whole. It was pressed by those who direct American businesses in Canada, by their professional advisers, by Canadian financiers whose interests were identified directly or indirectly with American investment in Canada, by influential members of the Canadian civil service, by some representatives of the university community, and by sections of the press." Gordon, *Choice for Canada*, p. xix. See also his *Political Memoir*, ch. 9.

    U.S. tax: Wright, "Persuasive Influence"; Safarian, "Web of Repercussions"; and Denis Smith, *Gentle Patriot*, pp. 172ff. Safarian suggests the American tax was a punishment directed at Canada for Gordon's unsuccessful budget, but this hypothesis was consistently rejected by both the prime minister and senior officials. At the same time, Canadian defence officials were negotiating to prevent Canada's defence sales to the U.S. being damaged by Robert McNamara's "cost reduction program." Middlemiss, "Defence Co-operation," pp. 182–86.

72. Eugene Forsey's reaction to the NDP's two-nations position is in his *Life on the Fringe*, pp. 205–7.

73. "Soapbox": Trudeau, *Memoirs*, Les Productions La Fête, broadcast by CBC-TV, episode I.

74. On accountability: Wearing, "Old Dog," p. 275.

    Kept himself detached: Authors' interview with Mark MacGuigan, Oct. 29, 1992.

75. "Open to the left": Trudeau, "Pelletier et Trudeau," pp. 3–4. Authors' translation.

76. Temporized: Despite an initial news report (*Toronto Star*, Feb. 16, 1968, pp. 1, 2) in which Trudeau was quoted as saying he was opposed to Gordon's economic nationalism, and that "no trading nation should practise it," Gordon wrote in his memoirs: "I was asked, of course, how I could support Trudeau for the leadership in view of the fact he was supposed to be lukewarm on the independence issue about which I have always held strong views. I do not know whether Trudeau had thought deeply about this question. I do know that, after reading *A Choice for Canada*, he came to see me and said he agreed with it. And I gained the clear impression that he approved in principle the proposals contained in the Watkins Report. It is quite true that he played down this whole question during the leadership campaign. But while I was disappointed about this, I acknowledged that from his standpoint it was 'good politics' to do so at that time." *Political Memoir*, p. 300.

On Sharp's endorsement of Trudeau: Sharp, *Which Reminds Me*, pp. 161–62.

77. "We weren't Liberals": Authors' interview with Jean Marchand, June 6, 1978.

78. Lipstick kiss: Confidential interview, June 1991.

79. Barrelling along: In the five years from 1962 to 1966, real GNP growth recovered its earlier strength, averaging 6.5 per cent. Unemployment moderated somewhat, at 4.7 per cent over the same period. Although inflation began to pick up after 1964, increases in the CPI for the period 1962–66 averaged only 2.1 per cent. Averages calculated from R.M. Campbell, *Grand Illusions*, table 1, p. 219. Also Economic Council of Canada, *Fourth Annual Review*, ch. 2: "The Great Expansion."

# Chapter 3
## The Spectre at the Feast: Economic Decline

1. Angry and unfounded statements: Authors' interviews with Sylvia Ostry, Nov. 26, 1979, and July 23, 1984; and with Simon Reisman, June 24, 1974.

    Radicals on the right: "The truth was that Trudeau was basically ignorant about economics. He seemed to like it that way." Brimelow, *Patriot Game*, p. 68.

2. Bryce described him: Authors' interview with Robert Bryce, Nov. 21, 1979.

    "Free stuff": Bryden, *Old Age Pensions*, p. 176. This sort of comment reflected both Trudeau's own scepticism about the welfare state apparatus and his bureaucracy's alarm over the uncontrollable costs built into programs initiated under Pearson. Doern, "Recent Changes."

3. The average annual rate of increase of inflation was 4.4 per cent for 1947–56, and 2.0 per cent for 1957–66. Canada, Royal Commission on the Economic Union and Development Prospects for Canada, *Report*, vol. 2, table 7-2, p. 8.

    For 1968 and 1969, the CPI increased 4.0 per cent and 4.5 per cent respectively. Canada, Department of Finance, *Quarterly Economic Review* (June 1988), table 44.1, p. 79.

    The early Benson budgets concentrated on fighting inflation at the cost of aggravating unemployment. R.M. Campbell, *Grand Illusions*, pp. 168–74.

    Prices and Incomes Commission: Haythorne, "Prices and Incomes Policy."

    David Wolfe suggests the growing militancy of the Canadian trade union movement in the late 1960s added a structural element to the cyclical decline in business profits, reinforcing business and government concern with rising wages. Wolfe, "State and Economic Policy."

4. Uninterested: "On issues that he is not concerned about personally (such as those not related to the constitution or bilingualism!), the Prime Minister can stay aloof from the policy issue entirely, should he wish to. This seems entirely consistent with Mr. Trudeau's style and seemingly low threshold for boredom." Hartle, *Revenue Budget Process*, p. 67.

5. On business reaction to taxing capital gains: W.O. Twaits, president of Imperial Oil, asked rhetorically in 1967, "Is it consistent with equity to tax the man who works and saves as hard as the non-saver? Is it equity to tax the innovator, the entrepreneur, at the same rate as the drones in society?" Gardner, "Tax Reform," p. 250.

John Bulloch: Partridge, "Slugging It Out," p. 32.

6. Trudeau quote: *Canadian Annual Review: 1970*, p. 412.

On Finance's backdown: Eric Kierans recalled how finance officials manipulated the cabinet over tax reform. "The result was that, for a year and a half, we studied trees. We never saw the forest – we never saw the issue of tax reform – as a whole." Swift, *Odd Man Out*, p. 249.

On the fate of tax reform: Gardner, "Tax Reform." The business columnist Ronald Anderson observed: "The capitulation, on almost every proposal that had met substantial opposition, was far more complete than even the most vigorous critic of the white paper could have foreseen." "Pragmatic Bill Capitalizes on Major Tax Reform Proposals," *Globe and Mail* (June 19, 1971), p. B1. The political economist David Wolfe wrote much later: "The protracted effort at comprehensive tax reform, which followed closely after a decade of major social reforms, crystallized the growing dissatisfaction among the business community with the perceived leftward drift of the Liberal party." Wolfe, "Politics of the Deficit," p. 146. Also *Canadian Annual Review: 1971*, pp. 330–38.

7. On the creation of DREE: Kent, *Public Purpose*, ch. 33; Savoie, *Regional Economic Development*, ch. 3; and Careless, *Initiative and Response*, pp. 85–89.

8. On Mackasey and UI reforms: A.F. Johnson, "Agent of Policy Change." The 1971 changes "put Canada among the ranks of the world's most generous unemployment insurance programs." Pal, *State, Class and Bureaucracy*, p. 50.

On Ron Basford's introduction of Bill C-256, the Competition Act, in June 1971: W.T. Stanbury, *Business Interests*, ch. 8.

Revisions to Part V of the Canada Labour Code (Industrial Relations) passed on June 30, 1972. W.D. Wood, *Industrial Relations Scene*, pp. S–G–8–10.

9. Privileged access: Gillies, *Where Business Fails*, pp. 83–88. Paul Pross describes the "diffusion of power" that accompanied the expansion of government during the 1960s, and the accompanying proliferation of public pressure groups in *Group Politics*, pp. 66–71. The emergence of professional lobbyists to reconnect business with government is discussed in Sawatsky, *Insiders*.

Cabinet committee system: Matheson, "Canadian Bureaucracy," pp. 345–47; French, *How Ottawa Decides*, pp. 2ff; and Sharp, "Decision-Making."

10. On Bennett and Trudeau: Authors' interview with William Bennett, June 6, 1985.

11. Martin Goldfarb on business animosity towards Trudeau: "But Trudeau kept asking them, 'Where are the jobs you promised? Why aren't you out selling to the world? When are you going to do it? And if you can't do it, why do you blame us?' He opened up China for them, but they seemed to expect him to go and sell their products door to door . . . And the private sector hated him for telling them to get off their butts. He really rubbed their noses in it." Graham, *One-Eyed Kings*, p. 103.

"Upset CEOs the most": Authors' interview with Ouida Touche, June 26, 1976.

12. On Canada's reliance on the world-wide economic expansion made possible by the hegemonic status of the United States in the post-war period, as well as by the country's carefully cultivated economic links to the American colossus: Aitken, *American Capital*; Wolfe, "Economic Growth"; and Clark-Jones, *Staple State*, chs. 1, 5, 7.

Canada depended on an indulgently hegemonic America that "would never betray another English-speaking democracy, especially one as deferential, as well-behaved, as contemptuous of vulgar 'nationalism' (and as profitable) as postwar Canada." Stevenson, "Third Option," p. 426.

On economic consequences of the Vietnam War: "Military expenditures abroad have been the major contributor to the persistent government account deficits . . . The gross outflow on military accounts rose steadily from 1960 through 1970. It averaged $3 billion from 1960 to 1964, $3.9 billion from 1965 to 1968, and $4.9 billion in 1969 and 1970 . . . The Vietnam War, of course, was the major cause." International Economic Policy Association, *Balance of Payments*.

13. Forced its global partners: Gilpin, *Political Economy*, pp. 138, 140.

14. On the reception given to Nixonomics in Ottawa: Plumptre, *Three Decades of Decision*, ch. 10. "Although no reasons were given [by] the U.S. authorities . . . [t]he implication was conveyed that to overcome the U.S. deficit, it would be necessary to force Canada again into a deficit position. And since the United States needs Canadian raw materials, this means that all the cuts would have to be in manufactured goods." Dobell, *Canada's Search*, p. 84.

15. Americans' earlier strategy: G.T. Stewart, "America's Canadian Policy."

16. "Crime": Trudeau's speech to the U.S. Congress, *Canadian Annual Review: 1977*, p. 243.

17. Americanization: Steele and Mathews, "Universities."

Decline in the staff from the U.K.: Bissell, *Halfway Up Parnassus*, p. 186.

On decline of British history in the curriculum: Paul T. Phillips, *Britain's Past*, chs. 7, 8.

Economics: Over half of Canadian teachers and researchers were born, bred, or trained outside Canada. A. Scott, "Living in Canada," p. 26.

Anglo-American intellectual models: "With the accelerated integration of the economies of Canada and the United States the [economics] 'profession' came to accept itself as part of the North American establishment . . . There was an explosion in the output of Canadian economists but an implosion of Canadian economics." Neill and Paquet, "Canadian Economics," p. 11.

18. On growing Canadian nationalism in the 1970s: LeDuc and Murray, "Resurgence."

On the *Manhattan* incident: Maxwell Cohen, "Arctic and the National Interest," and Dosman, *National Interest*, ch. 4.

19. On the Tory shift to continentalism: J. Laxer and R. Laxer, *Liberal Idea*, pp. 113–16.

20. On ideological conflict in the NDP: Brodie, "From Waffles to Grits."

From the Waffle manifesto of Sept. 4, 1969, *For an Independent Socialist Canada*: "The major threat to Canadian survival today is American control of the Canadian economy. The major issue of our times is not national unity but national survival and the fundamental threat is external, not internal." Cited in Godfrey and Watkins, *Gordon to Watkins*, p. 103.

21. On Kierans's frustration: W. Stewart, "Cold Inside," and Swift, *Odd Man Out*, p. 303. Kierans's letter of resignation and the prime minister's response are reprinted in Kierans, *Globalism*, appendix C.

22. Davey report: Canada, Senate, Special Committee on Mass Media, *Uncertain Mirror*.

Wahn report: Canada, House of Commons, Standing Committee on External Affairs and National Defence, "Report."

23. On marginalizing nationalist opposition: Clarkson, "Democracy in the Liberal Party," p. 157.
24. English Canadians' turn-of-the-century British imperialism: Berger, *Sense of Power*.
25. In 1971, the committee gathered a petition with 170,000 signatures in support of restrictions on foreign investment. Denis Smith, *Gentle Patriot*, p. 352.

   Claude Ryan: Ryan was disturbed by a damaging story published in *The Toronto Star* concerning his activities during the October Crisis of 1970, and since the paper's publisher was closely linked with the CIC, equated its attitude with the committee's. McCall-Newman, *Grits*, pp. 282–83, 449.
26. Trudeau decided: Authors' interview with Joel Bell, June 13, 1989.
27. Trudeau's preferred choice: Johnson had served on Trudeau's constitutional committee in the Department of Justice and was then seconded to the PCO to give economic advice in the context of constitutional change. Authors' interviews with A.W. Johnson, Nov. 26, 1984, and Walter Gordon, July 19, 1986.
28. Reisman as communist: In 1937, when one new recruit who joined the YCL in Montreal had to take its compulsory course on Stalin's *History of the Communist Party of the Soviet Union*, she discovered the teacher for the class was Simon Reisman; confidential interview, June 1989. According to another party member, Reisman was still attending party meetings in Ottawa after the war; confidential interview, Dec. 1993.
29. Charges of subversion: English, *Worldly Years*, pp. 58, 164; and Barros, *No Sense of Evil*, p. 1.

   The Brecher-Reisman study acknowledged that U.S. capital occupied a dominant and growing position in the Canadian economy and made entry into some important industries by Canadian firms extremely difficult. Still the economic costs of American investment were far outweighed by its "uniquely heavy inflows of technology, entrepreneurial and managerial skills." As for the political issue – "whether a country can have a meaningful independent existence in a situation where nonresidents own an important part of that country's basic resources and industry, and are therefore in a position to make important decisions affecting the operations and development of the country's economy" – the authors demurred: "While these implications may go to the very heart of the matter, they are, as such, outside the scope of this study." Brecher and Reisman, *Canada-United States Economic Relations*, pp. 4, 161, 152, 131.
30. Gordon on Reisman: Authors' interviews with Walter Gordon, Aug. 22, 1977, and July 19, 1986.
31. "Bob Bryce with balls": Authors' interview with Sylvia Ostry, Nov. 16, 1975.

   Continued to fume: Authors' interviews with Simon Reisman, June 16, 1974, Oct. 19, 1975, and Nov. 26, 1975; and with Marshall Crowe, Apr. 22 and 23, 1974, Oct. 10, 1975, May 22, 1979, and July 9 and 19, 1984.
32. On Reisman in Washington: Authors' interviews with Richard O'Hagan, June 5 and 6, 1978.

   Reisman's skills were given high marks by academic analysts. "Reisman deserves credit for several changes in the Finance Department's personnel and structure and, contrary to his public reputation, for expanding the sources from which economic advice is sought within the government." Phidd and Doern, *Politics and Management*, p. 149.

33. "Quiet diplomacy" was coined in the celebrated 1965 report by U.S. ambassador Livingston Merchant and Canadian ambassador Arnold Heeney, "Principles for Partnership," p. 9. "Canadian authorities must have confidence that the practice of quiet diplomacy is not only neighborly and convenient to the United States but that it is in fact more effective than the alternative of raising a row and being unpleasant in public."

For the foreign-policy-making élite's "relatively benign image of the United States" and "somewhat ambiguous [feelings] about the degree of Canadian independence": P.V. Lyon and Leyton-Brown, "Image and Policy Preference," p. 649. Also Byers and Leyton-Brown, "Canadian Elite Images." The last half of the 1970s saw a resurgence of faith in American leadership. Stevenson, "Third Option," p. 430.

With Trudeau's concurrence: Authors' interview with Allan Gotlieb, Aug. 4, 1986.

34. Nixon on Canadian independence: "That doctrine rests on the premise that mature partners must have autonomous independent policies; each nation must define the nature of its own interests; each nation must decide the requirements of its own security; each nation must determine the path of its own progress." Canada, House of Commons, *Debates* (Apr. 14, 1972), p. 1328. Journalist Peter Brimelow claims, "Nixon's speech had indeed been written at least partially in Canada, by Ivan Head, Prime Minister Trudeau's foreign affairs advisor." *Patriot Game*, p. 111. But Rufus Z. Smith, the ranking State Department official in the U.S. embassy in Ottawa, privately acknowledged the responsibility of drafting the text. Authors' notes of conversation between Smith and John Holmes, n.d.

Gray report: *Foreign Direct Investment*.

35. On Sharp's evolution: Sharp, *Which Reminds Me*, pp. 180–86, and "Canada-U.S. Relations."

36. Details of David Lewis's life from Lewis, *Good Fight*, C. Smith, *Unfinished Journey*, and authors' interviews with David Lewis, Aug. 17, 1975, and Stephen Lewis, May 16, 1975.

37. On Trudeau and Lewis: Authors' interviews with David Lewis, Aug. 7, 1975, and C.M. Drury, Nov. 2, 1976.

38. On Lewis and minority government: *Canadian Annual Review: 1973*, pp. 3–24; and Morton, *New Democrats*, pp. 146–47. Trudeau has the chutzpah to claim in his memoirs that these left-of-centre moves were projects he "had been dreaming about for a long time" and had forced the NDP to support. *Memoirs*, pp. 164–65.

39. Public-sector unions: The rapid growth of post-war welfare programs had required a massive increase in the size of the state apparatus. With collective bargaining established in the private sector since 1948, blue-collar wages had outstripped incomes for public servants, whose staff associations' demands for legal collective bargaining rights were successfully forced onto the Pearson government's agenda by the NDP. The consequent unionization of the country's civil servants had transformed the Canadian labour movement by swinging the balance of power to Canadian-controlled, politically progressive groups and away from the American-controlled labour unions.

40. On FIRA: Bell, "Canadian Industrial Policy," pp. 93–95.

On the CDC: Brooks, "State as Entrepreneur."

On Petro-Canada: L. Pratt, "Petro-Canada" (1981).

On Berger and pipeline inquiry: Page, *Northern Development*, ch. 5.

41. Cultural institutions: Although such cultural nationalists as Susan Crean constantly denounced the inadequacy of government funding, the federal government sustained a broad array of operations that provided the infrastructure for English- and French-Canadian culture. Apart from its contribution to post-secondary education, there was the Canadian Broadcasting Corporation, which had sustained a cultural community from the 1930s; the Canadian Radio-television and Telecommunications Commission, which set content rules for broadcasters and ensured that they were Canadian-owned; Telefilm Canada and the National Film Board, which helped finance and produce movies; the Canada Council, which supported the arts and commercial publishing; and various scholarly councils, which funded the academic disciplines in the humanities and the social and physical sciences. Crean, *Who's Afraid*, and Audley, *Canada's Cultural Industries*.

42. "Best goddam minister": Authors' interview with Simon Reisman, Oct. 29, 1975.

43. Reisman's anti-interventionism was characteristic more generally of Finance's institutional philosophy. "Reisman was the uncompromising protagonist of a certain view of the economy and of the role of government within it, and hence, of a certain view of the Department of Finance. Reisman's ideas did not dominate by the force of his personality alone. Far from it. Although there were significant internal differences, Reisman's views represented a majority viewpoint within the Department, having more to do with the ideology of mainstream Western economics than with any kind of 'coerced consensus.' Reisman's lengthy and successful bureaucratic career, however, gave him the *savoir-faire* and personal contacts to be a formidable force in central decision-making." French, *How Ottawa Decides*, p. 28.

Insisted that Trudeau disband: Authors' interview with Albert Breton, Feb. 9, 1988.

44. Friedman's attack on Keynesianism: "Role of Monetary Policy," pp. 1–8.

On the fight between Finance and Health and Welfare: Haddow, *Poverty Reform*, pp. 107–10, 124–29. Also Guest, *Emergence of Social Security*, ch. 12, "Unfinished Business: The Social Security Review 1973-1976"; and Van Loon, "Reforming Welfare."

On indexing in the 1973 budget: *Canadian Annual Review: 1973*, pp. 13–17. Robert Stanfield had advocated indexing on the grounds that it would remove "the government's vested interest in inflation," and John Turner defended the measure "as a bold and sensitive response to a rather fundamental tax problem . . . [that] puts Canada in the vanguard of countries with advanced tax systems." Gillespie, *Tax, Borrow and Spend*, pp. 192–93.

45. Davey and Coutts are described more completely in McCall-Newman, *Grits*, parts 1 and 3.

46. Davey's nationalism was strong enough for him to push for and obtain from Trudeau after the 1974 election the passage of Bill C-58, which supported the Canadian advertising industry. Its effect was to eliminate *Time* magazine from the Canadian market, allow *Maclean's* to become a national weekly magazine, and provide enough revenue from commercials to sustain the private television network, CTV, as well as local stations such as Toronto's CITY-TV.

47. "Not my kind of guy": Authors' interview with Keith Davey, July 9, 1974.
48. On the 1974 campaign: Clarkson, "Trudeau and the Liberal Party," and McCall-Newman, *Grits*, pp. 157–58.
49. House of Commons standings were 141 Liberals to 95 Conservatives, 16 New Democrats, and 11 Créditistes.
50. On the shift from Keynesianism towards supply-side and monetarist approaches: R.M. Campbell, *Grand Illusions*, pp. 182–85; Lamontagne, *Business Cycles*, p. 77; Wolfe, "Politics of the Deficit," p. 148; and Maslove and Swimmer, *Wage Controls*, p. 7.

    "Ungovernable": Crozier, Huntington, and Watanuki, *Crisis of Democracy*.

    Inflation had risen from 2.9 per cent in 1971 to 10.9 per cent in 1974, though this was still below the average for the other OECD countries, which were more dependent on imported oil and suffering more severely from the oil price hike of 1971. International Monetary Fund, *Government Finance Statistics Yearbook, 1986*.
51. "Imprudent": Authors' interview with Robert Bryce, Nov. 21, 1979.
52. "Broadloom": Authors' interview with Grace Pitfield, Oct. 26, 1974.
53. "Interested in power": Authors' interview with Grattan O'Leary, Apr. 17, 1974.
54. "Michael would have organized it": Authors' interview with Marshall Crowe, May 22, 1979.
55. On the growing disenchantment with fiscal and monetary levers as instruments of macro-economic policy, and the accompanying movement towards more interventionist measures directed at controlling wage inflation: Maslove and Swimmer, *Wage Controls*, p. 7.

    Stagflation: Unemployment in 1974 and 1975 was a stubborn 5.3 and 6.9 per cent, while inflation had risen into the double-digit bracket at 10.9 and 10.7 per cent.

    No evil in rising deficits: Authors' interview with Ed Neufeld, Jan. 25, 1988.
56. Structural weakness: For a balanced assessment of Canada's industrial dilemma at the end of the 1970s, see Wilkinson, *Changing World Economy*.

    Canada as semi-industrialized economy: In terms of finished products as a proportion of trade, Canada ranked with Argentina, Australia, Brazil, and India. Williams, *Not for Export*, table 1, p. 8.
57. Career prospects: Of the thirty-one finance ministers from Alexander Galt to Edgar Benson, there were two – Sir Charles Tupper and R.B. Bennett – who subsequently became prime minister. Bryce, *Maturing in Hard Times*, appendix.
58. Purely mechanical scheme: Christina [McCall] Newman, "The Ottawa Oligarchy II: How a Decision Is Made in Trudeau Town," *Globe and Mail* (Dec. 16, 1975), p. 8.
59. *Economics and the Public Purpose*: Trudeau had read Galbraith's 1973 book while vacationing in Jamaica. R. Gwyn, *Northern Magus*, p. 198. Galbraith's chapter "Fiscal Policy, Monetary Policy, and Controls" is an explicit justification for selective state intervention in regulating the activities of firms and unions in the monopolistic sector of the economy.

    "Superb response": Authors' interview, May 14, 1991. Firestone confirmed that Galbraith's "writings have had a good deal of influence on the Canadian Anti-Inflation Program." Firestone, *Anti-Inflation Program*, p. 5.

    Typically, Trudeau denied being much influenced by Galbraith in an interview with *Fortune*'s Herb Meyer: "Canada's Nationalism," p. 183. According to Peter

Brimelow, Trudeau told Meyer he was actually more influenced by his former professors Wassily Leontief and Joseph Schumpeter. Letter to the authors, June 4, 1991.

60. On business and controls: One of the first activities of the newly created BCNI was to
meet with the CLC in February of 1977 in an effort to negotiate an early end to controls. Waldie, "Labour-Government Consultation," pp. 171ff.

Corporate control: "It was apparent that a major task of management in the
1980s was going to be to defend the legitimacy of the entire private sector as the principal producer of goods and services in society." Gillies, *Where Business Fails*, p. 59.

Tripartism in bizthink represented "the culmination of Trudeau's drive to
increase the power of the federal government. That dovetails neatly with his effort to
loosen ties with the U.S., because the third option's objectives cannot be accomplished until Ottawa gets the authority to guide and direct the country's economy.
Tripartism is a way to knit a weak, loosely connected group of provinces and private
enterprises into a coherent, rational, manageable organization – sort of Canada Inc.,
with the prime minister as chairman of the board." Meyer, "Canada's Nationalism,"
p. 186.

61. Vilified in Quebec: Rioux, *Pour prendre publiquement congé*, and Bergeron, *Du duplessisme*, pp. 613–24.

Cut off from intellectuals: According to Albert Breton, an acrimonious meeting
of some twenty academics at the historian Ramsay Cook's house after the War Measures Act was a watershed for Trudeau. It was typical of him to cut off a whole group
of individuals so abruptly because of one incident: another absolute. Authors' interview with Albert Breton, Feb. 9, 1988.

62. On the IRPP as Trudeau's personal project: Authors' interview with Albert Breton,
Feb. 9, 1988.

63. Voice on television: In an interview broadcast on CTV, Dec. 28, 1975, Trudeau
described controls as "a massive intervention into the decision-making power of the
economic groups and it's telling Canadians we haven't been able to make it work, the
free market system." *Canadian Annual Review: 1975*, p. 97.

Paranoid business community: *Canadian Annual Review: 1975*, p. 351.

64. Near autonomy: Granatstein, "Untouchables," and W. Stewart, "Banks' Bank." Also
Laidler, *How Shall We Govern*.

65. Conversion to monetarism: On hearing of Bouey's 1974 Saskatoon monetary manifesto, Milton Friedman called it "the best speech I have ever heard a central banker
give." Quoted in Lamontagne, *Business Cycles*, p. 84.

Central bankers everywhere: The Bundesbank took a more consensual
approach, adjusting its Keynesianism to monetarism more gradually by maintaining
an intellectual dialogue with trade unions and the Länder. P.A. Johnson, "Policy
Paradigm Changes," p. 23.

66. Criticism of Bouey's policy came from both interventionists and conservatives:
Gonick, *Great Economic Debate*, pp. 115–16; Donner and Peters, *Monetarist Counter-
Revolution*, p. 32; and Lamontagne, *Business Cycles*, pp. 84–86. For a conservative cri-
tique, see Courchene, *Money, Inflation, and the Bank of Canada*, ch. 11.

67. Productivity: According to the Macdonald commission, productivity increases during the period 1974–81 averaged only 0.1 per cent. Canada, Royal Commission on
the Economic Union and Development Prospects for Canada, *Report*, vol. 2, p. 9.

Real wages: While nominal wages increased during the latter half of the 1970s, inflation combined with wage and price controls resulted in the erosion of real wages for Canadian workers after 1977. Economic Council of Canada, *Legacies*, p. 39.

The Economic Council of Canada suggested that up until 1977 conditions in the labour market continued to improve, despite the massive entrance of women and youth. After this period, however, the council notes signs of a weakening and polarization of the labour market. Economic Council of Canada, *Good Jobs, Bad Jobs*.

Breakdown of the social contract: The federal government itself took a lead in attacking what it perceived as the excessive power of the unions during this period. As Tom Traves and John Saywell note, "Civil servant bashing was an important component of the politics of restraint." The arrest of CUPW leader Jean-Claude Parrot and four other union leaders in 1978 for defying a back-to-work order signalled an important new aggressiveness on the part of Ottawa in seeking to restrain public-sector wages and union militancy in general. Traves and Saywell, "Parliament and Politics," in *Canadian Annual Review: 1978*, p. 15. Also Panitch and Swartz, *Trade Union Freedoms*, pp. 30–32; and Calvert, *Government Limited*, pp. 13–14.

68. Eyeing the Finance job: Chrétien, *Straight from the Heart*, p. 102.
69. "Losing effective control": *Canadian Annual Review: 1976*, p. 27.

   "Lack of accountability": *Canadian Annual Review: 1978*, p. 338.

   On the 1978 tax cut fiasco: Chrétien, *Straight from the Heart*, pp. 117–18. Also Savoie, *Public Spending in Canada*, pp. 151–56.
70. On the BEDM, see French, *How Ottawa Decides*, chs. 5, 6.
71. Certainly, in aggregate terms, Canada seemed to fare quite well over the decade Trudeau was in power. In employment growth, Canada ranked first among the seven leading industrialized countries throughout the period 1968–79, while in real GDP growth over the period 1968–73, Canada ranked a respectable third (after Japan and France), rising to second place for the rest of the decade (after Japan). In terms of inflation, Canada averaged the lowest rate among the OECD countries during the period 1968–73 (4.6 per cent as against an average of 5.6 per cent). Although the country dropped to third place in the subsequent period, its rate of inflation still remained below the OECD average (9.2 per cent against 10.0 per cent). Finally, despite the hysteria of the business community, the size of government spending as a percentage of GDP in Canada remained close to average, with only the U.S. and Japanese state expenditures taking a smaller chunk.

   Other figures were less flattering. In productivity growth Canada ranked second to last (before only the United States) over the entire period 1968–79. In 1968–73, Canada had the second highest rate of unemployment after Italy, and the highest rate for the rest of the decade (7.2 per cent compared with an OECD average of 4.9 per cent for 1973–79). See statistics in Canada, Royal Commission on the Economic Union and Development Prospects for Canada, *Report*, vol. 2, table 7-30, pp. 48–50.

## Chapter 4
## The Restoration and the Strategic Prime Ministership

1. For a detailed account of Trudeau's vicissitudes in the summer and autumn of 1979, see vol. 1, ch. 7.

2. On media pronouncements about the end of liberalism: Jeffrey Simpson, writing shortly after the 1979 election, pointed to the apparent world-wide malaise of liberalism. "There is considerable evidence that liberal ideas, in whatever forms, are on the defensive in many Western countries. Of course, in Canada there are no longer any Liberal governments left." "A Question of Patronage and Principle: Liberals Ponder Their Future," *Globe and Mail* (May 28, 1979), p. 10.

   Even more apocalyptically, Richard Gwyn maintained that only John Turner stood between the Grits and oblivion: "The natural division among political parties is between the right (Conservatives) and the left (New Democrats). The Liberals occupy an unnatural and therefore inherently unstable middle." "Turner Stands Between Grits and Oblivion," *Toronto Star* (June 21, 1979), p. 10.

   Anthony Westell, while cautioning against drawing early conclusions, noted, "There is certainly evidence in the polls of opinion to support the view that public attitudes are turning against government, bureaucracy and taxation." "A Trend – but Where Is It Headed?" *Toronto Star* (June 2, 1979), p. B2.

   Out of power: The Nova Scotia election of September 1979 marked "the first since Confederation [that] the Liberal party was not in power in Ottawa or in a single provincial capital." McCormick, "Is the Liberal Party Declining?" p. 88.

   "Systems-altering": Meisel, "Larger Context," p. 54.

   "Fatal illness": In Bliss's opinion, the empty Liberal campaign "was symptomatic of the profound difficulty Canadian Liberals are having finding a rationale for their party in a period of intense voter conservatism, distrust of big government, and suspicion of proposals to extend the welfare state." "Liberals Fighting a 'Fatal Illness,'" *Toronto Star* (June 5, 1979), p. 8.

3. "Defeated, not destroyed": The phrase was part of the opposition discourse. "Liberals were defeated, but not destroyed. The crocodile tears of columnists and the puffed pretensions of the NDP that the fate of Lloyd-George-era British Liberals lay round the corner for Canadian Grits should be laid to rest," wrote Lloyd Axworthy in his post-mortem of the 1979 election. "Towards a New Phase," p. 13.

4. Coutts's career up to 1979: McCall-Newman, *Grits*, pp. 135–74.

5. Back into the Liberal fold: The Liberal Party had dominated Alberta politics for the first decade after the province's creation in 1905, but had lost its hold in the federal election of 1917 and the provincial election of 1921.

   Gardiner had used Saskatchewan: Ward and Smith, *Relentless Liberal*, pp. 226–30.

   Driven the Liberal machine: Clarkson, "Defeat of the Government," pp. 168–87.

6. Plurality: The Conservatives won 136 seats, the Liberals 114, the NDP 26, and the Socreds 6. Penniman, *Canada at the Polls*, pp. 406–7.

7. Information on the Axworthys' background, motivation, and careers: Authors' interviews with Lloyd Axworthy on July 13, 1979, June 11, 1985, June 7, 1986, and Feb. 8, 1993; Tom Axworthy on Oct. 26, 1977, Nov. 9 and 10, 1978, Aug. 30, 1979, Feb. 22, 1980, Nov. 7, 1980, Nov. 14, 1981, Apr. 5, 1983, May 1 and 18, 1984, July 11, 1984, Jan. 14, 1985, Jan. 23, 1986, Dec. 2, 1988, Dec. 3, 1989, July 22, 1990, and Aug. 26, 1991; David Walker, Nov. 13, 1978, and Apr. 25, 1980; and Keith Davey, July 15, 1979, Mar. 10, 1980, and Sept. 24, 1981.

8. Base in the working class: Labour leaders supported the NDP because most trade unions were affiliated with it, but more trade unionists voted Liberal than New Democrat. In 1974, 53 per cent of skilled and 57 per cent of unskilled labour had voted Liberal (compared with 14 per cent of each group who had supported the NDP). H.D. Clarke et al., *Political Choice*, p. 109.

   Government should help: The post-Depression generation believed that institutions and systems in society could be improved and expanded, and could work for them. J. Kettle, *Big Generation*, p. 34.

9. MA thesis: T. Axworthy, "Innovation and the Party System."

10. Steadily losing ground: Liberal support in the four western provinces recovered its pre-Diefenbaker level briefly in the wake of Trudeaumania (27 seats and 36 per cent of the popular vote in 1968, as compared with 25 seats and 36 per cent of the vote in 1953). Despite a relatively strong showing in 1974 (13 seats and almost 30 per cent of the vote), Liberal support in the west declined steadily thereafter (3 seats and 22.7 per cent in 1979; 2 seats and 23.7 per cent in 1980). Thorburn, *Party Politics in Canada*, appendices. On the reasons behind the Liberals' secular decline in the west: David E. Smith, *Regional Decline*.

    Coutts's flirtation with the right: Liberal activists maintained that, given the choice, voters would always prefer the real Conservatives to an imitation.

11. "Second-rate men of action": Authors' interview with Pierre Trudeau, July 21, 1979.

    Perrier incident: Authors' interview with David Walker, Mar. 4, 1980.

12. The other shadow cabinet posts were held by Robert Andras, Treasury Board and Government Spending; Ursula Appolloni, Employment (Women); Warren Allmand, Indian Affairs; Jean-Jacques Blais, Justice; Rob Blaker, Supply and Services; Herb Breau, UI and Atlantic Provinces; Judd Buchanan, National Defence; Charles Caccia, Environment; Jim Fleming, Secretary of State; Dennis Dawson, Youth; Pierre De Bané, DREE; Louis Duclos, Science and Technology; John Evans, Corporate Affairs and Competition; Francis Fox, Employment; Jean-Robert Gauthier, Treasury Board and Public Service; Len Hopkins, Veterans Affairs; Don Johnston, National Revenue; Bob Kaplan, Immigration and Citizenship; Gilles Lamontagne, Post Office; Bernard Loiselle, Parks and Tourism; Mark MacGuigan, Solicitor General; John Munro and Jean-Luc Pepin, Industry, Trade and Commerce; Aideen Nicholson, Consumer Affairs; Jacques Olivier, Labour; André Ouellet, Public Works; Irénée Pelletier, Fitness and Amateur Sport; Keith Penner, Northern Development; Art Phillips, Small Business and Mining; Marcel Prud'homme, CIDA; John Reid, Privy Council Office; Ken Robinson, Urban Transit; Peter Stollery, Multiculturalism; Ian Watson, Constitutional Development of the North. "Liberal Caucus Policy Groups."

13. "Kick at the can": Authors' interview with Marc Lalonde, May 31, 1985.

      The caucus members of Lalonde's committee were Lloyd Axworthy, Jean-Jacques Blais, Pierre Bussières, John Evans, Maurice Foster, Jacques Guilbault, Roméo LeBlanc, Bernard Loiselle, Gary McCauley, Paul McRae, Art Phillips, and Marcel Roy. "Liberal Caucus Policy Groups," p. 1.

14. On the Tories' policy divisions under Clark: Simpson, *Discipline of Power*, ch. 2.

15. Precipitated an election: Vol. 1, pp. 159–81.

16. Extra-parliamentary Liberals: Wearing, *L-Shaped Party*, pp. 206–14; Clarkson, "Democracy in the Liberal Party." Also authors' interview with Gordon Dryden, June 4, 1994.

17. The "party should appoint an operating platform committee once an election is called," Axworthy wrote, careful to leave full power in the leader's hands: "The Leader and the Campaign Chairmen would have the final veto on any policy announcements, but the platform committee would suggest items based on past policy resolutions." T. Axworthy, "Renewal of the Liberal Party: Suggestions for a Program" (Nov. 12, 1979), p. 9. Authors' archive.

      Caucus-party parity on the committee was symbolized by the fact that Céline Hervieux-Payette, the party policy chair, and Lorna Marsden, a party vice-president, shared the chairmanship with Allan MacEachen, the senior member of the caucus.

18. Particularly offensive: "When Jim Higgins . . . from Dome Petroleum . . . heard the term 'utility pricing,' he went for his verbal gun, rose angrily to his feet and said that the suggestion was just *bullshit*. Marc Lalonde was heard afterward to suggest that Higgins should be locked in a cupboard and the key thrown away." Foster, *Sorcerer's Apprentices*, p. 13.

19. On the platform committee's deliberations: Authors' interviews with Lloyd Axworthy, June 11, 1985; Tom Axworthy, Feb. 22, 1980; Vince Borg, Jan. 7, 1980; Audrey Gill, Feb. 15 and 18, 1980, July 19 and 20, 1989, and June 16, 1991; Marc Lalonde, May 31, 1985; Fred Lazar, July 11, 1989; Nate Laurie, May 17, 1984; Lorna Marsden, March 2 and 3, 1980; and Barbara Sulzenko, May 14, 1984.

      Surprisingly difficult: "Allan MacEachen, who chaired the party's newly formed policy group, kept their recommendations under lock and key throughout the winter campaign." Sheppard and Valpy, *National Deal*, p. 22. Also Milne, *Tug of War*, p. 79.

20. Not convinced: Coutts's disagreement was tactical, not strategic. He had veered towards energy nationalism after the first OPEC crisis, becoming a staunch backer of Petro-Canada's expansion through take-overs during the late 1970s. One device he developed for outflanking the NDP on the prairies was federal government support for the creation of Coenerco, a co-op venture in the petroleum business.

21. Appointing Jack Austin: When offering him the position of deputy minister of energy, mines and resources, Trudeau had discussed with him the possibility of using energy as a "positive lever," one by which a society, "in the way it uses energy, can move its nature and character and its ability to respond." Olsen, *State Elite*, p. 90.

22. National unity: Trudeau's objective, according to Martin Goldfarb, was "to bring some federal authority back to the table, because the country will fragment and disintegrate if we allow the provinces to fight for their own territorial self-interest. We

sold the NEP to the public as a nationalist thing, but in Trudeau's mind it was something else." Cited in Graham, *One-Eyed Kings*, pp. 86–87.

Transnationals: In early 1979, following political upheaval in Iran, Exxon cut Imperial Oil's Venezuelan imports by a quarter (this was in addition to the 40,000-barrel-per-day shortfall in Iranian imports the country was already experiencing). Foster, *Blue-Eyed Sheiks*, pp. 64–65; and Doern and Toner, *Politics of Energy*, p. 254, n. 7. In response to the diversion the Liberal energy minister, Alastair Gillespie, delivered a series of ultimatums to Imperial, which came to nothing and were treated by industry observers as an election ploy.

On Lalonde's lack of qualms: "The major factor behind the NEP wasn't Canadianization or getting more from the industry or even self-sufficiency . . . *The* determinant factor was the fiscal imbalance between the provinces and the federal government in the scenario in which the provincial revenues would go up with the price of oil while Ottawa's share of the larger and larger pie got smaller and smaller . . . So we foresaw a situation in which the federal government would have no way of ever restoring the balance." Graham, *One-Eyed Kings*, p. 81.

23. The core of Trudeau's energy speech: "The Liberal plan seeks to achieve energy security at a fair price for all Canadians. Our energy program for the 1980s consists of 7 major commitments. We would start at once to: (1) Set a Made in Canada pricing policy to secure adequate supplies of energy at reasonable prices. (2) Achieve energy security through the accelerated development of Canada's domestic potential and the ensuring of Canada's off-shore supply. (3) Develop a more balanced energy program through the replacement of oil by natural gas and other energy forms. (4) Strengthen and expand Petro-Canada as an instrument of national policy. (5) Place a new emphasis on conservation and the promotion of energy alternatives. (6) Ensure that Canada's energy sector becomes more Canadian-owned and controlled. (7) See that energy becomes part of the larger economic strategy, forming the core of any industrial or regional development approach." "Notes for Remarks" (Jan. 25, 1980), p. 5.

24. The term "low-bridging" was used by Davey at a conference at Erindale College the following September: Authors' notes. Also Davey, *Rainmaker*, pp. 265–66.

Plan he had sent to party candidates: Davey, "Memorandum to All Liberal Candidates," Jan. 15, 1980. Authors' archive.

On the *Star* and Liberals in 1972: "After Fifty Years Liberals have Forfeited Our Support," *Toronto Star* (Oct. 16, 1972), editorial, p. 6. In the 1980 election the Liberals received the endorsement of only *The Toronto Star* and *La Presse*. *Canadian Annual Review: 1980*, p. 12.

25. "Part of his paradigm": Authors' interview with Tom Axworthy, Feb 22, 1980.
Countervailed: Milne, *Tug of War*, p. 117.

26. On Trudeau's campaign commitments: Lorna Marsden, then LPC vice-president, claimed that "all of Trudeau's policy announcements on energy, foreign ownership and western agriculture, for example, originated with the platform committee and none conflicted with resolutions passed at the 1978 convention." Wearing, *L-Shaped Party*, p. 244.

27. "Strategic prime ministership": Confidential interview, Oct. 1989.

28. Official commitments: Authors' interview with Tom Axworthy, Feb. 22, 1980. Jeffrey Simpson, "The Craft of the Cabinet Maker," *Globe and Mail* (Mar. 6, 1980), pp. 1–2.

29. Speech from the throne: Canada, House of Commons, *Debates* (Apr. 14, 1980), pp. 4–7.

30. Third National Policy: Bruce Doern commented that the set of constitutional, social, and economic initiatives undertaken by the Liberals represented the "most coherent assertion of political belief and principle by the Liberals since the early years of the Pearson Government." "Liberal Priorities," pp. 1–2. Donald Smiley subsequently extended Doern's assessment by referring to the Liberal program as a "Third National Policy." "Dangerous Deed," p. 74. Also Milne, *Tug of War*, p. 117. Leslie traces the "Third National Policy" back to the mid-1970s, culminating in the NEP. *Federal State*, pp. 8–10. Some scholars consider the forty years from 1941 to be the second National Policy. Eden and Molot, "National Policies," pp. 235–41; and Fowke, "National Policy."

31. The "post-Keynesian" approach was summarized by the senior mandarin Ian Stewart in 1981 as "a continuation of the process of gradualism with a twist – with a reinforced direction of funds to some of the structural and economic development problems of the Canadian economy." "Post-Keynesian World," p. 97.

# Chapter 5
# The National Energy Program and National Disunity

1. Biographical information on Lalonde: Authors' interviews Apr. 11, 1979, and May 31 and Dec. 18, 1985.

    Peter Foster claimed Lalonde was "ninth generation farming stock from Île Parrot." *Sorcerer's Apprentices*, p. 13. Lalonde himself told writer Malcolm Reid, "Our house was passed from father to son for five generations." "Understanding Lalonde," p. 31.

2. For a more complete account of Lalonde's upbringing and early career in politics: McCall-Newman, *Grits*, pp. 272–301.

    "Carbuncle": Authors' interview, Apr. 11, 1979.

3. "Typical Rotarian": Authors' interview, Apr. 11, 1979.

4. The Liberals won seventy-three out of seventy-five seats on February 18, 1980, in Quebec, while the Conservatives captured one seat. As the result of the death of a Social Credit candidate, the election in Frontenac riding was deferred until March 24, at which time the Liberals' victory brought their seats in the province to a record seventy-four.

5. On Lalonde's hatred for the 1970s: Authors' interviews with Marc Lalonde, Apr. 1, 1978, Apr. 11, 1979, and May 31, 1986; and Patrice Merrin, Apr. 21, 1978, and Apr. 11, 1979.

6. Doctrinally opposed: In March 1980, when the deputy ministers were summoned as a group to the Privy Council Office to discuss the new government's priorities, they pooh-poohed the Liberals' energy promises to a man (no women being present to break ranks). Authors' interview with Tom Axworthy, Feb. 22, 1980. Ottawa's officialdom was agreed only on the need to get a larger share of increased energy revenues in order to prevent severe fiscal imbalances. L. Pratt, "Energy: The Roots."

7. Funny-money populism: The direct source of Social Credit's economic theory was the Englishman Major C.H. Douglas (Macpherson, *Democracy in Alberta*, pp. 120–24), but easy-money thinking was embedded in a political culture steeped in the American debate over the unlimited coinage of silver that had been championed by the great Democrat, populist, and fundamentalist William Jennings Bryan, in the two decades before the Great War. Authors' interview with Kenneth McNaught, Mar. 13, 1994.

Social Credit's regulatory regime was "profoundly conservative in its emphasis upon property rights and strongly influenced by the regulatory tradition of the Southwest United States." Richards and Pratt, *Prairie Capitalism*, p. 79.

8. The Borden commission was established in October 1957. Its first report, delivered in 1958, recommended the creation of the National Energy Board; the second, in 1959, rejected the proposed Alberta-Montreal oil pipeline, thus setting in motion the continental integration of the industry that was endorsed by the Conservatives' subsequent National Oil Policy. McDougall, *Fuels and the National Policy*, ch. 5.

Oil to Montreal: "Though only an extremely small minority was against the Montreal pipeline, the minority opinion represented the continental option and received wider official audience." But "Canadian policy-making officials hung on every word that Imperial spokesmen uttered . . . Imperial apparently represented the voice of power and influence, the 'insider' that could manipulate the proper channels in Washington to open American markets." Clark-Jones, *Staple State*, pp. 49, 41.

Concerned that Venezuela might nationalize American petroleum corporations in response to the restrictions on its oil exports that Washington introduced in 1959, the U.S. State Department was pressing to keep the Canadian market open for Venezuelan oil. Continued Canadian dependence on imported Venezuelan oil satisfied both Washington's interests and those of the oil majors – who were thus able to exploit their more profitable but vulnerable Venezuelan holdings at a faster rate. Shaffer, *Canada's Oil*, pp. 156–60.

Free world: Cold War ideology played a key role in facilitating the continental integration of the Canadian petroleum industry and the disintegration of the Canadian oil market: "The military security of the continent was invoked on numerous occasions to justify reliance upon U.S. capital or the approval of controversial exports of gas to Montana and the Pacific Northwest. Alberta's resources were to be committed to the free world's struggle with Godless communism." Richards and Pratt, *Prairie Capitalism*, p. 82.

9. Suddenly: In March 1973, Imperial Oil's annual report maintained, "Canada is not in any way deficient in energy resources. Our present energy reserves, using present technology, are sufficient for our requirements for several hundred years." A year later, the company was peddling a very different line: "Within the next ten years,

production rates from existing reserves in Western Canada will be inadequate to supply markets now being served." Quoted in GATT-Fly, *Power to Choose*, pp. 29–32.

10. On Lougheed's state-building and his response to the OPEC crisis: L. Pratt, "State and
Province-Building," and Richards and Pratt, *Prairie Capitalism*, ch. 9, "Empire
Alberta: The Province as Entrepreneur."

On Lougheed's western common front: Westmacott and Dore, "Intergovernmental Cooperation," and D.G. Wood, *Lougheed Legacy*, pp. 106–10.

11. On the September 1973 announcement: "This price freeze marked a major conjunc-
ture in Canadian energy politics. It . . . transferred for the first time in Canada the
price-setting function from the industry, and in particular Imperial Oil, to the federal
government." Doern and Toner, *Politics of Energy*, p. 172.

Incensed: Alberta was also upset with Turner for making royalty payments non-
deductible from corporate income tax: D.G. Wood, *Lougheed Legacy*, pp. 154–55.

12. Clark's high-powered Economic and Policy Analysis Sector: Desveaux, *Designing
Bureaucracies*, pp. 76–80.

13. Most wasteful: McDougall, *Fuels and the National Policy*, p. 128.

Get tougher with Alberta: Already under Joe Clark's ministry, there was a
consensus within EMR that prices had to rise in order to facilitate domestic self-
sufficiency. On the issue of Canadianization, EMR acknowledged the need for Petro-
Canada as an essential aspect of the strategy of extending federal control over the
industry and countering Alberta's power. L. Pratt, "Petro-Canada" (1981),
pp. 102–3. For details of the Conservative government's failed attempt to resolve the
Canadian energy dilemma, see Simpson, *Discipline of Power*, ch. 7.

14. Heartened . . . the energy bureaucrats: Anticipating the organizational disruption
that the rapid concoction of the radical new energy policy would cause EMR, Michael
Pitfield appointed Art Collins to be associate deputy minister entrusted with the job
of reorganizing the department to "do" the NEP. Authors' interview with Art Collins, June 3, 1986.

15. Functionalism: The French title of the 1964 Trudeau-Lalonde group's manifesto,
"An Appeal for Realism in Politics," was "Manifeste pour une politique fonctionnelle."

16. For a more thorough description of the Pitfield reforms: McCall-Newman, *Grits*,
pp. 209ff. Also Lalonde, "Changing Role."

17. Douglas Hartle provides a thorough description of the federal decision-making
structure in the 1970s in *The Expenditure Budget Process*, ch. 1. The post-Clark government changes are detailed in Van Loon, "Ottawa's Expenditure Process."

18. Uncontrollable increases: By 1976, when Michael Pitfield was the chief civil servant
responsible for making the system work, expenditure control was a problem
throughout the industrialized world: Economic Council of Canada, *Toward Full
Employment*.

On the envelope system: Borins, "Ottawa's Expenditure Envelopes," pp. 63–64,
and Van Loon, "Policy and Expenditure Management." On the accompanying reorganization of the committee system: Aucoin, "Organizational Change," and Van
Loon, "Kaleidoscope in Grey."

19. On the NEP in the context of Ottawa's envelope system: Doern and Toner, *Politics of*

*Energy*, pp. 373–76, and Doern, "Energy Expenditures." One officer from the PCO was attached to the EnFin committee to ensure that the negotiations with Alberta over energy were consistent with the positions taken by Ottawa on the constitution.

EnFin and *enfin*: Foster, *Sorcerer's Apprentices*, p. 143n.

20. On the concentration of power within EnFin and the consequent political and bureaucratic animosity towards the NEP: Doern and Toner, *Politics of Energy*, pp. 40–41. Tom Axworthy's reflection on this problem: Graham, *One-Eyed Kings*, p. 80. The consequences of not playing the game by the rules: Van Loon, "Ottawa's Expenditure Process," pp. 109–10.

Never given a chance: Feedback from cabinet was kept to a minimum. On the wording on the proposed Western Development Fund, for instance, in order to preclude any suggestion that the premiers would participate in the spending of these funds, the phrase "the people in Western Canada" was changed to "Westerners."

21. Incentives: Besides the Department of Finance's growing concern throughout the late 1970s and early 1980s that the tax system was being overloaded with incentives, there were legal obstacles, Canada-U.S. tax treaties in particular, to using the tax system to discriminate in favour of Canadian-owned firms. "The only major way in which one could give greater support to Canadian firms was through direct grants, where international rules and conventions were less strict. The federal government wanted to favour Canadian firms because it feared that foreign ownership would otherwise increase, not decrease . . . The need to use grants also coincided with, and mutually reinforced, the larger Liberal visibility strategy." Doern and Toner, *Politics of Energy*, p. 49.

Appropriate use: One misunderstanding did cause an uproar. Finance moved to end a tax incentive encouraging the capping of newly drilled oil wells since it felt the incentives to drill then cap gas wells was overdriving the system. Although a relatively small issue, this cut the NEP's political support among the small Canadian firms whose cash flow was badly squeezed by the measure.

22. On the private sector's phobia about Ed Clark: Much was made at the Canadian Petroleum Association of the fact that his thesis had been on socialism in Tanzania. In the winter of 1980-81, abridged and highlighted copies of Clark's Harvard doctoral thesis, "Socialist Development and Public Investment in Tanzania," were circulated among oilmen. Deborah McGregor, "The Man Oilmen Love to Hate," *Financial Times* (Feb. 9, 1981), pp. 1, 27. Peter Foster did the most to mythologize Clark's role in the development of the NEP. *Sorcerer's Apprentices*, pp. 74–79. Also Doern and Toner, *Politics of Energy*, pp. 46–56.

23. On Lalonde's selection of Cohen: Appointing deputy ministers is a prime ministerial prerogative, but Lalonde's relationship with Pierre Trudeau was so close that he was the one minister who could name his own deputy.

Feverish atmosphere: Rationality among policy-makers is bounded by all kinds of constraints of time and information. EnFin's effort to redesign Canadian energy policy within a matter of months was a casebook example of what social scientists identify as "satisficing," when leaders maximize their goals within the limits imposed by deadlines, opposition, and so on. March, *Handbook of Organizations*, p. xiii, and March and Simon, *Organizations*, pp. 140ff. The notion of satisficing was applied in a famous study to the Cuban Missile Crisis by Allison, *Essence of Decision*, p. 72.

Security: Two versions of the draft legislation were maintained, the one containing an export tax on oil being kept under even closer guard. So concerned were energy officials that details of the NEP not be leaked in advance that "key energy people designed a detailed false shadow program which was actually discussed at high-level meetings as if it were the real thing. Sure enough, it was leaked in late September, 1980. A month later, the true NEP was released." Deborah McGregor, "The Man Oilmen Love to Hate," *Financial Times* (Feb. 9, 1981), pp. 1, 27.

24. Read every draft: Once when Lalonde scolded his deputy, Mickey Cohen, for missing an error Lalonde had found in a draft, Cohen shot back, "Oh, I just put it in to keep you on your toes." Authors' interview with Mickey Cohen, July 24, 1984.

"For good reason": Authors' interview with Serge Joyal, June 4, 1985.

25. Federal policies throughout the 1970s: Canada, Department of Energy, Mines and Resources, Energy Policy Sector, *Energy Strategy*; and Simpson, *Discipline of Power*, ch. 7.

26. On Lalonde's warning: Canada, Department of Energy, Mines and Resources, *National Energy Program*, pp. 17–19.

27. All-encompassing: The NEP was "the most significant act of government intervention in the Canadian economy since the Second World War. It was the most ambitious effort ever undertaken by Ottawa to reverse the foreign control of a major industry in favour of Canadian control." J. Laxer, *Oil and Gas*, pp. 73–74. Nationalist support varied from very warm in Ontario – Watkins, "National Energy Program" – to more critical in the periphery: Milne, *Tug of War*, pp. 87–95; and L. Pratt, "Petro-Canada" (1981), p. 101.

Despite its explicit goal of self-sufficiency and independence from the international market, the NEP failed to question the fundamentally continentalist, market-based assumptions upon which post-war energy policy has been founded: "From the days of the Borden Commission, the Canadian nationalist position has always been that proven, low-cost, and readily accessible reserves of natural gas in western Canada should not be exported, leaving Canadians to depend on costlier and more remote supplies for their future requirements. The worst fears of such nationalists were confirmed by two policies adopted almost simultaneously by the government in 1980: the approval of increased exports of Alberta natural gas via new pipelines to the United States (pre-build) and increased public subsidization of the accelerated development of still-inaccessible, high-cost fuel supplies in the frontier regions of Canada." McDougall, *Fuels and the National Policy*, p. 150.

28. Depletion allowances had been attacked by the Gordon commission in 1957 as unfairly discriminating against Canadian petroleum companies in favour of the integrated transnationals. They had come under fire from the Carter commission on tax reform in 1967 but had survived both scrutinies intact.

29. "Provincial duchies": Authors' interview with Marc Lalonde, Apr. 1, 1978.

30. Unilateral constitutional initiative: See vol. 1, chs. 13–14.

31. "Outright attempt": Alberta, *Ninth Annual Report*, p. 19. On October 30, 1980, Premier Lougheed appeared on prime-time television in Alberta to attack the NEP and what he saw as its extreme centralization of power in Ottawa. Doern and Toner, *Politics of Energy*, p. 267.

Alberta support for Lougheed was not the same as support for the petroleum companies. A poll taken by the Canada West Foundation in 1980 revealed that west-erners' "support for the oil industry is relatively weak, even among Albertans," with the vast majority of westerners, including 70 per cent of Albertans, agreeing that oil companies made excessive profits. Jeff Sallot, "Albertans Shock Lalonde: They're with Him," *Globe and Mail* (Sept. 23, 1981), p. 8.

Reprisals: "The cutbacks were designed to show the federal government how much more expensive imported oil was than that from Alberta. However, this ploy misfired because, under the National Energy Program, the Liberals had shifted the burden for subsidizing expensive imports from their own treasury directly onto the consumer via the Petroleum Compensation Charge. Marc Lalonde was therefore able to up the domestic oil price at the retail level to compensate for additional imports and then call the extra burden the 'Lougheed levy.'" Foster, *Sorcerer's Apprentices*, p. 167. Also Doern and Toner, *Politics of Energy*, pp. 266–67.

32. Alberta's alienation: "Bumper stickers and cap badges flourished, much of the frus-tration being directed at Ottawa's progeny, Petro-Canada. Typical of this mood was a bumper sticker on a huge Buick that stated: 'I'd rather push this thing a mile than buy gas from PetroCan.'" J. Lyon, *Dome*, p. 6. Bumper stickers from the mid-1970s read: "Let the Eastern Bastards freeze in the dark." D.G. Wood, *Lougheed Legacy*, p. 151.

33. "Drink together": Authors' interview with Merv Leitch, June 2, 1986.

34. Mellon-Cohen meetings: Authors' interview with Barry Mellon, June 3, 1986.

35. "Fabulously wealthy": Confidential interview, June 1986.

On price increases and the post-NEP fiscal regime: Doern and Toner, *Politics of Energy*, pp. 313, 328–35.

36. On negotiating positions: P. James, "Energy Politics."

On Cohen's tactics: Confidential interview.

$600 million: Foster, *Sorcerer's Apprentices*, p. 178; *Canadian Annual Review: 1981*, pp. 231–34.

37. The negotiating advantage was on the federal side: P. James, "Energy Politics," pp. 11–12. EMR's 200 economists, with their sophisticated econometric model, gave the federal negotiators a superior capacity to respond to alternative proposals. Desveaux, *Designing Bureaucracies*, ch. 5.

38. Export tax: Formally the hated duty was reduced to zero, thus maintaining Ottawa's claim to have the right to levy one.

"Balanced agreement": Lalonde, "Riding the Storm," p. 67.

Champagne: Lougheed regretted ever afterwards being graphically linked to the hated Trudeau in the gesture of a governmental deal at the expense of business. "In political terms it was a dumb thing for me to toast the signing of the agreement with Mr. Trudeau." D.G. Wood, *Lougheed Legacy*, p. 181.

39. Energy revenues: J. Laxer, *Oil and Gas*, p. 147; according to the memorandum of agreement signed in September and reproduced in the *Canadian Annual Review*, Alberta would receive $64.3 billion in oil and gas revenues for the period 1981-86, while Ottawa would get $54.3 billion. *Canadian Annual Review: 1981*, table 7, p. 233; and Foster, *Sorcerer's Apprentices*, p. 178.

"We've won!" Authors' interview with Tom Axworthy, Nov. 14, 1981.

40. "Split the profits": Authors' interview with Nick Taylor, June 3, 1986. The *actual* dis-tribution of revenues as compiled by the Petroleum Industry Monitoring Survey and

quoted in Milne, *Tug of War*, p. 85, shows that it was the producing provinces that experienced the most significant loss of revenues, while the share of industry remained essentially unchanged between 1979 and 1982:

|           | 1979   | 1980   | 1981   | 1982   |
|-----------|--------|--------|--------|--------|
| Industry  | 41.2%  | 45.4%  | 39.7%  | 40.3%  |
| Provinces | 45.7%  | 42.4%  | 37.3%  | 32.3%  |
| Ottawa    | 13.1%  | 12.2%  | 23.0%  | 27.4%  |

41. Refused to involve the industry: "In Calgary and Toronto, the oil companies offered their services to Alberta . . . but Alberta wasn't interested. Whether it was because the provincial mandarins thought they could do the job themselves, or whether it was because they mistrusted the industry is uncertain. All that is certain is that they failed to avail themselves of the industry's information and for six months locked themselves into a rarified world of economic assumptions and bureaucratic, computer projections with their Ottawa counterparts." Foster, *Sorcerer's Apprentices*, p. 169. Also Doern and Toner, *Politics of Energy*, p. 462.

    On the pro-Canadianization oilmen: Authors' interview with Prof. Larry Pratt, Sept. 29, 1981; and Doern and Toner, *Politics of Energy*, p. 43.

    On Dome's relationship with Ottawa over the NEP: President Bill Richards labelled the NEP "confiscation without compensation." J. Lyon, *Dome*, p. 9. Despite extensive contacts with Ottawa prior to the fall of 1980, Dome executives really did not know what to expect and were "horrified" when they finally read the NEP legislation. Foster, *Other People's Money*, pp. 88–92.

    Sour memories: Authors' interview with Marc Lalonde, Oct. 30, 1981.

    On the deep roots of free-enterprise ideology in Alberta's oil patch: House, *Last of the Free Enterprisers*, ch. 7.

42. Pressure on Edmonton: Authors' interview with Merv Leitch, June 2, 1986.

    Limit contacts: Feigenbaum, Samuels, and Weaver, "Innovation," p. 74.

43. Lalonde in Alberta: Jeff Sallot, "Lalonde Stumping Alberta to Stop the Spread of 'Distortions,'" *Globe and Mail* (Jan. 23, 1981), p. 9.

44. The NEP's proposal to phase out the depletion allowance for domestic exploration expenditures outside the Canada lands was also opposed by the juniors. Doern and Toner, *Politics of Energy*, pp. 247–48. The PGRT, which was imposed at the wellhead and allowed for no write-offs, imposed a considerable burden on small producers who were subsequently relieved in the May 1982 update through a $250,000 corporate tax credit designed to go primarily to small producers. Krukowski, *Canadian Taxation*.

    A further insult came in the 1981 MacEachen budget, which threatened to remove the drilling fund tax expenditures that had been built into the tax system in the late 1970s and that provided the juniors with a significant part of their working capital. Doern and Toner, *Politics of Energy*, pp. 246–47.

45. On Canadian-American free-enterprise solidarity: "Both the Canadian companies and the MNCs deeply resented the federal government's foray into their niche of the economy, viewing this intervention as an impingement on their ability to conduct business . . . [Canadian business] regarded itself as an international business community allied with U.S. investors. It regarded anything attacking the U.S. business community as an attack on themselves." Jenkins, "'Obsolescing Bargain,'" p. 156.

The majors quickly learned how to live with the new energy framework, using the massive government funding of their partner Canadian firms to subsidize entirely their riskier exploration activities in the Canada lands, thus allowing them to expand into safer, and more profitable, upstream activities. "Adaptation to economic nationalism and state intervention is part of the international oil companies' stock-in-trade. As an example of nationalist policy, the NEP has been a costly, divisive failure." L. Pratt, "Energy, Regionalism and Canadian Nationalism," p. 178.

The drilling rigs actually started moving south several months before the NEP was unveiled. Jenkins, "'Obsolescing Bargain,'" p. 160.

# Chapter 6
# Hurricane Ronnie: American Retaliation

1. Schlesinger on the New Right: "As program, however, neo-conservatism is very much *recherche du temps perdu*. It repeats conservative themes not just of the 1950s and 1920s but of the 1890s and before: the exaltation of laissez-faire and the unfettered market (Herbert Spencer's *Social Statics*, 1850); the crusade against government regulation (which began after the passage of the Interstate Commerce Act in 1887); the faith in trickle-down, now rebaptized supply-side, economics (Calvin Coolidge and Andrew Mellon); the call for the devolution of authority from Washington to the states (Eisenhower). Far from being bold new ideas, these constitute the boilerplate of every epoch of private interest. Neo-conservative zealots even want to return to the gold standard – and succeeded in inserting that thought into the 1984 Republican platform." *Cycles of American History*, p. 38.

On Reagan's career by a conservative observer: Wills, *Reagan's America*.

The ideologue's view from the right: Buckley, *Did You Ever See*. A response from the left: Coser and Howe, *New Conservatives*. From the centre: Crawford, *Thunder on the Right*. An insider's account of the growth of neo-conservatism in the U.S.: Rusher, *Rise of the Right*. A more objective conservative's view: Wills, *Confessions*. Also Robert W. Whitaker, *New Right Papers*.

On the make-up of the new conservative coalition: K. Phillips, *Emerging Republican Majority*.

2. "Bring out the Mounties": Authors' interview with Tom Axworthy, Nov. 14, 1981.

3. Threatening note: A few days later, the note was withdrawn at the instance of the Canadian ambassador. Authors' interview with Peter Towe, Nov. 29, 1989.

4. The North American Accord: This late-twentieth-century version of Manifest Destiny had been seized on by Reagan's entourage to fit in with their candidate's own

vague notion that neighbours ought to get along with each other. Before his inauguration he had gone to Mexico, a country he was familiar with from having lived so long in California, in order to boost his North American Accord idea. Authors' interview with Myer Rashish, Sept. 7, 1989.

"Show him pictures": Confidential interview conducted by John Kirton and Robert Bothwell, June 1986, generously made available to the authors by John Kirton.

5. Reagan story of Israeli soldiers: Authors' interview with Myer Rashish, Sept. 7, 1989.

6. Reagan on peace in the Middle East: Authors' conversation and interview with James Coutts, July 21, 1981, and Feb. 17, 1988.

7. Acid rain: Clarkson, *Canada and the Reagan Challenge*, ch. 8.

Not as bad: Authors' interview with Myer Rashish, Sept. 7, 1989.

8. Targets: The biggest take-over binges were launched by the three fattest Canadian firms, which overextended themselves, going into debt by the billions at a time when interest rates were at unprecedented heights. The Canadian giants had benefitted the most from the PIP grants and the possibility of setting up joint ventures with the transnationals by farming in on their land. Dome Petroleum went after Hudson's Bay Oil and Gas for $4 billion, Nova's Husky Oil purchased Uno-Tex for $371 million, and the publicly financed Petro-Canada bought Belgian-owned Petrofina for $1.45 billion, with money coming in from the consumer tax on refined gas, as well as on gasoline and petroleum products. Doern and Toner, *Politics of Energy*, p. 222. Larry Pratt described the PIP grants as the "richest fiscal incentives in the world" in "Energy: The Roots," p. 41.

9. "Odd man out": Confidential interview by John Kirton and Robert Bothwell, July 1986.

10. On clashes between the American and Canadian leaders: Martin, *Presidents and the Prime Ministers*, chs. 12–14.

11. "Rearguard action": Ball, *Discipline of Power*, p. 113. Walter Gordon thought Ball's views should be taken very seriously. From the reports he received as minister of finance he became convinced that "people in the State and Treasury Departments held decidedly imperialistic views about Canada." Gordon, *Political Memoir*, p. 165.

In the furore surrounding the NEP, Ball resurfaced at a House of Representatives subcommittee hearing in December 1980 to attack the NEP and FIRA, warning, "I hope that the Canadian government and the Canadian people will recognize realistically that discrimination begets retaliation. So long as such manifest unfairness continues, it generates pressures for restrictionist and protectionist measures." Crane, *Controlling Interest*, p. 28.

On the Auto Pact as interim measure, and "wait out this period": Authors' interview with Philip Trezise, former State Department official and American negotiator of the Auto Pact, Sept. 7, 1989.

Continental energy arrangement: The "idea of a coordinated North American energy policy by late 1973 was dead." Frank and Schanz, *U.S.-Canadian Energy Trade*, p. 25. Washington (and business and political élites in Canada) continued to pursue continental energy strategies. Both the 1970 Shultz report and President Nixon's subsequent strategy for energy security, Project Independence, envisioned the further continental integration of Canadian resources, as did plans for the development of the Mackenzie Valley gas pipeline and the Alberta tar sands in the mid-1970s. L. Pratt, *Tar Sands*, chs. 4, 5; Dosman, *National Interest*; and Bregha, *Blair's Pipeline*.

12. "Whatever our reservations": Authors' interview with Philip Trezise, Sept. 7, 1989.

13. "Slippery slope": Authors' interview with Daryl Johnson, Sept. 8, 1989.

14. "Who the hell": Confidential interview, Sept. 1989.

15. Called to a meeting: Authors' interview with Myer Rashish, Sept. 7, 1980.

    "Heard about it yesterday": Authors' interview with Raymond Waldmann, Sept. 18, 1981.

16. "Mistress and a wife": Authors' interview with Myer Rashish, Sept. 7, 1989.

17. Anthony Westell caught the prevailing mood in the Canadian business community: "The sooner we recognize that, for better or worse, we share not only a continent with the United States, but also an economy, a popular culture, and a society, and that nothing is likely to change the situation, the sooner we can set about creating with the United States the binational institutions which will give us a more influential voice in the development of the continent." Westell, "Sharing the Continent," pp. 10–14.

    Out of control: Americans were angry that Canada had squeezed offset commitments from its deal with McDonnell Douglas for the F-18A Hornet fighter plane worth 120 per cent of the contract. Atkinson and Nossal, "Bureaucratic Politics."

    Xenophobic passions: "Canada's Dry Hole," *Wall Street Journal* (June 5, 1981), editorial, p. 24.

18. On Lalonde and the back-in: "The final choice belonged to Marc Lalonde, who made it explicitly and willingly, urged on by senior Petro-Canada officials as well as some EMR officials. At the same time it followed . . . principles under regulations initiated by the Conservative government of John Diefenbaker." Doern and Toner, *Politics of Energy*, p. 54.

    Accusatory statements: "Sentiment is strong in favor of countermeasures against Canadian investment and energy policies . . . The dangers are real." "US Lashes Canada on Energy Curbs," *Toronto Star* (Sept. 23, 1981), p. A1 (report on speech by Myer Rashish).

    The inch he had given: It was Ian Stewart who had been fooled by a U.S. official who had told him that some symbolic gesture by Ottawa would quiet the oilmen's complaints. Once the *ex gratia* concession had been made, the U.S. took the Canadian move as an admission of the principle that compensation should be made for the Crown taking one-quarter ownership rights and moved to demand compensation for the full value of the back-in or withdrawal of the measure.

19. "Crisette": Authors' interview with Marc Lalonde, Oct. 30, 1981.

    "You wouldn't believe the pressure": Quoted by Robert Laxer in interview with authors, June 21, 1989.

20. "Fire-sale prices": Coming as they did when the price of oil had reached its peak, Canadian take-overs in fact gave U.S. companies top dollars for their assets.
21. "Have to adjust": Authors' confidential interview, June 1986.

    To heel: One young official in the United States Trade Representative's Office expressed the banana-republic attitude with which the Reaganites regarded Canada. Pointing to the dossiers he had been studying, he explained that they didn't want to do anything that would damage Alberta, since Alberta was the friend of the United States. They were looking for a way to "put a squeeze on" Ontario and Quebec as the Liberal Party's electoral fortress. The trick was going to be how not to cause so much damage that it would provoke an anti-American reaction bolstering the Liberals but just enough so that, "at the next election, Trudeau will be overthrown." Authors' confidential interview, Sept. 1981. Interagency disagreements within the U.S. administration over the appropriate response to the Liberal initiatives seriously confused Washington's responses to the NEP and FIRA. Wonder, "US Government Response."
22. In the vision of Niccolò Machiavelli the more a prince possessed Virtù – political knowledge, skill, prudence, strength of mind, judgement, and wisdom – the more he could vanquish Fortuna, those uncontrollable actions and unforeseen events others call luck, good or bad. Machiavelli, "The Prince," pp. 159ff.
23. Implicit nationalism: Trudeau's acceptance of the NEP's subsidization of a small group of Canadian capitalists contradicted his earlier anti-nationalism. Larry Pratt echoed Breton's 1960s critique of narrow economic nationalism (though from a different perspective): "We should also be skeptical, in my opinion, of nationalist programs such as the NEP since they involve a transfer of income and benefits to the national bourgeoisie, and this transfer is typically paid for by the taxpayer at the expense of foregone social programs. Not infrequently, investments in nationalism involve a redistribution of wealth from the working class to capital or to a rising middle class." L. Pratt, "Energy, Regionalism and Canadian Nationalism," pp. 195–96.

    National unity: Trudeau's perception of the NEP conflated the pressing fiscal needs of the federal government with those of the nation. Certainly the NEP's dramatic redistribution of energy rents from Alberta to the federal government (which Lalonde acknowledged as the program's central aim) did little to foster good relations between Ottawa and the regions.
24. Anti-militarism: Trudeau, "Pearson," pp. 7–12.
25. Respected Nixon's acuity: In the television version of his *Memoirs*, episode 2, Trudeau comments that Nixon was smooth in public, but insecure in private, "stiff, perspiring, not at ease in his skin," and dependent on Kissinger to explain things.

    Trudeau had appreciated the Nixon administration's help in rebuffing an attempt by France to obtain access via the European satellite *Symphonie* to the Quebec television audience – and with it, the potential to broadcast pro-separatist programming: Dewitt and Kirton, *Principal Power*, pp. 335–36.

    Trudeau as an "asshole": Martin, *Presidents and the Prime Ministers*, p. 256; and R. Gwyn, *49th Paradox*, p. 122.

    "Priceless asset": S. Gwyn, "Where Are You," p. 32.

26. "Tuned out": Confidential interview, Sept. 1989.
27. Puzzlement: Fremon, "Margaret Trudeau," pp. 115–16.

    On Trudeau's indifference to mass culture: Authors' interview with Tom Axworthy, Apr. 5, 1983.
28. "Interest in the exotic": Authors' interview with Jean Le Moyne, Nov. 26, 1986.
29. "You know damn well": Authors' interview with Keith Davey, July 15, 1979.

    "Sooner read *Le Monde*": Authors' interview with Richard O'Hagan, Feb. 28, 1979.
30. Never shown any embarrassment: Allan Gotlieb maintains Trudeau wanted the U.S. relationship left out. Authors' interview, Aug. 4, 1986.
31. "Woolly-minded": Richard Gwyn, "A Victory of Sorts for PM," *Toronto Star* (July 22, 1981), pp. A1, A20.
32. On Meese at the Montebello summit: Conversation with the authors, July 21, 1981.
33. Test case: Quoted in Clarkson, *Canada and the Reagan Challenge*, p. 35.

    An example of the Reaganites' perception of Canada's investment policies as a bad example for the Third World is Assistant Secretary of the Treasury Paul Craig Roberts's illuminating memos to Donald Regan and Richard V. Allen. "Trudeau should be told that the Reagan Administration believes that income-redistribution policies have received too much emphasis, both in industrial and in Third World countries, to the detriment of policies of income growth." Roberts, *Supply-Side Revolution*, p. 155.

    The assistant U.S. trade representative for investment policy, Harvey Bale, charged that Ottawa was pursuing "a policy of back-door expropriation." Canadianization "is an absolutely intolerable precedent should other countries choose to follow it." Glynn, "Uncle Sam," pp. 16, 21. Also: "In the eyes of the Reagan Administration, the core issue raised by the NEP and other related Canadian policies is that of Canadian derogation from the principle of national treatment of foreign investment . . . The US regards this situation as undesirable not only in itself, but particularly in terms of the encouragement it might give to less developed countries." Wonder, "US Government Response," pp. 482, 483.
34. "Bore the brunt": Authors' interview with Philip Trezise, Sept. 7, 1989.

# Chapter 7
# Ottawa Complains, Compromises, and Complies

1. Davey-Trudeau conversation and the Spadina seat: Authors' interviews with Keith Davey, Sept. 24, 1981, and Ethel Teitelbaum, Aug. 18, 1981.

     $4 million: McCall-Newman, *Grits*, appendix notes, p. 428.
2. "Kids for HQ": Authors' interview with Lorna Marsden, Aug. 18, 1981.
3. Academic brilliance: Harry Ferns, the political scientist who taught Gotlieb at United College in Winnipeg, said he never again had a student as good. Authors' interview, Aug. 15, 1973. Donovan Waters, speaking at the University of Toronto on Sept. 21, 1989, to a gathering of Oxonians, confirmed that Gotlieb had taken Oxford's legal community by storm.
4. On Gotlieb's career: Authors' interview with Allan Gotlieb, Aug. 4, 1986.
5. On Trudeau's view of External: Thordarson, *Trudeau and Foreign Policy*, pp. 91–92; Nossal, *Politics of Canadian Foreign Policy*, pp. 133–34; and Dobell, *Canada's Search*, ch. 2.
6. "Only one dazzling intellect": Authors' confidential interview, May 1979.
7. First-class mind: Authors' interview with Michael Pitfield, June 29, 1977.

     "Never dined at Sussex": Authors' interview with Allan Gotlieb, Aug. 4, 1986.
8. "Dispirited and disorganized": Authors' interview with Allan Gotlieb, Aug. 4, 1986.
9. On External's standing in the bureaucracy: Kirton, "Foreign Policy Decision-making"; Protheroe, *Imports and Politics*; and Wright, "Bureaucratic Politics."
10. "Bureaucratic imperialism": Authors' interview with Allan Gotlieb, Aug. 4, 1986.

      For Flora Macdonald's own recollections of this period: "Minister and the Mandarins." The Tory interregnum: Cox, "Leadership Change."
11. "'Soft' on the Americans": Authors' interview with Allan Gotlieb, Aug. 4, 1986.
12. In a public explanation of this "bilateral" strategy, Gotlieb wrote that "national economic development objectives" were becoming increasingly well defined in Ottawa. "The priority in foreign policy becomes the development of an external framework that facilitates the accomplishment of these objectives. Closer and stronger bilateral relations need to be pursued with several countries. Above all, this objective requires the successful management of the U.S. relationship to which it is intimately linked." Gotlieb and Kinsman, "Sharing the Continent."

      "My life was going by": Authors' interview with Allan Gotlieb, Aug. 4, 1986.
13. "Not going to invade": Authors' interview with Myer Rashish, Sept. 7, 1989.
14. Paul Heron Robinson, Jr., as ambassador: McCall and Clarkson, "Unquiet American."
15. "Carried away": Authors' confidential interview.
16. Labour unrest: On June 29, 1981, twenty-three thousand inside postal workers began a strike that would last forty-two days, tying the previous record set in 1975 by CUPW. The final agreement, ratified on August 10, 1981, was for two years.
17. "Two-by-four": Authors' interview with Myer Rashish, Sept. 7, 1989. Rashish's

speech caught more attention in Canada than in New York. "Canada's Policies Attacked by US," *Globe and Mail* (Sept. 23, 1981), p. 1.

18. "Stubborn buggers": Authors' confidential interview, July 1984.

"Rattling the hell": Authors' interview with Allan Gotlieb, Aug. 4, 1986.

19. There have been a variety of attempts to explain Canada's failure to develop the sort of corporatist and state-interventionist arrangements characteristic of the smaller West European nations. Atkinson and Coleman, *Industrial Change in Canada*, part 1; G. Laxer, *Open for Business*; and Williams, *Not for Export*. Among those who argue that Canada does exhibit features of what they call "state capitalism" are Laux and Molot, *State Capitalism*. Technological sovereignty: Britton and Gilmour, *Weakest Link*.

On the tortured history of Canada's search for an industrial strategy: Doern and Phidd, *Canadian Public Policy*, ch. 15; Blais, "Canadian Industrial Policy," ch. 2; French, *How Ottawa Decides*, chs. 5, 6; and Gillies, *Facing Reality*, ch. 4.

On the acceptance of an industrial strategy approach by the CLC: M. Smith, "Canadian Labour Congress," pp. 48–52.

20. For a description of the Swedish model and the crisis it has experienced since the mid-1970s: Rivlin, "Overview," and Weaver, "Political Foundations."

21. "Coup d'état": Seminar by Tom Axworthy at the University of Toronto, Jan. 14, 1985. The contents of the speech were finalized the night before Trudeau gave it by James Coutts, Tom Axworthy, and Herb Gray while they were negotiating with Beland Honderich for *The Toronto Star's* editorial endorsement: Authors' confidential interview, May 1988.

22. "For the first time": Herb Gray to the authors, Feb. 12, 1980.

Speech from the throne: Canada, House of Commons, *Debates* (Apr. 14, 1980), pp. 4–7.

23. Gray document: "Implementing the New National Industrial Development Policy" (marked "Secret," July 2, 1980).

"Perform to world standards": "Framework for Implementing the Government's New Industrial Development Policy," confidential document (n.d.), p. 13.

Internal government documents cited in this chapter are in the authors' archive.

24. $2.75 billion: "Olson Seen Moderating Gray's Plan of Economy," *Globe and Mail* (Sept. 17, 1980), p. 4; and Collison, "Have the Interventionists," p. 33.

Summing up the Ottawa bureaucracy's view of industrial strategy, Gordon Robertson, former clerk of the Privy Council, described it as "a catchword that is not likely to help. To provide a coherent, structured basis for a national policy of industrial guidance may be inconsistent with the kind of country and economy we have." *The Institute*, p. 1. Given this mind-set, it is no wonder that Gray's cabinet paper "caused a sensation in upper-level Ottawa": Williams, *Not for Export*, p. 166.

On Johnstone's disagreement with Gray: Authors' confidential interview, July 1986. According to a senior PCO official, Trudeau had appointed Johnstone as deputy minister in IT&C "to keep Gray under control." Confidential interview, Oct. 1989.

25. On Lalonde and Gray: The tough-love treatment Gray's document proposed for declining industries particularly threatened the labour-intensive textile and shoe manufacturers that were concentrated in Lalonde's Quebec, where jobs had long been protected by Ottawa's tariffs and quotas.

26. On the industrial strategy debate in 1981: Doern, "Mega-Project Episode."

Mackintosh compared with Innis: Nelles, "Looking Backward."

The Blair-Carr task force: Canada, Major Projects Task Force, *Major Canadian Projects: Major Canadian Opportunities*.

27. "Unblight": Authors' interview with David Bond, Nov. 26, 1986.

28. Letter from Pierre Elliott Trudeau to certain cabinet colleagues (July 6, 1981).

29. On the July 14 cabinet meeting: Confidential memorandum (July 17, 1981).

30. On his side: Confidential memorandum (July 14, 1981).

Fighting off a rival: Confidential memorandum (Aug. 24, 1981).

Ministers' position papers: Axworthy: "Western Economic Strategy" (July 22, 1981) and "Labour Market Strategy" (July 28, 1981); Lumley: "Export-Led Growth – Summary" (June 11, 1981); Roberts: "Note on Sectoral Approach, Sector Identification Assessment and Prioritization" (n.d.).

31. "Namby-pamby": Confidential memorandum (Aug. 24, 1981).

"May get the feeling": Unsigned memorandum to Gordon Osbaldeston (Aug. 21, 1981).

Canadianization: Osbaldeston sidetracked the nationalist threat by proposing an anodyne amendment to the Corporations and Labour Unions Returns Act instead of the promised performance reviews of foreign-owned firms by FIRA, which might "cause the United States Government to respond quickly and forecefully [*sic*] even if a mandatory reporting requirement for performance review were to apply to both Canadian-owned and foreign-owned corporations." Memorandum from G.F. Osbaldeston to Hon. Allan J. MacEachen (Sept. 5, 1981).

Apologized too abjectly: Memorandum from Lloyd Axworthy to Allan MacEachen (Aug. 25, 1981).

Another minister had cause to be upset: "It's very evident that GFO [Osbaldeston] has once again shafted De Bané." Confidential memorandum (Aug. 24, 1981).

32. "Leadership without dirigisme": Confidential memorandum (Aug. 13, 1981).

The budget document *Economic Development for Canada in the 1980s* called cautiously for "only a reasoned pace" of development for "local indigenous manufacturing and service industries" (p. 5). Where Gray sought an active government role in directly and indirectly influencing the pace and directions of industrial development, the Olson/MSED philosophy embodied in the November budget document eschewed an increased state role in *shaping* investment for the classical Canadian pattern of public *support* for private investment. "The message of *Economic Development for Canada* was not that industrial development lacks consequence or relevance, but rather that the engine of economic recovery must be resource exploitation." Williams, *Not for Export*, pp. 167–68.

The statement was quickly dismissed in the media: David Crane, "'Platitudes' but No Real Policy," *Toronto Star* (Nov. 19, 1981), p. A8; and Richard Gwyn, "Budget Book Amounts to an Economic Whiteout," Ottawa *Citizen* (Nov. 17, 1981), p. 8.

33. MacEachen's preference for a market-driven economy had been made clear in his 1980 budget, when he rejected the position that the government "intervene broadly, not only in shaping our industrial purposes, but in controlling the setting of prices, wages and the distribution of economic benefits generally." Canada, Department of Finance, *Budget* (Oct. 28, 1980), p. 3.

34. No "son of NEP": This assurance was not enough to satisfy the Reagan administration. U.S. Ambassador Robinson demanded that the hydra of economic nationalism be ceremoniously killed off in public. Clarkson, *Canada and the Reagan Challenge*, pp. 38–40. In his budget two months later, the finance minister accordingly ate humble pie on behalf of the government, declaring that the 1980 election promise to expand FIRA's powers would not be kept "at this time" – a phrase Tom Axworthy managed to insert as a sop to the party's nationalists and his own hopes. Authors' interview with Tom Axworthy, Nov. 14, 1981.

The day after the budget was released, David Bond, from Osbaldeston's economic development secretariat, and Gerry Shannon of Finance flew off to Washington, New York, and Chicago, where they assured American government officials and money market mavens that the industrial strategy idea was finished. Authors' interview with David Bond, Nov. 26, 1986.

# Chapter 8
# The Disastrous Budget and
# the End of the Dream

1. Details about Allan MacEachen's life and political career are derived from a formal interview on May 23, 1984; several conversations between him and the authors over a period of twenty years; interviews with Senators John Stewart and Keith Davey; and the following published material: Enright, "New Number Two"; MacIntyre, "Lonely Stranger"; and Dewar, "Most Hated Man." Assorted newspaper articles are credited in the notes that follow as well as memoirs of the Pearson years by Lester Pearson, Tom Kent, Walter Gordon, Judy LaMarsh, and Keith Davey and interviews conducted for the National Archives by the journalist Peter Stursberg and published in part as *Lester Pearson and the Dream of Unity*.

   "Little tick": Bruce Ward, "Hometown Loves MacEachen," *Toronto Star* (Dec. 20, 1981), p. A6.

2. For insights into Moses Coady, the Antigonish Movement, and their relationship to Allan MacEachen's political ideas, we are indebted to Professor Jordan Bishop of the Centre for International Studies, University College of Cape Breton, and to Senator John Stewart, formerly a Liberal MP and professor of political science at Barnard College, Columbia University, and St. Francis Xavier University.

   The Antigonish Movement's vision is described in Coady, *Masters of Their Own Destiny*; its class character is detailed in Sacouman, "Antigonish Movement Co-Operatives."

   "Not immutable": Enright, "New Number Two," p. 32.

3. According to Jack Pickersgill, his initial recommendation to hire MacEachen was not enthusiastically received by Pearson: "I suggested to Pearson that he invite MacEachen to join his staff. Despite some reservations on the ground that MacEachen had a reputation for laziness, Pearson agreed." Pickersgill, *Road Back*, p. 31.

4. Pearson prided himself: "I had begun in 1958 to create a small but excellent staff of

advisers. I had only three, my experts on research, politics, and policy. Maurice Lamontagne, Allan MacEachen, and, later, Tom Kent. These were idea men, with ideas very much in harmony with my own. In the terminology of 1960, they would have been regarded as left-wing Liberals." Pearson, *Mike*, vol. 3, p. 54.

MacEachen's special place in Pearson's circle is described by Judy LaMarsh with both envy and astonishment: *Gilded Cage*, p. 176.

"Two Scotches under par": Authors' interview with Keith Davey, Mar. 10, 1980.

Labour code: Tom Kent describes the 1965 federal labour code as MacEachen's "great legislative achievement." *Public Purpose*, p. 352.

SOAP, CAP, etc.: LaMarsh called this set of welfare measures "a strong interlocking system of security for Canadians disabled by age or mental or physical disability." *Gilded Cage*, p. 124.

5. Eight serious candidates: There was a ninth name on the first ballot, that of Lloyd Henderson, but he was not a certified delegate and failed to earn a single vote.

6. The history of CBDC (Devco) is detailed in George, "Cape Breton Development Corporation," and Tupper, "Public Enterprise."

   "G stands for God": Enright, "New Number Two."

7. "Black backdrop": Authors' interview with Keith Davey, May 15, 1984.

8. "Loyalty": Authors' interview with Senator John Stewart, Oct. 12, 1989.

9. "Electric effect": Confidential interview, March 1980.

10. MacEachen's prime ministerial possibilities: Andrew Szende, "MacEachen: More Than a Right-hand Man," *Toronto Star* (Oct. 18, 1980), p. B4.

11. Symbiosis: Authors' conversation with Grant Reuber, Aug. 6, 1988; and authors' interview with Walter Gordon, Aug. 22, 1977.

12. Six teams had served as minister and deputy in Finance from 1968 to 1979: Edgar Benson and Robert Bryce, Edgar Benson and Simon Reisman, John Turner and Simon Reisman, John Turner and Tommy Shoyama, Donald Macdonald and Tommy Shoyama, and Jean Chrétien and Tommy Shoyama. Colin Campbell discusses the relationship between Trudeau and the Department of Finance in *Governments Under Stress*, pp. 158–63.

13. Whatever misgivings the Trudeauites may have had originally about Finance's power, by the early 1980s the direction of institutional reform was towards a reinforcement of the department's authority not only in setting the broad fiscal framework, but in specific policy areas such as the social field. Gillespie, "Department of Finance and PEMS," and Van Loon, "Policy and Expenditure Management."

   Details of Ian Stewart's career are derived from interviews with him on July 11 and 19, 1984, and from Collison, "Economist with Trudeau's Ear" and "Ottawa's Policy Entrepreneurs."

14. Stewart in PCO: C. Campbell and Szablowski, *Super-Bureaucrats*, and French, *How Ottawa Decides*, p. 68.

   Stewart's paper on the post-controls Canada, *The Way Ahead* (published as a federal government document), was the subject of considerable controversy even among active Liberals. Logan, *Way Ahead*.

15. Soaring interest rates: In early August, the Canadian dollar hit a fifty-year low of 80.31 cents U.S. In response, the Bank of Canada interest rate reached a peak in late summer of 21.24 per cent, with the prime lending rate of chartered banks reaching

22.75 per cent and five-year mortgage rates at 21.75 per cent. "Dollar Still Rising," *Globe and Mail* (Nov. 18, 1981), p. B1; and Canada, Department of Finance, *Budget in More Detail*, p. 11.

16. Keltic Lodge: Authors' interviews with Robert Rabinovitch, Jan. 25, 1991, and Ian Stewart, July 19, 1984; McQuaig, *Behind Closed Doors*, p. 217.

17. Stewart's solution: I. Stewart, "Post-Keynesian World."

"Tax expenditures": In its December 1979 budget, the federal Department of Finance estimated that the revenue forgone in the fiscal year 1980–81 as a result of discretionary changes to the tax system since 1972 totalled $8.89 billion. Wolfe, "Politics of the Deficit," p. 120. Also Maslove, "Tax Expenditure," p. 248.

18. Reason to be pleased: When Simon Reisman briefed a group of businessmen about the 1981 budget and told them that, though loopholes were being closed, their tax rate would fall from 65 to 50 per cent, there was a big guffaw. "Who pays taxes?" came the query from an audience affluent enough to employ accountants who could find loopholes enough to reduce their taxes to zero. Confidential interview, Aug. 1989.

The revenue loss of $1.3 billion from lowering the top tax rate was to be offset by gains of $2.1 billion from eliminating tax expenditures. Gillespie, *Tax, Borrow and Spend*, p. 197.

On debt reduction as the chief goal of the 1981 budget: Wolfe, "Politics, the Deficit and Tax Reform," and Gillespie, "1981 Federal Budget." The decision to reduce taxes only for a minority of Canadians in the upper-income brackets was dictated by the two real goals of tax reform, a supply-side lowering of marginal tax rates and deficit reduction. Doern, "Liberal Priorities," pp. 8–10.

19. "Old smoothie": Pearson, *Mike*, vol. 3, p. 97.

20. This story in Graham, *One-Eyed Kings*, p. 108, was confirmed by the authors' interview with Michael Pitfield, Dec. 9, 1989.

21. Tax-based income policy: Donner and Peters, *Monetarist Counter-Revolution*, pp. 46–48.

Big players: Galbraith, *Economics and the Public Purpose*, ch. 3.

22. Directorship of the tax-policy section: Authors' interview with Ed Neufeld, Jan. 25, 1988.

Failed to consult: Authors' interview with Ed Clark and George Tough, July 3, 1984.

23. In the furore following the release of the budget, much was made of the fact that one of Stewart's key advisers was Osgoode Hall professor Neil Brooks. "Brooks has no 'business' experience except for acting as an adviser to groups (mostly government-financed) attacking the tax system. He is on record as having said that business has too much of a voice in tax policy-making." Arthur Drache, "What Really Went Wrong Inside Finance," *Financial Post* (Dec. 19, 1981), pp. 1, 2.

John Bulloch's small-business lobby group, the Canadian Federation of Independent Business, counted 163 tax changes that business would have to cope with in their paperwork. Baetz, "Canadian Federation of Independent Business," p. 347.

24. A number of commentators noted the philosophical similarities between the MacEachen budget and the Reagan tax reforms. "Taking a page out of President Reagan's economics textbook, he has lowered [the wealthy's] tax rates at the same

time as he has taken away their tax shelters." Richard Gwyn, "The Very Rich Look at the Budget and Chortle," Ottawa *Citizen* (Nov. 24, 1981), p. 8. In *Maclean's* John Hay offered an only slightly different interpretation: "Unlike Reagan, MacEachen took care to give his tax cuts the appearance of justice . . . Where Reagan's favoured the very rich, MacEachen's are aimed further down the scale." Hay, "Budget '81."

25. "Hoops": Authors' interview with Robert Rabinovitch, Mar. 24, 1993.

26. "Coalition of losers": Authors' interview with Robert Rabinovitch, Nov. 26, 1986.

27. Keynesians' view: At the infamous seven-course lunch he hosted for journalists to explain his austerity budget, Allan MacEachen distanced himself from Keynesianism: Keynes's "models and his analysis were built in situations where there was a shortage of demand or spending capacity or spending potential . . . I question whether the solution to our problem is to push up the deficit a bit more to recover the economy, when the recovery is there if we let it work." Thomas Walkom, "Lavish Lunch Embarrasses Minister," *Globe and Mail* (Nov. 17, 1981), p. 9.

28. Trudeau's Vancouver speech: "Transcript" (Nov. 24, 1981), pp. 20–21.

29. Later MacEachen was to recall, in his elliptical manner, that "the vehemence with which the attack was launched is still a matter of recollection in my head." As for his colleagues, "I don't think the Liberals added to their status by failing to support the budget's liberal principles." Authors' interview, May 12, 1984.

The successive changes to the budget provisions: Gillespie, "1981 Federal Budget." There was strong pressure from business in the aftermath of the 1981 budget for an opening up of the budgetary process. R.A. Young, "Business and Budgeting."

## Chapter 9
## The Liberals Regroup: Trudeau Gets Going

1. Ostry comments: Authors' interview, Feb. 25, 1982.

   Deteriorating economic situation: The OECD report, couched in doublespeak, did not hold out much hope that the Canadian government had room for manoeuvre. "Given the current stagflationary situation, countermeasures to offset the operation of these [Keynesian] stabilizers may not be appropriate, but nor would there appear to be room for discretionary reflationary measures." OECD Economic Surveys, *Canada*, p. 43.

2. On economic indicators: *Canadian Annual Review: 1982*, pp. 103, 106, 101.

3. Minimal prior consultation: Authors' interview with Robert Johnstone, July 11, 1986.

   On MacEachen's absenteeism: Confidential interview, Nov. 1986.

4. The Margaret memoirs, *Beyond Reason* and *Consequences*, were ghosted by the English writer Caroline Moorehead.

5. Trudeau on the miracle of his children: "Frost over Canada," television interview by David Frost, broadcast by CTV, Feb. 23, 1982.

   "Trudeau Transcendent": Authors' interview with Sylvia Ostry, Feb. 25, 1982.

6. Renamed constitution: Canada, Department of Justice, *Consolidation*.

7. Banting and Simeon, *And No One Cheered*.

8. Douglas Fisher, "Worthy of Note," *Toronto Sun* (May 3, 1982), p. 11; John Gray, "Choice of Architect 'Change in Policy,' PM Tells Commons," *Globe and Mail* (Apr. 30, 1982), p. 1; "Taxpayers Footed First-Class Bill for Pitfield's Travel," *Globe and Mail* (Apr. 30, 1982), p. 3; John Gray, "Forsey Cites Attitude, Quits the Liberal Party," *Globe and Mail* (May 1, 1982), p. 11.

9. "We were at our nadir": Authors' interview with Tom Axworthy, May 20, 1984.

10. Recessions are generally defined as three successive quarters of negative growth. Since the end of World War II, Canada had not exceeded two consecutive negative-growth quarters: in 1951 with −7.0 and −2.0 per cent; in 1957 with −1.8 and −0.7 per cent; in 1970 with −0.8 and −2.0 per cent. The last two quarterly declines of 1981 (−3.5 and −2.8 per cent) were to be followed by four more consecutive shrinkages: −4.5, −4.8, −2.8, and −3.2 per cent, making the longest decline since the Great Depression. Statistics Canada and Government of Ontario.

11. Laurie's brief recommended "a cap on public service increases, say CPI minus two, as well as on indexed transfers; an adjustment to full indexation of the personal tax to take account of any erosion in our competitive position vis-à-vis the U.S.; guidelines for *federal regulatory bodies and marketing boards* on acceptable price increases which they control; and a threat to members of the business community that if they do not conform, the window of *all* government assistance programs will be closed." "The Pitfalls of Current Macroeconomic Policy and Some Alternatives" (marked "Secret," Apr. 22, 1982), p. 14. Authors' archive.

12. Axworthy's labour-market policy review was commissioned from David Dodge, whom he had known at Princeton. The report of the Task Force on Labour Market Development, called *Labour Market Development in the 1980s*, was published in July 1981, just before the onslaught of the recession, which sidelined its ambitious proposals.

13. The $400 million became the NEED program: Authors' interviews with Lloyd Axworthy, Oct. 20, 1985, and June 1, 1993; Gaetan Lussier, June 12, 1985; and David Dodge, Nov. 25, 1981; and Dodge's seminar "Labour Market Policy and Economic Growth," University of Toronto, Nov. 25, 1981.

14. New limits on Ottawa's fiscal transfers: Ottawa did not actually reduce its level of support for health and post-secondary education, although the fact that eliminating the 1972 revenue guarantee would save the federal government an estimated $5.7 billion over the period 1982–87 led the provinces to believe "the 'feds' were cutting the EPF agreement proper." Perry, "Federal-Provincial Fiscal Arrangements," p. 37. Also Canada, Department of Finance, *Fiscal Arrangements*; Canada, Parliamentary Task Force on Federal-Provincial Fiscal Arrangements, *Fiscal Federalism*, pp. 76ff; Maslove and Rubashewsky, "Cooperation and Confrontation," ch. 3.

Desire to spend: In the debate within the Liberal caucus over the direction of economic policy, Tom Axworthy and Jim Coutts also urged a shift in direction, advocating "some strategic spending as a way of bolstering the Liberal party's flagging fortunes." Deborah McGregor, "In Ottawa, a Widening Liberal Rift," *Financial Times* (May 24, 1982), p. 2.

D'Aquino pushed hard against Liberal MPs' demands for lowering interest rates and the dollar. Deborah McGregor, "In Ottawa, a Widening Liberal Rift," *Financial Times* (May 24, 1982), p. 2.

15. On Trudeau's behaviour in the Six & Five exercise: Authors' interviews with David Ablett, May 14, 1984, Mar. 26 and June 4, 1993; Nate Laurie, May 14 and 17, 1984, Aug. 1 and 2, 1989, Nov. 16, 1989, and Mar. 26, 1993; and Robert Rabinovitch, Oct. 4, 1989, Jan. 25 and Apr. 19, 1991, and Mar. 24, 1993.

16. Indexing: The social security programs that had been indexed included family allowances, old-age security, the guaranteed income supplement, veterans' pensions, and the child tax credit.

17. Social spending was not out of control; it was interest payments on the public debt that accounted for almost half the projected increase in expenditures between the November 1981 and June 1982 budgets. Maslove, "Ottawa's New Agenda," p. 12; Moscovitch, "Welfare State," p. 82. The ratio of social program expenditures to GNP declined from a peak of 22.9 per cent in 1975–76 to 20.8 per cent in 1981–82, with a reduction in transfers to persons accounting for most of this decline. Wolfe, "Politics of the Deficit," p. 120; also Calvert, *Government Limited*, p. 78.

    The Breau report noted that federal transfers to the provinces and municipalities had been "fairly constant since 1970": Canada, Parliamentary Task Force on Federal-Provincial Fiscal Arrangements, *Fiscal Federalism*, p. 33. The Economic Council agreed and pointed instead to other factors – the country's poor economic performance, the indexation of the personal income tax, and the growth of tax expenditures – as the cause of the federal deficit. Economic Council of Canada, *Financing Confederation*, p. 121.

18. On Schmidt's comment to a meeting of finance and economic ministers: Henning, *Macroeconomic Diplomacy*, p. 16.

19. "Very damaging": Trudeau, "Transcript" (May 18, 1982), pp. 8–9.

    Propping up: A fixation with the value of the Canadian dollar was misplaced, since at this time almost all other major currencies experienced a sharp decline relative to the U.S. dollar. "The Canadian dollar, far from being chronically weak, as the U.S. dollar exchange rate alone suggests, was indeed one of the world's stronger currencies during [1969–84]. Its depreciation against the U.S. dollar . . . was symptomatic of the strength of the U.S. currency . . . and not of any specific weakness in the Canadian economy." Canada, Royal Commission on the Economic Union and Development Prospects for Canada, *Report*, vol. 2, p. 323. Nevertheless, "there was a widespread belief in the foreign exchange market that the Canadian dollar was about to depreciate . . . By May 1982, this state of expectations was having a large effect on the value of the Canadian dollar." Howitt, *Monetary Policy*, p. 99.

20. Inflation: The Canadian rate was 11.6 per cent and 11.5 per cent in the first two quarters of 1982, so the differential between Canadian and American inflation rates for the first quarter of 1982 was 3.9 per cent, reaching 4.7 per cent by the second quarter. Courchene, *No Place to Stand*, table 1, p. 27.

    On U.S. policy and Bouey's adherence to it: D. Kettle, *Leadership at the Fed*, p. 185; D. Cameron, "Monetary Relations." For Tom Courchene, Bouey's policies were an explicit attempt to implement Reaganomics in Canada: "The Bank's policy was, in my view, dominated by events south of the border . . . The discipline imposed on the Americans had to be transferred to Canada, and the obvious way of doing so was . . . by tying ourselves to the U.S. dollar." *No Place to Stand*, pp. 6–7. In doing this, the Bank was undermining its own effort a decade earlier to claim more autonomy in managing Canadian monetary policy by untying the Canadian dollar from its fixed relationship with the U.S. dollar and letting it float.

21. "Awkward": Authors' interview with Gerald Bouey, July 24, 1984.

22. Miffed: Bouey had warned the Liberals in 1980 that buy-outs of foreign petroleum companies by Canadian companies responding to the NEP's incentives and the subsequent repatriation of foreign capital in 1981 would depress the Canadian dollar: Authors' interview with Gerald Bouey and colleagues, Oct. 28, 1981.

   Social pain: Perhaps the most striking indicator was the re-emergence of widespread hunger, as suggested by the proliferation of food banks. Between 1981, when the first food bank was created in Edmonton, and 1984, seventy-five food banking operations were begun. Moscovitch, "Welfare State," p. 90.

23. On Stewart, Bouey, and monetary restraint: I. Stewart, "Post-Keynesian World," p. 97; authors' interview with Stewart, July 11, 1984; and Stewart's seminar at the University of Toronto, Nov. 19, 1984.

   On the budgetary impact of the Bank's policies: Maslove, Prince, and Doern, *Federal and Provincial Budgeting*, pp. 53–54.

   Bear the brunt: Public-sector wage settlements were already trailing private settlements. Swimmer, "'Six and Five,'" p. 244. "Wage increases in the federal public-service settlements in the first quarter of this year were 11.5 per cent compared to 13.1 per cent in the private sector." Wilfred List, "Wage Curbs Could Work: Johnston," *Globe and Mail* (June 18, 1982), p. 3. "There is a widespread perception in the business community that public-sector wages are an important factor in the rapid rise in wage settlements," one secret memo to Ian Stewart said. "This perception is incorrect: public-sector wage settlements are not 'leading' the private sector. Nevertheless, the misconception remains, and there is considerable pressure from the business community for the federal government to show more restraint with respect to employee compensation."

   There *was* some evidence that wages in general were rising faster than those in other countries, particularly the United States. By the fourth quarter of 1981, wage inflation in Canada was outpacing that in the U.S. by over four percentage points, and this gap continued to widen during the first half of 1982. Courchene, *No Place to Stand*, p. 28.

   The largest rollback under Six & Five hit the lowest-paid workers. Panitch and Swartz, *Trade Union Freedoms*, p. 35. If the government really accepted the Galbraithian explanation for inflation, controlling only wages and not prices was perverse. Economic Council of Canada, *Legacies*, pp. 39–40. The inflation that continued to build during the early 1980s should have suggested that corporate concentration had something to do with rising prices. Calvert, *Government Limited*, ch. 3.

24. On old-age security and the family allowance as basic cuts, with the guaranteed income supplement and child tax credit as supplements: Banting, *Welfare State*, ch. 2. The de-indexation of the basic programs, combined with the preservation and augmentation of the targetted GIS and CTC, introduced "through the back door" a higher degree of selectivity into the welfare system, undermining the principle of universality. Moscovitch, "Welfare State," pp. 83–85.

   The trade-off between cutbacks to universal social programs and job creation measures seems more of a capitulation on the part of the left-wing elements in the

Liberal caucus than a compromise. The spending on job creation, which was to come out of the erosion of social programs, was significantly lower compared with the funds committed by Ottawa in the 1970s, and ultimately was employed in the most partisan manner. Muszynski, "Labour Market Policy," p. 289; also Hugh Winsor, "Political Slush Funds Neither Create Jobs nor Win Elections," *Globe and Mail* (Oct. 27, 1986), p. 2.

25. Pre-budget consultations: Business and its allies had played a central role in pressing senior cabinet ministers for public-sector wage controls. Controls were "recommended" to the government by the chairman of the Royal Bank of Canada in his appearance before the House of Commons committee investigating bank profits. D. Cameron, "Wage Earners," p. 33.

    Tom d'Aquino boasted that, in the June 28 budget, the federal government "not only agreed with our advice but went even further." Middleton, "D'Aquino," p. 20. Also Bob Hepburn, "Why Ottawa Imposed Its 6 and 5 Program," *Toronto Star* (Dec. 6, 1983), p. A12.

26. First verse from "The Six & Five Song," Johnston, *Up the Hill*, p. 59.

27. Third way: "One is to control everything – and you can do it for a while until the lid jumps off. I have rejected that way. Another is to cause such abundant misery that expectations really disappear, and after enough bankruptcies, mortgage foreclosures, people going out of business and unemployment reaching again much higher records, then people will lower their expectations . . . And the third way is an exercise of national will . . . lower inflation and put ourselves in a better position to compete when the recovery comes." Trudeau, "Transcript" (July 9, 1982), pp. 13–15.

    Backed up by the PCO's staff: Authors' interview with David Ablett, Mar. 26, 1993.

28. Trudeau quote: "Transcript" (July 23, 1982), p. 19.

    Premiers: By October 1982, Ontario, Nova Scotia, New Brunswick, Newfoundland, Quebec, Saskatchewan, and British Columbia had taken steps to follow the federal lead. Within a year of the June 1982 federal budget, every province except Manitoba had instituted some form of wage restraint for public-sector workers. Panitch and Swartz, *Trade Union Freedoms*, pp. 35–40.

29. "Declaration of war": *Canadian Annual Review: 1982*, p. 133. Also Warrian, "Controls for Whom?"

    Lagging behind inflation: After 1977, "real incomes were stagnant or falling while productivity grew, albeit slowly, in both goods-producing and service sectors." Economic Council of Canada, *Legacies*, pp. 39–40.

    Interest rates: By the end of the year the bank rate stood at 10.25 per cent, compared with 21 per cent at its peak in August 1981. Howitt, *Monetary Policy*, table 13, p. 79.

30. Kid who cared: Trudeau, "The Province of Quebec at the Time of the Strike," in *Asbestos Strike*. On Trudeau's early support of the Quebec labour movement as a democratic opposition to nationalist ideology: Reginald Whitaker, "Reason, Passion and Interest," pp. 19–20.

    Alienated francophone labour leaders: Daniel Drache's introduction to Drache, *Quebec*, pp. xiii-xxv; and Saywell, *Parti Québécois*, pp. 55–67. This mutual alienation did not deter Trudeau from sending a telegram on behalf of Pelletier, Marchand, and himself to "express our feeling of solidarity" and "sympathy to your cause" during an asbestos workers' strike in Quebec a few years later. "L'Asbestos Corp. trouve étrange l'appui de Trudeau aux grévistes de Thetford," *Le Devoir* (Apr. 1, 1975), p. 3.

Whittling away: Pal, "Revision and Retreat." Also Muszynski, "Labour Market Policy," pp. 285–88; A.F. Johnson, "Agent of Policy Change," p. 624; and Moscovitch, "Welfare State."

Whitaker notes that the imposition of controls in 1975 had unintended consequences. "Wage controls finally precipitated the labour movement into close and open electoral support of the NDP, while identifying Trudeau, once of Asbestos Strike fame, as the primary enemy of the Canadian labour movement." Reginald Whitaker, "Reason, Passion and Interest," p. 26. Also M. Smith, "Canadian Labour Congress," p. 37.

31. On the advent of collective bargaining in the public service: Heron, *Canadian Labour Movement*, pp. 96–107; Craig, *Industrial Relations*, p. 229.

Towards greater autonomy: M. Smith, "Canadian Labour Congress," and Craig, *Industrial Relations*, pp. 97–98.

32. The real consequence of Six & Five was not to restrain inflation but to undermine the post-war industrial relations system. Panitch and Swartz, *Trade Union Freedoms*, ch. 3; Bercuson, "Ottawa Strikes Back"; and Swimmer, "'Six and Five.'"

33. Token consultations: "Not only do we not have tripartism, we have not even been able to develop social mechanisms which provide for effective communication among the national actors in the system." Adams, "Federal Government and Tripartism," p. 614; Giles, "Canadian Labour Congress."

34. Antipathetic: Authors' interview with Peter Warrian, Dec. 19, 1989.

"Assholes": Present for these accolades were Charles Caccia (Labour), Lloyd Axworthy (Employment), Herb Gray (Industry), John Munro (Indian Affairs), Judy Erola (Mines), Francis Fox (Communications), Hazen Argue (Wheat Board), and Bud Olson (Economic Development). "Labour Escalates Confrontation Politics."

35. No clout: Gillespie and Maslove, "Volatility and Visibility," ch. 2.

Bargaining rights: Bill C-124, the Public Sector Compensation Restraint Act introduced by Johnston in August 1982, suspended the rights of trade unions to collective bargaining for the duration of the controls period.

On the decision to "designate" the air traffic controllers: Johnston, *Up the Hill*, pp. 79–80. This move came in the wake of the increasing use of the strike weapon by federal public servants during the 1970s. Swimmer, "Changes," pp. 294–96; also Goar, "Trudeau's Capitalist," whose banner read, "Business has no better friend in the cabinet than Don Johnston. The really good news is that he seems headed for political stardom."

36. "Terrible summer of 1982": Authors' interview with Monique Bégin, Mar. 21, 1986.

# Chapter 10
# Restructuring Government, Inc.

1. On the mood in Trudeau's circle: Authors' interviews with Robert Rabinovitch, Jan. 25, 1991; David Ablett, Mar. 26, 1993; Alan Nymark, Apr. 20, 1993; and Tom Axworthy, May 1, May 18, and July 11, 1984.
2. On Lumley at FIRA: Jenkins, "Canada: A Small State," p. 116.
3. On Johnston as business Liberal: Johnston, *Up the Hill*, p. 53.
    On Chrétien at EMR: Confidential interview, Jan. 1986.
4. Tackling the fisheries and the western grain transportation system represented a major reorientation of thinking by the state managers, a significant realignment of the institutional basis of their policy process, and an attempt to eliminate the huge financial strains created by the ever-growing subsidies demanded by farmers and fishermen.
    Government had pumped hundreds of millions of dollars into the fisheries. Barrett and Davis, "Floundering," p. 125. The proposal to rescue the troubled fish companies made by LeBlanc and his DFO officials in 1981 was considered "the ultimate madness" by the PCO, not just because it would be costly but because it favoured the small, inshore fishermen over the big, integrated fish-processing companies who were now lobbying hard against the DFO. Royce, "Creating Troubled Waters," pp. 40–41; and Pross and McCorquodale, *Economic Resurgence*, pp. 68, 80–81. In an astonishing internal putsch that put the DFO in a kind of trusteeship, Pitfield had Michael Kirby charged with an independent task force to study the crisis and recommend action to a special committee of cabinet dominated by business Liberals. The task force report was the basis for shifting federal policy away from maximizing employment in the "social fishery" to favouring economic viability. Canada, Task Force on Atlantic Fisheries, *Navigating Troubled Waters*.
    The cost to Ottawa of maintaining the railways' guaranteed "Crow Rate" for grain shipments had amounted to $1 billion over the 1970s. Gilson, "Quid Pro Crow," p. 5. The Pepin-Kroeger project to eliminate the statutory basis for the Crow was daring because it incurred the wrath of powerful farm organizations in both the west and Quebec (Skogstad, *Agricultural Policy-Making*, p. 140), but Pepin viewed the proposed $20-billion reconstruction of the transportation system as a new industrial strategy for the west. Authors' interview with Jean-Luc Pepin, Nov. 28, 1986.
5. Unemployment: *Canadian News Facts* 16, no. 16 (Sept. 19, 1982), p. 2749.
    Agri-food strategy: *Challenge for Growth: An Agri-food Strategy for Canada* had been approved by cabinet, but Whelan was not effective in getting support from his colleagues for the money needed to achieve a major reorientation of Canadian agriculture. Authors' interviews with J.P. Connell, June 10, 1985, and Gaetan Lussier, June 12, 1985; and letter to the authors from J.P. Connell, July 31, 1985.
6. Merger mania: There had been more mergers in the period 1969–80 than in the previous seventy years, and 1982 was to produce another record. Linda McQuaig, "Corporate Mergers Increasing in Canada," *Globe and Mail* (May 5, 1984), p. 20. Apart from a bill to clean up the most unacceptable business practices, such as fraud,

the corporate community objected so vociferously and effectively to all proposals to tackle corporate concentration in the economy that the five other bills put forward by the previous nine ministers of consumer and corporate affairs from 1968 to 1979 had been stymied. Brecher, *Competition Policy*, p. 52.

Acid rain: Clarkson, *Canada and the Reagan Challenge*, pp. 183–203, 345–46.

The make-up of the Priorities and Planning Committee of cabinet showed that it still had a significant left-nationalist contingent. Herb Gray, Roméo LeBlanc, John Roberts, Lloyd Axworthy, and Jack Austin might not outnumber Jean Chrétien, Gerry Regan, Yvon Pinard, Don Johnston, Judy Erola – and Marc Lalonde and Allan MacEachen in their new incarnations – on P&P, but their presence would be felt in several crucial jousts that lay ahead. "Release," p. 4. Hay, "Little Shuffle," p. 13.

7. "Dangerous statist": Charlotte Montgomery, "Ottawa's Economic Policy to Continue, Lalonde Says," *Globe and Mail* (Sept. 11, 1982), p. 2.

8. Lalonde's reputation: Authors' interviews with Peter Lougheed and Merv Leitch, June 4, 1986.

9. "I needed to re-establish": Authors' interview with Marc Lalonde, May 31, 1985. "Fundamentally": Anderson, "Oil War," p. 43.

10. "On the road": Authors' interviews with Marc Lalonde, May 31 and Dec. 18, 1985.

11. Restored to primacy: Authors' interview with Marc Lalonde, May 31, 1985.

Stewart, whom Lalonde respected, was allowed to save face by announcing that he had asked to be relieved of his post. In his letter, Stewart gallantly defended the competence and integrity of the public service in general and his own department in particular by accepting personal responsibility for the "advice" to the minister and cabinet that had resulted in the November 12, 1981, budget. James Rusk, "PM's Top Economic Adviser Resigns," *Globe and Mail* (Oct. 22, 1982), p. 1.

12. "The kind of guy": "Cohen's Appointment Praised by Business," *Globe and Mail* (Oct. 23, 1982), p. 11.

13. On Pitfield as stimulus to the BCNI: A 1976 article by the clerk of the Privy Council concluded with the provocative suggestion that the key issue of the 1980s would be government growth, and the possible threat that such expansion posed to the very existence of the private-enterprise economy. Pitfield, "Shape of Government."

14. On the raison d'être of the BCNI: Langille, "Business Council on National Issues"; Doern and Phidd, *Canadian Public Policy*, p. 425; and Gillies, *Where Business Fails*, p. 72.

15. On bank presidents and baby bonuses: There were only a dozen or so bank presidents in the whole country; most of them were deep into middle age and their children were well past the baby bonus stage. But even if each president was succouring ten squalling infants and was paid by the state for the privilege, the total expenditure involved would add so little to the national deficit (and would be taxed back in any case because of their high income) that number-crunchers would write it off as inconsequential.

16. On BCNI's approach: Langille, "Business Council on National Issues," pp. 54–55.

17. "Scrapped": Ann Silversides, "Lalonde Speech Received Favorably," *Globe and Mail* (Oct. 28, 1982), p. B6. The government's retreat from the tax equity philosophy embraced in MacEachen's 1981 budget had taken place in three stages: MacEachen's immediate modifications of Dec. 18, 1981, his Six & Five budget of June 28, 1982,

and Lalonde's statement of October 27, 1982. Gillespie, *Tax, Borrow and Spend*, p. 199.

18. Three speeches: Trudeau, "Prime Minister's Broadcasts" (Oct. 19, 20, 21, 1982), pp. 1–3. Authors' interviews with Allan Nymark, Apr. 20, 1993; and David Ablett, Mar. 26 and June 4, 1993.

19. Fired off: Clarkson, *Canada and the Reagan Challenge*, pp. 42–49.

20. On Haig's replacement by Shultz: Schieffer and Gates, *Acting President*, p. 139.

21. Bilateral issues: *Canadian Annual Review: 1984*, pp. 145–57.

22. Reston, "Talk with Trudeau."

   Visitation to Ottawa: Sun Oil, du Pont, Quaker Oats, Standard Oil, Gillette, Procter & Gamble, and American Express were among the corporations who sent their presidents or chairmen to check out whether Canada was still safe for capitalism. James Rusk, "FIRA to be Revised, U.S. Executives Told," *Globe and Mail* (Oct. 21, 1982), p. 1.

   Lapdog: Canadian Club of Chicago, Jan. 28, 1983, authors' notes.

23. "Wasn't wildly keen": Authors' interview with Michael Pitfield, Jan. 13, 1990.

24. "I was asked": Authors' interview with Michael Pitfield, Jan. 13, 1990.

25. Tailored to the personality: The "agencies of the government of Canada and the key individuals who operate them reflect the preferences of one man to a degree usually attained only in one-party regimes." C. Campbell, *Governments Under Stress*, p. 99. Also Aucoin, "Organizational Change," pp. 3, 6–17.

26. On insiders' view of Pitfield: Authors' interviews with Michael Kirby, Feb. 26, 1986; James Coutts, May 9, 1984; and Tom Axworthy, July 11, 1984.

27. On the Program and Expenditure Management System: Borins, "Ottawa's Expenditure Envelopes," pp. 72–73; Aucoin, "Organizational Change," p. 12; and Doern and Phidd, *Canadian Public Policy*, pp. 266–70.

   One indicator of the envelope system's success in controlling expenditures was its maintenance by the Mulroney government. Doern, Maslove, and Prince, *Public Budgeting in Canada*, pp. 119–26.

28. Rompkey disempowered: In retaliation for complaining against him to Pitfield, the deputy minister launched an audit of the fishermen in Rompkey's riding. Authors' interview with David Smith, May 17, 1984.

   On Lloyd Axworthy's free-wheeling approach to administration: By August 1983 he had one hundred people working for him in his ministerial offices in Ottawa and Winnipeg. Bakvis, *Regional Ministers*, p. 191. Axworthy even challenged bureaucrats in another minister's department by instructing his immigration officials in Latin America to be more receptive to applications from political refugees than External Affairs officials wanted them to be. Authors' interview with Meyer Brownstone, June 2, 1994.

29. "Manipulator": Authors' interview with Douglas Hartle, Oct. 24, 1989.

30. "Lowly assistant": Authors' interview with Allan Gotlieb, Aug. 4, 1986.

   18.5 kilograms: Authors' interview with Donald Tansley, Nov. 19, 1985.

31. National interest: Authors' interview with Michael Pitfield, Jan. 13, 1990.

   "You did what you could": Confidential interview, July 1985. Morgan describes the morale problems and organizational contradictions of the civil service in *Nowhere to Go* and *Implosion*.

32. "Whiz kids": Authors' interview with Eugene Forsey, Nov. 29, 1986.
33. Irrationally complex: Authors' interview with Allan Gotlieb, Aug. 4, 1986.
34. Cover story: McCall-Newman, "Michael Pitfield."
    "My right arm": Authors' interview with Michael Pitfield, Jan. 13, 1990.

## Chapter 11
## The Last Liberal Optimist Defends the Cause

1. Axworthy's memo concluded on the need for an activist role for government with an improved welfare system, more surveillance of the private sector, profit-sharing to give workers a higher stake in their firms, more federal entrepreneurial activity in resources (Petro-Canada providing the model), more security for the aged, and a dynamic foreign policy: in short, "a new phase of reform-Liberalism." T. Axworthy, "Liberalism, Neo-Conservatism, and the Challenges of the 80's" (Sept. 27, 1979), pp. 11–13. Authors' archive.
    "Right-wing tide": Authors' interview with Tom Axworthy, July 11, 1984.
2. On British Liberalism since the Great War: Dangerfield, Strange Death, foreword; and since World War II: Dutton, "Brink of Oblivion."
    On European Liberal parties' anti-collectivism: Bolkestein, Modern Liberalism, pp. 255–78; and von Hayek-like laissez-faire: J.H. MacCallum Scott, Experiment in Internationalism, pp. 49ff.
    Liberal International: Authors' interview with Lorna Marsden, July 1, 1993.
3. On Mitterrand's economic orthodoxies: Fonteneau and Muet, La gauche, chs. 1, 2; Friend, Seven Years, pp. 104–8; Hall, Governing the Economy, ch. 8; and Ritchie, "France," pp. 25–26.
4. Thatcher's fierce attack: H. Young, One of Us, chs. 9, 11, 12.
5. Democrats had no answers: Galbraith, Who Needs the Democrats, pp. 8, 29, 47.
6. Negative connotations: On the left, see Beiner's description of privatized, anti-political liberal society's moral emptiness. "We are barbarized by an empty public culture, intimidated by bureaucracies, numbed into passivity by absence of opportunity for meaningful deliberation, inflated by absurd consumption, stripped of dignity by a way of living that exceeds a human scale." What's the Matter, p. 34. For a conservative demolition of liberalism, see Pangle, Ennobling of Democracy, p. 180, where university education is described in terms of "corrosive intellectual and moral fashions that pervade the academic élite and seek vents through every college classroom."
    Liberalism was even blamed by the McGill, then Harvard professor Ruth Wisse for betraying the Jews, in If I Am Not for Myself. Rights-based individualist liberalism, renamed atomism, is attacked by Charles Taylor as anarchist in "Atomism."
    For samples of the vast literature of American social criticism: Lasch, Culture of Narcissism and Haven in a Heartless World.
7. On the evolution of Canada's liberal ethic as traced through its policies: Manzer, Public Policies.
8. Not nearly leftward enough: J. Laxer and R. Laxer, Liberal Idea, ch. 3.
9. Losing their electoral alliance: According to the Tories' pollster, Allan Gregg, fewer

voters identified themselves as Liberal than as Conservative after the recession of 1981–82 – a historic shift in the Canadian electorate. Authors' interview with Allan Gregg, Oct. 31, 1984.

10. On how Trudeau's handlers obsessed about his public presentation: P. Gossage, *Close to the Charisma*, pp. 109–30.

11. "Political central agency": Tom Axworthy, "The Strategic Prime Ministership," seminar at University of Toronto, Jan. 14, 1985; and authors' interview with Tom Axworthy, Jan. 23, 1986.

12. Western provinces dead set against them: Federally, D.E. Smith, *Regional Decline*; and provincially, in Saskatchewan, Wilson, *Politics of Defeat*.

    Government largesse: "The party system remained an . . . alternative means of redistributing resources from centre to periphery . . . [since] the Maritime provinces have become increasingly dependent on federal monies." Bickerton, "Party System," p. 470.

    Volatile voters: H. Clarke et al., *Absent Mandate*, pp. 174–83. The same phenomenon had emerged in Britain, where there was no longer a loyal following for any party, the electorate having become completely volatile. Clemens, *Polls, Politics and Populism*, pp. 182–83.

13. On the role of business in financing the party in the King–St. Laurent era: Reginald Whitaker, *Government Party*, pp. 74–77, 102–11, 121–28, 162–64, 196–201, 287–88.

    The election expense legislation of 1974 had opened up the raising of funds to public scrutiny, put controls on election spending, set up quite effective limits on political advertising, and introduced handsome public subsidies for parties and their candidates. The number of corporate donors to the Conservatives had outnumbered corporate donors to the Liberals since 1977; by 1983 the figures were 18,067 and 7,536, respectively. The Tories had also surpassed the Grits since 1977 in individual donors, the figures for 1983 rising to 99,264 compared with 33,649. W.T. Stanbury, "Mother's Milk," pp. 804, 807.

14. Suffocated creativity: Such stalemate characterized an effort made by the Grindstone Group to rethink the party's economic policies and set up a Liberal policy institute by holding at Mont Sainte-Marie, in the Laurentians, a weekend colloquium of some fifty intellectuals (along with a young officer from the U.S. embassy), Nov. 16-18, 1980. Authors' notes.

15. "Only way to go is up!": Tom Axworthy to Christina McCall, Sept. 25, 1981.

16. "Real action": Authors' interview with James Fleming, Jan. 15, 1986.

17. "Best man": Authors' interview with Ed Lumley, June 24, 1986. How masterful Trudeau had been in presiding over cabinet became clear to his colleagues only in the next ministry: "It was a shock to all of us to see John Turner in action: he was so loose." Authors' interview with Gerald Regan, Nov. 26, 1986.

18. Information on cabinet politics: Various confidential interviews with members of the Trudeau government.

19. On Bégin and Joyal's revolt: Iain Hunter, "PM Shrugs Off Caucus Wrath," Ottawa *Citizen* (Feb. 10, 1982), p. 1; and Ben Tierney, "PM Warns He'll Lower Boom If Any More Public Criticism," Ottawa *Citizen* (Feb. 12, 1982), p. 4.

20. "Stay out of trouble": Authors' interview with James Fleming, Jan. 15, 1986.

21. Threat to Keith Davey: At the time of the Restoration, the Liberals had established

the Canadian Media Corporation as the agency of record that bought space and time for government advertising. Three of the four owners of CMC were the agencies (Vickers & Benson and Ronalds-Reynolds of Toronto, and BCP of Montreal) that had created the Liberals' advertising for the 1980 campaign. That these were large-L Liberal firms was confirmed by the fact that they had each contributed to the Liberal Party in 1979 but had given the Conservatives no donations. Another Liberal agency, MacLaren's, went on to get the constitutional advertising campaign. Within a year of the 1980 election the three Toronto agencies making up Red Leaf Communications were sharing $12 million in government contracts. Keith Davey had more than just a partisan interest in keeping control over the government's rich advertising patronage: he was president of Analytical Communications Inc. and Associates, the public relations arm of Vickers & Benson. On the Liberal ad agency network: "Davey Joins V&B's ACI"; Smyka, "Liberals Axe MBS": Smyka, "Four-Agency Consortium"; and "Liberal AOR System." Contracts to MacLaren's and the Red Leaf Communications agencies: Smyka, "Feds Turn $8m Spotlight"; and "Goodis Lauds Merit as Criterion for Landing Ottawa's Business," *Globe and Mail* (Feb. 4, 1981), p. B4.

22. "Trust me, Jim": Letter to the authors from James Fleming, Feb. 2, 1986.
23. Almost all the Quebeckers still described themselves as Roman Catholics, and adherents to that faith by then equalled the combined number of Protestants and Anglicans among the MPs from the other provinces. Among MPs from outside Quebec, a growing proportion were Roman Catholics: in 1951, 20 of 125 MPs declared themselves to be RC, compared with 33 of 82 MPs in 1982. *Canadian Parliamentary Guide*, 1951 and 1982.
24. Unsung ombudsmen: Constituency work took, on average, 68 per cent of the backbenchers' time, loading, in Mark MacGuigan's experience, about 3,000 cases per year on his Windsor riding office and 2,500 on his House of Commons office. Richard Price, "Representation by Members of Parliament," seminar presented at the University of Toronto, Dec. 4, 1989; and Tower, "Put Power Back."

    Harried stints: The 1968 expansion of the standing committees' functions led to the backbenchers' being organized in "flying squads" to keep a numerical majority of Liberals on each committee as it held hearings on government bills. Rick Van Loon commented wryly, "We can assume that any Government will continue to strengthen the committee system because it wastes so well the talents of MPs." "The Frustrating Role of Ottawa Backbenchers," *Globe and Mail* (Apr. 5, 1971), p. 7; also John Stewart, "Reform of House of Commons Committee System," seminar presented at the University of Toronto, Oct. 6, 1986. Committees in 1980–81 heard 3,326 witnesses: Pross, "Parliamentary Influence," p. 260.
25. Wasted: Authors' interview with Pierre Deniger, Dec. 18, 1985. Breau's diligence in producing his report, *Fiscal Federalism in Canada*, was not entirely unproductive: he was briefly a minister in 1984 after Trudeau elevated LeBlanc to the Senate.
26. "Fan out": Confidential interview with a member of the Liberal caucus, kindly provided by Paul Thomas from his research material for "National Party Caucuses."
27. "As good a reading": Authors' interview with Tom Axworthy, Jan. 14, 1985.
28. Six & Five exercise: Thomas, "National Party Caucuses," p. 108.
29. First among unequals: Canadian political science has been reluctant to admit that the prime minister's power massively outweighs that of his allegedly equal colleagues

around the cabinet table. Although Fred Schindeler ("The Prime Minister and the Cabinet") has argued that the prime ministership under Pierre Trudeau achieved a new stage of dominance through the expansion of the PMO and PCO, and Denis Smith ("President and Parliament") has pointed out that the Canadian is more powerful than the British PM because of being selected by a party convention rather than by parliamentarians, the discipline's main texts on the subject – *The Prime Minister in Canadian Government and Politics* by Punnett and *The Prime Minister and the Cabinet* by Matheson – espouse the traditional view that the centre of power is the cabinet, whose leader is constrained within the parliamentary system.

On Trudeau in caucus: Authors' interview with David Collenette, July 15, 1985.

30. Done well by parliamentarians: The reforms Trudeau brought about included the election of caucus committee chairs by the MPs, rather than their appointment by the prime minister, and the creation of a caucus research bureau: Thomas, "National Party Caucuses," p. 87. A contemporary judgement was that "he has done more than any prime minister for years to assist his backbenchers." Anthony Westell, "Trudeau Helps to Increase Influence of Backbenchers," *Toronto Star* (Apr. 16, 1970), p. 10. For a partisan overview of Trudeau's reforms: Marsden, "Party and Parliament," pp. 263–67.

31. "I made sure" and "In response to complaints": Authors' interview with Pierre Trudeau, July 21, 1979.

32. On morale in the Quebec caucus: Authors' interviews with Warren Allmand, Mar. 23, 1986; Monique Bégin, June 14, 1984; Rémi Bujold, Oct. 9, 1985; Pierre Bussières, Mar. 17, 1986; Dennis Dawson, Apr. 6, 1986; Pierre Deniger, Dec. 18, 1985; and Louis Duclos, Mar. 18, 1986.

33. On Marchand's assault on Créditiste ridings and Lalonde's power in caucus: Bakvis, *Regional Ministers*, pp. 103, 268–70.

34. On Lalonde's authoritarianism: Authors' interview with Louis Duclos, Sept. 28, 1993, and other confidential interviews.

35. Axworthy and LeBlanc's weak relations with their provincial parties: Bakvis, *Regional Ministers*, pp. 233 and 98.

MacEachen's role: "MacEachen, for his part, never built up a powerful Nova Scotia base as Nova Scotia lieutenants before him had done, in spite of being a Nova Scotia MP for over twenty years. The Liberals did not win more than two of the eleven or twelve federal seats in Nova Scotia in any election between 1958 and 1978, except for 1963, when they won five." Wearing, *L-Shaped Party*, p. 95.

Jimmy Gardiner: Ward and Smith, *Relentless Liberal*.

36. Favourite stratagem: Authors' interview with Dennis Dawson, Apr. 24, 1986.

37. For the perks (and scams) enjoyed by MPs in the strange world of the House of Commons: S. Cameron, *Ottawa Inside Out*, ch. 6, and Woods, *Sauvé*, ch. 8.

38. "Giant among pygmies": Authors' interview with Charles Caccia, June 18, 1981, while still a backbencher, before he was elevated to the cabinet.

## Chapter 12
## The Grits Gather in Convention and Contention

1. Liberal loyalists: For one thing, they were the prime source of party candidates and its core support. As local opinion leaders, they could be counted on to discuss the government's performance in their communities – positively if they felt connected to the Liberal centre, negatively if they were disaffected. Even this late in the Trudeau era, some of them still had fresh policy energy unconstrained by the bureaucratically imposed caution that infected the cabinet and caucus.

2. "Subjective reason": Authors' interview with Pierre Trudeau, July 21, 1979.

    "Directly into the decision-making processes": Trudeau, "Excerpts from Public Statements" (Mar. 14, 1968), p. 7. Authors' archive.

    "Real, organic power": Trudeau, "Notes for the Prime Minister's Address" (Nov. 10, 1968), pp. 3–5.

    Encouraged: Trudeau had told the party policy chair, Allen Linden, that he hoped the party would start with a clean slate and work out its policies from first principles, asking such basic questions as whether Canada should belong to NATO, and whether the CPR should be nationalized or the CBC privatized. Linden, "Memorandum: Liberal Federation of Canada," report of conversation on Oct. 26, 1968. Authors' archive.

    "Modern mass party": R.J. Stanbury, *Liberal Party*, pp. 41–42.

3. "Shock the nation": Allen Linden, "Memorandum: Liberal Federation of Canada," report of conversation on Oct. 26, 1968, pp. 2–3. Authors' archive.

    Most ambitious: D.E. Smith, *Regional Decline*, p. 72.

4. "Society's radar": Trudeau, "Notes for Remarks" (Nov. 21, 1969), p. 4.

    "Policy is for nuts": Authors' confidential interview with the president of a Liberal riding association in Toronto, Jan. 1971.

5. "Who the fuck?" and "We've been had": Authors' interview with Allen Linden, May 16, 1972.

6. Insulted: During a meeting with eight disenchanted Liberals on May 14, 1973, Trudeau asked a challenger, "What about Harold Laski?" implying that the activists' hopes, which Trudeau had himself raised, of having their prime minister accept their policies were as futile as Laski's failed attempts to get British prime minister Clement Attlee to follow the Labour Party's dictates. Authors' notes.

    "Gives a damn": Clarkson, "Feedback from Active Liberals: Survey of 1000 Most Prominent Members of the Liberal Party in Ontario," July 1973, p. 29. Authors' archive. The failure of the participatory effort: Clarkson, "Democracy in the Liberal Party."

7. Details of Marsden's life: Authors' interviews with Lorna Marsden, Oct. 30, 1978, Mar. 3, 1979, Sept. 16, 1982, and Oct. 30, 1984.

8. Publish: Marsden, *Population Probe*; Marsden and Harvey, *Canadian Population Concerns* and *Fragile Federation*.

    The usual marital arrangement: This was shrewdly discussed by the literary critic

Carolyn Heilbrun under her pseudonym, Amanda Cross, when she wrote that academic wives play the role of barely acknowledged but crucially important assistant, "often to an extent unknown or unsuspected . . . Queenie Leavis, the wife of that most terrifying and influential critic of his time, F.R. Leavis, admitted in an interview years after his death that she had done all the research for his famous books and written the greater part of them." *Players Come Again*, p. 65.

9. "Acts like a man": Confidential interview.

10. Ridiculed: [McCall] Newman, "What's So Funny."

11. On radical feminists: Smillie, "Judy Rebick."

   On the radical (compared with liberal) feminist wave: Bashevkin, *Toeing the Lines*, ch. 1.

12. The way for women: Marsden, "Political Women in Canada."

   "Her feminist friends": Authors' interview with Lynn McDonald, Sept. 16, 1982.

   "Typical of those": Authors' interview with Lorna Marsden, Apr. 19, 1979.

13. Academic disdain: In Canadian social science the quality and quantity of scholarship on political parties varied inversely with their size and significance. Compared with the many volumes about the already defunct Social Credit Party of Alberta, there was by the mid-1970s only one substantial work – Reginald Whitaker's *The Government Party* – on the Liberal Party of Canada.

   "Sound of his own voice": Authors' interview with Bernard Ostry, May 13, 1979.

14. Turnover rate: Only 17 per cent of all the delegates at the 1978 convention had attended three previous party conventions. Clarkson, "1978 Convention, Liberal Party of Canada; Report of Perlin/Clarkson Survey" (1978), p. 4. Authors' archive.

   By the hundreds: The 3,500 delegates at the 1978 Liberal Party convention "debated" 1,100 resolutions. Marsden, "Party and Parliament," p. 275.

15. Moved the crucial motion: Authors' interview with Vincent Borg, Jan. 7, 1980.

16. Acknowledged backroom broker: Gray, "New Backroom Girls," p. 69.

   How brutal: Jackie Smith, "Aideen Nicholson, Stalwart Liberal," *Toronto Star* (Sept. 10, 1984), p. C1.

17. Document describing actions: "Report on 1980 Resolutions."

   Details on Marsden's activities: Marsden and Bujold, "Report of the Steering Committee."

18. Roused by the controversy: Authors' interviews with Lorna Marsden, Sept. 16, 1982; Helen Wilson, Feb. 15, 18, and 22, 1982; and Judy Erola, May 24, 1984. Also Collins, "Which Way to Ottawa?" and Kome, *Taking of Twenty-Eight*.

   Wording: For the lawyer Mary Eberts, who took many cases about women's rights to the Supreme Court on behalf of LEAF, the Legal Education and Action Fund, the improvements made in the charter's section 15 on equality rights were particularly valuable. Eberts, "Court and Its Leadership."

19. Weak position: "It's simply a power differential and a voluntary organization will always lack clout." Memorandum from Lorna Marsden to Greg Schmidt, President's Committee for Reform of the LPC (Aug. 10, 1983), p. 6. Authors' archive.

20. On the Carleton conference: Doucet, *Confessions*, p. 27.

   On the Faulkner-Coutts exchange: Authors' notes, June 7, 1981.

21. Outraged letter: Ben Tierney, "Capital Accounts," Ottawa *Citizen* (Jan. 16, 1982), p. 4.
22. Racking her brains: Authors' interview with Lorna Marsden, Sept. 16, 1982.
23. Debt: Bob Hepburn, "Campagnolo Promises Liberal Revival, Reform," *Toronto Star* (Nov. 8, 1982), p. A1.
    Lalonde's telephoning: Authors' interview with Iona Campagnolo, May 17, 1984.
24. Resolution 40: "Priority Resolutions."
    Iron law of oligarchy: Michels, *Political Parties*, part VI, ch. 2.
25. Stalking-horse: Authors' interview with Peter Donolo, Dec. 18, 1985.
26. On Turner's convention behaviour: Authors' notes, Nov. 6-7, 1982.
27. "Greatest success story": Trudeau, "Prime Minister's Remarks" (Nov. 7, 1982), p. 4; and John Gray, "Liberals Cheer, Applaud on Cue but Old Fire Missing," *Globe and Mail* (Nov. 8, 1982), p. 9.
    "Bursting with ideas": Trudeau, "Notes for Remarks" (Nov. 5, 1982), pp. 1, 9.
    Regional meetings: Trudeau had made appearances earlier that year at policy meetings held in Banff (June), Kingston (July), and Quebec (October), and at the platform committee (September), leading Jim Coutts to claim that Trudeau paid more attention to his party than had Lester Pearson. Seminar at the University of Toronto, Nov. 10, 1986.
28. Rebuff to Lalonde: "'The party sent a signal not to abandon the principle of universality, and I'm a good party man,' he told the Post." Giles Gherson and Deborah Dowling, "Concern over Debt Overshadows Liberal 'Summit,'" *Financial Post* (Nov. 13, 1982), p. 5.
    PMO strategy on Apps: Authors' interview with Keith Davey, Nov. 6, 1982.
29. Apps's resolution was one of only thirty-two resolutions that were actually debated in plenary session; the other forty-nine were passed without debate. Authors' notes, Nov. 6, 1982.
30. Transition to older age: Levinson et al., *Seasons of a Man's Life*, p. 34.
    "Who knows?" Trudeau, "Frost over Canada," television interview by David Frost, broadcast by CTV, Feb. 23, 1982.
31. Public support for patriation package: A Gallup poll reported in *La Presse* on June 19, 1982, revealed that 49 per cent of Quebeckers felt the 1982 constitution was a good thing, compared with 16 per cent who thought the opposite. Dion, "La sécession du Québec," p. 8.
32. *P'tit coq*: Authors' interview with Jean-Luc Pepin, Nov. 28, 1986.
33. On the Axworthy-Trudeau relationship: Authors' interviews with Tom Axworthy, July 11, 1984; Keith Mitchell, May 29, 1986; Heather Peterson, July 12, 1979; and Robert Rabinovitch, Nov. 26, 1986.
34. "What's in it for you guys?" Authors' interviews with Keith Davey, July 9, 1974; and Jerry Grafstein, July 12, 1974.
    "Foxy": Authors' interview with Pierre Trudeau, Sept. 27, 1978.
35. Political solution: Munro, "Crow's Nest," p. 106, and authors' interviews with Hazen Argue, Nov. 27, 1986; Lloyd Axworthy, Oct. 28, 1985; Doug Campbell, June 7, 1986; Murray Cormack, June 6, 1986; Pierre Deniger, Dec. 18, 1985; Gary Duke, May 30, 1986; Leroy Fjordbotten, June 10, 1986; Jean Garon, Mar. 18, 1986; Clay

Gilson, June 6, 1986; Ralph Goodale, June 5, 1986; Arthur Kroeger, July 17, 1984; Claude Lemelin, July 12, 1984; Gaetan Lussier, June 12, 1985; Alan Macpherson, June 2, 1986; Chris Mills, June 2, 1986; David Miller, May 22, 1986; Lorne Parker, June 7, 1986; Jean-Luc Pepin, Nov. 28, 1986; Hugh Planche, May 21, 1986; Doug Radke, June 11, 1986; Clarence Roth, June 4, 1986; Barry Wilson, July 23, 1984; and G.R. Withers, June 11, 1985.

In private hands: The consolidation of fish firms as Fishery Products International still left Ottawa holding 60 per cent, the Newfoundland government 26 per cent, and the Bank of Nova Scotia 14 per cent. Forty-seven per cent of Nova Scotia's National Sea was in private hands, and 14 per cent with the Bank of Nova Scotia, although 65 per cent of its financing came from government. Pross, "Fishery," p. 92. Michael Harris, "Fishery Deal Nets Big Dollars," *Globe and Mail* (Feb. 10, 1984), p. 10. Authors' interviews with Cy Abery, Nov. 7, 1985; Herb Breau, Jan. 13, 1986; Pierre De Bané, Nov. 14, 1985; Coline Campbell, Nov. 10, 1985; Richard Cashin, Nov. 6, 1985; Joseph Gough, July 26, 1984; Anthony Hampson, Jan. 24, 1986; Jack Hart, Nov. 4, 1985; Michael Kirby, Dec. 20, 1985; Arthur Kroeger, Nov. 21, 1985; Roméo LeBlanc, Nov. 20, 1985; Sandy MacLean, Nov. 8, 1985; David Mann, Nov. 9, 1985; A.W. May, June 11, 1985; Susan McCorquodale, Nov. 6, 1985; William Morrow, Nov. 7, 1985; Peter Nicholson, Oct. 30, 1985; Paul Pross, Nov. 8, 1985; Victor Rabinovitch, July 26, 1984, and Jan. 14, 1986; William Rompkey, Jan. 13, 1986; Gordon Slade, Nov. 7, 1985; Janet Smith, Nov. 21, 1985; Donald Tansley, Nov. 14, 1985; and Rick Williams, Nov. 10, 1985.

36. Controversial bill: The McDonald royal commission on the RCMP spy service's behaviour during and after the October Crisis of 1970 had concentrated on the "inherent contradiction" between the RCMP's role in intelligence, which led it to break laws in tracking spies or infiltrating subversive activities, and its role as the country's senior law enforcement agency. Canada, Commission of Inquiry Concerning Certain Activities of the Royal Canadian Mounted Police, *Third Report*, p. 35. Kaplan's office had drafted legislation that purported to implement McDonald's recommendations for creating a security intelligence service separated from the RCMP and accountable to Parliament, but when Bill C-157 was tabled in May 1983 it sparked an outcry from civil libertarians, the attorney general of Ontario, Roy McMurtry, and Peter Russell, the McDonald commission's research director. Littleton, *Target Nation*, p. 152.

Long-overdue: The McGill economist Irving Brecher ranked "the story of competition reform among the saddest experiences in Canadian public policy." Merger law, which was "once grossly inadequate," had been rendered a "farce" by court interpretation. Brecher, "Sad Story of Competition Reform," pp. 1, 2. Canadian business was among the most concentrated in the world. As the UBC economist William Stanbury put it, big business "had paradise. Any change in competition law was paradise lost." This meant that the reforms proposed by the Trudeau government in the decade following the Economic Council's proposals in 1969 (*Interim Report*) were seen as dangerous state intervention in the workings of the marketplace. Authors' interview with William Stanbury, May 30, 1985.

37. Film and television: Although it was not one of the strategic prime ministership's top three priorities, considerable efforts had been expended to develop a comprehensive

strategy for culture and information. Responsibility for culture and communications policies had been brought together under the Department of Communications, the forceful Pierre Juneau was made its deputy minister, and the Federal Cultural Policy Review Committee (Hébert-Appelbaum) was established to review the whole gamut of Canada's cultural policies. The committee's privatization thrust was echoed in the DOC's 1983 broadcasting policy, which was oriented to developing a branch-plant television industry. The CRTC's decisions on pay-television also continued the process of making Canadian broadcasting a conduit for American programming. Authors' interviews with Francis Fox, Dec. 17, 1985; and Pierre Juneau, June 20, 1984. Also Magder, *Canada's Hollywood*, ch. 10; and Clarkson, *Canada and the Reagan Challenge*, pp. 341–45.

Moral pressure: Clarkson, *Canada and the Reagan Challenge*, pp. 346–47.

## Chapter 13
## One More Time? The International Year of Pierre Trudeau

1. A quarter-century of travelling: From May 1948 to April 1949, he visited Germany, Austria, Czechoslovakia, Hungary, Poland, Yugoslavia, Bulgaria, Lebanon, Transjordan, Syria, Iraq, Turkey, Afghanistan, Pakistan, India, Burma, Thailand, Indo-China, China, and Japan; in 1951, "most of Africa"; in 1952, the Soviet Union; in 1955, Pakistan, India, Ceylon, Indonesia, Australia, and New Zealand; in 1957, Nigeria, Ghana, and Togo; in 1959, Japan and Vietnam; in 1960, China again. T. Axworthy, "'To Stand Not So High,'" p. 388, n. 17.

Conferences in the First, Second, and Third Worlds: Trudeau joined a delegation of left-wing economists led by Cambridge's Joan Robinson in 1952 to the Moscow Economic Conference where he was able to observe the reality of Stalin's regime. Wiles, "Soviet Economica," pp. 133–38. Also letter to the authors from Peter Wiles, Sept. 20, 1991; and interview with Morris Miller, July 23, 1991. As part of a Canadian delegation to a conference in Lahore, Pakistan, in 1954, he joined in the debates about poverty in Asia and apartheid in South Africa. Authors' interview with Frank Peers, Dec. 10, 1993. In 1955, while working in Paris on *The Asbestos Strike*, he wangled an introduction from Frank Scott to a "big-wig in the Labour Party" so he could attend the British socialists' annual conference. Djwa, *Politics of the Imagination*, p. 322. He went to West Africa with a group of Canadians for a World University Students conference in 1957. Authors' interview with Lionel Tiger, Feb. 19, 1992.

A world-view: At his press conference a few hours after winning the 1968 convention, Trudeau showed that his critique of Canada's foreign policy was clear ("based on either pre-war premises or immediate post-war premises") and that he had formulated his vision for its new direction ("complete reassessment is needed" for peacekeeping and participation in NATO). "Transcript" (Apr. 7, 1968), p. 18.

2. Public statements: Trudeau's key foreign-policy speeches had been constructed by Jean Beetz, Allan Gotlieb, and Ivan Head: "Canada and the World" (May 29, 1968);

"A Defence Policy for Canada" (Apr. 3, 1969); "The Relation of Defence Policy to Foreign Policy" (Apr. 12, 1969).

Private statements to Trudeau's supporters: In 1968 he told Al Linden, the Liberal Party's policy chairman, that in a couple of years he would be ready to "shock the nation" by asking such questions as whether Canada should "get completely out of NATO and pour all of our defence money into improving the life of our people within the country, like the Indians and the poor." Linden, "Memorandum: Liberal Federation of Canada," report of conversation on Oct. 26, 1968, pp. 2–3. Authors' archive.

3. "Providing him with policy advice: This was the first time a Canadian prime minister had appointed such an adviser to his entourage from outside the ranks of the foreign service.

Aid to francophone Africa: Canada's aid to francophone Africa increased from $10.7 million in 1967 to $195.8 million in 1984. Canadian International Development Agency, *Annual Review*, 1966 to 1986.

Affinity with Latin America: "The region was identified as a focus for Canadian foreign policy for the first time in history." Rochlin, *Discovering the Americas*, p. 71.

Sovereignty over the Northwest Passage: Kirton and Munton, "*Manhattan* Voyages," pp. 85, 91–94.

Extricate Canada: "You have no idea the pressures I'm under!" Trudeau confided to the anti-war demonstrator Claire Culhane, following her fast on Parliament Hill in 1968. Lowe, *One-Woman Army*, p. 191.

Trudeau's personal agenda: According to Head, Trudeau "knew exactly what to do with foreign policy" when he came to office. Harbron, "Canada Recognizes China," p. 2.

U.S. economic power: Interview with Jay Walz, *New York Times* (Nov. 22, 1968), cited in Radwanski, *Trudeau*, p. 182.

4. "Something to say": Cited in Thordarson, *Trudeau and Foreign Policy*, p. 73.

5. Warnings from parliamentarians and bureaucrats: The Departments of National Defence and External Affairs, SCEAND (the Standing Committee on External Affairs and National Defence), which held extensive hearings in Canada and Europe, and STAFFEUR, an interdepartmental special task force on relations with Europe, all favoured the status quo. Only "Canadian Defence – A Study" (cited in Angell, "Trudeau Doctrine," pp. 36–37), a cabinet discussion paper prepared secretly by Ivan Head, seemed to have any impact on Trudeau. Also Bland, *Administration of Defence Policy*, pp. 56–58.

Deeply divided on the issue: On the final day of cabinet's weekend-long, fiercely argued defence policy debate in 1969, with Kierans and Macdonald battling Sharp and Cadieux, one minister remarked sardonically, "By noon we were aligned and by four o'clock we were in NATO." Bothwell, *Canada and the United States*, p. 101. Trudeau announced the partial withdrawal immediately rather than informing his NATO allies via diplomatic channels. According to Mitchell Sharp, this tactical error caused lasting bad feeling towards Trudeau within the alliance. *Which Reminds Me*, p. 175.

6. Trudeau was determined: "Only the force of Pierre Trudeau's personality and his determination to deal with this matter made it possible. To him must go credit for

cutting a hoary old Gordian knot by deciding that Canada would go it alone." Andrew, *Rise and Fall*, p. 92. Also Frolic, "Trudeau Initiative," pp. 192–98.

Despite objections: Sharp, *Which Reminds Me*, pp. 203–7. In his television memoirs Trudeau says Nixon tried to dissuade him from recognizing China but did not threaten (*Memoirs*, Les Productions La Fête, broadcast by CBC-TV, episode III); in his published version he boasts of recognizing China "to the displeasure of the United States." *Memoirs*, p. 164. Trudeau had stolen the limelight from Nixon's breakthrough on China, which was "probably the most significant and prudent American foreign policy initiative since the launching of the Marshall Plan and the creation of NATO." Isaacson, *Kissinger*, p. 333.

7. Deep antipathy: When Nixon proceeded himself to treat with communist China, he refused to let Canada provide the channel of communication between the Chinese and American negotiators. Starr, *Kissinger*, p. 56. Following Trudeau's abrogation of civil liberties with the War Measures Act, Nixon wrote on his news summary of October 17, 1970, for Bob Haldeman, "Watch the Press – they will defend their liberal friend!" Lisée, *Eye of the Eagle*, p. 79.

8. Irritated Nixon: "He disdained Trudeau's clear enjoyment of social life; he tended to consider him soft on defense and in his general attitude toward the East." Kissinger, *White House Years*, p. 383.

Compliance: Or, in the words of one high-ranking External officer with long experience in Washington, "They wanted loyalty, support, predictability." Confidential interview, Mar. 1985.

9. Reprieve: Former ambassador Arthur Andrew judges "the damage [of defying Nixon over China] to our relations with the United States was minimal." *Rise and Fall*, p. 93.

10. Canada's standing: James Eayrs, doyen of foreign policy scholars, declared Canada a "foremost power." "We have what it takes, since we have all it takes . . . The resources are there, or waiting, too – animal, vegetable *and* mineral. Hardly a month elapses without the revelation of some new bonanza in our larder. (We need only decide how fast to develop them, how much to charge for them.)" "Defining a New Place," p. 24. Other academics followed suit: Hillmer and Stevenson, *Foremost Nation*. By the end of the decade Canada had become, in the phrase of David Dewitt and John Kirton, *A Principal Power*. Kim Nossal responds, however, that the "paradox of unrealized power" means Canada's great resources do not necessarily make it a great power. *Politics of Canadian Foreign Policy*, pp. 18–19.

11. Tokyo in 1970: Confidential interview, Sept. 1989. For more on Trudeau's insistence on experiencing exotica during his official forays abroad: P. Gossage, *Close to the Charisma*, pp. 201–12.

12. On Trudeau's encounter with Malraux: Authors' interviews with Madeleine Gobeil, Apr. 18, 1985, and Charles Lussier, June 6, 1991; Madsen, *Malraux*; and Galente, *Malraux*.

13. Trip to Beijing: During the official banquet, Premier Zhou Enlai said, "We are very glad to entertain our old friend here again" – the expression connoting rapport, understanding, and sympathy for the Chinese way. Harbron, "Canada Recognizes China," p. 2. Also Frolic, "Trudeau Initiative."

Ming vase: Alsop, "Architectural Digest," p. 110.

Economic summits: It was not until 1977 that Canada was regarded as a permanent member of the G-7. Nossal, *Politics of Canadian Foreign Policy*, pp. 82–85.

14. Empathetic colleagues: Helmut Schmidt wrote of his colleague, "I have always found Pierre Trudeau full of insights in regard of current international affairs. He clearly was devoted to the cause of the West, but this devotion did not hamper him from understanding the motivations of the Moscowian leaders, nor did it prevent him from maintaining national Canadian interests vis-à-vis our mutual superpower-ally U.S.A." Letter to the authors, Apr. 8, 1994.

On Carter at London summit: Confidential interview, Sept. 1989, and Martin, *Presidents and the Prime Ministers*, p. 262.

15. "Frustration and anger": "Notes for Remarks . . . at the Mansion House," in Trudeau, *Lifting the Shadow*, p. 20.

Grown substantially: CIDA's budget grew at the prodigious rate of over 21 per cent per year from 1969/70 to 1974/75, reaching its high of 0.54 per cent of GNP in 1975 but falling back to 0.42 per cent by 1980. Helleiner, "Developing Countries," p. 20; Hitchins and Liander, "Patterns of Trade and Aid," p. 23; and Islam, "For Whose Benefits," table 8.1.

Effectiveness: After the Parti Québécois victory in 1976, Jean Chrétien, as minister of industry, trade, and commerce, was charged with protecting jobs in Quebec towns dependent on textile or shoe factories and raised trade barriers against imports produced in destitute countries such as Bangladesh. By 1983 Canada had imposed 179 separate restraint agreements under the Multi-Fibre Arrangement, affecting fifteen textile products and sixteen types of clothing coming from thirteen developing and five East European countries. C. Pratt, "Internationalism," pp. 47–48.

What Canadian companies could sell: C. Pratt, "Internationalism," pp. 39–40.

When it came to supporting commodity agreements that would keep up the price of raw materials produced in the Third World, Canada was supportive only when its own staple exports of lead, zinc, and copper would benefit. It stonewalled when such accords threatened to increase consumer prices in Canada for imported coffee, cocoa, or rubber. Cranford Pratt, lecture, University of Toronto, Feb. 13, 1985.

16. "Stop condemning": Redekop, "Commerce over Conscience," p. 84. Also Freeman, *South Africa*, chs. 3–5.

On comparison of Canada's record: In 1980 Canadian ODA as a percentage of GNP was more than double that of the U.S. but less than half that of Sweden or the Netherlands. Redekop, "Commerce over Conscience," p. 92; Thérien, "Canadian Aid," p. 14.

17. On government responses to Brandt report: *Canadian Annual Review: 1980*, pp. 206, 212.

18. Two dozen: B. Wood, "Canada's Views," p. 1; and C. Pratt, "Internationalism," pp. 35–36.

Structural change: The prime minister declared at a press conference, "I don't think increased bilateral aid is really the solution to the much deeper underlying problem of the gap between the North and the South. It's a matter of sharing power in the economic institutions and sharing technology and then sharing political power, too." "Transcript" (Nov. 17, 1980), pp. 6–7.

Moderate their negotiating stance: Nossal, "Personal Diplomacy," p. 288.

19. Manage to persuade: Margaret Thatcher also claimed credit for persuading Reagan to attend Cancún. *Downing Street Years*, p. 168.

20. "Ask Al": Martin, *Presidents and the Prime Ministers*, p. 284; Jeffrey Simpson, "Trudeau Takes Break After Frustrating Trip," *Globe and Mail* (June 14, 1982), p. C16.

21. Goldfarb's polling: Authors' interview with Martin Goldfarb, Nov. 13, 1984.

For the *coureur de bois* analogy, we are indebted to Yolande Grisée of the Université d'Ottawa.

22. High-priced pedlar: Bryan Johnson, "PM Gets Bouquets in Lotus Land," *Globe and Mail* (Jan. 5, 1983), pp. 1–2; "Brunei's Oil Wealth Lures Canadian Visitors," *Globe and Mail* (Jan. 14, 1983), p. 4; and "Intangible Benefits: Trudeau Raised Profile of Canada in Asia," *Globe and Mail* (Jan. 20, 1983), pp. 1–2.

23. On Trudeau and the media: Authors' interviews with Andrew Szende, July 17, 1984; Manfred von Nostitz, July 20, 1984; and Ted Johnson, May 22, 1984.

24. "Unemployment in Sudbury": Bryan Johnson, "Can't Risk Trade Ties for Filipino Nun, Aide Says," *Globe and Mail* (Jan. 15, 1983), p. 1.

25. Trudeau quote: Nossal, "Cabin'd, Cribb'd, Confin'd," p. 52.

26. "Tory syndrome": Perlin, *Tory Syndrome*.

27. Comprehensive test ban: "While Canada could encourage the nuclear powers to act . . . she could not overcome their principal constraint, the absence of political will." Angell, "Trudeau Doctrine," p. 48.

Impotence: Canada was more successful in efforts aimed at staving off armaments escalations such as the militarization of the seabed than in having existing systems disarmed. Gotlieb and Dalfen, "National Jurisdiction," pp. 231, 251.

28. On the spat with Indira Gandhi: Trudeau, *Memoirs*, pp. 214–15.

West Germany: Dunn, *Controlling the Bomb*, p. 36.

29. Greater military contribution: Byers, "Defence and Foreign Policy," p. 331.

Substantial annual increase: The defence structure review launched in 1974 led to cabinet approval in 1975 for a long-range program to acquire new military equipment. Byers, "Canadian Defence and Defence Procurement," p. 157; Leyton-Brown and MacDonald, "Industrial Preparedness," p. 142; and Shadwick, "Canadian Defence Policy," p. 8. The funding formula was made inflation-proof in 1976. Treddenick, "Arms Race," p. 89.

Principally: The most significant exception was the German Leopard tank that Schmidt, "after long discussion," helped persuade Trudeau was needed for the Canadian forces in Europe. Authors' interview with Pierre Trudeau, Dec. 18, 1985.

30. Peace-promoting polemicist: In 1951, when still in the PCO, Trudeau had attacked Pearson's involvement in the Korean War in a long anonymous article – "Positions sur la présente guerre [Positions on the Current War]." His more courageous diatribe was "Pearson ou l'abdication de l'esprit [Pearson or the Abdication of Conscience]" – more courageous because his vitriol cost him his candidacy in the 1963 election.

31. Strangelovian dream: In the words of the eminent mathematician and conflict analyst Anatol Rapoport, completely automated weaponry of this kind let the military "destroy everybody without hating anybody." Lecture at the University of Toronto, Mar. 7, 1994.

32. The importance of arms production was underlined by the positive export balance

of $1.2 billion from 1959 to 1983. Byers, "Canadian Defence and Defence Procurement," p. 163. "Since the mid-1970s Ottawa had increasingly viewed technological innovation in the military sphere as a cutting edge for advances in Canadian civilian high technologies." Tucker, "Canadian Security Policy," p. 211, n. 69. Military factors were subordinated to "the more pressing economic and political considerations relating to . . . the maintenance of an important sector of Canadian manufacturing." Middlemiss, "Defence Industrial Preparedness," p. 715.

33. Community of interests: Reinforcing this governmental lobby was an expanding network of military-industrial organizations including the Conference of Defence Associations, the Federation of United Military Services, the Canadian Defence Preparedness Association, the NATO Industrial Advisory Group, the Canadian Institute of Strategic Studies, and the Aerospace Industries Association of Canada. On policy communities and policy networks, see Coleman and Skogstad, *Policy Communities*, ch. 1.

34. External's press release emphasized that CANUSTEP could cover a wide range of military equipment besides "the guidance system for unarmed cruise missiles." In the exchange of notes constituting the agreement, Ambassador Gotlieb's text included the sentence "Canada may refuse any T&E projects proposed under this Agreement." Canada, Department of External Affairs, "Agreement," p. 1.

35. Trudeau letter: Langille, *Changing the Guard*, p. 44, n. 25.

   Unsuspecting politicians: "DND would not have gone out of its way to raise the political implications of the umbrella agreement," a Department of National Defence official later admitted. Authors' confidential interview, Jan. 1986.

36. Casual comment: Sellar, "How Canada Took the Cruise."

   "That's the way": Authors' conversation with Pierre Trudeau, Dec. 18, 1985.

   The original suffocation speech: Trudeau, "Notes for a Speech" (May 26, 1978).

37. Trudeau's speech: "Transcript" (June 18, 1982).

   Andropov peace offensive: Walker, *Cold War*, pp. 272–73.

38. "Evil empire": Gaddis, *End of the Cold War*, p. 249, n. 11.

39. Little reason to trust: Richard Perle and Edward Teller of the White House Science Council made public statements confirming that the administration would be reluctant to exchange scientific information with the Soviet Union: Walker, *Cold War*, p. 275. Well before the administration unveiled its Star Wars scheme, independent security analysts had been worrying about the "self-made web of palpable contradictions" it had woven around its commitment to waging nuclear war till victory. Draper, "How Not to Think," p. 40.

40. Urgently wanted: Authors' interview with Marcel Massé, June 11, 1985.

41. "La bouche de Marilyn": H. Young, *One of Us*, p. 383.

42. On de Gaulle and separatism: Clarkson, "Vive le Québec Libre!" and D.C. Thomson, *Vive le Québec libre*, pp. 210–11. For the Gaullist perspective, see Mallen, *Vivre le Québec libre*, p. 172. For De Gaulle's speeches and statements, see Lescop, *Le pari québécois*. For a French analyst's assessment of de Gaulle's voyage, Lacouture, *De Gaulle*, ch. 19, "La dette de Louis XV."

   On Trudeau's French policy: Authors' interviews in Paris with MM. Fred Bild and Gilles Duguay at the Canadian Embassy; the former Gaullists Maurice Couve de Murville, Xavier Deniau, Martial de la Fournière, Jean de Lipkowski, Pierre

Maillard, and Pierre-Louis Mallen; Bernard Garcia, François de Laboulaye, François Leduc, and Jean-Marie Soutou from the Quai d'Orsay; the political scientist Alfred Grosser; the journalists Claude Julien, Jean Lacouture, Georges Many, and Pierre-Henri Menthon; the director of the budget, Michel Prada; Claude Roquet at the Délégation générale du Québec, during April 1986; and, in Canada, Allan Gotlieb, Canadian ambassador to the U.S.; Louise Beaudoin, André Dufour, and Gérard Pelletier in Quebec; John English and Krystyne Griffin in Toronto in 1986 and 1987.

On Mitterrand at Williamsburg: Trudeau found considerable common ground with Mitterrand, who was alarmed at Reagan's anti-communism and astonished at his ignorance. "Is this guy for real?" Trudeau quotes him as saying in astonishment after the president had uncorked one of his anecdotes about a priest who had been trained in Moscow as a secret agent. *Memoirs*, Les Productions La Fête, broadcast by CBC-TV, episode V.

43. Trudeau criticized NATO summits for "rubber stamping a communiqué which has been cooked, pre-cooked . . . [so that] there is no exchange, there is no deepening of the consensus within the Alliance, there is no effort at persuading each other." *Canadian Annual Review: 1982*, p. 188.

44. In tune with the Europeans: Confidential External Affairs documents, June 1983.

45. Foreign affairs advisers: H. Young, *One of Us*, p. 171.

On Schmidt feigning sleep and Giscard d'Estaing on Thatcher as "la fille d'épicier": H. Young, *One of Us*, p. 187. Her press secretary, Bernard Ingham, once said of Thatcher, "She has but one emotion: fury." Cited by Robert Boyce during lecture at the University of Toronto, Feb. 22, 1993.

46. Details of Williamsburg summit: Confidential External Affairs memoranda and authors' interviews with Pierre Trudeau, Dec. 18, 1985; W. Allen Wallis, Feb. 9, 1994; Marshall Casse, Mar. 3, 1994; and Thomas Delworth, Feb. 20, 1994.

"Solace to the Soviets": Authors' interview with Pierre Trudeau, Dec. 18, 1985.

Reagan's anger: Reagan, *American Life*, pp. 353–54. The Americans' view of the contretemps with Trudeau and Mitterrand is more fully described in Shultz, *Turmoil and Triumph*, pp. 354–57. Also Thatcher, *Downing Street Years*, p. 300.

47. Trudeau and Mitterrand: Mitterrand's reflection on Reagan and Thatcher after the morning's argument was, "Vraiment, ils n'en comprennent rien." Authors' confidential interview, Mar. 1994.

"Our full political resources": *Canadian Annual Review: 1983*, pp. 191–92. Trudeau claimed credit for winning this addition to the communiqué. "Transcript . . . at the London Economic Summit" (June 9, 1984), in Trudeau, *Lifting the Shadow*, p. 113.

Civility restored: The Americans were enormously pleased with the summit's results. Authors' interview with Richard Burt, June 3, 1994.

48. Flood of protest mail: Between November and May the PMO had received 6,570 telegrams and letters plus 20,000 write-in forms and petitions on the Cruise issue. By January 1983, 52 per cent of Canadians aware of the issue were opposed to its testing. Bromke and Nossal, "Tensions," p. 341.

On the Canadian public's greater willingness to blame *both* the U.S. and the U.S.S.R. for escalating the arms race: Byers and Munton, "Canadian Defence," p. 26.

"Natural allies": Lecture by Tom Axworthy at the University of Toronto, Jan. 14, 1985.

49. "Pounding the shit": Langille, *Changing the Guard*, p. 52.

50. "Testing us": Joe O'Donnell, "Liberal Party President Opposes Cruise Missile Tests in Canada," *Toronto Star* (Feb. 24, 1983), cited in Byers and Munton, "Canadian Defence," p. 22.

Threats: Don Sellor, "Pentagon Plans to Bar Canada from New Deal," Ottawa *Citizen* (Apr. 23, 1983), pp. 1, 10, quoted in Langille, *Changing the Guard*, p. 54.

Interviews on the politics of the Cruise were held with Lloyd Axworthy, Apr. 10, 1985, and Oct. 28, 1985; Jean-Jacques Blais, June 11, 1985; Charles Caccia, Jan. 19, 1994; Kenneth Calder, Jan. 14, 1986; Ross Francis, June 11, 1985; Allan Gotlieb, Aug. 4, 1986; Darel Johnson, Sept. 8, 1989; Jeremy Kinsman, Nov. 20, 1985; Marc Lalonde, Dec. 18, 1985; George Lindsey, Jan. 13, 1986; John Roberts, Dec. 12, 1985; Gérard Thériault, Apr. 11, 1987; and Ramsey Withers, June 11, 1985.

51. "Nothing else": Authors' interview with Lloyd Axworthy, June 1, 1993.

"We just couldn't afford": Authors' interview with Marc Lalonde, Dec. 18, 1985.

52. Trudeau insisted on Schmidt's role in his decision: Authors' interview, Dec. 18, 1985. The air-launched Cruise was not actually related to NATO's nuclear modernization, and no treaty obligation committed Canada to this action. Naidu, "Cruise Missile," p. 10.

On Trudeau's casuistry with Bush: "You may get some benefit of our testing the Cruise – but it is not to help you; it is because the Europeans have asked us to do this for them." Quoted in May, "Testing the Cruise," p. 26.

53. "Play politics with peace": Authors' interview with Tom Axworthy, Jan. 14, 1985. Nevertheless, it was already known in the Department of National Defence that the prime minister was interested in making some original proposals for arms control. Confidential interview, Jan. 1986.

54. Axworthy kept searching: He had even canvassed the Chief of Defence Staff for suggestions. Confidential interview, Apr. 1987.

On the Caldicott lunch: R. Gwyn and S. Gwyn, "Politics of Peace," p. 23.

McNamara had written in an article that created a stir at the time that "*nuclear weapons serve no military purpose whatsoever. They are totally useless – except only to deter one's opponent from using them*" (emphasis in original). "Military Role," p. 79.

55. Val Morin ministers' seminar: Authors' interview with Franklyn Griffiths, Jan. 20, 1994.

56. Access to American intelligence: The National Security Agency shared its information with Canada's Communications Security Establishment. Granatstein and Bothwell, *Pirouette*, p. 264.

Denounced the Soviets: "Soviets Liars, Terrorists, U.S. President Charges," *Globe and Mail* (Sept. 3, 1983), p. A1.

Persons interviewed or heard in seminar for this section: Lloyd Axworthy, Apr. 10, 1985, and Oct. 28, 1985; Tom Axworthy, Jan. 14, 1985; Jean-Jacques Blais, June 11, 1985; Wilhelm Bleek, Oct. 18, 1984; Charles Caccia, Jan. 19, 1994; Kenneth Calder, Jan. 14, 1986; Thomas Delworth, Apr. 19, 1985, and Feb. 20, 1994; Louis Delvoie, Feb. 20, 1984, and May 17, 1984; D.B. Dewar, June 13, 1985; Peter Dobell,

July 18, 1984; Robert Fowler, May 22, 1984; Patrick Gossage, Dec. 3, 1985; Allan Gotlieb, Aug. 4, 1986; Franklyn Griffiths, Jan. 18, 1994; James Harlick, July 12, 1984; Ivan Head, May 23, 1984, and Jan. 26, 1994; Serge Joyal, June 4, 1985; Jeremy Kinsman, Nov. 20, 1985; John Kirton, Apr. 25, 1984, and May 21, 1994; George Lindsey, Jan. 13, 1986; Marcel Massé, June 11, 1985; James Medas, Sept. 7, 1989; Robert Montgomery, July 25, 1984; Kim Nossal, May 11, 1994; Geoffrey Pearson, July 24, 1984; Sean Riley, May 17, 1984; John Rouse, July 11, 1984; Jacques Roy, Aug. 4, 1986; Mitchell Sharp, July 26, 1984; Sonja Sinclair, Jan. 17, 1985; Janice Stein, May 19, 1994; Gérard Thériault, Apr. 11, 1987; Pierre Trudeau, Dec. 18, 1985; Manfred von Nostitz, July 20, 1984; and Martin Walker, Mar. 15, 1994.

57. Urged the prime minister: Authors' interview with Ivan Head, Jan. 26, 1994.
58. On Trudeau's interlocutors: Canada, Department of External Affairs, "Prime Minister's Initiative on East-West Relations and International Security," p. 3, cited in Angell, "Trudeau Doctrine," p. 100.

Kennan, the former ambassador to Moscow and architect of American containment policy towards the U.S.S.R., had already told an audience in 1981 that the administration's view of the Soviet Union was "so extreme, so subjective, so far removed from what any sober scrutiny of external reality would reveal that it is not only ineffective but dangerous as a guide to political action." He went on to warn that the "endless series of distortions and oversimplifications, systematic dehumanization of the leadership of another great country, and routine exaggeration of Moscow's military capabilities and of the supposed iniquity of its intentions" imperilled chances for a "more hopeful world." Brownstein and Easton, *Reagan's Ruling Class*, p. 562.

59. Trudeau was vexed: Authors' interview with Allan Gotlieb, Aug. 4, 1986.
60. Ignatieff: He had been bypassed for the governor-generalship by Trudeau, who had all but offered him the job. Even though his remarkable wife, Alison Ignatieff – the granddaughter of a famous Queen's University principal and the sister of the nationalist philosopher George Grant – had trained for the role of vice-regal spouse by spending time as the Queen's lady-in-waiting, Trudeau had jilted Ignatieff in favour of the former Manitoba premier Ed Schreyer. Authors' interviews with Alison Ignatieff, Jan. 22, 1982, and George Ignatieff, Apr. 1, 1979.
61. "Ominous rhythm of crisis": Trudeau, "Reflections on Peace and Security" (Oct. 27, 1983).
62. Inadequate preparation: "Successful statecraft involves more than shuttling between the capitals of the great powers for several months urging global negotiations . . . To be effective, diplomacy directed at the great powers requires sustained efforts over a period of years. And such efforts are impossible without a professional organization which can act continuously to give concrete expression to both the broad and narrow interests of a state in the international system." Nossal, *Politics of Canadian Foreign Policy*, p. 125.
63. Neither for turning: Thatcher's PR advisers had already suggested she say this herself. H. Young, *One of Us*, p. 209.
64. "Corporal at the top": H. Young, *One of Us*, p. 331.

Respected: Authors' interview with Sir Francis Pym, Apr. 22, 1986.

65. Her high commissioner: Sir John Ford had caused a diplomatic incident by intervening in Canadian politics because he had become convinced that Trudeau would declare Canada a republic. Vol. 1, pp. 324–26.

Taking the side: Trudeau did actually come through in the Falklands War with Canadian support for the British position.

Blot on Trudeau's copy-book: Authors' interview with Bernard Ingham, Apr. 23, 1986.

66. "Only when you are wrong": "Thatcher Dismisses Differences with PM," *Toronto Star* (Sept. 28, 1983), p. A1.

"Megaphone diplomacy": "Transcript of a Toast," in Trudeau, *Lifting the Shadow*, pp. 65–66.

67. "The French in him": Authors' interview with Bernard Ingham, Apr. 23, 1986.

68. Five-part program: Trudeau, "Remarks" (Nov. 13, 1983).

69. "Balanced set of proposals": Kirton, "Trudeau and the Diplomacy of Peace," p. 4.

70. "Intoxicated": Authors' interview with Allan Gotlieb, Aug. 4, 1986.

71. Soviets' paranoia: Walker, *Cold War*, pp. 276–77.

72. Infiltrated: S. Gotlieb, *Washington Rollercoaster*, p. 162. Also S. Gotlieb, *Wife of.*

73. Trudeau was a communist: Penned by the Red-baiting Toronto *Sun* columnist Lubor Zink, it noted that "although he himself was not a regular Communist Party member," Trudeau's writings from the 1950s and such acts as his recognition of China demonstrated that the "Communists' shrewd bet on the young Montreal radical paid off." "Unpenetrated Problem," pp. 753, 756.

74. "On the front end": Authors' interview with Derek Burney, Sept. 6, 1989.

View . . . had hardened: Authors' interview in the Pentagon with Darel Johnson, Sept. 8, 1989.

75. Viciously sarcastic: Authors' interview with Darel Johnson, Sept. 8, 1989.

76. Perle's idea of arms control: Brownstein and Easton, *Reagan's Ruling Class*, pp. 498–503, 526–27.

77. Pentagon had advised the White House: Authors' interview in the Pentagon with Darel Johnson, Sept. 8, 1989.

Reception in Cuba: R. Gwyn, *Northern Magus*, p. 307.

78. On the State Department's view: "We were trying to keep everyone calm and wanted to be sure the public felt we were listening, so we'd have had to be nuts to give Pierre Trudeau a cold fish in the face." Authors' interview with Richard Burt, June 3, 1994, and confidential interview in the State Department, Sept. 1989.

79. Margot Kidder: Authors' interviews with Martin Knelman, Mar. 7 and Apr. 13, 1994.

80. Shown restraint: Trudeau had nevertheless raised hackles in Washington by admonishing both superpowers at his convocation address to Notre Dame University in 1982. Granatstein and Bothwell, *Pirouette*, p. 365.

Hold his tongue: Confidential interview, June 1985.

81. "Man of peace": Authors' interview with Allan Gotlieb, Aug. 4, 1986. Also R. Gwyn and S. Gwyn, "Politics of Peace," p. 29; and Trudeau, *Memoirs*, p. 338.

82. Advance pleading: P. Gossage, *Close to the Charisma*, p. 157.

"Godspeed" had been proposed for the president's lips by Robert Montgomery, one of the "pipsqueaks" from the State Department who had been reported as critical of the Trudeau caper. Authors' interview with Robert Montgomery, July 25, 1984.

83. "Great step forward": "Statements" (Dec. 15, 1983), in Trudeau, *Lifting the Shadow*, p. 91.

"Pipsqueaks": *Memoirs*, Les Productions La Fête, broadcast by CBC-TV, episode V. The high-level State Department official Lawrence Eagleburger had dismissed Trudeau's initiative at a Carnegie Endowment luncheon in Washington, saying, "Whoever thinks we would agree to that must have been smoking something pretty funny." Richard Burt of the State Department said, "If your Trudeau thinks he can contribute anything to world peace, he's out of his mind." Authors' interview with Patrick Gossage, Dec. 3, 1985.

Let the word out: Richard Burt and Lawrence Eagleburger deliberately undermined Trudeau's impact with the media. Authors' interview with Patrick Gossage, Dec. 3, 1985, and Gossage's *Close to the Charisma*, p. 259.

# Chapter 14
# The Era Ends: Resignation and Replacement

1. Ostry quote: Authors' interview with Bernard Ostry, Mar. 14, 1984.
2. Controversial: The House of Commons Committee on Privileges and Elections had conducted two inquiries in 1983 into news reports alleging that Mackasey had received an extravagant sum from an obscure Montreal company to act as a lobbyist while sitting as an MP and had also received unusual financial support from the Bank of Montreal. Although the committee exonerated him, his credibility was compromised. Palango, *Above the Law*, ch. 14.
3. "Sweet Canadians": The character is Dr. Minnow in Atwood, *Bodily Harm*, pp. 124–38.
4. High on pot: Carl Millins, "'Pot' Remark on Trudeau Initiative Made by 3rd Senior U.S. Diplomat," *Globe and Mail* (Dec. 22, 1983), p. 1. Also P. Gossage, *Close to the Charisma*, p. 260.
5. Whole armour of God: The phrase is from Ephesians 6: 11, 12, 14–15. "Put on the whole armour of God. For we wrestle not against flesh and blood, but against principalities, against powers, against the rulers of the darkness of this world, against spiritual wickedness in high places . . . Stand therefore, having your loins girt about with truth, and having on the breastplate of righteousness; and your feet shod with the preparation of the gospel of peace." Michael Pitfield confirmed the spiritual basis of Trudeau's motivation: "It was a gift of God to be given the position of prime minister of Canada whose unique location as a neighbour with vital airspace gave him real leverage to press the American president." Authors' interview, June 3, 1994. In his interview with the *New York Times* editorial board, Trudeau spoke of the politician as having "a godly role." Trudeau, *Shadow of War*, p. 99.
6. *The New York Times*: Transcript of Jan. 20, 1984, interview in Trudeau, *Shadow of War*, pp. 96–100.

Outraged Raymond Barre: "Do you think the President of the United States, in answer to an overrunning of Europe by conventional Soviet forces, will want to start World War III, an atomic war?" Trudeau asked Barre. "You have to believe that in order to not have a credibility gap." "I will never put the question because if I put the question," Barre replied, "there is no longer credibility." Trudeau, *Shadow of War*, p. 103.

"Old self": Authors' interview with Gwenyth Grube, Dec. 25, 1983.

"True colors": Authors' interview at the Pentagon with Darel Johnson, Sept. 8, 1989.

7. "The shadow of war": Canada, House of Commons, *Debates* (Feb. 9, 1984), pp. 1213, 1216.

8. Moderation of rhetoric: Reagan's discourse started to contain more peaceable references in November 1983. Fisher, "Reagan Reversal," ch. 6.

9. "No one else": Authors' interview with Janice Stein, May 19, 1994.

10. Critics: Adam Bromke and Kim Nossal considered that Trudeau's disarmament proposals had inadequately exploited Canadian academic expertise, had underutilized the diplomatic resources of External Affairs, and had attacked the symptoms, not the causes, of East-West tension. Bromke and Nossal, "Trudeau Rides," pp. 4–5.

Crippling defence expenditures: Access to Soviet archives resulting from *glasnost* suggests that the Reaganites' hang-tough theory did not work. Soviet defence expenditures did not in fact escalate in the 1980s to match Star Wars. Lebow and Stein, "Reagan and the Russians," p. 35.

11. Post-national citizen: Kim Nossal's argument about Trudeau's efforts on the "North-South issues as representing an outgrowth of a personal commitment by an individual who was able to use his position as the head of the Canadian government to advance interests that were defined in global, rather than national, terms . . . a personal transcendence of the very nation-state" could be applied with even more validity to his peace initiative. Nossal, "Personal Diplomacy," p. 290.

12. American discourse: The president's rhetoric was moderated both for political reasons – the White House wanted Reagan re-elected, and speeches about the evil empire alarmed public opinion – and because Reagan had become genuinely alarmed about nuclear war. Authors' interview with Richard Burt, June 3, 1994; and Fisher, "Reagan Reversal," ch. 6.

Persuading foreign ministers: Michael Tucker credited German, not Canadian, diplomacy for this achievement. "Politics of Peace," p. 10.

13. The Gallup poll of October 1983 had the Liberals at 26 to the Conservatives' 55 per cent; the February 1984 figures were 32 to 52 per cent.

14. "My destiny": Charlotte Montgomery, "PM to Review Own Future, Peace Plan," *Globe and Mail* (Feb. 3, 1984), p. 2.

15. "Protect him from the yahoos": Authors' interview with Tom Axworthy, July 11, 1984. It was more than the brutes in the party who had been pressing for Trudeau to resign. Dennis Dawson, the talented chairman of the Quebec caucus, had publicly endorsed the calling of a leadership convention as "the only way for the Liberal Party to stay in power." "Trudeau Must Go or Party Beaten, Liberal MPs State," *Globe and Mail* (Aug. 19, 1983), p. 1.

"Superior lawyer": Authors' interview with Charles Taylor, Jan. 21, 1991.

16. Taken his place: The veteran columnist W.A. Wilson wrote that for months Lalonde

"has been virtually a behind-the-scenes prime minister, filling the vacuum created by Mr. Trudeau's long loss of interest in domestic affairs." "A Problem for Mr. Turner," *Winnipeg Free Press* (Mar. 9, 1984), p. 6. When, as one example, Judy Erola was pressed by women wanting to know if she supported their position on the inclusion of homemakers in the Canada Pension Plan, she replied, "I ideally probably would like to say I advocate it as well. But I have to live with reality . . . I answer to the Minister of Finance." Canada, House of Commons, Special Committee on Pension Reform, *Proceedings*, p. 21.

17. Corporate concentration: The all-time high of 576 mergers in 1982 was surpassed by 1983's figure of 628. Linda McQuaig, "Corporate Mergers Increasing in Canada," *Globe and Mail* (May 5, 1984), p. 20.

Competitive abroad: The idea that monopolies were needed at home if they were to succeed in the global economy had been given official legitimacy by the 1978 *Report* of the Royal Commission on Corporate Concentration.

Become a Liberal: Authors' interview with Judy Erola, May 24, 1984.

"Bent over backwards": W.T. Stanbury, "Half a Loaf," p. 33. Also authors' interviews with Robert Bertrand, Jan. 14, 1986; Mark Daniels, Jan. 6, 1986; Lawson Hunter, Jan. 13, 1986; George Post, June 7, 1985; and W.T. Stanbury, May 30, 1985.

18. Federal study: Canada, Task Force on Retirement Income Policy, *Retirement Income System*. It also warned that an impending funding crisis was threatening workers with a substantial decline in living standard in retirement unless contributions were quadrupled. More relevant for federal politicians concerned about their electoral prospects was the fact that income security was "the only direct link between Ottawa and the individual citizen – besides taxation." Banting, "Institutionalized Conservatism," pp. 67–68.

Anglophone business executives were particularly opposed because of the recession to making increases in their contributions to their employees' retirement funds. They were ideologically against any expansion of the Canada Pension Plan that would make possible the kind of government participation in the economy achieved by Quebec's Caisses de dépôt, which had become the country's largest single holder of common stock.

Second government report: Canada, Department of National Health and Welfare, *Better Pensions for Canadians*.

19. Would soon double: Although not permitted in federal law, subsidiaries of foreign banks had set up in Canada in the early Trudeau years by exploiting loopholes in provincial regulations. Fifty-seven new banks were licensed in the eighteen months after the 1980 legislation. They joined the chartered banks' exclusive club, the Canadian Bankers' Association, which then supported their demands. Pauly, *Opening Financial Markets*, pp. 94-118; and Pauly's seminar at the University of Toronto, Feb. 27, 1987.

20. On the 1984 budget: Canada, House of Commons, *Debates* (Feb. 15, 1984), pp. 1423–33.

On Lalonde as Keynesian: Lecture by Marc Lalonde at the University of Toronto, Apr. 1, 1985.

Job creation: The Special Recovery Capital Program, which Lalonde had first launched with $2.4 billion in his 1983 budget, was designed to short-circuit the bureaucratic safeguards of the Pitfield system. Allocation of the funds was the responsibility of Donald Johnston, the minister responsible for the Ministry of State for Economic and Regional Development, but regional ministers were able to direct the money towards ridings where Liberal MPs were fighting for their political lives. Bakvis, *Regional Ministers*, pp. 165–81.

Electorally smart: On hearing of the GIS increase, Jacques Parizeau, Quebec's finance minister at the time, quipped, "Thank God for elections in Canada. It's always at that time that old age pensions are raised." *Globe and Mail* (Feb. 16, 1984), p. 10.

One of the greatest enthusiasts for the 1984 budget was Lorna Marsden, who documented the large number of resolutions from the party's 1982 convention that found expression in its pages. Marsden, "Budget '84," pp. 2–3.

21. Trudeau could stay: Authors' interviews with Tom Axworthy, July 11, 1984; and Marc Lalonde, May 31, 1985.

22. Pitfield had joined them: Bob Hepburn, "He Made His Decision After Walk in Blizzard," *Toronto Star* (Mar. 1, 1984), pp. A1, A5.

23. Briefing style: Authors' interviews with Tom Axworthy, May 18, May 20, and July 11, 1984; and James Coutts, May 9, 1984.

24. Detailed election strategy: T. Axworthy, "A Strategy for Fighting the Next Election" (Nov. 26, 1983), authors' archive; and T. Axworthy, "Towards the Next Election," pp. 26–31.

25. Speech from the throne: Canada, House of Commons, *Debates* (Dec. 7, 1983), pp. 1–5.

26. "Emotional conflict": Authors' interview with Tom Axworthy, July 11, 1984.
    "Quantum shift": Authors' interview with James Coutts, June 7, 1994.

27. Weekend privacy: Authors' interview with Tom Axworthy, May 20, 1984.

28. On Margaret Trudeau's new marriage: S. Cameron, "Maggie: Happy at Last!," p. 57.

29. On Pitfield's belief: Authors' interview with Michael Pitfield, June 3, 1994.

30. "That was never true": Quoted in Graham, "Man with a Mission," p. 19.

31. Fondness for Davey: Authors' interview with Pierre Trudeau, Sept. 27, 1978.

32. "Odd piece of pie": Authors' interview with Keith Davey, Sept. 24, 1981.

33. Visited Washington: Authors' interview with Keith Davey, Sept. 24, 1981.

34. "Okay, okay": Authors' interview with Keith Davey, Mar. 10, 1980.

35. "Peace thing": Authors' interview with Keith Davey, Oct. 30, 1984.

36. On Trudeau's attitude to journalists: Authors' interview with Keith Davey, Oct. 30, 1984. After interviewing Trudeau on his Meech Lake intervention, Frum said to the authors: "He's never liked me and it's getting worse. Now he really hates me." Authors' interviews with Barbara Frum, June 14, 1987, and Oct. 2, 1990.

37. "In great spirits": Davey, *Rainmaker*, p. 301.

38. "Movie star": Authors' interview with Paul Plant, May 3, 1979.
    On Campagnolo as minister: Authors' interviews with Abby Hoffman, June 10, 1985; Bruce Kidd, July 24, 1985; and Peter Lesaux, June 18, 1985.
    "Dynamite": Authors' interview with Keith Davey, June 30, 1977.

39. Biographical details: Authors' interview with Iona Campagnolo, May 17, 1984, and June 22, 1985; and Ferrante, "Iona Campagnolo."

40. Details of the Ashworth-Campagnolo quarrel: Authors' interviews with Keith Davey, May 15, 1984; David Smith, May 17, 1984; and Gordon Dryden, June 4,

1994; and letter to the authors from Iona Campagnolo, June 9, 1994. Also Rosemary Speirs, "The Man Behind the Peterson Machine," *Toronto Star* (July 8, 1987), p. A19.

41. The party's anger at the prime minister's gatekeepers had shifted from Coutts-and-Davey to Davey-and-Axworthy. The British Columbian Ray Perrault, a former cabinet minister and colleague of Davey's in the Senate, had told the press in December that Davey and the PMO under Axworthy were "increasingly out of touch" with party members, "pushing buttons that aren't wired anymore." "PM, Top Advisers Impeding Party Reform, Ex-ministers Say," *Globe and Mail* (Dec. 1, 1983), p. 13.

42. "Political orphan": Letter to the authors from Iona Campagnolo, June 9, 1994.

43. "Sea of disloyalty": Authors' interview with Philippe Deane Gigantes, May 16, 1984. Also authors' interview with Michel Rochon, July 19, 1984.

44. "I patted his hand": Letter to the authors, June 9, 1994.

45. "Things are written": Authors' interview with Pierre Trudeau, June 6, 1985.

46. "What can you do?": Authors' interview with Martin Goldfarb, Apr. 17, 1979.

47. Cultural dissonance: Authors' interview with Martin Goldfarb, Nov. 11, 1984. "As any capable cultural anthropologist knows – and a capable pollster is a sophisticated student of cultural behavior – deciphering the nuances of attitudes, opinions and behaviors in a context of cultural complexity is a difficult task." Goldfarb and Axworthy, *Different Drummer*, p. xiii.

48. Authors' interview with Pierre Trudeau, June 6, 1985.

49. "You do it!": Letter to the authors from Iona Campagnolo, June 9, 1994.

50. The following responses to Trudeau's resignation appeared in *The Toronto Star* (Mar. 1, 1984), pp. A3, A4. From Ontario and Quebec premiers: Stephen Handelman, "History Will Look Kindly on Trudeau, Davis Says"; "Trudeau Dream of Bilingualism 'A Failure,' Levesque Charges." The article "'A Voice for Sanity': The World Pays Tribute to PM" contained assessments by Brandt: Trudeau "brought Canada into the centre of world affairs, thus successfully making the country a viable factor for peace and equality." By Eban: "He was among a select group of Western statesmen . . . who are particularly conscious of the problems of underdeveloped countries." By Wilson: "He was a committed Commonwealth statesman." By Callaghan: "Canada's voice was listened to with respect when he spoke . . . he was a bridge-builder who enjoyed a special empathy with the leaders of the poorer countries." By Nixon: "While we did not agree on some foreign policy issues, I would rate him as one of the ablest leaders of the Western world." By Kissinger: "A remarkable leader for whom I have the greatest respect." State Department response: Carl Mullins, "Resignation Surprises, Puzzles U.S. Officials."

51. "Not to succeed myself": Lawrence Martin, "'I Was My Best Successor,' Trudeau Says at Fundraiser," *Globe and Mail* (Nov. 21, 1984), p. 1.

52. The expert commentator was Daniel Cappon, professor of psychology at York University. Roy MacGregor, "Why They're Lining Up to Lose," *Toronto Star* (Mar. 31, 1984), p. B1.

53. On Macdonald's decision: Authors' interview with Keith Davey, May 15, 1984. When Macdonald was asked in December 1980 by a Liberal activist what had happened to his leadership plans, he remarked bleakly, "I was fucked. Coutts and Davey double-crossed me by talking Trudeau into returning." Authors' confidential interview, Dec. 1980.

On Campagnolo's decision: Authors' interviews with Iona Campagnolo, May 17, 1984, and June 22, 1985; and Lorna Marsden, Mar. 26, 1984.

On Coutts's decision: Authors' interviews with Jim Coutts, May 9, 1984, and Keith Davey, May 15, 1984. Also Davey, *Rainmaker*, pp. 320–22.

54. "We that have loved him so": Browning, *Poems*, p. 11. Axworthy neglected to use the famous opening lines: "Just for a handful of silver he's left us, / Just for a riband to stick in his coat."

55. "Irreversible": Authors' interview with Tom Axworthy, July 11, 1984.

56. On the CIIPS: Authors' interviews with Peter Dobell, July 18, 1984, and Geoffrey Pearson, July 24, 1984.

Canada Health Act: Authors' interviews with Monique Bégin, Mar. 21, 1986; David Kirkwood, Nov. 27, 1986; Claude Lemelin, July 12, 1984; Michael Mendelson, June 6, 1986; and Richard Van Loon, May 23, 1984. Resistance from cabinet: Allan MacEachen was the centre of ministerial opposition; only Jean Chrétien, Roméo LeBlanc, and Gene Whelan supported Bégin originally. Authors' interview with Monique Bégin, Mar. 21, 1986. Trudeau's support: Bégin, *Medicare*, p. 109. Provincial hostility: The provincial governments were already furious at Ottawa for the unilateral cutbacks it had been making in its transfer payments to them for the education, health, and social programs in whose financing it participated; the extra-billing threat was so much more salt in the wound. For some federal politicians, the Canada Health Act was brilliant since it was popular social policy that did not cost Ottawa money. Prince, "Whatever Happened," p. 97. The Canada Health Act was consistent with Ottawa's strategy of reducing federal expenditures. Brown, "Health Care Financing," p. 112.

57. Deep convictions: Palango, *Above the Law*, pp. 134–35.

On Pitfield and Bill C-157: Littleton, *Target Nation*, p. 158.

The Young Offenders Act had been passed in 1982 but not proclaimed because of provincial opposition to the reform. Authors' interview with Roger Tassé, June 12, 1985.

58. Choosing judges: Trudeau also showed non-partisan professionalism in the selection of important governmental figures such as the auditor general. Authors' interview with Kenneth Dye, Jan. 18, 1985.

Beyond political favouritism: A study by the Canadian Bar Association found that from 1979 to 1984 partisanship played no role in Supreme Court appointments. *Report*, p. 57. Also Peter Russell, "Staffing the Judiciary," lecture at the University of Toronto, Oct. 27, 1986.

59. On Order-in-Council appointments: Simpson, *Spoils of Power*, p. 352.

60. "Peacenik statement": Authors' interview with Richard Burt, June 3, 1994.

"I was horrified": Reagan, *American Life*, p. 354.

"For God's sake, Pierre": Jamieson, *No Place for Fools*, p. 10.

61. "Collective grief": Authors' interview with Judy Erola, May 24, 1984.

62. Ahead of the Conservatives: From a 12-point deficit (Conservatives at 48 per cent, Liberals at 36 per cent) in March's Gallup poll, the Liberals had moved to a 6-point lead in June (Conservatives at 40 per cent, Liberals at 46 per cent).

63. Taunting: A sample exchange in the House between the two pugilists:

**Mr. Crosbie:** Well, Mr. Speaker, we know it is 1984 when we have Big Brother over there answering. Heil Schickelgrubber!

**Mr. Trudeau:** The Reichstag was burned down by guys like you. (House of Commons, *Debates* [Feb. 16, 1984], p. 1464.)

Glum: Authors' interview with John Crosbie, June 14, 1984.

The better the Grits: Authors' interviews with many delegates at the Liberal convention, June 13-16, 1984.

64. Maximum publicity: Authors' interview with Michael Kirby, Apr. 26, 1984.

"No choice": Authors' interview with Monique Bégin, June 14, 1984.

65. Idealized: Walter Stewart's paeans were typical. "In appearance, he is perfect. Central casting, looking for the man to play the Senator from Rocky Ridge, would bung him into the part without hesitation. It's all there – the trim, exercised body, still, at 54, the body of an athlete; the face, handsome enough for a shirt ad, but not weak, dominated by a firm jaw, an engaging grin and those remarkable eyes – baby blue one minute, icy grey the next. He has the voice, the carriage, the manners, the polish, the brains. He is bilingual, charming and hard-working. He chats as easily with tycoons as with janitors, smiles a lot, laughs a lot, and is guaranteed not to fade, rust or drip on the carpet." "The Natural," p. 30.

Endorsing women's demands was one thing, understanding what they meant was another. When the young Liberal who had drafted the policy material on contract compliance – firms with government contracts would have to comply with stipulated employment and wage standards – congratulated Turner for adopting the position, he appeared puzzled. "Contract appliance?" he responded. Authors' interview with Janice Rubin, July 16, 1985.

66. "Outnumber us": Authors' interview with Céline Hervieux-Payette, Oct. 9, 1985.

67. "Mr. Blunder": Peter Lennon, "Mr. Blunder or Mr. Backwoods?" London *Times* (June 25, 1984), p. 10.

68. Carstairs on the 1984 leadership race: *Not One of the Boys*, pp. 72–76.

69. Chrétien outranked Turner 55 per cent to 19 as "personally likeable" but Turner prevailed otherwise: "appealing image on television" (56 to 22 per cent), "sound views on policy" (32 to 25 per cent), "overall ability and competence" (45 to 28 per cent), "can unite party" (52 to 26 per cent), "can make tough decisions" (44 to 31 per cent), "can earn respect from international leaders" (57 to 21 per cent), "can appeal to different regions" (55 to 24 per cent), and "best able to help the party win the next election" (63 to 19 per cent). George Perlin, "Liberal Leadership Convention Questionnaire," survey conducted for the CBC (June 6, 1984), p. 11. Authors' archive. As Joseph Wearing of Trent University reported, Turner's victory was "pre-ordained": two-thirds of the ex-officio delegates and a majority of the constituency delegates his students polled on the convention floor intended to vote for the winner. Joseph Wearing, "What Made Turner's Selection a Pre-ordained Conclusion," *Financial Post* (June 30, 1984), p. 7.

70. "TV variety show": Rick Groen, "Passing the Baton in Prime Time," *Globe and Mail* (June 18, 1984), p. 14.

71. Eulogists' quotes: Authors' notes from the convention coverage.

72. "If our cause was right" and "Our hopes are high": Trudeau, "Remarks" (June 14, 1984), p. 6.

73. State of exalted exhaustion: Authors' interviews with Eddie Goldenberg, May 22 and July 10, 1984.

"A real Liberal": Christina Spencer and Chris Hall, "Deals, Rumors, Sudden Shifts All Part of the Race," Ottawa *Citizen* (June 17, 1984), p. 24.

"Final shaft": Charles Lynch, "It Was Over Even Before It Started," Ottawa *Citizen* (June 17, 1984), p. 23.

74. Winnability: The front page of Canada's national newspaper carried a story reporting that a Goldfarb poll of voters showed the Liberals could win an election with Chrétien as leader. Lawrence Martin, "Poll Says Chrétien Best Bet to Beat Mulroney," *Globe and Mail* (June 16, 1984), p. 1.

75. "Until that moment": Authors' interview with Tom Axworthy, July 11, 1984.

# Conclusion
## Trudeau in the Afterlife, Canada After Trudeau

1. Cell of malcontents: Authors' interview with Bill Macdonald, Sept. 9, 1983.

2. Comic chaos: Authors' interviews with Rick Alway, Oct. 23, 1984; John Payne, May 30 and Nov. 14, 1984, and May 31, 1985; Dan Gagnier, Aug. 20, 1986; and Rose Gagnier, Aug. 20, 1986.

3. On Turner's managerial style: Clarkson, "Dauphin and the Doomed," pp. 104–5.

4. Weak, weak, weak: Authors' confidential interview, July 1984.

5. Ego-expanding: Authors' interview with John Payne, Nov. 14, 1984.

Far from ready: Clarkson, "Dauphin and the Doomed," pp. 105–17.

6. Obsessively anti-Trudeau: Authors' interviews with Bill Lee, May 18 and July 18, 1984.

7. On Turner as reformer: [McCall] Newman, "Turner," p. 20.

8. Big Blue Machine: Authors' interviews with Norman Atkins, Nov. 7, 1984; and Lowell Murray, May 23 and 24, 1984, and June 6, 1985.

On Gregg's research: Authors' interview with Allan Gregg, Oct. 31, 1984.

9. "A"-list dinner: S. Gotlieb, *Washington Rollercoaster*, p. 180.

On Brian Mulroney as lightweight: Authors' interview with Dalton Robertson, Dec. 6, 1983.

10. Liberal machine in Quebec: Authors' interviews with Warren Allmand, Mar. 21, 1986; Pierre Bastien, Oct. 9, 1985; Rémi Bujold, Oct. 9, 1985; Joan Fraser, June 5, 1985; Eddie Goldenberg, Apr. 22, 1985; Pierre-Marc Johnson, Mar. 19, 1986; Gérard D. Lévesque, Mar. 17, 1986; Paul Martin, June 3, 1985; and Jean Paré, June 3, 1986.

The NDP secured 19 per cent of the popular vote and thirty seats in the 1984 federal election, compared with 20 per cent and thirty-two seats in 1980.

11. Better front man: Authors' interview with Robert Hurlbut, Dec. 6, 1983.

12. Transnational capital: Gilpin, *Political Economy*, ch. 6; J.E. Thomson and Krasner, "Global Transactions," pp. 201–2.

Canadian business increasingly hostile: Clarkson, "Disjunctions," pp. 112–14.
13. Horrors: Weston, *Reign of Error*, chs. 8–18.
14. On free trade as panacea: Economic Council of Canada, *Looking Outward*; R. Wonnacott and P. Wonnacott, *Free Trade Between the United States and Canada*; P. Wonnacott and R. Wonnacott, *U.S.-Canadian Free Trade*; H.G. Johnson, Wonnacott, and Shibata, *Harmonization of National Economic Policies*.

On support of the U.S. ambassador and the BCNI: Doern and Tomlin, *Faith and Fear*, pp. 46–48, 103–8, 217–19; Langille, "Business Council on National Issues," p. 72; Inwood, "Nationalism Versus Continentalism," ch. 7; and authors' interview with David Langille, Nov. 21, 1987.

Trade policy officials: Authors' interviews with Allan Gotlieb, Oct. 31, 1989; A. Halliday, July 20, 1984; Michael Hart, Feb. 1, 1994; Robert Latimer, June 7, 1985; Ed Lumley, Jan. 14, 1986; Sylvia Ostry, Feb. 16, 1986; Gerald Regan, Nov. 26, 1986; and Colin Robertson, Feb. 3, 1985.
15. Outmuscled: Doern and Tomlin, *Faith and Fear*, pp. 276–85, 288–89.

Dictated: "The private sector basically got what it wanted in the final text." Rugman, "Why Business Supports," p. 96. Also Doern and Tomlin, *Faith and Fear*, pp. 108–11.

Charter of rights for continental business: Clarkson, "Constitutionalizing."

On Quebec and the FTA: Latouche, "Le petit, le gros," pp. 148–59. "Quebec's peculiar circumstances had produced a nationalist movement that saw close relations with the United States as not only compatible with its independence project but indeed an essential part of it." Chodos and Hamovitch, *Quebec and the American Dream*, p. 198; see also pp. 10–13, 196–97, 221, 225. According to Courchene, the province's desire to "decrease dependency on and economic ties to Ottawa and the rest of Canada" is merely the logical economic extension of the Quiet Revolution. "What Does Ontario Want," pp. 8–11.

Prevent another NEP: Doern and Tomlin, *Faith and Fear*, pp. 50–52.

Sell it out: Authors' interview with Lloyd Axworthy, Jan. 18, 1993.
16. Pro-Canada movement: The Pro-Canada Network consisted of more than thirty national organizations, including the Assembly of First Nations, Canadian Auto Workers, Canadian Environmental Law Association, Canadian Labour Congress, Canadian Teachers' Federation, Canadian Union of Postal Workers, Canadian Union of Public Employees, Centrale de l'enseignement du Québec, Confederation of Canadian Unions, Confédération des syndicats nationaux, Council of Canadians, Friends of the Earth, Ecumenical Coalition for Economic Justice, National Action Committee on the Status of Women, National Anti-Poverty Organization, National Farmers' Union, National Federation of Nurses' Unions, One Voice Seniors' Network, Union des producteurs agricoles, United Steelworkers of America, and Alliance of Canadian Cinema, Television, and Radio Artists. *Pro-Canada Dossier*, p. 2. Many of these organizations were themselves umbrellas for other groups; NAC had some five hundred affiliates at the time. Total membership was estimated at several million Canadians. Bashevkin, *True Patriot Love*, p. 110.

Political economists: D. Cameron, *Free Trade Papers*, and Marjorie Cohen, *Free Trade*.

On John Turner in the 1988 federal election: Clarkson, "Liberals: Disoriented."

17. All alone at Stornoway: Authors' confidential interview, Apr. 1988.

18. Business community: Niosi, "Rise of French-Canadian Capitalism"; Fournier, "New Parameters"; Fraser, *Quebec Inc.*, chs. 5–11.

19. Celebrated prodigal son: Authors' interviews with Lise Bissonnette, Dec. 17, 1985; Denise Bombardier, June 2, 1985; Madeleine Gobeil, Apr. 8, 1985; Leo Kolber, Jan. 24, 1991; and Wanda O'Hagan, June 5, 1985.

20. "Polemics": Authors' interview with Pierre Trudeau, June 6, 1985.

21. Diatribe: Trudeau, "'Say Goodbye.'"

22. On the Meech Lake Accord, from start to finish: A. Cohen, *Deal Undone.*

23. On Charlottetown and aftermath: Russell, *Constitutional Odyssey*, ch. 11; also Blais, "Quebec Referendum."
   Denunciation: Trudeau, *"A Mess."*

24. On Chrétien's fall and rise: Frizzell, Pammett, and Westell, *Canadian General Election*, pp. 227–32.

25. Thinkers' conference: *Finding Common Ground.*

26. Extended the original FTA: Continentalists saw NAFTA as a move towards greater liberalization (Globerman and Walker, *Assessing NAFTA*), whereas nationalists saw it as further weakening the Canadian state (Grinspun and Cameron, *Political Economy*; D. Cameron and Watkins, *Canada Under Free Trade*).

27. On the 1993 federal election: Frizzell, Pammett, and Westell, *Canadian General Election.*

28. "Too early to tell": Pierre Trudeau's address at the University of Toronto, Mar. 5, 1984, authors' notes.

29. Disappointment: Conway, "Inadequate Defense." The contents of *Memoirs* revealed that Trudeau had grown more obdurate with the years. "No regrets" was the text's recurring motif as he defended his intellectual turf by refusing to modify the positions he had assumed thirty years before.

# BIBLIOGRAPHY

Acton, Lord, *Essays on Freedom and Power* (Lester, Mass.: Peter Smith, 1972).

Adams, Roy J., "The Federal Government and Tripartism," *Relations industrielles* 37, no. 3 (1982), pp. 606–17.

Aitken, Hugh G.J., *American Capital and Canadian Resources* (Cambridge, Mass.: Harvard University Press, 1961).

———, "The Changing Structure of the Canadian Economy, with Particular Reference to the Influence of the United States," in Hugh G.J. Aitken et al., *The American Economic Impact on Canada* (Durham, N.C.: Duke University Press, 1959), pp. 3–35.

———, "Defensive Expansionism: The State and Economic Growth in Canada," in Hugh G.J. Aitken, ed., *The State and Economic Growth* (New York: Social Sciences Research Council, 1959), pp. 79–114.

Aitken, Hugh G.J., et al., *The American Economic Impact on Canada* (Durham, N.C.: Duke University Press, 1959).

Alberta, *Ninth Annual Report to March 31, 1982* (Edmonton: Department of Federal and Intergovernmental Affairs, 1982).

Allen, Ralph, *Ordeal by Fire: Canada, 1910–1945* (Toronto: Doubleday, 1961).

Allison, Graham T., *Essence of Decision: Explaining the Cuban Missile Crisis* (Boston: Little, Brown, 1971).

Alsop, S.M., "Architectural Digest Visits Pierre Trudeau," *Architectural Digest* (Jan. 1986), pp. 106–113.

Anderson, Ian, "The Oil War Is the First War," *Maclean's* (Apr. 17, 1981), pp. 42–44.

Andrew, Arthur, *The Rise and Fall of a Middle Power: Canadian Diplomacy from King to Mulroney* (Toronto: Lorimer, 1993).

Angell, David J.R., "The Trudeau Doctrine and Canadian Arms Control and Defence Policy, 1968–1984," senior essay, Yale University, 1986.

Annan, Noel, *Our Age: Portrait of a Generation* (London: Weidenfeld and Nicolson, 1990).

Atkinson, Michael M., and William D. Coleman, *The State, Business, and Industrial Change in Canada* (Toronto: University of Toronto Press, 1989).

Atkinson, Michael M., and Kim Richard Nossal, "Bureaucratic Politics and the New Fighter Aircraft Decisions," *Canadian Public Administration* 24, no. 4 (Winter 1981), pp. 531–62.

Atwood, Margaret, *Bodily Harm* (Toronto: McClelland and Stewart, 1981).

Aucoin, Peter, "Organizational Change in the Machinery of Canadian Government: From Rational Management to Brokerage Politics," *Canadian Journal of Political Science* 19, no. 1 (Mar. 1986), pp. 3–27.

Audley, Paul, *Canada's Cultural Industries: Broadcasting, Publishing, Records and Film* (Toronto: Canadian Institute for Economic Policy, 1983).

Axworthy, Lloyd, "Towards a New Phase," *The Canadian Forum* 59, no. 692 (Sept. 1979), pp. 13–14.

Axworthy, Thomas, "Innovation and the Party System: An Examination of the Career of Walter L. Gordon and the Liberal Party," MA thesis, Queen's University, 1970.

———, " 'To Stand Not So High Perhaps but Always Alone': The Foreign Policy of Pierre Elliott Trudeau," in Thomas S. Axworthy and Pierre Elliott Trudeau, eds., *Towards a Just Society: The Trudeau Years* (Toronto: Viking, 1990), pp. 12–48.

————, "Towards the Next Election," script of video presentation to the annual meeting of the Liberal Party of Ontario, Toronto, Mar. 24, 1984.

Axworthy, Thomas S., and Pierre Elliott Trudeau, eds., *Towards a Just Society: The Trudeau Years* (Markham, Ont.: Viking, 1990).

Baetz, Mark C., "The Canadian Federation of Independent Business and the MacEachen Budget," in M.C. Baetz and D.H. Thain, *Canadian Cases in Business-Government Relations* (Toronto: Methuen, 1985), pp. 325–47.

Bakvis, Herman, *Regional Ministers: Power and Influence in the Canadian Cabinet* (Toronto: University of Toronto Press, 1991).

Ball, George, *Discipline of Power* (Boston: Little, Brown, 1968).

Banting, Keith, "Institutionalized Conservatism: Federalism and Pension Reform," in Jacqueline S. Ismael, ed., *Canadian Social Welfare Policy: Federal and Provincial Dimensions* (Montreal: McGill-Queen's University Press, 1985), pp. 48–74.

————, *The Welfare State and Canadian Federalism*, 2nd ed. (Montreal and Kingston: McGill-Queen's University Press, 1987).

Banting, Keith, and Richard Simeon, *And No One Cheered: Federalism, Democracy and the Constitution Act* (Toronto: Methuen, 1983).

Barrett, Gene, and Anthony Davis, "Floundering in Troubled Waters: The Political Economy of the Atlantic Fishery and the Task Force on Atlantic Fisheries," *Journal of Canadian Studies* 19, no. 1 (Spring 1984), pp. 124–37.

Barros, James, *No Sense of Evil: Espionage, the Case of Herbert Norman* (Toronto: Deneau, 1986).

Barzini, Luigi, *The Europeans* (New York: Simon and Schuster, 1983).

Bashevkin, Sylvia B., *Toeing the Lines: Women and Party Politics in English Canada* (Toronto: University of Toronto Press, 1985).

————, *True Patriot Love: The Politics of Canadian Nationalism* (Toronto: Oxford University Press, 1991).

Bégin, Monique, *Medicare: Canada's Right to Health* (Montreal: Optimum, 1987).

Beiner, Ronald, *What's the Matter with Liberalism?* (Los Angeles: University of California Press, 1992).

Bélanger, Yves, and Pierre Fournier, *L'entreprise québécoise: Développement historique et dynamique contemporaine* (LaSalle, Que.: Editions Hurtubise HMH, 1987).

Bell, Joel, "Canadian Industrial Policy in a Changing World," in Thomas S. Axworthy and Pierre Elliott Trudeau, eds., *Towards a Just Society: The Trudeau Years* (Toronto: Viking, 1990), pp. 78–106.

Bercuson, David J., "Ottawa Strikes Back," *Saturday Night* (Mar. 1983), pp. 48–52.

Berger, Carl, *The Sense of Power: Studies in the Ideas of Canadian Imperialism 1867-1914* (Toronto: University of Toronto Press, 1970).

————, ed., *Imperialism and Nationalism, 1884-1914: A Conflict in Canadian Thought* (Toronto: Copp Clark, 1969).

Bergeron, Gérard, *Du duplessisme à Trudeau et Bourassa, 1956-1971* (Montreal: Parti pris, 1971).

Bickerton, James, "The Party System and the Representation of Periphery Interests: The Case of the Maritimes," in Alain G. Gagnon and Brian A. Tanguay, eds., *Canadian Parties in Transition: Discourse, Organization, Representation* (Toronto: Nelson, 1989), pp. 461–84.

Bissell, Claude, *Halfway up Parnassus: A Personal Account of the University of Toronto 1932-1971* (Toronto: University of Toronto Press, 1974).

Black, Conrad, *Duplessis* (Toronto: McClelland and Stewart, 1977).

Blais, André, "The Debate on Canadian Industrial Policy," in André Blais, ed., *Industrial Policy* (Toronto: University of Toronto Press, 1986), pp. 55–82.

————, "The Quebec Referendum: Quebeckers Say No," in Kenneth McRoberts and Patrick J. Monahan, eds., *The Charlottetown Accord, the Referendum, and the Future of Canada* (Toronto: University of Toronto Press, 1993), pp. 200–207.

Bland, Douglas, *The Administration of Defence Policy in Canada, 1947 to 1985* (Kingston, Ont.: Ronald Frye, 1987).

Bliss, Michael, *Northern Enterprise: Five Centuries of Canadian Business* (Toronto: McClelland and Stewart, 1987).

Bolkestein, F., *Modern Liberalism: Conversations with Liberal Politicians* (New York: Elsevier, 1982).

Borins, Sandford F., "Ottawa's Expenditure Envelopes: Workable Rationality at Last?" in G. Bruce Doern, ed., *How Ottawa Spends Your Tax Dollars, 1982: National Policy and Economic Development* (Toronto: Lorimer, 1982), pp. 63–85.

————, "World War Two Crown Corporations: Their Wartime Role and Peace-time Privatization," *Canadian Public Administration* 25, no. 3 (Fall 1982), pp. 380–404.

Bothwell, Robert, *Canada and the United States: The Politics of Partnership* (Toronto: University of Toronto Press, 1992).

Bothwell, Robert, and William Kilbourn, *C.D. Howe: A Biography* (Toronto: McClelland and Stewart, 1979).

Bothwell, Robert, Ian Drummond, and John English, *Canada Since 1945: Power, Politics, and Provincialism* (Toronto: University of Toronto Press, 1981).

Brecher, Irving, *Canada's Competition Policy Revisited: Some New Thoughts on an Old Story* (Montreal: Institute for Research on Public Policy, 1981).

————, "The Flow of United States Investment Funds into Canada Since World War II," in Hugh G.J. Aitken et al., *The American Economic Impact on Canada* (Durham, N.C.: Duke University Press, 1959), pp. 100–126.

————, "The Sad Story of Competition Reform," *Choices* (Feb. 1982), pp. 1–3.

Brecher, Irving, and S.S. Reisman, *Canada-United States Economic Relations*, Background Studies for Royal Commission on Canada's Economic Prospects, no. 29 (Ottawa: Minister of Supply and Services, 1957).

Bregha, François, *Bob Blair's Pipeline: The Business and Politics of Northern Energy Development Projects* (Toronto: Lorimer, 1979).

Breslin, Catherine, "The Other Trudeaus," *Chatelaine* (Sept. 1969), pp. 32–33, 108–11; (Oct. 1969), pp. 42, 78–87.

Breton, Albert, "The Economics of Nationalism," *Journal of Political Economy* 72, no. 4 (Aug. 1964), pp. 376–86.

Breton, Albert, et al., "An Appeal for Realism in Politics," *The Canadian Forum* (May 1964), pp. 29–33.

Breton, Albert, Claude Bruneau, Yvon Gauthier, Marc Lalonde, Maurice Pinard, and Pierre E. Trudeau, "L'agriculture au Québec," *Cité libre* 78 (July 1965), pp. 9–16.

Breton, Albert, Raymond Breton, Claude Bruneau, Yvon Gauthier, Marc Lalonde, Maurice Pinard, and Pierre E.-Trudeau, "Manifeste pour une politique fonctionnelle," *Cité libre* 67 (May 1964), pp. 11–17.

Brimelow, Peter, *The Patriot Game* (Toronto: Key Porter, 1986).

Britton, John N.H., and James M. Gilmour, *The Weakest Link: A Technological Perspective on Canadian Industrial Underdevelopment*, Science Council of Canada Study no. 43 (Ottawa: Science Council of Canada, 1978).

Brodie, M. Janine, "From Waffles to Grits: A Decade in the Life of the New Democratic Party," in Hugh G. Thorburn, ed., *Party Politics in Canada*, 5th ed. (Scarborough: Prentice-Hall Canada, 1985), pp. 205–17.

Bromke, Adam, and Kim Nossal, "Tensions in Canada's Foreign Policy," *Foreign Affairs* 62, no. 2 (Winter 1983/84), pp. 335–53.

———, "Trudeau Rides the 'Third Rail,'" *International Perspectives* (May-June 1984), pp. 3–6.

Brooke, Janet M., *Discerning Tastes: Montreal Collectors, 1880-1920* (Montreal: Montreal Museum of Fine Arts, 1989).

Brooks, Stephen, "The State as Entrepreneur: From CDC to CDIC," *Canadian Public Administration* 26, no. 4 (Winter 1983), pp. 525–43.

Brown, Malcolm C., "Health Care Financing and the Canada Health Act," *Journal of Canadian Studies* 21, no. 2 (Summer 1986), pp. 111–32.

Browning, Robert, *Poems of Robert Browning*, Edward Shanks, ed. (London: Macmillan, 1961).

Brownstein, Ronald, and Nina Easton, *Reagan's Ruling Class: Portraits of the President's Top One Hundred Officials* (Washington, D.C.: Presidential Accountability Group, 1982).

Bryce, Robert, *Maturing in Hard Times: Canada's Department of Finance Through the Great Depression* (Montreal: McGill-Queen's University Press, 1986).

Bryden, Kenneth, *Old Age Pensions and Policy-Making in Canada* (Montreal: McGill-Queen's University Press, 1974).

Buckley, William F., Jr., *Did You Ever See a Dream Walking?* (New York: Bobbs-Merrill, 1970).

Byers, R.B., "Canadian Defence and Defence Procurement: Implications for Economic Policy," in Denis Stairs and Gilbert R. Winham, eds., *Selected Problems in Formulating Foreign Economic Policy* (Toronto: University of Toronto Press, 1985), pp. 131–95.

———, "Defence and Foreign Policy in the 1980s: The Demise of the Trudeau Doctrine," *International Journal* 33 (Spring 1978), pp. 312–38.

Byers, R.B., and David Leyton-Brown, "Canadian Elite Images of the International System," *International Journal* 32, no. 3 (Summer 1977), pp. 608–39.

Byers, R.B., and Don Munton, "Canadian Defence, Nuclear Arms and Public Opinion: Consensus and Controversy," paper presented at the annual meeting of the Canadian Political Science Association, June 1983.

Calvert, John, *Government Limited: The Corporate Takeover of the Public Sector in Canada* (Ottawa: Canadian Centre for Policy Alternatives, 1984).

Cameron, Duncan, "Monetary Relations in North America," *International Journal* 42, no. 1 (Winter 1986-7), pp. 170–98.

———, "Wage Earners, the Liberals, and the Canadian Economy," *OUR Generation* 15, no. 4 (Spring 1983), pp. 29–34.

———, ed., *The Free Trade Papers* (Toronto: Lorimer, 1986).

Cameron, Duncan, and Mel Watkins, eds., *Canada Under Free Trade* (Toronto: Lorimer, 1993).

Cameron, Stevie, "Maggie: Happy at Last!" *Chatelaine* (June 1985), pp. 57, 98, 106–10.

———, *Ottawa Inside Out: Power, Prestige and Scandal in the Nation's Capital* (Toronto: Key Porter, 1989).

Campbell, Colin, *Governments Under Stress: Political Executives and Key Bureaucrats in Washington, London, and Ottawa* (Toronto: University of Toronto Press, 1983).

Campbell, Colin, and George J. Szablowski, *The Super-Bureaucrats: Structure and Behaviour in Central Agencies* (Toronto: Macmillan of Canada, 1979).

Campbell, Robert M., *The Full-Employment Objective in Canada, 1945-85: Historical,*

*Conceptual and Comparative Perspectives* (Ottawa: Economic Council of Canada, 1991).

————, *Grand Illusions: The Politics of the Keynesian Experience in Canada, 1945-1975* (Peterborough, Ont.: Broadview Press, 1987).

Canada, *Economic Development for Canada in the 1980s* (Ottawa: November 1981).

————, *The Way Ahead: A Framework for Discussion* (Ottawa: Oct. 1976), working paper, 32 pages.

Canada, Commission of Inquiry Concerning Certain Activities of the Royal Canadian Mounted Police, *Third Report: Certain R.C.M.P. Activities and the Question of Governmental Knowledge* (Ottawa: Supply and Services Canada, 1981). [McDonald Report.]

Canada, Department of Agriculture, *Challenge for Growth: An Agri-food Strategy for Canada* (Ottawa: n.p., 1981).

Canada, Department of Energy, Mines and Resources, *The National Energy Program, 1980* (Ottawa: Energy, Mines and Resources Canada, 1980).

————, Energy Policy Sector, *An Energy Strategy for Canada: Policies for Self-Reliance* (Ottawa: Supply and Services Canada, 1976).

Canada, Department of External Affairs, "Agreement with the United States of America on Test and Evaluation of US Defence Systems in Canada," Communiqué No. 15 (Feb. 10, 1983).

————, *Foreign Policy for Canadians* (Ottawa: Information Canada, 1970).

Canada, Department of Finance, *The Budget* (Ottawa: Department of Finance, Oct. 28, 1980).

————, *The Budget in More Detail* (Ottawa: Department of Finance, 1981).

————, *Fiscal Arrangements in the Eighties – Proposals of the Government of Canada* (Ottawa: Department of Finance, 1981).

Canada, Department of National Health and Welfare, *Better Pensions for Canadians* (Ottawa: Minister of Supply and Services, 1982).

Canada, Department of Justice, *A Consolidation of the Constitution Acts 1867 to 1982* (Ottawa: Supply and Services, 1983).

Canada, House of Commons, Special Committee on Pension Reform, *Proceedings* no. IV (Apr. 21, 1983).

Canada, House of Commons, Standing Committee on External Affairs and National Defence, "Report of the Special Committee Respecting Canada-U.S. Relations," *Proceedings* No. 33 (July 13-27, 1970). [Wahn Report.]

Canada, Major Projects Task Force, *Major Canadian Projects: Major Canadian Opportunities: A Report . . . on Major Capital Projects in Canada to the Year 2000* (Ottawa: Industry, Trade and Commerce, 1981).

Canada, Parliamentary Task Force on Federal-Provincial Fiscal Arrangements, *Fiscal Federalism in Canada* (Ottawa: Minister of Supply and Services, 1981). [Breau Report.]

Canada, Royal Commission on Canada's Economic Prospects, *Final Report* (Ottawa: Minister of Supply and Services, 1957). [Gordon Report.]

Canada, Royal Commission on Corporate Concentration, *Report . . .* (Ottawa: Supply and Services, 1978). [Bryce Report.]

Canada, Royal Commission on the Economic Union and Development Prospects for Canada, *Report . . .* , 3 vols. (Ottawa: Minister of Supply and Services, 1985). [Macdonald Report.]

Canada, Royal Commission on Financial Management and Accountability, *Final Report* (Ottawa: Minister of Supply and Services, 1979). [Lambert Report.]

Canada, Senate, Special Committee on Mass Media, *The Uncertain Mirror: Report . . .* , vol. I (Ottawa: Information Canada, 1970). [Davey Report.]

Canada, Task Force on Atlantic Fisheries, *Navigating Troubled Waters: A New Policy for the Atlantic Fisheries* (Ottawa: Ministry of Supply and Services, 1983). [Kirby Report.]

Canada, Task Force on Labour Market Development, *Labour Market Development in the 1980s: A Report . . .* (Ottawa: Department of Employment and Immigration, 1981). [Dodge Report.]

Canada, Task Force on Retirement Income Policy, *The Retirement Income System in Canada: Problems and Alternative Policies for Reform*, 2 vols. (Ottawa: n.p., 1979). [Lazar Report.]

*Canadian Annual Review of Politics and Public Affairs*, John T. Saywell, ed. (1971-78), R.B. Byers, ed. (1978-1986) (Toronto: University of Toronto Press, annual).

Canadian Bar Association, *Report of the Canadian Bar Association Committee on the Appointment of Federal Judges in Canada* (Ottawa: Canadian Bar Foundation, 1985).

Careless, Anthony, *Initiative and Response: The Adaptation of Canadian Federalism to Regional Economic Development* (Montreal: McGill-Queen's University Press, 1977).

Carstairs, Sharon, *Not One of the Boys* (Toronto: Macmillan Canada, 1993).

Chodos, Robert, and Eric Hamovitch, *Quebec and the American Dream* (Toronto: Between the Lines, 1991).

Chrétien, Jean, *Straight from the Heart* (Toronto: Key Porter, 1986).

Clarke, Harold D., et al., *Absent Mandate: The Politics of Discontent in Canada* (Toronto: Gage, 1984).

————, *Political Choice in Canada* (Toronto: McGraw-Hill, 1979).

Clarke, Peter, *The Keynesian Revolution in the Making, 1924-1936* (Oxford: Oxford University Press, 1988).

Clark-Jones, Melissa, *A Staple State: Canadian Industrial Resources in Cold War* (Toronto: University of Toronto Press, 1987).

Clarkson, Stephen, *Canada and the Reagan Challenge: Crisis and Adjustment 1981-1985* (Toronto: Lorimer, 1985).

————, "Constitutionalizing the Canadian-American Relationship," in Duncan Cameron and Mel Watkins, eds., *Canada Under Free Trade* (Toronto: Lorimer, 1993), pp. 1–20.

————, "The Dauphin and the Doomed: John Turner and the Liberal Party's Debacle," in Howard Penniman, ed., *Canada at the Polls, 1984: A Study of the Federal General Elections* (Durham, N.C.: American Enterprise Institute, 1988), pp. 97–119.

————, "The Defeat of the Government, the Decline of the Liberal Party, and the (Temporary) Fall of Pierre Trudeau," in Howard R. Penniman, ed., *Canada at the Polls, 1979 and 1980: A Study of the General Elections* (Washington, D.C.: American Enterprise Institute, 1981), pp. 152–89.

————, "Democracy in the Liberal Party: The Experiment with Citizen Participation under Pierre Trudeau," in Hugh G. Thorburn, ed., *Party Politics in Canada*, 4th ed. (Scarborough: Prentice-Hall, 1979), pp. 154–60.

————, "Disjunctions: Free Trade and the Paradox of Canadian Development," in Daniel Drache and Meric S. Gertler, eds., *The New Era of Global Competition: State Policy and Market Power* (Montreal: McGill-Queen's University Press, 1991), pp. 103–26.

————, "The Liberals: Disoriented in Defeat," in Alan Frizzell, Jon H. Pammett, and Anthony Westell, eds., *The Canadian General Election of 1988* (Ottawa: Carleton University Press, 1989), pp. 27–41.

————, "Pierre Trudeau and the Liberal Party: The Jockey and the Horse," in Howard R. Penniman, ed., *Canada at the Polls: The General Election of 1974* (Washington, D.C.: American Enterprise Institute, 1975), pp. 57–96.

————, "Vive le Québec Libre! Or Putting the Leader Back In," in David P. Shugarman and Reg Whitaker, eds., *Federalism and Political Community: Essays in Honour of Donald Smiley* (Peterborough, Ont.: Broadview, 1990), pp. 55–69.

Clemens, John, *Polls, Politics and Populism* (London: Gower, 1983).

Clement, Wallace, *The Canadian Corporate Elite: An Analysis of Economic Power* (Toronto: McClelland and Stewart, 1975).

Coady, Moses, *Masters of Their Own Destiny* (New York: Harper, 1939).

Cohen, Andrew, *A Deal Undone: The Making and Breaking of the Meech Lake Accord* (Vancouver: Douglas and McIntyre, 1990).

Cohen, Marjorie Griffin, *Free Trade and the Future of Women's Work: Manufacturing and Service Industries* (Toronto: Garamond, 1987).

Cohen, Maxwell, "The Arctic and the National Interest," *International Journal* 26, no. 1 (Winter 1970-71), pp. 52–81.

Coleman, William D., and Grace Skogstad, eds., *Policy Communities and Public Policy in Canada: A Structural Approach* (Mississauga, Ont.: Copp Clark Pitman, 1990).

Collins, Anne, "Which Way to Ottawa?" *City Woman* (Dec. 1981), pp. 11–32.

Collison, Robert, "The Economist with Trudeau's Ear," *Canadian Business* 53, no. 10 (Oct. 1980), pp. 114–27.

————, "Have the Interventionists Lost Their Nerve?" *Canadian Business* 55, no. 1 (Jan. 1982), pp. 31–37.

————, "Ottawa's Policy Entrepreneurs," *Canadian Business* 55, no. 1 (Jan. 1982), pp. 40–42.

Conway, John, "An Inadequate Defence Before the Bar of History," review of *Memoirs*, by Pierre Elliott Trudeau, *Compass* (Mar./Apr. 1994), pp. 36–38.

Cook, Chris, *A Short History of the Liberal Party, 1900-1988* (London: Macmillan, 1989).

Cooper, R.N., *The Economics of Interdependence* (New York: McGraw-Hill, 1968).

Coser, Lewis A., and Irving Howe, *The New Conservatives: A Critique from the Left* (New York: Quadrangle/New York Times, 1974).

Courchene, Thomas J., *Money, Inflation, and the Bank of Canada: An Analysis of Monetary Gradualism, 1975-80*, vol. II (Montreal: C.D. Howe Institute, 1981).

————, *No Place to Stand? Abandoning Monetary Targets: An Evaluation* (Toronto: C.D. Howe Institute, 1983).

————, *What Does Ontario Want?* (Toronto: Robarts Centre for Canadian Studies, York University, 1989).

Cox, David, "Leadership Change and Innovation in Canadian Foreign Policy: The 1979 Progressive Conservative Government," *International Journal* 37, no. 4 (Autumn 1982), pp. 555–83.

Craig, Alton W.J., *The System of Industrial Relations in Canada* (Scarborough, Ont.: Prentice-Hall, 1990).

Crane, David, *Controlling Interest: The Canadian Oil and Gas Stakes* (Toronto: McClelland and Stewart, 1982).

Crawford, Alan, *Thunder on the Right* (New York: Pantheon, 1980).

Crean, Susan M., *Who's Afraid of Canadian Culture?* (Toronto: General, 1976).

Cregier, Don M., *Decline of the British Liberal Party: Why and How?* (Murray, Ky.: Lorrah & Hitchcock, 1985).

Creighton, Donald, *The Forked Road: Canada 1939-1957* (Toronto: McClelland and Stewart, 1976).

Crépeau, P.-A., and C.B. Macpherson, eds., *The Future of Federalism; L'avenir du fédéralisme* (Toronto: University of Toronto Press, 1965).

Cross, Amanda [pseud.], *The Players Come Again* (New York: Ballantine Books, 1990).

Crozier, Michel J., Samuel P. Huntington, and Joji Watanuki, *The Crisis of Democracy: Report on the Governability of Democracies to the Trilateral Commission* (New York: New York University Press, 1975).

Cuff, R.D., and J.L. Granatstein, *American Dollars – Canadian Prosperity: Canadian-American Economic Relations, 1945-1950* (Toronto: Samuel-Stevens, 1978).

———, *Canadian-American Relations in Wartime: From the Great War to the Cold War* (Toronto: Hakkert, 1975).

———, "The Rise and Fall of Canadian-American Free Trade, 1947-8," *Canadian Historical Review* 58, no. 4 (Dec. 1977), pp. 459–82.

Dangerfield, George, *The Strange Death of Liberal England* (New York: Harrison Smith & Robert Haas, 1935).

Davey, Keith, *The Rainmaker: A Passion for Politics* (Toronto: Stoddart, 1986).

"Davey Joins V&B's ACI," *Marketing* (Nov. 26, 1979), p. 1.

Dawson, R. MacGregor, *William Lyon Mackenzie King: A Political Biography*, vol. I, *1874-1923* (Toronto: University of Toronto Press, 1958).

Delisle, Esther, *The Traitor and the Jew: Anti-Semitism and the Delirium of Extremist Right-wing Nationalism in French Canada from 1929-1939* (Montreal: Robert Davies, 1993).

Desveaux, James A., *Designing Bureaucracies: Institutional Capacity and Large-Scale Problem Solving* (Berkeley, Cal.: Stanford University Press, 1994).

Deutsch, John J., "Recent American Influence in Canada with Particular Reference to Economic Factors and Canadian Reaction," in Hugh G.J. Aitken et al., *The American Economic Impact on Canada* (Durham, N.C.: Duke University Press, 1959), pp. 36–50.

Dewar, Elaine, "The Most Hated Man in Canada," *Today Magazine*, supplement to the *Toronto Star* (June 19, 1982), pp. 11–14.

Dewitt, David B., and John J. Kirton, *Canada as a Principal Power: A Study in Foreign Policy and International Relations* (Toronto: Wiley & Sons Canada, 1983).

Dion, Stéphane, "La sécession du Québec: Evaluation des probabilités après les élections fédérales du 25 octobre 1993," paper presented at "Les élections au Canada, 1993: Changement et continuité," Mexico City, Nov. 12, 1993.

Djwa, Sandra, *The Politics of the Imagination: A Life of F.R. Scott* (Toronto: McClelland and Stewart, 1987).

Dobell, Peter C., *Canada's Search for New Roles: Foreign Policy in the Trudeau Era* (Toronto: Oxford University Press, 1972).

Doern, G. Bruce, "Energy Expenditures and the NEP: Controlling the Energy Leviathan," in Allan M. Maslove, ed., *How Ottawa Spends, 1984: The New Agenda* (Toronto: Methuen, 1984), pp. 31–78.

———, "Liberal Priorities 1982: The Limits of Scheming Virtuously," in G. Bruce Doern, ed., *How Ottawa Spends Your Tax Dollars, 1982: National Policy and Economic Development* (Toronto: Lorimer, 1982), pp. 1–36.

———, "The Mega-Project Episode and the Formulation of Canadian Economic

Development Policy," *Canadian Public Administration* 26, no. 2 (Summer 1983), pp. 219–38.

———, "Recent Changes in the Philosophy of Policy-Making in Canada," *Canadian Journal of Political Science* 4, no. 2 (June 1972), pp. 243–64.

Doern, G. Bruce, and Richard W. Phidd, *Canadian Public Policy: Ideas, Structure, Process* (Toronto: Methuen, 1983).

Doern, G. Bruce, and Brian W. Tomlin, *Faith and Fear: The Free Trade Story* (Toronto: Stoddart, 1991).

Doern, G. Bruce, and Glen Toner, *The Politics of Energy: The Development and Implementation of the NEP* (Toronto: Methuen, 1985).

Doern, G. Bruce, Allan M. Maslove, and Michael J. Prince, *Public Budgeting in Canada: Politics, Economics and Management* (Ottawa: Carleton University Press, 1988).

Donner, Arthur W., and Douglas D. Peters, *The Monetarist Counter-Revolution: A Critique of Canadian Monetary Policy 1975-1979* (Toronto: Canadian Institute for Economic Policy and Lorimer, 1979).

Dosman, Edgar J., *The National Interest: The Politics of Northern Development, 1968-75* (Toronto: McClelland and Stewart, 1975).

Doucet, Gerald, *Confessions of a Distant Liberal* (n.p., 1990).

Dow, James, *The Arrow* (Toronto: Lorimer, 1979).

Drache, Daniel, ed., *Quebec: Only the Beginning, The Manifestoes of the Common Front* (Toronto: New Press, 1972).

Draper, Theodore, "How Not to Think About Nuclear War," *New York Review of Books* (July 15, 1982), pp. 35–43.

Dunn, Lewis, *Controlling the Bomb: Nuclear Proliferation in the 1980s* (New Haven, Conn.: Yale University Press, 1982).

Dutton, David, "On the Brink of Oblivion: The Post-War Crisis of British Liberalism," *Canadian Journal of History* 27 (Dec. 1992), pp. 425–50.

Eayrs, James, "Defining a New Place for Canada in the Hierarchy of World Power," *International Perspectives* (May/June 1975), pp. 15–24.

Eberts, Mary, "The Court and Its Leadership (or Lack Thereof) on Social Issues, Including Women's Issues," paper given at a Political Economy Workshop at the University of Toronto, Mar. 5, 1990.

Economic Council of Canada, *Financing Confederation: Today and Tomorrow* (Ottawa: Minister of Supply and Services, 1982).

———, *Fourth Annual Review: The Canadian Economy from the 1960s to the 1970s* (Ottawa: Queen's Printer, 1967).

———, *Good Jobs, Bad Jobs: Employment in the Service Economy* (Ottawa: Minister of Supply and Services, 1989).

———, *Interim Report on Competition Policy* (Ottawa: Queen's Printer, 1969).

———, *Legacies: 26th Annual Review* (Ottawa: Minister of Supply and Services, 1989).

———, *Looking Outward: A New Trade Strategy for Canada* (Ottawa: Supply and Services Canada, 1975).

———, *Toward Full Employment and Price Stability: A Report to the OECD by a Group of Independent Experts* (Paris: Organisation for Economic Co-operation and Development, 1977).

Eden, Lorraine, and Maureen Appel Molot, "Canada's National Policies: Reflections on 125 Years," *Canadian Public Policy* 19, no. 3 (Sept. 1993), pp. 232–51.

Eisler, Riane, *The Chalice and the Blade* (New York: HarperCollins, 1988).

English, John, *Shadow of Heaven: 1897-1948*, vol. 1 of *The Life of Lester Pearson* (Toronto: Lester and Orpen Dennys, 1989).

————, *The Worldly Years: 1949-1972*, vol. 2 of *The Life of Lester Pearson* (Toronto: Knopf, 1992).

Enright, Michael, "The New Number Two," *Maclean's* (Nov. 1, 1976), pp. 26–40.

Esberey, Joy E., *Knight of the Holy Spirit: A Study of William Lyon Mackenzie King* (Toronto: University of Toronto Press, 1980).

Fanon, Frantz, *The Wretched of the Earth* (New York: Grove Press, 1963), originally published as *Les damnés de la terre* (Paris: Maspero, 1961).

Feigenbaum, Harvey, Richard Samuels, and Kent Weaver, "Innovation, Coordination, and Implementation in Energy Policy," in R. Kent Weaver and Bert A. Rockman, eds., *Do Institutions Matter?* (Washington, D.C.: Brookings Institution, 1993).

Ferrante, Angela, "The Prime of Iona Campagnolo," *Chatelaine* (May 1983), pp. 53, 70–74.

Ferns, H.S., *Reading from Left to Right: One Man's Political History* (Toronto: University of Toronto Press, 1983).

Ferns, H.S., and B. Ostry, *The Age of Mackenzie King: The Rise of the Leader* (London: William Heinemann, 1955).

*Finding Common Ground: The Proceedings of the Aylmer Conference*, Jean Chrétien, ed. (Hull, Que.: Voyageur Publishing, 1992).

Firestone, O.J., *Canada's Anti-Inflation Program and Kenneth Galbraith* (Ottawa: University of Ottawa Press, 1977).

Fisher, Elizabeth, "The Reagan Reversal: America's Soviet Policy, 1981-1985," PhD thesis, University of Toronto, 1994.

Fonteneau, Alain, et Pierre-Alain Muet, *La gauche face à la crise* (Paris: Presses de la Fondation Nationale des Sciences Politiques, 1985).

*Foreign Direct Investment in Canada* (Ottawa: Information Canada, 1972). [Gray Report.]

Forsey, Eugene, *A Life on the Fringe: The Memoirs of Eugene Forsey* (Toronto: Oxford University Press, 1990).

Foster, Peter, *The Blue-Eyed Sheiks* (Toronto: Collins, 1979).

————, *Other People's Money: The Banks, the Government and Dome* (Don Mills, Ont.: Totem Books, 1984).

————, *The Sorcerer's Apprentices* (Toronto: Collins, 1982).

Fournier, Pierre, "The New Parameters of the Quebec Bourgeoisie," in Alain G. Gagnon, ed., *Quebec: State and Society* (Scarborough, Ont.: Methuen, 1984), pp. 201–227.

Fowke, V.C. "The National Policy – Old and New," *Canadian Journal of Economics and Political Science* 18, no. 3 (Aug. 1952), pp. 271–86.

Frank, Helmut J., and John J. Schanz, Jr., *U.S.-Canadian Energy Trade: A Study of Changing Relationships*, Westview Special Studies in Natural Resources and Energy Management (Boulder, Col.: Westview Press, 1978).

Fraser, Matthew, *Quebec Inc.: French-Canadian Entrepreneurs and the New Business Elite* (Toronto: Key Porter, 1987).

Freeman, Linda, *Canadian Policy Towards South Africa* (forthcoming).

Fremon, Celeste, "Margaret Trudeau," *Playgirl* (Sept. 1979), pp. 34–37, 88–91, 104, 115–20, 124.

French, Richard D., *How Ottawa Decides: Planning and Industrial Policy-Making, 1968-1980* (Toronto: Canadian Institute for Economic Policy and Lorimer, 1980).

Friedman, Milton, "The Role of Monetary Policy," *American Economic Review* 58, no. 1 (Mar. 1968), pp. 1–17.

Friend, Julius W., *Seven Years in France: François Mitterrand and the Unintended Revolution, 1981-1988* (Boulder, Col.: Westview, 1989).

Frizzell, Alan, Jon H. Pammett, and Anthony Westell, *The Canadian General Election of 1993* (Ottawa: Carleton University Press, 1994).

Frolic, B. Michael, "The Trudeau Initiative," in Paul M. Evans and B. Michael Frolic, eds., *Reluctant Adversaries: Canada and the People's Republic of China, 1949-1970* (Toronto: University of Toronto Press, 1991), pp. 189–216.

Furbank, P.N., *E.M. Forster: A Life* (Oxford: Oxford University Press, 1979).

Gaddis, John Lewis, *The United States and the End of the Cold War: Implications, Reconsiderations, Provocations* (New York: Oxford University Press, 1992).

Galbraith, John Kenneth, *The Affluent Society* (Boston: Houghton Mifflin, 1958).

———, *The Age of Uncertainty* (Boston: Houghton Mifflin, 1977).

———, *Economics and the Public Purpose* (Boston: Houghton Mifflin, 1973).

———, *A Life in Our Times: Memoirs* (New York: Ballantine, 1981).

———, *Who Needs the Democrats? And What It Takes to be Needed* (Garden City, N.Y.: Doubleday, 1970).

Galente, Pierre, *Malraux* (New York: Cowles, 1971).

Gardner, Robert, "Tax Reform and Class Interests: The Fate of Progressive Reform, 1967-72," *Canadian Taxation* 3, no. 4 (Winter 1981), pp. 245–57.

GATT-Fly, *Power to Choose: Canada's Energy Options* (Toronto: Between the Lines, 1981).

George, Roy, "The Cape Breton Development Corporation," in Allan Tupper and G. Bruce Doern, eds., *Public Corporations and Public Policy in Canada* (Montreal: Institute for Research on Public Policy, 1981), pp. 365–88.

Giles, Anthony, "The Canadian Labour Congress and Tripartism," *Relations industrielles* 37, no. 1 (1982), pp. 93–125.

Gillespie, W. Irwin, "The Department of Finance and PEMS: Increased Influence or Reduced Monopoly Power?" in Allan M. Maslove, ed., *How Ottawa Spends, 1984: The New Agenda* (Toronto: Methuen, 1984), pp. 189–214.

———, "The 1981 Federal Budget: Muddling Through or Purposeful Tax Reform?" *Canadian Tax Journal* 31, no. 6 (Nov.-Dec. 1983), pp. 975–1002.

———, *Tax, Borrow and Spend: Financing Federal Spending in Canada, 1867-1990* (Ottawa: Carleton University Press, 1991).

Gillespie, W. Irwin, and Allan M. Maslove, "Volatility and Visibility: The Federal Revenue and Expenditure Plan," in G. Bruce Doern, ed., *How Ottawa Spends Your Tax Dollars, 1982: National Policy and Economic Development* (Toronto: Lorimer, 1982), pp. 37–62.

Gillies, James, *Facing Reality: Consultation, Consensus and Making Economic Policy for the 21st Century* (Montreal: Institute for Research on Public Policy, 1986).

———, *Where Business Fails* (Montreal: Institute for Research on Public Policy, 1981).

Gilpin, Robert, *The Political Economy of International Relations* (Princeton, N.J.: Princeton University Press, 1987).

Gilson, J.C., "The Quid Pro Crow," paper prepared for the Western Business Outlook Conference, Conference Board of Canada, Edmonton, June 8, 1983.

Globerman, Steven, and Michael Walker, eds., *Assessing NAFTA: A Trinational Analysis* (Vancouver: Fraser Institute, 1992).

Glynn, Lenny, "Why's Uncle Sam Becoming Uncle Scrooge? Try FIRA and the NEP," *Canadian Business* 54, no. 11 (Nov. 1981), pp. 16, 21.

Goar, Carol, "Trudeau's Capitalist," *Canadian Business* 55, no. 11 (Nov. 1982), pp. 66–68.

Godfrey, Dave, and Mel Watkins, eds., *Gordon to Watkins to You, A Documentary: The Battle for Control of Our Economy* (Toronto: New Press, 1970).

Goldfarb, Martin, and Thomas Axworthy, *Marching to a Different Drummer: An Essay on the Liberals and Conservatives in Convention* (Toronto: Stoddart, 1988).

Gonick, Cy, *The Great Economic Debate: Failed Economics and a Future for Canada* (Toronto: Lorimer, 1987).

Goodman, Bernard, *Industrial Materials in Canadian-American Relations* (Detroit: Wayne State University Press, 1961).

Gordon, Walter L., *A Choice for Canada* (Toronto: McClelland and Stewart, 1966).

———, *A Political Memoir* (Toronto: McClelland and Stewart, 1977).

Gossage, Carolyn, *A Question of Privilege* (Toronto: Peter Martin, 1977).

Gossage, Patrick, *Close to the Charisma: My Years Between the Press and Pierre Elliott Trudeau* (Toronto: McClelland and Stewart, 1986).

Gotlieb, Allan, and Charles Dalfen, "National Jurisdiction and International Responsibility: New Canadian Approaches to International Law," *American Journal of International Law* 67 (1973), pp. 229–58.

Gotlieb, Allan, and Jeremy Kinsman, "Sharing the Continent: Reviving the Third Option," *International Perspectives* (Jan.-Feb. 1981), pp. 2–5.

Gotlieb, Sondra, *Washington Rollercoaster* (Toronto: Doubleday Canada, 1990).

———, *Wife of . . . An Irreverent Account of Life in Washington* (Toronto: Macmillan of Canada, 1985).

Gouin, Jacques, *Sir Lomer Gouin, 1861-1929* (Montreal: Marie-France, 1981).

Graham, Ron, "Man with a Mission," *Saturday Night* (Aug. 1982), pp. 15–24.

———, *One-Eyed Kings: Promise and Illusion in Canadian Politics* (Toronto: Totem Books, 1987).

Granatstein, J.L., *How Britain's Weakness Forced Canada into the Arms of the United States*, 1988 Joanne Goodman Lectures (Toronto: University of Toronto Press, 1989).

———, *A Man of Influence: Norman A. Robertson and Canadian Statecraft, 1929-68* (Ottawa: Deneau, 1981).

———, *The Ottawa Men: The Civil Service Mandarins, 1935-1957* (Toronto: Oxford University Press, 1982).

———, "The Untouchables," *Saturday Night* (Apr. 1983), pp. 32–43.

Granatstein, J.L., and Robert Bothwell, *Pirouette: Pierre Trudeau and Canadian Foreign Policy* (Toronto: University of Toronto Press, 1990).

Grant, George, *Lament for a Nation* (Toronto: McClelland and Stewart, 1965).

Gray, Charlotte, "Women in Politics, 1980: The New Backroom Girls," *Chatelaine* (July 1980), pp. 25–26, 80–88.

Gray Report. See *Foreign Direct Investment in Canada*.

Grinspun, Ricardo, and Maxwell A. Cameron, eds., *The Political Economy of North American Free Trade* (New York: St. Martin's Press, 1993).

Guest, Dennis, *The Emergence of Social Security in Canada* (Vancouver: University of British Columbia Press, 1980).

Gwyn, Richard, *The 49th Paradox: Canada in North America* (Toronto: McClelland and Stewart, 1985).

———, *The Northern Magus: Pierre Trudeau and Canadians*, ed. by Sandra Gwyn (Toronto: McClelland and Stewart, 1980).

Gwyn, Richard, and Sandra Gwyn, "The Politics of Peace," *Saturday Night* (May 1984), pp. 19–32.

Gwyn, Sandra, *The Private Capital: Ambition and Love in the Age of Macdonald and Laurier* (Toronto: McClelland and Stewart, 1984).

————, "Where Are You, Mike Pearson, Now That We Need You? Decline and Fall of Canada's Foreign Policy," *Saturday Night* (Apr. 1978), pp. 27, 29–30.

Haddow, Rodney S., *Poverty Reform in Canada, 1958-1978* (Montreal: McGill-Queen's University Press, 1993).

Hall, Peter A., *Governing the Economy: The Politics of State Intervention in Britain and France* (New York: Oxford University Press, 1986).

————, *The Political Power of Economic Ideas: Keynesianism Across Nations* (Princeton, N.J.: Princeton University Press, 1989).

Hamelin, Jean, and Jean Provencher, *Brève histoire du Québec* (Montreal: Boréal Express, 1981).

Hansen, Alvin, *Fiscal Policy and Business Cycles* (New York: W.W. Norton, 1941).

Harbron, John D., "Canada Recognizes China: The Trudeau Round, 1968-1973," *Behind the Headlines* 33, no. 5 (Oct. 1974), pp. 1–29.

————, *This Is Trudeau* (Toronto: Longmans Canada, 1968).

Hart, Michael, "Almost but Not Quite: The 1947-48 Bilateral Canada-US Negotiations," *American Review of Canadian Studies* 19, no. 1 (Spring 1989), pp. 25–58.

Hartle, Douglas, *The Expenditure Budget Process in the Government of Canada* (Toronto: Canadian Tax Foundation, 1978).

————, *The Revenue Budget Process of the Government of Canada: Description, Appraisal, and Proposals* (Toronto: Canadian Tax Foundation, 1982).

Hay, John, "Budget '81: The Gathering Storm," *Maclean's* (Nov. 23, 1981), pp. 34–35.

————, "A Little Shuffle on the Deck," *Maclean's* (Sept. 20, 1982), pp. 13–14.

Haythorne, George V., "Prices and Incomes Policy: The Canadian Experience, 1969-72," *International Labour Review* 108, no. 6 (Dec. 1973), pp. 485–503.

Helleiner, G.K., "Canada, the Developing Countries and the International Economy: What Next?" *Journal of Canadian Studies* 19, no. 4 (Winter 1984-5), pp. 16–27.

Henning, C. Randall, *Macroeconomic Diplomacy in the 1980s: Domestic Politics and International Conflict among the United States, Japan, and Europe*, Atlantic Paper no. 65 (London: Croom Helm for The Atlantic Institute for International Affairs, 1987).

Heron, Craig, *The Canadian Labour Movement* (Toronto: Lorimer, 1989).

Higgins, Larratt, "The Alienation of Canadian Resources: The Case of the Columbia River Treaty," in Ian Lumsden, ed., *Close the 49th Parallel, Etc.: The Americanization of Canada* (Toronto: University of Toronto Press, 1970), pp. 223–40.

Hillmer, Norman, and Garth Stevenson, eds., *A Foremost Nation: Canadian Foreign Policy and a Changing World* (Toronto: McClelland and Stewart, 1977).

Hitchens, Christopher, *Blood, Class, and Nostalgia: Anglo-American Ironies* (London: Chatto and Windus, 1990).

Hitchins, Diddy R.M., and Bertil Liander, "Post World War II Patterns of Trade and Aid: Canada, USA and EEC," *Canadian Issues* 11 (1990), pp. 13–42.

Holmes, John, *Living with Uncle: The Canadian-American Relationship* (Toronto: University of Toronto Press, 1981).

————, *The Shaping of Peace: Canada and the Search for World Order*, vol. 2, *1943-1957* (Toronto: University of Toronto Press, 1982).

Holroyd, Michael, *Bernard Shaw* (London: Chatto and Windus, 1988).

House, J.D., *The Last of the Free Enterprisers: The Oilmen of Calgary* (Toronto: Macmillan, 1980).

Howitt, Peter, *Monetary Policy in Transition: A Study of Bank of Canada Policy, 1982-85*, Policy Study no. 1 (Toronto, Montreal, Calgary: C.D. Howe Institute, 1986).

Hughes, Everett C., and Margaret L. McDonald, "French and English in the Economic Structure of Montreal," *Canadian Journal of Economics and Political Science* 7, no. 4 (Nov. 1941), pp. 493–505.

Iglauer, Edith, *The Strangers Next Door* (Madeira Park, B.C.: Harbour, 1991).

Innis, Harold A., "Economic Trends in Canadian-American Relations, " in Mary Q. Innis, ed., *Essays in Canadian Economic History* (Toronto: University of Toronto Press, 1956), pp. 233–41. Originally published in 1938.

———, "Recent Developments in the Canadian Economy," in Mary Q. Innis, ed., *Essays in Canadian Economic History* (Toronto: University of Toronto Press, 1956), pp. 291–308.

International Economic Policy Association, *The United States Balance of Payments: From Crisis to Controversy* (Washington, D.C.: IEPA, 1972), quoted in John Bellamy Foster, "The Uncoupling of the World Order: A Survey of Global Crisis Theories," in M. Gottdiener and Nicos Komninos, eds., *Capitalist Development and Crisis Theory: Accumulation, Regulation and Spatial Restructuring* (London: Macmillan, 1989), pp. 99–122.

International Monetary Fund, *Government Finance Statistics Yearbook, 1986* (Washington, D.C.: IMF, 1986).

Inwood, Greg, "Nationalism Versus Continentalism: Ideology in the Mirror of the Macdonald Royal Commission," PhD thesis, University of Toronto, forthcoming.

Isaacson, Walter, *Kissinger: A Biography* (New York: Simon and Schuster, 1992).

Islam, Nasir, "For Whose Benefits? Smoke and Mirrors: CIDA's Development Assistance Program in the 1980s," paper presented at the annual meeting of the Canadian Political Science Association, June 9, 1988.

Jacobs, Jane, *Canadian Cities and Sovereignty Association* (Toronto: Canadian Broadcasting Corporation, 1980).

James, Patrick, "Energy Politics in Canada, 1980-81: Threat Power in a Sequential Game," paper, McGill University, n.d.

James, R. Warren, *Wartime Economic Co-operation: A Study of Relations Between Canada and the United States* (Toronto: Ryerson, 1949).

Jamieson, Don, *No Place for Fools: The Political Memoirs of Don Jamieson* (St. John's: Breakwater, 1989).

Janeway, Elizabeth, *Powers of the Weak* (New York: Knopf, 1980).

Jebb, Richard, *Studies in Colonial Nationalism* (London: Edward Arnold, 1905).

Jenkins, Barbara, "Canada: A Small State with a Hegemon's Mentality," in Fen Osler Hampson and Christopher J. Maule, eds., *Canada Among Nations, 1990-91: After the Cold War* (Ottawa: Carleton University Press, 1991), pp. 110–53.

———, "Reexamining the 'Obsolescing Bargain': A Case Study of Canada's National Energy Program," *International Organization* 40, no. 1 (Winter 1986), pp. 139–65.

Johnson, Andrew F., "A Minister as an Agent of Policy Change: The Case of Unemployment Insurance in the Seventies," *Canadian Public Administration* 24, no. 4 (Winter 1981), pp. 612–33.

Johnson, Harry G., "Canada's Economic Prospects," review of *Preliminary Report* of the Royal Commission on Canada's Economic Prospects, *Canadian Journal of Economics and Political Science* 24, no. 1 (Feb. 1958), pp. 104–10.

———, "A Theoretical Model of Economic Nationalism in New and Developing States," *Political Science Quarterly* 80, no. 2 (June 1965), pp. 169–85.

Johnson, Harry G., Paul Wonnacott, and Hirofumi Shibata, *Harmonization of*

*National Economic Policies Under Free Trade* (Montreal: Private Planning Association of Canada, 1968).

Johnson, Peter A., "Policy Paradigm Changes: Between Institutions and Environments," paper presented to the annual meeting of the Canadian Political Science Association, 1992.

Johnston, Donald, *Up the Hill* (Montreal: Optimum, 1986).

Kent, Tom, *A Public Purpose: An Experience of Liberal Opposition and Canadian Government* (Montreal and Kingston: McGill-Queen's University Press, 1988).

Kettle, Donald F., *Leadership at the Fed* (New Haven, Conn.: Yale University Press, 1986).

Kettle, John, *The Big Generation* (Toronto: McClelland and Stewart, 1980).

Kierans, Eric W., *Globalism and the Nation-State* (Toronto: CBC Enterprises, 1984).

———, "The Tax Reform Process: Problems of Tax Reform," *Canadian Taxation* 1, no. 4 (Winter 1979), pp. 22–24, quoted in Jamie Swift, *Odd Man Out: The Life and Times of Eric Kierans* (Toronto: Douglas and McIntyre, 1988), p. 249.

Kilbourn, William, *The Firebrand: William Lyon Mackenzie and the Rebellion in Upper Canada* (Toronto: Clarke, Irwin, 1964).

Kirton, John J., "The Consequences of Integration: The Case of the Defence Production Sharing Agreements," in W. Andrew Axline et al., *Continental Community? Independence and Integration in North America* (Toronto: McClelland and Stewart, 1974), pp. 116–36.

———, "Foreign Policy Decision-Making in the Trudeau Government: Promise and Performance," *International Journal* 33, no. 2 (Spring 1978), pp. 287–311.

———, "Trudeau and the Diplomacy of Peace," *International Perspectives* (July-Aug. 1984), pp. 3–5.

Kirton, John, and Don Munton, "The *Manhattan* Voyages and Their Aftermath," in Franklyn Griffiths, ed., *The Politics of the Northwest Passage* (Montreal: McGill-Queen's University Press, 1987), pp. 67–97.

Kissinger, Henry, *The White House Years* (Boston: Little, Brown, 1979).

Kome, Penney, *The Taking of Twenty-Eight: Women Challenge the Constitution* (Toronto: Women's Educational Press, 1983).

Krukowski, John V., *Canadian Taxation of Oil and Gas Income* (Don Mills, Ont.: CCH Canadian, 1987).

Kuttner, Robert, "The Poverty of Economics," *Atlantic Monthly* 255 (Feb. 1985), pp. 74–84.

"Labour Escalates Confrontation Politics," *The Labour Scene* 3, no. 10 (Jan. 1982), pp. 73–74.

Lacouture, Jean, *De Gaulle*, vol. III (Paris: Seuil, 1986).

Laidler, David E.W., *How Shall We Govern the Governor? A Critique of the Governance of the Bank of Canada* (Toronto: C.D. Howe Institute, 1991).

Lalonde, Marc, "The Changing Role of the Prime Minister's Office," *Canadian Public Administration* 14, no. 4 (Winter 1971), pp. 509–35.

———, "Riding the Storm: Energy Policy, 1968-1984," in Thomas S. Axworthy and Pierre Elliott Trudeau, eds., *Towards a Just Society: The Trudeau Years* (Toronto: Viking, 1990).

LaMarsh, Judy, *Memoirs of a Bird in a Gilded Cage* (Toronto: McClelland and Stewart, 1969).

Lamontagne, Maurice, *Business Cycles in Canada: The Postwar Experience and Policy Directions* (Ottawa: Canadian Institute for Economic Policy, 1984).

Langille, David, "The Business Council on National Issues and the Canadian State," *Studies in Political Economy* no. 24 (Autumn 1987), pp. 41–85.

———, *Changing the Guard: Canada's Defence in a World in Transition* (Toronto: University of Toronto Press, 1990).

Lasch, Christopher, *The Culture of Narcissism: American Life in an Age of Diminishing Expectations* (New York: Norton, 1978).

———, *Haven in a Heartless World: The Family Besieged* (New York: Basic Books, 1977).

Laski, Harold J., *A Grammar of Politics*, 5th ed. (London: George Allen Empress and Unwin, 1967).

Latouche, Daniel, "Le petit, le gros et le moyen," in Marc Gold and David Leyton-Brown, eds., *Trade-Offs on Free Trade: The Canada-U.S. Free Trade Agreement* (Scarborough, Ont.: Carswell, 1988), pp. 148–59.

Laux, Jeanne Kirk, and Maureen Appel Molot, *State Capitalism: Public Enterprise in Canada* (Ithaca, N.Y.: Cornell University Press, 1988).

Laxer, Gordon, *Open for Business: The Roots of Foreign Ownership in Canada* (Don Mills, Ont.: Oxford University Press, 1989).

Laxer, James, *Oil and Gas: Ottawa, the Provinces and the Petroleum Industry* (Toronto: Lorimer, 1983).

Laxer, James, and Robert Laxer, *The Liberal Idea of Canada: Pierre Trudeau and the Question of Canada's Survival* (Toronto: Lorimer, 1977).

Lebow, Richard Ned, and Janice Stein, "Reagan and the Russians," *Atlantic Monthly* (Feb. 1994), pp. 35–36.

LeDuc, Lawrence, and J. Alex Murray, "A Resurgence of Canadian Nationalism: Attitudes and Policy in the 1980s," in Allan Kornberg and Harold D. Clarke, eds., *Political Support in Canada: The Crisis Years* (Durham, N.C.: Duke University Press, 1983), pp. 270–90.

Lescop, Renée, *Le pari québécois du général de Gaulle* (Montreal: Boréal Express, 1981).

Leslie, Peter M., *Federal State, National Economy* (Toronto: University of Toronto Press, 1987).

Levine, Marc V., *The Reconquest of Montreal: Language Policy and Social Change in a Bilingual City* (Philadelphia: Temple University Press, 1990).

Levinson, Daniel, et al., *The Seasons of a Man's Life* (New York: Ballantine Books, 1978).

Lewis, David, *The Good Fight: Political Memoirs, 1909-1958* (Toronto: Macmillan of Canada, 1981).

Lewis, David, and Frank Scott, *Make This Your Canada: A Review of C.C.F. History and Policy* (Toronto: Central Canada Publishing Company, 1943).

Leyton-Brown, David, and Brian MacDonald, "Industrial Preparedness," in R.B. Byers, ed., *The Canadian Strategic Review, 1982* (Toronto: Canadian Institute of Strategic Studies, 1982).

"Liberal AOR System Is 'Farce' Says Swain," *Marketing* (July 14, 1980), p. 2.

"Liberal Caucus Policy Groups," Office of the Leader of the Opposition, Ottawa, July 19, 1979.

Lijphart, Arend, "Cultural Diversity and Theories of Political Integration," *Canadian Journal of Political Science* 4, no. 1 (Mar. 1971), pp. 1–14.

Linteau, Paul-André, et al., *Quebec: A History 1867-1929*, translated by Robert Chodos (Toronto: James Lorimer, 1983).

———, *Quebec Since 1930*, translated by Robert Chodos and Ellen Garmaise (Toronto: James Lorimer, 1991).

Lisée, Jean-François, *In the Eye of the Eagle* (Toronto: HarperCollins, 1990).

Littleton, James, *Target Nation: Canada and the Western Intelligence Network* (Toronto: Lester and Orpen Dennys, 1986).

Logan, Robert K., ed., *The Way Ahead for Canada: A Paperback Referendum* (Toronto: Lester and Orpen, 1977).

Lowe, Mick, *One-Woman Army: The Life of Claire Culhane* (Toronto: Macmillan of Canada, 1992).

Lower, A.R.M., "Canada, the Second Great War, and the Future," *International Journal* 1, no. 2 (Spring 1946), pp. 97–111.

Lyon, Peyton V., and David Leyton-Brown, "Image and Policy Preference: Canadian Elite Views on Relations with the United States," *International Journal* 32, no. 3 (Summer 1977), pp. 640–71.

Lyon, Jim, *Dome: The Rise and Fall of the House That Jack Built* (Toronto: Macmillan of Canada, 1983).

McCall, Christina [McCall-Newman], *Grits: An Intimate Portrait of the Liberal Party* (Toronto: Macmillan of Canada, 1982).

————[Newman], "Growing Up Reluctantly," *Maclean's* (Aug. 1972), pp. 21–22, 56–60.

————[Newman], "How to Spot the Ottawa Man: A Concise Guide," *Maclean's* (Oct. 6, 1962), p. 3.

————[McCall-Newman], "Michael Pitfield and the Politics of Mismanagement," *Saturday Night* (Oct. 1982), pp. 24–44.

————[Newman], "Turner: The Once and Future Contender," *Maclean's* (May 1971), pp. 19–21, 54–56.

————[Newman], "What's So Funny About the Royal Commission on the Status of Women?" *Saturday Night* (Jan. 1969), pp. 21–24.

————[McCall Newman], "The Year They Created Modern Canada," *Saturday Night* (June 1977), pp. 20–22.

McCall, Christina, and Stephen Clarkson, "Unquiet American," *Saturday Night* (Nov. 1984), pp. 9–10, 12.

McCallum, John, *Unequal Beginnings: Agriculture and Economic Development in Quebec and Ontario Until 1870* (Toronto: University of Toronto Press, 1980).

MacCallum Scott, John H., *Experiment in Internationalism: A Study in International Politics* (London: George Allen & Unwin, 1967).

McCormick, Peter, "Is the Liberal Party Declining? Liberals, Conservatives, and Provincial Politics, 1867-1980," *Journal of Canadian Studies* 18, no. 4 (Winter 1983-84), pp. 88–107.

Macdonald, Flora, "The Minister and the Mandarins," *Policy Options* 1, no. 3 (Sept.-Oct. 1980), pp. 29–32.

McDougall, John N., *Fuels and the National Policy* (Toronto: Butterworths, 1982).

MacDowell, Laurel Sefton, "The Formation of the Canadian Industrial Relations System During World War II," *Labour/Le Travailleur* 3 (1978), pp. 175–96.

Machiavelli, Niccolò, "The Prince," in *The Portable Machiavelli*, Peter Bondanella and Mark Musa, eds. and trans. (Harmondsworth, Eng.: Penguin, 1979), pp. 77–166.

MacIntyre, Linden, "The Lonely Stranger Who Is Finance Minister," *Saturday Night* (May 1980), pp. 47–49.

Mackintosh, W.A., "Canadian Economic Policy from 1945 to 1957 – Origins and Influences," in Hugh G.J. Aitken et al., *The American Economic Impact on Canada* (Durham, N.C.: Duke University Press, 1959), pp. 51–68.

————, "Dependence on Export Markets Overseas," in J. Douglas Gibson, ed., *Canada's Economy in a Changing World* (Toronto: Macmillan of Canada, 1948), pp. 130–51.

MacLennan, Hugh, *Two Solitudes* (Toronto: Macmillan, 1969).

McLin, Jon B., *Canada's Changing Defense Policy, 1957-1963: The Problems of a Middle Power in Alliance* (Baltimore, Md.: Johns Hopkins Press, 1967).

McNamara, Robert, "The Military Role of Nuclear Weapons: Perceptions and Misperceptions," *Foreign Affairs* 62, no. 1 (Fall 1983), pp. 59–80.

McNaught, Kenneth [S.W. Bradford, pseud.], "The CCF Failure in Foreign Policy," *The Canadian Forum* 30, no. 356 (Sept. 1950), pp. 127–28.

McNaughton, A.G.L., "The Proposed Columbia River Treaty," *International Journal* 18, no. 2 (Spring 1963), pp. 148–65.

Macpherson, C.B., *Democracy in Alberta: Social Credit and the Party System*, 2nd ed. (Toronto: University of Toronto Press, 1962).

McQuaig, Linda, *Behind Closed Doors* (Markham, Ont.: Penguin Canada, 1987).

Madsen, Abel, *Malraux: A Biography* (New York: Morrow, 1976).

Magder, Ted, *Canada's Hollywood: The Canadian State and Feature Films* (Toronto: University of Toronto Press, 1993).

Mallen, Pierre-Louis, *Vivre le Québec libre: Les secrets de de Gaulle* (Paris: Plon, 1978).

Mannoni, O., *Prospero and Caliban: The Psychology of Colonization* (New York: Praeger, 1956).

Manzer, Ronald, *Public Policies and Political Development in Canada* (Toronto: University of Toronto Press, 1985).

March, James, *Handbook of Organizations* (Chicago: Rand McNally, 1965).

March, James, and Herbert Simon, *Organizations*, with the collaboration of Harold Guetzkow (New York: Wiley, 1958).

Marsden, Lorna, "Budget '84: Party Policy Voices Heard . . . Again," *Liberal Policy Newsletter* (Feb.-Mar. 1984), pp. 2–3.

———, "The Party and Parliament: Participatory Democracy in the Trudeau Years," in Thomas S. Axworthy and Pierre Elliott Trudeau, eds., *Towards a Just Society: The Trudeau Years* (Toronto: Viking, 1990), pp. 262–81.

———, "Political Women in Canada: Women and Partisan Politics," talk to a conference on the Canadian women's movement, Stong College, York University, Sept. 30, 1977.

———, *Population Probe: Canada*, foreword by Edward Harvey (Toronto: Copp Clark, 1972).

Marsden, Lorna, and Rémi Bujold, "Report of the Steering Committee of the Standing Committee on Policy," National Liberal Convention, Ottawa, Nov. 5-7, 1982.

Marsden, Lorna R., and Edward B. Harvey, *Fragile Federation: Social Change in Canada* (Toronto: McGraw-Hill, 1979).

———, eds., *Canadian Population Concerns* (Toronto: Population Research Foundation, 1977).

Martin, Lawrence, *The Presidents and the Prime Ministers* (Toronto: Doubleday Canada, 1982).

Maslove, Allan M., "Ottawa's New Agenda: The Issues and the Constraints," in Allan M. Maslove, ed., *How Ottawa Spends, 1984: The New Agenda* (Toronto: Methuen, 1984), pp. 1–30.

———, "Tax Expenditure, Tax Credits and Equity," in G. Bruce Doern, ed., *How Ottawa Spends Your Tax Dollars: Federal Priorities, 1981* (Toronto: Lorimer, 1981), pp. 232–54.

Maslove, Allan M., and Bohodar Rubashewsky, "Cooperation and Confrontation: The Challenges of Fiscal Federalism," in Michael J. Prince, ed., *How Ottawa Spends, 1986-87: Tracking the Tories* (Toronto: Methuen, 1986), pp. 95–118.

Maslove, Allan M., and Gene Swimmer, *Wage Controls in Canada, 1975-78: A Study of Public Decision Making* (Montreal: Institute for Research on Public Policy, 1980).

Maslove, Allan M., Michael J. Prince, and G. Bruce Doern, *Federal and Provincial Budgeting* (Toronto: University of Toronto Press, 1986).

Matheson, William A., "The Cabinet and the Canadian Bureaucracy," in W.D.K. Kernaghan and A.M. Willms, eds., *Public Administration in Canada: Selected Readings*, 2nd ed. (Toronto: Methuen, 1971), pp. 339–48.

———, *The Prime Minister and the Cabinet* (Toronto: Methuen, 1976).

May, John, "Testing the Cruise: To Defend or Disarm?" *Maclean's* (May 30, 1983), pp. 22–26.

Meisel, John, "The Formulation of Liberal and Conservative Programmes in the 1957 Canadian General Election," *Canadian Journal of Economics and Political Science* 26, no. 4 (Nov. 1960), pp. 565–74.

———, "The Larger Context: The Period Preceding the 1979 Election," in Howard R. Penniman, ed., *Canada at the Polls, 1979 and 1980: A Study of the General Elections* (Washington, D.C.: American Enterprise Institute, 1981), pp. 24–54.

Merchant, Livingston T., and A.D.P. Heeney, "Canada and the United States: Principles for Partnership," *Department of State Bulletin* (Aug. 2, 1965), pp. 1–16.

Meyer, Herbert E., "Canada's Nationalism Exacts a High Price," *Fortune* (Aug. 1976), p. 186.

Michels, Robert, *Political Parties: A Sociological Study of the Oligarchical Tendencies of Modern Democracy*, reprint (New York: Dover, 1959).

Middlemiss, Dan, "Canada and Defence Industrial Preparedness: A Return to Basics?" *International Journal* 42, no. 4 (Autumn 1987), pp. 707–30.

———, "Defence Co-operation," in Norman Hillmer, ed., *Partners Nevertheless: Canadian-American Relations in the Twentieth Century* (Toronto: Copp Clark Pitman, 1989), pp. 167–93.

———, "Economic Defence Co-operation with the United States 1940-63," in Kim Richard Nossal, ed., *An Acceptance of Paradox: Essays on Canadian Diplomacy in Honour of John W. Holmes* (Toronto: Canadian Institute of International Affairs, 1982), pp. 86–109.

Middleton, Jan, "Thomas d'Aquino: The Voice of Business in the Halls of Power," *Canadian Business* 56, no. 3 (Mar. 1983), pp. 17, 20.

Milne, David, *Tug of War* (Toronto: Lorimer, 1984).

Moggridge, D.E., *Keynes*, 3rd ed. (Toronto: University of Toronto Press, 1993).

Morgan, Nicole, *Implosion: An Analysis of the Growth of the Federal Public Service in Canada, 1945-1985* (Montreal: Institute for Research on Public Policy, 1986).

———, *Nowhere to Go? Possible Consequences of the Demographic Imbalance in Decision-making Groups of the Federal Public Service* (Montreal: Institute for Research on Public Policy, 1981).

Morton, Desmond, *The New Democrats, 1961-1986: The Politics of Change* (Toronto: Copp Clark Pitman, 1986).

Morton, Desmond, and J.L. Granatstein, *Marching to Armageddon: Canadians and the Great War 1914-1919* (Toronto: Lester and Orpen Dennys, 1989).

Morris, James, *Farewell the Trumpets* (London: Faber and Faber, 1978).

———, *Heaven's Command* (London: Faber and Faber, 1973).

———, *Pax Britannica* (London: Faber and Faber, 1968).

Moscovitch, Allan, "The Welfare State Since 1975," *Journal of Canadian Studies* 21, no. 2 (Summer 1986), pp. 77–94.

Mounier, Emmanuel, *Traité du caractère: Anthologie* (Paris: Editions du Seuil, 1974).

Muirhead, B.W., *The Development of Postwar Canadian Trade Policy: The Failure of the Anglo-European Option* (Toronto: University of Toronto Press, 1992).

———, "Trials and Tribulations: The Decline of Anglo-Canadian Trade, 1945-50," *Journal of Canadian Studies* 24, no. 1 (Spring 1989), pp. 50–65.

Munro, Gary, "Changing the Crow's Nest Freight Rate," *Journal of Canadian Studies* 22, no. 4 (Winter 1987-88), pp. 93–114.

Muszynski, Leon, "The Politics of Labour Market Policy," in G. Bruce Doern, ed., *The Politics of Economic Policy* (Toronto: University of Toronto Press, 1985), pp. 251–305.

Naidu, M.V., "Canada, NATO and the Cruise Missile," *Peace Research* (May 1983), pp. 1–10.

Neatby, H. Blair, *William Lyon Mackenzie King*, vol. II, *1924-1932* (Toronto: University of Toronto Press, 1963).

Neill, Robin, and Gilles Paquet, "L'économie hérétique: Canadian Economics before 1967," *Canadian Journal of Economics* 26, no. 1 (Feb. 1993), pp. 3–13.

Nelles, H.V., "Looking Backward: Interpreting Canada's Economic Development," in John Lennos, ed., *Se connaître: Politics and Culture in Canada* (North York, Ont.: York University, 1985), pp. 24–29.

Newman, Christina. See McCall, Christina.

Newman, Peter C., *The Canadian Establishment*, vol. 1 (Toronto: McClelland and Stewart, 1975).

———, *Flame of Power* (Toronto: Longmans, 1959).

Nicolson, Nigel, *Vita and Harold: The Letters of Vita Sackville-West and Harold Nicolson, 1910-1962* (London: Weidenfeld, 1992).

Niosi, Jorge, "The Rise of French-Canadian Capitalism," in Alain G. Gagnon, ed., *Quebec: State and Society* (Scarborough, Ont.: Methuen, 1984), pp. 186–200.

Noel, S.J.R., "Consociational Democracy and Canadian Federalism," *Canadian Journal of Political Science* 4, no. 1 (Mar. 1971), pp. 15–18.

Nossal, Kim Richard, "Cabin'd, Cribb'd, Confin'd?: Canada's Interests in Human Rights," in Robert O. Matthews and Cranford Pratt, eds., *Human Rights in Canadian Foreign Policy* (Montreal: McGill-Queen's University Press, 1988), pp. 46–58.

———, "Personal Diplomacy and National Behaviour: Trudeau's North-South Initiatives," *Dalhousie Review* 62, no. 2 (Summer 1982), pp. 279–91.

———, *The Politics of Canadian Foreign Policy* (Scarborough, Ont.: Prentice-Hall, 1985).

Odier, Charles, *Les deux sources consciente et inconsciente de la vie morale*, 2nd ed. (Neuchatel: Éditions de la baconnière, 1946).

OECD Economic Surveys, *Canada* (Paris: Organisation for Economic Co-operation and Development, June 1982).

Olsen, Dennis, *The State Elite* (Toronto: McClelland and Stewart, 1980).

Owram, Doug, *The Government Generation: Canadian Intellectuals and the State, 1900-1945* (Toronto: University of Toronto Press, 1986).

Page, Robert, *Northern Development: The Canadian Dilemma* (Toronto: McClelland and Stewart, 1986).

Pal, Leslie A., "Revision and Retreat: Canadian Unemployment Insurance, 1971-1981," in Jacqueline S. Ismael, ed., *Canadian Social Welfare Policy: Federal and Provincial Dimensions* (Montreal and Kingston: McGill-Queen's University Press, 1985), pp. 75–104.

———, *State, Class and Bureaucracy: Canadian Unemployment Insurance and Public Policy* (Montreal: McGill-Queen's University Press, 1988).

Palango, Paul, *Above the Law: The Crooks, the Politicians, the Mounties, and Rod Stamler* (Toronto: McClelland and Stewart, 1994).

Pangle, Thomas L., *The Ennobling of Democracy: The Challenge of the Postmodern Era* (Baltimore, Md.: Johns Hopkins University Press, 1992).

Panitch, Leo, and Donald Swartz, *The Assault on Trade Union Freedoms* (Toronto: Garamond Press, 1988).

Partridge, John, "Slugging It Out for the Little Guy," *Canadian Business* 55, no. 2 (Feb. 1982), pp. 30–37, 91–95.

Pauly, Louis B., *Opening Financial Markets: Banking Politics on the Pacific Rim* (Ithaca, N.Y.: Cornell University Press, 1988).

Pearson, Lester B., *Mike: The Memoirs of the Right Honourable Lester B. Pearson*, John A. Munro and Alex I. Inglis, eds., vol. 2, *1948-1957*; vol. 3, *1957-1968* (Toronto: University of Toronto Press, 1973-75).

Peden, Murray, *Fall of an Arrow* (Stittsville, Ont.: Canada's Wings, 1978).

Penniman, Howard R., ed., *Canada at the Polls, 1979 and 1980: A Study of the General Elections* (Washington, D.C.: American Enterprise Institute, 1981).

Perlin, George C., *The Tory Syndrome: Leadership Politics in the Progressive Conservative Party* (Montreal: McGill-Queen's University Press, 1980).

Perry, David B., "The Federal-Provincial Fiscal Arrangements for 1982-87," *Canadian Tax Journal* 31, no. 1 (Jan.-Feb. 1983), pp. 30–47.

Phidd, Richard, and G. Bruce Doern, *The Politics and Management of Canadian Economic Policy* (Toronto: Macmillan of Canada, 1978).

Phillips, Kevin P., *The Emerging Republican Majority* (New Rochelle, N.Y.: Arlington House, 1969).

Phillips, Paul, "National Policy, Continental Economics, and National Disintegration," in David Jay Bercuson, ed., *Canada and the Burden of Unity* (Toronto: Macmillan of Canada, 1977), pp. 19–43.

Phillips, Paul T., *Britain's Past in Canada: The Teaching and Writing of British History* (Vancouver: University of British Columbia Press, 1989).

Pickersgill, J.W., *The Mackenzie King Record*, vol. 1, *1939-44* (Toronto: University of Toronto Press, 1960).

———, *My Years with Louis St. Laurent: A Political Memoir* (Toronto: University of Toronto Press, 1975).

———, *The Road Back: By a Liberal in Opposition* (Toronto: University of Toronto Press, 1986).

Pickersgill, J.W., and D.F. Forster, *The Mackenzie King Record*, vol. 2, *1944-45*; vol. 3, *1945-46*; vol. 4, *1947-48* (Toronto: University of Toronto Press, 1968-70).

Piet, Louisa W., *Canada: New World Power* (Toronto: George J. McLeod, 1945).

Pitfield, Michael, "The Shape of Government in the 1980s," *Canadian Public Administration* 19, no. 1 (Spring 1976), pp. 8–20.

Plumptre, Wynne [A.F.W.], "Exports to the United States," in J. Douglas Gibson, ed., *Canada's Economy in a Changing World* (Toronto: Macmillan of Canada, 1948), pp. 208–43.

———, *Three Decades of Decision: Canada and the World Monetary System, 1944-1975* (Toronto: McClelland and Stewart, 1977).

Pratt, Cranford, "Canada: An Eroding and Limited Internationalism," in R. Cranford Pratt, ed., *Internationalism Under Strain: The North-South Policies of Canada, the Netherlands, Norway, and Sweden* (Toronto: University of Toronto Press, 1988).

Pratt, Larry, "Energy, Regionalism and Canadian Nationalism," *Newfoundland Studies* 1, no. 2 (Fall 1985), pp. 175–99.

————, "Energy: The Roots of National Policy," *Studies in Political Economy* 7 (Winter 1982), pp. 31–32.

————, "Petro-Canada," in Allan Tupper and G. Bruce Doern, eds., *Public Corporations and Public Policy in Canada* (Montreal: Institute for Research on Public Policy, 1981), pp. 95–148.

————, "Petro-Canada: Tool for Energy Security or Instrument of Economic Development?" in G. Bruce Doern, ed., *How Ottawa Spends Your Tax Dollars, 1982* (Toronto: Lorimer, 1982), pp. 87–113.

————, "The State and Province-Building: Alberta's Development Strategy," in Leo Panitch, ed., *The Canadian State: Political Economy and Political Power* (Toronto: University of Toronto Press, 1977), pp. 133–62.

————, *The Tar Sands: Syncrude and the Politics of Oil* (Edmonton: Hurtig, 1976).

Prince, Michael J., "Whatever Happened to Compassion? Liberal Social Policy, 1980-84," in Allan M. Maslove, ed., *How Ottawa Spends, 1984: The New Agenda* (Toronto: Methuen, 1984), pp. 79–121.

"Priority Resolutions Amendments by Caucuses of Sponsoring Groups and National Youth Commission Priority Resolutions," National Liberal Convention, Ottawa, Nov. 5-7, 1982.

*The Pro-Canada Dossier* no. 23 (special issue, Jan. 1, 1990).

Pross, A. Paul, "The Fishery: Ali versus Frazier," in Barbara Jamieson, ed., *Governing Nova Scotia: Policies, Priorities and the 1984-85 Budget* (Halifax: Dalhousie School of Public Administration, 1984).

————, *Group Politics and Public Policy* (Toronto: Oxford University Press, 1986).

————, "Parliamentary Influence and the Diffusion of Power," *Canadian Journal of Political Science* 18, no. 2 (June 1985), pp. 235–66.

Pross, A. Paul, and Susan McCorquodale, *Economic Resurgence and the Constitutional Agenda: The Case of the East Coast Fisheries* (Kingston: Queen's University Institute of Intergovernmental Relations, 1987).

Protheroe, David R., *Imports and Politics: Trade Decision-Making in Canada, 1968-1979* (Montreal: Institute for Research on Public Policy, 1980).

Punnett, R.M., *The Prime Minister in Canadian Government and Politics* (Toronto: Macmillan of Canada, 1977).

Radwanski, George, *Trudeau* (Toronto: Macmillan of Canada, 1978).

Reagan, Ronald, *An American Life* (New York: Simon and Schuster, 1990).

Redekop, Clarence G., "Commerce over Conscience: The Trudeau Government and South Africa, 1968-84," *Journal of Canadian Studies* 19, no. 4 (Winter 1984-85), pp. 82–105.

Reid, Escott, *Radical Mandarin: The Memoirs of Escott Reid* (Toronto: University of Toronto Press, 1989).

————, *Time of Fear and Hope: The Making of the North Atlantic Treaty* (Toronto: McClelland and Stewart, 1977).

Reid, Malcolm, "Understanding Lalonde," *Saturday Night* (June 1981), pp. 27–37.

"Release [regarding cabinet shuffle]," Office of the Prime Minister, Ottawa, Oct. 27, 1982.

"Report on 1980 Resolutions," National Liberal Convention, Ottawa, Nov. 5-7, 1982.

Resnick, Philip, *The Land of Cain: Class and Nationalism in English Canada 1945-1975* (Vancouver: New Star Books, 1977).

Reston, James, "A Talk with Trudeau," *New York Times Magazine* (Oct. 3, 1982), pp. 40–41, 54–56, 70–71.

Richards, John, and Larry Pratt, *Prairie Capitalism: Power and Influence in the New West* (Toronto: McClelland and Stewart, 1979).

Rioux, Marcel, *Pour prendre publiquement congé de quelques salauds* (Montreal: L'Héxagone, 1980).

Ritchie, Ella, "France," in Martin Harrop, ed., *Power and Policy in Liberal Democracies* (Cambridge: Cambridge University Press, 1992), pp. 23–47.

Rivlin, Alice M., "Overview," in Barry P. Bosworth and Alice M. Rivlin, eds., *The Swedish Economy* (Washington, D.C.: Brookings Institution, 1987), pp. 1–21.

Roberts, Paul Craig, *The Supply-Side Revolution: An Insider's Account of Policymaking in Washington* (Cambridge, Mass.: Harvard University Press, 1984).

Robertson, Gordon, [Untitled], *The Institute* (Institute for Research on Public Policy) 6, no. 2 (Apr./May, 1984), p. 1.

Rochlin, James, *Discovering the Americas: The Evolution of Canadian Foreign Policy Towards Latin America* (Vancouver: University of British Columbia Press, 1994).

Royce, Diana M., "Creating Troubled Waters: Public Policy-Making and the Task Force on Atlantic Fisheries," MA thesis, Queen's University, 1985.

Rugman, Alan, "Why Business Supports Free Trade," in John Crispo, ed., *Free Trade: The Real Story* (Toronto: Gage, 1988), pp. 95–104.

Rusher, William A., *The Rise of the Right* (New York: William Morrow, 1984).

Sabine, George H., *A History of Political Theory*, rev. ed. (New York: Holt, Rinehart and Winston, 1950).

Sacouman, R. James, "Underdevelopment and the Structural Origins of Antigonish Movement Co-Operatives in Eastern Nova Scotia," in Robert J. Brym and R. James Sacouman, eds., *Underdevelopment and Social Movements in Atlantic Canada* (Toronto: New Hogtown Press, 1979), pp. 107–26.

Safarian, A.E., "The Web of Repercussions," in Stephen Clarkson, ed., *An Independent Foreign Policy for Canada?* (Toronto: McClelland and Stewart, 1968), pp. 48–51.

Savoie, Donald J., *The Politics of Public Spending in Canada* (Toronto: University of Toronto Press, 1990).

————, *Regional Economic Development: Canada's Search for Solutions* (Toronto: University of Toronto Press, 1986).

Sawatsky, John, *The Insiders: Government, Business, and the Lobbyists* (Toronto: McClelland and Stewart, 1987).

Saywell, John, *The Rise of the Parti Québécois, 1967-1976* (Toronto: University of Toronto Press, 1977).

Scheinberg, Stephen, "The Indispensable Ally: Canadian Resources and the Cold War," paper delivered to Canadian Historical Association annual meeting, Edmonton, Alberta, June 1975.

Schieffer, Bob, and Gary Paul Gates, *The Acting President* (New York: E.P. Dutton, 1989).

Schindeler, Fred, "The Prime Minister and the Cabinet: History and Development," in Thomas Hockin, ed., *Apex of Power: The Prime Minister and Political Leadership in Canada* (Scarborough, Ont.: Prentice-Hall, 1971), pp. 22–49.

Schlesinger, Arthur M., Jr., *The Cycles of American History* (Boston: Houghton Mifflin, 1986).

Scott, Anthony, "Does Living in Canada Make One a Canadian Economist?" *Canadian Journal of Economics* 26, no. 1 (Feb. 1993), pp. 26–38.

Scott, Frank R. [pseud. S], "Embryo Fascism in Quebec," *Foreign Affairs* 16, no. 3 (Apr. 1938), pp. 454–66.

Scott, Frank R., "Nationalism in French Canada," in F.R. Scott, *Essays on the*

*Constitution: Aspects of Canadian Law and Politics* (Toronto: University of Toronto Press, 1977), pp. 82–89. Originally published in 1936.

Sellar, Don, "How Canada Took the Cruise," in Thomas Perry, ed., *The Prevention of Nuclear War* (Vancouver: Physicians for Social Responsibility, 1983), pp. 194–98.

Shadwick, Martin, "Canadian Defence Policy," *International Perspectives* (Sept.-Oct. 1983), pp. 7–10.

Shaffer, Ed, *Canada's Oil and the American Empire* (Edmonton: Hurtig, 1983).

Sharp, Mitchell, "Canada-U.S. Relations: Options for the Future," *International Perspectives* (special issue, Autumn 1972), pp. 1–24.

———, "Decision-Making in the Federal Cabinet," *Canadian Public Administration* 19, no. 1 (Spring 1976), pp. 1–7.

———, *Which Reminds Me . . . A Memoir* (Toronto: University of Toronto Press, 1994).

Shaw, E.D., *There Never Was an Arrow* (Toronto: Steel Rail, 1979).

Sheppard, Robert, and Michael Valpy, *The National Deal: The Fight for a Canadian Constitution* (Toronto: Fleet, 1982).

Shultz, George P., *Turmoil and Triumph: My Years as Secretary of State* (New York: Macmillan, 1993).

Simpson, Jeffrey, *Discipline of Power: The Conservative Interlude and the Liberal Restoration*, rev. ed. (Toronto: Macmillan of Canada, 1984).

———, *Spoils of Power: The Politics of Patronage* (Toronto: Collins, 1988).

Skogstad, Grace, *The Politics of Agricultural Policy-Making in Canada* (Toronto: University of Toronto Press, 1987).

Smillie, Christine, "Judy Rebick," *Briarpatch* 23, no. 2 (Mar. 1994), pp. 13–20.

Smiley, Donald V., "Canada and the Quest for a National Policy," *Canadian Journal of Political Science* 8, no. 1 (Mar. 1975), pp. 40–62.

———, "A Dangerous Deed: The Constitution Act, 1982," in Keith Banting and Richard Simeon, eds., *And No One Cheered: Federalism, Democracy and the Constitution Act* (Toronto: Methuen, 1983), pp. 74–95.

Smith, Cameron, *Unfinished Journey: The Lewis Family* (Toronto: Summerhill, 1989).

Smith, David E., *The Regional Decline of a National Party: Liberals on the Prairies* (Toronto: University of Toronto Press, 1981).

Smith, Denis, *Gentle Patriot: A Political Biography of Walter Gordon* (Edmonton: Hurtig, 1973).

———, "President and Parliament: The Transformation of Parliamentary Government in Canada," in Thomas Hockin, ed., *Apex of Power: The Prime Minister and Political Leadership in Canada* (Scarborough: Prentice-Hall, 1971), pp. 224–41.

Smith, Miriam, "The Canadian Labour Congress: From Continentalism to Economic Nationalism," *Studies in Political Economy* 38 (Summer 1992), pp. 35–60.

Smyka, Mark, "Feds Turn $8m Spotlight on the Constitution," *Marketing* (Aug. 4, 1980), p. 1.

———, "Four-Agency Consortium to Handle Ottawa AOR Millions," *Marketing* (July 7, 1980), pp. 1, 4.

———, "Liberals Axe MBS: Now What Happens?" *Marketing* (Mar. 24, 1980), p. 1.

Soward, F.H., *Canada in World Affairs: From Normandy to Paris, 1944-1946* (Toronto: Oxford University Press, 1950).

Spencer, Robert A., *Canada in World Affairs: From UN to NATO 1946-1949* (Toronto: Oxford University Press, 1959).

Stacey, Charles P., *A Very Double Life: The Private World of Mackenzie King* (Toronto: Macmillan of Canada, 1976).

Stairs, Denis, *The Diplomacy of Constraint: Canada, the Korean War, and the United States* (Toronto: University of Toronto Press, 1974).

Stanbury, Richard J., *Liberal Party of Canada: An Interpretation*, Liberal Federation of Canada, Ottawa, June 15, 1969, mimeographed, 59 pages.

Stanbury, W.T., *Business Interests and the Reform of Canadian Competition Policy, 1971-75* (Toronto: Carswell-Methuen, 1977).

———, "Half a Loaf: Bill C-29, Proposed Amendments to the Combines Investigation Act," *The Canadian Business Law Journal* 10, no. 1 (Feb. 1985), pp. 1–34.

———, "The Mother's Milk of Politics: Political Contributions to Federal Parties in Canada, 1974-1984," *Canadian Journal of Political Science* 19, no. 4 (Dec. 1986), pp. 795–821.

Starr, Harvey, *Henry Kissinger: Perceptions of International Politics* (Lexington, Ky.: University Press of Kentucky, 1984).

Steele, James, and Robin Mathews, "The Universities: Takeover of the Mind," in Ian Lumsden, ed., *Close the 49th Parallel, etc.: The Americanization of Canada* (Toronto: University of Toronto Press, 1970), pp. 169–78.

Stevenson, Garth, "The Third Option," *International Journal* 33, no. 2 (Spring 1978), pp. 424–31.

Stewart, Gordon T., "America's Canadian Policy," in Norman Hillmer, ed., *Partners Nevertheless: Canadian-American Relations in the Twentieth Century* (Toronto: Copp Clark Pitman, 1989), pp. 11–31.

Stewart, Greig, *Shutting Down the National Dream* (Scarborough, Ont.: McGraw-Hill, 1988).

Stewart, Ian, "Ottawa and the Post-Keynesian World," in David Crane, ed., *Beyond the Monetarists: Post-Keynesian Alternatives to Rampant Inflation, Low Growth and High Unemployment* (Toronto: Canadian Institute for Economic Policy, 1981), pp. 90–98.

Stewart, Walter, "Baby, It Was Cold Inside," *Maclean's* (July 1971), pp. 32, 63–66.

———, "The Banks' Bank," *Saturday Night* (Sept. 1982), pp. 26–36.

———, "The Natural," *Toronto Life* (June 1983), pp. 29–31, 59–60.

Stone, Frank, *Canada, the GATT and the International Trade System* (Montreal: Institute for Research on Public Policy, 1984).

Struthers, James, *No Fault of Their Own: Unemployment and the Canadian Welfare State, 1914-1941* (Toronto: University of Toronto Press, 1983).

Stursberg, Peter, *Lester Pearson and the Dream of Unity* (Toronto: Doubleday, 1978).

Swift, Jamie, *Odd Man Out: The Life and Times of Eric Kierans* (Vancouver: Douglas and McIntyre, 1988).

Swimmer, Gene, "Changes to Public Service Labour Relations Legislation: Revitalizing or Destroying Collective Bargaining?" in Michael J. Prince, ed., *How Ottawa Spends, 1987-88: Restraining the State* (Toronto: Methuen, 1987), pp. 293–316.

———, "'Six and Five': Part Grandstanding and Part Grand Plan," in Allan M. Maslove, ed., *How Ottawa Spends, 1984: The New Agenda* (Toronto: Methuen, 1984).

Taylor, Charles, "Atomism," in Alkis Kontos, ed., *Powers, Possessions and Freedom: Essays in Honour of C.B. Macpherson* (Toronto: University of Toronto Press, 1979), pp. 39–61.

Thatcher, Margaret, *The Downing Street Years* (New York: HarperCollins, 1993).

Thérien, Jean-Philippe, "Canadian Aid: A Comparative Analysis," paper presented to the Canadian Political Science Association, June 1992.

Thomas, Paul, "The Role of National Party Caucuses," in Peter Aucoin, ed., *Party*

*Government and Regional Representation in Canada* (Toronto: University of Toronto Press, 1985).

Thomson, Dale C., *Louis St. Laurent: Canadian* (Toronto: Macmillan of Canada, 1967).

———, *Vive le Québec libre* (Toronto: Deneau, 1988).

Thomson, Janice E., and Stephen D. Krasner, "Global Transactions and the Consolidation of Sovereignty," in Ernst-Otta Czempiel and James N. Rosenau, eds., *Global Changes and Theoretical Challenges: Approaches to World Politics for the 1990s* (Lexington, Mass.: Lexington Books, 1989), pp. 195–219.

Thorburn, Hugh G., ed., *Party Politics in Canada*, 5th ed. (Toronto: Prentice-Hall, 1985).

Thordarson, Bruce, *Trudeau and Foreign Policy: A Study in Decision-Making* (Toronto: Oxford University Press, 1972).

Tower, Courtney, "Let's Put Power Back in Parliament," *Reader's Digest* (Oct. 1979), pp. 53–57.

Treddenick, John M., "The Arms Race and Military Keynesianism," *Canadian Public Policy* 11, no. 1 (Mar. 1985), pp. 77–92.

Trudeau, Margaret, *Beyond Reason* (New York: Paddington, 1979).

———, *Consequences* (Toronto: McClelland and Stewart, 1982).

Tucker, Michael, "Canadian Security Policy," in Maureen Appel Molot and Brian T. Tomlin, eds., *Canada Among Nations, 1985: The Conservative Agenda* (Toronto: Lorimer, 1986).

———, "Trudeau and the Politics of Peace," *International Perspectives* (May-June 1984), pp. 7–10.

Tupper, Allan, "Public Enterprise and Social Welfare: The Case of the Cape Breton Development Corporation," *Canadian Public Policy* 4, no. 4 (Autumn 1978), pp. 530–46.

Van Loon, Richard J., "Kaleidoscope in Grey: The Policy Process in Ottawa," in Michael S. Whittington and Glen Williams, eds., *Canadian Politics in the 1980s*, 2nd ed. (Toronto: Methuen, 1984), pp. 412–33.

———, "Ottawa's Expenditure Process: Four Systems in Search of Co-ordination," in G. Bruce Doern, ed., *How Ottawa Spends: The Liberals, the Opposition and Federal Priorities, 1983* (Toronto: Lorimer, 1983), pp. 93–120.

———, "The Policy and Expenditure Management System in the Federal Government: The First Three Years," *Canadian Public Administration* 26, no. 2 (Summer 1983), pp. 255–85.

———, "Reforming Welfare in Canada," *Public Policy* 27, no. 4 (Fall 1979), pp. 469–504.

Van Steenburg, Robert, "An Analysis of Canadian-American Defence Economic Cooperation: The History and Current Issues," in David G. Haglund, ed., *Canada's Defence Industrial Base: The Politics of Preparedness and Procurement* (Kingston, Ont.: Ronald P. Frye, 1988), pp. 189–219.

Wade, Mason, *The French Canadians 1760-1967*, vol. 1, *1760-1910*; vol. 2, *1911-1967* (Toronto: Macmillan of Canada, 1968 and 1983).

Waldie, K.G., "The Evolution of Labour-Government Consultation on Economic Policy," in W. Craig Riddell, ed., *Labour-Management Cooperation in Canada* (Toronto: University of Toronto Press, 1985), pp. 151–201.

Walker, Martin, *The Cold War and the Making of the Modern World* (London: Fourth Estate, 1993).

Ward, Norman, and David Smith, *Jimmy Gardiner, Relentless Liberal* (Toronto: University of Toronto Press, 1990).

Warrian, Peter, "Controls for Whom?" *The Canadian Forum* 62, no. 721 (Sept. 1982), pp. 10–11.

Watkins, Mel, "In Defence of the National Energy Program," *The Canadian Forum* 61, no. 710 (June-July, 1981), pp. 6–9.

Wearing, Joseph, "Can An Old Dog Teach Itself New Tricks? The Liberal Party Attempts Reform," in Alain G. Gagnon and A. Brian Tanguay, eds. *Canadian Parties in Transition: Discourse, Organization, Representation* (Toronto: Nelson, 1989), pp. 272–86.

———, *The L-Shaped Party: The Liberal Party of Canada, 1958-1980* (Toronto: McGraw-Hill, 1981).

Weaver, R. Kent, "Political Foundations of Swedish Economic Policy," in Barry P. Bosworth and Alice M. Rivlin, eds., *The Swedish Economy* (Washington, D.C.: Brookings Institution, 1987), pp. 289–324.

Webber, Jeremy, "The Malaise of Compulsory Conciliation: Strike Prevention in Canada During World War II," *Labour/Le Travail* 15 (Spring 1985), pp. 57–88.

Westell, Anthony, "Sharing the Continent: Canada's Investment Capital Moves South of the Border," *International Perspectives* (Jan.-Feb. 1981), pp. 10–14.

Westley, Margaret W., *Remembrance of Grandeur: The Anglo Protestant Elite of Montreal 1900-1950* (Montreal: Éditions Libre Expression, 1990).

Westmacott, M., and P. Dore, "Intergovernmental Cooperation in Western Canada: The Western Economic Opportunities Conference," in J. Peter Meekison, ed., *Canadian Federalism: Myth or Reality*, 3rd ed. (Toronto: Methuen, 1977), pp. 340–52.

Weston, Greg, *Reign of Error: The Inside Story of John Turner's Troubled Leadership* (Scarborough, Ont.: McGraw-Hill Ryerson, 1988).

Whitaker, Reginald, *The Government Party: Organizing and Financing the Liberal Party of Canada, 1930-1958* (Toronto: University of Toronto Press, 1977).

———, "Reason, Passion and Interest: Pierre Trudeau's Eternal Liberal Triangle," *Canadian Journal of Political and Social Theory* 4, no. 1 (Winter 1980), pp. 5–31.

Whitaker, Robert W., ed., *The New Right Papers* (New York: St. Martin's, 1982).

Wiles, Peter, "Soviet Economica," *Soviet Studies* 2, no. 2 (Oct. 1952), pp. 133–38.

Wilkinson, B.W., *Canada in the Changing World Economy* (Montreal: C.D. Howe Institute, 1980).

Williams, Glen, *Not for Export: Toward a Political Economy of Canada's Arrested Industrialization*, updated ed. (Toronto: McClelland and Stewart, 1986).

Wills, Garry, *Confessions of a Conservative* (New York: Doubleday, 1979).

———, *Reagan's America: Innocents at Home* (New York: Doubleday, 1987).

Wilson, Barry, *Politics of Defeat: The Decline of the Liberal Party in Saskatchewan* (Saskatoon: Western Producer Prairie Books, 1980).

Wisse, Ruth R., *If I Am Not for Myself . . . The Liberal Betrayal of the Jews* (New York: Free Press, 1992).

Wolfe, David, "Economic Growth and Foreign Investment: A Perspective on Canadian Economic Policy, 1945-1957," *Journal of Canadian Studies* 13, no. 1 (Spring 1978), p. 3–20.

———, "The Politics of the Deficit," in G. Bruce Doern, ed., *The Politics of Economic Policy* (Toronto: University of Toronto Press, 1985), pp. 111–62.

———, "Politics, the Deficit and Tax Reform," *Osgoode Hall Law Journal* 26, no. 2 (Summer 1988), pp. 347–65.

———, "The State and Economic Policy in Canada, 1945-75," in Leo Panitch, ed., *The Canadian State: Political Economy and Political Power* (Toronto: University of Toronto Press, 1977), pp. 251–88.

Wonder, Edward, "The US Government Response to the Canadian National Energy Program," *Canadian Public Policy* 8 (1982), supplement, pp. 480–93.

Wonnacott, Paul, and Ronald J. Wonnacott, *U.S.-Canadian Free Trade: The Potential Impact on the Canadian Economy* (Montreal: Private Planning Association of Canada, 1968).

Wonnacott, Ronald J., and Paul Wonnacott, *Free Trade Between the United States and Canada: The Potential Economic Effects* (Cambridge, Mass.: Harvard University Press, 1967).

Wood, Bernard, "Canada's Views on North-South Negotiations," *Third World Quarterly* 3, no. 4 (Oct. 1981), pp. 1–8.

Wood, David G., *The Lougheed Legacy* (Toronto: Key Porter, 1985).

Wood, W. Donald, *The Current Industrial Relations Scene in Canada (1973)* (Kingston, Ont.: Industrial Relations Centre, Queen's University, 1973).

Woods, Shirley E., *Her Excellency, Jeanne Sauvé* (Toronto: Macmillan of Canada, 1986).

———, *Ottawa: The Capital of Canada* (Toronto: Doubleday Canada, 1980).

Wright, Gerald, "Bureaucratic Politics and Canada's Foreign Economic Policy," in Denis Stairs and Gilbert R. Winham, eds., *Selected Problems in Formulating Foreign Economic Policy* (Toronto: University of Toronto Press, 1985), pp. 9–58.

———, "Persuasive Influence: The Case of the Interest Equalization Tax," in W. Andrew Axline et al., *Continental Community? Independence and Integration in North America* (Toronto: McClelland and Stewart, 1974), pp. 137–63.

Young, Hugo, *One of Us: A Biography of Margaret Thatcher* (London: Macmillan, 1989).

Young, Robert A., "Business and Budgeting: Recent Proposals for Reforming the Revenue Budgeting Process," *Canadian Public Policy* 9, no. 3 (Sept. 1983), pp. 347–61.

Young-Bruehl, Elizabeth, *Hannah Arendt* (New Haven, Ct.: Yale University Press, 1982).

Zink, Lubor J., "The Unpenetrated Problem of Pierre Trudeau," *National Review* (June 25, 1982), pp. 751–56.

## Works by Pierre Elliott Trudeau

[Anonymously] "Faites vos jeux," *Cité libre* 1, no. 1 (1950), p. 38.

[Anonymously] "Positions sur la présente guerre," *Cité libre* 1, no. 3 (May 1951), pp. 1–11.

"De libro, tributo . . . et quibusdam aliis" [About a book, taxes . . . and certain other matters], *Cité libre* 10 (Oct. 1954), pp. 1–16. [Reprinted in *Federalism and the French Canadians* (Toronto: Macmillan of Canada, 1968), pp. 63–78.]

*Mémoire . . . à la Commission royale d'enquête sur les problèmes constitutionelles*, 2nd ed. (Montreal: Fédération des Unions industrielles du Québec, 1955).

"À propos de 'domination économique,'" *Cité libre* 20 (May 1958), pp. 7, 11–13, 15.

"Some Obstacles to Democracy in Quebec," *Canadian Journal of Economics and Political Science* 24, no. 3 (Aug. 1958), pp. 297–311. [Reprinted in *Federalism and the French Canadians* (Toronto: Macmillan of Canada, 1968), pp. 103–23.]

"New Treason of the Intellectuals," in *Federalism and the French Canadians* (Toronto: Macmillan of Canada, 1968), pp. 151–81. Translated from "La nouvelle trahison des clercs," *Cité libre* 46 (Apr. 1962), pp. 3–16.

"Economic Rights," *McGill Law Journal* 8, no. 2 (June 1962), pp. 121, 123, 125.

"Pearson ou l'abdication de l'esprit," *Cité libre* 56 (Apr. 1963) pp. 7–12.

[With others] "Manifeste pour une politique fonctionnelle," *Cité libre* 67 (May 1964), pp. 11–17.

[With others] "An Appeal for Realism in Politics," *The Canadian Forum* (May 1964), pp. 29–33.

[With others] "L'agriculture au Québec," *Cité libre* 78 (July 1965), pp. 9–16.

[With Gérard Pelletier] "Pelletier et Trudeau s'expliquent," *Cité libre* 80 (Oct. 1965), pp. 3–5.

"Federalism, Nationalism, and Reason," in P.-A. Crépeau and C.B. Macpherson, eds., *The Future of Canadian Federalism/L'avenir du fédéralisme canadien* (Toronto: University of Toronto Press, 1965), pp. 16–35. [Reprinted in *Federalism and the French Canadians* (Toronto: Macmillan of Canada, 1968), pp. 182–203.]

"Quebec and the Constitutional Problem," Brief to the Constitution Committee of the Quebec Legislative Assembly, 1965, in *Federalism and the French Canadians* (Toronto: Macmillan of Canada, 1968), pp. 3–51.

"Separatist Counter-Revolutionaries," in *Federalism and the French Canadians* (Toronto: Macmillan of Canada, 1968).

*Approaches to Politics*, translated by I.M. Owen (Toronto: Oxford University Press, 1970).

[As editor] *The Asbestos Strike*, translated by James Boake (Toronto: James Lewis & Samuel, 1974).

*Lifting the Shadow of War*, C. David Crenna, ed. (Edmonton: Hurtig, 1987).

"'Say Goodbye to the Dream of One Canada,'" in Donald Johnston, ed., *With a Bang, Not a Whimper: Pierre Trudeau Speaks Out* (Toronto: Stoddart, 1988), pp. 8–22.

[As co-editor, with Thomas S. Axworthy] *Towards a Just Society: The Trudeau Years* (Toronto: Viking, 1990).

*"A Mess that Deserves a Big No,"* translated by George Tombs (Montreal: Robert Davies, 1992).

*Memoirs* (Toronto: McClelland and Stewart, 1993).

## Speeches and Interviews

These transcripts are in the Library of Parliament.

"Transcript of Press Conference with Pierre E. Trudeau," National Press Building, Ottawa, Apr. 7, 1968.

"Canada and the World," *Statements and Speeches* no. 68/17 (May 29, 1968).

"Notes for the Prime Minister's Address to the Liberal Federation of Canada (Quebec)," Nov. 10, 1968.

"A Defence Policy for Canada," *Statements and Speeches* no. 69/7 (Apr. 3, 1969).

"The Relation of Defence Policy to Foreign Policy," *Statements and Speeches* no. 69/8 (Apr. 12, 1969).

"Notes for Remarks by the Prime Minister at the Harrison Liberal Conference, Harrison Hot Springs, British Columbia," Nov. 21, 1969.

"Notes for a Speech by Pierre Elliott Trudeau, Prime Minister of Canada, to the United Nations General Assembly Special Session on Disarmament," New York, May 26, 1978.

"Notes for Remarks by the Right Honourable P.E. Trudeau," Halifax Board of Trade, Halifax, Jan. 25, 1980.

"Transcript of the Prime Minister's News Conference en Route from Riyadh to Jeddah," Nov. 17, 1980.

"Transcript of the Prime Minister's Speech at the Liberal Party of Canada (British Columbia) Fundraising Dinner, Vancouver, November 24, 1981."

"Transcript of Prime Minister's Interview with Jim Hoagland, Washington Post, published May 18, 1982."

"Transcript of the Prime Minister's Address to the Second United Nations Special Session on Disarmament," New York, June 18, 1982.

"Transcript of the Prime Minister's News Conference," National Press Theatre, Ottawa, July 9, 1982.

"Transcript of the Prime Minister's News Conference," National Press Theatre, Ottawa, July 23, 1982.

"The Prime Minister's Broadcasts to the Nation on the Economy," Oct. 19, 20, 21, 1982, Office of the Prime Minister.

"Notes for Remarks by the Prime Minister at the National Convention of the Liberal Party," Hull, Quebec, Nov. 5, 1982.

"The Prime Minister's Remarks at the Closing Sessions of the Liberal Party of Canada Policy Convention," Château Laurier, Ottawa, Nov. 7, 1982.

"Reflections on Peace and Security," Remarks by the Prime Minister to the Conference on Strategies for Peace and Security in the Nuclear Age, University of Guelph, Ontario, Oct. 27, 1983.

"Remarks by the Prime Minister on Peace and Security," Queen Elizabeth Hotel, Montreal, Nov. 13, 1983.

"Remarks by Prime Minister Pierre Elliott Trudeau," Liberal Party of Canada Leadership Convention, Ottawa, June 14, 1984.

# LIST OF INTERVIEWS

In addition to drawing on material provided by the more than five hundred people listed in Volume 1, our research for this book benefitted from interviews with, or lectures given by, the following protagonists and observers of the period, as well as several people who did not want their names listed.

Rosalie Abella
Elly Alboim
Michael Atkinson
Robert Baldwin
James Barros
A.W. Beairsto
E.J. Benson
André Bernard
Elaine Bernard
Jagdish Bhagwati
Anne Bohm
Robert Boyce
Catherine Breslin
Meyer Brownstone
Richard Burt
Alan Cairns
Pierre Carignan
Pat Carney
Kenneth Carty
Jean-Michel Catta
Egan Chambers
Sherrill Cheda
Jean Chrétien
Wallace Clement
Marjorie Cohen
Penny Collenette
Robert Cox
John Crosbie
John Curtis
Rufus Davis
Thérèse Gouin Décarie
Vianney Décarie
Thomas Delworth
Andrée Désautels
Ronald Dick
Stéphane Dion
Colin Dobell
I.M.B. Dobell

Arthur Donner
Charles Doran
Daniel Drache
Patricia Dumas
George Elliott
Harry Ferns
Elizabeth Fisher
D'Iberville Fortier
Allan Fotheringham
Jean Fournier
Joan Fox
Paul Fox
Barbara Frum
Robert Fulford
John Kenneth Galbraith
Stephen Gill
Sam Gindin
John Grant
Franklyn Griffiths
Larry Grossman
Gwenyth Grube
Michael Hart
Michael Hawes
Alfred Hero
John Honderich
W.H. Hopper
Gorse Howarth
Michael Howlett
Adèle Hurley
Mel Hurtig
William Irvine
Peter Katzenstein
Robert Keohane
William Kilbourn
Allan King
Jeff King
Martin Knelman
Leo Kolber

Michael Kusner
Andrée Lajoie
Bernard Landry
Otto Lang
David Langille
Peter Langille
Jean Laponce
John Laschinger
Camille Laurin
Dominic LeBlanc
Suzanne Le Moyne
Peter Leslie
Malcolm Lester
Georges-Henri Lévesque
David Lewis
James Lightbody
Allen Linden
Evert Lindquist
Richard Lipsey
Jim Littleton
Patricia Lortie
Charles Lussier
Doug McArthur
Lynn McDonald
Barbara McDougall
Ian McDougall
Steven McDowell
Heather MacIvor
Kenneth McNaught
Kay Macpherson
Kenneth McRae
Rianne Mahon
Harald Malmgren
Ronald Manzer
de Montigny Marchand
Elie Martell
Shelley Martell
Lawrence Martin
Paul Martin, Sr.
Thomas Maxwell
Tony Merchant
William Merkin
Patrice Merrin
Ralph Miliband
Morris Miller
Pamela Miller

William Mingo
D.W. Minion
Jacques-Yvan Morin
William Mulholland
Ted Mumford
William Neville
Edward Ney
James Nininger
Kim Richard Nossal
Alan Nymark
Wanda O'Hagan
H.A. Olson
Jon Pammett
Louis Pauly
Ross Perry
Douglas Peters
Paul Plant
John Porter
Cranford Pratt
Richard Price
David Rayside
Louis Rasminsky
Escott Reid
Simon Reisman
John Reshetar
Michel Robert
Edward Roberts
Colin Robertson
Dalton Robertson
Gerald Robinson
Lukin Robinson
Peter Robinson
François Rocher
Roger Rolland
Jeff Rose
Jeffrey Sachs
Liora Salter
Maurice Sauvé
Gerald Schwartz
Rodger Schwass
Robin Sears
Brian Segal
Tom Shillington
Grace Skogstad
David Slater
Richard Smith

Richard Stanbury
Janice Stein
Davie Steuart
Don Stevenson
Tom Sweeney
Kenneth Taylor
Tom Taylor
William Taylor
Hugh Thorburn
Janis Thordarson
William Thorsell
Lionel Tiger
Alexander Tomlinson
John Tory
Ouida Touche
Adam Ulam

Pierre Vadeboncoeur
Ian Waddell
Raymond Waldmann
W. Allen Wallis
Gabriel Warren
Leonard Waverman
Joseph Wearing
David Weatherhead
William Westfall
Peter Wiles
Lynn Williams
Seymour Wilson
Gilbert Winham
Henry Wiseman
Ruth Wisse

# ACKNOWLEDGEMENTS

Besides those thanked in the acknowledgements in Volume 1, we would like to express our gratitude to John Grant of Wood Gundy, Bruce Wilkinson of the University of Alberta, and Don Moggridge and David Wolfe of the University of Toronto, for their expert comments on all or part of the political economy sections of this book; and to John Kirton, Kim Nossal, and Janice Stein for giving careful readings to Chapter 13. All of them offered collegial advice with great generosity; the authors are, of course, responsible for the analysis and any factual errors it inadvertently contains.

William Toye was kind enough to cast his practised editorial eye on an early draft of this material and to make several helpful suggestions. Ashley McCall and David Trick each brought to their perusal of the completed manuscript special strengths and offered us their keen insights. Darlene Money addressed with great intelligence the difficult task of preparing a comprehensive index for both volumes.

William Lee, John Payne, and several senior bureaucrats and Liberal Party officials generously offered us access to their personal archives of notes and memoranda from the period.

Christopher Boyle and Bruce Jones made valuable contributions to the political economy research, and Peter Biro undertook research in Montreal. Blaise Clarkson took on the daunting labour of ordering our ballooning files and creating the large bibliography, displaying in both jobs her remarkable competence and depth of character. Ayesha Anklesaria worked cheerfully and exactingly under deadline duress at checking the notes for accuracy.

Kyra Clarkson heartened us often by long-distance phone from Paris, Berlin, and New Haven. And once again our good friends sustained us. For their sensitivity and constancy we would like to salute in particular Ann Charney, Alec Havrlant, and James Reed.

Toronto, July 1994                                    Christina McCall &
                                                      Stephen Clarkson

# INDEX

This index covers both volumes of *Trudeau and Our Times*.

Abbott, Douglas, 1.220; 2.115-16

Abbott, Tony, 1.420; 2.115-16

Académie Querbes, 1.29, 395; 2.29

acid rain, 1.191; 2.191, 265, 273, 328

Action catholique canadienne, 1.61, 85, 203-5, 213, 401, 403

Action libérale nationale, 2.39

Acton, Lord, 1.54, 205; 2.68, 156, 449

advertising, 2.62, 100, 114, 146, 155, 274, 294, 459, 495-6; political, 1.223-4, 288, 442; 2.83, 117, 418, 423

Africa, 1.101; 2.334, 342-3, 395

agriculture, 1.302-3, 306, 308; 2.221, 265, 491

Agriculture, Department of, 1.191, 192; 2.265

agri-food strategy, 2.265, 328

Aitken, Jonathan, 1.320

Aitken, Max, 2.120

Alberta, 1.225, 279, 288-9, 296, 299, 302-3, 307, 329, 331, 335, 365, 371, 373, 437-8, 444-5; 2.100, 114, 152, 157, 220; amending formula proposal, 1.368-9, 374-5, 381; American investment, 1.302, 443-4; 2.167, 191; attitude to central Canada, 1.299-302, 306-8, 358, 426-7; 2.182; energy resources, 1.158, 301, 303-5, 364; 2.166-70, 176, 177-81, 199, 216, 234, 470; and federal government, 1.301-5; 2.166-82, 198, 216, 234, 266, 327, 360, 470

Alberta Heritage Savings Trust Fund, 1.308-9, 446; 2.169

Alberta Petroleum Marketing Commission, 1.304

amending formula, 1.250-1, 255, 258, 266-8, 271, 273, 285, 293-4, 307, 338, 359, 368-9, 374-5, 377-8, 381, 385; 2.10, 164, 425

Anderson, Doris, 2.308, 313

Anderson, George, 1.432

Anderson, Rick, 2.428

Andras, Robert, 2.464

Andropov, Yuri, 2.354, 355, 372, 383

anglophones, 1.81, 207, 212, 240, 283, 312, 438

Anti-Inflation Board, 2.125, 126, 130, 175, 250

anti-Semitism, 2.30-1, 68, 286

anti-strike legislation, 1.53

Appolloni, Ursula, 2.464

Apps, Alf, 2.314-17, 319-20, 326, 408

Arbatov, Georgii, 2.364

Arctic, Canadian sovereignty in, 2.110

Argue, Hazen, 1.292

arms control, 2.355, 371, 382, 384, 506

Armstrong, Jane, 1.448

Armstrong, Willis, 2.193, 198

Aron, Raymond, 1.48

Asbestos strike (1949), 1.53-4, 65, 69; 2.68

Ashworth, Gordon, 2.396

Asia, 1.50, 147, 204; 2.202, 210, 334, 343, 349

Atlantic provinces, 1.191, 307-9, 359; 2.102, 152, 260, 264, 289

Austin, Jack, 2.153, 231, 265

Australia, 1.249, 354; 2.193

automobile industry, 1.179; 2.97, 104, 157, 167, 292

Automobile Owners' Association, 1.27, 395; 2.27

autonomy, provincial, 1.84, 254, 274, 370; 2.39

Auto Pact, 2.97, 104, 193, 360, 475

Axworthy, Lloyd, 1.165, 191, 292,
    381, 426; 2.140-3, 148, 152, 159,
    221, 223, 250-2, 260, 265, 279,
    292-3, 301, 309, 311-13, 318,
    326-8, 361, 408
Axworthy, Tom, 1.139, 148, 152, 154,
    168-71, 188-9, 192, 420, 422;
    2.137, 140-53, 158-60, 177, 181,
    188, 201, 218, 228, 284, 303, 306,
    309, 311, 324, 388, 390; as
    Trudeau's principal secretary,
    1.381; 2.248, 249, 262, 288, 291,
    295, 301, 306, 314, 318-19, 324-5,
    327, 345, 362-3, 385-6, 394, 396,
    397, 401-2, 414, 416

Baker, James, 2.375
balance of trade, 2.53, 130, 346, 352,
    444
Balfour report, 1.249
Ball, George, 2.193, 475
Ballem, John, 1.301
Balthazar, Louis, 1.433
Bank of Canada, 1.187; 2.15, 90,
    127-8, 232, 234, 244, 254-5, 268,
    435, 487-8
Banting, Keith, 2.247
Barlow, Maude, 2.405
Barre, Raymond, 2.382, 512-13
Barrette, Antonio, 1.458
Basford, Ron, 2.94
Beaufort Sea, 2.182
Beaupré, Ernest, 2.31, 89
Becker, Ernest, 1.399
Beetz, Jean, 1.260, 353
Bégin, Monique, 1.191, 228-9, 234;
    2.148, 251, 261, 265, 293-4, 312,
    326, 328, 387, 402-3, 408
Beige Paper, 1.210, 214-16, 230
Bell, Joel, 2.102, 181
Benda, Julien, 1.409
Bennett, R.B., 1.300, 303, 444
Bennett, W.A.C., 1.438
Bennett, William (B.C. premier),
    1.290, 311, 352, 354-6, 375, 381,
    384

Bennett, William (Iron Ore Co.),
    2.95
Benoit, Jeanne, 1.61-2, 403. See also
    Sauvé, Jeanne
Benson, Edgar, 1.118; 2.90-3, 106,
    111, 267, 454
Benson White Paper, 2.92-3, 95, 103
Bentham, Jeremy, 2.43
Berger, Thomas, 2.110
Bergeron, Gérard, 1.244, 290, 380,
    435
Bernard, Louis, 1.370; 2.30
Bernier, Robert, 1.38; 2.29-31
Bertrand, Jean-Jacques, 1.385
Big Blue Machine, 1.365-6; 2.419
bilateralism, 2.214, 216, 273, 360,
    361
bilingualism, 1.118, 122, 137, 224,
    264, 284, 350-1, 367; 2.86, 129,
    391, 419, 431
Bill 101, 1.226, 291, 351, 385
bill of rights, 1.260, 290, 322. See also
    charter of rights
Bissell, Claude, 2.98
Bissonnette, Lise, 1.193, 233-4
Black, Conrad, 1.32, 67; 2.204
Blair, Bob, 2.181, 221
Blais, Jean-Jacques, 1.443
Blakeney, Allan, 1.225, 289, 311-12,
    337, 371-3, 375, 377, 445
Blaker, Rob, 2.464
Bliss, Michael, 2.137-8
Bloc populaire canadien, 2.39, 41
Bloc Québécois, 2.427
Bockstael, Robert, 1.426; 2.301
Bombardier, Denise, 1.386, 402
Bond, David, 2.221, 222
Borden, Sir Robert, 1.300; 2.18
Borden royal commission, 2.167, 468
Borduas, Paul-Émile, 1.57-8; 2.33, 68
Bouchard, Lucien, 2.427, 429
Bouey, Gerald, 2.128, 254-5, 461,
    487-8
Bourassa, Henri, 1.39, 84, 231, 261,
    264, 437-9; 2.41, 438
Bourassa, Robert, 1.124, 137, 201,

206-7, 232, 266-9, 369, 385; 2.391, 420, 431
Boyd, Liona, 1.147
branch plants, 2.54, 76-8, 86, 97, 100, 106, 131, 218, 219
Brandt, Willy, 2.343-4, 400
Braque, Georges, 1.48; 2.35
Breau, Herb, 2.297, 487
Brecher, Irving, 2.104
Breton, Albert, 1.87, 409-10; 2.79-80, 98, 126, 452, 461
Breton, Raymond, 1.409-10, 452
Bretton Woods Agreement, 2.96
British Columbia, 1.285, 290-2, 306, 311, 343, 371, 375; 2.110
British North America Act, 1.83, 101-2, 118, 142, 246, 248-50, 256, 260, 274, 347, 367, 437-8; amendments, 1.253, 295, 311, 315, 318-20, 327, 340, 347, 353, 359, 383; 2.246; patriation, 1.101-2, 142, 245, 248, 252, 298, 307, 317, 359, 383, 385; 2.245-6; and Quebec, 1.252, 254; renewal, 1.101-2, 142, 245, 262, 264
Broadbent, Ed, 1.326, 328, 339, 371-2, 449; 2.132, 259, 399, 423
Brock, William, 2.190, 215, 272
Brooks, Neil, 2.484
Bruneau, Claude, 1.410
Bryce, Robert, 2.56, 58-9, 89, 90, 92, 103-4, 119, 447
Buchanan, John, 1.308, 312, 371
Buchanan, Judd, 2.395
budgets, 1.160-2, 164, 172, 424; 2.15, 16, 83, 93, 150, 155, 174-5, 180, 232-40, 243, 257-8, 260, 271, 275, 280, 287, 322, 326, 387-8, 473, 484
Bujold, Rémi, 2.299
Bulloch, John, 2.93, 484
Burelle, André, 1.420
Burke, Edmund, 2.71
Burnham, Libby, 2.120
Burns, Robert, 1.237
Burt, Richard, 2.406, 512
Bush, George, 2.191, 362, 375, 383

business community, 1.52, 53, 59, 187, 190-1, 273, 293; 2.17, 31, 94-5, 107, 111, 157, 197, 235, 244, 256-7, 287, 349, 376, 379, 381, 408, 418-19; anti-Trudeau, 2.90, 92, 111, 124, 125, 126, 208, 263; and Liberal Party, 1.137, 138, 220; 2.62, 87, 137, 181, 208, 227, 293, 315, 320, 328, 386, 387, 416, 420; in Quebec, 1.196, 198, 206, 225, 232, 269, 272; 2.39
Business Council on National Issues, 2.252, 269-71, 352-3, 386, 421, 461
Bussières, Pierre, 2.279
by-elections, federal, 1.139, 143, 419, 425; 2.19, 206-9, 288, 291

cabinet committees, 1.117, 122, 136, 157, 227-8, 230; 2.94, 105, 171-3, 294-5, 353, 432, 455
cabinets: of King, 2.54, 70; of Pearson, 2.87, 111-12, 141, 226, 493; of St. Laurent, 2.59, 60, 76; of Trudeau, 1.291-2; 2.89, 91, 100, 106, 218-22, 227, 250, 252, 256, 263, 291-5, 325, 416, 495; of Turner, 2.416, 495
Caccia, Charles, 2.328, 410
Cadieux, Fernand, 1.414
Cadieux, Leo, 2.503
Cadieux, Marcel, 1.100; 2.210
Cafik, Norman, 1.420
Caldicott, Helen, 2.362, 363, 365
Calgary, 1.299, 301
Calgary Herald, 1.341
Calgary Petroleum Products, 1.300
Callaghan, James, 2.341, 344
camarilla (palace guard), 1.150, 152, 421
Cameron, David, 1.288, 441
Cameron, Duncan, 2.422
Camp, Dalton, 1.309, 366; 2.202
Campagnolo, Iona, 1.419; 2.312, 315-16, 320, 361, 394-7, 399-401, 413, 414, 419, 428

Campbell, Kim, 2.428-9
Canada, 1.97-8, 101, 103-4, 123, 361;
    2.105; American influence, 1.95-6,
    115, 121; 2.11, 96, 105, 167, 203,
    305, 335; British connection, 1.95,
    114; 2.51, 53, 437, 439; economy,
    1.96-8, 123, 188, 219, 267, 283,
    358, 417; 2.67, 82, 89, 132, 167,
    208, 210, 217-19, 243-61, 273,
    305, 421-3, 462; foreign
    investment, 2.54, 72, 76-7, 99-100,
    102, 106, 176, 197, 217, 226, 305,
    422, 439, 446, 457; foreign policy,
    1.97, 119, 121, 412, 417; 2.203,
    211-13, 304, 333-5, 338, 341-2,
    349, 502-3; international role,
    1.95-6, 97, 114; 2.209, 214, 335,
    381, 412; relations with U.S., 2.9,
    51-2, 106, 187, 192-3, 200, 203,
    206, 214-16, 232, 244, 272-4,
    336-8, 373, 381, 419, 421-3, 444
Canada Assistance Plan, 2.226
Canada Council, 1.195; 2.459
Canada Development Corporation,
    2.110, 121
Canada Health Act, 2.402-3, 517
Canada Lands, 2.176, 177, 182, 192,
    474
Canada Pension Plan, 1.100; 2.514
Canada-United States Free Trade
    Agreement (FTA), 2.421-3, 428
Canada-United States Test and
    Evaluation Program (CANUSTEP),
    2.353-4, 507
Canada West Foundation, 2.472
Canadian Advisory Council on the
    Status of Women, 2.313
Canadian Bar Association, 1.105, 261,
    270
Canadian Broadcasting Corporation
    (CBC), 1.23, 98; 2.235, 272, 393-4,
    459
Canadian Council for Fair Taxation,
    2.93
Canadian Defence Association, 2.352
Canadian Forum, 1.87; 2.120

Canadian High Commission, 2.47, 60
Canadian Institute for International
    Peace and Security, 2.402
Canadian International Development
    Agency (CIDA), 2.213, 342-3, 505
Canadianization, of energy industry,
    2.176, 180-1, 183, 223, 287, 469,
    481
Canadian Labour Congress, 1.430;
    2.217, 259-61, 461
Canadian Manufacturers'
    Association, 2.386
Canadian Pacific Railway, 1.303
Canadian Petroleum Association,
    2.182
Canadian Radio-television and
    Telecommunications
    Commission, 2.295, 459
Canadian Security and Intelligence
    Service Act (1984), 2.403
Canadian Transport Commission,
    2.380
Canadian Unity Information Office,
    1.223, 270, 441
Cape Breton, 2.224, 227
Cape Breton Development
    Corporation, 2.227
capital, 2.76; American, 2.54-5, 75,
    77-8, 86, 111, 223, 446; Canadian,
    2.87, 128, 268; international, 2.254
capital gains tax, 2.93
capitalism, 1.54, 58, 188, 254; 2.11,
    19, 22-3, 40, 43, 57, 69, 71, 78, 93,
    110, 112, 225, 284
capital punishment, 1.139; 2.145-6
Caplan, Gerald, 1.363
capping, of inflationary increases,
    2.253, 256
Caro, Robert, 2.202
Carr, Shirley, 2.221
Carrington, Lord, 1.322, 383; 2.369
Carstairs, Sharon, 2.410
Carter, Jimmy, 2.138, 187, 189,
    194-5, 200, 341, 344, 424
Carter, Kenneth LeMoyne, 2.92, 93
Cartier, George-Étienne, 1.200

Casgrain, Thérèse, 1.71, 88-9, 234; 2.70, 73

Castonguay, Claude, 1.267

Castro, Fidel, 1.77, 133

CCF. *See* Co-operative Commonwealth Federation

central Canada, 1.299, 302, 304-6; 2.84, 135, 140, 142, 178, 226; source of western anger, 1.187, 303, 305, 307; 2.182

Chaput-Rolland, Solange, 1.234

charisma, 1.102-3, 412-13, 415; 2.271, 306

charitable foundations, 2.235, 237

Charlottetown Accord, 2.426

Charpentier, Georges, 2.47

Charron, Claude, 1.211, 370-1, 373; 2.323

charter of rights, 1.110, 245, 256-7, 263-4, 266, 279, 292-4, 296-7, 328, 337, 339, 342, 347, 349, 366, 373, 378; 2.298, 313, 422; entrenched in constitution, 1.106, 142, 260-2, 271, 274, 285, 291, 311, 318, 322-3, 358, 359, 369, 371-2, 383, 385, 449; 2.10, 159, 199, 247, 287, 327, 432

Chernenko, Konstantin, 2.383

Chevrier, Lionel, 1.91

child tax credit, 2.256, 487-8

China, 1.147, 405; 2.337, 502, 504

Chong, Denise, 2.405

Choquette, Raymond, 1.395

Chouinard, Julien, 1.350, 353

Chrétien, François, 1.216, 329

Chrétien, Jean, 1.216-18, 352, 368; 2.326, 400, 416-17, 423; as cabinet minister, 1.191, 218, 362, 431; 2.148, 156, 292-3, 327, 395, 505; as Liberal Party leader, 2.426, 427; as prime minister, 2.429-30; in Quebec referendum Non campaign, 1.223-4, 226, 243, 335, 431-2, 434; 2.165, 172; role in constitutional reform, 1.245, 362, 381-2, 440-1

*Cité libre*, 1.62-5, 67, 69, 76-7, 80, 83-4, 86, 119, 403-5, 410-11; 2.64, 68, 72, 78, 86, 157, 163, 194, 426

Citélibristes, 1.66-7, 70, 80, 203, 268, 403, 405

civil liberties, 1.61, 68, 123, 206, 256, 292-3; 2.69, 126, 285, 499, 504

civil rights, 1.255-6, 260, 274, 347

civil service, 2.51, 63, 110, 279-80

Clark, Joe, 1.55, 329-30, 332-3; as Conservative leader, 1.140, 155, 187, 272, 277, 331-2; 2.132, 247, 265, 349; and constitutional debate, 1.335-40, 344, 351; and the media, 1.157, 330, 336-7, 450; as opposition leader, 1.142, 329-30, 333, 335; 2.132, 319, 326; as prime minister, 1.154, 156-8, 161, 164, 179-80, 286, 334-5, 365, 449-51; 2.138, 146, 149-50, 152, 155, 170, 172-3, 213, 230-1, 243, 306, 469

Clark, S.D., 2.174-5

Clark, William Edmund (Ed), 2.169-70, 174-5, 236, 470

Clarke, Gwen, 1.416

class, in Quebec, 1.25, 27, 52-4, 59-60, 62, 68-9, 80-1, 245-6; 2.21-2, 30-1

Claxton, Brooke, 2.317

Clay, Lucius, 1.247

Clear Grits, 2.144, 145

Clippingdale, Richard, 1.335

Coady, Father Moses, 2.82, 224-5, 453

Cohen, Marjorie, 2.422

Cohen, Mickey, 1.192; 2.175, 179-80, 267

Cold War, 2.166, 253, 334, 336-7, 351, 373, 383-4, 446-8, 468

collective bargaining, 2.52, 57, 94, 259, 261, 488

Collège Jean-de-Brébeuf, 1.30-2, 38-40, 44, 46, 54, 58, 112, 268-9; 2.29-31, 33, 73, 412

Collenette, David, 2.295, 410

colonialism, 2.63, 101
Columbia River Treaty, 2.76
Comité pour une politique
   fonctionnelle, 1.87, 410-11
Commission of Inquiry into Certain
   Activities of the RCMP
   (McDonald), 2.248, 403, 501
Committee for an Independent
   Canada, 1.207; 2.102
Committee of Public Safety, 1.206
Committee on Economic and
   Regional Development, 2.292
Committee on Social Development,
   2.292
Commons standing committees,
   2.96-7, 101, 496
Commonwealth conferences, 1.354;
   2.340, 369, 371-2
Communications, Department of,
   1.191-2; 2.211, 328, 502
communism, 1.58, 65, 402, 404; 2.55,
   57, 67, 334, 356, 358, 372, 374,
   457
Company of Young Canadians, 2.94
competition, 2.94, 168, 195, 217, 268,
   381
competition law, 2.328, 501
competition policy, 1.191; 2.286
Confederation, 1.105, 107, 256,
   307-8, 311, 346, 349, 360; 2.16-17,
   85-6
Confédération des syndicats
   nationaux, 1.78, 430; 2.258
Confederation of Tomorrow
   conference (1967), 1.258, 259
Conquest, the, 1.56, 200; 2.22-3, 29
conscription crises, in Quebec: in
   World War I, 1.28, 334; 2.18, 38,
   65; in World War II, 1.42, 231,
   245-6, 398; 2.33-4, 40, 65, 69,
   70
Conservative Party, 1.300, 330; in
   Canada, 1.300, 301, 330, see also
   Progressive Conservative Party; in
   Quebec, 2.33-4; in United
   Kingdom, 1.319

consociational élites, 2.51, 54, 76, 90,
   112, 382, 400, 412, 415, 443
constitution, of Canada, 1.170, 173;
   2.107, 128, 165, 287, 327, 418, see
   also British North America Act,
   Constitution Act; amendments,
   1.294, 307, 346-7, 349, 351, 354,
   371-2, 374-5, see also amending
   formula; division of powers, 1.252,
   253-7, 285, 293, 309, 347, 351,
   373, 375; patriation, 1.142, 245,
   248-50, 252, 258, 266, 268, 272-4,
   298, 344, 357-9; 2.139, 159, 180,
   199, 207, 229, 245-7, 275, 298,
   342, 343-4, 403, 431; 2.368, 369;
   reform, 1.101, 106, 118, 239,
   242-5, 253, 256-8, 275, 278; 2.86,
   89, 120, 159, 160, 172; Trudeau's
   unilateral patriation proposal,
   1.278-9, 285, 292-5, 310, 317, 322,
   359, 361, 366, 373, 383, 385
Constitution Act (1982), 1.457;
   2.246-7, 321, 327
constitutional committees, 1.102,
   117, 256; 2.57
constitutional conferences, 1.142,
   243; 2.69, 208, 397; **1968**,
   1.109-10, 262-3, 265, 439; **1971**,
   1.124, 206-7, 266-7, 279, 294, 307,
   311, 359, 369, 439; **1978**, 1.142,
   271, 310, 365; **1979**, 1.310, 365;
   **1980**, 1.285-6, 288-9, 291, 313;
   **1981**, 1.359
constitutional law, 1.50, 67, 246, 348;
   2.91
constitutional theory, 1.79, 246-7,
   260, 283
Consumer and Corporate Affairs,
   Department of, 1.191, 228; 2.94,
   112, 265
consumer demand, 2.57, 123, 171
consumer goods, 2.53, 54
consumer price index, 2.91, 113
continentalism, 2.54-5, 76, 83-4, 91,
   97-8, 100, 104, 107, 193, 217, 223,
   268-9, 351, 415, 421-2, 432-3, 446

Continuing Committee of Ministers
  on the Constitution (CCMC),
  1.265, 286, 362, 439
convention, in constitutional matters,
  1.295, 346-7, 349, 353
Cook, Ramsay, 1.112, 415; 2.310, 461
Co-operative Commonwealth
  Federation (CCF), 1.88, 245, 252,
  400; 2.34, 40-1, 52, 84, 100, 103,
  107, 114, 145, 248. See also New
  Democratic Party
co-operative movement, 1.60; 2.82,
  159, 225
Coote, Alice, 2.64
Copps, Sheila, 2.427
"corporate welfare bums," 2.107-8,
  109
Council for Canadian Unity, 1.432
courts, 1.275, 294, 344, 432
Coutts, James, 1.117, 124, 155;
  2.114-17, 206-9, 288, 295; as
  Trudeau's principal secretary,
  1.138-40, 151-6, 159, 164, 167-73,
  179, 189, 192, 420, 425; 2.125,
  137-8, 142, 144-9, 157, 228, 284,
  288-9, 291, 303, 314, 388, 390
Coyne, Deborah, 2.433
Coyne, James, 2.127
Créditiste Party, 1.89, 162, 164, 169,
  423-4, 450
credit supply, 2.91, 127, 244
Creighton, Donald, 1.71-2
Criminal Code amendments, 1.107
Croll, David, 1.416
Crosbie, John, 1.157, 161, 426, 450;
  2.150-1, 407, 413, 518
Crowe, Marshall, 2.90, 105, 121
Crown corporations, 1.78, 264; 2.52,
  150, 330
Crow's Nest Pass Rate, 1.303; 2.327,
  491
Cruise missile testing, 2.351-5, 360-2,
  374-6, 508-9
CTV Television Network, 1.125, 363;
  2.461
Cuban Missile Crisis, 2.193, 364

Culhane, Claire, 2.503
Cullen, Bud, 1.420
cultural organizations, 2.52, 111, 459
currency, 2.53, 88, 96
Cyrano de Bergerac, 1.43-4, 273,
  278, 341, 383; 2.199, 442

Danson, Barnett, 1.416, 420; 2.293,
  380
d'Aquino, Thomas, 2.252, 270-1,
  486, 489
Davey, Jim, 1.117, 414
Davey, Keith, 1.124, 169, 172, 422;
  2.100-1, 141, 147, 206-8, 226, 227,
  257, 294-5, 303, 324, 345-6,
  392-4, 395, 396, 399, 401, 411,
  418, 459, 496; as campaign
  organizer, 1.117, 138-40, 179, 190;
  2.83, 114-15, 116, 151-2, 155-6,
  202
Davis, Rufus, 2.46
Davis, William, 1.158, 225, 290, 294,
  310, 312, 331, 337, 359, 361-9,
  381, 382-3, 384, 446; in
  constitutional negotiations,
  1.362-3, 366-9, 382-3
Dawson, Dennis, 2.299, 408, 513
Dawson, MacGregor, 2.18-19, 436
Day, Sir Derek, 1.324
Deaver, Michael, 2.196, 373, 376
De Bané, Pierre, 2.221, 222, 264, 280
debates, in election campaigns,
  2.418-19, 423, 429
de Bellefeuille, Pierre, 1.23
Décarie, Thérèse Gouin, 1.399;
  2.34-5, 39-41, 44-5, 47, 59, 87-8
Décarie, Vianney, 2.45
decentralization, 1.272, 335, 370
Defence Industries Productivity
  Program, 2.352
defence policy, 2.335-6, 349, 353, 506
defence production-sharing
  agreement, 2.77, 193
deficits, 2.56, 65, 123, 134, 150-1,
  232, 244, 252-4, 271, 387, 397,
  418, 420, 428

de Gaulle, Charles, 1.21, 100, 103-5, 107, 115, 414; 2.334, 356-7, 424
de Grandpré, Jean, 1.44-5, 112-13
Delvoie, Louis, 2.365
democracy, 1.67-9, 118, 121, 150, 246, 248, 254, 257, 264, 357; 2.11, 64, 70, 85, 88
Democratic Party, in United States, 1.47; 2.286
Deniger, Pierre, 2.299
DePoe, Norman, 1.412-13
Depression, the, 1.32, 39, 62; 2.39, 40, 56, 82, 141, 225
Désautels, Andrée, 2.48
Desbarats, Peter, 1.97
Desmarais, Paul, 1.160; 2.427
Deutsch, John, 2.90
development, of resources, 2.183, 192
Devoir, Le, 1.42, 53, 60, 65, 67, 78, 174, 193, 203-4, 208, 215, 224, 233, 256, 334, 373, 429, 441; 2.33, 102
Dickie, Bill, 2.169
Dickson, Brian, 1.353
Diefenbaker, John, 1.85, 91, 98, 102, 163, 260, 303, 330, 333, 451; 2.77, 79, 82, 115, 120, 127, 167, 171, 193, 209
Dion, Léon, 1.373, 434, 456
disarmament, 2.349, 354, 356, 362, 366, 374-5, 382, 513
distribution of powers, 1.68, 253-5, 257-8, 266, 293, 309, 347, 351, 372-3, 375, 438, 447
Dome Petroleum, 2.181-2, 473-5
dominion-provincial conferences, 2.61. See also constitutional conferences, federal-provincial conferences, first ministers' conferences
Don Juanism, 1.73, 130
Donner, Arthur, 2.235
Donolo, Peter, 2.428
Douglas, Tommy, 1.372
Drache, Daniel, 2.99
Drapeau, Jean, 1.42, 206

Drury, Charles (Bud), 1.137, 431; 2.293
Dryden, Gordon, 1.167; 2.396
Dubé, Father Rodolphe (François Hertel), 2.29-31
Duclos, Louis, 1.338; 2.299, 300
Dunham Ladies' College, 2.25-26
Dunton, Davidson, 1.86, 259
Duplessis, Maurice, 1.32, 39, 52-3, 59-61, 65-9, 76, 81, 84, 90, 200, 217, 251-2, 254, 333, 385, 401, 404-5, 410; 2.34, 39, 64, 73, 79, 163, 177, 204, 323
Duplessisism, 1.54, 82; 2.71
Dupuy, Michel, 2.365

Eagleburger, Lawrence, 2.381, 512
East Coast Fishery Treaty, 2.189
East-West relations, 2.357-8, 364, 366-7, 370, 376, 383
École libre de sciences politiques, 1.48, 49, 51, 247, 400; 2.44
Economic Council of Canada, 2.126, 252, 462
economic management, 1.254-5; 2.91-2, 113, 229
economic nationalism, 1.412; 2.78-9, 86, 100, 108, 110, 145-6, 199, 222-3, 274, 451
economic policy, 2.173, 213, 222, 249-50, 253, 264, 267-8, 315, 319, 429, 446, 486
economics, 1.46-7, 49-50, 67, 79; 2.41-2, 69, 98, 220, 231, 452; free-market, 2.11, 78, 89, 104, 113, 126, 182, 183, 225, 239; neo-classical, 2.79, 86, 123; Trudeau's knowledge of, 2.72, 89, 447
economic strategy, 2.57, 107, 130-2, 266
economic summits, 1.315; 2.191, 196, 204, 209, 214, 254, 340-1, 343-5, 356-8, 366, 373, 375, 504-5, 508
economic union, 1.285, 364; 2.268
economy: Canadian, 1.96-8, 123, 188, 283, 358, 417; 2.82, 89, 130,

208, 210, 230, 243-61, 265, 268,
386; global, 1.129; 2.96, 130, 244
education, 1.264, 292-4, 351, 364;
2.67; in Quebec, 1.29, 38, 78-9,
84; 2.25-6, 29, 37-8, 78-9
education rights, 1.259, 264, 292,
293, 366, 381, 385, 457
elections, federal, 1.226; 2.385, 388-9,
397, 400, 411; **1949**, 1.250; **1957**,
2.82; **1958**, 1.163; 2.82, 225; **1962**,
2.140; **1963**, 1.85, 217; 2.83; **1968**,
1.113-14, 205, 263, 415; 2.90, 98,
116; **1972**, 1.124, 132, 418; 2.106,
116, 203; **1974**, 1.125, 133, 207,
267, 268; 2.117-18, 142, 153;
**1979**, 1.15-18, 23, 143-4, 154, 214,
272, 273, 334-5, 393, 419-20;
2.132-3, 137-9, 144-6, 149, 153,
165, 306, 311, 395; **1980**,
1.178-80, 188, 273, 282, 334-5,
365, 370, 425-7; 2.165, 206, 218,
229, 249, 300, 306; **1984**, 1.393;
2.417-19; **1988**, 2.422-3; **1993**,
2.429
elections, provincial, 2.425; Ontario,
**1981**, 1.367; Quebec, 1.226, 401;
**1944**, 1.401; **1948**, 1.401; **1952**,
1.61, 401; **1956**, 1.61, 69, 401;
**1960**, 1.76, 81, 407; **1962**, 1.78;
**1970**, 1.428; **1976**, 1.207, 269-70,
428, 435; 2.164, 194; **1981**, 1.374,
456
electoral reforms, 1.78, 242, 408;
2.289, 495
élites, dominating French Canada,
1.59, 65-66, 68, 80, 358, 408
Elizabeth II, 1.268, 274, 316, 323,
324, 360, 439, 447, 448; 2.247, 275
Elliott, Allan, 1.26, 394; 2.25
Elliott, Edward, 2.25
Elliott, Gordon, 1.26, 27, 48, 51; 2.25
Elliott, Grace, 1.25-32, 127, 237;
2.25-7. *See also* Trudeau, Grace
Elliott
Elliott, Philip Armstrong, 1.26; 2.25
Elliott, Sarah Sauvé, 1.26; 2.24-5

employment, 2.149, 461
Employment and Immigration,
Department of, 1.191; 2.251, 265
Enders, Thomas, 1.147
Energy, Mines and Resources,
Department of, 1.157, 190, 192,
229; 2.165, 169-70, 174, 181, 229,
231-2, 264, 267. *See also* EnFin
energy conservation, 2.170-1, 177
energy costs, 1.364; 2.258
energy crises, 1.304, 305, 307;
2.152-4
energy industry, 2.110, 151, 154, 177,
199
energy policy, 1.364; 2.152-3, 155,
156, 165, 169, 171, 172, 174-5,
192, 199, 213-14, 216, 231, 233,
249, 262-3, 327, 465
energy resources, 1.157-8, 161-2,
284, 301, 303-7, 309; 2.221, 341
Energy Resources Conservation
Board, 1.304
energy self-sufficiency, 1.179; 2.154,
199, 220, 445, 471
energy supply, 2.166, 171, 176
energy taxes, 1.161, 162, 164, 304,
307; 2.152, 176-7
EnFin, 2.172-3, 213, 470
English language, 1.38, 41, 81, 86-7,
115, 201, 225, 256; 2.23, 32, 64-5.
*See also* anglophones
"envelope" system, in government
spending, 2.251, 265, 278, 280,
292, 469, 492
Environment, Department of, 1.191;
2.265
environmentalism, 2.110
Epp, Jake, 1.335, 338, 452
Erickson, Arthur, 1.147; 2.15, 248,
435
Erikson, Erik, 1.24, 396; 2.436
Erola, Judy, 2.312, 313, 386, 407, 514
*Esprit*, 1.62, 63; 2.45, 64
Estey, Willard, 1.350, 353
ethnic minorities, 1.82, 292; 2.420,
431

ethnic nationalism, 1.83, 260

Europe, 1.32, 48–50; 2.55, 63, 67, 103, 124, 193–4, 201, 210, 215, 285, 310

European Economic Community, 2.203, 341

Evans, John, 2.464, 465

exploration, for energy resources, 2.177–8, 183, 192, 473

Expo 67, 1.98, 103–4

exports, 2.76, 128, 167, 217, 268, 342, 352, 360, 422, 445

External Affairs, Department of, 1.121, 192, 222, 260, 289; 2.49, 59–61, 65, 94, 97, 166, 189, 198, 203, 209–14, 228, 244, 263, 272–4, 326, 334–5, 337, 339, 346, 349, 365, 421

Ezrin, Hershell, 1.441–2

Fabianism, 2.40, 49, 51

Fainsod, Merle, 1.247

Fairbairn, Joyce, 1.164, 190, 416, 423; 2.228, 399, 405, 414

Fairweather, Gordon, 1.422

family allowances, 1.267; 2.43, 67, 110, 256, 412, 450, 487, 488

family law, 1.107, 272; 2.389

Faribault, Marcel, 1.404

farming, 1.302–3; 2.18, 75, 137, 225, 265, 327–8, 422, 491. See also agriculture

fascism, 2.58, 70, 103

Faulkner, Hugh, 1.420; 2.314

Favreau, Guy, 1.91, 255

Federal Economic Development Coordinators, 2.280

Federal and Intergovernmental Affairs Department, Alberta, 1.303–4

federalism, 1.54, 79, 83, 105, 158, 224, 228, 260, 284; 2.72, 81, 125–6, 138, 142, 154, 163, 391, 426, 431–2; Canadian, 1.67–8, 83, 87, 106, 109–10, 118, 174, 244, 249, 254–5, 259, 263; 2.171; and the Quebec referendum, 2.202–3,

211, 213–14, 223; federal-provincial conferences, 1.201, 251–2, 265, 269, 271, 308, 327. See also constitutional conferences; first ministers' conferences

federal-provincial relations, 1.158, 189, 249–51, 265, 269, 270–1, 273, 282, 284, 288, 304, 306–7, 324, 340, 359–60, 370; 2.61, 148, 164, 199, 207, 216, 313, 432

Federal-Provincial Relations Office (FPRO), 1.223–5, 282–3, 286–9, 298, 345, 363, 431–2, 441–2; 2.129

Federal Reserve Board, 2.128, 254

Fédération des travailleurs du Québec, 1.430

Fédération libérale du Québec, 1.61

feminism, 1.233, 329; 2.110, 265, 307–9, 313, 315, 326

Filion, Gérard, 1.60

Finance, Department of, 1.190, 192, 219; 2.56, 58–9, 61, 91–2, 96, 102–4, 112, 114, 123–4, 130, 132, 168, 170, 183, 213, 222, 229–40, 249, 255–6, 263, 265–7. See also EnFin

Finestone, Sheila, 1.234

finished goods, 2.53, 122

first ministers' conferences, 1.265–9, 299, 310, 315, 359, 375, 439; 2.37, 323, 425, 432

Fisher, Douglas, 1.218, 413; 2.248

fisheries, 1.285, 308, 311, 446; 2.227, 264, 301, 327–8, 491, 501

Fisheries, Department of, 1.191

Fisheries and Oceans, Department of, 2.264

Fleming, James, 1.191, 441; 2.294–5

food strategy, 2.265, 328

Ford, Gerald, 2.200, 340

Ford, Sir John, 1.324–7, 337, 448; 2.510

foreign aid, 2.334, 342–3, 412

Foreign and Commonwealth Office, United Kingdom, 1.314, 322–4, 326; 2.49

foreign investment, 1.179; 2.75, 77-8, 83, 85-6, 104, 106, 108, 217, 422, 457

Foreign Investment Review Agency (FIRA), 2.110, 157, 196, 198, 215-16, 218, 220, 223, 244, 264, 269, 272, 274, 360, 372, 475, 481

foreign policy, 1.97, 119, 121, 249, 412, 417; 2.105-7; of Quebec, 1.81, 100, 137, 255, 257, 412

forestry resources, 2.221, 360

Forget, Claude, 1.216

Forsey, Eugene, 1.271, 282, 352, 436; 2.108, 248, 281, 453

Foster, Maurice, 2.464, 465

Fournier, Jean, 2.64-5, 438, 448-9

Fowler, Robert, 2.406

Fox, Francis, 1.191; 2.293-4, 328

Fox, Joan, 2.47-8

Fox, Paul, 2.46, 47-8, 68

France, 1.59, 101, 103, 105-7, 137, 185, 247; 2.44-7, 66, 285, 356-7, 366; relations with Quebec, 1.81, 100, 103, 105-6, 137, 255

francophones, 1.103, 115, 117-18, 201, 261, 283, 292, 312, 351, 360, 367, 391; 2.431

Fraser, Graham, 1.211, 428

Freedman, Samuel, 1.346

free enterprise, 2.20, 80, 183, 198, 268, 284, 286-7, 369, 386-7

Freeland, Sir John, 1.324

free trade, 2.53-4, 85, 122, 428, 433, 445. *See also* Canada–United States Free Trade Agreement; North American Free Trade Agreement

freight rates, 2.327-8

French language, 1.36-7, 41, 59, 78, 201, 258, 261, 291, 438, 443; 2.31-2, 62-3, *see also* francophones; anglophones' inability to speak, 1.86, 205, 273; 2.18, 62-3, 64, 65; as an official language, 1.259, 264

Friedman, Milton, 2.113, 128

Friedrich, Carl, 1.46-7, 123, 247

Front de libération du Québec (FLQ), 1.85, 122-3, 206, 256

Front de libération nationale (Algeria), 1.85

Frost, David, 1.401; 2.245-6

Frum, Barbara, 1.450; 2.393, 515

Frum, Murray, 1.159

Fulton, E. Davie, 1.255; 2.120

Fulton-Favreau formula, 1.255; 2.164

functionalism, 1.68, 263, 439; 2.91, 171

Gagnon, Lysiane, 1.234, 433-4

Galbraith, J.K., 1.120; 2.57, 70, 78, 124-5, 236, 460

Gallagher, Jack, 2.181-2

Gandhi, Indira, 2.350, 371

Gang of Eight, 1.338, 340, 359, 368-9, 371-3, 375-9, 383

Gardiner, Jimmy, 1.421; 2.139, 301

Gardom, Garde, 1.343

Garneau, Raymond, 1.208; 2.420

gasoline taxes, 1.161-2; 2.176-7, 475

Gauthier, Jean-Robert, 2.464

Gauthier, Yvon, 1.410

Geller-Schwartz, Linda, 1.441

General Agreement on Tariffs and Trade (GATT), 2.73, 104, 111, 118, 244, 268, 273, 421

General Bureau of International Security and Arms Control, 2.365

Gérin-Lajoie, Paul, 1.77, 255

Germany, 1.247; 2.285, 350, 353

Gibson, Fred, 1.381, 441; 2.63

Gibson, Gordon, 1.117, 414

Gigantes, Philippe Deane, 2.132, 380, 397, 515

Gill, Audrey, 2.311-12, 314, 315, 320

Gillespie, Alastair, 1.420; 2.293

Gilson, Étienne, 2.44

Giscard d'Estaing, Valéry, 2.358

Gladstone, William, 2.43, 435

globalization, 2.268-9, 381

*Globe and Mail*, 1.107, 276, 325, 337, 448, 450; 2.202, 235, 252, 271, 393, 411

Gobeil, Charlotte, 2.338
Gobeil, Madeleine, 1.74, 185-6;
    2.310
Golden, David, 1.416
Goldenberg, Carl, 1.117, 220, 259,
    261, 282
Goldenberg, Eddie, 1.220, 224;
    2.156, 413
Goldfarb, Martin, 1.139-40, 160, 166,
    168, 190, 358, 422; 2.116, 117,
    152, 155, 295, 298, 329, 345, 388,
    343, 398-9, 401
Goldschlag, Klaus, 2.106
Goodman, Eddie, 1.365
goods and services tax, 2.428
Gordon, Alison, 1.416
Gordon, John King, 1.416
Gordon, Walter L., 1.85, 91, 96, 117,
    207, 410; 2.76-7, 82, 84-7, 90, 98,
    102, 104-5, 107, 115, 141, 143,
    145-6, 160, 226, 230, 305, 392,
    451, 453
Gossage, Patrick, 1.190, 420
Gotlieb, Allan, 1.100, 192, 260, 326,
    415-16; 2.209-17, 223, 273, 339,
    364-5, 371-3, 375-8, 419
Gouin, Léon-Mercier, 2.36-7, 40, 42
Gouin, Paul Nérée, 2.39
Gouin, Sir Lomer, 1.29; 2.29, 36-8,
    88
Gouin, Thérèse, 1.399; 2.34-5, 39-41,
    44-5, 47, 59, 87-8
government contracts, 2.62
government intervention, 2.58, 104,
    113, 124-6, 166, 176, 180, 214,
    217-20, 222, 233, 252, 261, 284,
    286, 328, 420
government spending, 1.188, 190;
    2.56, 130, 253, 271, 292, 381, 387,
    461
Goyer, Jean-Pierre, 1.414
Grafstein, Jerry, 1.139-40, 178, 190,
    422; 2.116-17, 294, 318, 380, 418
Graham, Alasdair, 1.151-2, 168; 2.316
grain, in western economy, 1.306;
    2.264, 327-8, 491

Grandy, James, 2.122
Grant, George, 2.99
Gray, Herb, 1.179, 190-2, 416; 2.102,
    148, 152, 218-22, 251, 263, 268,
    301, 326, 408, 480
Gray report, 2.106, 218
Green, Joe, 1.415
Greene, T.H, 2.43
Gregg, Allan, 1.163, 336; 2.419
Grenada invasion, 2.366-7, 376
Grindstone Group, 1.149-50, 155,
    421; 2.311, 427
Gromyko, Andrei, 2.383
Gropius, Walter, 1.47
Groulx, Abbé Lionel, 1.28, 40, 200,
    394-5; 2.30
guaranteed annual income, 2.112-13,
    152, 165, 287
guaranteed income supplement,
    2.226, 256, 388, 487-8
Guilbault, Jacques, 1.167-8
Guindon, Hubert, 1.403, 408-9
Gulf Canada, 2.183
Gwyn, Richard, 1.413, 421; 2.248,
    463
Gwyn, Sandra, 1.147
Gzowski, Peter, 1.410; 2.394

Haberler, Gottfried, 2.58, 447
Haggan, Reeves, 1.441
Haig, Alexander, 2.189-90, 273, 345
Halberstam, David, 2.202
Halifax, 1.281
Hansen, Alvin, 1.47; 2.58, 447-8
Harper, Elijah, 2.426
Harrington Lake, 1.128, 146
Harris, Lou, 2.83
Harris, Seymour, 2.56, 447
Hartle, Douglas, 2.280
Hartz, Louis, 1.47, 400; 2.43
Harvard Nuclear Study Group, 2.364
Harvard University, 1.19, 41, 42-4,
    46-9, 54, 56-8, 67-9, 79, 189,
    246-7, 254, 269, 301, 305, 313,
    400; 2.80, 103, 114, 116, 441
Harvey, Edward, 2.307

Hatfield, Heber, 1.360
Hatfield, Richard, 1.288, 290, 312,
    325-6, 359-61, 365-7, 382-3; 2.425
Hays, Harry, 1.296, 298, 328, 337
Hays-Joyal committee, 1.296, 337,
    449
Head, Ivan, 1.117, 259; 2.212, 310,
    334-5, 338, 340, 342, 364
Health and Welfare, Department of,
    1.191, 228; 2.265, 328
Heap, Dan, 2.208
Heath, Edward, 2.340
Hébert, Jacques, 1.67, 168, 172,
    405-6; 2.380, 390
Hellyer, Paul, 1.205; 2.116, 293
Hertel, François, 2.29-31
Hervieux-Payette, Céline, 2.409,
    465
Hibernia oil field, 1.308; 2.192,
    198
Hilton, David, 2.239-40
Hnatyshyn, Ray, 2.170
Hobbes, Thomas, 1.69; 2.43
homosexuals, 1.73, 107, 293
Honderich, Beland, 2.87, 135, 155,
    393
Hood, William, 1.423
Hopkins, Len, 2.464
Hopper, Bill, 2.181
Horner, Jack, 1.419, 422
Hošek, Chaviva, 2.428-9
Houde, Camillien, 1.32, 42, 395; 2.34
House of Commons, Canada, 1.55,
    102, 107, 121, 160, 291, 293, 295,
    319-20, 325-6, 338-9, 452; 2.15,
    16, 89, 106, 109, 126
housing, 1.119, 161; 2.67, 148, 150,
    152, 233, 389
Howard, Frank, 2.395
Howarth, Gorse, 2.220
Howe, C.D., 1.138, 220; 2.54, 75, 77,
    94, 269, 317, 352, 446
Hudson's Bay Oil and Gas Company,
    2.99, 475
Hurley, Jim, 1.441
Hurtig, Mel, 2.101, 305

hydroelectric power, 1.305; 2.24, 76,
    177
Hydro-Quebec, 1.78

Iglauer, Edith, 1.36
Ignatieff, George, 2.366, 510
immigration, 1.261; 2.21, 289, 296,
    329, 431
imperialism, 2.51, 63, 101, 193, 437
Imperial Oil Company, 1.31, 300;
    2.26, 183
imports, 2.54, 97, 113, 128, 217, 229,
    258
incentives, economic, 2.75, 97, 113
income, 2.75, 83, 387
income tax, 2.110, 115, 253, 256
Independent Petroleum Association
    of Canada, 2.183
indexing, 2.113, 253, 256, 459, 487
India, 2.350, 371-2
Indian Affairs and Northern
    Development, Department of,
    1.192, 237
individualism, 1.48, 263; 2.11, 32
industrialism, 2.43, 99
industrialization, of Canada, 2.20, 23,
    38, 51, 218
industrial strategy, 1.191; 2.106, 108,
    124, 131, 152, 156, 158, 160, 176,
    216-18, 221-3, 259, 268, 480-2
Industry, Department of, 2.104, 122,
    129, 131
Industry, Trade and Commerce,
    Department of, 1.190, 192; 2.166,
    213, 218, 219, 222, 244, 250, 267,
    505
inflation, 1.124, 136, 143, 190; 2.91,
    97, 113, 118, 122, 124-5, 128, 132,
    230, 232, 235-6, 244, 252-4, 256,
    258-60, 262-3, 268, 271, 322, 327,
    381, 387, 454, 460-2, 488
infrastructure, 2.56, 62
Ingham, Bernard, 2.369
Innis, Harold, 2.55, 98, 175, 217, 220
Institut canadien des affaires
    publiques (ICAP), 1.69; 2.73, 120

Institute for Research on Public Policy, 1.77, 189, 281; 2.126

Institute of Commonwealth Studies, 1.320

insurance companies, 2.24, 239

interest rates, 2.128, 208, 230, 232, 234, 254-5, 258, 261, 381, 387, 389, 475, 482-3, 487

International Development Research Centre, 2.213, 364

internationalism, 2.52, 63, 76, 91, 110

International Monetary Fund, 2.58, 348, 380

International Trade Ministry, 1.191; 2.222

interprovincial trade, 1.284, 293, 364

Iron Ore Company of Canada, 1.76, 332; 2.105

Irwin, Ron, 2.410

Jackman, Hal, 2.120

Jamieson, Don, 2.339

Japan, 2.54-5, 123, 203, 210, 215

Jécistes, 1.61-3, 404; 2.163

Jennings, Sir Ivor, 2.60

Jeunesse étudiante catholique, 1.61, 403; 2.162-3

Jewett, Pauline, 2.405

Jews, in government, 1.118, 415-16, 453; 2.296

job creation, 2.75, 91, 93, 253, 256, 294, 387, 488-9, 514-15

Johnson, Albert W. (Al), 1.260; 2.103, 112-13, 457

Johnson, Daniel, 1.100, 103-4, 110, 255, 259, 263, 385

Johnson, H.G., 2.452

Johnson, Lyndon, 2.193, 200

Johnson, Pierre-Marc, 1.237, 385

Johnson, Ted, 1.190; 2.390, 396, 399

Johnston, Donald, 1.169, 190, 381; 2.152, 250, 252, 257, 261, 264, 292, 401, 413, 515

Johnstone, Robert, 1.192; 2.220, 480

Joyal, Serge, 1.296, 298, 328, 337, 424, 449; 2.257, 294

Juneau, Pierre, 1.192, 403, 432; 2.500

Jungian psychology, 1.70, 72, 74, 396, 417

Justice, Department of, 1.86-7, 101, 107, 117, 191-2, 221-2, 259-60, 265, 345, 441; 2.63, 112, 120, 164, 281

Just Society, 1.14, 115, 118, 122, 422; 2.70, 88, 92, 93

Kaplan, Robert, 2.328

Kennan, George, 2.364, 510

Kennedy, Edward, 1.135

Kennedy, John F., 2.192-3

Kenny, Colin, 1.139

Kent, Tom, 1.85, 100, 118, 410; 2.82-4, 93

Kershaw committee, 1.320, 324, 327, 337

Keynes, John Maynard, 1.46; 2.56-8

Keynesian economic theory, 1.46, 47, 51, 254; 2.52, 56-8, 72, 74, 79, 82, 91, 103, 113, 118, 159, 219, 231-3, 251-2, 268, 286-7, 485

Kidder, Margot, 2.363, 376, 385

Kierans, Eric, 2.100, 293, 456

Kilbourn, William, 1.415; 2.68

King, William Lyon Mackenzie, 1.39, 42, 180, 250, 416, 444; 2.16, 19, 20, 34, 39, 43, 50, 52-4, 61, 70, 77, 87, 139, 141, 145, 159, 192, 284, 286, 289, 317, 321, 336, 412, 436, 445-6

Kingston, Ontario, 2.64, 83

Kirby, Michael, 1.189, 281-4, 288, 319-20, 326, 345-6, 362-3, 368, 381, 382, 384, 441, 443; 2.172, 276, 328, 380, 408, 491

Kirton, John, 2.371

Kissinger, Henry, 1.120; 2.200, 212-13, 337-8, 340, 400, 430

kitchen accord, on the constitution, 1.381

Kohl, Helmut, 2.356, 367

Korea, 1.354-5; 2.76

Korean Airlines crisis, 2.363-4, 366, 369, 373
Kraft, Joseph, 2.202
Kroeger, Arthur, 1.192; 2.264
Kroeker, Hal, 2.221
Kübler-Ross, Elisabeth, 1.397

Labelle, Huguette, 1.192
Laberge, Louis, 2.258
labour, 2.123, 128-9; mobility of, 1.284, 293, 311, 351
Labour, Department of, 1.191; 2.94, 103
labour disputes, 1.220; 2.52
labour law, 1.69, 78, 201, 242, 348
labour leaders, 2.270, 323
labour movement, 1.53-4, 78, 143, 271, 430; 2.40, 52, 57, 91, 108, 125, 127, 129, 259, 489
Labour Party, in United Kingdom, 1.316, 319, 321, 411, 417; 2.46, 47, 49, 51, 72
labour unions, 1.53-4, 68-70, 143, 206, 253, 266; 2.19, 46, 52-4, 67-70, 72, 75, 84, 87, 94, 100, 110, 125, 129, 187, 221, 235, 259, 261, 402, 422, 458, 464, 479
LaFlèche, Léo, 1.42
Lafontaine, Louis-Hippolyte, 1.200
La Forest, Gerard, 1.259
laissez-faire economics, 2.20, 38, 86, 93, 183
L'Allier, Jean-Paul, 1.267, 434
Lalonde, Marc, 1.85-7, 91, 99, 100, 105, 108, 116, 143, 161, 166, 172, 192, 214, 296; 2.91-2, 120, 288, 299-300, 316, 326, 399, 411, 413, 414, 417; as cabinet minister, 1.137, 189-90, 206, 228-9, 267, 270-1, 381-2; 2.112, 129, 166, 170, 172-5, 179, 197, 216, 220, 231-2, 244, 248, 263, 265-6, 271, 274-5, 293, 312, 319, 328, 361, 376-7, 386, 390, 395; as Trudeau's ally, 1.205; 2.163-5, 262, 390
LaMarsh, Judy, 2.405

Lambert Report, 2.131
Lamer, Antonio, 1.353
Lamontagne, Gilles, 1.191-2; 2.353, 363, 365
Lamontagne, Maurice, 1.87, 91; 2.82, 83-4
Lang, Otto, 1.419, 421; 2.293
Langevin, Hector, 2.73
language law, 1.351, 367; 2.426
language rights, 1.41-2, 88, 91, 106, 159, 267, 274, 283, 285, 292, 329, 355, 366, 438, 457; 2.408
Lapalme, Georges Émile, 1.61, 65; 2.73, 79
Lapierre, Jean, 2.299
Lapointe, Charles, 1.443
Lapointe, Ernest, 1.200
Laporte, Pierre, 1.77, 90, 122
LaSalle, Roch, 1.451
Lasch, Christopher, 2.310
Laski, Harold, 1.49, 65, 121, 417; 2.46-7, 64, 114, 368, 441-2
Laskin, Bora, 1.348, 350-2, 416, 453, 454
Latin America, 2.335
Latouche, Daniel, 1.377, 434, 435
Laurendeau, André, 1.60, 78, 86, 197, 203, 259, 410, 437; 2.41
Laurie, Nate, 2.151, 156, 249-50, 252, 253, 256, 380
Laurier, Wilfrid, 1.89, 200, 216, 231, 238, 303; 2.19, 38, 39, 41, 43, 412
Laval University, 1.60, 71, 373, 404
Law of the Sea Conference, 2.189
law reform, 1.107, 258, 260, 311; 2.389
Laxer, James, 2.109
Leader of the Opposition's Office (LOO), 1.154, 170; 2.139, 145-8, 151, 157, 249, 288, 428
League for Social Reconstruction (LSR), 2.51, 74-5
LeBlanc, Roméo, 1.191; 2.148, 251, 264, 297, 301, 326
LeDain, Gerald, 1.259
Lee, William, 2.318, 417, 418

Leeson, Howard, 1.443
Léger, Paul-Émile, 1.66-7, 404
Leitch, Merv, 2.179
Lemelin, Claude, 1.431, 441
Le Moyne, Jean, 1.56-7, 64-5, 117, 394, 402; 2.201-2
Lennon, John, 1.120
Leontief, Wassily, 1.47; 2.58, 447, 461
LePan, Douglas, 2.63
Lesage, Jean, 1.61, 76-8, 81, 99-100, 197, 232, 254-6, 263, 385; 2.64, 79, 84
Levasseur, Pierre, 1.117
Lévesque, Corinne, 1.242
Lévesque, Dominique, 1.199-200
Lévesque, Father Georges-Henri, 1.60; 2.82, 453
Lévesque, René, 1.60, 77-8, 90, 98, 104-5, 137, 197-200, 234, 259, 311; 2.323; in constitutional negotiations, 1.269, 272, 311, 369-70, 374-80, 384-6; as PQ leader, 1.198, 207, 241, 266; 2.338; as premier of Quebec, 1.19, 137, 201-2, 211-13, 219, 223, 230, 242, 269, 280, 288-9, 294, 359, 368, 374, 424, 429, 431; 2.165, 247; in referendum fight, 1.170-2, 196, 212, 223, 230, 232, 235-6, 241-2, 429, 431; as television broadcaster, 1.60, 77, 197, 198
Levinson, Daniel, 1.396-9, 426
Levitt, Kari, 2.99
Lewis, David, 1.125; 2.34, 100, 107-10, 117
Liberal International, 2.285, 315
Liberalism, 2.11, 16, 19, 37, 40-1, 43, 49, 66, 73, 80, 82, 84, 86, 109, 114, 261-2, 265, 284-5, 287, 301, 314, 325, 330, 368, 389, 391, 393-4, 401-2, 415, 420-1, 423
liberalism, 1.47-8, 68, 79, 313, 400; 2.31-2, 39-41, 43, 49, 66, 68, 71-2, 74, 80, 150, 188, 195, 204, 265, 284-7, 326, 433

Liberal Party, in Alberta, 1.303; 2.181, 401, 410, 462
Liberal Party, in Europe, 2.284-5, 492
Liberal Party, of British Columbia, 1.151; 2.395
Liberal Party, of Ontario, 2.401-2
Liberal Party, of Quebec, 1.32, 61, 76-8, 81, 104, 197, 201, 207-8, 214, 216, 224, 243, 267, 373, 407; 2.164-5, 263, 391; leadership, 1.61, 65, 81, 207-10, 214, 224, 232, 263, 373; 2.29, 38, 73, 79, 84, 88; and neo-federalism, 1.207, 210, 214, 256, 267; women in, 1.122, 234
Liberal Party, of United Kingdom, 2.18, 19, 284, 435-6, 441, 494
Liberal Party of Canada, 1.16-18, 61, 109, 151, 154, 180, 309; 2.11, 16, 18, 34, 51, 61-2, 64, 73, 83, 90, 101, 142, 144, 206-7, 306, 308, 429
— anglophone wing, 1.149, 167, 186-7; 2.85, 397
— backbenchers, 2.291, 295-302, 496
— backroom loyalists, 1.117, 124, 138-9; 2.311, 317, 418
— business Liberals. See Liberal Party of Canada, right wing
— caucus, 1.164-6, 167-8, 214, 291-2; 2.86, 100, 148-9, 151, 264-5, 274, 276, 291, 295-302, 304, 325, 417, 423, 496-7
— conventions, 1.109, 149, 151-2; 2.304-6, 310, 312, 314-21, 346
— extra-parliamentary wing, 1.118, 138, 149-50, 167; 2.85, 100-1, 146, 148, 149, 151, 291, 303-4, 310-12, 313-21, 401, 420
— francophone wing, 1.20, 109, 144, 149, 167, 227-8, 257, 268, 373; 2.289, 311, 391, 417
— fundraising, 2.290, 316, 396
— leadership, 1.108-14, 116, 148, 149-50, 164-9, 170-2, 205, 218; 2.62, 84, 102, 112, 116, 129, 151, 311, 312, 315, 317, 318

— leadership contests, 1.111, 116, 128, 149, 151-2; 2.82, 87, 150, 206, 207, 211, 226-7, 229, 251, 293, 304, 311, 397, 400-14, 417, 418
— left wing, 2.82, 250-1, 287, 317-18, 326, 329, 380, 400, 401-2, 429, 491
— under Lester Pearson, 1.85-6, 99-101, 105-8; 2.81, 82, 84, 90, 140, 282, 304, 308
— national director, 2.62, 114, 312-13, 316, 320, 396
— nationalism in, 2.82, 93, 156, 223, 284
— national organization, 1.149, 151-2, 155, 167-8, 172; 2.83, 147, 151, 304, 310-11, 315-16, 325, 361, 428, 463-4
— as official opposition, 1.145, 148, 155; 2.18, 77, 114, 137, 139, 140, 145-6, 149, 218, 225, 228, 276, 420-3
— policy and policy-making, 1.109; 2.85, 141, 146-9, 151-7, 161, 304-6, 310-16, 319-20, 346, 402, 428
— president, 2.315-16, 320, 395-6, 401, 413
— right wing, 2.82, 219, 223, 229, 250, 317-18, 329, 401
— Toronto advisers, 1.125, 138-40, 143-4; 2.83, 113-14, 301, 315, 317
— welfare Liberals. See Liberal Party of Canada, left wing
— women's participation, 2.312
— youth wing, 2.316-17
liberty, 1.358; 2.32, 64, 358
Linden, Allen, 2.304-6
linguistic rights, 1.41-2, 106, 267, 274, 283, 285, 292, 329, 355, 366, 438, 457
Local Initiatives Program, 2.94
Locke, John, 1.69, 248; 2.43
Loiselle, Bernard, 2.464, 465
Loiselle, Gilles, 1.317-21

London School of Economics, 1.49, 51, 54, 65, 67, 79, 121, 247, 254, 313, 400, 417; 2.46, 103, 164, 412
Lougheed, Peter, 1.158, 225, 300-2, 341, 364, 367, 368, 377; 2.173, 472; and Alberta energy resources, 1.301-6, 308-9, 364; 2.169-70, 178, 469, 471, 472; in constitutional negotiations, 1.288-90, 304, 307-8, 310-11, 320, 341, 368, 371, 374, 381, 384, 446, 457
Lumley, Ed, 1.164, 169, 191; 2.221-2, 250, 264, 292
Lussier, André, 1.36
Lussier, Charles, 1.41-2, 64, 246, 403; 2.31, 33, 34, 41, 440
Lussier, Gaétan, 1.192
Lyon, Sterling, 1.278, 288, 311-12, 368, 457

McCall, Storrs, 1.225-6
McCulley, Joe, 2.32
McDermott, Dennis, 2.260
MacDonald, Daniel, 1.420
Macdonald, Donald, 1.137, 159, 165, 414; 2.124, 129, 153, 169, 206, 207, 247, 274, 283, 293, 318, 322, 326, 379, 401, 421, 516
MacDonald, Flora, 2.213
Macdonald, Sir John A., 1.180, 300, 302, 362, 438; 2.16, 22, 99-100, 159, 321
Macdonald, William, 2.318, 409
Macdonell, James, 2.130
MacDougall, Hartland C., 2.119
MacEachen, Allan, 1.137, 161, 165-9, 172, 424; 2.82, 84, 225, 226, 413-14, 465, 482; as cabinet minister, 1.190, 192, 381; 2.148, 174, 221, 226-30, 232, 245, 272-4, 293, 301, 326, 339, 361, 363, 365, 373, 481; and 1981 budget, 2.15, 17, 233-6, 238-40, 243, 251, 260, 271, 275, 280, 287, 326, 473, 483-5
McGill Law Journal, 2.78

McGill University, 1.61, 79, 225, 245-6, 408; 2.34, 36, 69, 71, 74, 98, 103, 108, 119

MacGuigan, Mark, 1.192, 259, 321, 323, 326, 381, 383, 448; 2.214, 293, 354, 401, 413

McIlwain, Charles, 1.47, 247, 435

McIntyre, William, 1.353

Mackasey, Bryce, 2.94, 259, 380, 512

McKenna, Frank, 2.425

McKenzie, Robert, 1.49, 51, 400; 2.47

Mackenzie Valley pipeline, 2.110, 475

McKibbon, James, 1.322

Mackintosh, W.A., 2.220, 445

Mackness, William, 2.271

MacLaren, Roy, 2.152, 267

MacLeod, Norman, 2.315-16, 396, 408

McLuhan, Marshall, 1.112, 120, 126-7

McMurtry, Roy, 1.349, 362, 365, 368, 381

McNair, John, 2.46

McNally, Ed, 1.305-6

McNamara, Kevin, 1.319-20

McNamara, Robert, 2.363

McNaught, Kenneth, 2.76

McNaughton, General A.G.L., 2.76

Macpherson, C.B., 2.78, 452

McRae, Paul, 2.464, 465

macroeconomics, 2.57, 72, 159

McTeer, Maureen, 1.426

magazines, Canadian, 2.100

Malépart, Jean-Claude, 2.408

Maloney, Ron, 1.237

Malraux, André, 1.120; 2.340

mandarinate, 2.50-3, 57, 61, 70, 77, 111, 119, 209, 216, 280-1, 322, 324, 444, 447

Manion, John, 1.192

Manitoba, 1.264, 278, 288, 302, 311, 350, 355, 371, 373, 426, 438; 2.29, 61, 63, 142, 250, 260, 391, 410, 426

Manitoba Court of Appeal, 1.338, 344-6

Manning, Preston, 2.428, 429

Manpower and Immigration, Department of, 2.211, 227

manufactured goods, 2.18, 53, 57, 97, 123, 217

manufacturing, 2.123, 131, 217-18, 451

Mao Zedong, 2.337, 340

Marchak, Patricia, 2.99

Marchand, Jean, 1.53, 60, 63, 70, 78, 82, 88, 89-94, 99, 101, 108-9, 113, 118, 137, 143, 149, 166, 172, 174, 186-7, 190, 197, 228, 255-6, 275, 394; 2.74, 84, 87, 91, 93, 163, 293, 300, 321, 380, 390

Marchand, Leonard, 1.419

markets, 2.54-5, 66, 76, 89, 99, 105, 106, 161, 169, 195, 198, 217-19, 221-2, 265, 268, 421

Marsden, Lorna, 1.167; 2.208, 306-16, 319-20, 380, 408, 465, 513

Martin, Paul, 1.105, 414; 2.293

Martin, Paul, Jr., 2.408, 427, 428, 429

Martland, Ronald, 1.353

Marxism, 1.48, 402; 2.47, 78, 79, 366

media, 1.120-1, 123-4, 133, 143, 148, 152, 156, 191, 208, 219, 262-3; 2.17, 100, 115, 127, 137, 146, 155, 237, 240, 247-8, 288-9, 308, 315-17, 319-20, 345-6, 373, 381, 393, 399, 413, 418-20, 427

medicare, 2.57, 83, 85, 226, 265, 319, 328, 391, 402, 412, 429

Meech Lake Accord, 2.425-7, 515

Meekison, Peter, 1.304, 381, 384

Meese, Ed, 2.205

Megarry, Roy, 1.448

Meighen, Arthur, 1.300

Mellon, Barry, 2.179

Mercier, Honoré, 2.37

Mercier, Léonce, 1.228

mergers and take-overs, 2.83, 265, 386, 475, 491, 514

Mexico, 2.189, 205, 343, 428

Michels, Robert, 1.150
Middle East, 1.50, 157; 2.190-1
Miliband, Ralph, 2.46, 441
Mill, John Stuart, 2.43
Miller, Morris, 2.46-7, 68
Millican, Harold, 1.299
mining, 2.55, 74, 221, 225
Ministry of State for Economic and
    Regional Development, 1.192;
    2.173, 264, 280, 515
Ministry of State for
    Multiculturalism, 1.191, 192;
    2.294, 295
Ministry of State for Social
    Development, 2.265, 280
minorities and the disadvantaged,
    2.327, 329; disabled persons,
    1.158; francophones, 1.264, 283,
    292-3; native people, 1.293, 297,
    339, 385; 2.158; Quebec
    anglophones, 1.225, 283, 292-3;
    rights of, 1.246, 250, 261, 283,
    292-4, 355, 381, 385, 457; 2.94,
    389, 432; women, 2.158-9
minority governments: Conservative,
    **1957**, 1.163; **1979**, 1.145; 2.139;
    Liberal, **1963**, 1.85, 217; 2.85, 114;
    **1972**, 1.124; 2.108-9, 112, 168,
    338
Mitterrand, François, 2.204, 285, 344,
    356-7, 359, 367, 406, 424, 508
Mobil oil company, 2.192
Molgat, Gil, 1.168
monarchy, 1.313, 360
Mondale, Walter, 2.200
monetarism, 1.137; 2.127-8, 233, 287
monetary policy, 1.187; 2.127, 232,
    252, 460
money supply, 2.127, 244
Montaigne, Michel Eyquem, 2.32, 37
Montebello, Quebec, 2.191, 196,
    204, 209, 344
Montesquieu, Charles-Louis de
    Secondat, 2.32, 37, 443
Montreal, 1.25-31, 35-8, 98, 104,
    165, 176, 197, 228, 232, 234, 236,

268, 272, 286, 296, 304, 332; 2.50,
    63, 65, 67, 108, 114, 436; English
    in, 1.21-4, 32-3, 53, 66, 68, 70, 74,
    196, 232, 385; 2.24, 38, 39, 59, 66,
    424, 436-7
Montreal Royals baseball club, 1.31,
    33; 2.31
Moore, Jim, 1.420
Moorehead, Caroline, 1.394, 418
Morin, Claude, 1.201-2, 212, 219,
    288-9, 317, 369-70, 375, 379, 384,
    385, 424, 429, 430, 434
Morin, Jacques-Yvan, 1.370
Mounier, Emmanuel, 1.58-9, 62,
    205, 402; 2.44-5, 64, 200
Mulroney, Brian, 1.277, 290, 330,
    331-3; 2.95, 120, 349, 367, 376,
    391, 399, 418-19, 425-6, 428,
    432-3; as prime minister, 2.379,
    419-21
multiculturalism, 2.389
Munro, John, 2.400, 413
Murray, Lowell, 1.156, 163, 331-4;
    2.120

National Action Committee, 2.308
National Assembly, Quebec, 1.195,
    228, 234, 256, 296, 457
national debt, 2.252, 255, 387, 397,
    429
National Defence, Department of,
    1.192, 351, 352, 353, 365
National Energy Board, 2.165
National Energy Program, 1.189-90,
    311, 328, 358, 366, 372; 2.174-83,
    196-7, 205, 208, 213-16, 219-20,
    222-3, 232, 244, 255, 263-4,
    266-8, 272, 298, 360, 375, 422,
    466, 470-2, 475-7; back-in
    provision, 2.176, 192, 197, 215,
    274, 474
National Film Board, 1.98, 195, 456
nationalism, 1.260, 303; 2.83, 193-4,
    217, 264, 393; French-Canadian,
    1.12-15, 80, 82, 84, 101, 109, 113,
    122, 181, 195, 197, 254, 259,

394-5, 409, 411; 2.11, 58, 85, 101, 110, 126, 156
nationalization, 1.78; 2.55, 178, 285
National Liberal Federation, 2.39
National Liberal Women's Commission, 2.395
National Oil Policy, 1.303; 2.468
National Policy, 1.302, 455; 2.16, 22, 100, 159, 269, 284, 328, 467
National Training Act, 2.260
national unity, 1.179, 205, 298-9, 333-5, 340; 2.116, 138, 139, 154, 157, 199-201, 207, 426, 477
native peoples, 1.119, 237, 293, 297, 316, 318, 339, 385, 457; 2.32, 94, 110, 158, 245, 397, 425-6, 429
natural gas, 1.303-4, 306, 308; 2.110, 166, 177-8, 180, 183, 360, 446
natural resources, 1.284, 303-7, 444, 449; 2.23, 66, 99, 269, 327, see also resources; exploitation of, 2.54, 66
neo-conservatism, 1.129, 187; 2.187-8, 192, 195, 247, 270, 330, 367, 380, 420, 432-3, 474
neo-federalism, 1.203-4, 207, 210, 212, 215, 229, 239, 256, 266-7, 269, 334, 372, 434-5; 2.84, 431
neo-Marxism, 2.98-9
neo-nationalism, 1.261
Neufeld, Ed, 2.236
New Brunswick, 1.288, 308, 312, 325, 359, 360, 367, 382, 446; 2.297, 301, 425
New Democratic Party (NDP), 1.124, 163, 321, 339, 363, 371-2, 449; 2.85, 100, 107, 109, 114, 132, 141, 145, 150, 155, 159, 168, 208, 248, 259-60, 286, 289, 329, 423, 429, 456, 465
Newfoundland, 1.285, 307-8, 312, 371; 2.150, 179, 192, 327-8, 410, 426; Court of Appeal of Supreme Court of, 1.344, 346-8, 452-3
newly industrializing countries (NICS), 2.123, 346
New York Times, 2.202, 274, 382

New Zealand, 1.249; 2.193
Nicholson, Aideen, 2.464
Nigeria, 1.121; 2.343
Nixon, Richard, 1.121; 2.96, 105, 107, 188, 200, 273, 337-8, 341, 350, 400, 411, 457, 477, 504
Nixon, Robert, 2.410
Nixonomics, 1.129; 2.96-7, 102, 106, 110, 337-8
Non campaign, in Quebec referendum, 1.223-25, 229, 234-5, 432
NORAD, 2.77, 336
North American Free Trade Agreement (NAFTA), 2.428, 521
North Atlantic Treaty Organization (NATO), 1.323-4; 2.55, 159, 194, 204, 336, 340, 345, 349-51, 355, 357, 361-3, 365-6, 372, 374, 382, 412, 503
North-South relations, 2.204, 214, 505
Northwest Passage, 2.99, 335
notwithstanding clause, 1.381, 383, 385; 2.426
Nova Corporation, 2.181, 475
Nova Scotia, 1.280, 308, 312, 371; 2.82, 99, 225, 259, 278, 328
nuclear non-proliferation, 2.349, 350, 371-2
nuclear war, 2.355, 370, 375, 382-5
nuclear weapons, 2.349-50, 355

O'Connell, Martin, 1.420
October Crisis (1970), 1.122-3, 206, 265, 266; 2.98, 102, 126, 259, 411, 457, 501
Office of the Opposition. See Leader of the Opposition's Office (LOO)
Official Languages Act, 1.117-18, 264
O'Hagan, Richard, 2.142-3, 146, 202
oil: in Alberta, 1.303-4, 306, 309; 2.167-9, 178-81, 221; Hibernia field, 1.309; 2.192, 198; prices, 1.229; 2.110, 132, 153-4, 168-70, 176, 179-81, 263, 268, 327;

royalties, 1.304; 2.168, 169; oil and gas industry, 1.301, 303, 304, 307, 444; 2.151-3, 166, 168-9, 174, 177, 180-2, 236, 446, 471-4; American, 2.191-2, 196, 198, 205, 223; Canadianization, 2.176, 180-1, 199, 223, 287; junior and independent companies, 2.183, 471, 473

oil crises, 1.129, 157, 304, 305; 2.110, 118, 124, 131, 151, 168, 170

old age security, 2.487, 488

O'Leary, Grattan, 2.120-1

Olivier, Jacques, 2.464

Olson, Bud, 2.220, 292

O'Malley, Martin, 1.107

O'Neill, Louis, 1.237

Ono, Yoko, 1.120

Ontario, 1.279, 293, 294, 300, 302-3, 305, 307, 309-11, 312, 359, 362, 368, 382, 455; 2.18, 34, 68, 100, 103, 114, 144-5, 150, 274, 289, 360, 389, 400, 419

Ontario Committee on the Status of Women, 2.308

OPEC, 1.129, 157, 304, 364; 2.110, 118, 124, 132, 153, 168, 169, 176, 231

Opportunities for Youth, 2.94

opting out, of federal programs, 1.100, 374-5, 377, 379, 383, 385, 457

Organisation for Economic Co-operation and Development, 2.132, 243, 245

Osbaldeston, Gordon, 1.192; 2.173-4, 220-3, 244, 268, 280, 282, 416, 481

Osgoode Hall, Toronto, 1.259

Ostry, Bernard, 1.416; 2.94, 104, 309-10, 379-80

Ostry, Sylvia, 1.159, 416; 2.69, 243, 246, 406

O'Sullivan, J.P., 1.346

Ottawa, 1.15, 54, 286, 299-300, 357; 2.15, 50, 61-5, 114, 443

Ouellet, André, 1.191, 228-9, 381; 2.265, 293, 328, 386

Outremont, 1.29, 30, 42, 44, 45, 48, 71, 72, 238, 395; 2.28, 35, 68, 74

override, provincial, of constitutional amendments, 1.381, 383, 385

Owen, David, 1.175

pan-Canadianism, 1.39, 84, 239, 261, 336, 371, 374; 2.199, 268, 388, 400, 432

Panitch, Leo, 2.99

Papineau, Louis-Joseph, 1.200

Parizeau, Jacques, 1.219, 424; 2.515

Parliament, British, 1.275, 279, 286-7, 291, 293-5, 298, 312, 315-16, 318, 320, 322, 346, 361; 2.32

Parliament, Canadian, 1.148, 272, 291, 298, 317, 320, 355

participatory democracy, 1.118, 121, 150; 2.87, 88, 91, 92, 101, 127, 146, 303-4, 306, 310, 313, 314, 323

Parti pris, 1.80

Parti Québécois, 1.198, 201, 202, 207, 224, 226-7, 236, 266, 269, 270, 289, 293, 296, 319, 351, 370-1, 373, 401, 428, 456; 2.129, 154, 164-5, 194, 245, 322, 338, 390, 391, 403, 505; and referendum on sovereignty-association, 1.142, 194, 209, 210, 227, 230, 233, 237, 240, 291, 370, 434

Paterson, Alex, 1.225-6

patronage, 1.52-3, 221, 331; 2.62, 290, 317, 318, 380, 417, 418

pay equity, 2.307

Payette, Lise, 1.233-4, 242, 433

Payne, John, 2.318, 409, 417

peace movement, 2.335, 360, 381-2

Pearson, Geoffrey, 2.365, 372

Pearson, Lester B. (Mike), 1.153; 2.60, 81-2, 160, 209, 225, 234, 333, 334, 335; as prime minister, 1.85-6, 90, 91, 98, 100, 105, 107,

109, 217, 255, 257-8, 259, 262,
265, 277; 2.83-4, 87, 92-4, 100,
112, 120, 140-2, 164, 171, 193,
211, 226, 228, 286, 351, 412, 414;
and Trudeau, 1.93, 99, 101, 105,
106, 108, 109, 257-8

Peckford, Brian, 1.311, 314, 368,
384-5; 2.425

Pelletier, Alec, 1.60, 403

Pelletier, Gérard, 1.53, 63-6, 78, 88,
92-3, 99, 118, 137, 168, 172, 190,
197, 257, 267, 380, 403; 2.70, 74,
84-7, 91, 94, 293, 310, 357, 365,
380, 390, 391

Pelletier, Irénée, 2.464

Pelletier, Jean, 2.248

Penner, Keith, 2.464

pensions, 1.229, 267; 2.57, 67, 110,
158, 226, 256, 307, 329, 387, 412,
485

Pentagon, 2.55, 77, 194, 351, 352,
353, 360, 375, 382

Pepin, Jean-Luc, 1.191, 271, 441, 442;
2.129-30, 250, 264, 293-4, 326,
327, 491

Pepin-Robarts task force, 1.271, 441

Perle, Richard, 2.374, 507

Perlin, George, 2.349

Perrault, Ray, 1.443

Perroux, François, 1.48

Perry, Suzanne, 1.420

personalism, 1.56, 58-61, 63-4, 85-6,
204-5, 402-3, 405; 2.44-5, 64,
162-3, 165, 246, 325, 335

Peterson, Kevin, 1.341

Petro-Canada, 1.157; 2.110, 146, 148,
154, 166, 168, 176, 177, 181, 191,
205, 269, 465, 469, 475; back-in
provision in NEP, 2.176, 192, 197,
274, 476

petrochemical industry, 1.301, 304,
307; 2.166, 174

petroleum, 1.303, 307, 444; 2.166-70,
177, 181, 191, 446, 470-1

petroleum and gas revenue tax
(PGRT), 2.176

Petroleum Incentive Payments (PIP
grants), 2.177, 180, 183, 475

Philippines, 2.348

Phillips, Art, 2.464, 465

Picard, Gérard, 1.60

Pickersgill, Jack, 1.55, 250, 436; 2.17,
60-1, 63

Pinard, Maurice, 1.410; 2.452

Pinard, Yvon, 2.295

pipelines, for oil and gas, 2.110, 167,
360, 468

PIP grants, 2.177, 180, 183, 475

Pitfield, Grace MacDougall, 2.26-7,
119

Pitfield, Michael, 1.87, 99, 100, 168,
189, 192, 229, 260, 281-3, 288,
326, 355, 381, 411; 2.71, 91-2,
119-22, 142, 146, 157, 211-2, 214,
233, 235, 248, 262-3, 274-83, 310,
324-5, 328, 388, 391, 512; and
bureaucratic organization,
1.116-17, 136, 157, 265; 2.171-3,
221, 244, 269, 272, 278-81, 416,
432, 469

Pitfield, Ward Chipman, 2.71, 119-20

Plant, Paul, 2.395

Plommer, Leslie, 1.448

PMO/PCO, 1.122, 281, 381; 2.112,
231, 237, 250, 262, 275-6, 278,
281, 289, 365. See also Prime
Minister's Office; Privy Council
Office

Point de mire, 1.98

Poland, 2.356

political economy, 1.79; 2.98, 175,
217, 220

political science, 1.47, 49-50; 2.42

polls, opinion, 1.160, 163, 166, 168,
173, 179, 235, 272, 298, 338, 358,
366, 442; 2.34, 83, 117-18, 131,
152, 289, 291, 295, 297, 298, 314,
317, 329, 345, 348, 360, 367, 379,
385, 388, 394, 397, 419; on the
constitution, 336; in the Quebec
referendum campaign, 1.214, 235

populism, 2.77, 92, 94, 114, 145, 167

Porteous, Tim, 1.117
Porter, John, 1.112, 408
Positive Action Committee, 1.225, 434
positivism, 1.47, 247, 413
potash, 1.306, 307, 308
poverty, 2.94, 113, 158, 159, 204, 270, 329, 342, 343, 488
prairies, 2.18, 92, 114, 145
Presse, La, 1.78, 220, 234
Prices and Incomes Commission, 2.91
Prime Minister's Office (PMO), 1.55, 100, 116, 125, 150, 152, 381; 2.59, 61, 87, 102, 120, 132, 172, 206, 212, 270-1, 288, 291, 294, 399, 402, 415. See also PMO/PCO
Prince Edward Island, 1.308, 312, 371
Priorities and Planning Committee, 2.173, 174, 213, 244, 251, 252, 253, 255-7, 292-3, 295, 492
Priority Resolution 40, 2.316-17, 320, 326
private sector, 2.56, 222, 256, 271, 275, 386-7, 488
privatization, 2.330, 381, 420
Privy Council, of Great Britain, 1.250, 454
Privy Council Office (PCO), 1.54, 60, 99, 100, 102, 116-17, 189, 223, 260, 265, 280, 431-2, 439; 2.59, 60-1, 64, 105, 120, 121, 212, 221, 238, 249, 255, 271, 280, 281, 291, 294, 416; young Trudeau as policy analyst, 1.54-5, 64, 99, 119, 204, 248, 251, 280; 2.49-50, 57, 58-63, 65-6, 69. See also PMO/PCO
Pro-Canada Network, 2.520
procurement policies, 2.157, 219
productivity, 2.67, 118, 128, 132, 160, 461
program cuts, 2.272
Progressive Conservative Party, 1.85, 91, 98, 187, 325; 2.77, 99, 109, 113, 114, 116, 120, 132, 145, 146, 159, 286, 381, 429; in Alberta,

1.158; and business, 2.381, 418-23; and the constitution, 1.284, 335-6, 339-40; filibuster on unilateral constitutional bill, 1.338-40; in the House of Commons, 1.160-2, 164, 172, 339-40, 424; 2.150, 155; internal conflict, 1.98, 156, 330-3, 349; leadership, 1.329-30; 2.349; as minority government (1979-80), 1.145, 148, 156-7, 162, 283, 329; 2.170, 228; of New Brunswick, 1.361; in Nova Scotia, 1.308; in Ontario, 1.158, 293, 337, 363-6; as opposition, 1.98, 295, 329, 333; 2.247-8; and Quebec, 1.32, 52, 68-9, 156, 334-5, 451; Red Tories in, 1.330, 366; right wing, 1.330, 333-4; 2.146
progressivism, 2.18, 225
protectionism, 1.284, 293, 455; 2.30, 53, 99, 111, 160, 218, 219, 226, 421, 445
provinces, 1.81, 225; 2.93, 157, 280, 402; coalition of, 306-10, 312, 316, 340, 341-3, 348, 370-1, 375-9, see also Gang of Eight; control over resources, 1.303-5, 307, 308, 311, 364; 2.168; power struggle with federal government, 1.284-5, 290, 294, 298-9, 304-5, 307, 309-12, 347, 359-69, 371-5, 376-8, 381-5; 2.313
provincial courts, 1.312, 343-4
provincial premiers, 1.225, 306, 336, 358; 2.177-8, 252, 258, 402-3, 412, 431, 432; anglophone, 1.225, 230, 258, 264, 267, 270, 272, 275, 277, 279, 309, 310, 316, 368, 369, 371, 374-9, 425, 438; conferences of, 1.258, 263, 265-6, 271-2, 274, 312, see also constitutional conferences, federal-provincial conferences, first ministers' conferences; opposed to Trudeau's constitutional proposal (1981), 1.285-6, 288-91, 294, 298-9,

306-12, 316-21, 324-7, 338, 340,
342-4, 353, 363, 371, 374, 383;
2.208
Prud'homme, Marcel, 2.464
public sector, 2.253, 256, 258, 387,
462, 479, 488
Public Works, Department of, 1.221
*puer aeternus* (eternal youth), 1.34,
36-7, 70, 74, 406, 412
pulp and paper, 2.55
Pym, Sir Francis, 1.322-3

Quebec, province, 1.23, 32, 67, 79,
81; 2.10, 24, 67, 145, 152, 400,
431; American investment, 1.52,
80; 2.66, 67; Anglo business
domination, 1.25, 52, 53, 59, 68,
80, 81; 2.27-9, 30, 66, 88;
constitutional status, 1.81, 203-4,
253, 283; controlling élites, 1.408,
409-10; 2.21, 22, 23, 24, 323;
crises of the 1960s and 1970s, 1.85,
105, 108, 122-3, 254, 256, 265-6;
federalism in, 2.84, 177-8, 391;
foreign investment, 1.52, 58, 80;
2.28, 38, 66, 67; foreign policy,
1.81, 100, 137, 412; 2.211, 335,
356, 357; nationalism, 1.39, 80;
2.79-81, 305, 323, 426, 429;
opposition to military service,
1.28, 41, 42, 43, 333-4; racial
tensions in, 1.28, 39-40; 2.27-9,
30, 31; separatism in, 1.19, 20,
82-3, 87, 100, 104-8, 113, 137,
173, 201, 203, 256, 265, 269, 307;
2.10, 79, 84, 94, 129, 154, 194,
200, 287, 334, 356, 391, 426; social
policy, 1.255, 267; 2.112; veto of
constitutional amendments, 1.294,
307, 311, 375, 377, 385
Quebec-Canada Committee, 1.432
Quebec City, 1.71, 232, 234, 268,
439; 2.24, 39, 69, 428
Quebec referendum (1980), 1.242-77;
2.10, 154, 287, 327, 382, 424;
federal involvement, 1.213-16,

221-32, 234-9, 274, 275-6; 2.165,
178, 179; the question, 1.210, 212,
226, 230, 233, 240, 429, 430, 433;
significance of, 1.240-1
Quebec referendum (1992), 2.426
Quiet Revolution, 1.23, 82, 84, 196,
254, 410, 428

Rabinovitch, Robert, 1.229, 431-2;
2.221, 238, 249, 250, 328
racism, 1.96, 235-6, 237, 273; 2.21,
22, 23, 24, 31, 259
Radwanski, George, 1.21; 2.393
Rae, Jennifer, 1.416
Rae, John, 1.220; 2.413
Rae, Saul, 1.220, 416
Rashish, Myer, 2.196-7, 214-15, 216,
273
Rasminsky, Louis, 1.416; 2.90, 435
Rassemblement provincial des
citoyens, 2.73
raw materials, 2.55, 123, 217, 505
*Reader's Digest*, 2.100
Reagan, Ronald, 1.358; 2.187-91,
196, 204-5, 247, 254, 285, 329,
344, 345, 353, 355, 356, 357-60,
367, 370, 372-8, 383, 385, 400,
406, 411, 508
recession, 2.132, 183, 249, 251, 265,
280, 287, 328, 329, 344, 381,
387-8, 486
Recherches sociales, 2.70
redistribution of wealth, 2.86, 91,
176, 329
referendums: national, 1.42, 270,
272-3, 294, 311, 338, 351, 376-80,
382, 383; 2.136, 145-6; in Quebec:
on sovereignty-association, 1.142,
149, 168, 170, 171, 172, 173, 202,
208, 210-12, 275, 335, 370, 378,
382. *See also* Quebec referendum
(1980)
Reform Party, 2.428
refugees, 2.67, 431
Regan, Donald, 2.223
Regan, Gerald, 1.191, 281; 2.259, 278

Regional and Industrial Expansion, Department of (DRIE), 2.263-4
Regional Economic Expansion, Department of (DREE), 2.93, 222, 244
regional equity, 2.91
Reid, John, 1.420, 421
Reisman, Simon, 1.416; 2.103-5, 106, 112-13, 119, 122, 193, 233, 236, 267, 419, 421, 457, 459, 484
Relève, La, 1.57
religious freedoms, 1.329
research and development, 2.131, 352
Reshetar, John, 2.43, 44
resource industries, 2.269
resource management, 1.307, 309, 311, 351, 449
resource megaprojects, 2.178, 181, 221, 251, 260, 268
resource policy, 1.301, 372; 2.218
resources, 1.304, 309; 2.57, 75, 76, 105, 123, 153, 166-70, 198, 231, 327, 446; export of, 2.75, 77, 105, 217, 268, 445, 450
Reston, James, 2.202, 274
retirement income, 2.387, 389, 514
Reuber, Grant, 1.192; 2.230
Revenue, Department of, 2.278-9
Ridley, Nicholas, 1.324
Riel, Louis, 1.334
rights, human, 1.246, 250, 256, 261, 283, 351, 359, 381, 385, 457; collective, 1.68, 82, 106, 283; individual, 1.47, 68, 82, 106, 241, 283, 359; 2.11, 20
Ritchie, Ed, 2.106
Ritchie, Roland, 1.353
Robarts, John, 1.258, 259, 271, 441
Robert, Michel, 1.208, 349, 429, 432
Roberts, John, 1.191, 321, 323, 381, 420; 2.221, 265, 326, 400, 413
Robertson, Gordon, 1.54, 100, 168-9, 248, 251, 253, 266, 270-1, 280-3, 404, 430, 436; 2.61, 65, 66, 119, 121, 204, 480
Robertson, Norman, 2.60, 61, 114

Robinette, John J., 1.349
Robinson, Ken, 2.464
Robinson, Paul H., Jr., 2.215, 274
Robinson, Svend, 1.443
Rockefeller, John D., 2.19
Rogers, General Bernard, 2.364
Rolland, Roger, 1.48, 58, 117, 403; 2.35-6, 44
Rolling Stones, 1.135, 140
Roman Catholic church, 1.28, 35, 39, 50, 53, 56, 57, 62, 80; 2.335; dominance in Quebec society, 1.39, 56, 58, 60, 66-9, 76, 78, 84, 358, 401; 2.23, 30, 66, 67, 72, 79; and personalism, 1.56, 58, 59; 2.44, 64, 142, 162-3, 165; repression of intellectuals and artists, 1.57, 66, 68, 402; 2.64; ties with politics, 1.52-3, 56, 58-9, 66-7, 68, 69, 401, 410; 2.37-8, 66, 67, 72, 79
Romanow, Roy, 1.362, 381
Rompkey, William, 2.278-9, 410, 493
Rosen, Harry, 1.425
Ross, Frank, 2.111
Rotstein, Abraham, 2.99
Rouleau, Suzette Trudeau, 1.119, 129, 394; 2.390. See also Trudeau, Suzette
Rousseau, Jean-Jacques, 1.69, 248; 2.304
Roy, Fabien, 1.162, 424, 450
Roy, Jean-Louis, 1.110, 456
Roy, Marcel, 2.464, 465
Roy, Michel, 1.373, 440
Royal Canadian Air Force, 2.38, 77
Royal Canadian Mounted Police, 2.248, 403, 501
Royal Commission on Bilingualism and Biculturalism (Laurendeau-Dunton), 1.86, 98, 103, 259, 264
Royal Commission on Canada's Economic Prospects (Gordon), 1.96; 2.76-77, 281-2, 318, 322, 326, 379, 401, 421, 451

Royal Commission on Economic Union and Development Prospects for Canada (Macdonald), 2.283, 318, 322, 326, 379, 401, 421

Royal Commission on Taxation (Carter), 1.87; 2.92, 93, 471

royal commissions, 1.86, 87, 96, 98, 103, 167, 259, 264; 2.76-7, 92, 93, 120, 167, 281-2, 283, 308, 318, 322, 379, 401, 421, 450, 468

Rubin, Ed, 1.117, 414

Russell, Bertrand, 1.426

Russell, Peter, 1.354, 410, 454; 2.102

Ryan, Claude, 1.203-7, 259; 2.457; Beige Paper, 1.210, 214, 215, 230, 430; as Quebec Liberal Party leader, 1.202, 207-9, 214, 224, 370, 373, 374, 456; 2.391, 431; in referendum campaign, 1.202, 210-11, 214-15, 223-4, 226, 229, 232, 233, 241-3, 335, 429, 432

Ryan, Madeleine, 1.233-4

Sabine, George, 2.43

St. Laurent, Louis, 1.55, 65, 89, 90, 138, 200, 250, 251, 252-3, 416; 2.50, 54, 59-62, 81, 87, 90-1, 225, 269, 286, 412

St. Lawrence Seaway, 2.62

Saskatchewan, 1.252, 279, 285, 289, 292, 301-3, 306, 307, 311, 312, 321, 337, 371, 373, 375, 377-8, 437, 449; 2.80, 139, 301; CCF government, 2.69, 103, 122

Sauvé, Jeanne Benoit, 1.61-2, 234, 339, 403, 452; 2.148, 312, 380, 405

Sauvé, Maurice, 1.34, 62, 87

Sauvé, Paul, 1.76, 458

Sauvé, Sarah, 1.26

Saywell, John, 1.112, 415

Schmidt, Helmut, 2.130, 200, 204, 205, 254, 285, 341, 344, 356, 358, 362, 424, 492, 505

Schreyer, Ed, 1.445; 2.158, 510

Schumpeter, Joseph, 1.47; 2.43, 58, 78, 84-5, 447, 461

Science and Technology, Department of, 1.191

Science Council of Canada, 2.126, 217

Scott, F.R. (Frank), 1.60, 67, 69, 79, 88, 115, 245, 246, 252, 282, 411, 436; 2.34, 69-71, 72, 74, 78, 85, 108, 114, 120, 449-50; as civil libertarian, 1.60-1, 245, 246, 256, 260; 2.69

Scott, Peter, 1.88, 394; 2.69, 450

Scowcroft, General Brent, 2.364

secularism, 1.80

Sedgwick, Gordon, 2.120

Segal, Hugh, 1.362-3, 365, 368, 382

Senate, of Canada, 1.271, 290, 291, 293, 295, 333, 338; 2.39, 40, 100, 116, 207, 282, 295, 297, 316, 380, 396, 417, 422; reform, 1.285, 309, 311, 372

Senegal, 2.343

senior citizens, 1.293, 297; 2.158, 328, 387, 388

separatism, in Quebec, 1.19, 20, 82-3, 87, 100, 104-6, 108, 113, 137, 173, 201, 203, 256, 265, 269, 289, 291, 316; 2.10, 79, 84, 97, 129, 154, 165, 179, 195, 200, 287, 327, 334, 356-7, 426, 431

Servan-Schreiber, Jean-Jacques, 2.310

sexism, 1.233; 2.259

sexual equality, 1.338

shadow cabinet, of Liberals, 2.148, 218, 464

Sharp, Daryl, 1.74

Sharp, Mitchell, 1.100, 137, 218, 220; 2.85, 87, 90, 106-7, 130, 226, 293, 337, 338, 430

Shoyama, T.K. (Tommy), 1.432; 2.122

Shultz, George, 2.273-4, 361, 366, 373, 377, 383

Simeon, Richard, 2.247

Simpson, Jeffrey, 2.202, 463

Sinclair, James, 1.126, 127, 129, 416; 2.95

Sinclair, Margaret, 1.123, 126-9, 185, 416, 418; 2.95. *See also* Trudeau, Margaret Sinclair

"Six and Five" principle, 2.256-8, 261, 263, 268, 271, 292, 298, 315, 327, 346, 387, 392, 486, 488-90

Small, Doug, 1.243

small business, 1.122; 2.17, 93, 159, 389

Smith, Gordon, 2.280

Smith, Mel, 1.384

Smith, Stuart, 1.175

social benefits, 2.67, 132, 226, 304, 419

social contract, 1.358; 2.129, 462

Social Credit Party, 1.301, 303, 424, 444; 2.114, 167, 220, 468. *See also* Créditiste Party

socialism, 1.49, 80, 88, 245, 372, 402; 2.11, 34, 40, 41, 43, 46, 79, 108, 175, 192, 286

social justice, 2.57, 108, 230, 233, 234, 237, 381

social policy, 2.387, 417-18, 419, 420, 429, 517

social programs, 2.270, 319, 328, 391, 402, 419, 429, 487-8

social security. *See* social welfare

social welfare, 2.52, 56, 75, 79, 82, 85, 90, 110, 112, 118, 172, 215, 253, 254, 256, 259, 264, 265, 270, 287, 381

Société Saint-Jean-Baptiste, 1.258-9

sociology, 1.79; 2.98

South Africa, 1.249; 2.342-3

Southeast Asia, 1.96; 2.246

sovereignty, 1.98, 101, 110, 122, 308; 2.189, 335, 337, 422, 428; of Quebec, 1.81-2, 107, 137, 202, 209, 210, 211, 214, 230, 236; 2.10, 84, 425, 429

sovereignty-association, 1.194, 202, 228-30, 239, 242, 269, 275, 279, 334-5, 370, 378, 382, 431; 2.179

Soviet Union, 2.204, 218, 334, 335, 353, 383-4, 510

Special Joint Committee of the Senate and the House of Commons on the Constitution of Canada, 1.296, 298, 337, 443, 449

special status, for Quebec, 1.81, 203, 204, 207, 256, 257, 262, 334, 375, 414, 442; 2.84

spending restraint, 2.130

Square Mile, 1.31; 2.22, 26, 28, 31, 34, 36, 71, 437

stagflation, 2.122-3, 130, 460

Stanbury, Richard, 2.304, 305

Stanfield, Robert, 1.124, 136, 140, 155, 205, 330, 415, 450-1; 2.99-100, 107, 116, 118, 125, 459

staple commodities, 2.53, 54, 55, 57, 131, 166, 168, 221, 244, 268, 340

Starowicz, Mark, 2.393

State Trading Corporation, 2.219

statism, 1.201-2, 242, 317, 429; 2.86, 263, 275, 285

Statute of Westminster, 1.39, 249, 327

Stein, Janice, 2.384

Stewart, Ian, 1.192, 346; 2.170, 174, 230-8, 249, 252, 255-6, 266, 275, 287, 380, 476, 482, 492

Stewart, John, 2.228

Stewart, Walter, 1.122

Stockholm, conference on European security, 2.383, 385

Stollery, Peter, 2.207

Stornoway, 1.146, 167, 169, 170, 171, 175, 176, 187

Strategic Air Command, U.S., 2.77

Strategic Defense Initiative (SDI), 2.355, 363

strategic prime ministership, 1.188-9; 2.16, 17, 232, 243

Strayer, Barry, 1.117, 259, 345, 441

Streisand, Barbra, 1.120; 2.385

strikes, 2.129, 208, 261, 271, 479, 490

Suez Crisis, 1.96

Sulzenko, Barbara, 2.149, 156

summit meetings. *See* economic summits

"supply-side" economic management, 2.113, 118, 233, 234, 237

Supreme Court of Canada, 1.250, 266, 271, 307, 310, 348, 372, 416, 441, 453, 454; 2.403-4, 426, 517; and the constitution, 1.338, 340, 343, 345, 347-55, 367, 371, 372, 375, 383, 453

Supreme Court of Newfoundland, 1.340

Sweden, 2.55, 217-18

Talmey, Lauris, 2.395

Tansley, Donald, 2.280

Tanzania, 2.175, 343

tariffs, 1.302; 2.18, 38, 53, 111, 118, 218, 219, 268

Taschereau, Louis-Alexandre, 1.200; 2.38, 39

Task Force on Canadian Unity, 1.271, 441, 442

task forces, on constitution, 1.118, 259-60; 2.211, 212

Tassé, Roger, 1.192, 346, 381, 432, 441

taxation, 1.81; 2.56, 57, 92, 103, 109, 113, 128, 229, 234-9, 428; of energy, 1.161, 162, 164, 304, 307; 2.152, 155, 161, 162, 169, 174, 178, 179, 180, 470, 472, 475

tax breaks and loopholes, 2.74-5, 92, 100, 113, 166, 233, 236, 238-9, 267, 483

tax credits, 1.229

tax incentives, 2.97, 174, 183, 219, 230, 232, 388, 471

tax reform, 1.118, 190; 2.92, 93, 173, 231, 267, 455

Taylor, Charles, 1.79, 88, 90, 93, 394; 2.74, 84, 386

Taylor, Nick, 2.181, 401

Taylor, Si, 2.365

Taylor Statten camp, 1.37, 397; 2.32

Teitelbaum, Ethel, 1.112, 415

Teitelbaum, Mashel, 1.112

television, 1.60, 125, 143, 242-3, 267; 2.126, 271, 274, 328, 377, 393, 411-13, 458, 501-2; coverage of hearings and conferences, 1.110, 263, 289, 295-6, 337, 339, 449; influence on political opinion, 1.110-12, 114, 211-13, 230; in political campaigns, 1.223; 2.117

Tellier, Paul, 1.192, 270, 431

terrorism, in Quebec, 1.85, 122-3, 206, 256

Texas Gulf Corporation, 2.110

Thatcher, Margaret, 1.278, 314-19, 321-2, 324, 337, 355, 447; 2.196, 205, 285, 329, 344, 356, 358-60, 367-70, 383, 506, 508

Third Option, 2.107, 203, 338, 461

Third World, 2.123, 128, 204, 214, 217, 316, 334, 340, 342, 343, 344, 348, 354, 371, 393, 401, 505

timber trade, 1.22, 24; 2.221, 360

*Time*, 1.413; 2.100, 270, 459

Tobin, Brian, 2.410

Toole, Barry, 1.326

Toronto, 1.112, 124, 196, 241, 272, 286, 305; 2.83, 116, 120, 124, 139, 147, 207-9, 288, 294, 436

*Toronto Star*, 2.87, 155-56, 202, 248, 393, 394

totalitarianism, 1.247

Touche, Ouida, 2.95

Tough, George, 2.170, 175, 236

Towe, Peter, 2.189

trade: interprovincial, 1.284, 293, 364; in natural resources, 1.284, 301-3, 304-11

Trade and Commerce, Department of, 1.218; 2.54, 57, 121-2, 129, 131

trade deficit, 2.53

Trans-Canada Highway, 2.62

transcontinental railroads, 1.302

transfer payments, to provinces, 2.245, 253, 403, 432, 487, 517

transnational corporations, 1.301;
2.420
Transport, Department of, 1.191,
192; 2.250, 264, 327
Treasury Board, 1.190, 192, 218, 260,
416, 431; 2.59, 103, 104, 231, 263,
264, 280
Tremblay, Arthur, 1.335, 336
Tremblay commission, 1.253-4; 2.72
Trezise, Philip, 2.193
trucking industry, 2.273
Trudeau, Charles Elliott (Tip), 1.28,
33, 34, 39, 47, 71, 129; 2.29
Trudeau, Charles-Émile (Charlie),
1.25, 26-37, 40, 44, 65, 71, 128,
394-5; 2.27, 31, 33-4, 37, 40, 442
Trudeau, Grace Elliott, 1.25, 26-32,
35-6, 38, 44, 70, 71, 72, 129, 418;
2.20, 27-9, 31, 34-6, 48
Trudeau, Joseph, 1.25
Trudeau, Justin, 1.315; 2.412
Trudeau, Malvina, 1.25-6
Trudeau, Margaret Sinclair, 1.24, 73,
125, 135, 173, 175-7, 426; 2.117,
201, 322, 324, 369, 412; books by,
1.126, 142, 146, 175, 418; 2.245;
careers, 1.141, 177; in 1972
election campaign, 1.133;
indiscretions, 1.132-5, 145-6,
147-8, 175, 394, 426; 2.245;
pregnancies and childbirth, 1.130,
132, 135; as prime minister's wife,
1.123, 125, 126, 131-2, 133;
remarriage, 2.391; separation from
Trudeau, 1.137, 140
Trudeau, Michel, 1.177; 2.412
Trudeau, Pierre Elliott, 1.17-18, 28,
110, 187, 205-6, 228, 263; 2.84,
109
— anti-nationalism, 1.51, 83-4,
89-90, 92, 101, 122, 181, 260, 408,
409, 410, 477
— arrogance, 1.102, 120-2, 123, 174,
198, 235, 277-8; 2.89, 248, 417
— athleticism, 1.37, 147, 200; 2.71,
424, 433

— attitude to Great Britain, 1.313-14
— awards, 1.69, 406
— biracial identity, 2.42-4, 45, 46,
164
— birth, childhood, adolescence,
1.19, 27-31, 32-7, 38, 40; 2.18, 22,
27, 28, 29-32
— and Cité libre, 1.62-9, 76, 83, 84,
86, 119, 403
— commitment to federalism, 1.83,
100, 105, 106-7, 109, 140, 230-1,
253, 254-5, 260-3, 283, 358, 366;
2.10, 120, 126, 129, 154, 163, 287,
426, 431
— constitutional goals, 1.285-7, 295,
297, 311, 336, 340, 342, 347-351,
357, 359, 362, 365-6, 368, 371,
376; 2.231, 245, 249, 262-3, 382
— and constitutional theory, 1.68,
77, 79, 102, 142, 170, 179, 245,
247, 253-4, 256-8, 260-2, 282,
343, 376; 2.231, 245, 249, 262-3,
382
— and Cyrano de Bergerac, 1.43-4,
273, 278, 341, 383, 442
— economic views, 2.72, 77-8, 80,
81, 86-7, 88
— education, 1.29, 30, 32, 36-42,
46-9, 204, 205, 395, 400; 2.29, 31,
32-3, 42-9, 58, 64, 164
— emotional detachment, 1.21,
35-6, 39, 70, 74
— father's untimely death, 1.33-4,
36, 38, 396-7, 399; 2.31, 164
— individualism, 1.36, 37, 59, 68
— integration late in life, 1.177-9,
277
— integrity, 1.139-40, 142, 358;
2.302, 326, 433
— intellectual force, 1.38, 48, 101,
102, 120, 140, 227, 349, 366,
368; 2.73, 291, 293, 302, 335, 338,
433
— in international affairs, 2.58, 63,
194, 203, 204, 214, 330, 333, 424,
502-12

— junior civil servant in PCO, 1.54-5, 64, 99, 119, 204, 248, 251, 280; 2.48-9, 57, 58-62, 63, 69

— and labour unions, 1.68, 69, 70, 143, 254

— leader of the opposition, 1.148, 174, 420, 421; 2.390

— and Lévesque, 1.170-1, 197, 202, 232, 235-7, 241, 376-80

— Liberal Party leader, 1.107, 108, 158-9, 164-73, 198, 263, 415, 423; 2.86, 87, 101, 120

— loyalty of followers, 1.151, 152-3; 2.318, 390

— marital problems, 1.126, 130-1, 136-42, 173-6; 2.125, 163, 165, 339, 369

— marriage, 1.24, 123, 126, 399, 426; 2.95

— media relations, 1.106, 110-12, 120-1, 123, 133, 187-8, 262, 358, 400, 412-13, 422; 2.393-4, 399, 515

— member of Parliament, 1.95, 97, 102-3, 257; 2.85, 116, 120, 162

— memoirs, 2.433, 521

— minister of justice, 1.101, 105-6, 109, 110, 258, 259, 260, 261; 2.85, 120, 163, 211

— paradoxical style, 1.36, 40, 50-1, 106, 129

— as parent, 1.141, 175, 186; 2.322, 391, 398, 399, 411, 433

— parental influences, 1.33, 35-40, 398; 2.31, 42, 48

— parliamentary secretary to Pearson, 1.93-4, 99, 257, 258; 2.85, 112, 120, 163, 210-11

— peace initiative, 2.355, 365-6, 369-78, 379, 380-2, 384, 388, 390, 393, 402, 513

— personalism, 1.55-6, 59-60, 64, 204, 403; 2.64, 324

— physical appearance, 1.45, 102, 107, 111, 178, 200, 231, 238; 2.16

— pledge to renew constitution, 1.238-9, 244, 245, 279-80

— political beliefs, 1.49, 79, 82-4, 436; 2.11, 33-4, 41, 43-6, 49, 72, 78-81, 95, 127, 146, 156-7, 323

— political charisma, 1.21, 102, 111, 114, 119-20, 140, 144, 277; 2.87, 271, 306

— professor of constitutional law, 1.77, 79, 197, 255; 2.79

— psychological and emotional development, 1.398-9

— *puer aeternus*, 1.70, 74, 101

— and Quebec referendum, 1.214-16, 221-2, 229-32, 235-9, 275, 276, 382

— relationships with women, 1.45, 72, 73-4, 77, 111-12, 119, 147, 185-6, 416, 418; 2.34-5, 36-7, 45, 71-2, 322, 363, 384-5, 398, 424, 433

— resignation (1984), 2.379-80, 385-6, 396-400, 514

— resignation and return (1979-80), 1.158, 159, 164, 167-73, 186, 214, 369, 422; 2.228, 251, 342

— reversal of normal life pattern, 1.398-9

— and Roman Catholic Church, 1.35, 38, 50, 56, 58, 64, 66-67, 68, 76; 2.246

— rumours about, 1.73, 237-8

— self-discipline, 1.30, 37, 50

— sense of privacy, 1.20-1, 114, 133

— shyness, 1.30, 33, 45, 101, 113, 114, 173

— and socialism, 2.34, 41, 46-7, 73, 78, 80, 89, 127

— speeches, 1.114, 231-3, 236-9, 243-4, 257, 261, 272-3, 295, 433, 434; 2.143-4, 153-4, 156-7, 201, 218, 239, 257, 272, 319, 342, 354, 366, 370, 412, 466, 480, 502

— spiritual sense, 1.35, 50, 56, 58-9; 2.382, 433, 512

— "street fighter," 1.106, 262, 268; 2.323
— successor to Pearson, 1.108-9, 110-13
— unconventional behaviour, 1.36, 45-6, 77, 79, 99, 102-3, 110-11, 114, 120, 178; 2.33, 323, 339-40, 369-70
— unilateral action to patriate constitution, 1.278, 285-90, 294, 310-12, 315, 320-1, 325, 327-8, 336-8, 340-1, 348, 354, 365-6, 370-3, 375, 378, 382-3, 442, 448; 2.178, 180, 245, 300
— wealth, 1.44-5, 59, 71, 112, 204, 205, 402, 411; 2.31, 45, 64, 67, 69, 79, 89
— writings, 1.49, 64-9, 82, 83, 112, 119, 406, 407, 408-10; 2.44, 68, 70, 72, 78, 81, 163, 194, 200
Trudeau, Sacha, 1.177; 2.347, 412
Trudeau, Suzette, 1.28, 33, 35, 44, 71; 2.29. *See also* Rouleau, Suzette Trudeau
Trudeaumania, 1.20, 111-12, 114, 123, 126, 425; 2.145
Trudeau trust, 2.69, 79, 89
Turner, John, 1.111, 137, 159, 160, 165, 169, 219, 290, 415; 2.95, 111-13, 122, 124, 129, 206, 247, 273, 293, 305, 317-20, 326, 329, 376, 391, 400, 427, 459, 495; as Liberal Party leader, 2.415-16, 419-23, 518
Turner, Phyllis, 2.111
Twaddle, Kerr, 1.350
24 Sussex Drive, 1.16, 17, 125, 134, 140, 146, 215, 299, 323, 426; 2.115, 121
"two-track" approach, 2.355, 357, 362, 374

Ulam, Adam, 2.43
unanimity principle, 1.279, 284, 350, 354, 371
Underhill, Frank, 2.108

unemployment, 1.124; 2.75, 78, 91, 113, 118, 123, 128, 132, 208, 230, 244, 251, 253, 254, 256, 259-60, 265, 322, 387, 454
unemployment insurance, 1.121-2; 2.43, 67, 94, 259, 328, 450
UNESCO, 1.185-6
unilingualism, in Quebec, 1.369, 373
Union des forces démocratiques, 2.74
Union Nationale, 1.32, 39, 62, 65, 76, 100, 109, 263, 266, 267, 333, 401, 407, 429, 432; 2.34, 39, 67, 72
United Farmers of Alberta, 1.303
United Kingdom, 1.49, 249, 314, 316, 319, 321, 353, 411, 417; 2.10, 53, 72, 138, 285, 341, 366, 420
United Nations, 2.52, 82, 189, 337, 354, 365, 372, 382, 391, 444
United States, 1.39, 188, 197; 2.16, 19, 50, 52, 55, 61, 76, 79, 86, 96-7, 166, 188-9, 193-5, 210, 254, 285-6, 351, 355, 366; Carter administration, 2.194, 201, 286; Department of Defense, 2.193-4, 351; economic domination in Canada, 2.86, 105, 110, 203; investment in Canada, 2.54, 75-6, 99-100, 104-5, 203; Nixon administration, 2.193; Reagan administration, 2.188, 193, 195-9, 205, 215-16, 234, 237, 254, 263, 265, 272-3, 328-9, 344, 355, 364, 372, 375-7, 383, 400, 419; State Department, 2.49, 106, 193-4, 196, 198, 205, 214, 273, 373, 375-6; trade representative's office, 2.190, 215, 272-3; Treasury Department, 2.196, 223
Université de Montréal, 1.40-2, 66, 77, 79, 185, 203, 245-6, 255, 259, 269, 404; 2.30, 32, 34, 40, 44, 67, 79, 87, 162
uranium, 1.306; 2.55, 99
U.S.S. *Manhattan*, 2.99

Vadeboncoeur, Pierre, 1.402, 403; 2.73

value-added industry, 2.251

Vancouver, 1.127-8, 286; 2.111, 153

Vanier, Georges, 2.65

Vastel, Michel, 1.227

Veilleux, Gérard, 1.432, 441; 2.237

Venezuela, 1.135; 2.167, 466, 468

vertical mosaic, 1.112, 118, 408

veto, of constitutional amendments, 1.294, 307, 311, 372, 375, 377, 385

Viau, Cécile, 1.420; 2.399

Vietnam, 2.96, 193-4, 203, 286, 335, 374, 456

Vignaux, Paul, 2.73

Vogel, Richard, 1.343

Volcker, Paul, 2.254, 255

von Franz, Marie-Louise, 1.72-3

von Hayek, Friedrich, 2.285

voting age, in Quebec, 1.78

*Vrai*, 1.67, 69, 406; 2.72, 442


Wadds, Jean, 1.326, 363, 447

Waffle, 2.100, 110, 456

wage and price controls, 1.137, 143, 187; 2.125, 129, 175, 231, 259, 287, 341, 461

wage-price spiral, 2.258

wages, 2.57, 75, 129, 253, 256-8, 261, 271, 461, 487-8

Wagner, Claude, 1.330, 422

Wahn, Ian, 2.100, 101

Walker, David, 2.147

*Wall Street Journal*, 2.197, 205

War Measures Act, 1.123, 206, 269; 2.461, 504

Warren, Jake, 2.193

Watkins, Mel, 2.87, 99, 100

Watson, Ian, 2.464

Watt, Charlie, 1.237

Watts, Ron, 1.441

weapons, 2.77, 349, 351, 353-5, 384, 506-7

Weber, Max, 1.99, 102-3, 140, 397-8, 413

Weinberger, Caspar, 2.214, 353, 377

welfare state, 2.46, 72, 107, 118, 132, 135, 165, 420, 433, 450, 454

Wells, Clyde, 1.347; 2.425, 426

Wells, Tom, 1.365

western Canada, 1.359, 445; 2.18, 39, 102, 145, 159, 289, 301, 428; alienation from central Canada, 1.187, 299-300, 302, 306-8, 358, 426-7; alienation from Liberal Party, 1.138, 426-7; 2.208-9, 416, 420, 422

Western Canada Sedimentary Basin, 2.167

Western Economic Opportunities Conference, 1.445

Western Europe, 2.193, 204

Western Grain Transportation Act, 2.328

West Germany, 2.285, 350

Whelan, Eugene, 1.191; 2.265, 293, 328, 401, 413, 491

Whitaker, Reg, 2.99

White, T.H., 2.116, 202

White Papers, 1.118, 122, 209, 210

Whyte, John, 1.340, 453

Wilkinson, Bruce, 2.123

Williams, Blair, 2.428

Williams, J.H., 2.58

Williamsburg, Va., 2.357, 360, 364, 366, 508

Wilson, Bertha, 1.453, 2.405

Wilson, George, 2.208

Wilson, Michael, 2.420

Winnipeg, 1.320, 421; 2.140-2, 301

*Winnipeg Free Press*, 2.82

Winters, Robert, 1.116, 415; 2.227

women, 1.233-4, 294, 297, 338; 2.158-9, 329, 387, 389; in government, 1.122; 2.296, 311, 313

women's issues, 2.405, 413, 429, 518

women's movement, 2.422, 425

women's rights, 1.338, 339, 457; 2.68, 251, 307-9, 313

Woodsworth, J.S., 1.260
workers, 1.80, 81; 2.75, 80, 86, 129,
    258, 285, 323, 330, 464
working conditions, 2.57
World Bank, 2.52, 348
World War I, 1.27, 28, 249; 2.18, 23,
    24, 38, 56, 101
World War II, 1.41, 313, 398; 2.33,
    39, 45, 76, 141, 176
Wylie, Torrance, 1.168

Young Communist League, 2.103
Young Offenders Act (1982), 2.403,
    517
Youth Opportunity Fund, 2.389
Yvette, symbol in Quebec
    referendum, 1.233-4, 433

zero option, 2.374-5
Zhou Enlai, 2.340, 504